Garfield
FAT CAT 3-PACK
VOLUME 14

Garfield
FAT CAT 3-PACK
VOLUME 14

BY
JIM DAVIS

BALLANTINE BOOKS · NEW YORK

2009 Ballantine Books Trade Paperback Edition

Published in the United States by Ballantine Books, an imprint of The Random House Publishing Group, a division of Random House, Inc., New York.

Originally published as three separate titles. *Garfield Survival of the Fatest, Garfield Older & Wider*, and *Garfield Pigs Out.*

BALLANTINE and colophon are registered trademarks of Random House, Inc.

ISBN 978-0-345-49175-6

Printed in the United States of America

www.ballantinebooks.com

9 8 7 6 5 4

Garfield
SURVIVAL of the FATTEST

BY JIM DAVIS

Ballantine Books • New York

Outrageous Outtakes

Never-before-seen, over-the-top strips saved from extinctio by our kooky comics conservationists

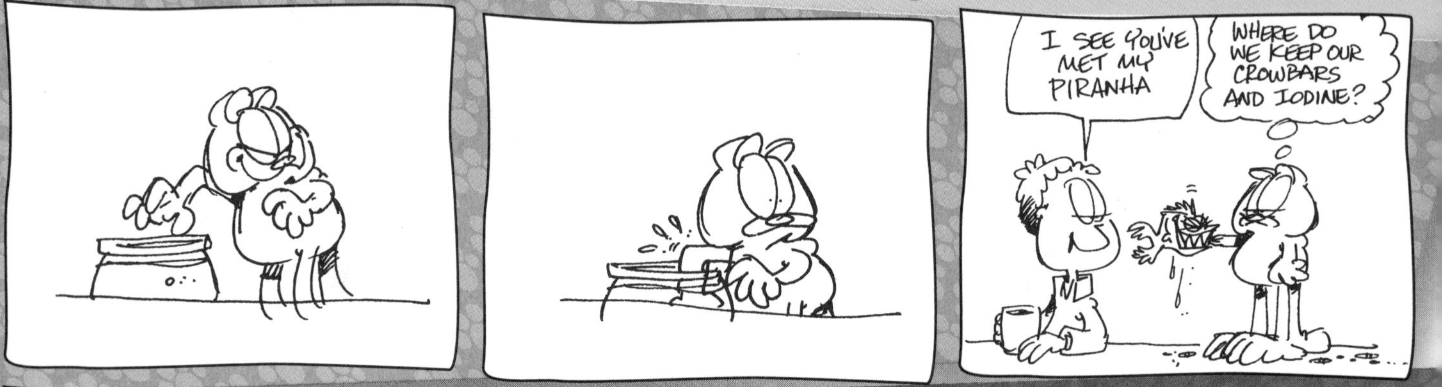
I SEE YOU'VE MET MY PIRANHA
WHERE DO WE KEEP OUR CROWBARS AND IODINE?

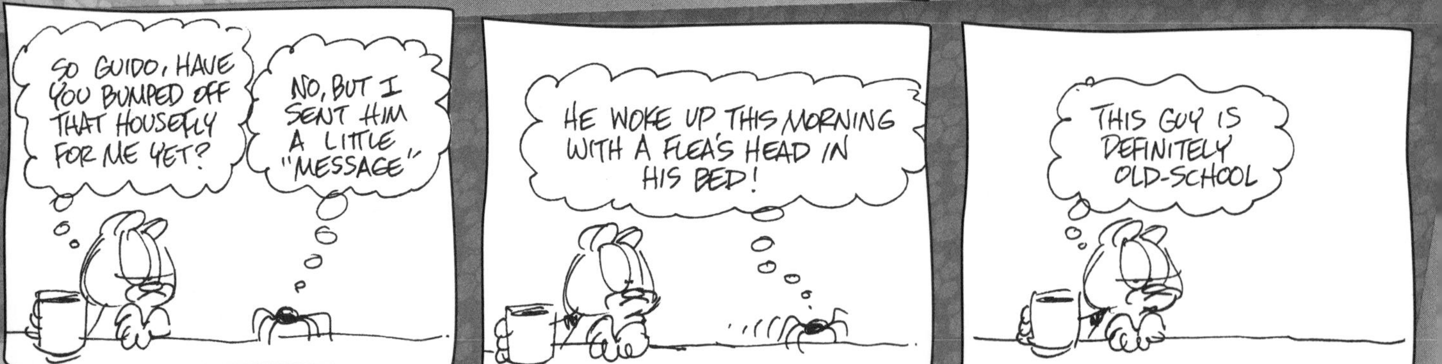
SO GUIDO, HAVE YOU BUMPED OFF THAT HOUSEFLY FOR ME YET?
NO, BUT I SENT HIM A LITTLE "MESSAGE"
HE WOKE UP THIS MORNING WITH A FLEA'S HEAD IN HIS BED!
THIS GUY IS DEFINITELY OLD-SCHOOL

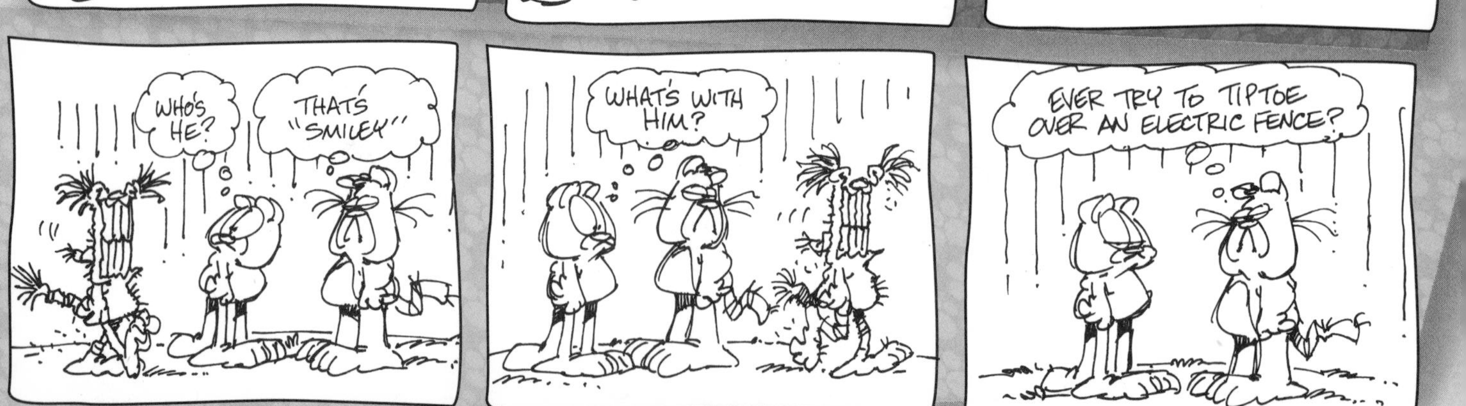
WHO'S HE?
THAT'S "SMILEY"
WHAT'S WITH HIM?
EVER TRY TO TIPTOE OVER AN ELECTRIC FENCE?

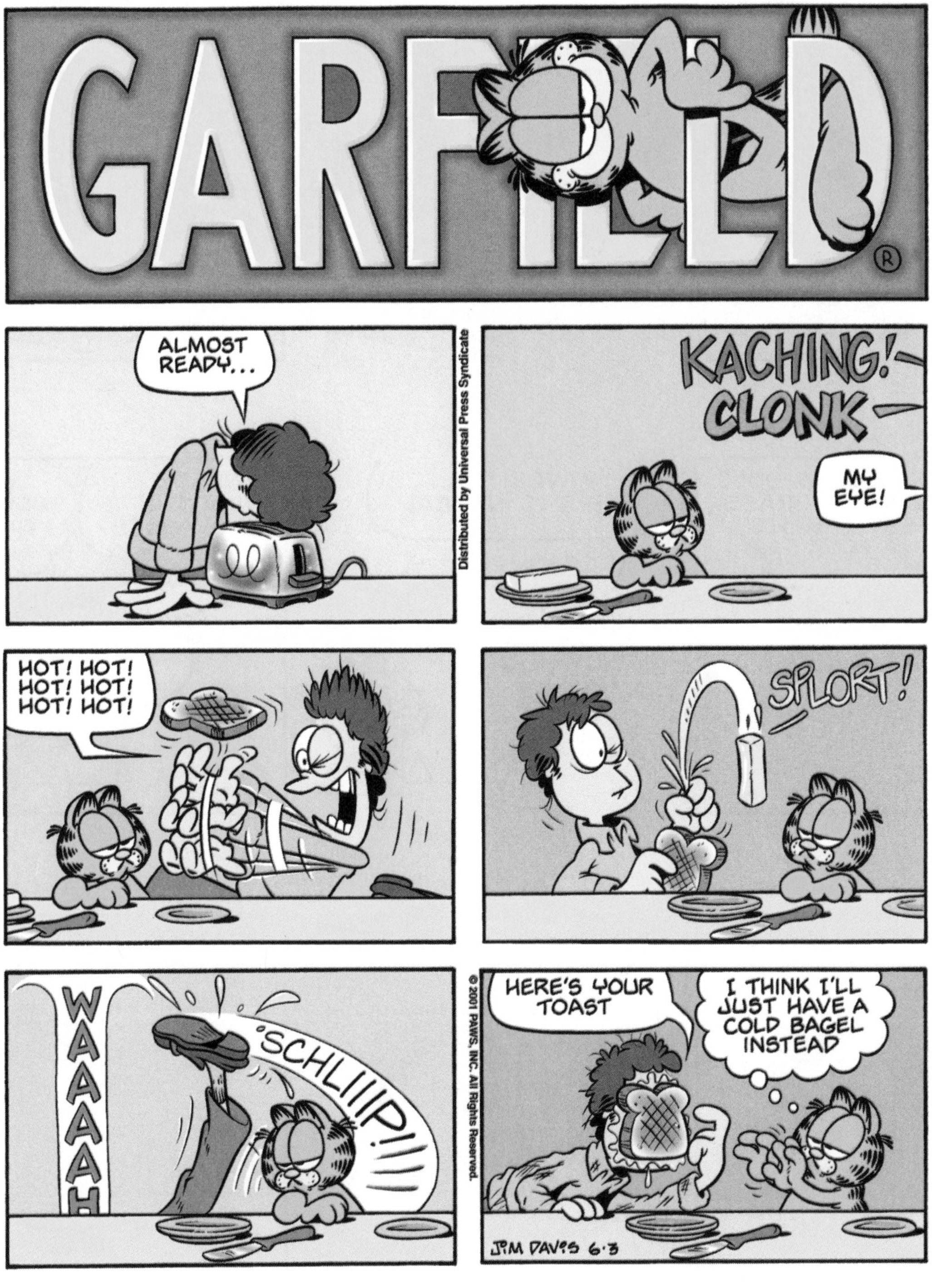
GARFIELD®
ALMOST READY...
Distributed by Universal Press Syndicate
KACHING!
CLONK
MY EYE!
HOT! HOT! HOT! HOT! HOT! HOT!
SPLORT!
WAAAAAH
SCHLIIIP!
© 2001 PAWS, INC. All Rights Reserved.
HERE'S YOUR TOAST
I THINK I'LL JUST HAVE A COLD BAGEL INSTEAD
JIM DAVIS 6-3

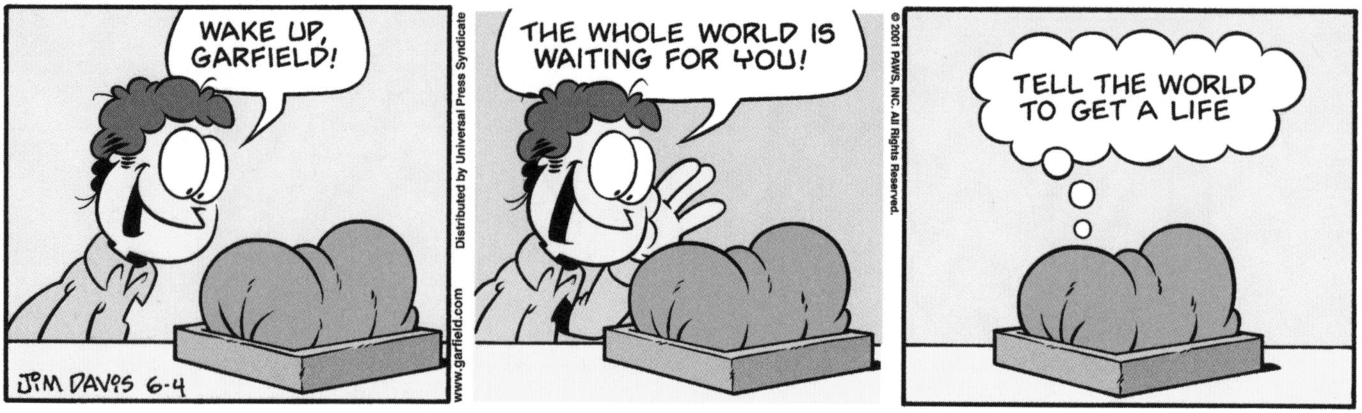
WAKE UP, GARFIELD!
JIM DAVIS 6-4
Distributed by Universal Press Syndicate www.garfield.com
THE WHOLE WORLD IS WAITING FOR YOU!
© 2001 PAWS, INC. All Rights Reserved.
TELL THE WORLD TO GET A LIFE

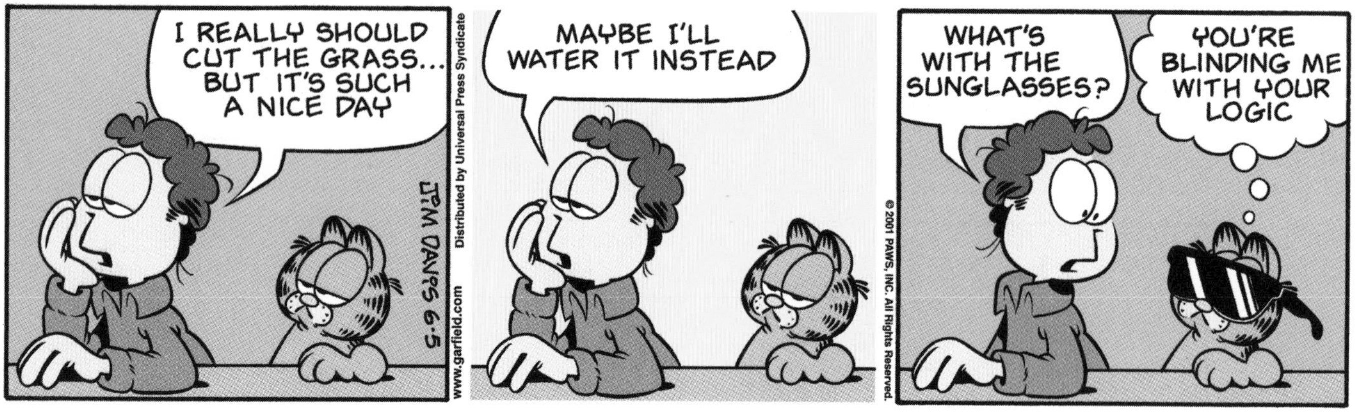
I REALLY SHOULD CUT THE GRASS... BUT IT'S SUCH A NICE DAY
JIM DAVIS 6-5
Distributed by Universal Press Syndicate www.garfield.com
MAYBE I'LL WATER IT INSTEAD
© 2001 PAWS, INC. All Rights Reserved.
WHAT'S WITH THE SUNGLASSES?
YOU'RE BLINDING ME WITH YOUR LOGIC

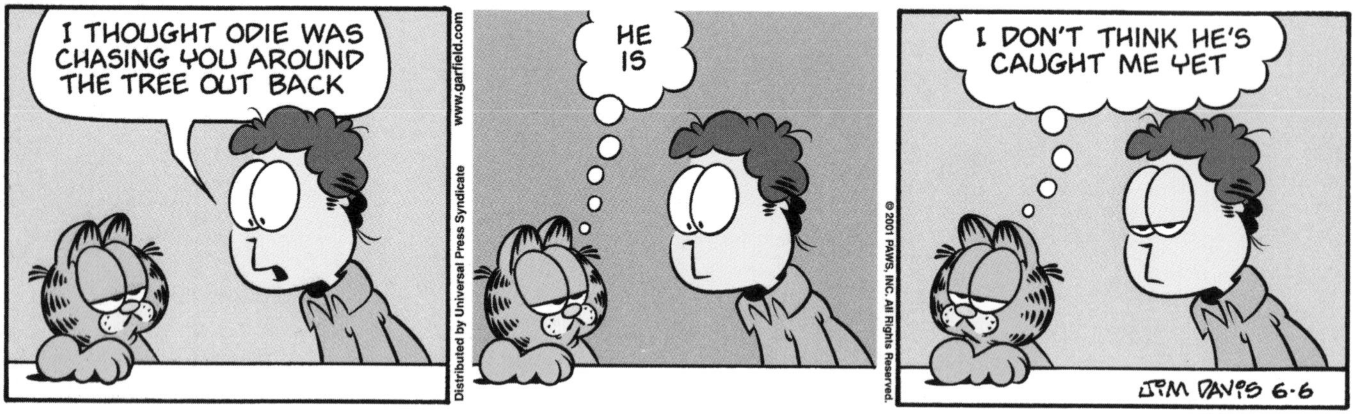
I THOUGHT ODIE WAS CHASING YOU AROUND THE TREE OUT BACK
Distributed by Universal Press Syndicate www.garfield.com
HE IS
© 2001 PAWS, INC. All Rights Reserved.
I DON'T THINK HE'S CAUGHT ME YET
JIM DAVIS 6-6

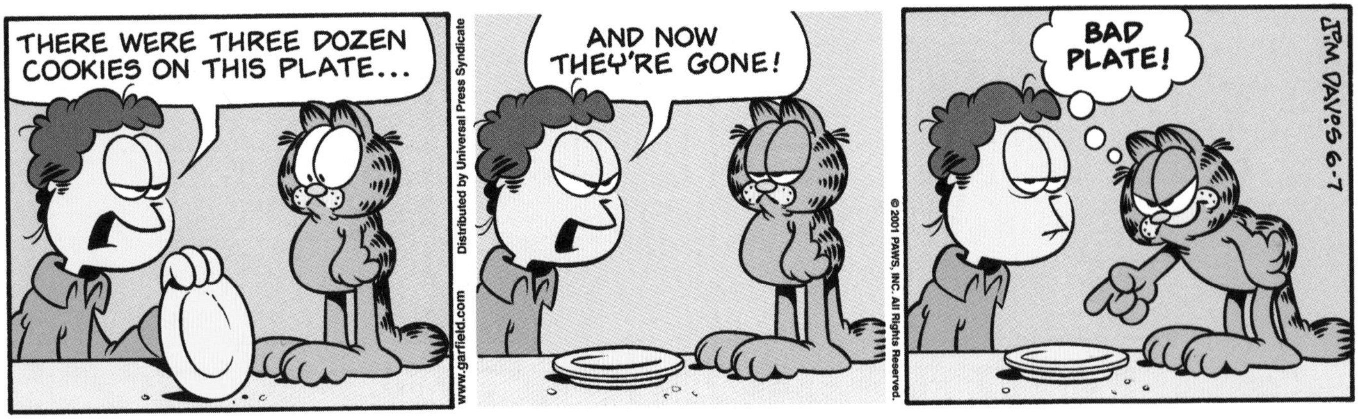
THERE WERE THREE DOZEN COOKIES ON THIS PLATE...
AND NOW THEY'RE GONE!
BAD PLATE!
JIM DAVIS 6-7
www.garfield.com Distributed by Universal Press Syndicate
© 2001 PAWS, INC. All Rights Reserved.

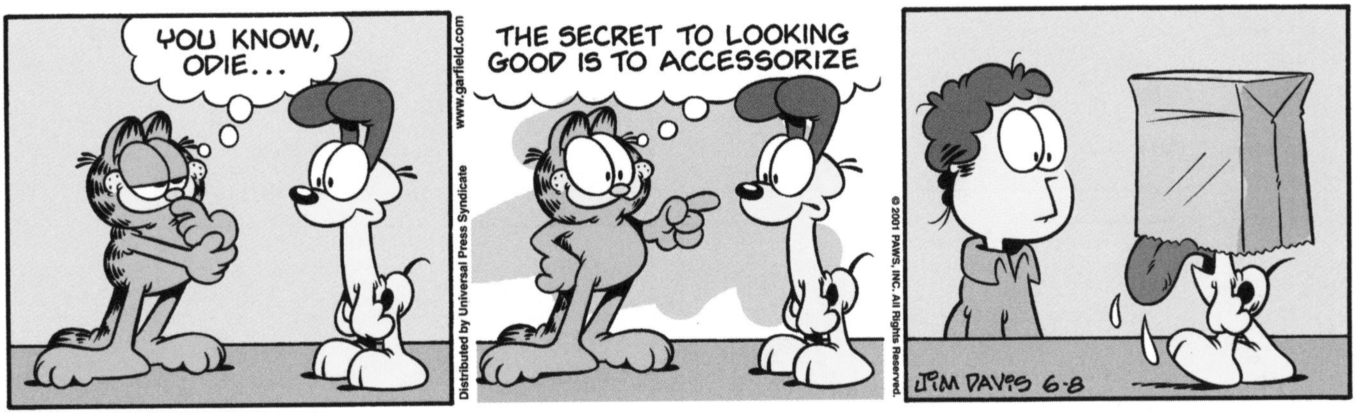
YOU KNOW, ODIE...
THE SECRET TO LOOKING GOOD IS TO ACCESSORIZE
JIM DAVIS 6-8
Distributed by Universal Press Syndicate www.garfield.com
© 2001 PAWS, INC. All Rights Reserved.

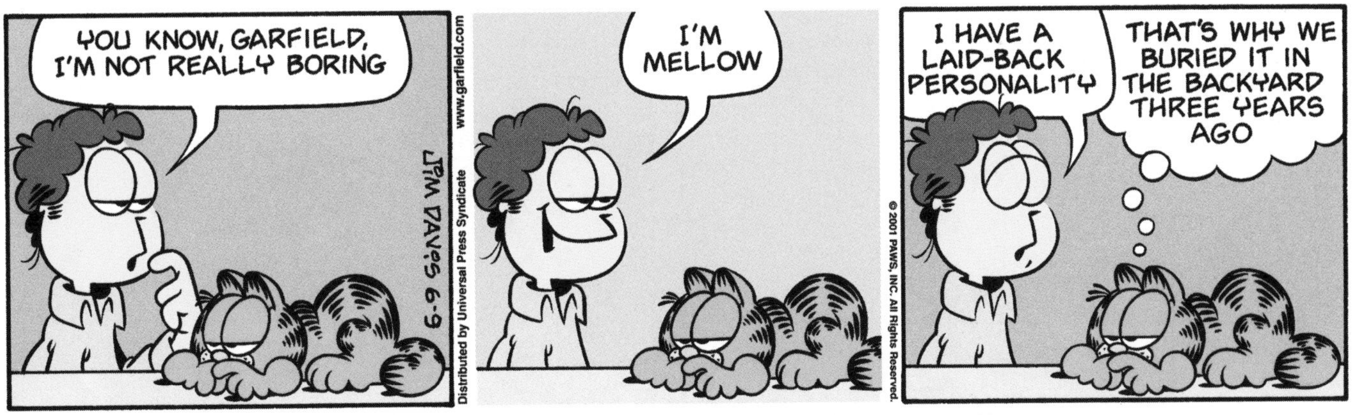
YOU KNOW, GARFIELD, I'M NOT REALLY BORING
I'M MELLOW
I HAVE A LAID-BACK PERSONALITY
THAT'S WHY WE BURIED IT IN THE BACKYARD THREE YEARS AGO
JIM DAVIS 6-9
Distributed by Universal Press Syndicate www.garfield.com
© 2001 PAWS, INC. All Rights Reserved.

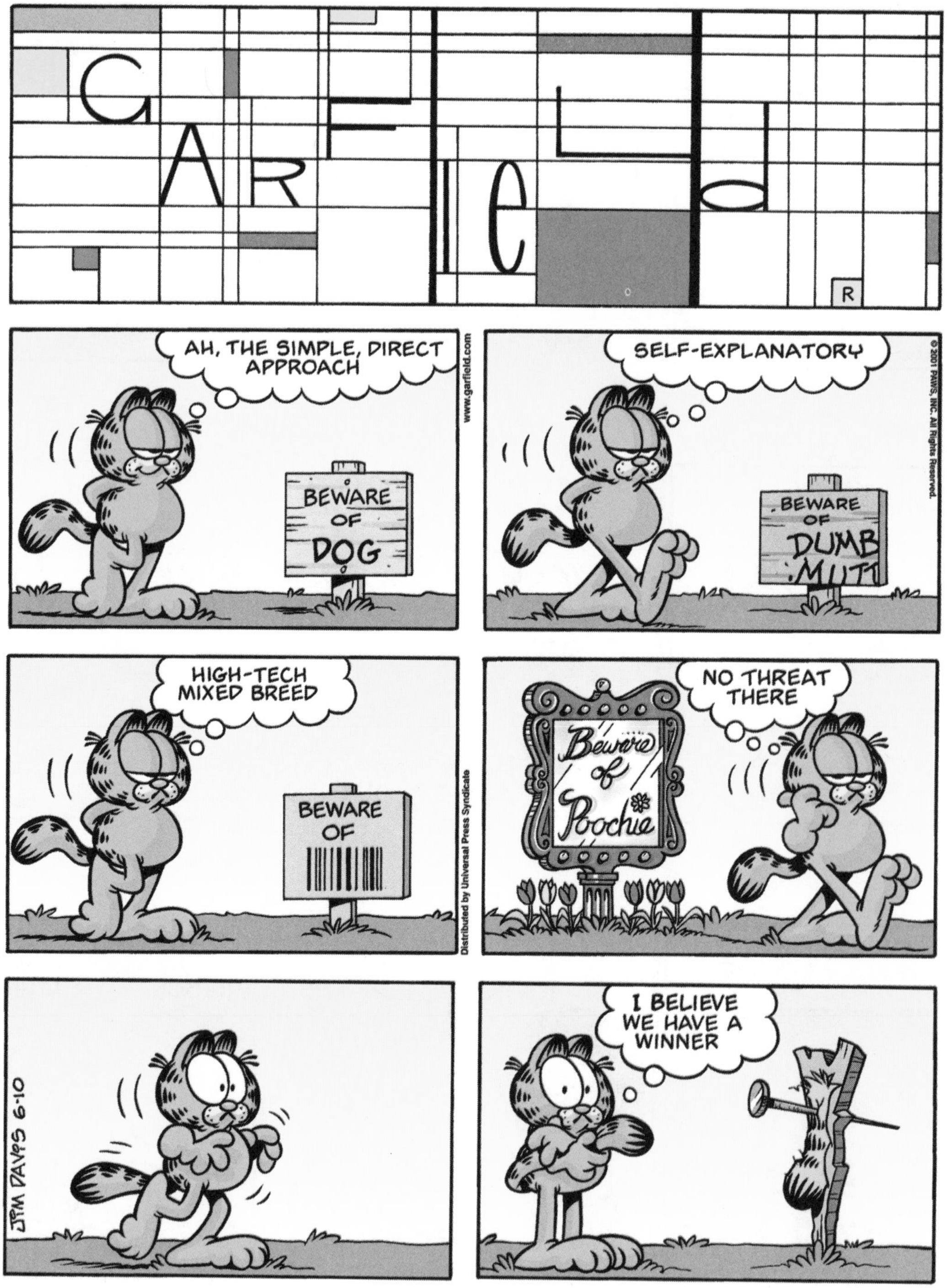
GARFIELD
AH, THE SIMPLE, DIRECT APPROACH
BEWARE OF DOG
www.garfield.com
SELF-EXPLANATORY
BEWARE OF DUMB MUTT
© 2001 PAWS, INC. All Rights Reserved.
HIGH-TECH MIXED BREED
BEWARE OF
Distributed by Universal Press Syndicate
NO THREAT THERE
Beware of Poochie
JPM DAVPS 6-10
I BELIEVE WE HAVE A WINNER

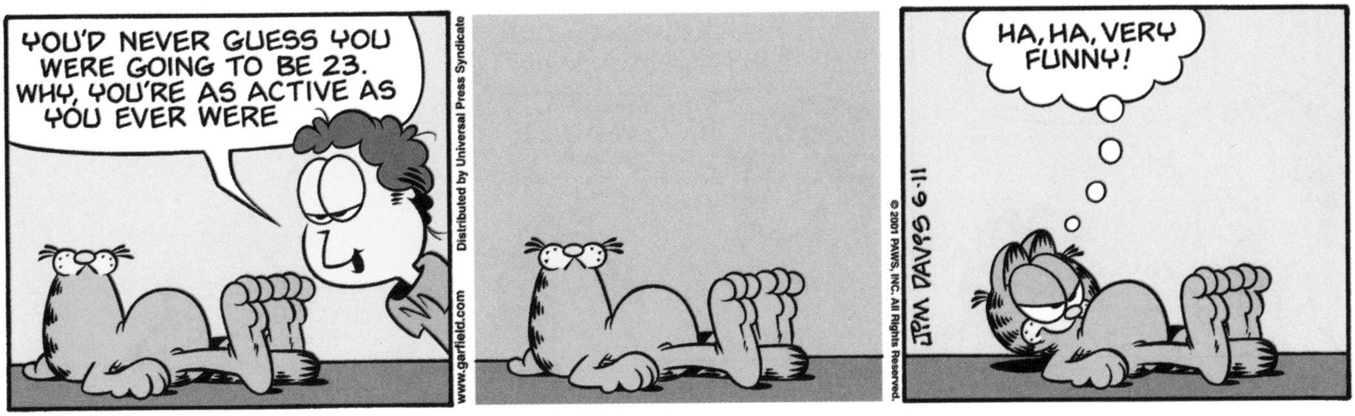
YOU'D NEVER GUESS YOU WERE GOING TO BE 23. WHY, YOU'RE AS ACTIVE AS YOU EVER WERE
HA, HA, VERY FUNNY!
JIM DAVIS 6-11
www.garfield.com Distributed by Universal Press Syndicate
© 2001 PAWS, INC. All Rights Reserved.

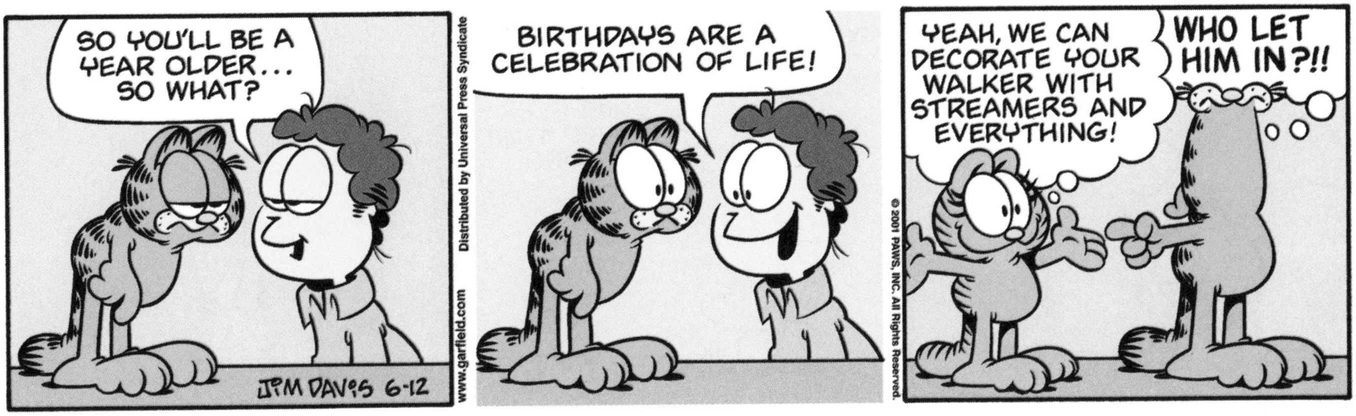
SO YOU'LL BE A YEAR OLDER... SO WHAT?
BIRTHDAYS ARE A CELEBRATION OF LIFE!
YEAH, WE CAN DECORATE YOUR WALKER WITH STREAMERS AND EVERYTHING!
WHO LET HIM IN?!!
JIM DAVIS 6-12
www.garfield.com Distributed by Universal Press Syndicate
© 2001 PAWS, INC. All Rights Reserved.

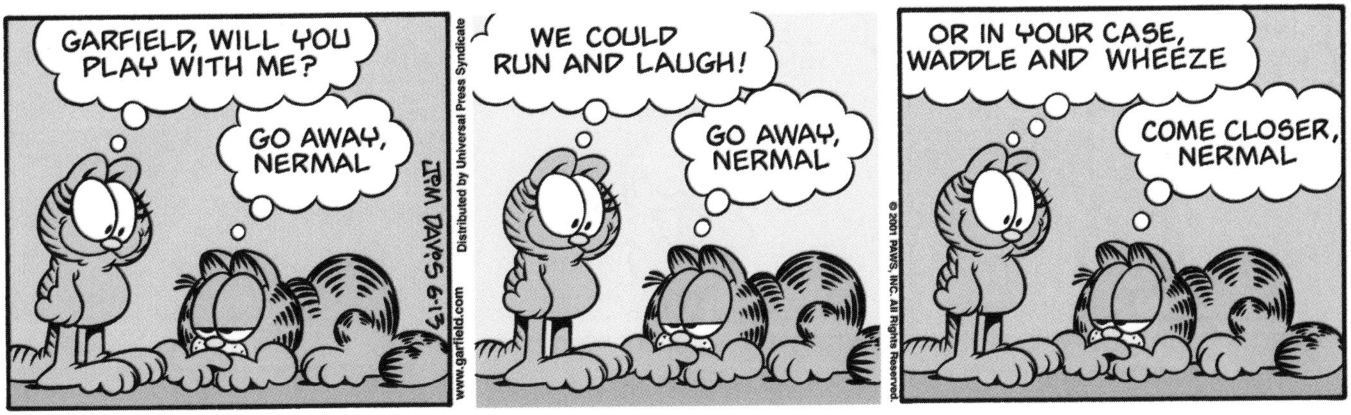
GARFIELD, WILL YOU PLAY WITH ME?
GO AWAY, NERMAL
WE COULD RUN AND LAUGH!
GO AWAY, NERMAL
OR IN YOUR CASE, WADDLE AND WHEEZE
COME CLOSER, NERMAL
JIM DAVIS 6-13
www.garfield.com Distributed by Universal Press Syndicate
© 2001 PAWS, INC. All Rights Reserved.

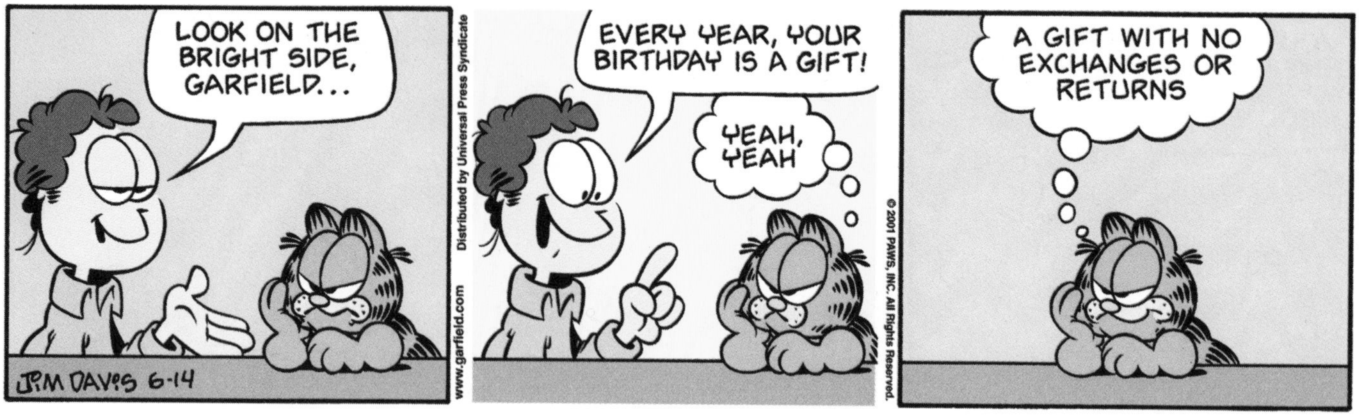
LOOK ON THE BRIGHT SIDE, GARFIELD...
JIM DAVIS 6-14
EVERY YEAR, YOUR BIRTHDAY IS A GIFT!
YEAH, YEAH
A GIFT WITH NO EXCHANGES OR RETURNS
www.garfield.com Distributed by Universal Press Syndicate
© 2001 PAWS, INC. All Rights Reserved.

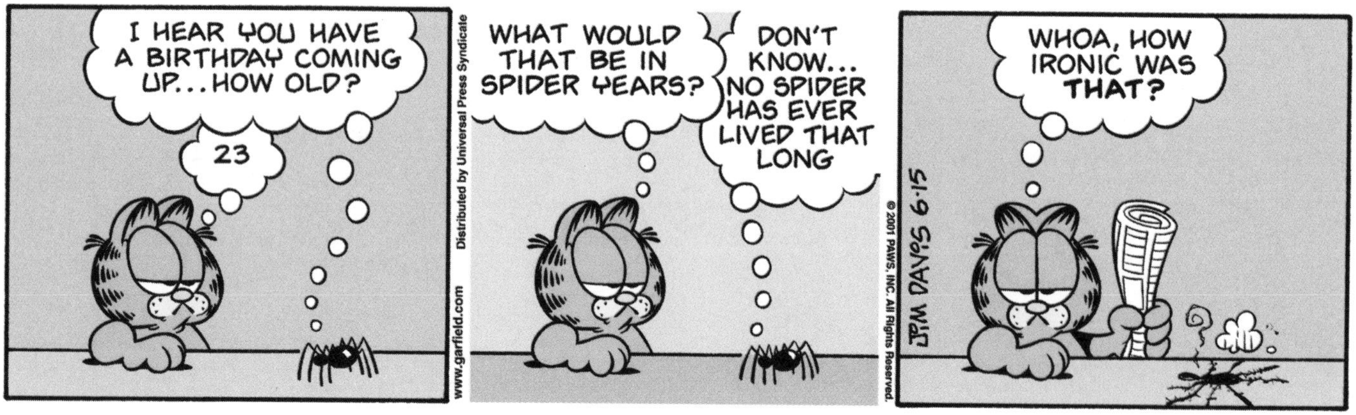
I HEAR YOU HAVE A BIRTHDAY COMING UP...HOW OLD?
23
WHAT WOULD THAT BE IN SPIDER YEARS?
DON'T KNOW... NO SPIDER HAS EVER LIVED THAT LONG
WHOA, HOW IRONIC WAS **THAT?**
JIM DAVIS 6-15
www.garfield.com Distributed by Universal Press Syndicate
© 2001 PAWS, INC. All Rights Reserved.

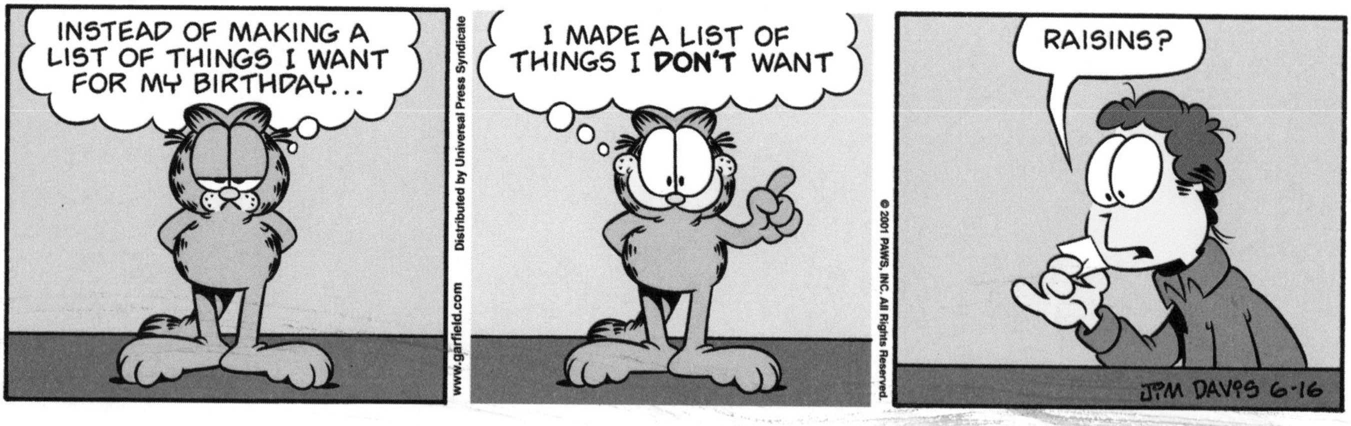
INSTEAD OF MAKING A LIST OF THINGS I WANT FOR MY BIRTHDAY...
I MADE A LIST OF THINGS I **DON'T** WANT
RAISINS?
JIM DAVIS 6-16
www.garfield.com Distributed by Universal Press Syndicate
© 2001 PAWS, INC. All Rights Reserved.

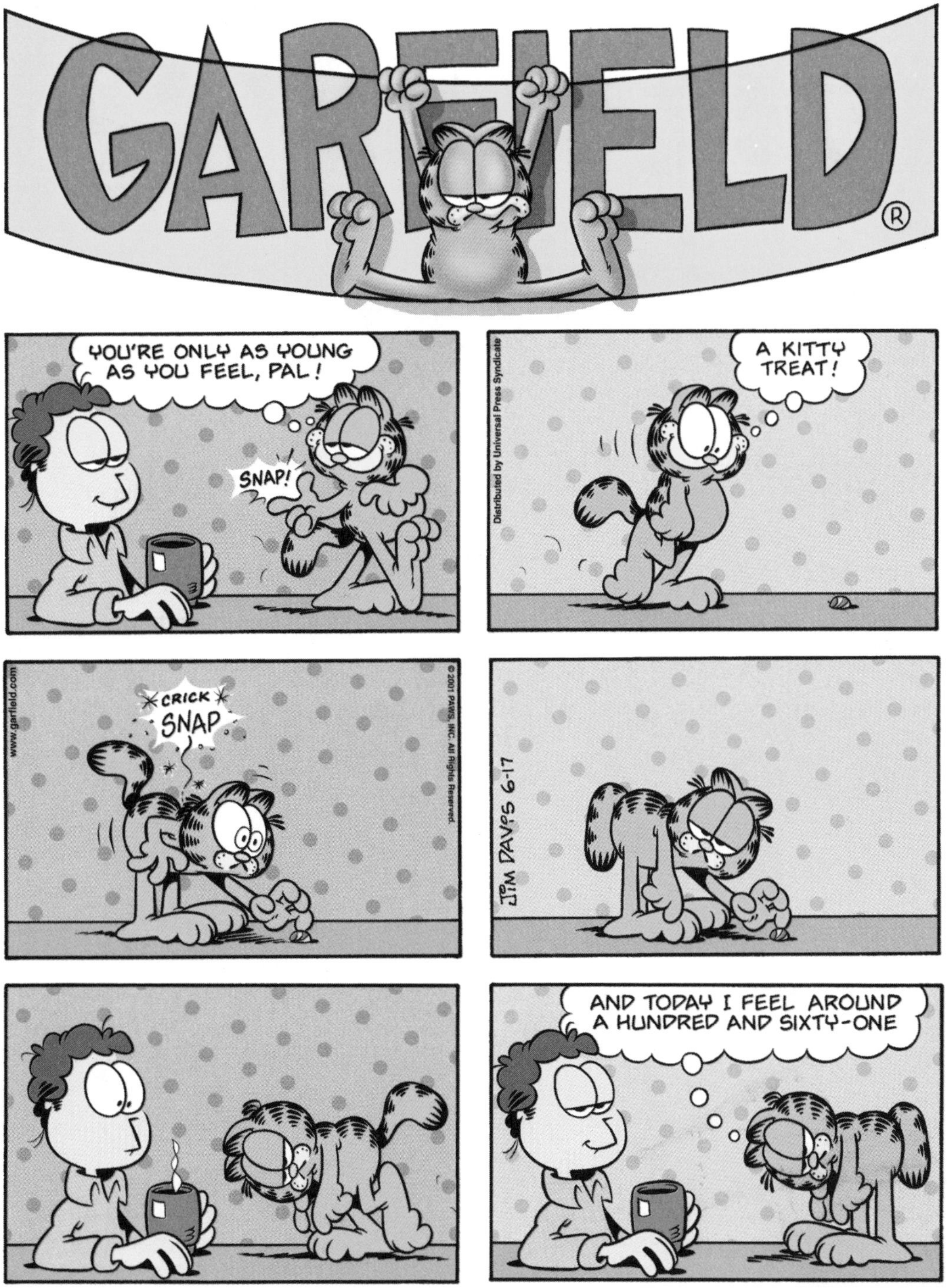
GARFIELD®
YOU'RE ONLY AS YOUNG AS YOU FEEL, PAL!
SNAP!
Distributed by Universal Press Syndicate
A KITTY TREAT!
www.garfield.com
CRICK SNAP
© 2001 PAWS, INC. All Rights Reserved.
JIM DAVIS 6-17
AND TODAY I FEEL AROUND A HUNDRED AND SIXTY-ONE

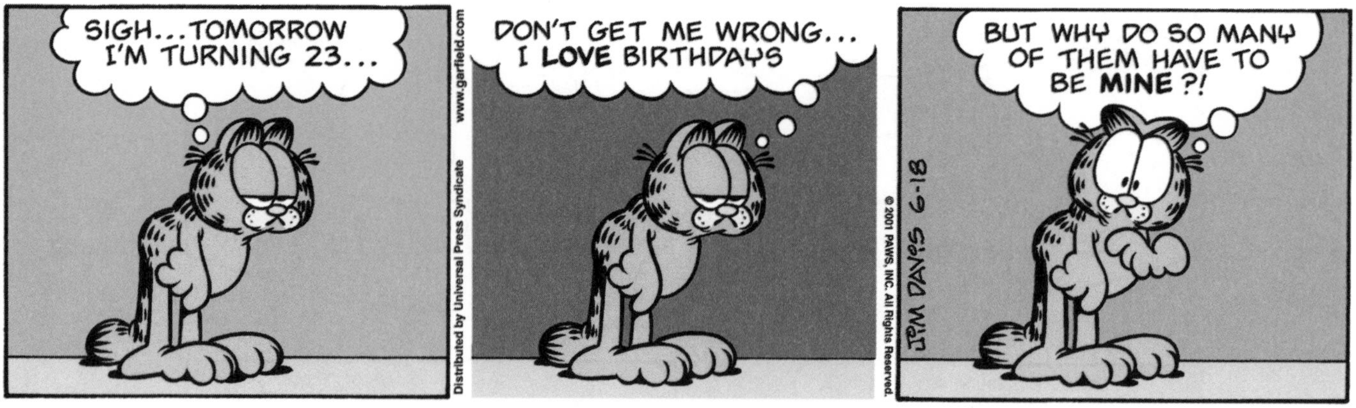
SIGH...TOMORROW I'M TURNING 23...
DON'T GET ME WRONG... I **LOVE** BIRTHDAYS
BUT WHY DO SO MANY OF THEM HAVE TO BE **MINE** ?!
Distributed by Universal Press Syndicate www.garfield.com
© 2001 PAWS, INC. All Rights Reserved.
JIM DAVIS 6-18

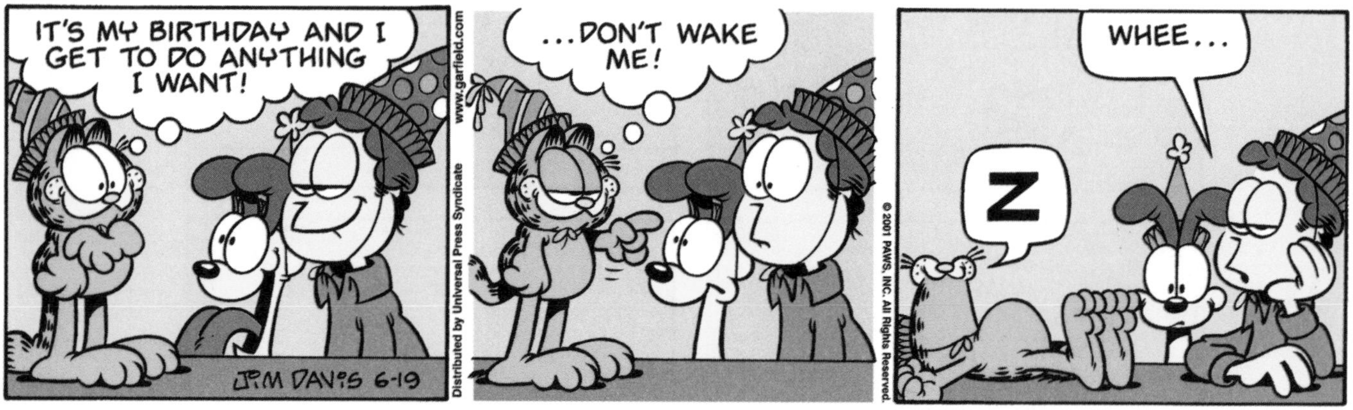
IT'S MY BIRTHDAY AND I GET TO DO ANYTHING I WANT!
...DON'T WAKE ME!
Z
WHEE...
JIM DAVIS 6-19
Distributed by Universal Press Syndicate www.garfield.com
© 2001 PAWS, INC. All Rights Reserved.

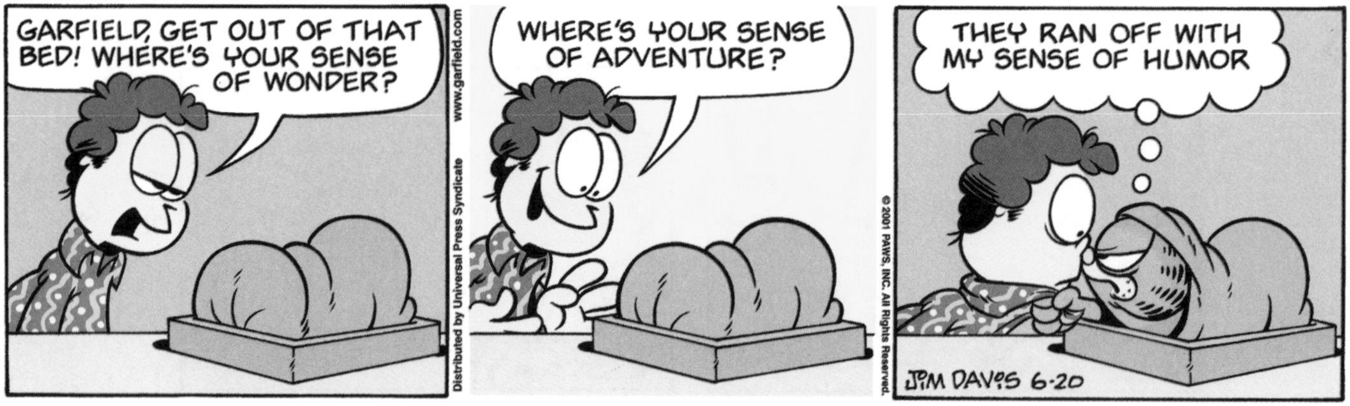
GARFIELD, GET OUT OF THAT BED! WHERE'S YOUR SENSE OF WONDER?
WHERE'S YOUR SENSE OF ADVENTURE?
THEY RAN OFF WITH MY SENSE OF HUMOR
Distributed by Universal Press Syndicate www.garfield.com
© 2001 PAWS, INC. All Rights Reserved.
JIM DAVIS 6-20

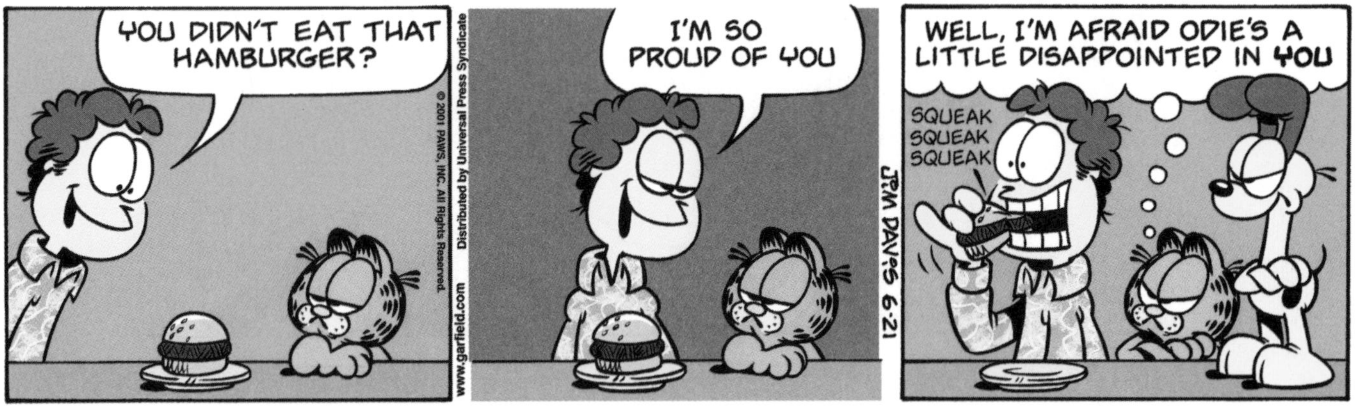
YOU DIDN'T EAT THAT HAMBURGER?
© 2001 PAWS, INC. All Rights Reserved.
Distributed by Universal Press Syndicate
www.garfield.com
I'M SO PROUD OF YOU
JIM DAVIS 6-21
WELL, I'M AFRAID ODIE'S A LITTLE DISAPPOINTED IN **YOU**
SQUEAK SQUEAK SQUEAK

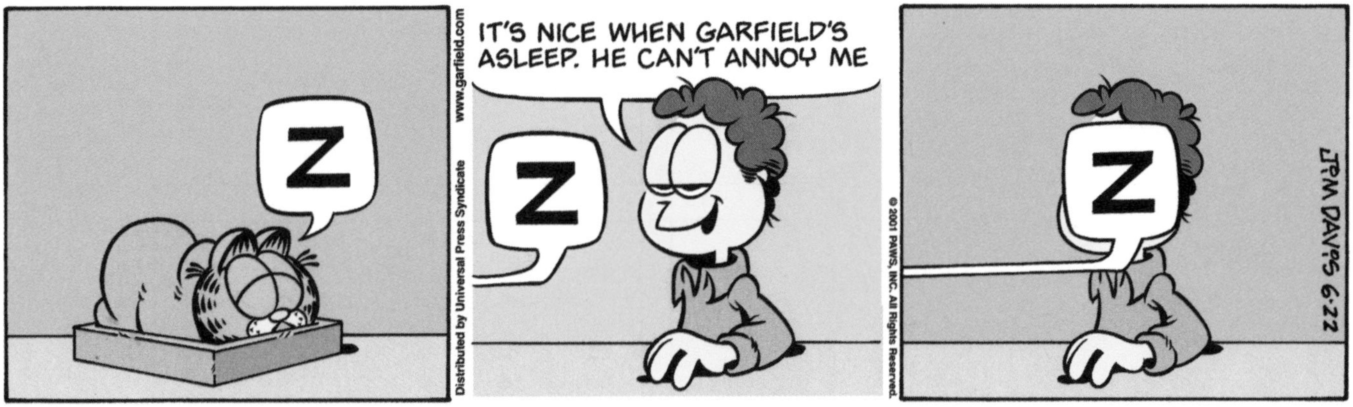
Z
Distributed by Universal Press Syndicate
www.garfield.com
IT'S NICE WHEN GARFIELD'S ASLEEP. HE CAN'T ANNOY ME
Z
© 2001 PAWS, INC. All Rights Reserved.
Z
JIM DAVIS 6-22

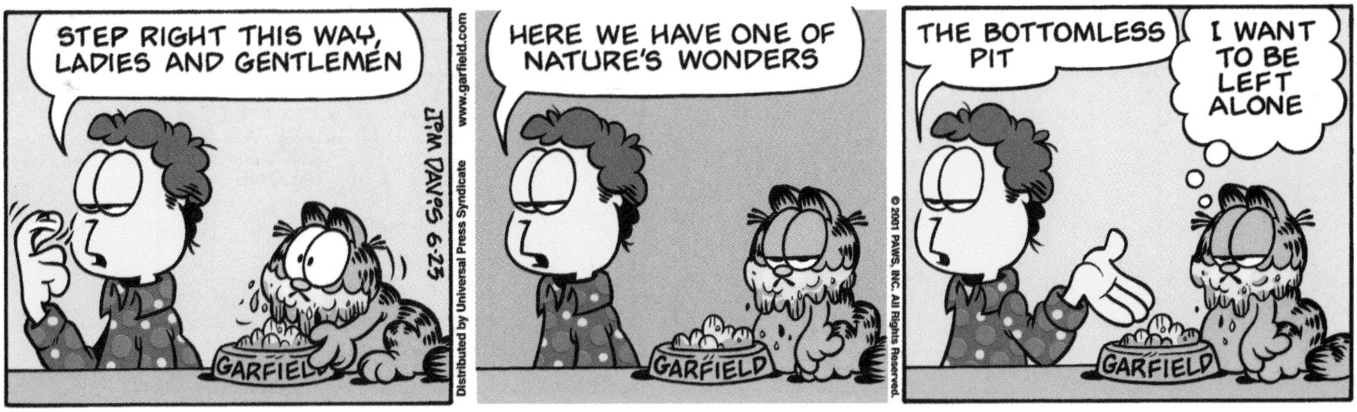
STEP RIGHT THIS WAY, LADIES AND GENTLEMEN
JIM DAVIS 6-23
GARFIELD
Distributed by Universal Press Syndicate
www.garfield.com
HERE WE HAVE ONE OF NATURE'S WONDERS
GARFIELD
© 2001 PAWS, INC. All Rights Reserved.
THE BOTTOMLESS PIT
I WANT TO BE LEFT ALONE
GARFIELD

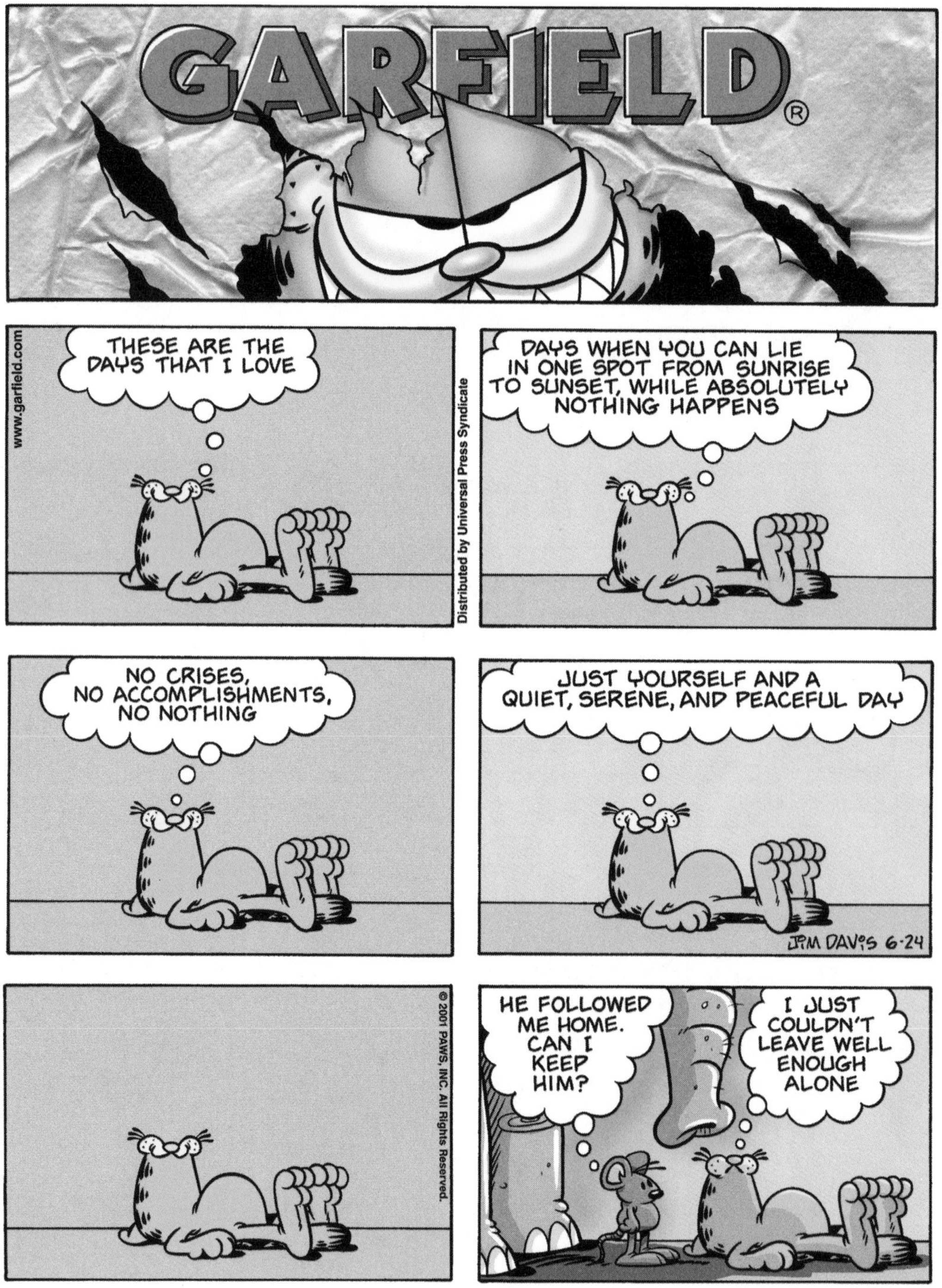
GARFIELD®
www.garfield.com
THESE ARE THE DAYS THAT I LOVE
Distributed by Universal Press Syndicate
DAYS WHEN YOU CAN LIE IN ONE SPOT FROM SUNRISE TO SUNSET, WHILE ABSOLUTELY NOTHING HAPPENS
NO CRISES, NO ACCOMPLISHMENTS, NO NOTHING
JUST YOURSELF AND A QUIET, SERENE, AND PEACEFUL DAY
JIM DAVIS 6-24
© 2001 PAWS, INC. All Rights Reserved.
HE FOLLOWED ME HOME. CAN I KEEP HIM?
I JUST COULDN'T LEAVE WELL ENOUGH ALONE

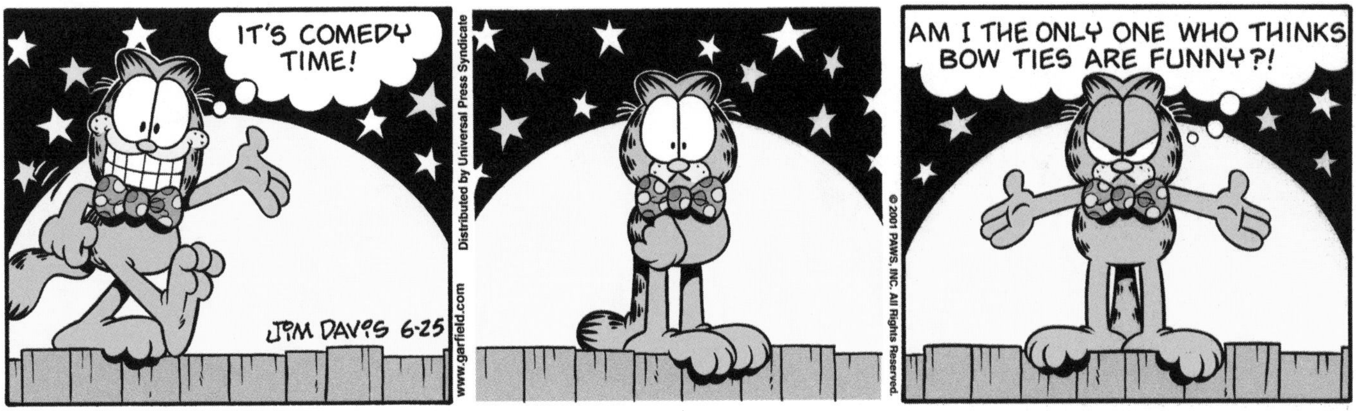
IT'S COMEDY TIME!
JIM DAVIS 6-25
Distributed by Universal Press Syndicate
www.garfield.com
© 2001 PAWS, INC. All Rights Reserved.
AM I THE ONLY ONE WHO THINKS BOW TIES ARE FUNNY?!

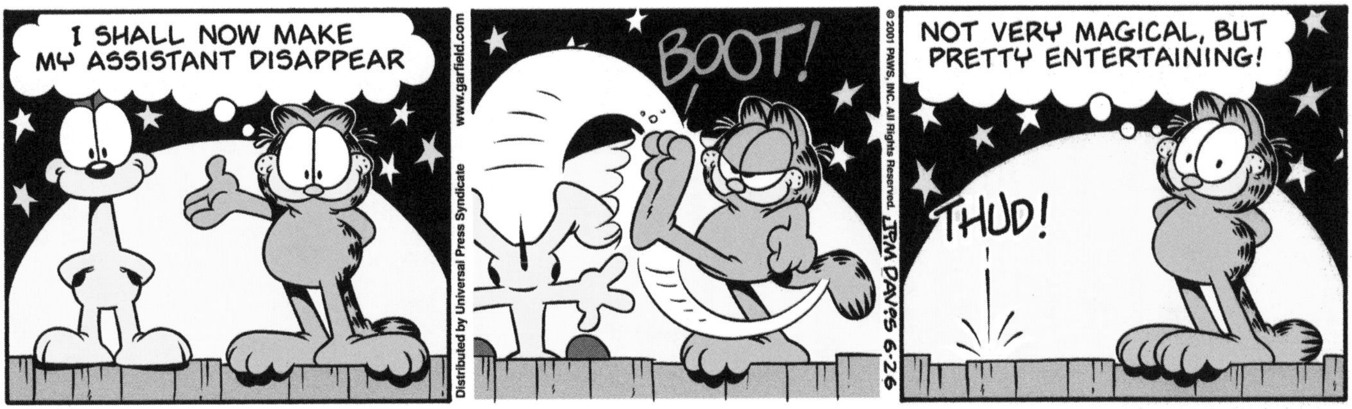
I SHALL NOW MAKE MY ASSISTANT DISAPPEAR
Distributed by Universal Press Syndicate
www.garfield.com
BOOT!
© 2001 PAWS, INC. All Rights Reserved.
JIM DAVIS 6-26
NOT VERY MAGICAL, BUT PRETTY ENTERTAINING!
THUD!

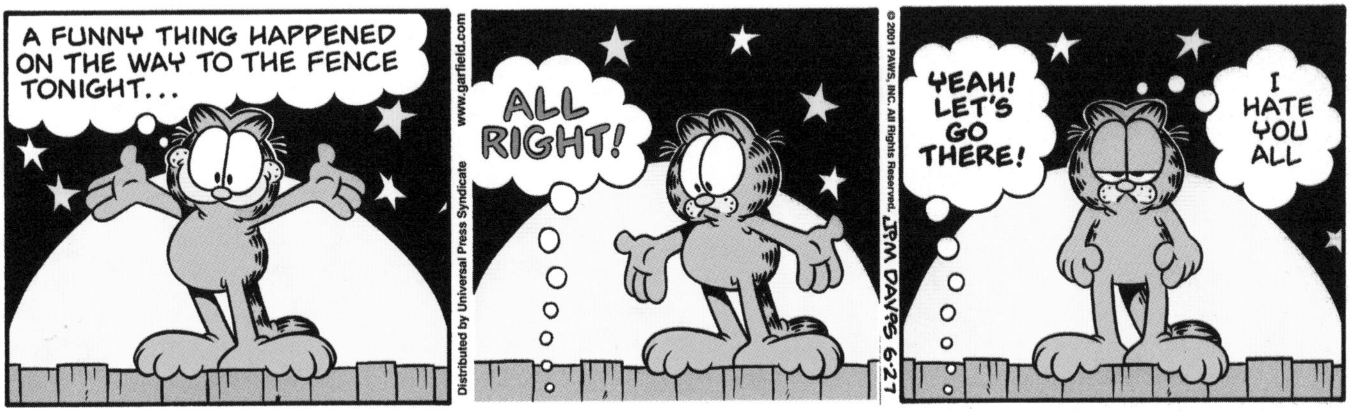
A FUNNY THING HAPPENED ON THE WAY TO THE FENCE TONIGHT...
Distributed by Universal Press Syndicate
www.garfield.com
ALL RIGHT!
© 2001 PAWS, INC. All Rights Reserved.
JIM DAVIS 6-27
YEAH! LET'S GO THERE!
I HATE YOU ALL

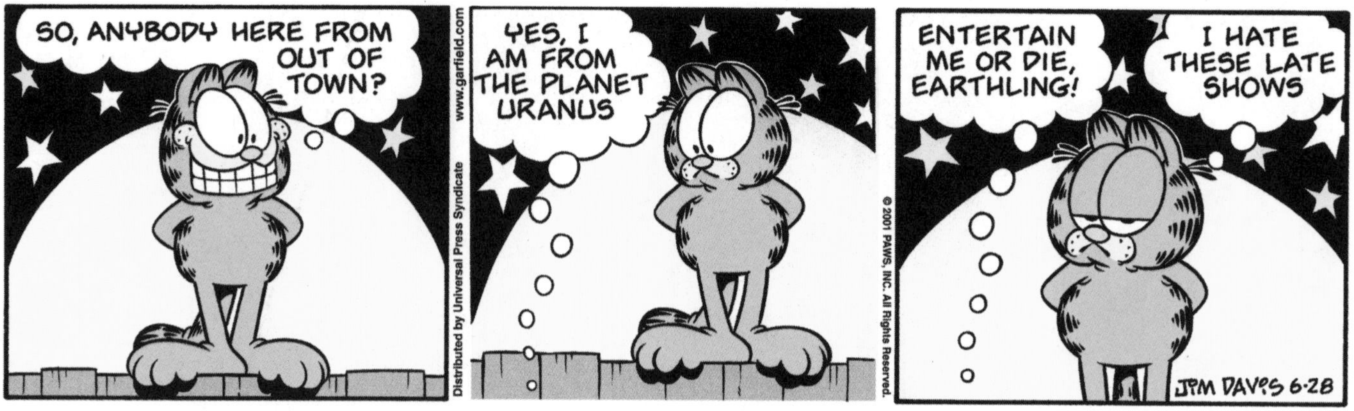
SO, ANYBODY HERE FROM OUT OF TOWN?
YES, I AM FROM THE PLANET URANUS
ENTERTAIN ME OR DIE, EARTHLING!
I HATE THESE LATE SHOWS
JIM DAVIS 6-28
Distributed by Universal Press Syndicate www.garfield.com
© 2001 PAWS, INC. All Rights Reserved.

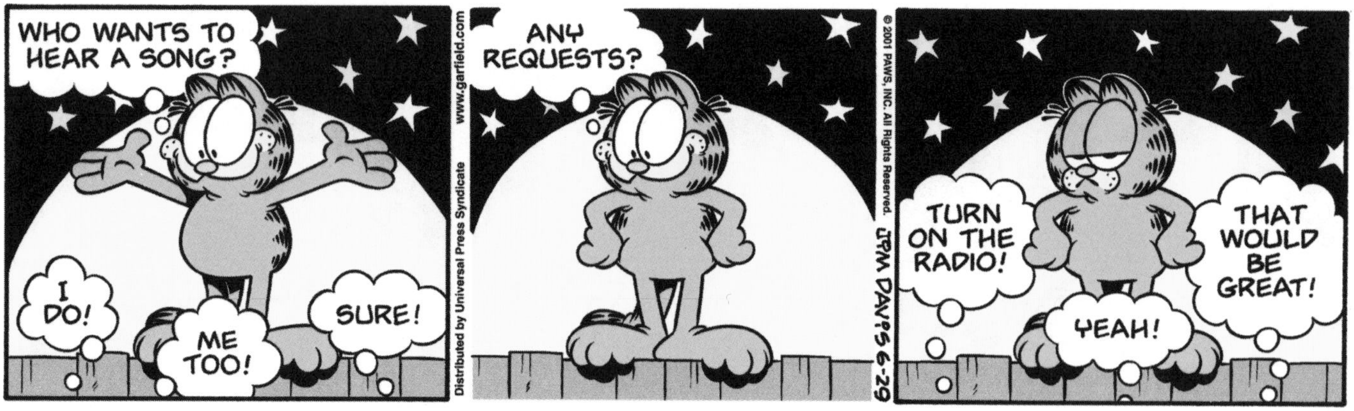
WHO WANTS TO HEAR A SONG?
I DO!
ME TOO!
SURE!
ANY REQUESTS?
TURN ON THE RADIO!
YEAH!
THAT WOULD BE GREAT!
JIM DAVIS 6-29
Distributed by Universal Press Syndicate www.garfield.com
© 2001 PAWS, INC. All Rights Reserved.

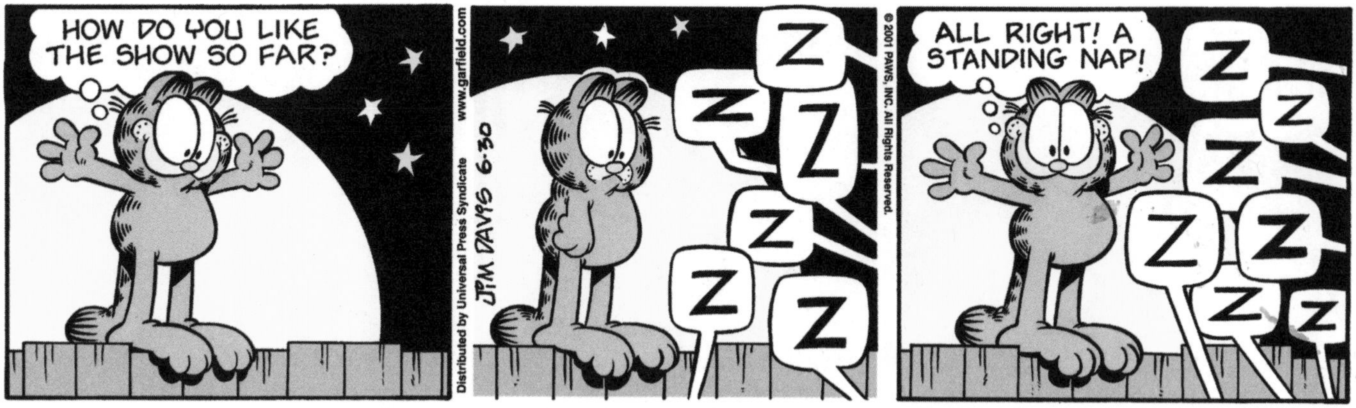
HOW DO YOU LIKE THE SHOW SO FAR?
Z Z Z Z Z Z
ALL RIGHT! A STANDING NAP!
Z Z Z Z Z Z Z
JIM DAVIS 6-30
Distributed by Universal Press Syndicate www.garfield.com
© 2001 PAWS, INC. All Rights Reserved.

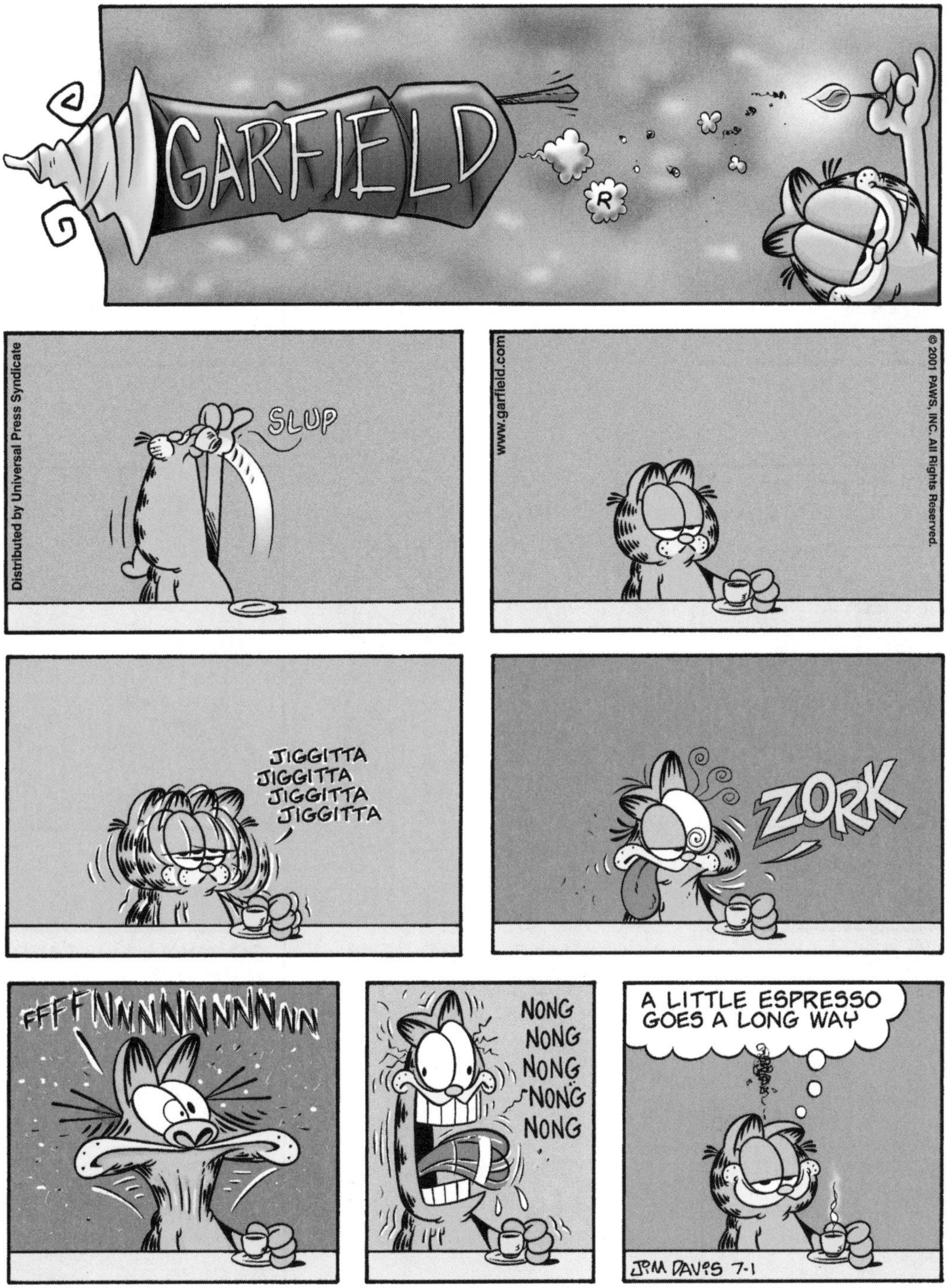
GARFIELD
R
Distributed by Universal Press Syndicate
SLUP
www.garfield.com
© 2001 PAWS, INC. All Rights Reserved.
JIGGITTA
JIGGITTA
JIGGITTA
JIGGITTA
ZORK
FFFFNNNNNNNNNNNN
NONG
NONG
NONG
NONG
NONG
A LITTLE ESPRESSO GOES A LONG WAY
JIM DAVIS 7-1

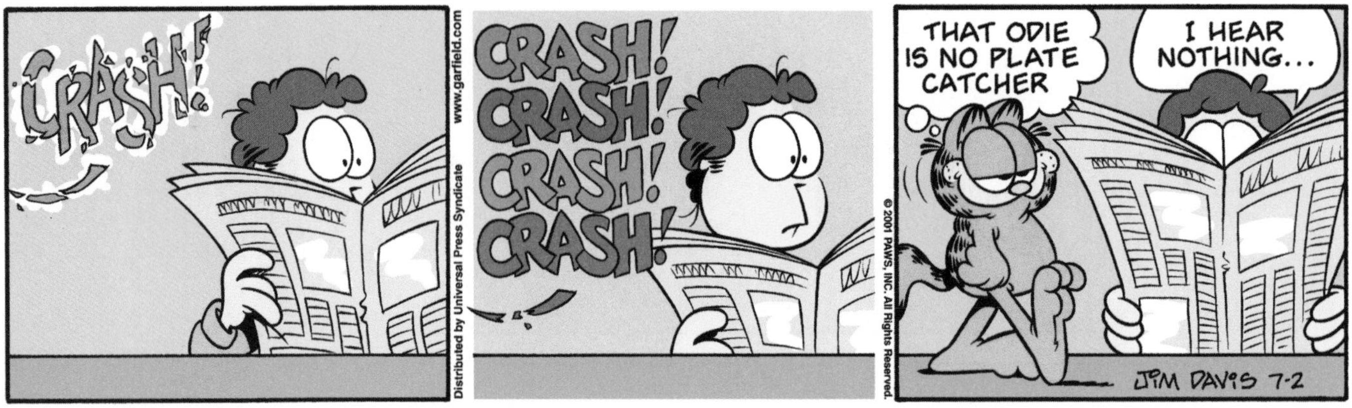
CRASH!
CRASH! CRASH! CRASH! CRASH!
THAT ODIE IS NO PLATE CATCHER
I HEAR NOTHING...
www.garfield.com
Distributed by Universal Press Syndicate
© 2001 PAWS, INC. All Rights Reserved.
JIM DAVIS 7-2

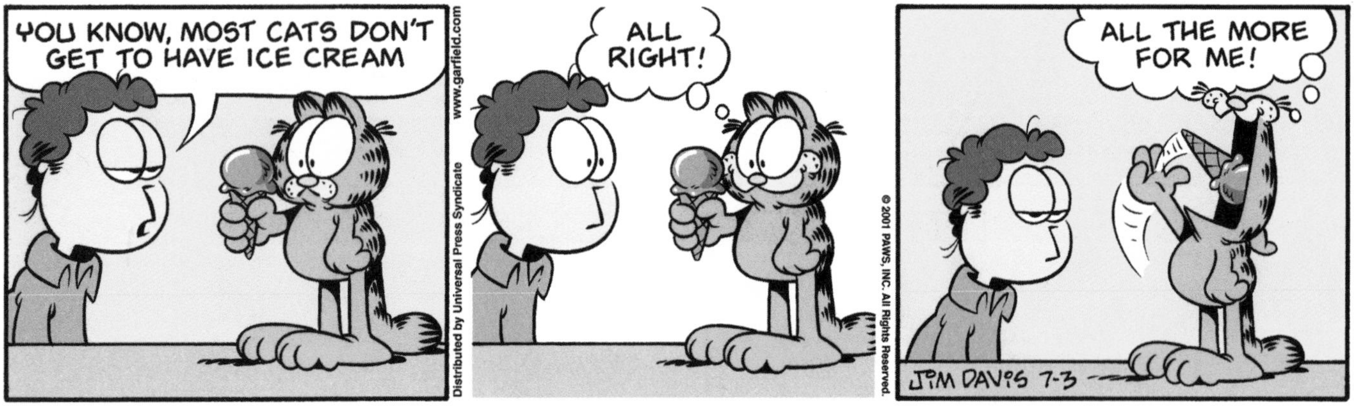
YOU KNOW, MOST CATS DON'T GET TO HAVE ICE CREAM
ALL RIGHT!
ALL THE MORE FOR ME!
www.garfield.com
Distributed by Universal Press Syndicate
© 2001 PAWS, INC. All Rights Reserved.
JIM DAVIS 7-3

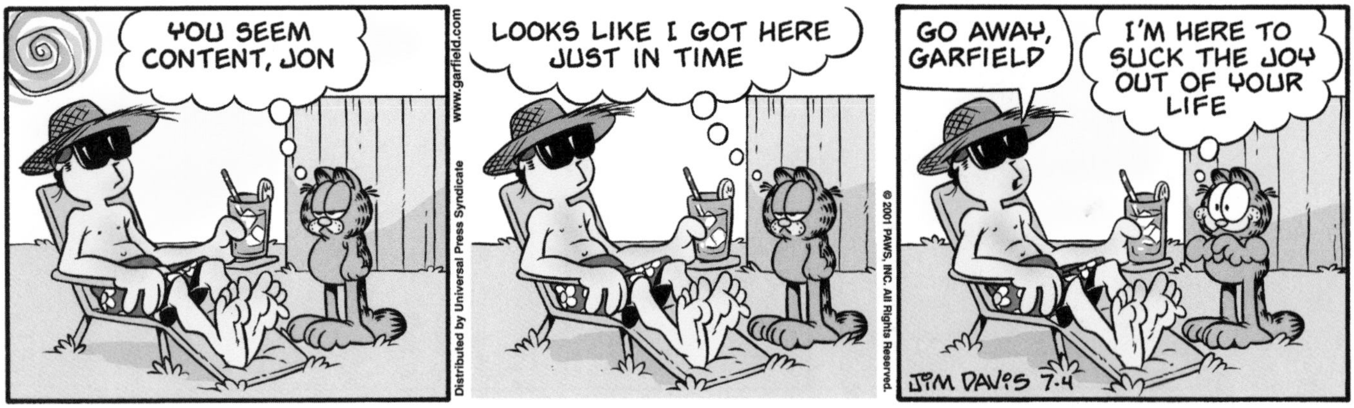
YOU SEEM CONTENT, JON
LOOKS LIKE I GOT HERE JUST IN TIME
GO AWAY, GARFIELD
I'M HERE TO SUCK THE JOY OUT OF YOUR LIFE
www.garfield.com
Distributed by Universal Press Syndicate
© 2001 PAWS, INC. All Rights Reserved.
JIM DAVIS 7-4

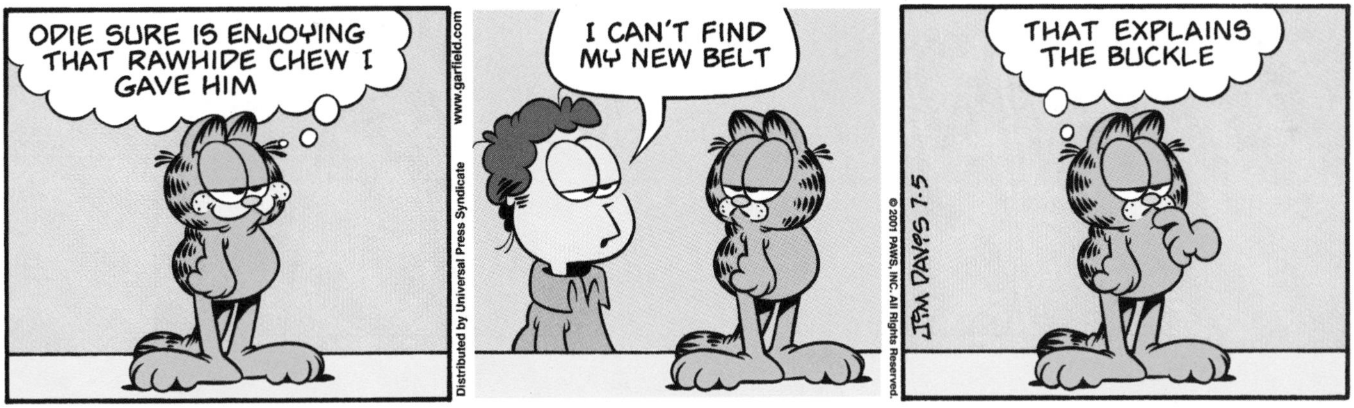
ODIE SURE IS ENJOYING THAT RAWHIDE CHEW I GAVE HIM
Distributed by Universal Press Syndicate www.garfield.com
I CAN'T FIND MY NEW BELT
© 2001 PAWS, INC. All Rights Reserved.
JIM DAVIS 7-5
THAT EXPLAINS THE BUCKLE

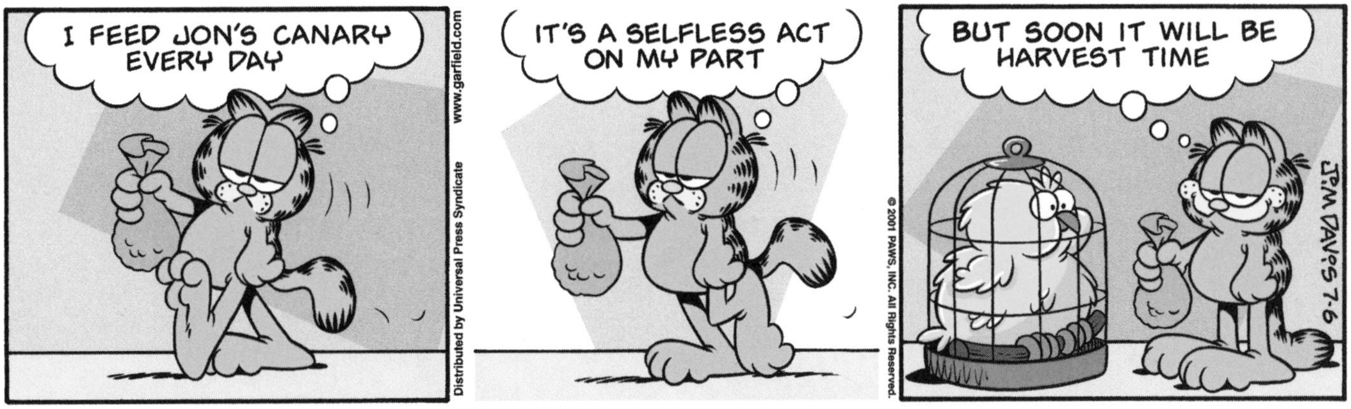
I FEED JON'S CANARY EVERY DAY
Distributed by Universal Press Syndicate www.garfield.com
IT'S A SELFLESS ACT ON MY PART
© 2001 PAWS, INC. All Rights Reserved.
BUT SOON IT WILL BE HARVEST TIME
JIM DAVIS 7-6

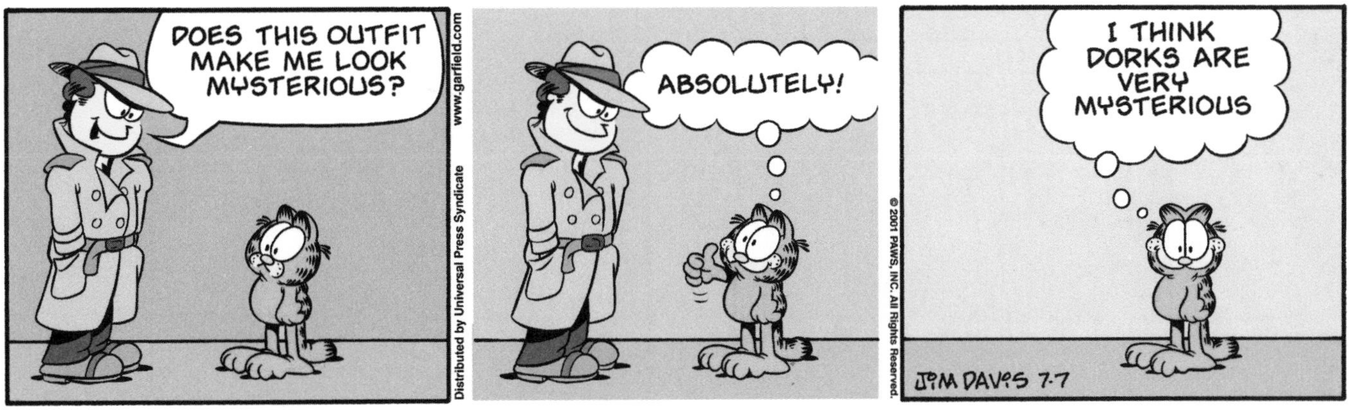
DOES THIS OUTFIT MAKE ME LOOK MYSTERIOUS?
Distributed by Universal Press Syndicate www.garfield.com
ABSOLUTELY!
© 2001 PAWS, INC. All Rights Reserved.
I THINK DORKS ARE VERY MYSTERIOUS
JIM DAVIS 7-7

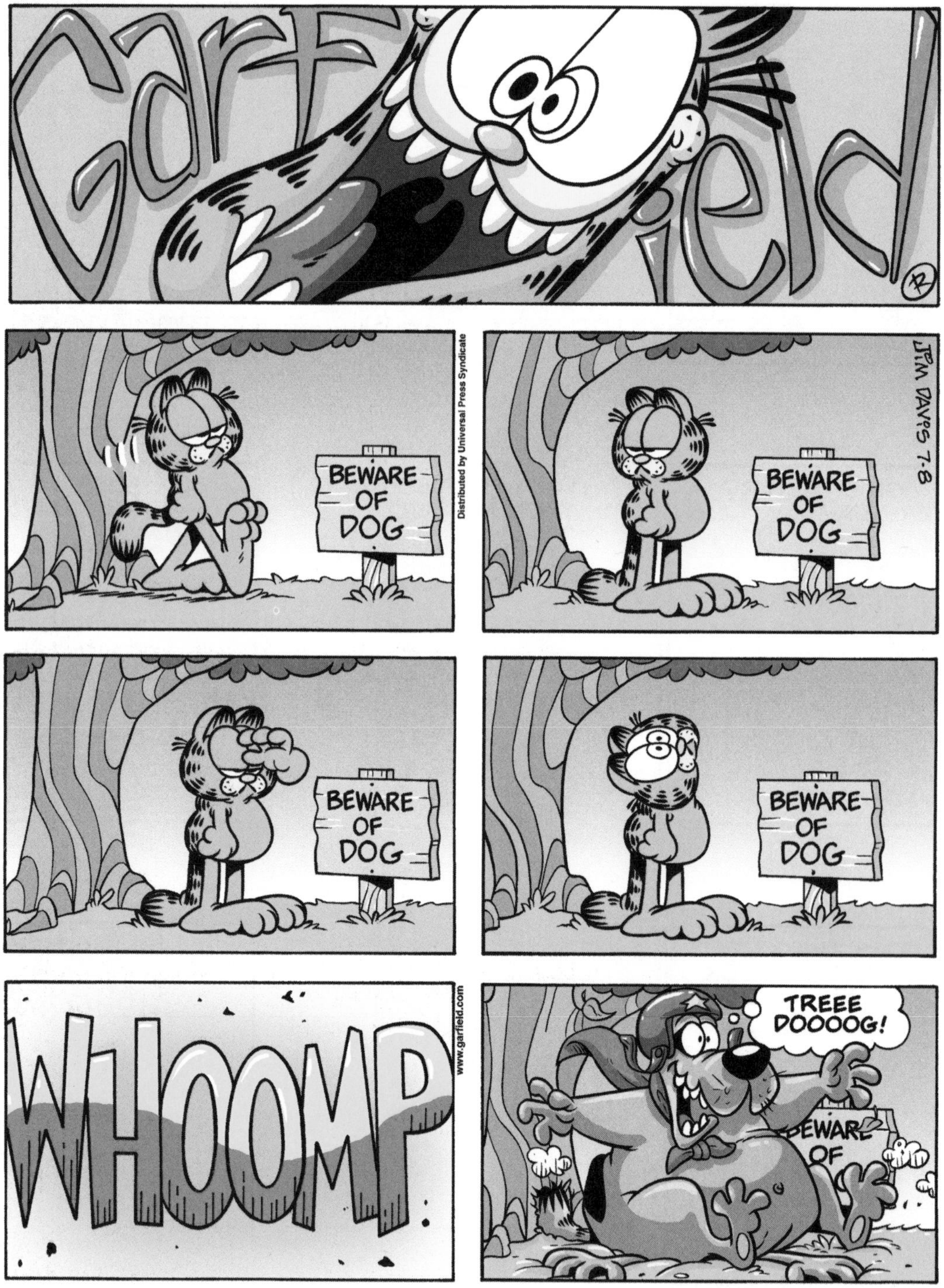
Garfield
JIM DAVIS 7-8
Distributed by Universal Press Syndicate
BEWARE OF DOG
BEWARE OF DOG
BEWARE OF DOG
BEWARE OF DOG
WHOOMP
www.garfield.com
TREEE DOOOOG!
BEWARE OF

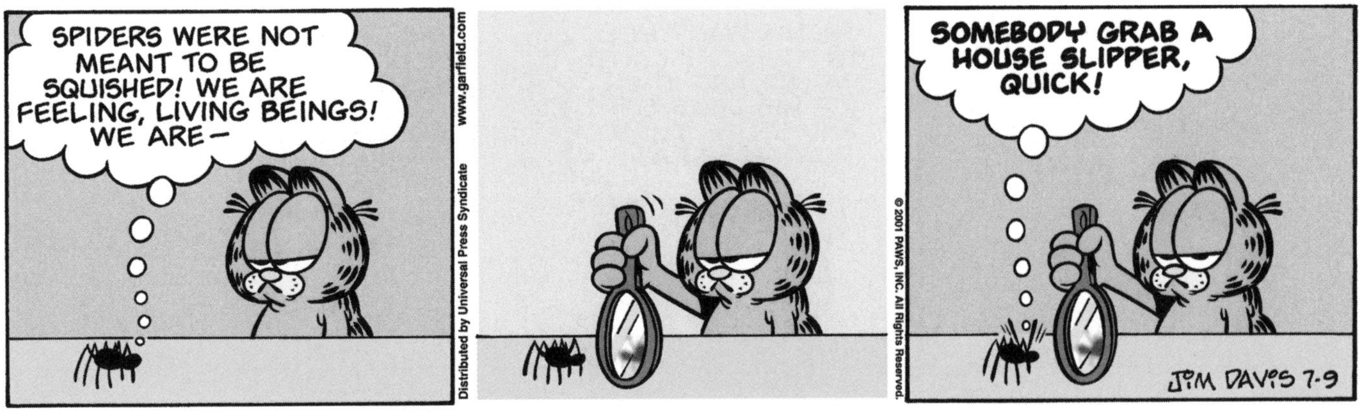
SPIDERS WERE NOT MEANT TO BE SQUISHED! WE ARE FEELING, LIVING BEINGS! WE ARE—
SOMEBODY GRAB A HOUSE SLIPPER, QUICK!
JIM DAVIS 7-9
Distributed by Universal Press Syndicate www.garfield.com
© 2001 PAWS, INC. All Rights Reserved.

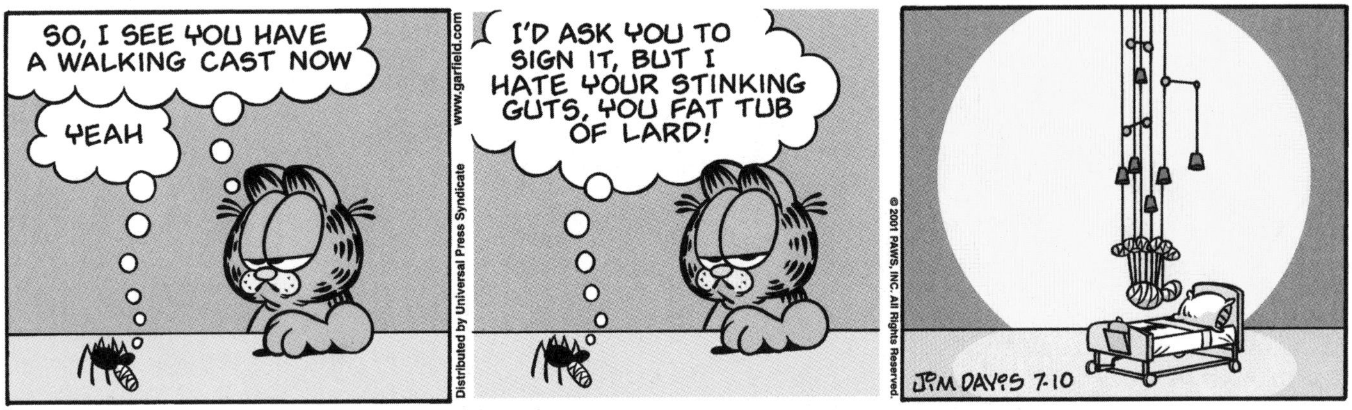
SO, I SEE YOU HAVE A WALKING CAST NOW
YEAH
I'D ASK YOU TO SIGN IT, BUT I HATE YOUR STINKING GUTS, YOU FAT TUB OF LARD!
JIM DAVIS 7-10
Distributed by Universal Press Syndicate www.garfield.com
© 2001 PAWS, INC. All Rights Reserved.

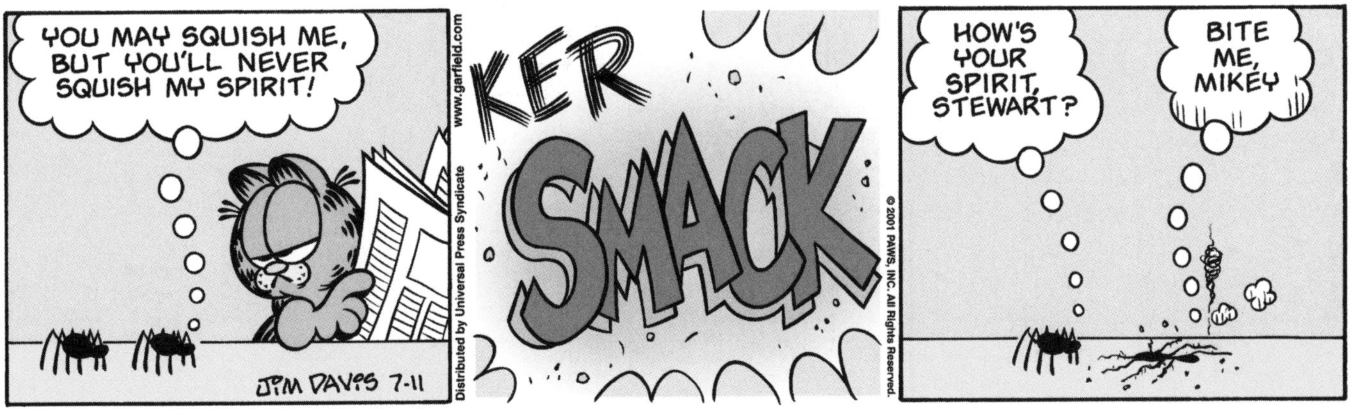
YOU MAY SQUISH ME, BUT YOU'LL NEVER SQUISH MY SPIRIT!
JIM DAVIS 7-11
KER SMACK
HOW'S YOUR SPIRIT, STEWART?
BITE ME, MIKEY
Distributed by Universal Press Syndicate www.garfield.com
© 2001 PAWS, INC. All Rights Reserved.

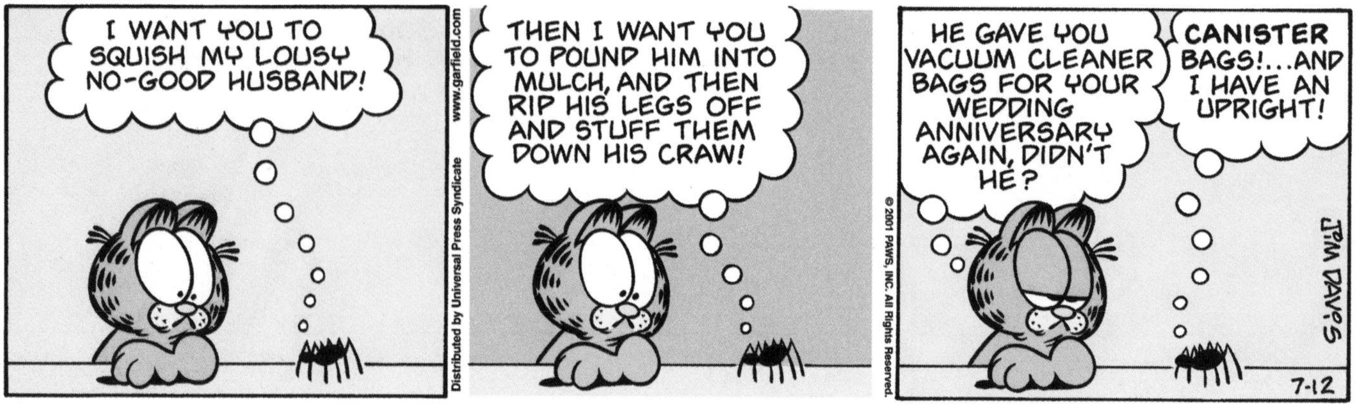
I WANT YOU TO SQUISH MY LOUSY NO-GOOD HUSBAND!
Distributed by Universal Press Syndicate www.garfield.com
THEN I WANT YOU TO POUND HIM INTO MULCH, AND THEN RIP HIS LEGS OFF AND STUFF THEM DOWN HIS CRAW!
© 2001 PAWS, INC. All Rights Reserved.
HE GAVE YOU VACUUM CLEANER BAGS FOR YOUR WEDDING ANNIVERSARY AGAIN, DIDN'T HE?
CANISTER BAGS!...AND I HAVE AN UPRIGHT!
JIM DAVIS
7-12

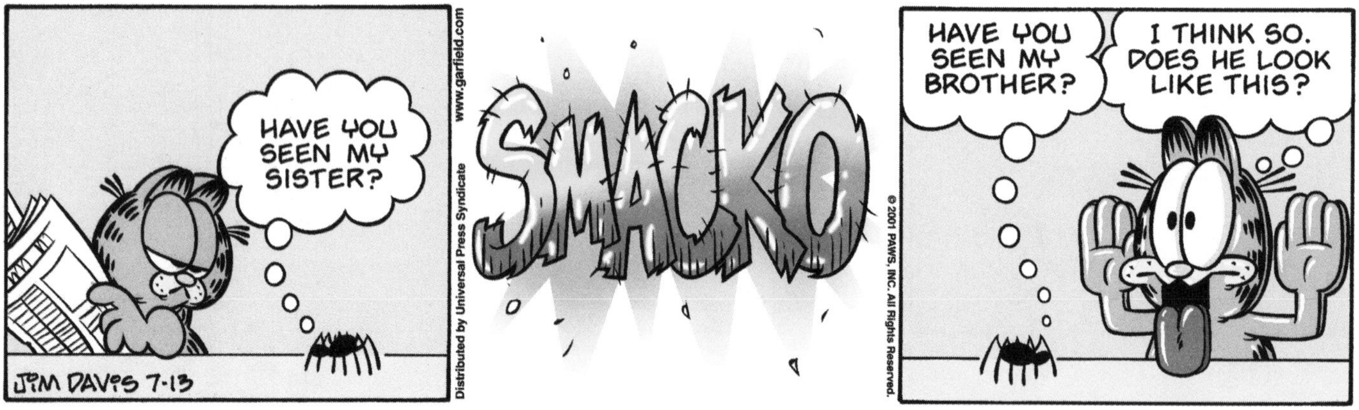
HAVE YOU SEEN MY SISTER?
JIM DAVIS 7-13
Distributed by Universal Press Syndicate www.garfield.com
SMACKO
© 2001 PAWS, INC. All Rights Reserved.
HAVE YOU SEEN MY BROTHER?
I THINK SO. DOES HE LOOK LIKE THIS?

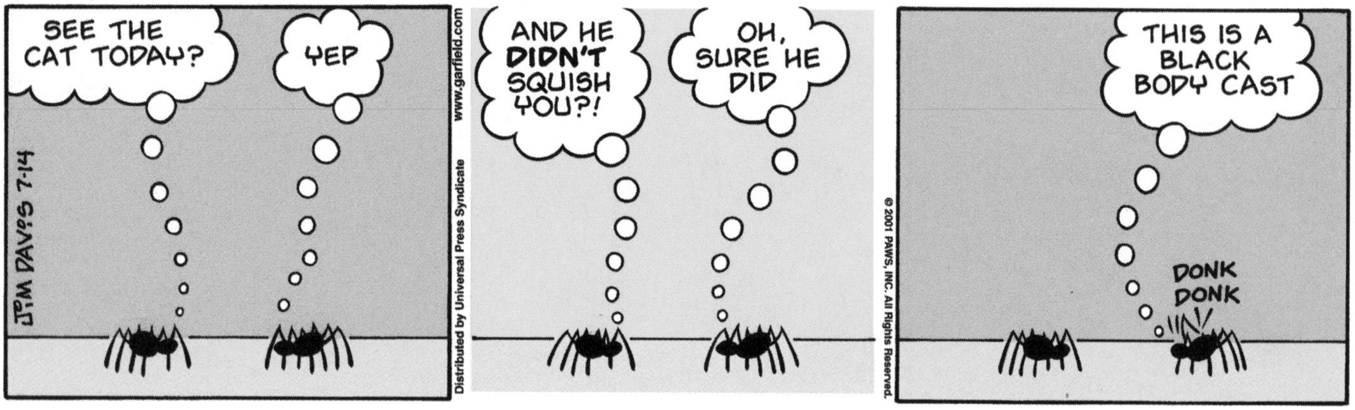
SEE THE CAT TODAY?
YEP
JIM DAVIS 7-14
Distributed by Universal Press Syndicate www.garfield.com
AND HE DIDN'T SQUISH YOU?!
OH, SURE HE DID
© 2001 PAWS, INC. All Rights Reserved.
THIS IS A BLACK BODY CAST
DONK
DONK

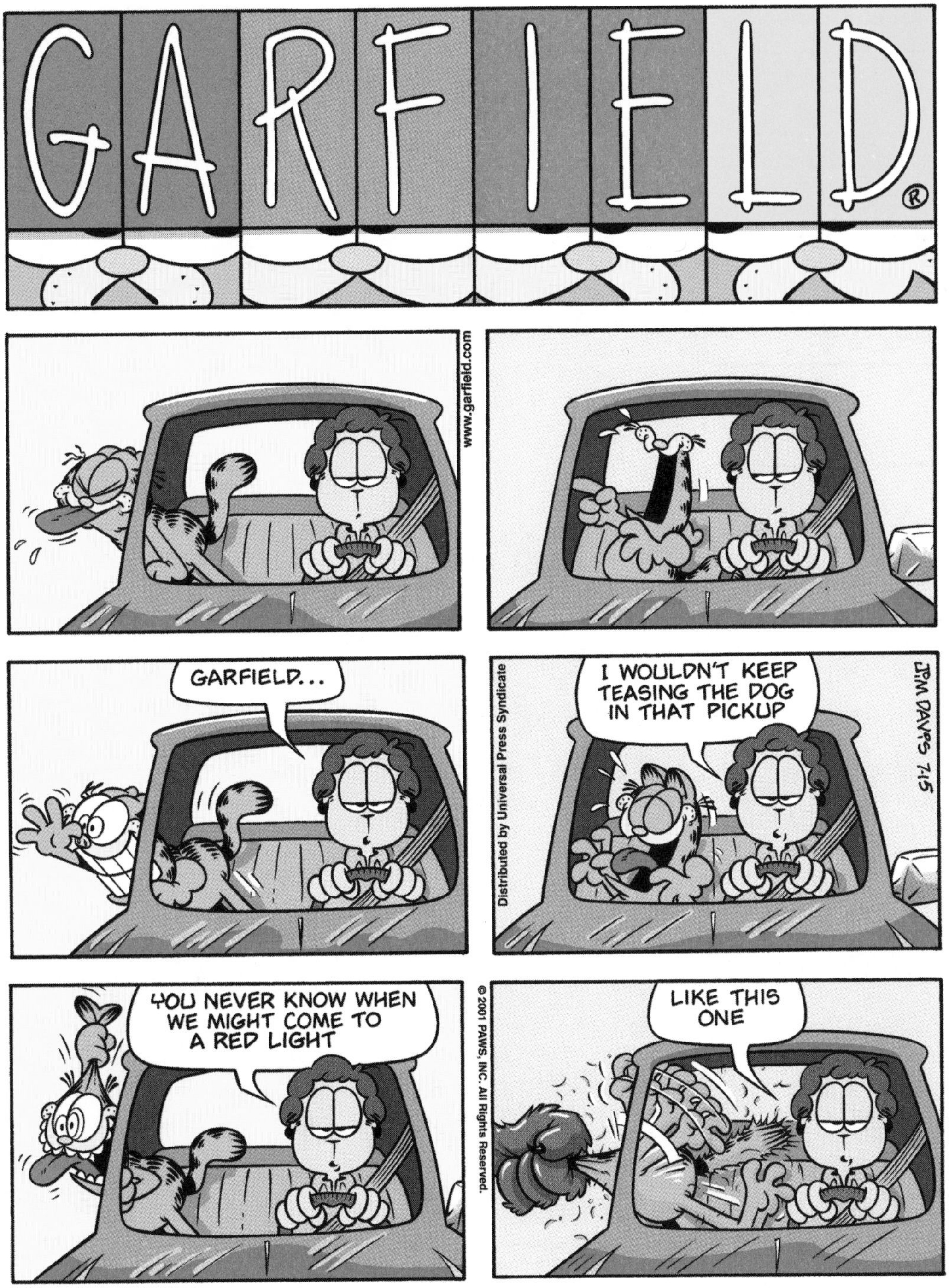
GARFIELD®
www.garfield.com
GARFIELD...
I WOULDN'T KEEP TEASING THE DOG IN THAT PICKUP
Distributed by Universal Press Syndicate
JIM DAVIS 7-15
YOU NEVER KNOW WHEN WE MIGHT COME TO A RED LIGHT
© 2001 PAWS, INC. All Rights Reserved.
LIKE THIS ONE

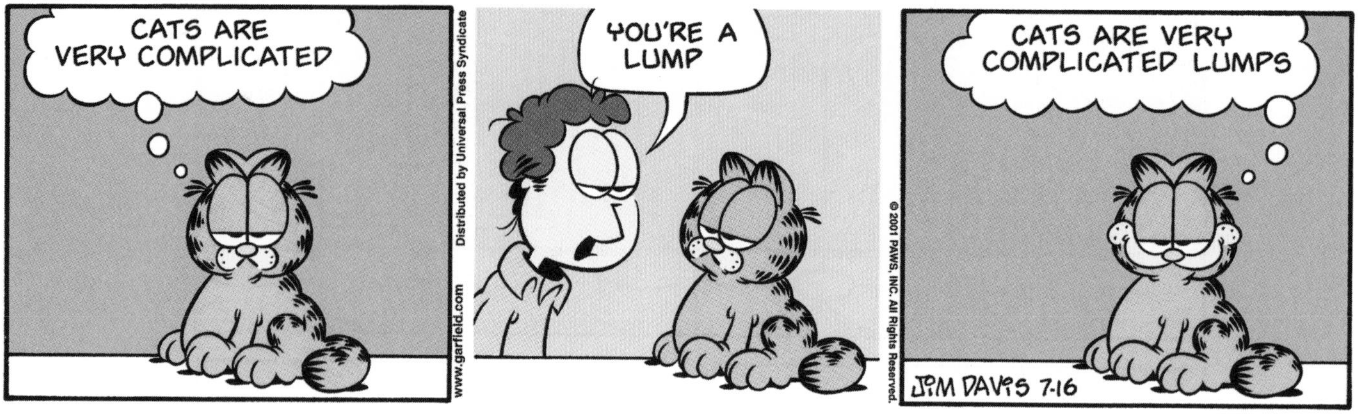
CATS ARE VERY COMPLICATED
www.garfield.com Distributed by Universal Press Syndicate
YOU'RE A LUMP
© 2001 PAWS, INC. All Rights Reserved.
CATS ARE VERY COMPLICATED LUMPS
JIM DAVIS 7-16

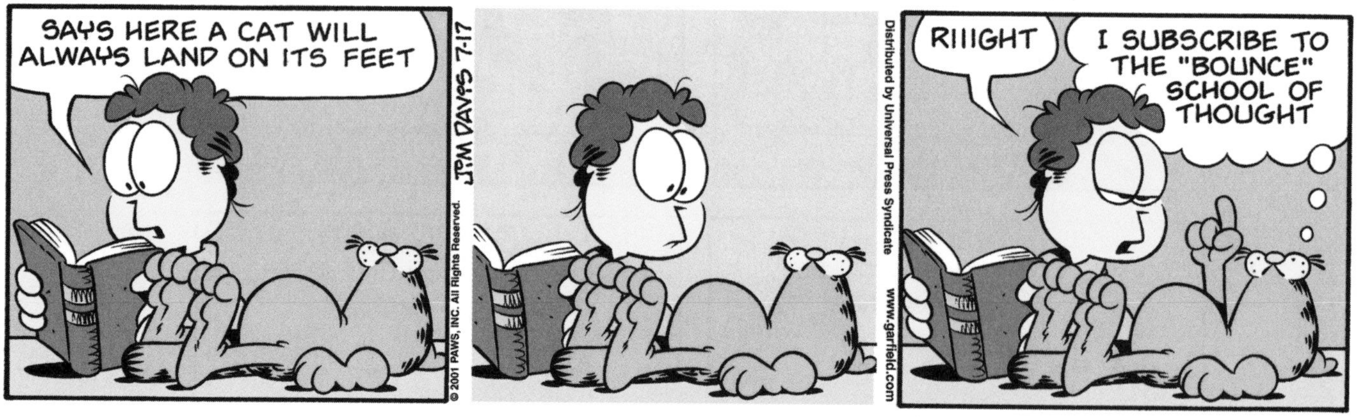
SAYS HERE A CAT WILL ALWAYS LAND ON ITS FEET
JIM DAVIS 7-17
© 2001 PAWS, INC. All Rights Reserved.
Distributed by Universal Press Syndicate www.garfield.com
RIIIGHT
I SUBSCRIBE TO THE "BOUNCE" SCHOOL OF THOUGHT

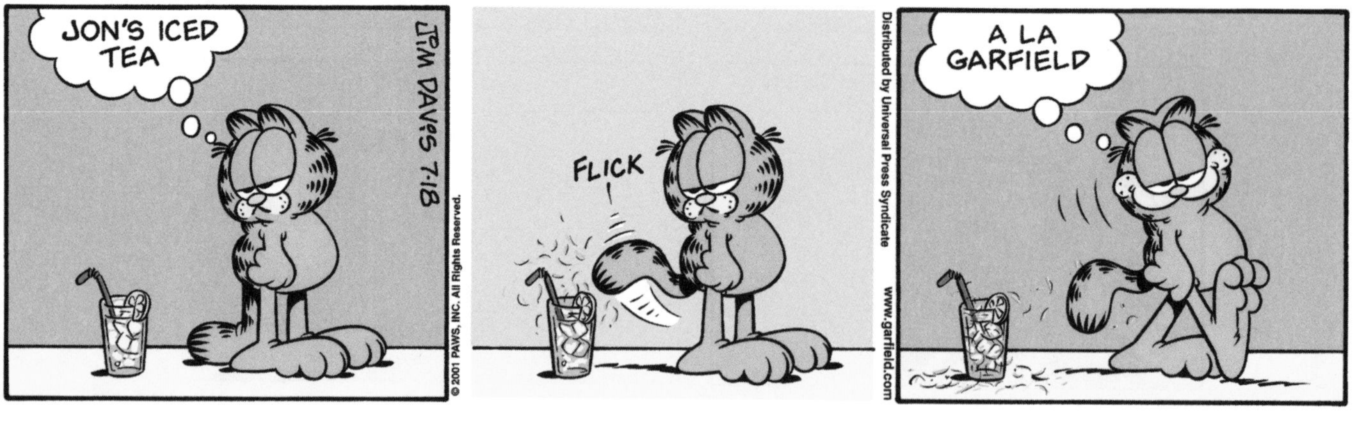
JON'S ICED TEA
JIM DAVIS 7-18
© 2001 PAWS, INC. All Rights Reserved.
FLICK
Distributed by Universal Press Syndicate www.garfield.com
A LA GARFIELD

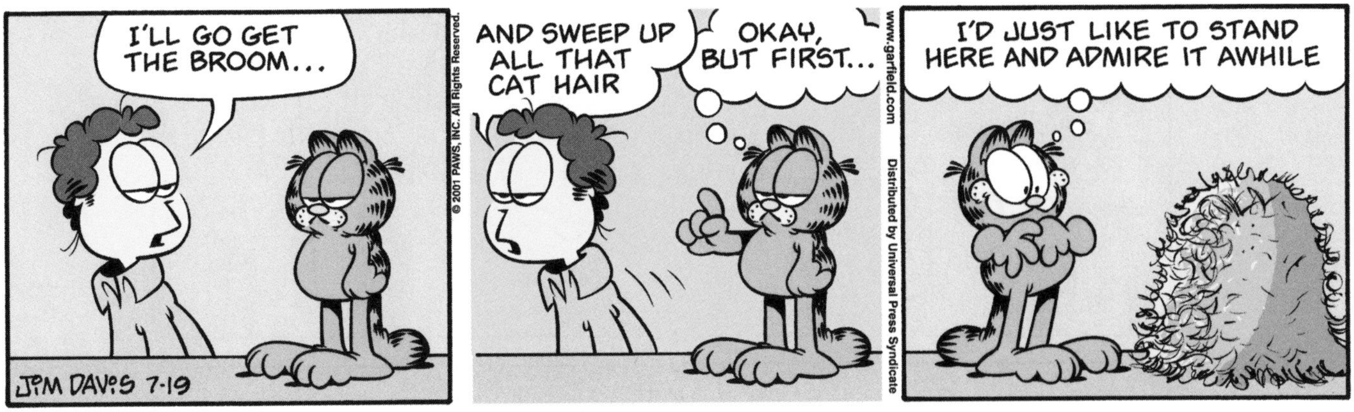
I'LL GO GET THE BROOM...
JIM DAVIS 7-19
© 2001 PAWS, INC. All Rights Reserved.
AND SWEEP UP ALL THAT CAT HAIR
OKAY, BUT FIRST...
www.garfield.com
Distributed by Universal Press Syndicate
I'D JUST LIKE TO STAND HERE AND ADMIRE IT AWHILE

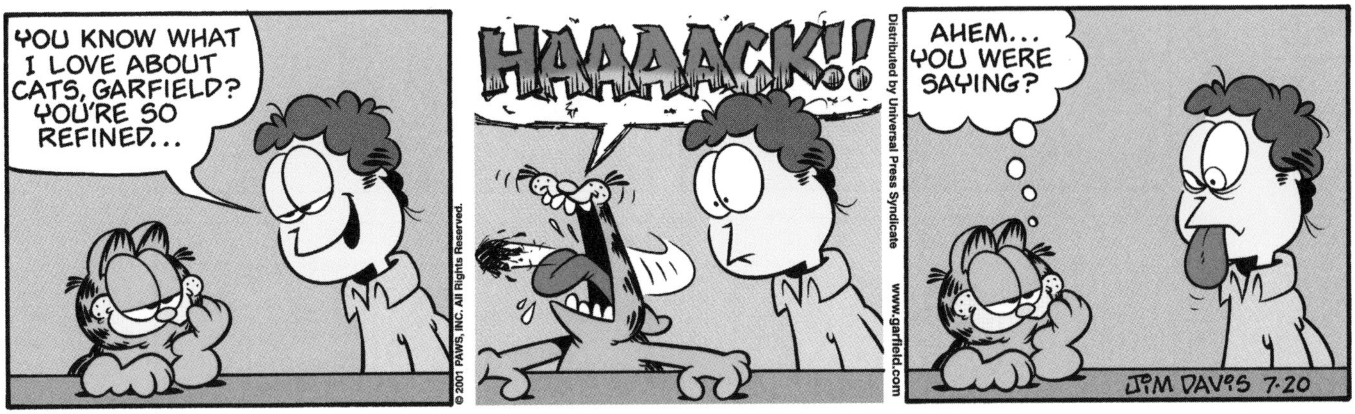
YOU KNOW WHAT I LOVE ABOUT CATS, GARFIELD? YOU'RE SO REFINED...
© 2001 PAWS, INC. All Rights Reserved.
HAAAACK!!
Distributed by Universal Press Syndicate
www.garfield.com
AHEM... YOU WERE SAYING?
JIM DAVIS 7-20

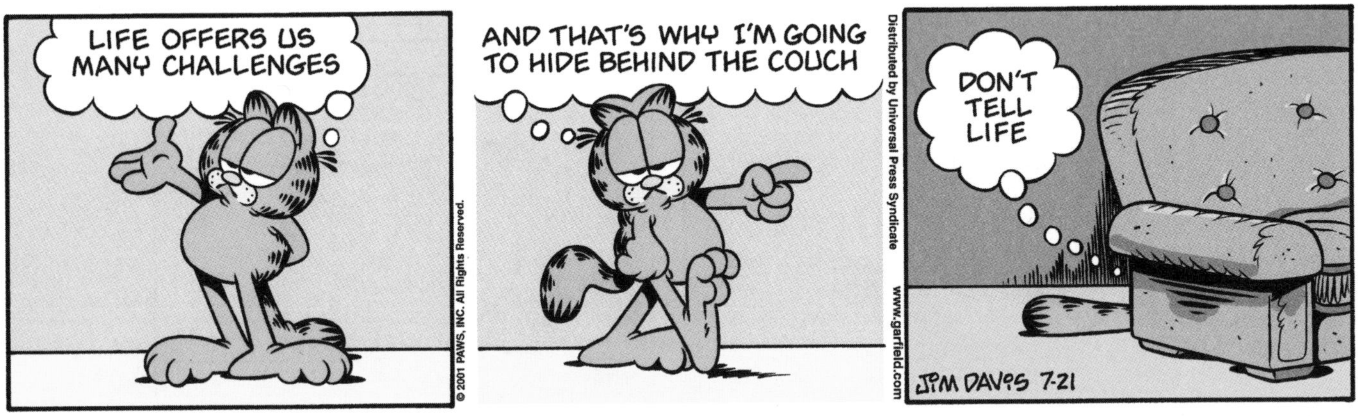
LIFE OFFERS US MANY CHALLENGES
© 2001 PAWS, INC. All Rights Reserved.
AND THAT'S WHY I'M GOING TO HIDE BEHIND THE COUCH
Distributed by Universal Press Syndicate
www.garfield.com
DON'T TELL LIFE
JIM DAVIS 7-21

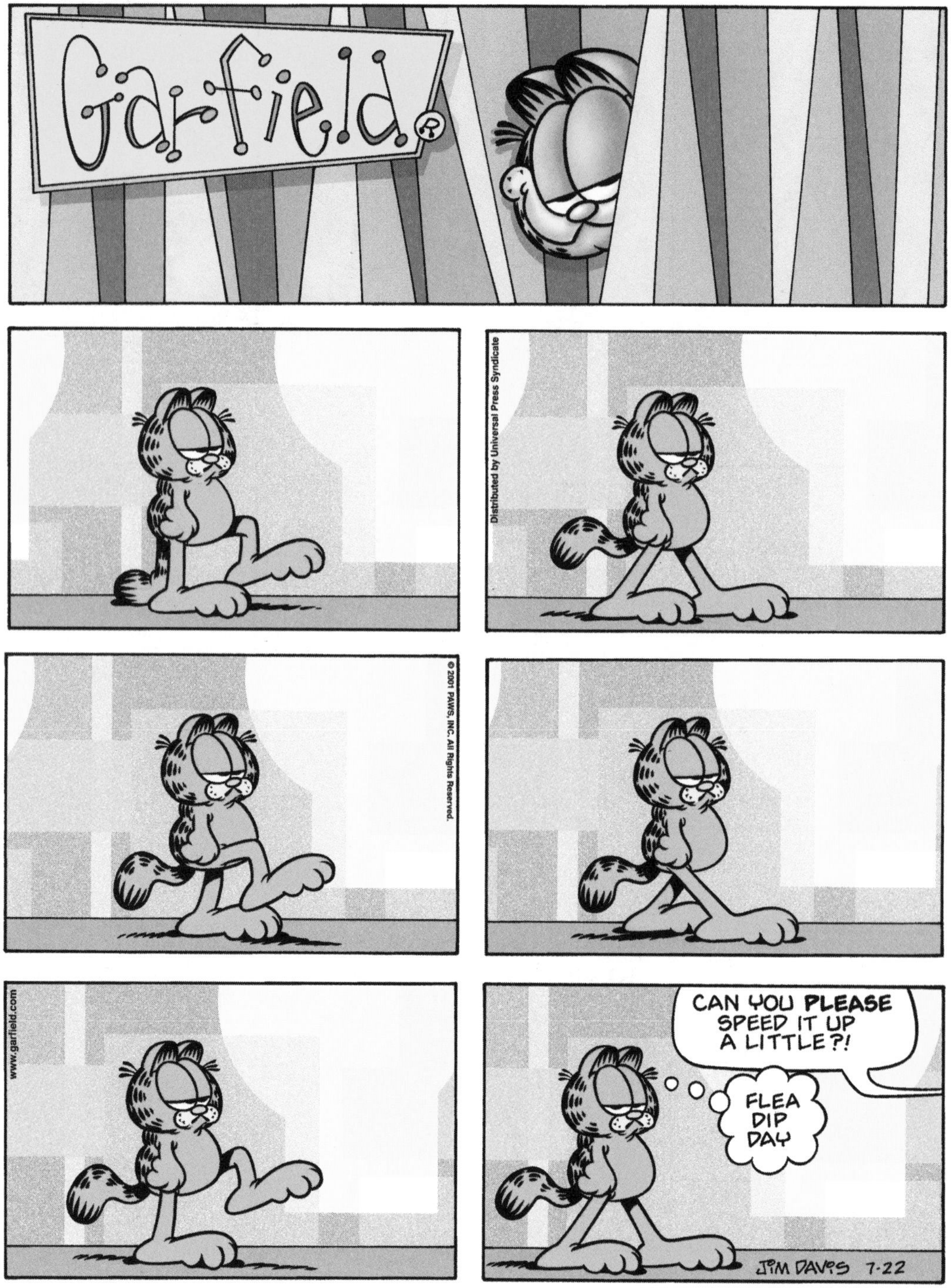
Garfield®
Distributed by Universal Press Syndicate
© 2001 PAWS, INC. All Rights Reserved.
www.garfield.com
CAN YOU PLEASE SPEED IT UP A LITTLE?!
FLEA DIP DAY
JIM DAVIS 7-22

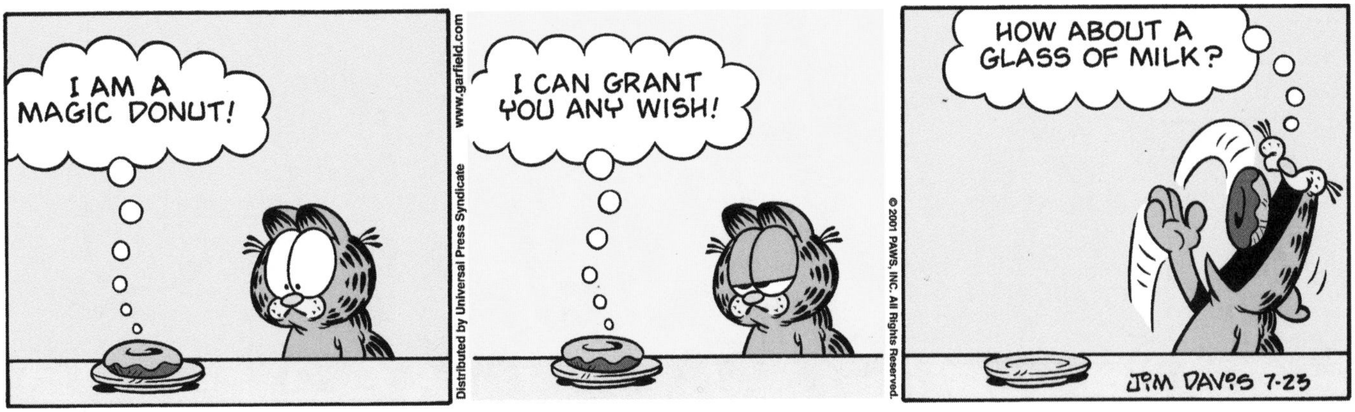
I AM A MAGIC DONUT!
I CAN GRANT YOU ANY WISH!
HOW ABOUT A GLASS OF MILK?
JIM DAVIS 7-23
www.garfield.com
Distributed by Universal Press Syndicate
© 2001 PAWS, INC. All Rights Reserved.

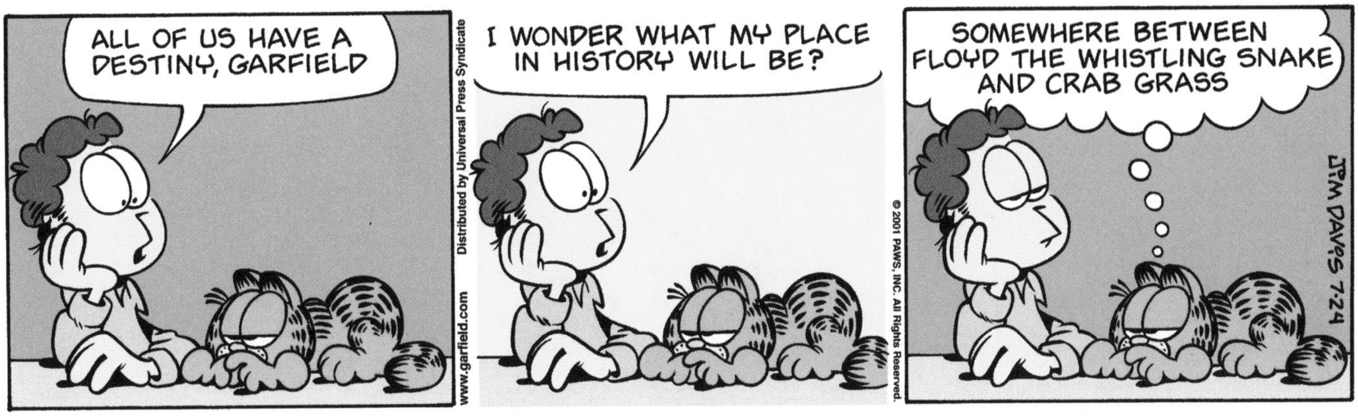
ALL OF US HAVE A DESTINY, GARFIELD
I WONDER WHAT MY PLACE IN HISTORY WILL BE?
SOMEWHERE BETWEEN FLOYD THE WHISTLING SNAKE AND CRAB GRASS
JIM DAVIS 7-24
www.garfield.com
Distributed by Universal Press Syndicate
© 2001 PAWS, INC. All Rights Reserved.

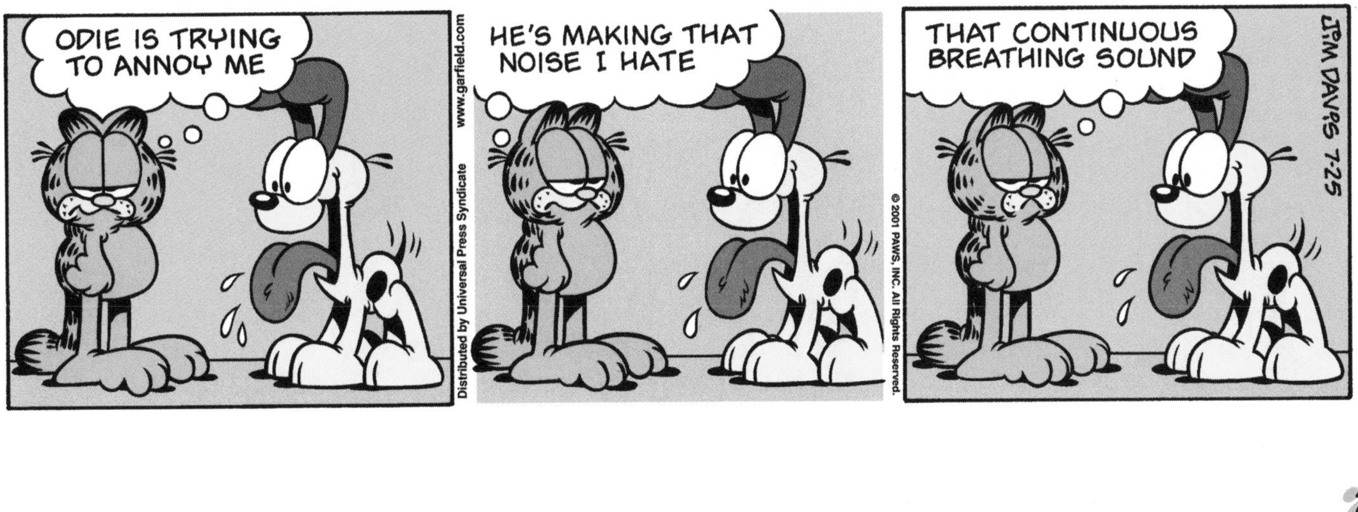
ODIE IS TRYING TO ANNOY ME
HE'S MAKING THAT NOISE I HATE
THAT CONTINUOUS BREATHING SOUND
JIM DAVIS 7-25
www.garfield.com
Distributed by Universal Press Syndicate
© 2001 PAWS, INC. All Rights Reserved.

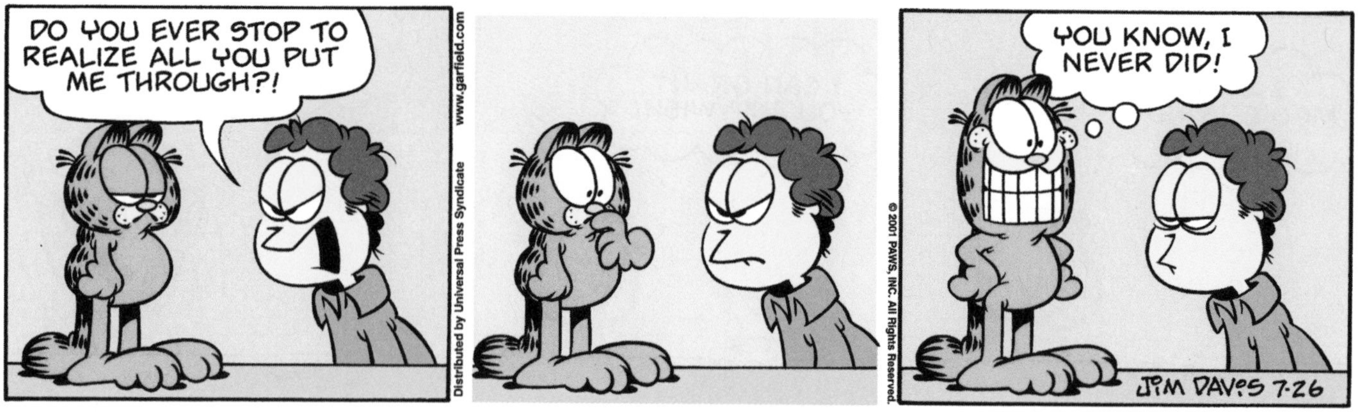
DO YOU EVER STOP TO REALIZE ALL YOU PUT ME THROUGH?!
Distributed by Universal Press Syndicate www.garfield.com
YOU KNOW, I NEVER DID!
© 2001 PAWS, INC. All Rights Reserved.
JIM DAVIS 7-26

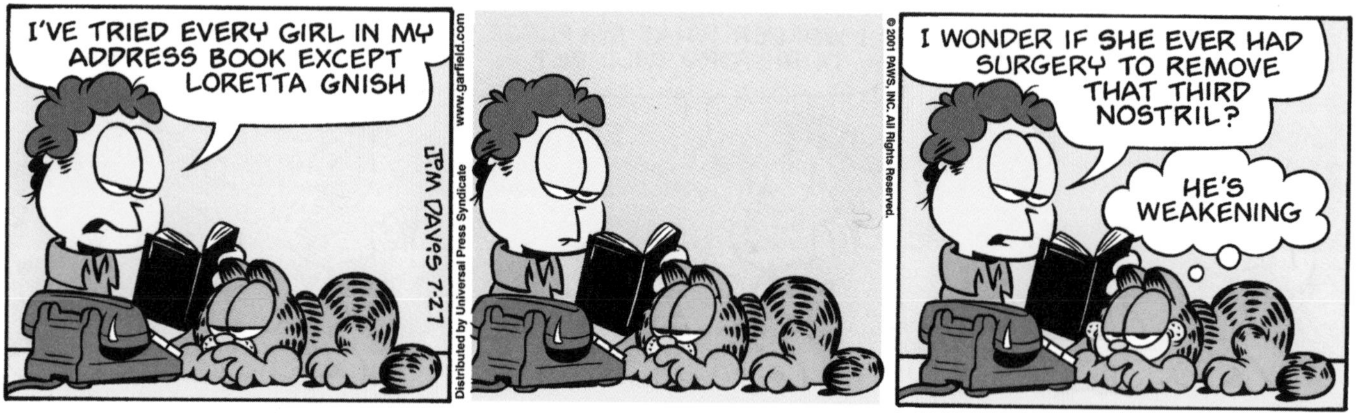
I'VE TRIED EVERY GIRL IN MY ADDRESS BOOK EXCEPT LORETTA GNISH
JIM DAVIS 7-27
Distributed by Universal Press Syndicate www.garfield.com
© 2001 PAWS, INC. All Rights Reserved.
I WONDER IF SHE EVER HAD SURGERY TO REMOVE THAT THIRD NOSTRIL?
HE'S WEAKENING

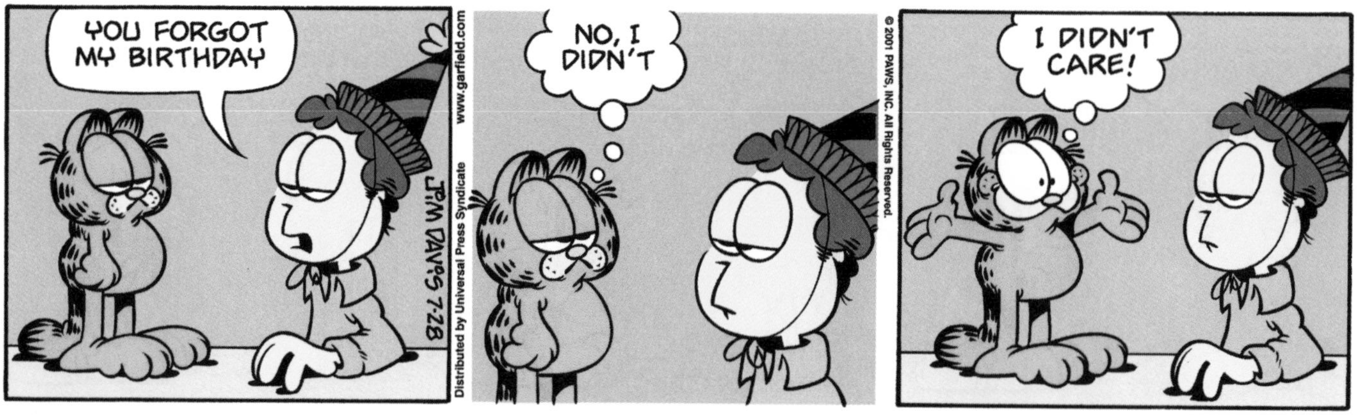
YOU FORGOT MY BIRTHDAY
JIM DAVIS 7-28
Distributed by Universal Press Syndicate www.garfield.com
NO, I DIDN'T
© 2001 PAWS, INC. All Rights Reserved.
I DIDN'T CARE!

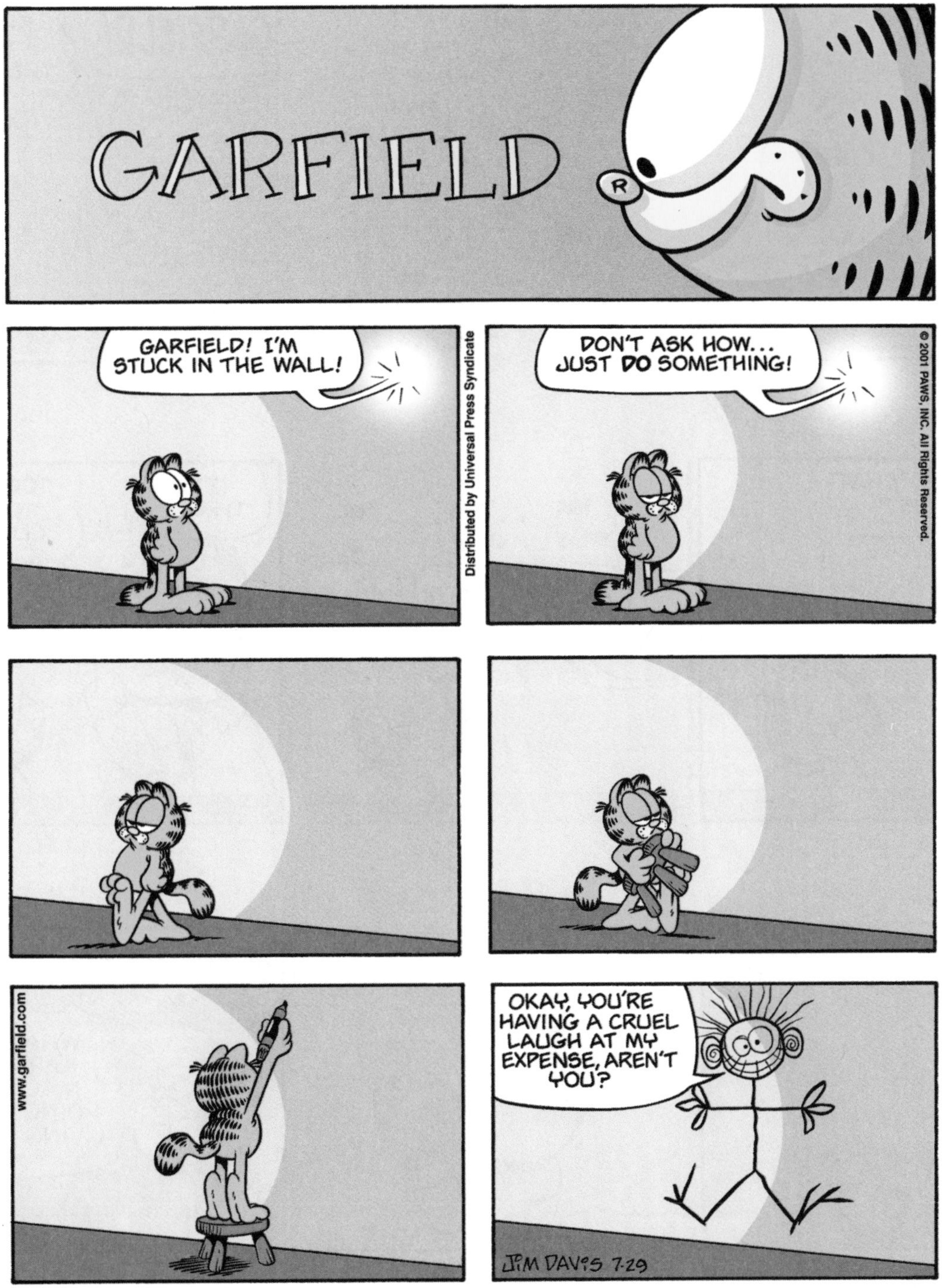
GARFIELD
GARFIELD! I'M STUCK IN THE WALL!
Distributed by Universal Press Syndicate
DON'T ASK HOW... JUST DO SOMETHING!
© 2001 PAWS, INC. All Rights Reserved.
www.garfield.com
OKAY, YOU'RE HAVING A CRUEL LAUGH AT MY EXPENSE, AREN'T YOU?
JIM DAVIS 7-29

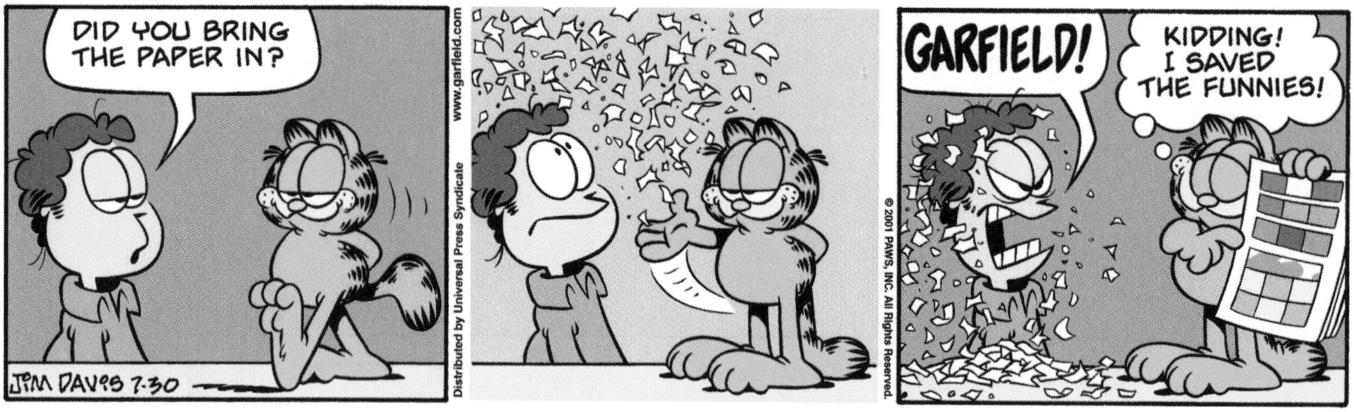
DID YOU BRING THE PAPER IN?
JIM DAVIS 7-30
www.garfield.com
Distributed by Universal Press Syndicate
GARFIELD!
KIDDING! I SAVED THE FUNNIES!
© 2001 PAWS, INC. All Rights Reserved.

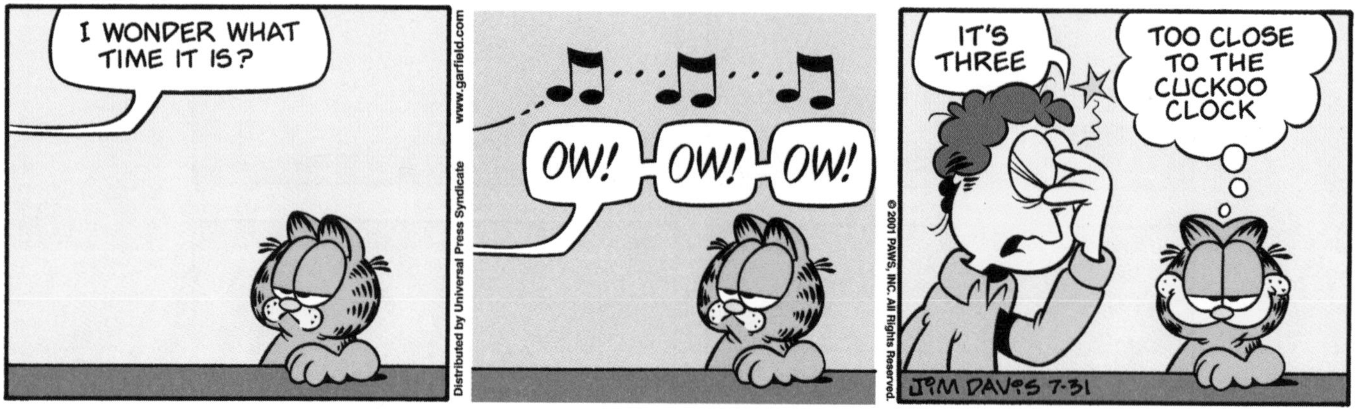
I WONDER WHAT TIME IT IS?
www.garfield.com
Distributed by Universal Press Syndicate
OW! OW! OW!
IT'S THREE
TOO CLOSE TO THE CUCKOO CLOCK
© 2001 PAWS, INC. All Rights Reserved.
JIM DAVIS 7-31

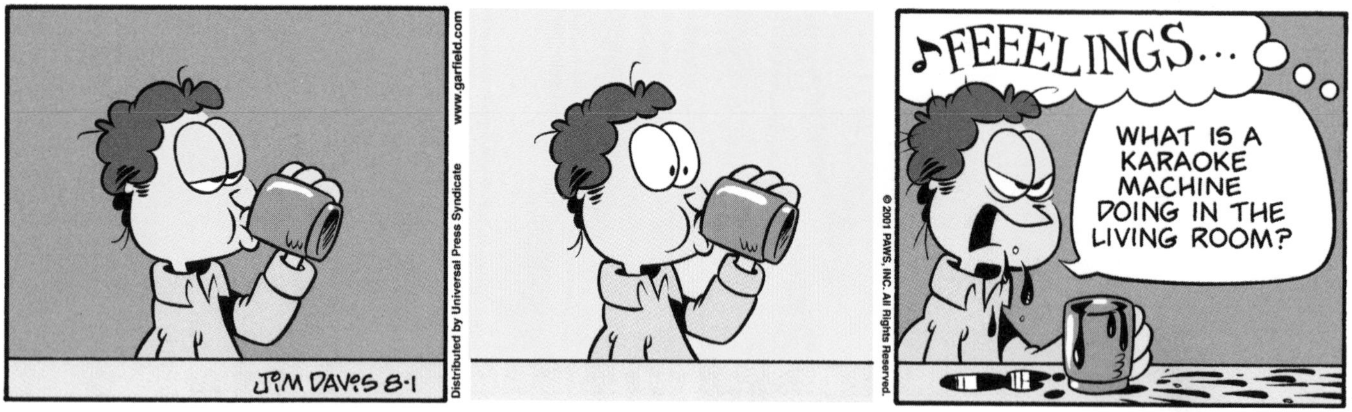
JIM DAVIS 8-1
www.garfield.com
Distributed by Universal Press Syndicate
♪FEEELINGS...
WHAT IS A KARAOKE MACHINE DOING IN THE LIVING ROOM?
© 2001 PAWS, INC. All Rights Reserved.

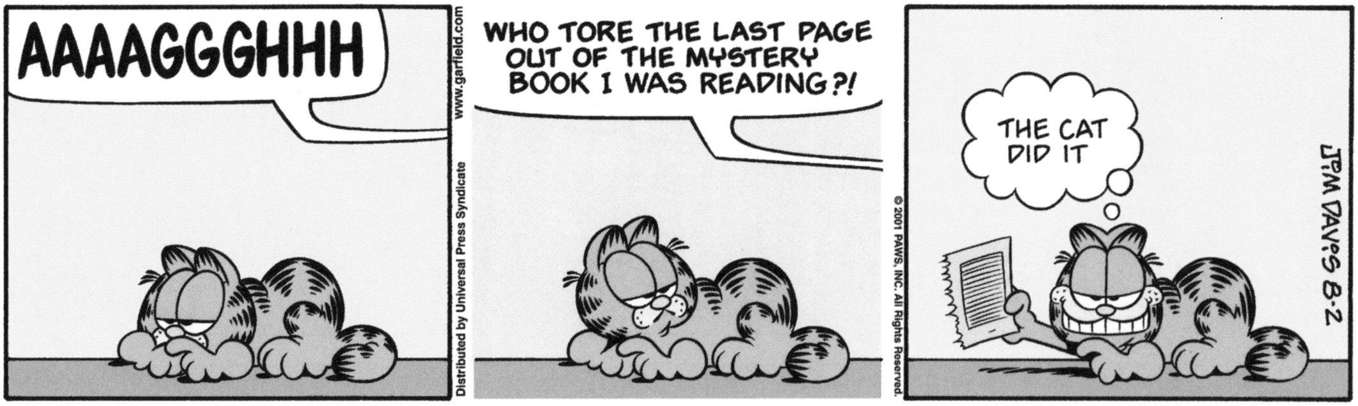
AAAAGGGHHH
www.garfield.com
Distributed by Universal Press Syndicate
WHO TORE THE LAST PAGE OUT OF THE MYSTERY BOOK I WAS READING?!
© 2001 PAWS, INC. All Rights Reserved.
THE CAT DID IT
JIM DAVIS 8-2

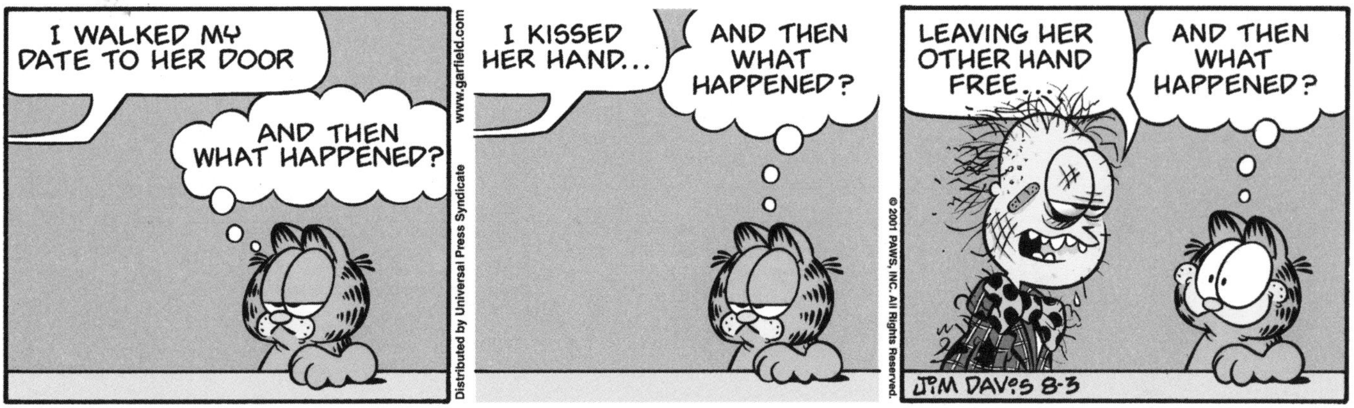
I WALKED MY DATE TO HER DOOR
AND THEN WHAT HAPPENED?
www.garfield.com
Distributed by Universal Press Syndicate
I KISSED HER HAND...
AND THEN WHAT HAPPENED?
© 2001 PAWS, INC. All Rights Reserved.
LEAVING HER OTHER HAND FREE...
AND THEN WHAT HAPPENED?
JIM DAVIS 8-3

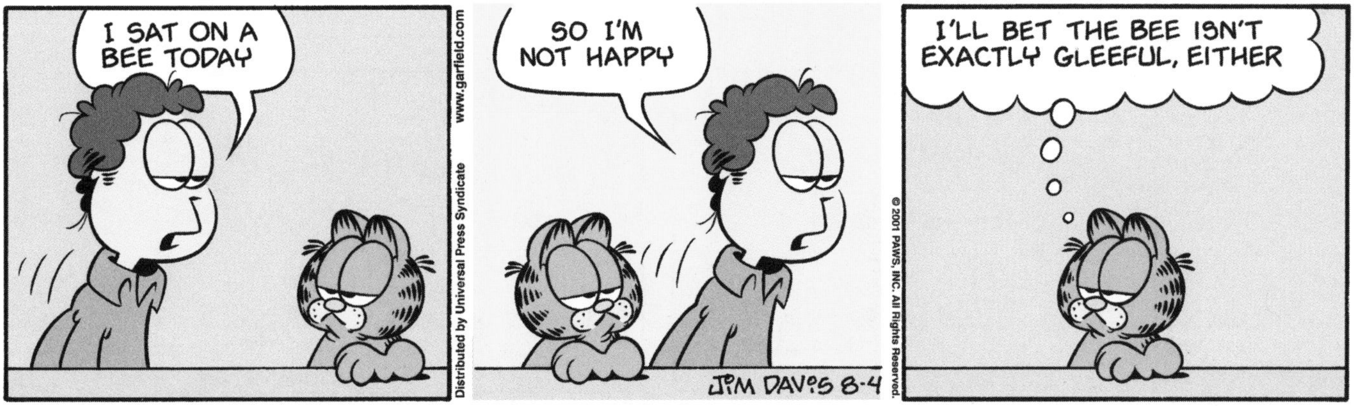
I SAT ON A BEE TODAY
www.garfield.com
Distributed by Universal Press Syndicate
SO I'M NOT HAPPY
JIM DAVIS 8-4
© 2001 PAWS, INC. All Rights Reserved.
I'LL BET THE BEE ISN'T EXACTLY GLEEFUL, EITHER

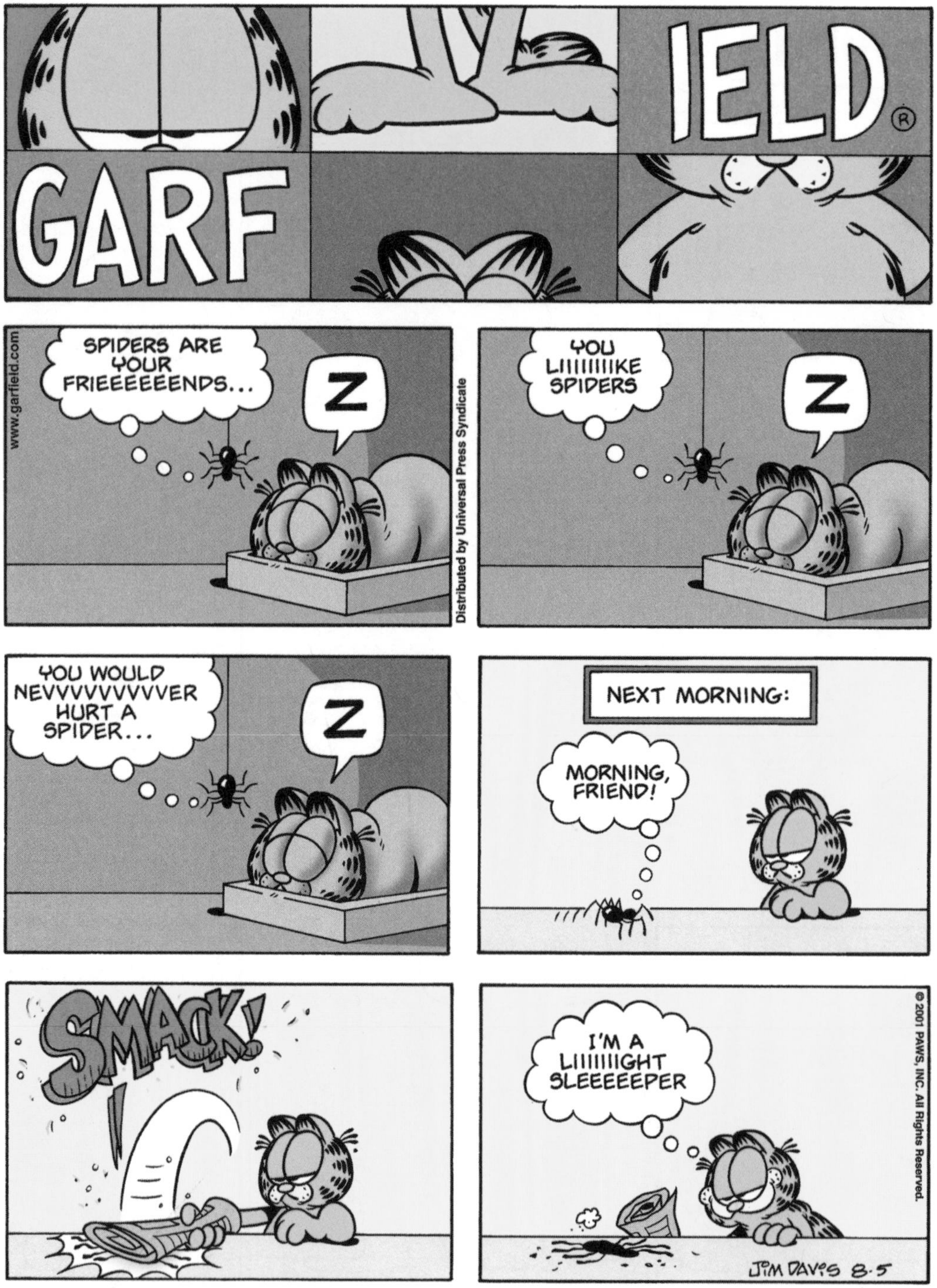
GARFIELD®
www.garfield.com
SPIDERS ARE YOUR FRIEEEEEEENDS...
Z
Distributed by Universal Press Syndicate
YOU LIIIIIIIKE SPIDERS
Z
YOU WOULD NEVVVVVVVVVER HURT A SPIDER...
Z
NEXT MORNING:
MORNING, FRIEND!
SMACK!
I'M A LIIIIIIGHT SLEEEEEPER
© 2001 PAWS, INC. All Rights Reserved.
JIM DAVIS 8-5

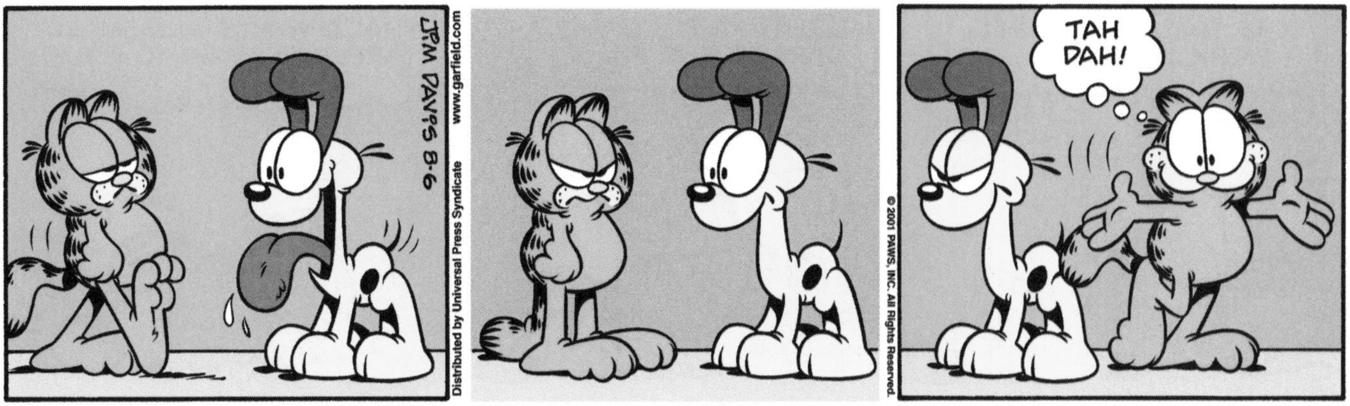
JIM DAVIS 8-6
www.garfield.com
Distributed by Universal Press Syndicate
© 2001 PAWS, INC. All Rights Reserved.
TAH DAH!

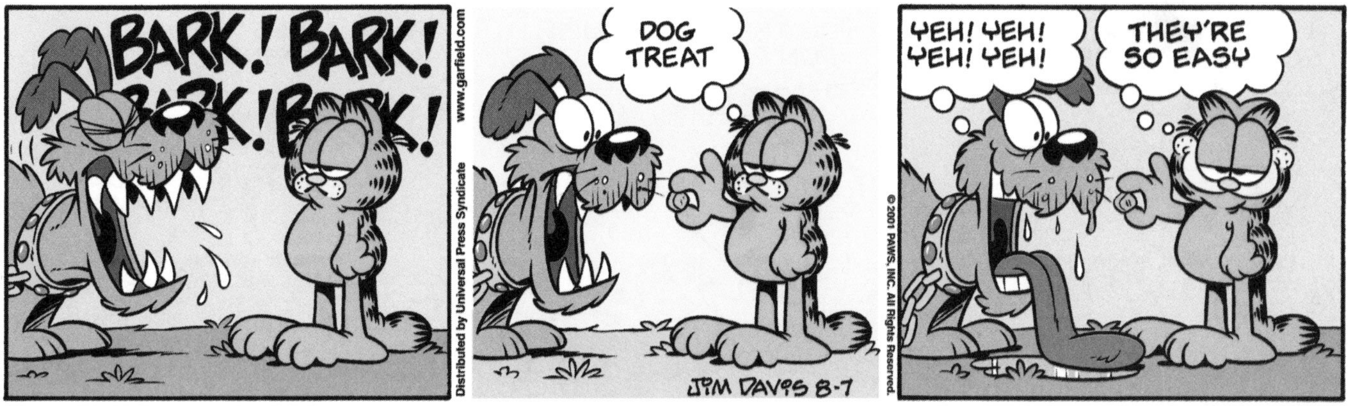
BARK! BARK! BARK! BARK!
www.garfield.com
Distributed by Universal Press Syndicate
DOG TREAT
JIM DAVIS 8-7
© 2001 PAWS, INC. All Rights Reserved.
YEH! YEH! YEH! YEH!
THEY'RE SO EASY

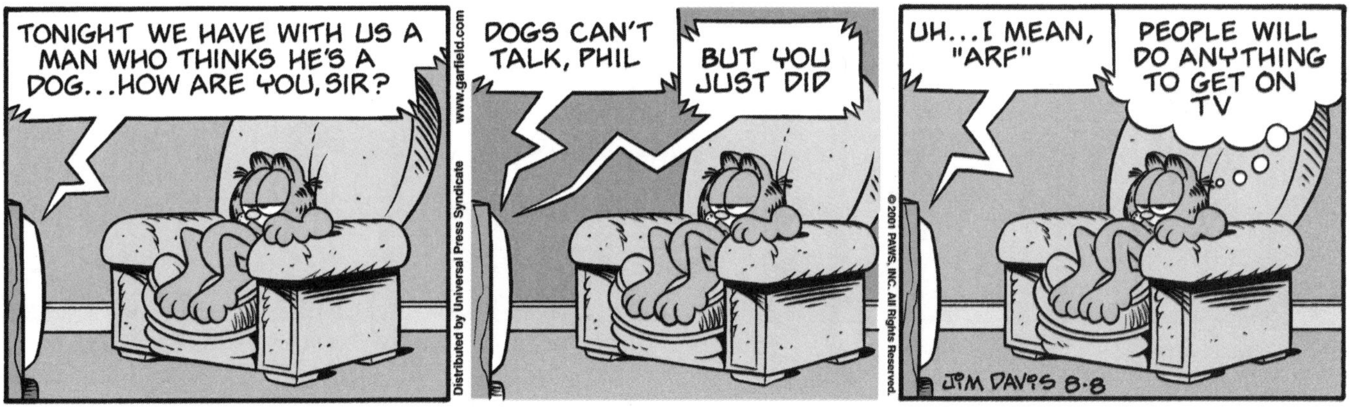
TONIGHT WE HAVE WITH US A MAN WHO THINKS HE'S A DOG...HOW ARE YOU, SIR?
www.garfield.com
Distributed by Universal Press Syndicate
DOGS CAN'T TALK, PHIL
BUT YOU JUST DID
© 2001 PAWS, INC. All Rights Reserved.
UH...I MEAN, "ARF"
PEOPLE WILL DO ANYTHING TO GET ON TV
JIM DAVIS 8-8

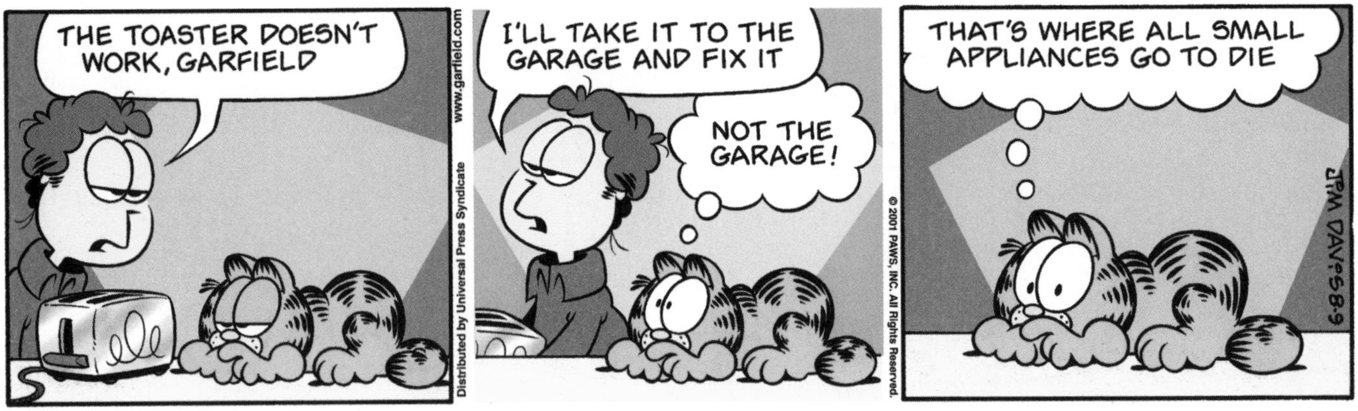
THE TOASTER DOESN'T WORK, GARFIELD
I'LL TAKE IT TO THE GARAGE AND FIX IT
NOT THE GARAGE!
THAT'S WHERE ALL SMALL APPLIANCES GO TO DIE
JIM DAVIS 8-9
www.garfield.com
Distributed by Universal Press Syndicate
© 2001 PAWS, INC. All Rights Reserved.

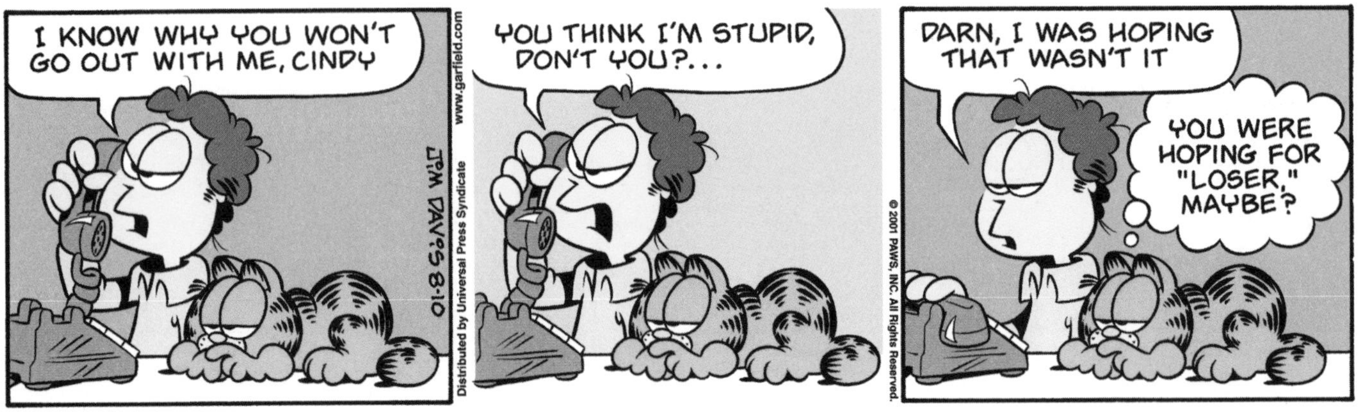
I KNOW WHY YOU WON'T GO OUT WITH ME, CINDY
JIM DAVIS 8-10
YOU THINK I'M STUPID, DON'T YOU?...
DARN, I WAS HOPING THAT WASN'T IT
YOU WERE HOPING FOR "LOSER," MAYBE?
www.garfield.com
Distributed by Universal Press Syndicate
© 2001 PAWS, INC. All Rights Reserved.

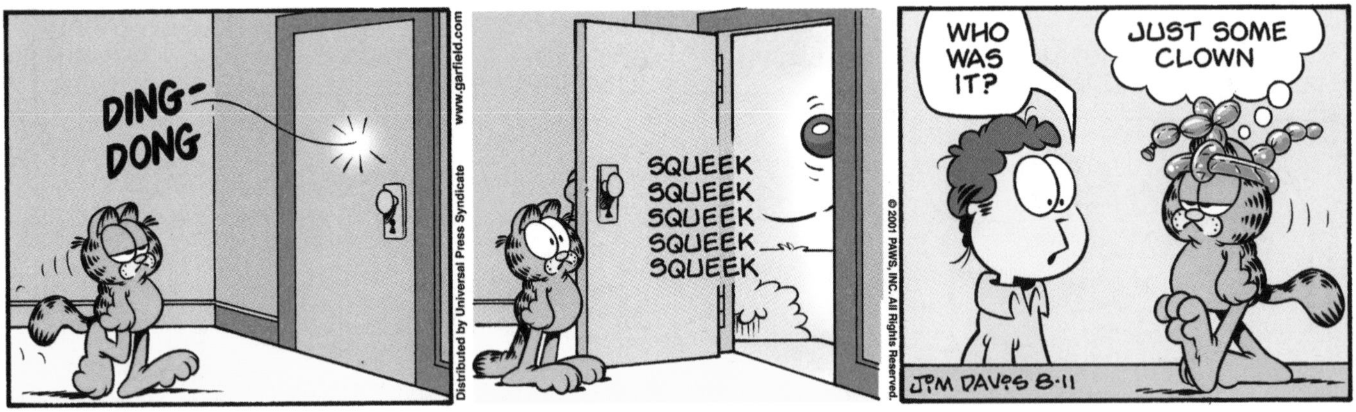
DING-DONG
SQUEEK
SQUEEK
SQUEEK
SQUEEK
SQUEEK
WHO WAS IT?
JUST SOME CLOWN
JIM DAVIS 8-11
www.garfield.com
Distributed by Universal Press Syndicate
© 2001 PAWS, INC. All Rights Reserved.

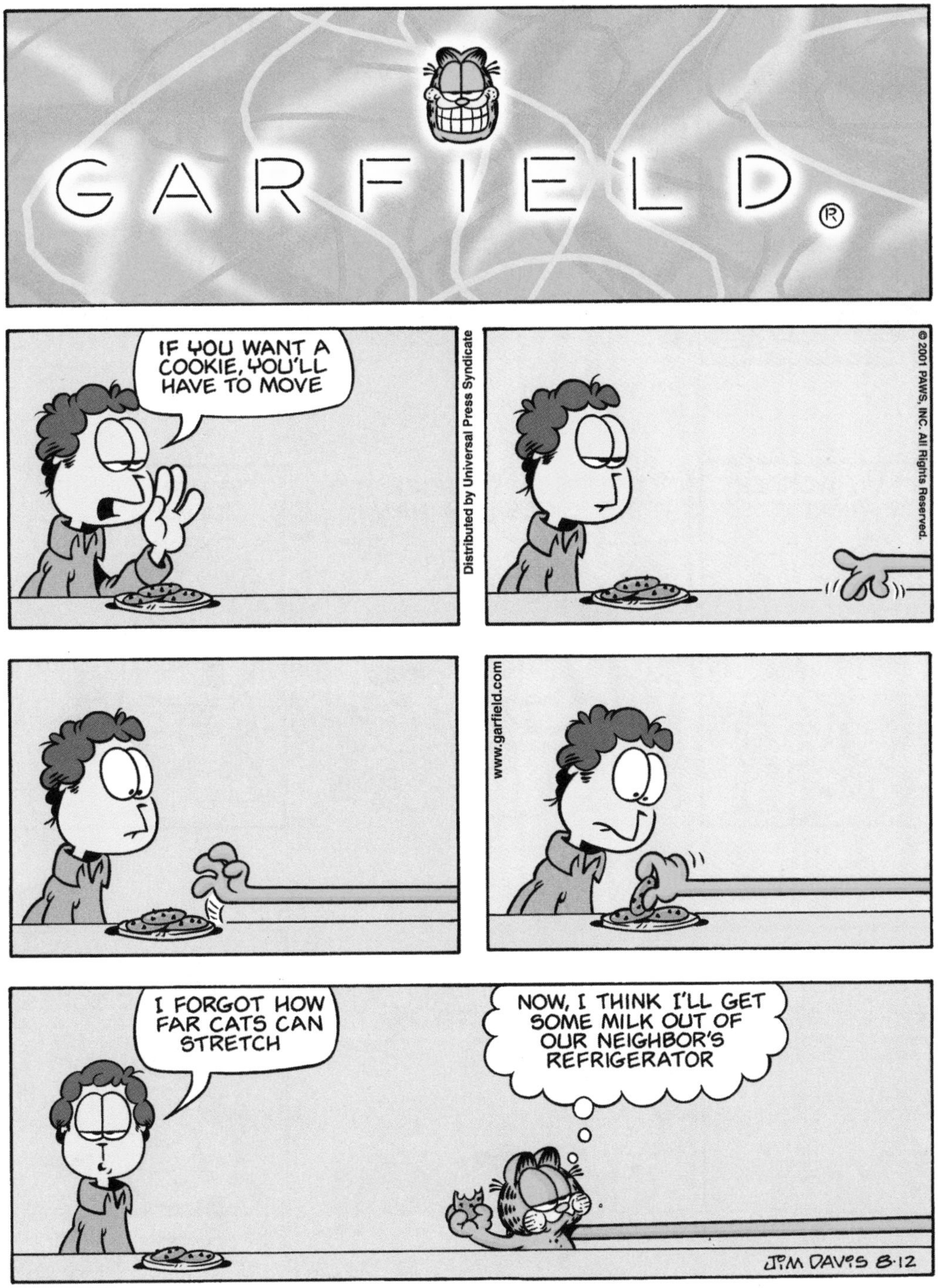
GARFIELD®
IF YOU WANT A COOKIE, YOU'LL HAVE TO MOVE
Distributed by Universal Press Syndicate
© 2001 PAWS, INC. All Rights Reserved.
www.garfield.com
I FORGOT HOW FAR CATS CAN STRETCH
NOW, I THINK I'LL GET SOME MILK OUT OF OUR NEIGHBOR'S REFRIGERATOR
JIM DAVIS 8-12

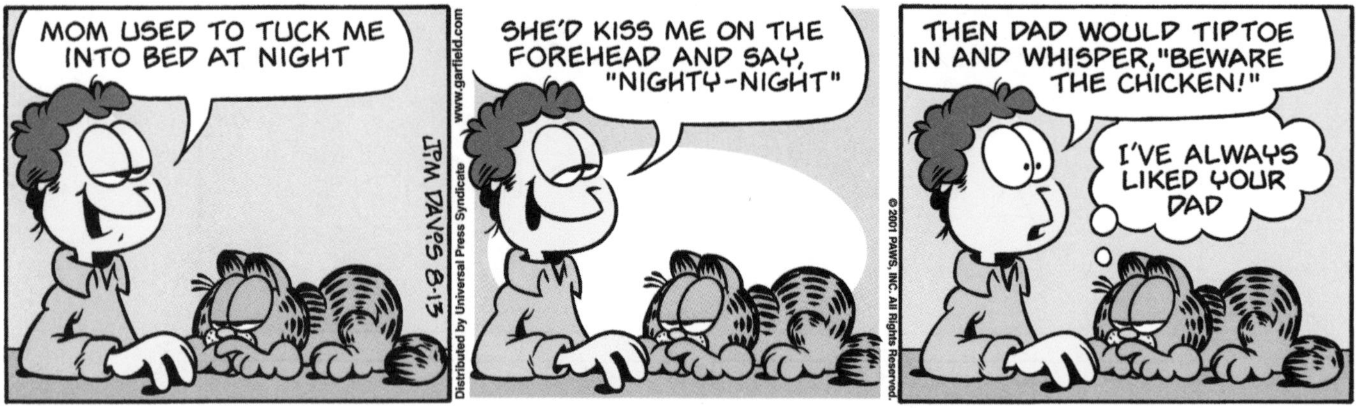
MOM USED TO TUCK ME INTO BED AT NIGHT
JIM DAVIS 8-13
Distributed by Universal Press Syndicate www.garfield.com
SHE'D KISS ME ON THE FOREHEAD AND SAY, "NIGHTY-NIGHT"
© 2001 PAWS, INC. All Rights Reserved.
THEN DAD WOULD TIPTOE IN AND WHISPER, "BEWARE THE CHICKEN!"
I'VE ALWAYS LIKED YOUR DAD

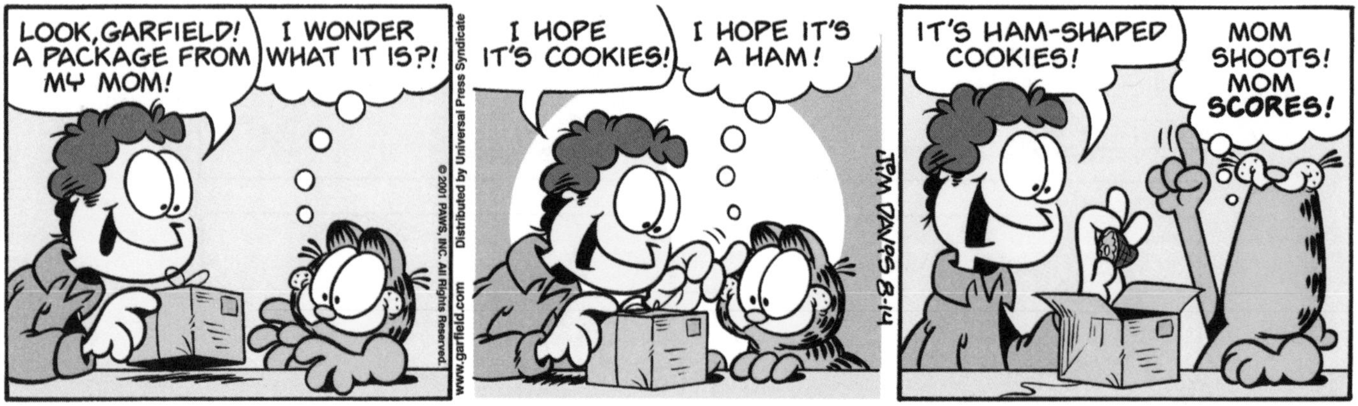
LOOK, GARFIELD! A PACKAGE FROM MY MOM!
I WONDER WHAT IT IS?!
© 2001 PAWS, INC. All Rights Reserved.
Distributed by Universal Press Syndicate www.garfield.com
I HOPE IT'S COOKIES!
I HOPE IT'S A HAM!
JIM DAVIS 8-14
IT'S HAM-SHAPED COOKIES!
MOM SHOOTS! MOM **SCORES!**

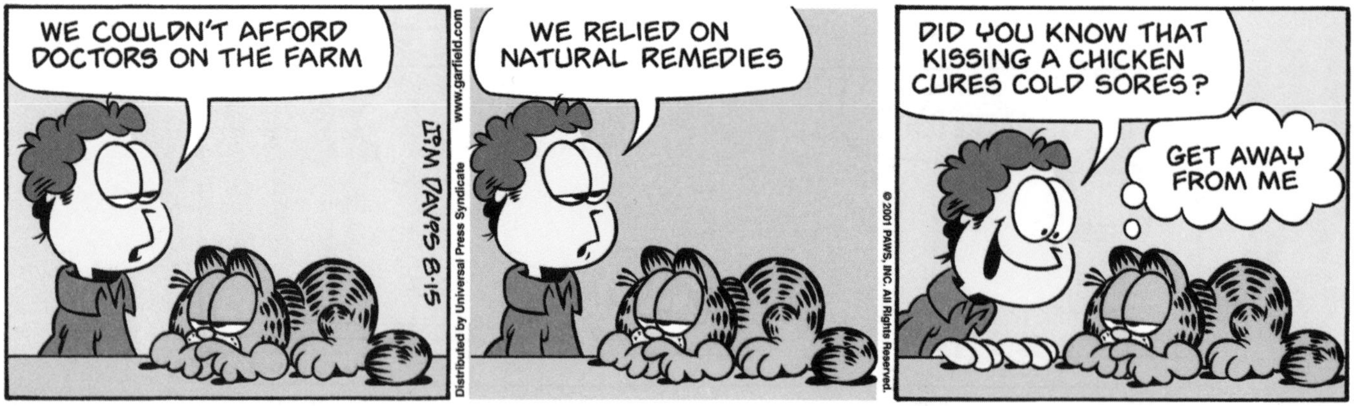
WE COULDN'T AFFORD DOCTORS ON THE FARM
JIM DAVIS 8-15
Distributed by Universal Press Syndicate www.garfield.com
WE RELIED ON NATURAL REMEDIES
© 2001 PAWS, INC. All Rights Reserved.
DID YOU KNOW THAT KISSING A CHICKEN CURES COLD SORES?
GET AWAY FROM ME

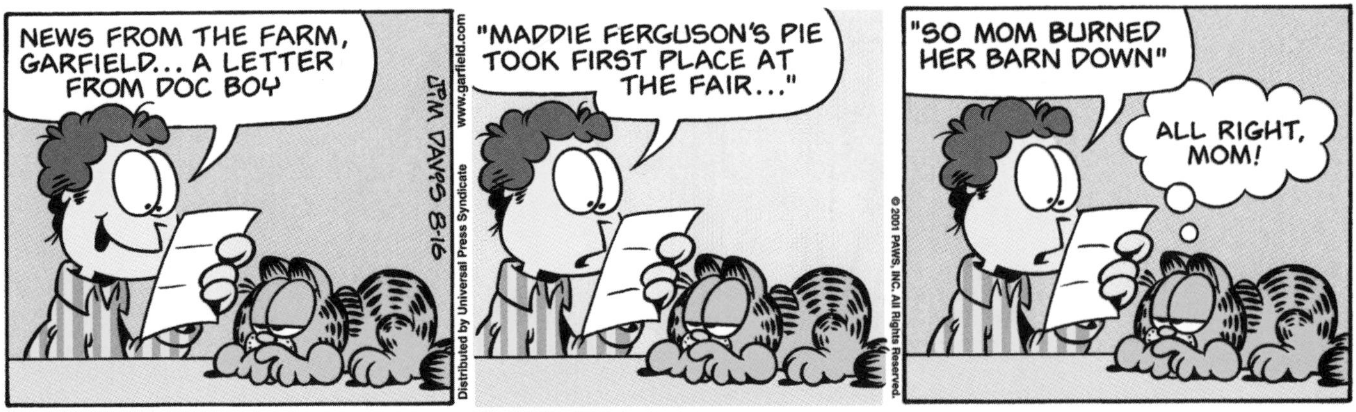
NEWS FROM THE FARM, GARFIELD... A LETTER FROM DOC BOY
JIM DAVIS 8-16
www.garfield.com
Distributed by Universal Press Syndicate
"MADDIE FERGUSON'S PIE TOOK FIRST PLACE AT THE FAIR..."
© 2001 PAWS, INC. All Rights Reserved.
"SO MOM BURNED HER BARN DOWN"
ALL RIGHT, MOM!

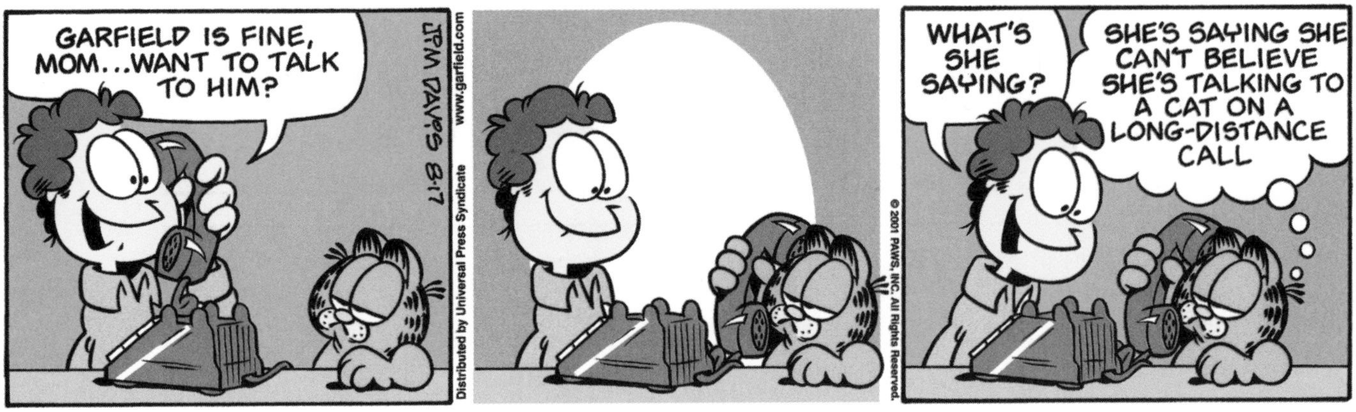
GARFIELD IS FINE, MOM...WANT TO TALK TO HIM?
JIM DAVIS 8-17
www.garfield.com
Distributed by Universal Press Syndicate
© 2001 PAWS, INC. All Rights Reserved.
WHAT'S SHE SAYING?
SHE'S SAYING SHE CAN'T BELIEVE SHE'S TALKING TO A CAT ON A LONG-DISTANCE CALL

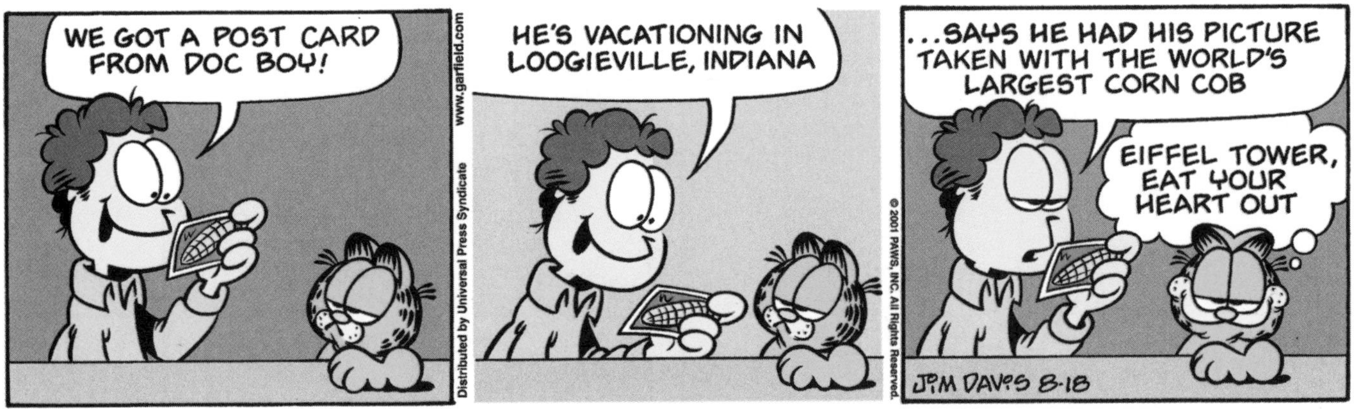
WE GOT A POST CARD FROM DOC BOY!
www.garfield.com
Distributed by Universal Press Syndicate
HE'S VACATIONING IN LOOGIEVILLE, INDIANA
© 2001 PAWS, INC. All Rights Reserved.
...SAYS HE HAD HIS PICTURE TAKEN WITH THE WORLD'S LARGEST CORN COB
EIFFEL TOWER, EAT YOUR HEART OUT
JIM DAVIS 8-18

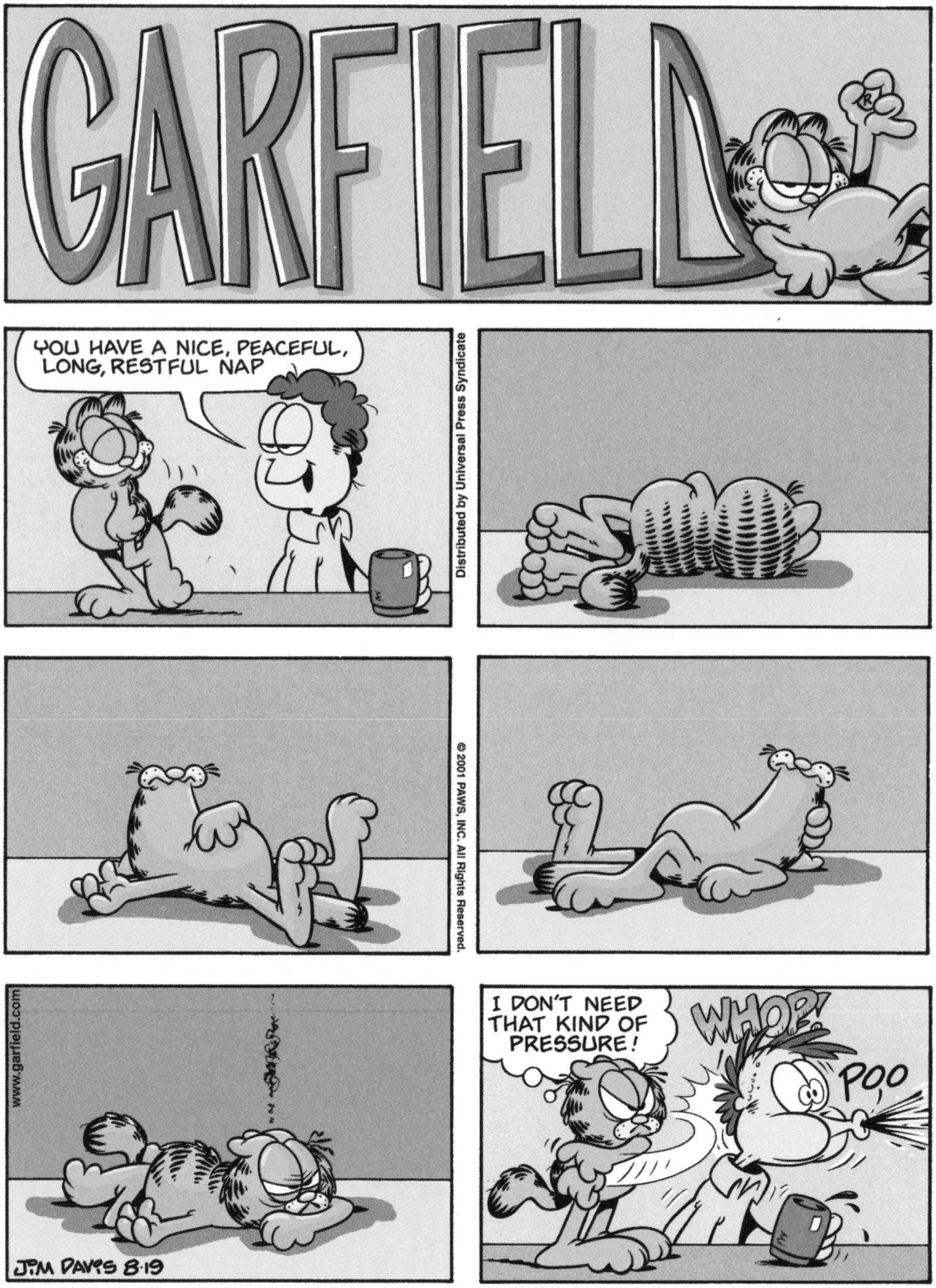
GARFIELD
YOU HAVE A NICE, PEACEFUL, LONG, RESTFUL NAP
Distributed by Universal Press Syndicate
© 2001 PAWS, INC. All Rights Reserved.
www.garfield.com
JIM DAVIS 8·19
I DON'T NEED THAT KIND OF PRESSURE!
WHOP!
POO

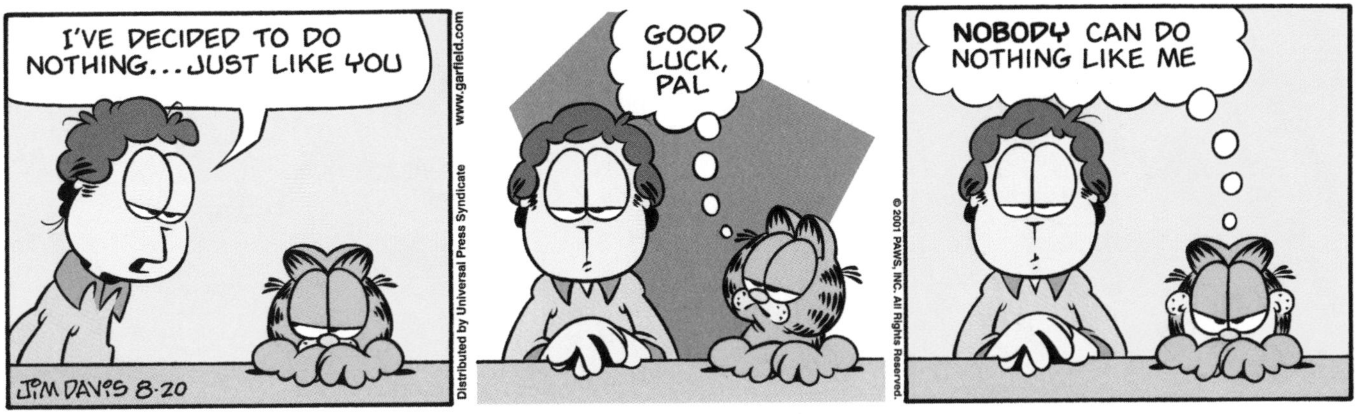
I'VE DECIDED TO DO NOTHING... JUST LIKE YOU
JIM DAVIS 8-20
www.garfield.com
Distributed by Universal Press Syndicate
GOOD LUCK, PAL
© 2001 PAWS, INC. All Rights Reserved.
NOBODY CAN DO NOTHING LIKE ME

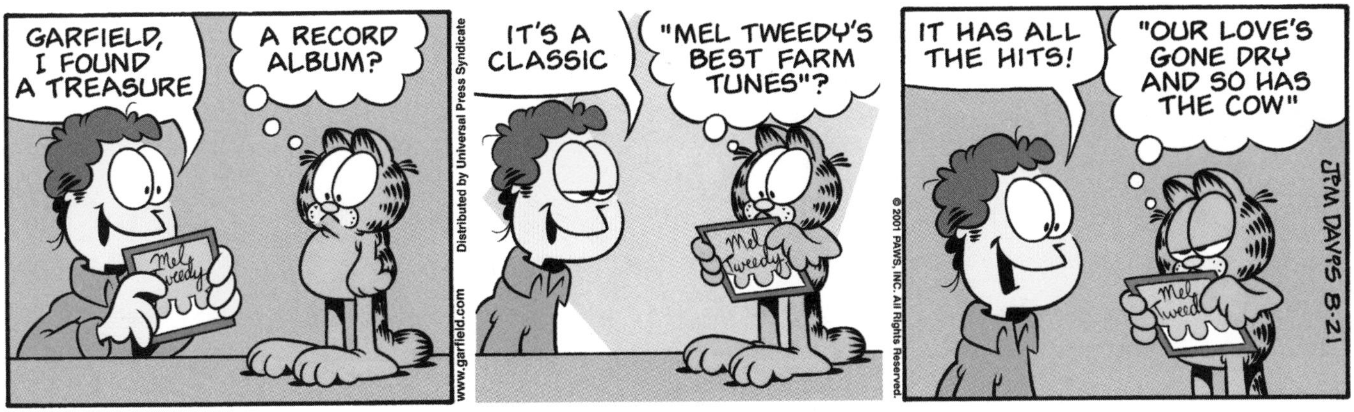
GARFIELD, I FOUND A TREASURE
A RECORD ALBUM?
Mel Tweedy
www.garfield.com
Distributed by Universal Press Syndicate
IT'S A CLASSIC
"MEL TWEEDY'S BEST FARM TUNES"?
© 2001 PAWS, INC. All Rights Reserved.
IT HAS ALL THE HITS!
"OUR LOVE'S GONE DRY AND SO HAS THE COW"
JIM DAVIS 8-21

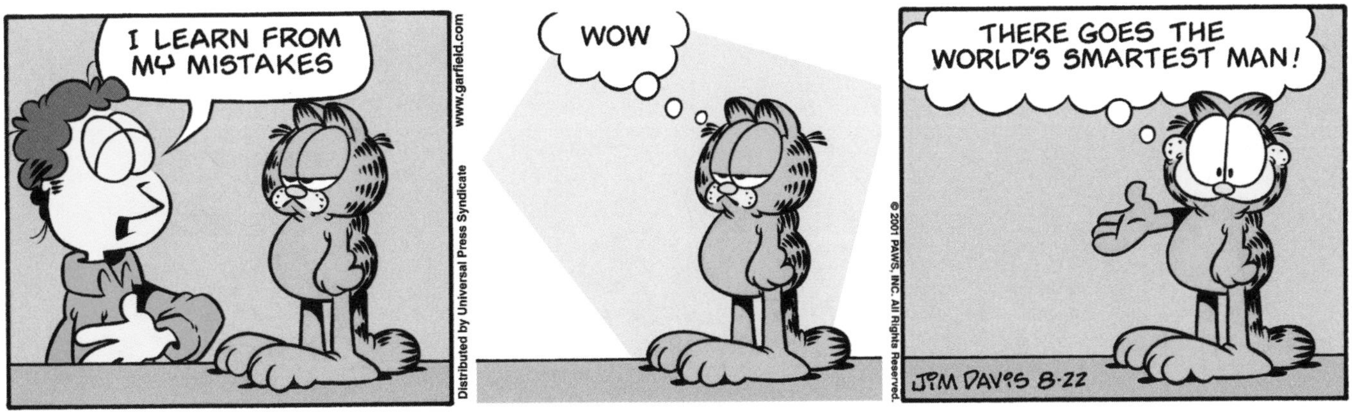
I LEARN FROM MY MISTAKES
www.garfield.com
Distributed by Universal Press Syndicate
WOW
© 2001 PAWS, INC. All Rights Reserved.
THERE GOES THE WORLD'S SMARTEST MAN!
JIM DAVIS 8-22

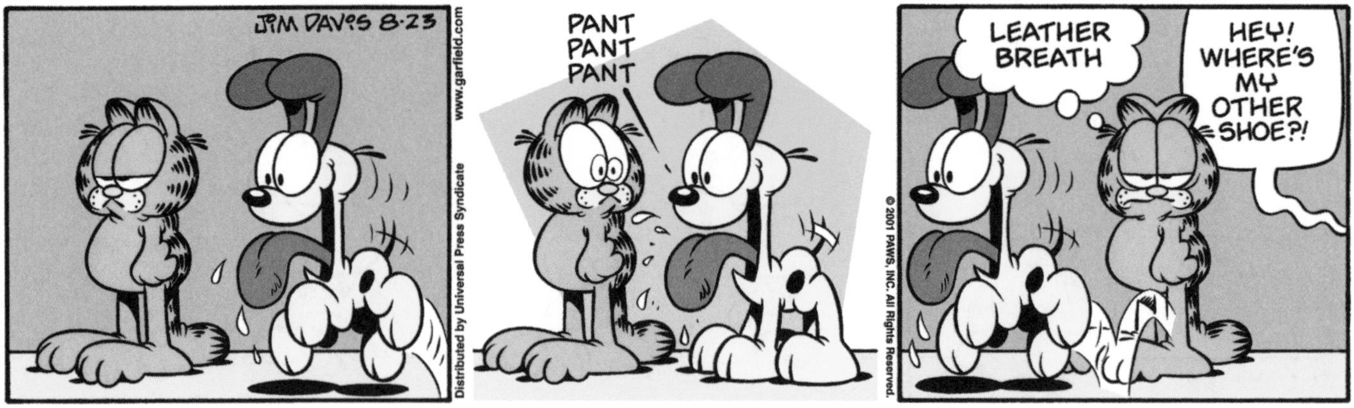
JIM DAVIS 8-23
www.garfield.com
Distributed by Universal Press Syndicate
PANT
PANT
PANT
© 2001 PAWS, INC. All Rights Reserved.
LEATHER BREATH
HEY! WHERE'S MY OTHER SHOE?!

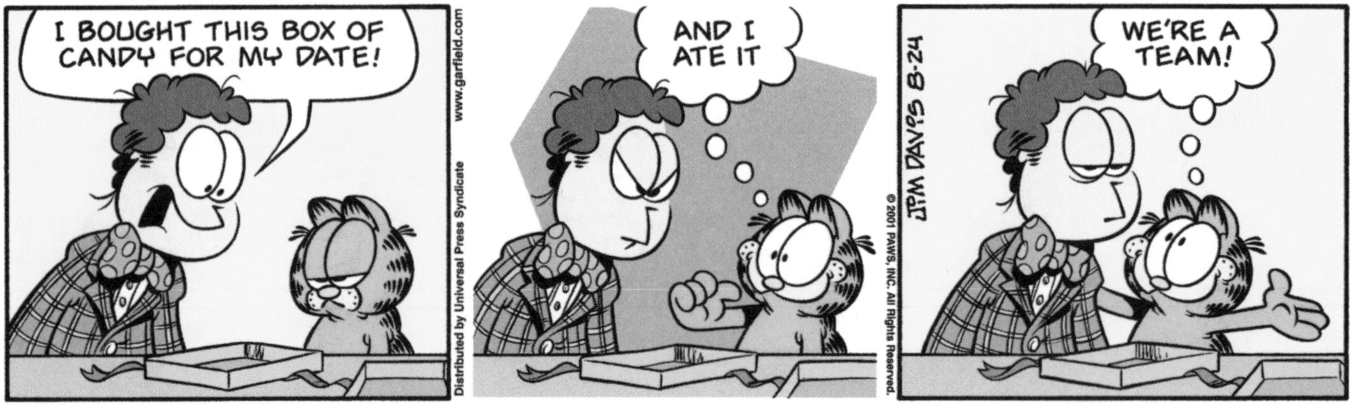
I BOUGHT THIS BOX OF CANDY FOR MY DATE!
www.garfield.com
Distributed by Universal Press Syndicate
AND I ATE IT
JIM DAVIS 8-24
© 2001 PAWS, INC. All Rights Reserved.
WE'RE A TEAM!

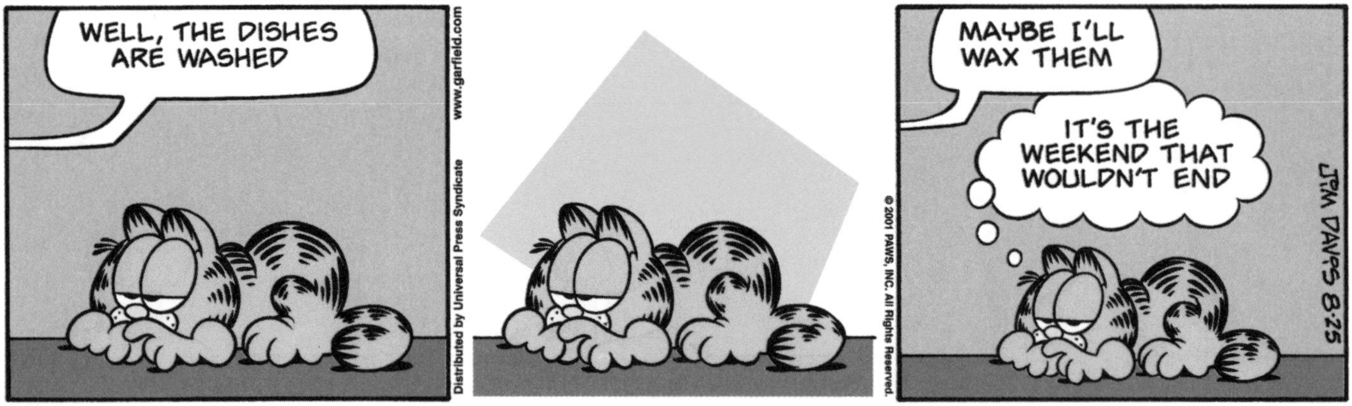
WELL, THE DISHES ARE WASHED
www.garfield.com
Distributed by Universal Press Syndicate
© 2001 PAWS, INC. All Rights Reserved.
MAYBE I'LL WAX THEM
IT'S THE WEEKEND THAT WOULDN'T END
JIM DAVIS 8-25

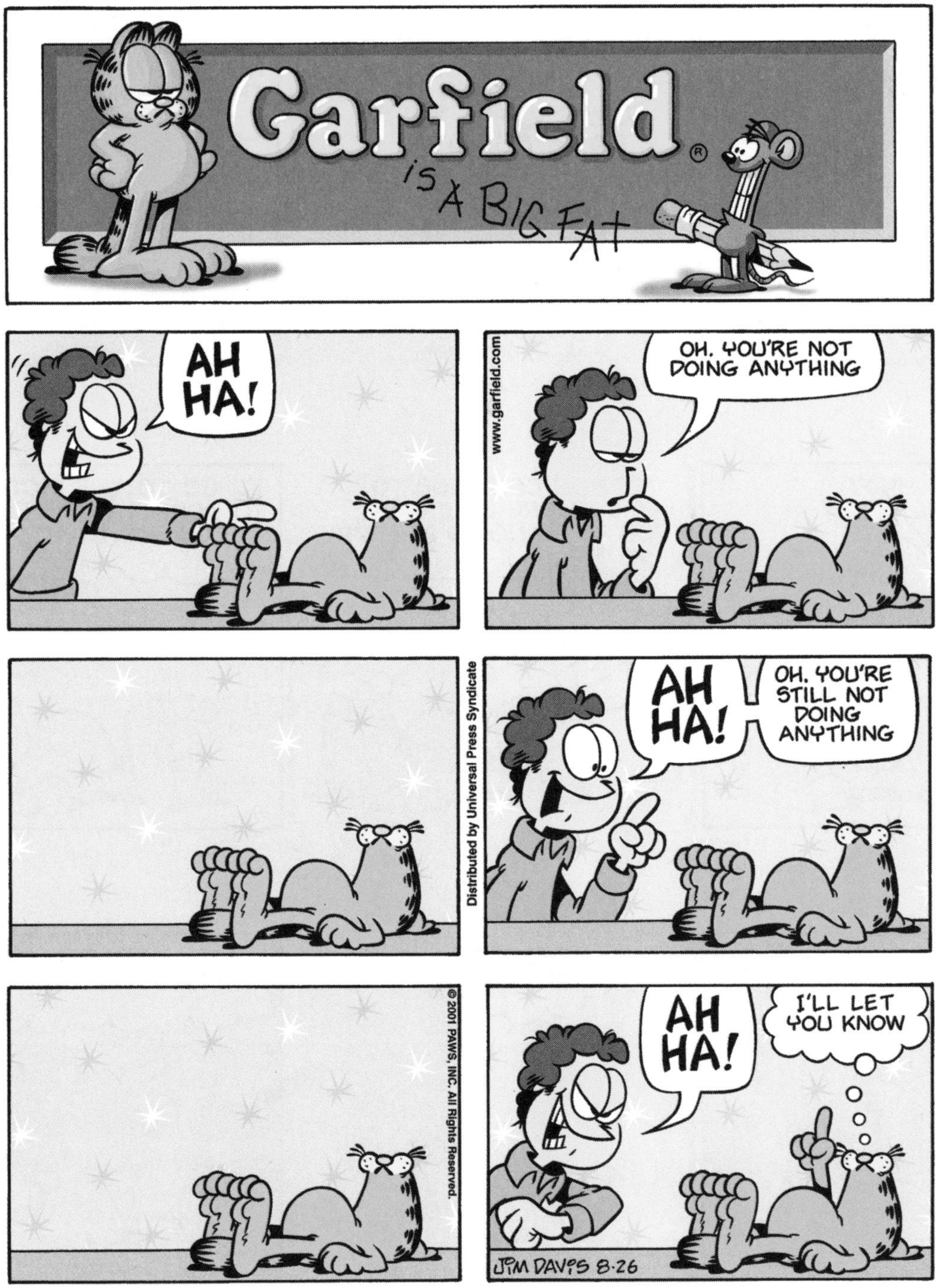
Garfield®
IS A BIG FAT
AH HA!
OH. YOU'RE NOT DOING ANYTHING
www.garfield.com
Distributed by Universal Press Syndicate
AH HA!
OH. YOU'RE STILL NOT DOING ANYTHING
© 2001 PAWS, INC. All Rights Reserved.
AH HA!
I'LL LET YOU KNOW
JIM DAVIS 8-26

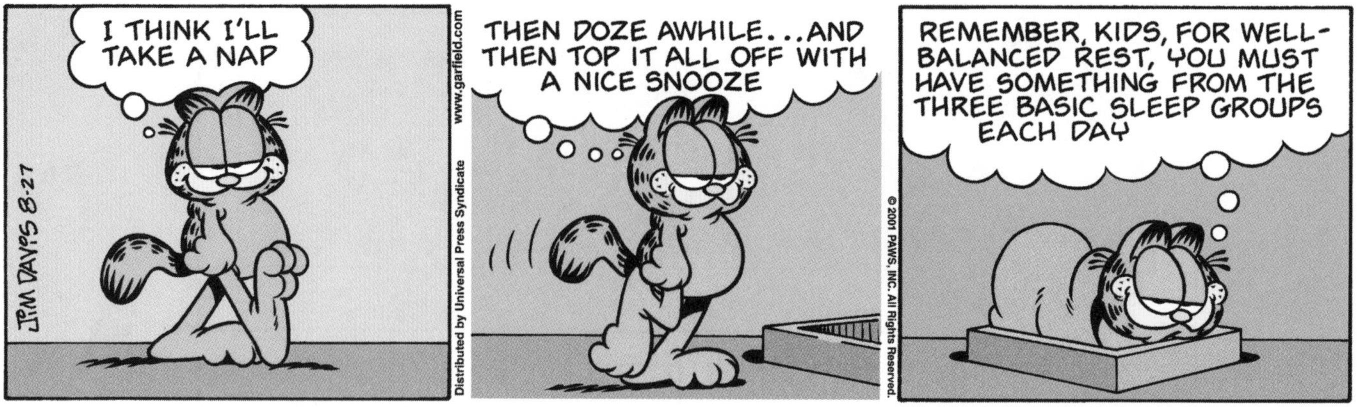
I THINK I'LL TAKE A NAP
JIM DAVIS 8-27
www.garfield.com
Distributed by Universal Press Syndicate
THEN DOZE AWHILE...AND THEN TOP IT ALL OFF WITH A NICE SNOOZE
© 2001 PAWS, INC. All Rights Reserved.
REMEMBER, KIDS, FOR WELL-BALANCED REST, YOU MUST HAVE SOMETHING FROM THE THREE BASIC SLEEP GROUPS EACH DAY

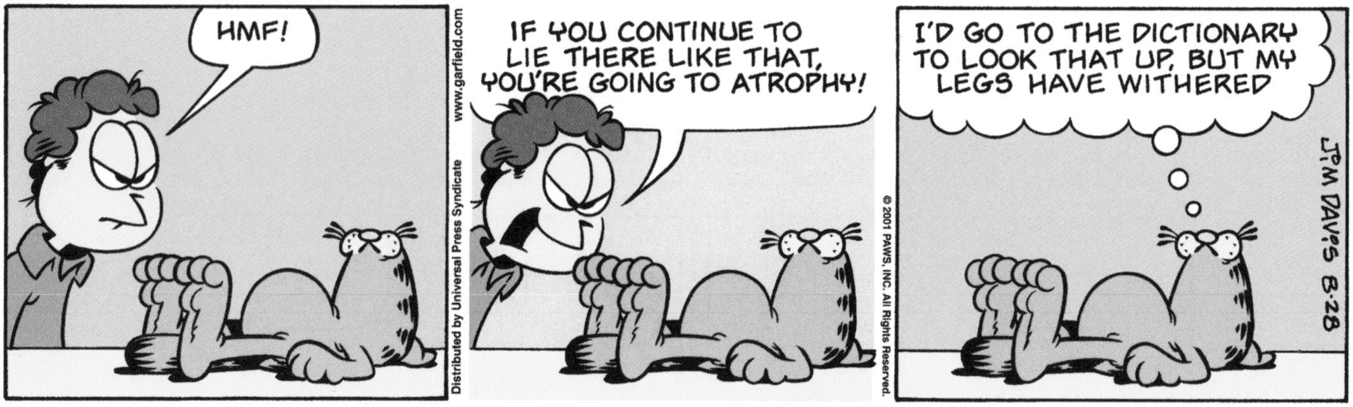
HMF!
www.garfield.com
Distributed by Universal Press Syndicate
IF YOU CONTINUE TO LIE THERE LIKE THAT, YOU'RE GOING TO ATROPHY!
© 2001 PAWS, INC. All Rights Reserved.
I'D GO TO THE DICTIONARY TO LOOK THAT UP, BUT MY LEGS HAVE WITHERED
JIM DAVIS 8-28

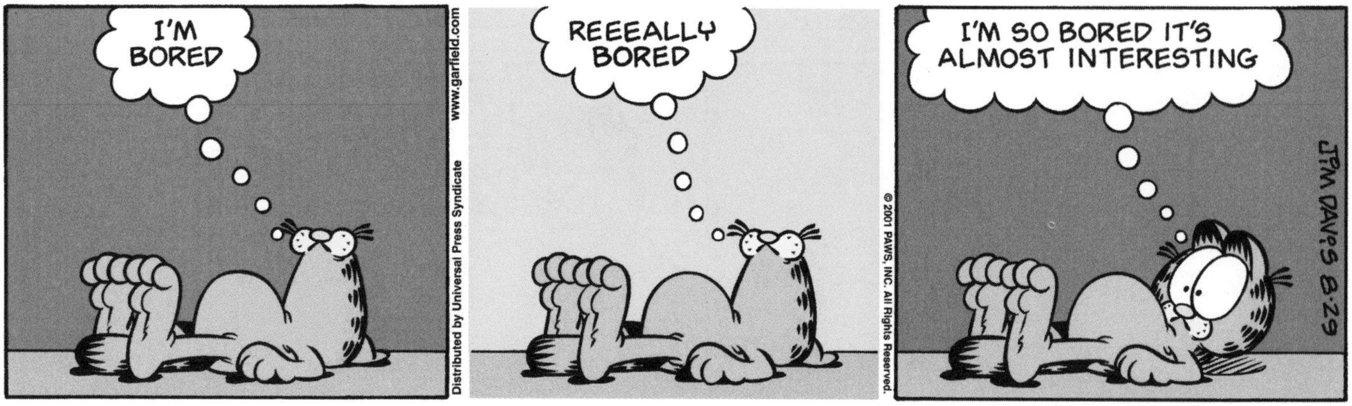
I'M BORED
www.garfield.com
Distributed by Universal Press Syndicate
REEEALLY BORED
© 2001 PAWS, INC. All Rights Reserved.
I'M SO BORED IT'S ALMOST INTERESTING
JIM DAVIS 8-29

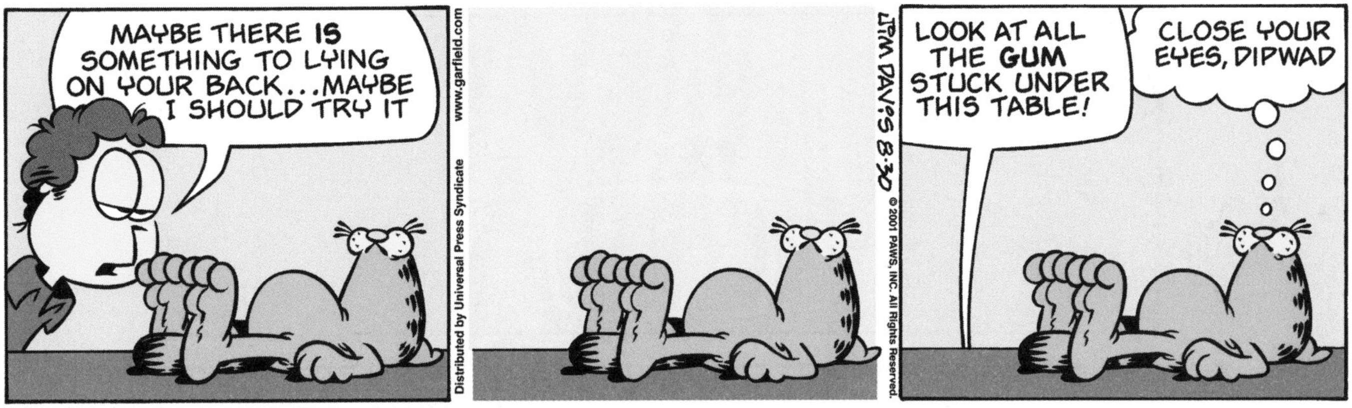
MAYBE THERE IS SOMETHING TO LYING ON YOUR BACK...MAYBE I SHOULD TRY IT
www.garfield.com
Distributed by Universal Press Syndicate
JIM DAVIS 8-30
© 2001 PAWS, INC. All Rights Reserved.
LOOK AT ALL THE GUM STUCK UNDER THIS TABLE!
CLOSE YOUR EYES, DIPWAD

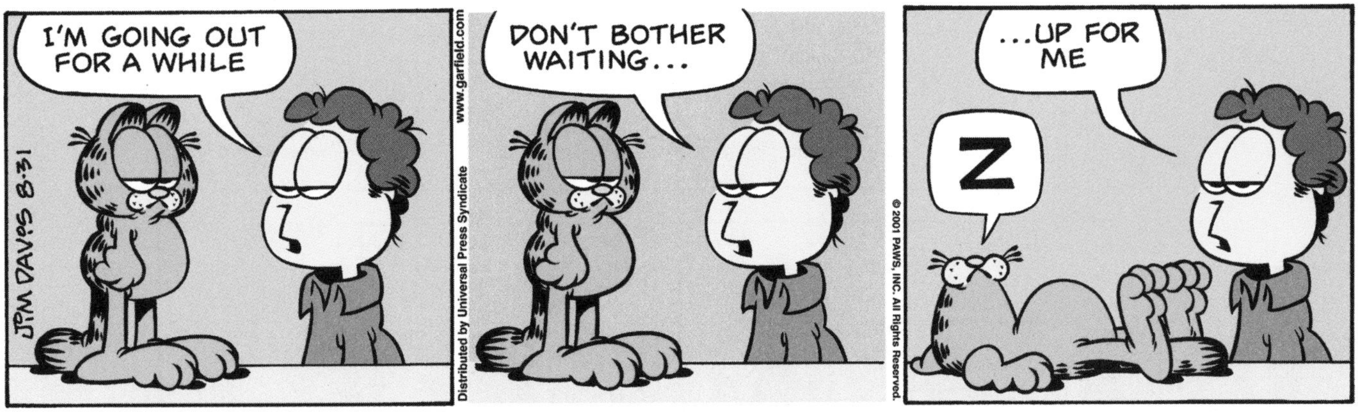
I'M GOING OUT FOR A WHILE
JIM DAVIS 8-31
www.garfield.com
Distributed by Universal Press Syndicate
DON'T BOTHER WAITING...
© 2001 PAWS, INC. All Rights Reserved.
Z
...UP FOR ME

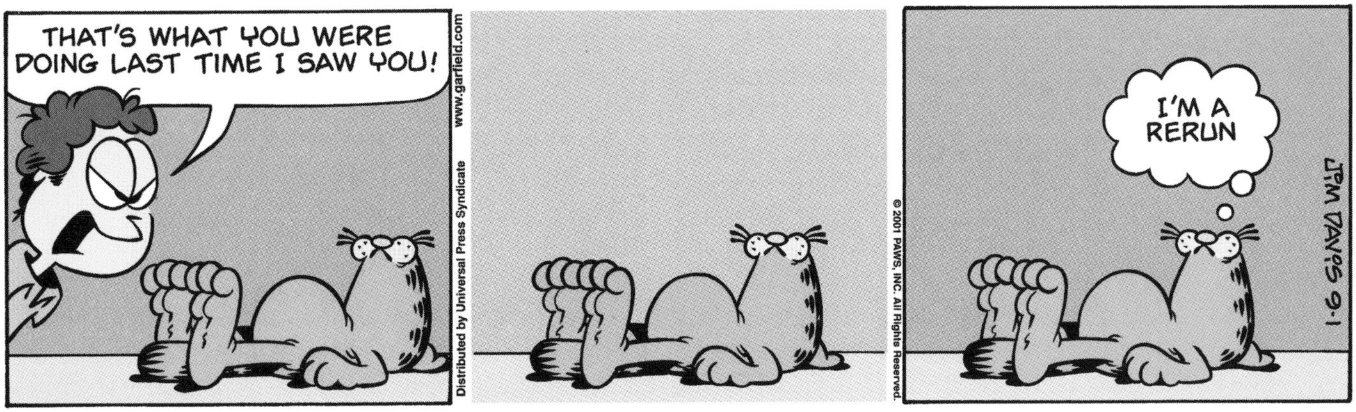
THAT'S WHAT YOU WERE DOING LAST TIME I SAW YOU!
www.garfield.com
Distributed by Universal Press Syndicate
© 2001 PAWS, INC. All Rights Reserved.
I'M A RERUN
JIM DAVIS 9-1

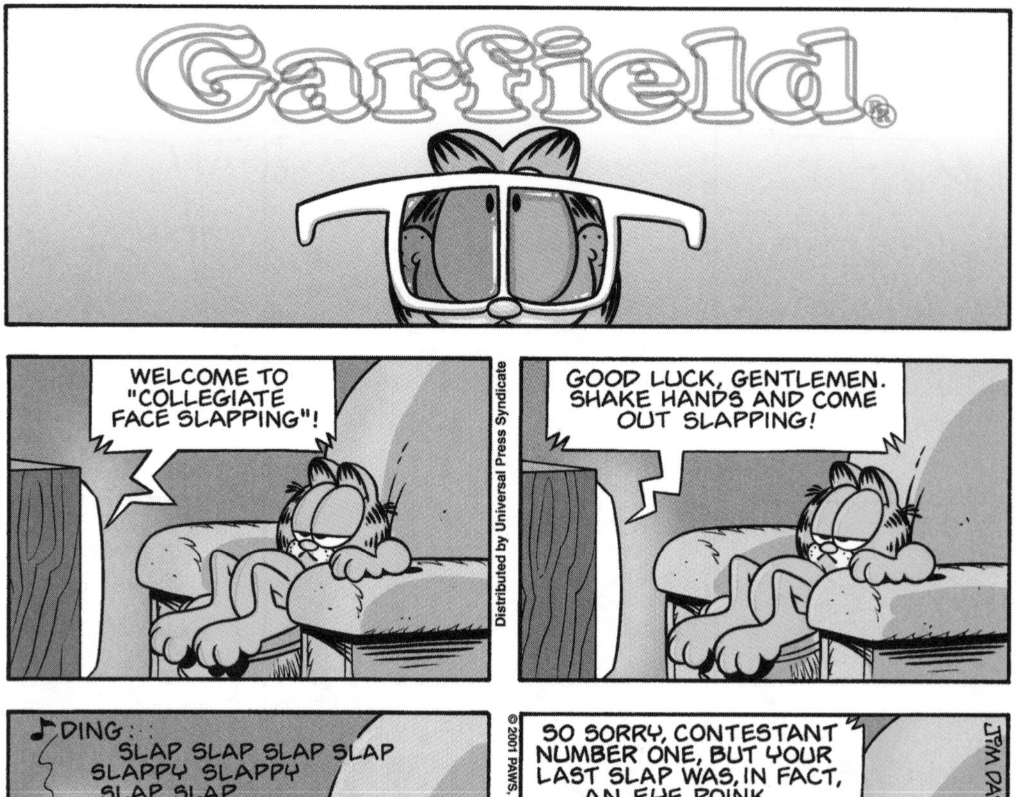
Garfield®
WELCOME TO "COLLEGIATE FACE SLAPPING"!
Distributed by Universal Press Syndicate
GOOD LUCK, GENTLEMEN. SHAKE HANDS AND COME OUT SLAPPING!
DING
SLAP SLAP SLAP SLAP SLAPPY SLAPPY SLAP SLAP SLAPPITY SLAPPITY SLAP*POINK*
UH-OH! WE HAVE A PENALTY FLAG
© 2001 PAWS, INC. All Rights Reserved.
SO SORRY, CONTESTANT NUMBER ONE, BUT YOUR LAST SLAP WAS, IN FACT, AN EYE POINK
JIM DAVIS 9-2
TWO POINTS OFF...
TWO POINTS?! THAT WASN'T AN EYE POINK! HERE'S AN EYE POINK!
POINK
AND THE REF GOES DOWN!
WHAT DID WE EVER DO BEFORE 32 SPORTS CHANNELS?

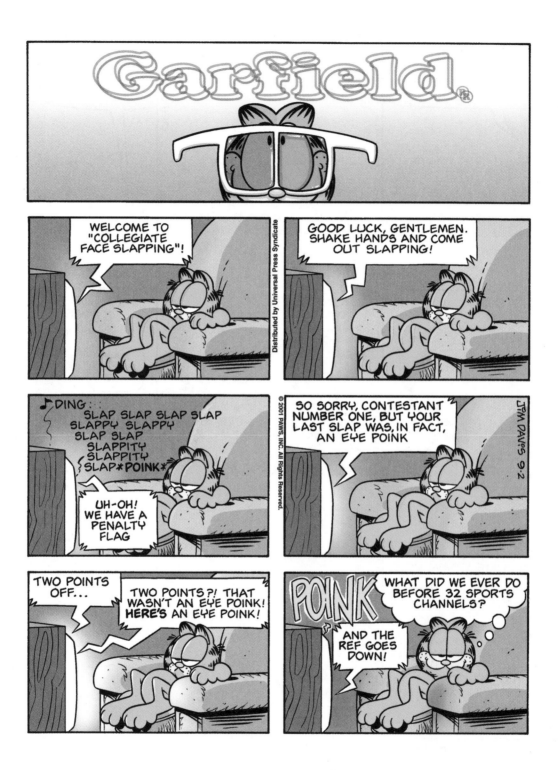

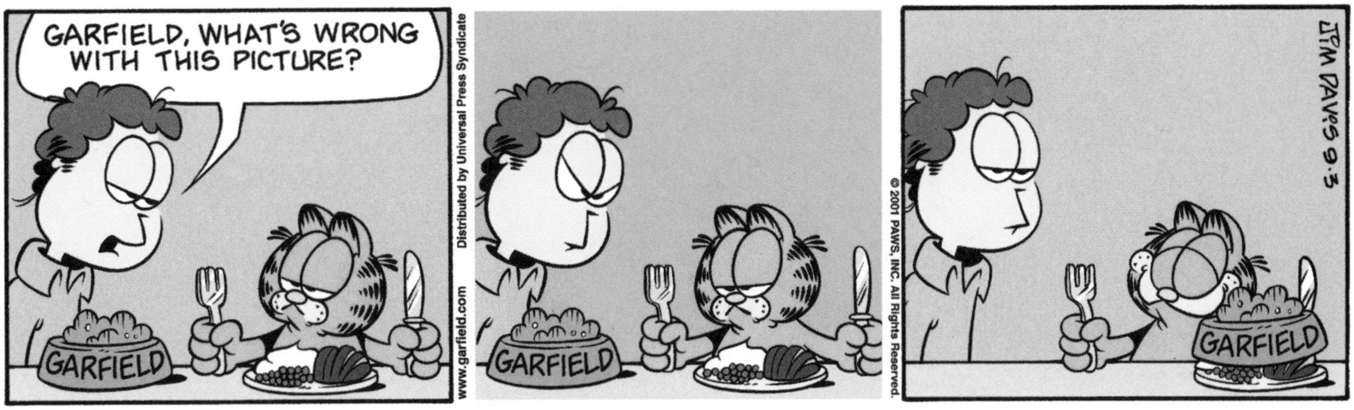
GARFIELD, WHAT'S WRONG WITH THIS PICTURE?
GARFIELD
www.garfield.com Distributed by Universal Press Syndicate
© 2001 PAWS, INC. All Rights Reserved.
JIM DAVIS 9-3

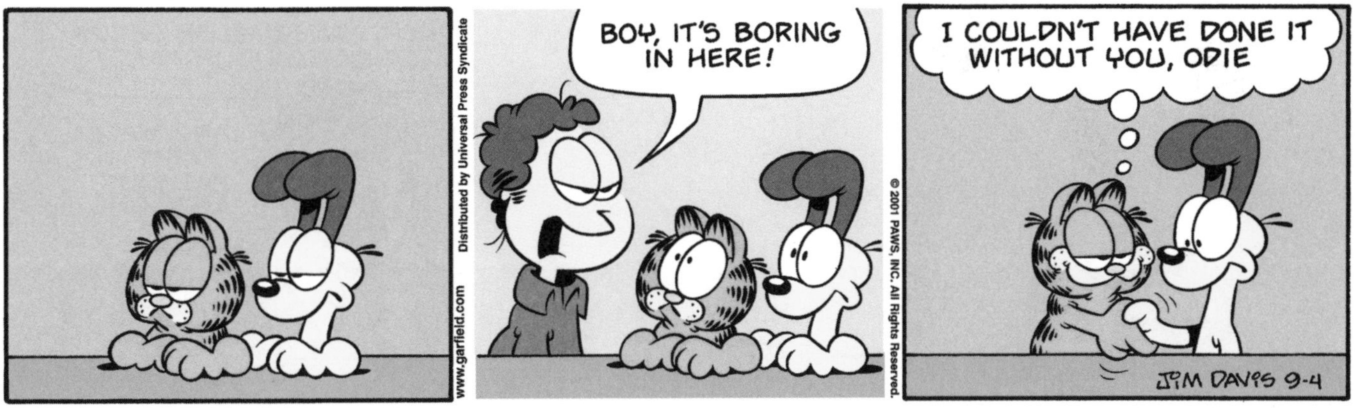
www.garfield.com Distributed by Universal Press Syndicate
BOY, IT'S BORING IN HERE!
© 2001 PAWS, INC. All Rights Reserved.
I COULDN'T HAVE DONE IT WITHOUT YOU, ODIE
JIM DAVIS 9-4

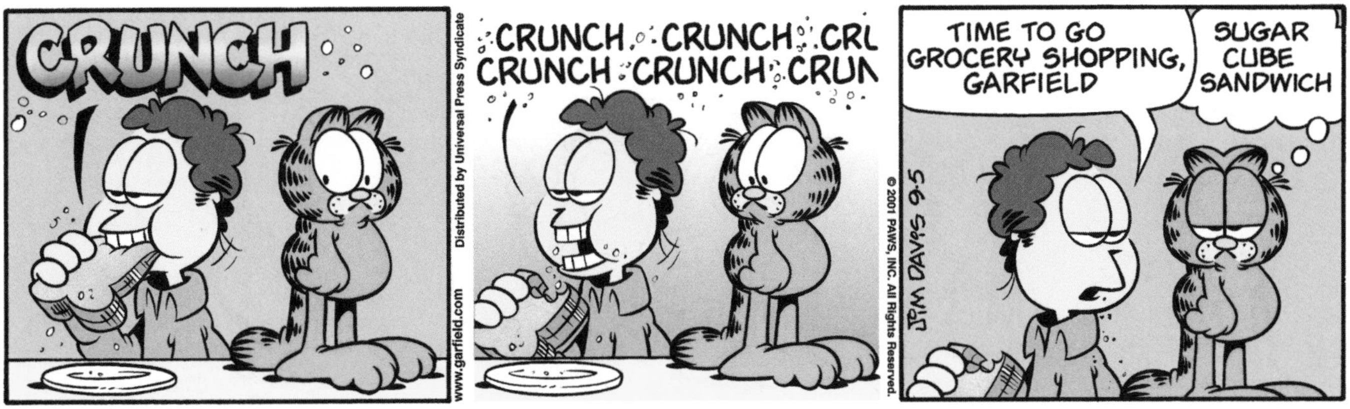
CRUNCH
www.garfield.com Distributed by Universal Press Syndicate
CRUNCH CRUNCH CRU
CRUNCH CRUNCH CRUN
© 2001 PAWS, INC. All Rights Reserved.
JIM DAVIS 9-5
TIME TO GO GROCERY SHOPPING, GARFIELD
SUGAR CUBE SANDWICH

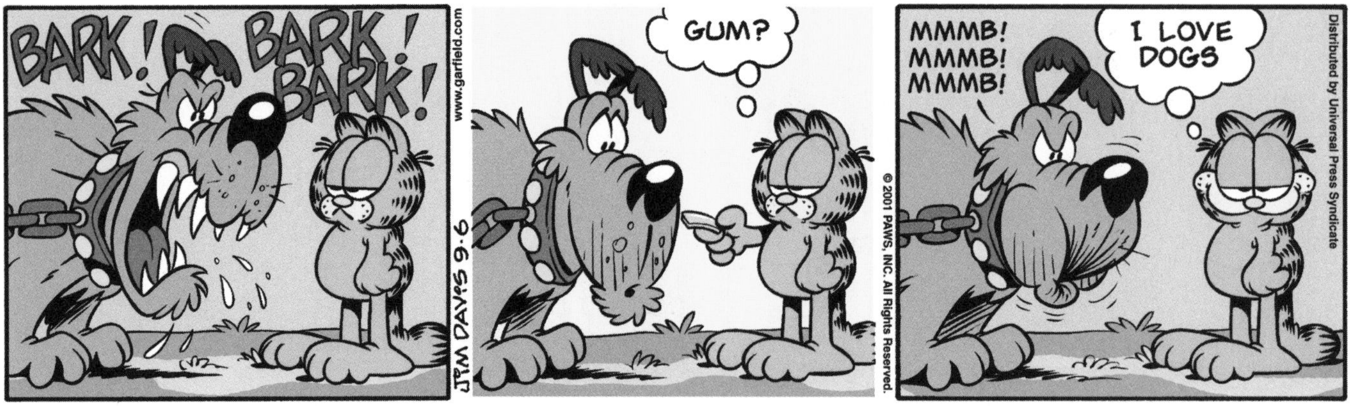
BARK! BARK! BARK!
JIM DAVIS 9·6
www.garfield.com
GUM?
© 2001 PAWS, INC. All Rights Reserved.
MMMB! MMMB! MMMB!
I LOVE DOGS
Distributed by Universal Press Syndicate

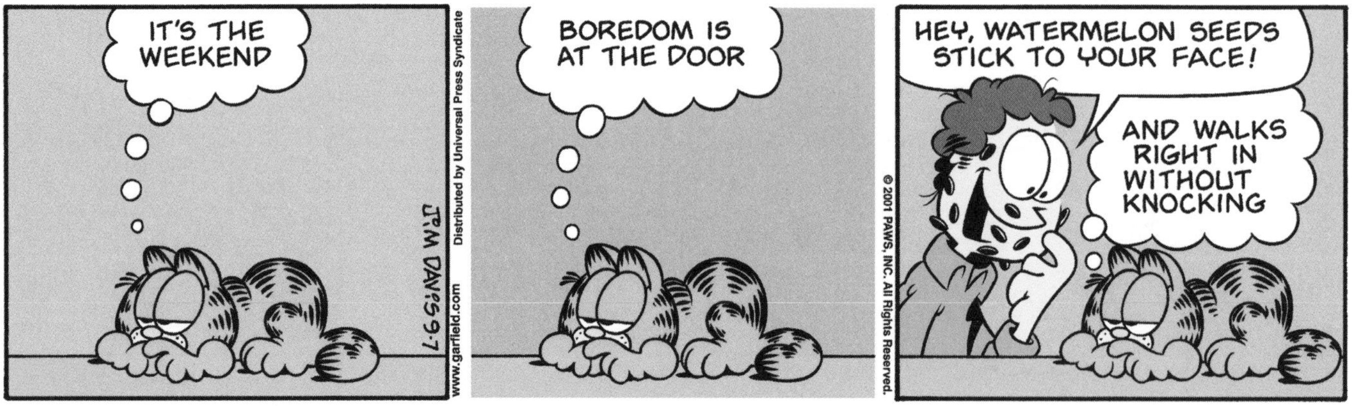
IT'S THE WEEKEND
JIM DAVIS 9·7
Distributed by Universal Press Syndicate
www.garfield.com
BOREDOM IS AT THE DOOR
© 2001 PAWS, INC. All Rights Reserved.
HEY, WATERMELON SEEDS STICK TO YOUR FACE!
AND WALKS RIGHT IN WITHOUT KNOCKING

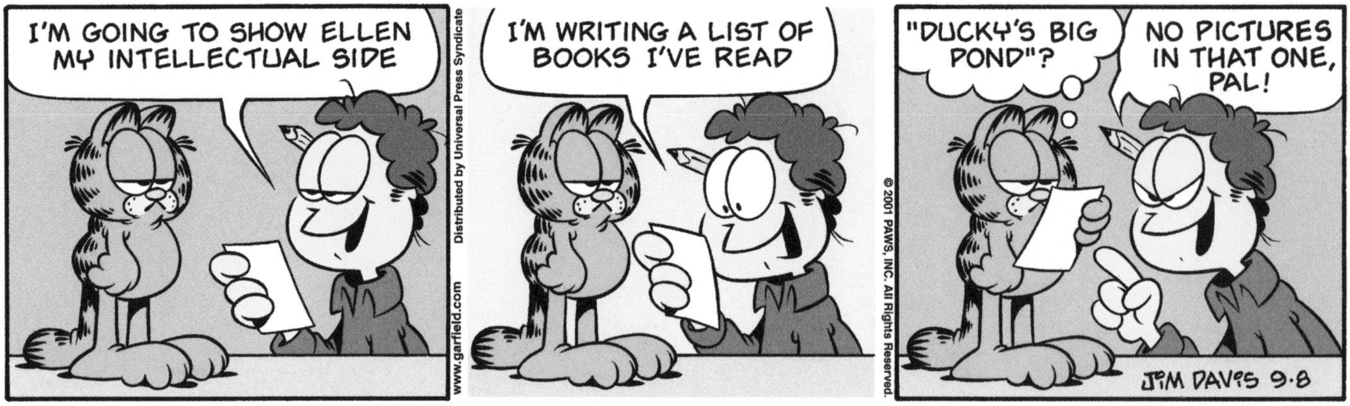
I'M GOING TO SHOW ELLEN MY INTELLECTUAL SIDE
Distributed by Universal Press Syndicate
www.garfield.com
I'M WRITING A LIST OF BOOKS I'VE READ
© 2001 PAWS, INC. All Rights Reserved.
"DUCKY'S BIG POND"?
NO PICTURES IN THAT ONE, PAL!
JIM DAVIS 9·8

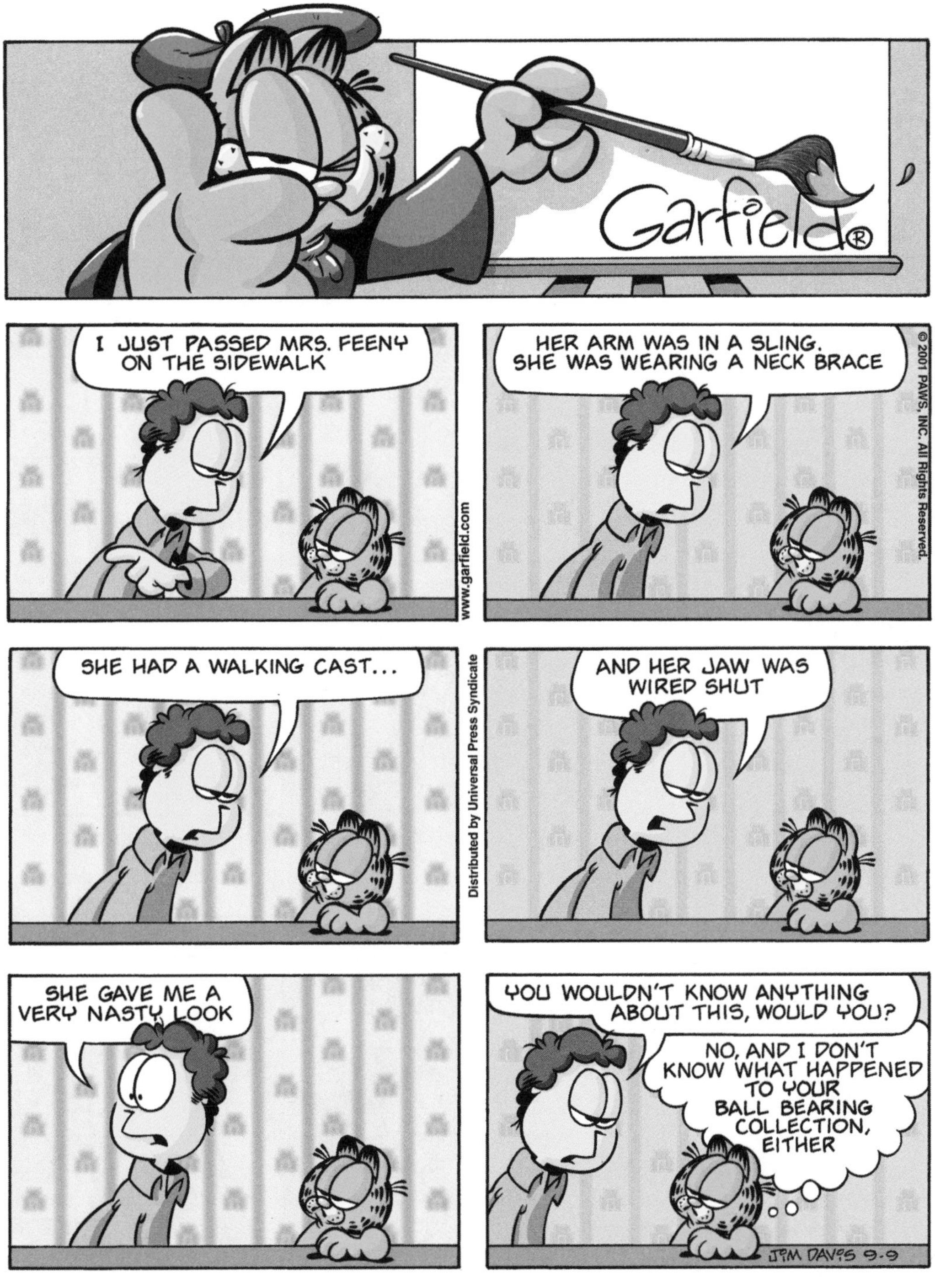

Garfield®
I JUST PASSED MRS. FEENY ON THE SIDEWALK
HER ARM WAS IN A SLING. SHE WAS WEARING A NECK BRACE
SHE HAD A WALKING CAST...
AND HER JAW WAS WIRED SHUT
SHE GAVE ME A VERY NASTY LOOK
YOU WOULDN'T KNOW ANYTHING ABOUT THIS, WOULD YOU?
NO, AND I DON'T KNOW WHAT HAPPENED TO YOUR BALL BEARING COLLECTION, EITHER
JIM DAVIS 9-9
www.garfield.com
Distributed by Universal Press Syndicate
© 2001 PAWS, INC. All Rights Reserved.

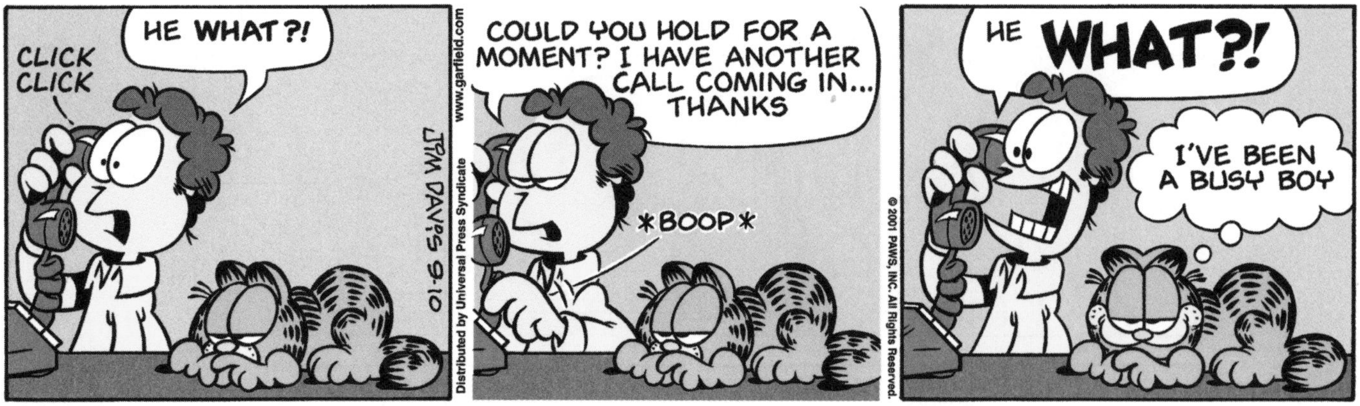
CLICK CLICK
HE WHAT?!
COULD YOU HOLD FOR A MOMENT? I HAVE ANOTHER CALL COMING IN... THANKS
BOOP
HE WHAT?!
I'VE BEEN A BUSY BOY
JIM DAVIS 9-10
www.garfield.com
Distributed by Universal Press Syndicate
© 2001 PAWS, INC. All Rights Reserved.

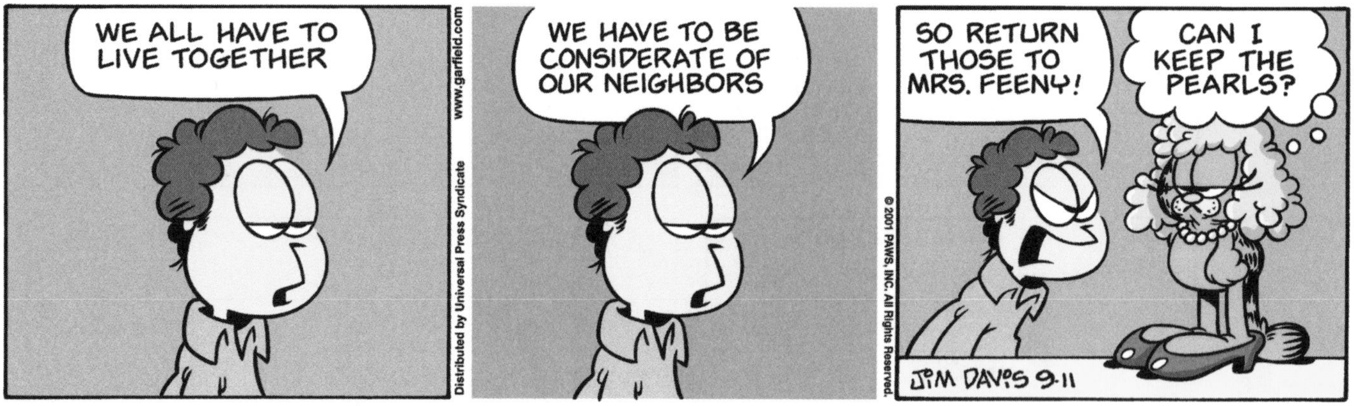
WE ALL HAVE TO LIVE TOGETHER
WE HAVE TO BE CONSIDERATE OF OUR NEIGHBORS
SO RETURN THOSE TO MRS. FEENY!
CAN I KEEP THE PEARLS?
JIM DAVIS 9-11
www.garfield.com
Distributed by Universal Press Syndicate
© 2001 PAWS, INC. All Rights Reserved.

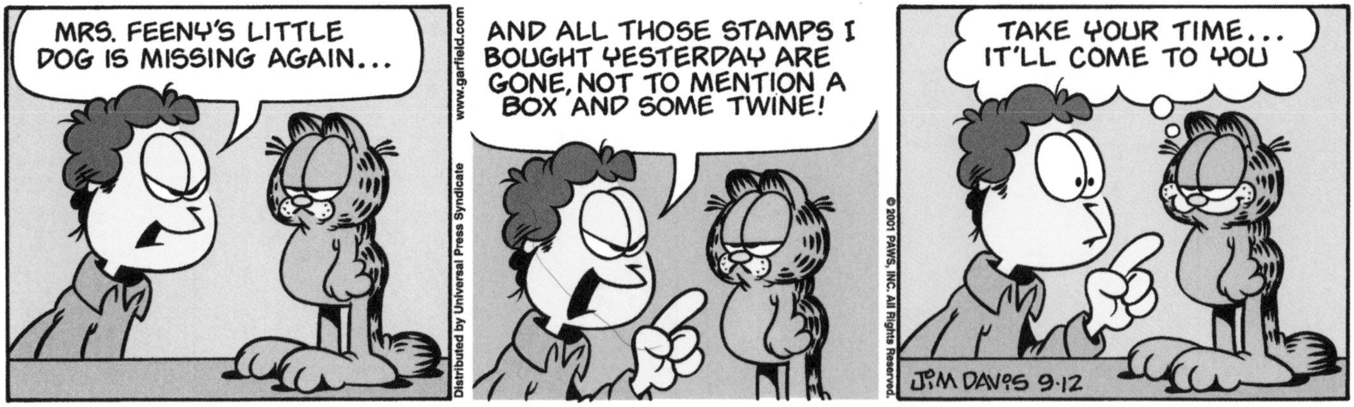
MRS. FEENY'S LITTLE DOG IS MISSING AGAIN...
AND ALL THOSE STAMPS I BOUGHT YESTERDAY ARE GONE, NOT TO MENTION A BOX AND SOME TWINE!
TAKE YOUR TIME... IT'LL COME TO YOU
JIM DAVIS 9-12
www.garfield.com
Distributed by Universal Press Syndicate
© 2001 PAWS, INC. All Rights Reserved.

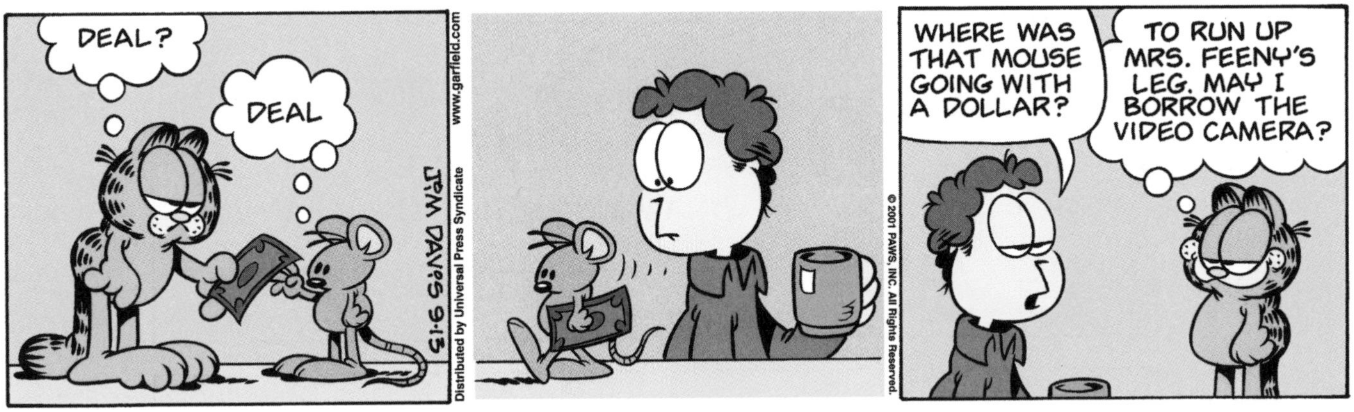
DEAL?
DEAL
JIM DAVIS 9-13
www.garfield.com
Distributed by Universal Press Syndicate
WHERE WAS THAT MOUSE GOING WITH A DOLLAR?
TO RUN UP MRS. FEENY'S LEG. MAY I BORROW THE VIDEO CAMERA?
© 2001 PAWS, INC. All Rights Reserved.

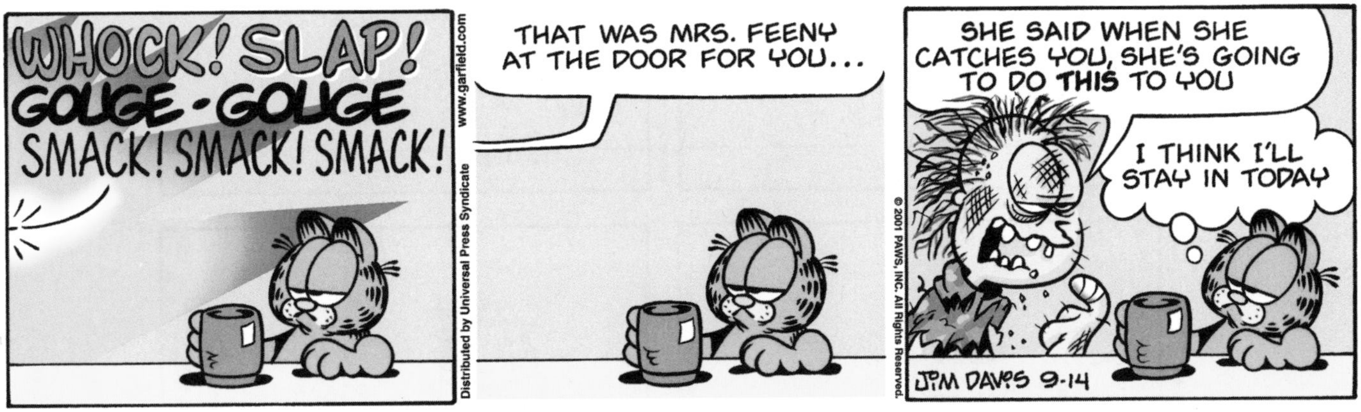
WHOCK! SLAP!
GOUGE-GOUGE
SMACK! SMACK! SMACK!
www.garfield.com
Distributed by Universal Press Syndicate
THAT WAS MRS. FEENY AT THE DOOR FOR YOU...
SHE SAID WHEN SHE CATCHES YOU, SHE'S GOING TO DO **THIS** TO YOU
I THINK I'LL STAY IN TODAY
© 2001 PAWS, INC. All Rights Reserved.
JIM DAVIS 9-14

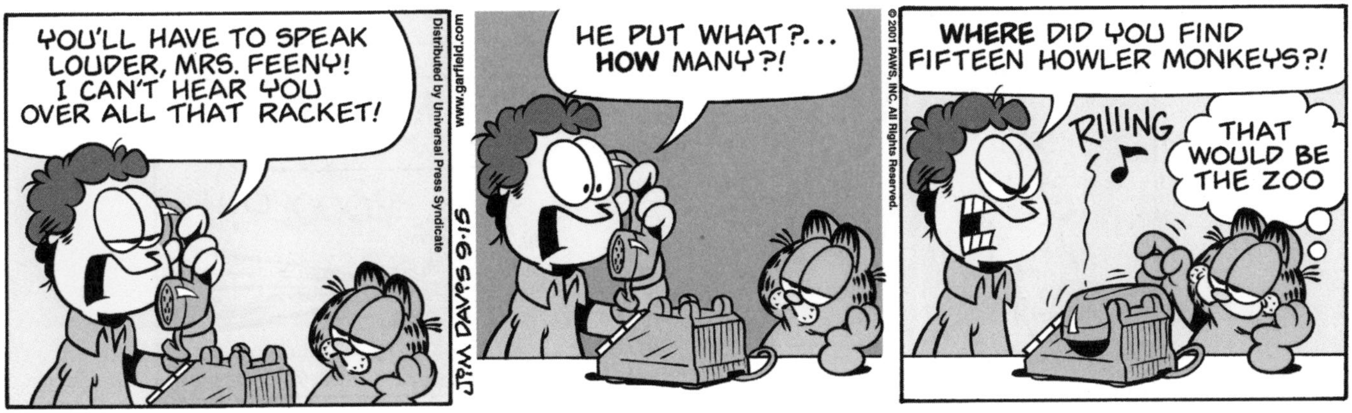
YOU'LL HAVE TO SPEAK LOUDER, MRS. FEENY! I CAN'T HEAR YOU OVER ALL THAT RACKET!
www.garfield.com
Distributed by Universal Press Syndicate
JIM DAVIS 9-15
HE PUT WHAT?... **HOW** MANY?!
WHERE DID YOU FIND FIFTEEN HOWLER MONKEYS?!
RIIIING
THAT WOULD BE THE ZOO
© 2001 PAWS, INC. All Rights Reserved.

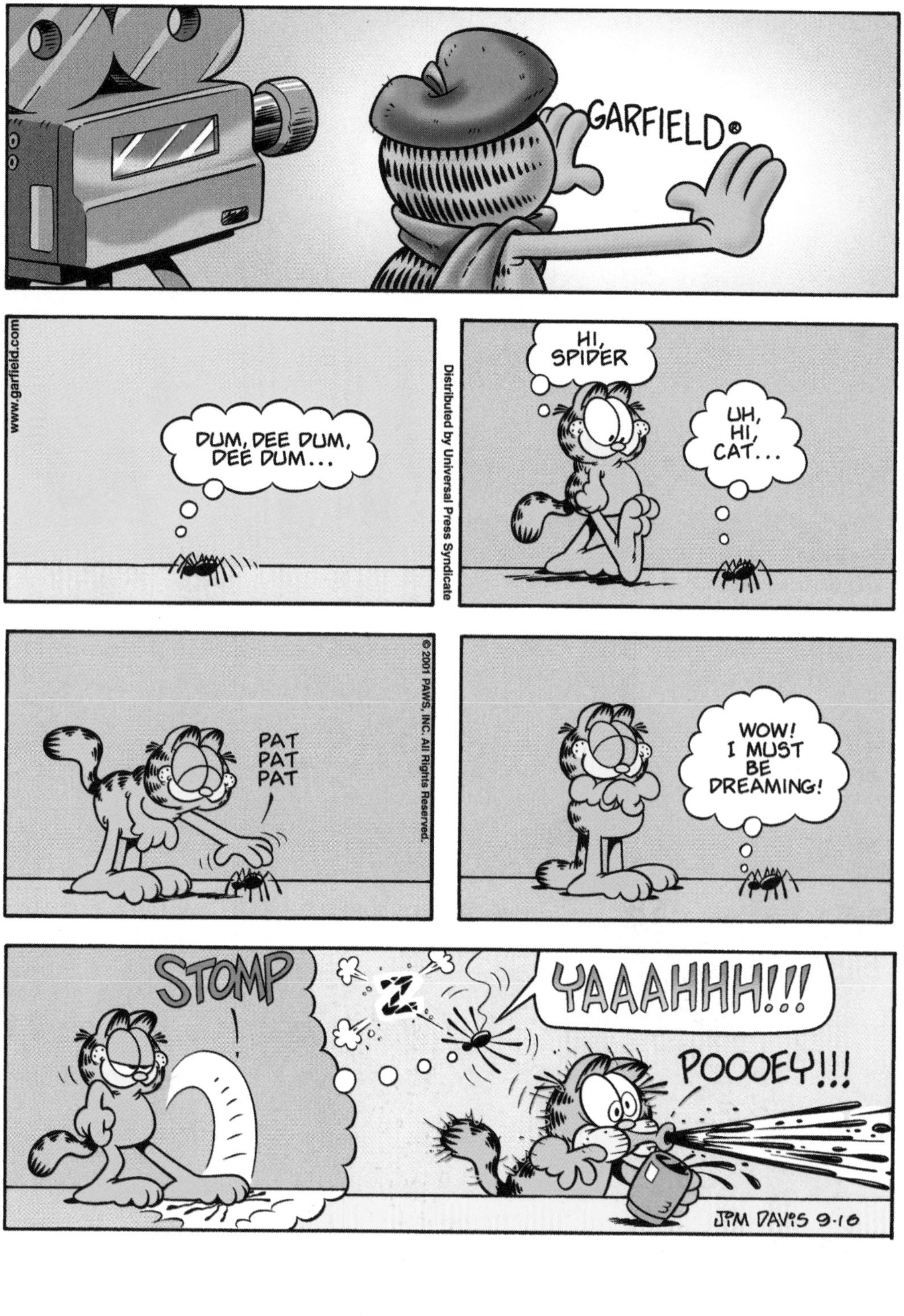
GARFIELD®
www.garfield.com
DUM, DEE DUM, DEE DUM...
Distributed by Universal Press Syndicate
HI, SPIDER
UH, HI, CAT...
© 2001 PAWS, INC. All Rights Reserved.
PAT PAT PAT
WOW! I MUST BE DREAMING!
STOMP
YAAAHHH!!!
POOOEY!!!
JIM DAVIS 9-16

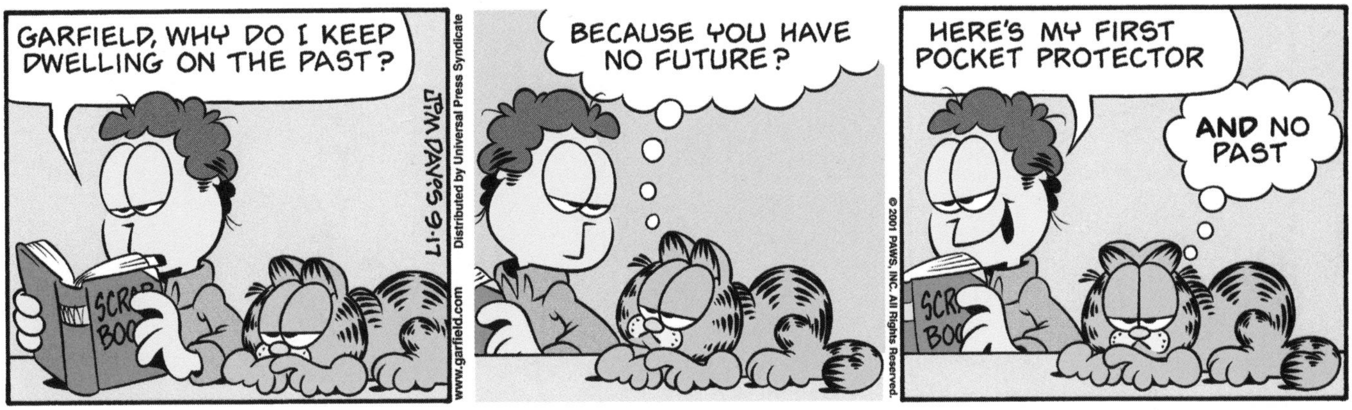
GARFIELD, WHY DO I KEEP DWELLING ON THE PAST?
JIM DAVIS 9-17
BECAUSE YOU HAVE NO FUTURE?
HERE'S MY FIRST POCKET PROTECTOR
AND NO PAST
Distributed by Universal Press Syndicate www.garfield.com
© 2001 PAWS, INC. All Rights Reserved.

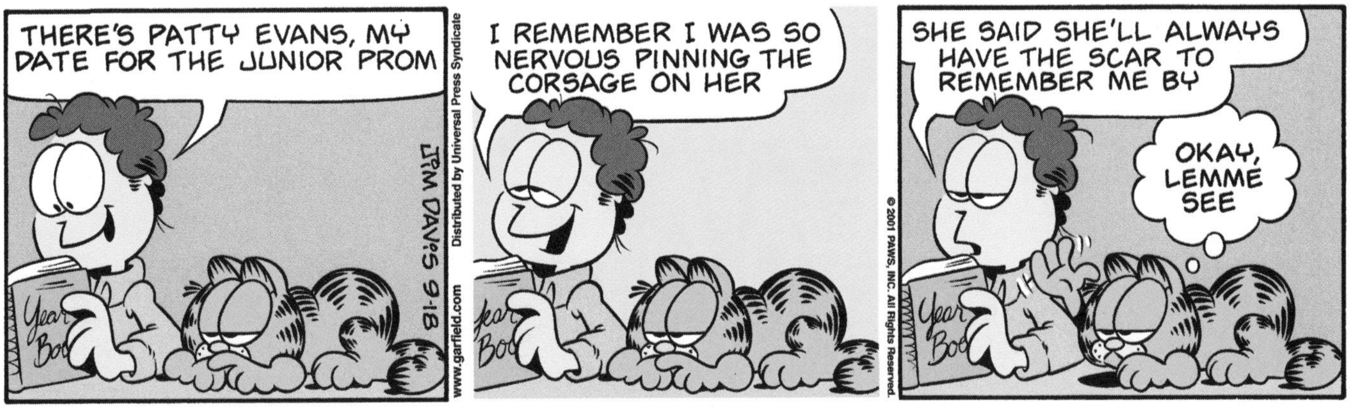
THERE'S PATTY EVANS, MY DATE FOR THE JUNIOR PROM
JIM DAVIS 9-18
I REMEMBER I WAS SO NERVOUS PINNING THE CORSAGE ON HER
SHE SAID SHE'LL ALWAYS HAVE THE SCAR TO REMEMBER ME BY
OKAY, LEMME SEE
Distributed by Universal Press Syndicate www.garfield.com
© 2001 PAWS, INC. All Rights Reserved.

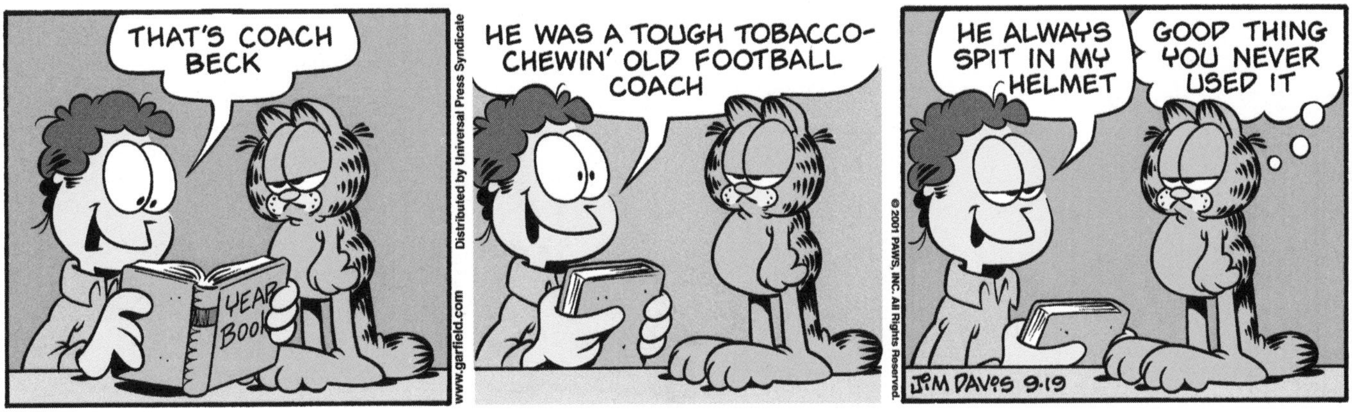
THAT'S COACH BECK
HE WAS A TOUGH TOBACCO-CHEWIN' OLD FOOTBALL COACH
HE ALWAYS SPIT IN MY HELMET
GOOD THING YOU NEVER USED IT
JIM DAVIS 9-19
Distributed by Universal Press Syndicate www.garfield.com
© 2001 PAWS, INC. All Rights Reserved.

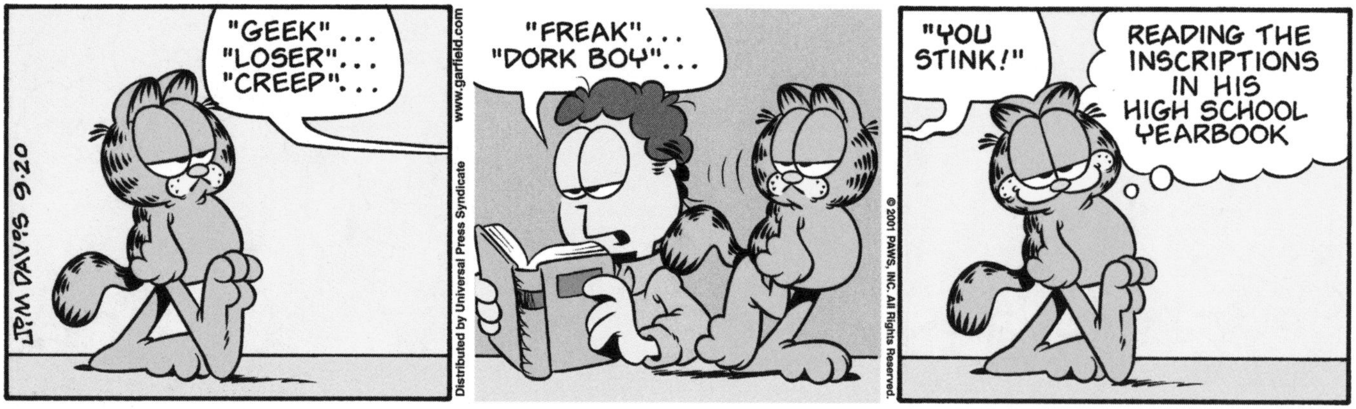
JIM DAVIS 9·20
"GEEK"... "LOSER"... "CREEP"...
www.garfield.com
Distributed by Universal Press Syndicate
"FREAK"... "DORK BOY"...
© 2001 PAWS, INC. All Rights Reserved.
"YOU STINK!"
READING THE INSCRIPTIONS IN HIS HIGH SCHOOL YEARBOOK

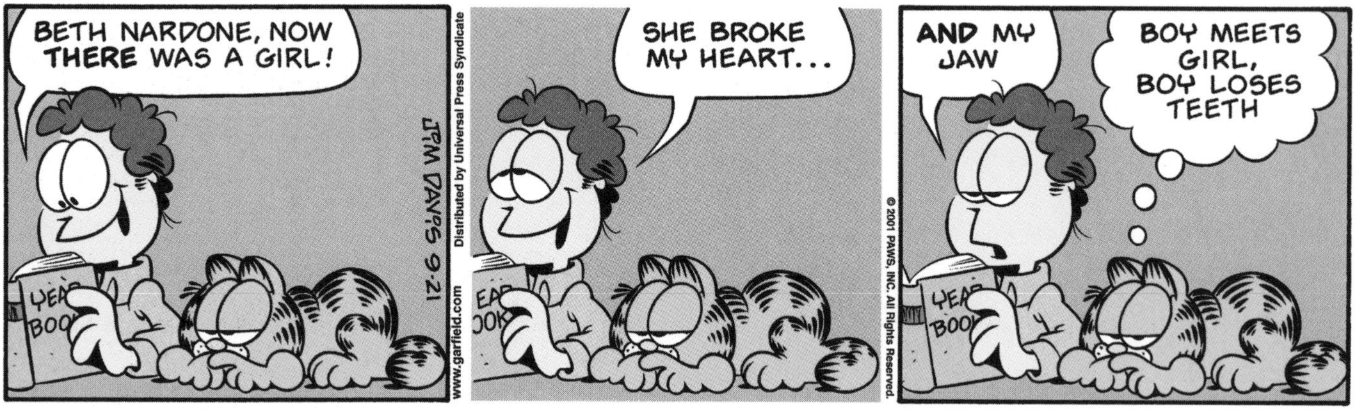
BETH NARDONE, NOW **THERE** WAS A GIRL!
YEAR BOOK
JIM DAVIS 9·21
Distributed by Universal Press Syndicate
www.garfield.com
SHE BROKE MY HEART...
© 2001 PAWS, INC. All Rights Reserved.
AND MY JAW
BOY MEETS GIRL, BOY LOSES TEETH

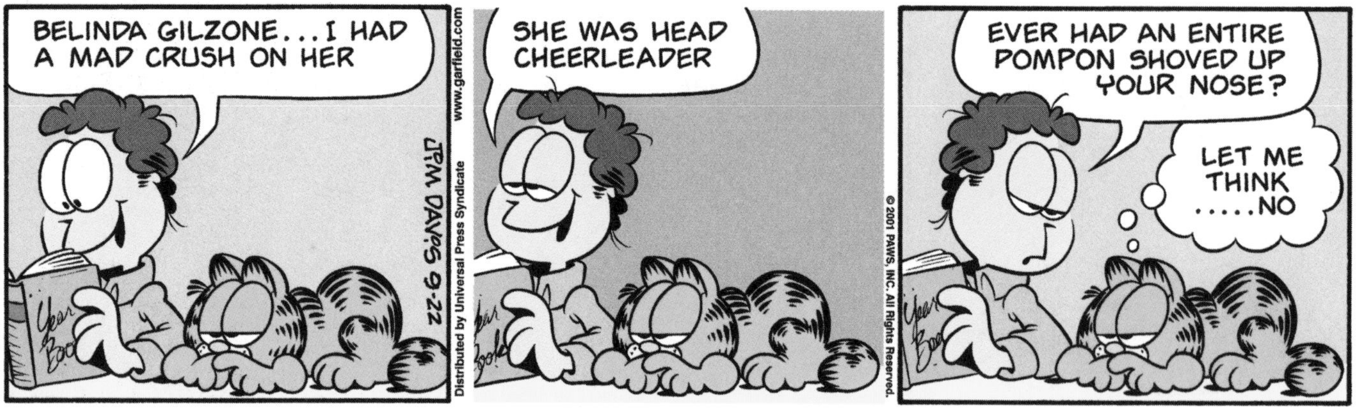
BELINDA GILZONE... I HAD A MAD CRUSH ON HER
Year Book
JIM DAVIS 9·22
www.garfield.com
Distributed by Universal Press Syndicate
SHE WAS HEAD CHEERLEADER
© 2001 PAWS, INC. All Rights Reserved.
EVER HAD AN ENTIRE POMPON SHOVED UP YOUR NOSE?
LET ME THINK .....NO

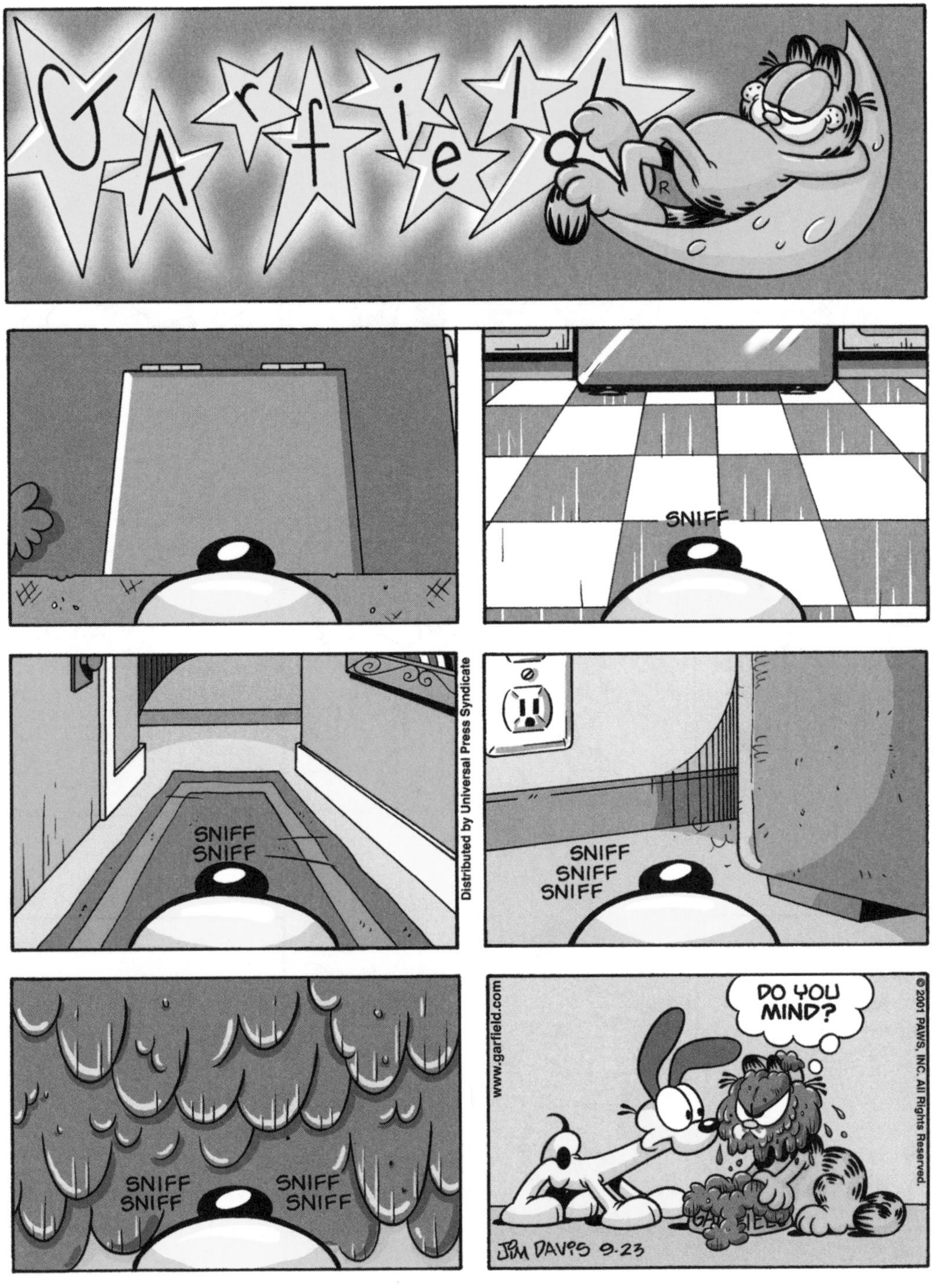
Garfield
SNIFF
SNIFF
SNIFF
SNIFF
SNIFF
SNIFF
SNIFF
SNIFF
SNIFF
SNIFF
SNIFF
DO YOU MIND?
JIM DAVIS 9.23
Distributed by Universal Press Syndicate
www.garfield.com
© 2001 PAWS, INC. All Rights Reserved.

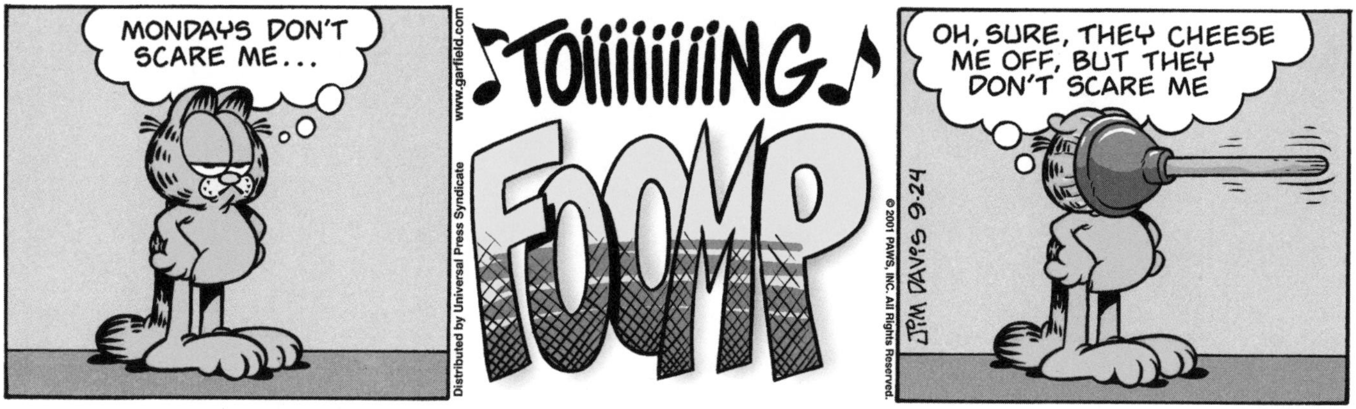
MONDAYS DON'T SCARE ME...
www.garfield.com
Distributed by Universal Press Syndicate
TOiiiiiiiiNG
FOOMP
© 2001 PAWS, INC. All Rights Reserved.
JPM DAVIS 9-24
OH, SURE, THEY CHEESE ME OFF, BUT THEY DON'T SCARE ME

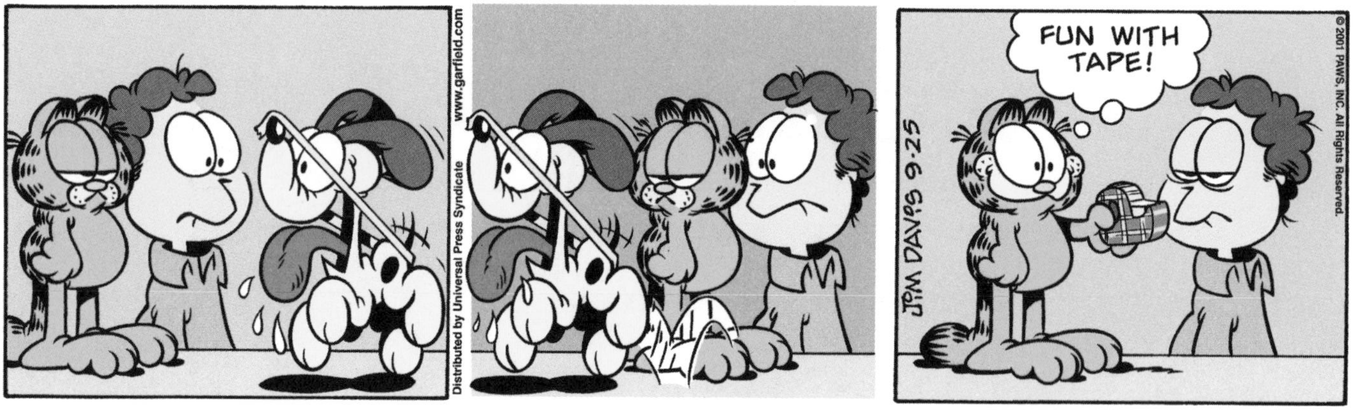
www.garfield.com
Distributed by Universal Press Syndicate
JPM DAVIS 9-25
FUN WITH TAPE!
© 2001 PAWS, INC. All Rights Reserved.

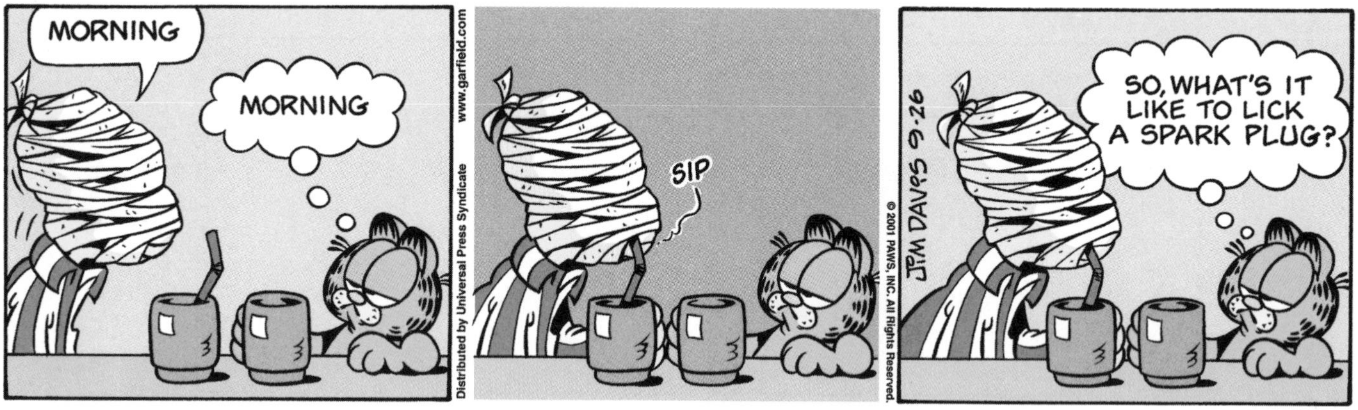
MORNING
MORNING
www.garfield.com
Distributed by Universal Press Syndicate
SIP
© 2001 PAWS, INC. All Rights Reserved.
JPM DAVIS 9-26
SO, WHAT'S IT LIKE TO LICK A SPARK PLUG?

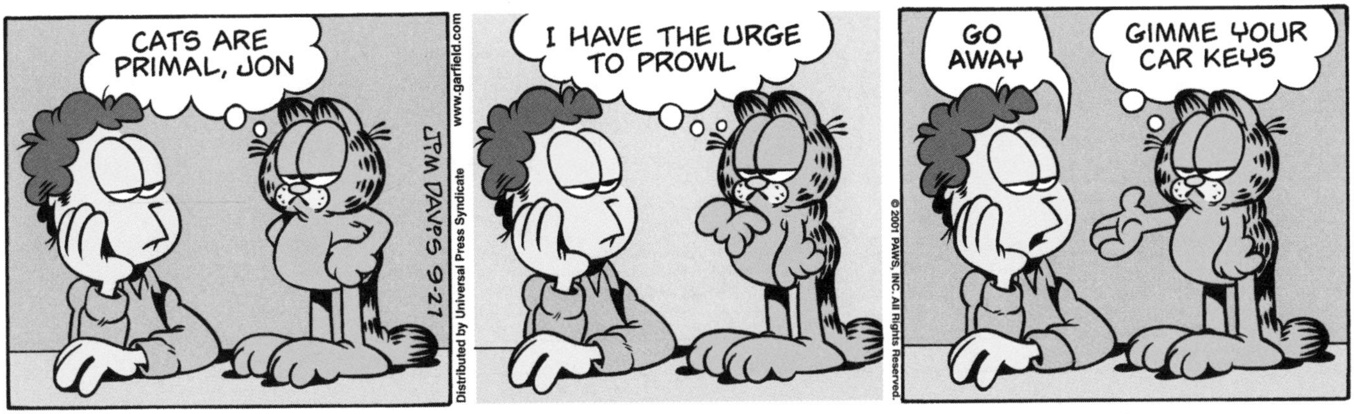
CATS ARE PRIMAL, JON
JIM DAVIS 9-27
www.garfield.com
Distributed by Universal Press Syndicate
I HAVE THE URGE TO PROWL
© 2001 PAWS, INC. All Rights Reserved.
GO AWAY
GIMME YOUR CAR KEYS

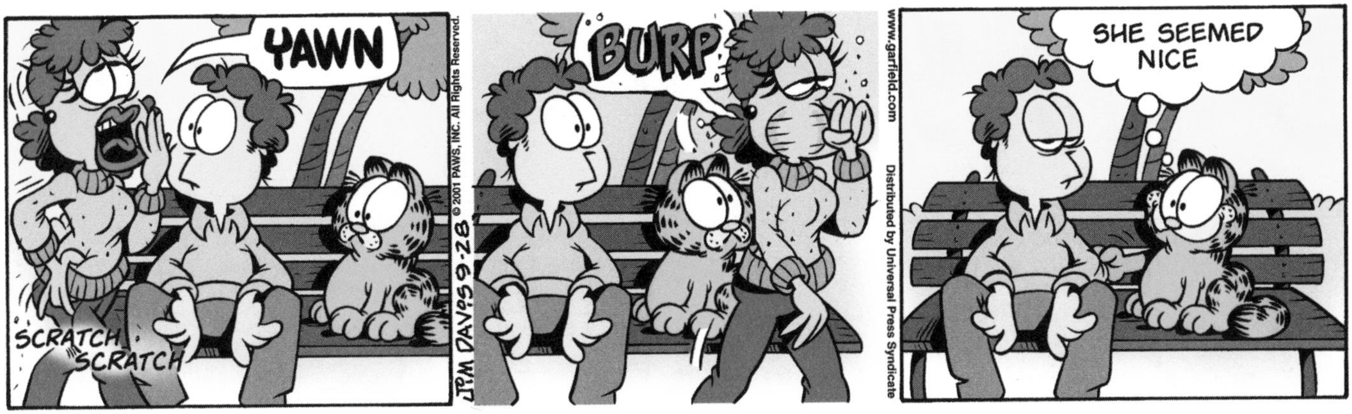
YAWN
SCRATCH SCRATCH
© 2001 PAWS, INC. All Rights Reserved.
JIM DAVIS 9-28
BURP
www.garfield.com
Distributed by Universal Press Syndicate
SHE SEEMED NICE

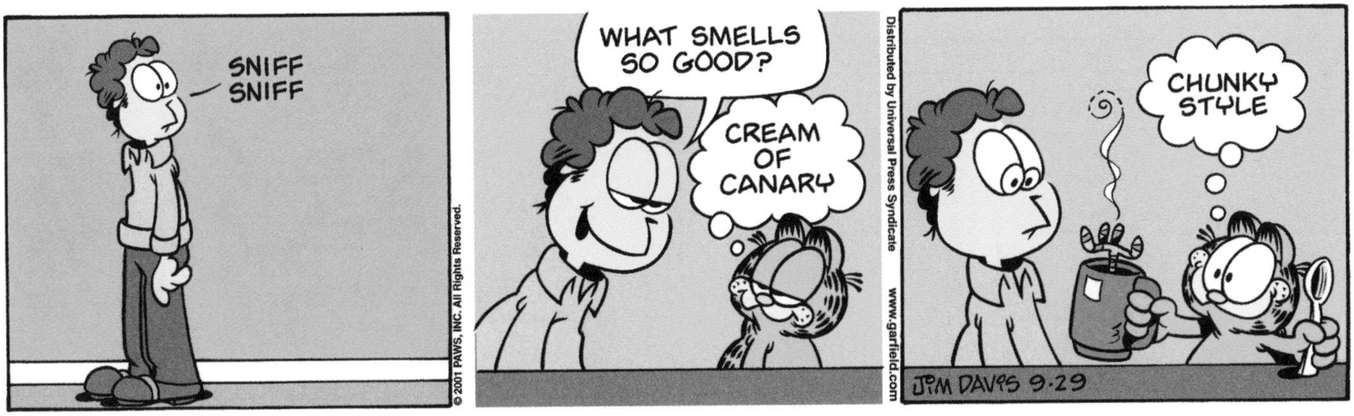
SNIFF SNIFF
© 2001 PAWS, INC. All Rights Reserved.
WHAT SMELLS SO GOOD?
CREAM OF CANARY
Distributed by Universal Press Syndicate
www.garfield.com
CHUNKY STYLE
JIM DAVIS 9-29

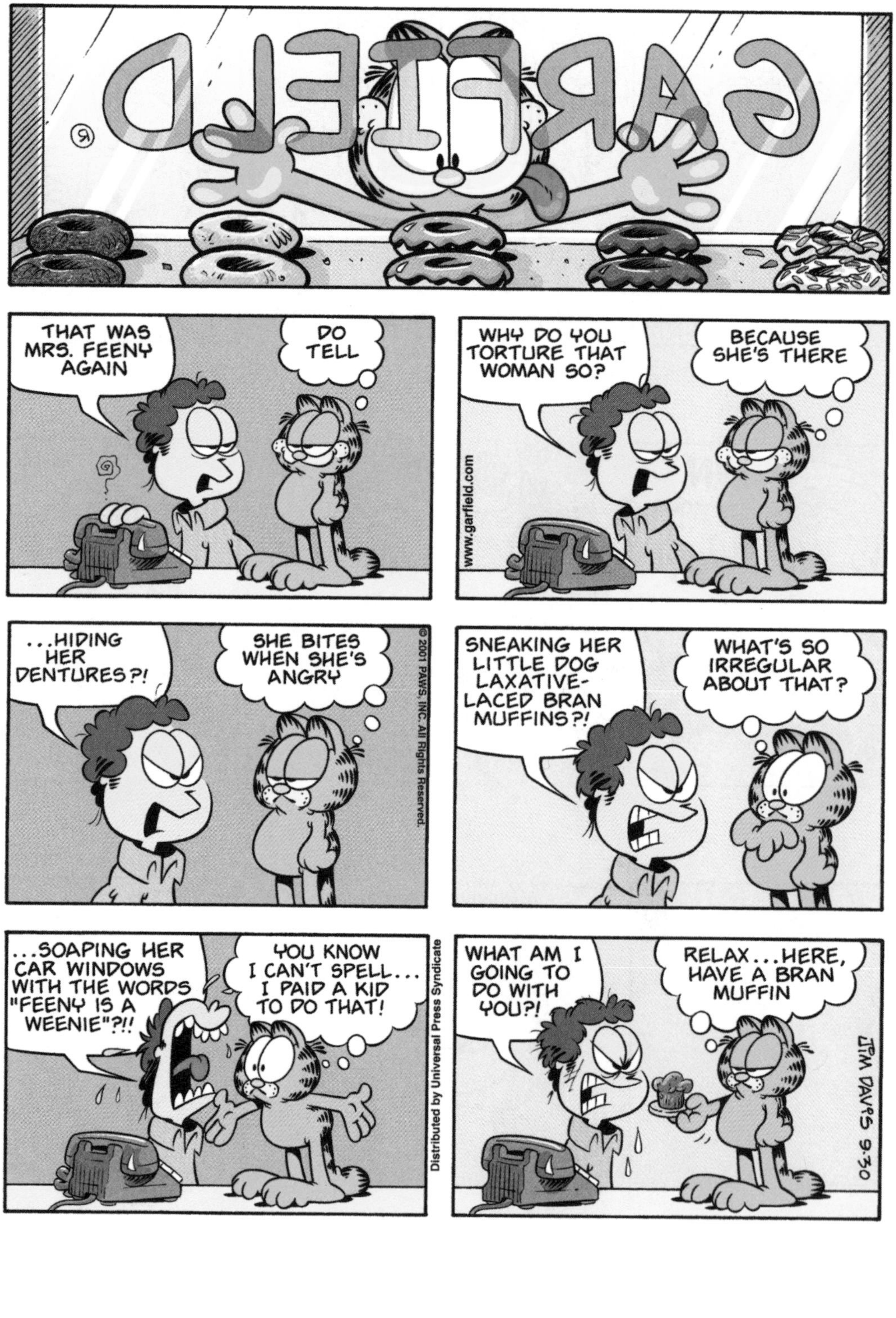
GARFIELD
THAT WAS MRS. FEENY AGAIN
DO TELL
WHY DO YOU TORTURE THAT WOMAN SO?
BECAUSE SHE'S THERE
www.garfield.com
...HIDING HER DENTURES?!
SHE BITES WHEN SHE'S ANGRY
© 2001 PAWS, INC. All Rights Reserved.
SNEAKING HER LITTLE DOG LAXATIVE-LACED BRAN MUFFINS?!
WHAT'S SO IRREGULAR ABOUT THAT?
...SOAPING HER CAR WINDOWS WITH THE WORDS "FEENY IS A WEENIE"?!!
YOU KNOW I CAN'T SPELL... I PAID A KID TO DO THAT!
Distributed by Universal Press Syndicate
WHAT AM I GOING TO DO WITH YOU?!
RELAX...HERE, HAVE A BRAN MUFFIN
JIM DAVIS 9-30

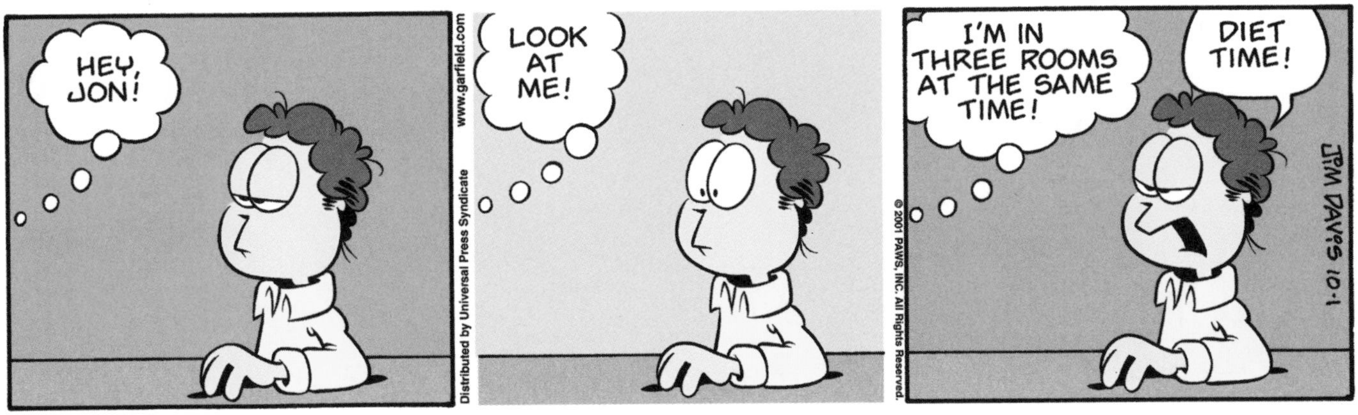
HEY, JON!
www.garfield.com
Distributed by Universal Press Syndicate
LOOK AT ME!
© 2001 PAWS, INC. All Rights Reserved.
I'M IN THREE ROOMS AT THE SAME TIME!
DIET TIME!
JIM DAVIS 10-1

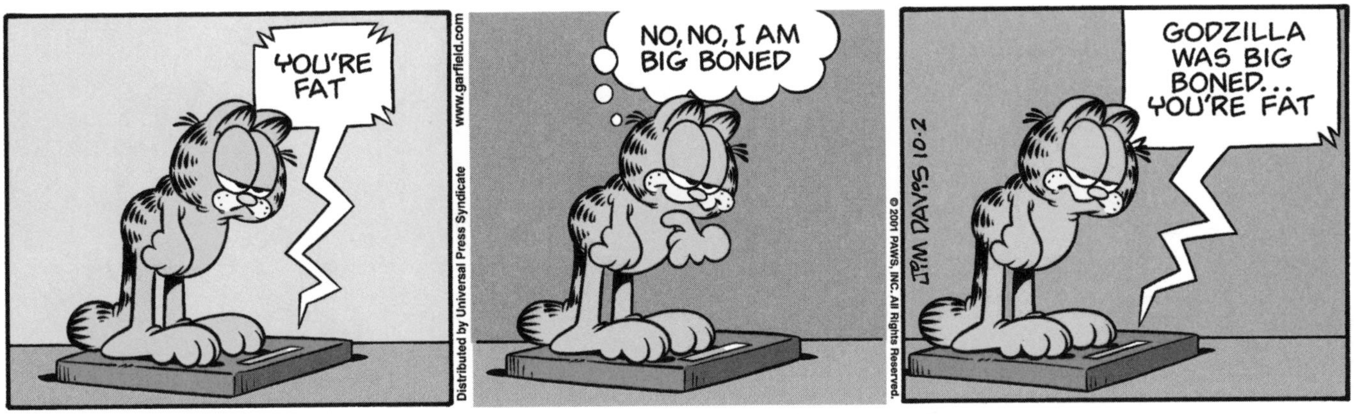
YOU'RE FAT
www.garfield.com
Distributed by Universal Press Syndicate
NO, NO, I AM BIG BONED
© 2001 PAWS, INC. All Rights Reserved.
JIM DAVIS 10-2
GODZILLA WAS BIG BONED... YOU'RE FAT

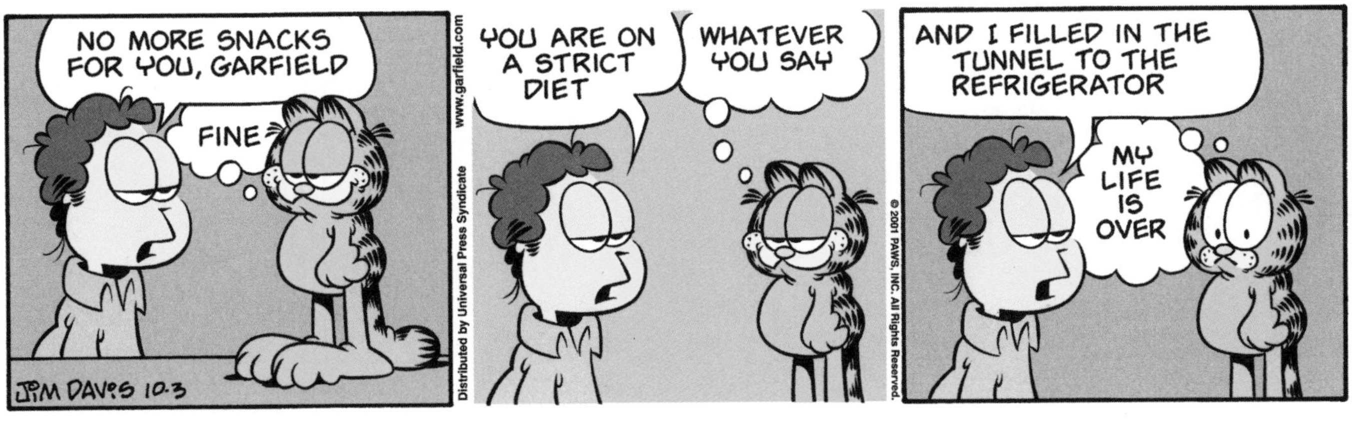
NO MORE SNACKS FOR YOU, GARFIELD
FINE
JIM DAVIS 10-3
www.garfield.com
Distributed by Universal Press Syndicate
YOU ARE ON A STRICT DIET
WHATEVER YOU SAY
© 2001 PAWS, INC. All Rights Reserved.
AND I FILLED IN THE TUNNEL TO THE REFRIGERATOR
MY LIFE IS OVER

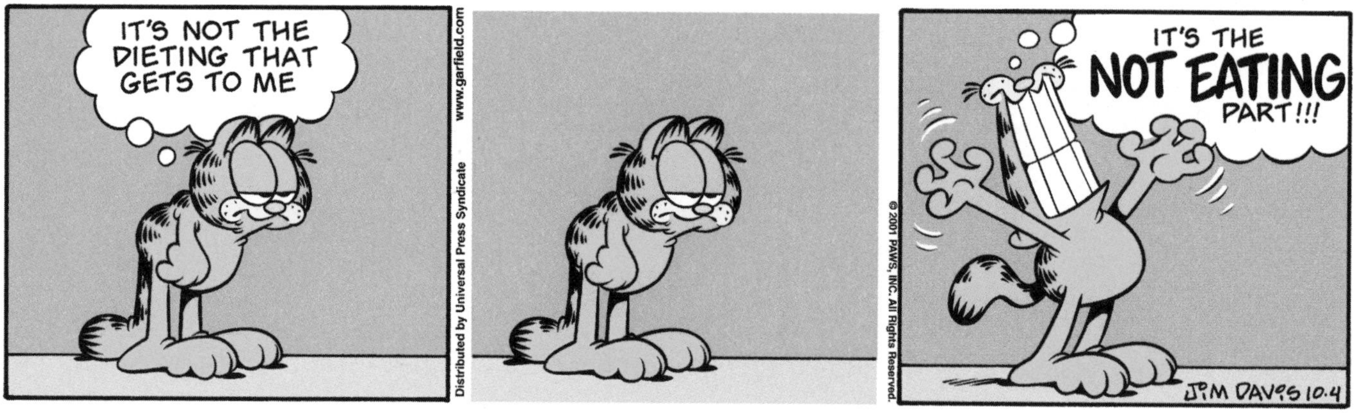
IT'S NOT THE DIETING THAT GETS TO ME
Distributed by Universal Press Syndicate www.garfield.com
IT'S THE NOT EATING PART!!!
© 2001 PAWS, INC. All Rights Reserved.
JIM DAVIS 10.4

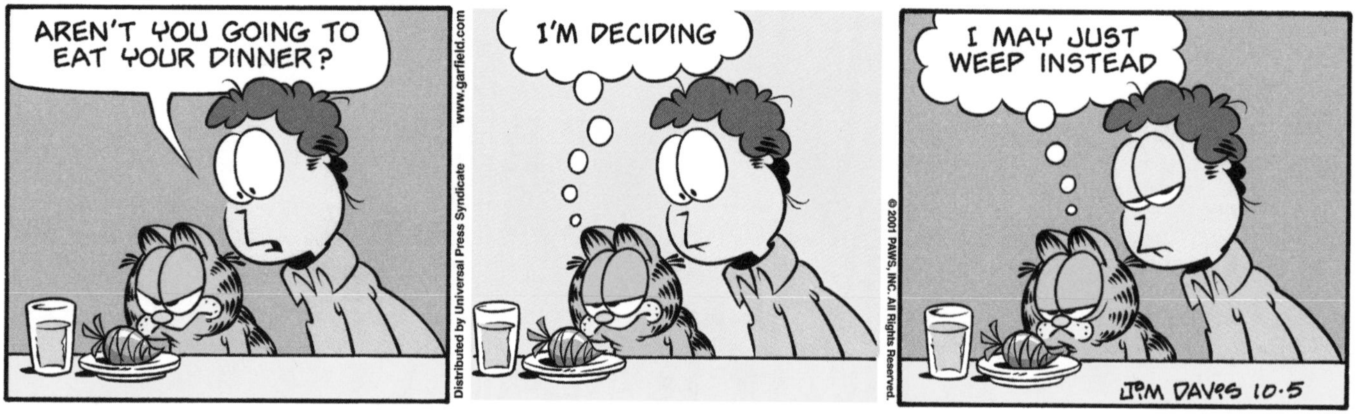
AREN'T YOU GOING TO EAT YOUR DINNER?
Distributed by Universal Press Syndicate www.garfield.com
I'M DECIDING
© 2001 PAWS, INC. All Rights Reserved.
I MAY JUST WEEP INSTEAD
JIM DAVIS 10·5

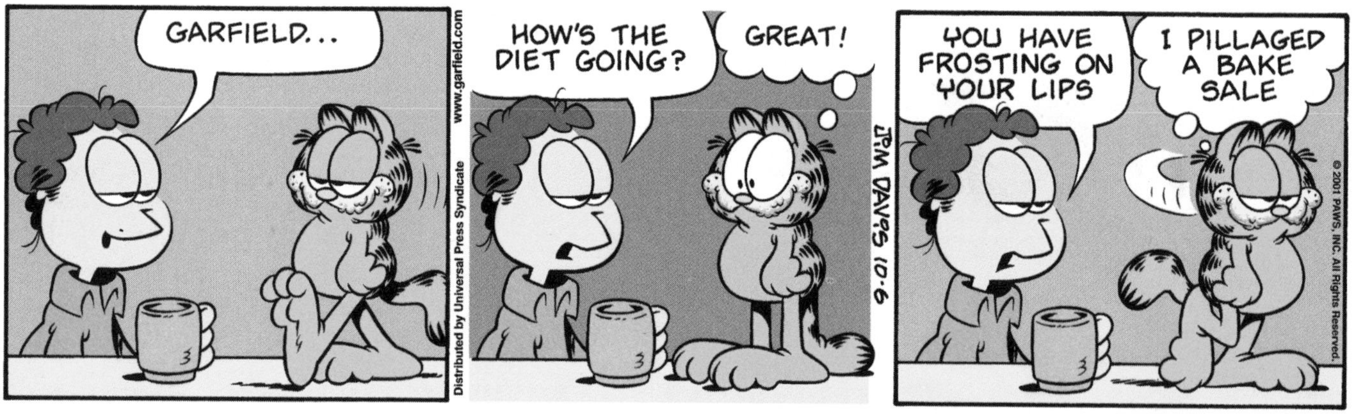
GARFIELD...
Distributed by Universal Press Syndicate www.garfield.com
HOW'S THE DIET GOING?
GREAT!
JIM DAVIS 10·6
YOU HAVE FROSTING ON YOUR LIPS
I PILLAGED A BAKE SALE
© 2001 PAWS, INC. All Rights Reserved.

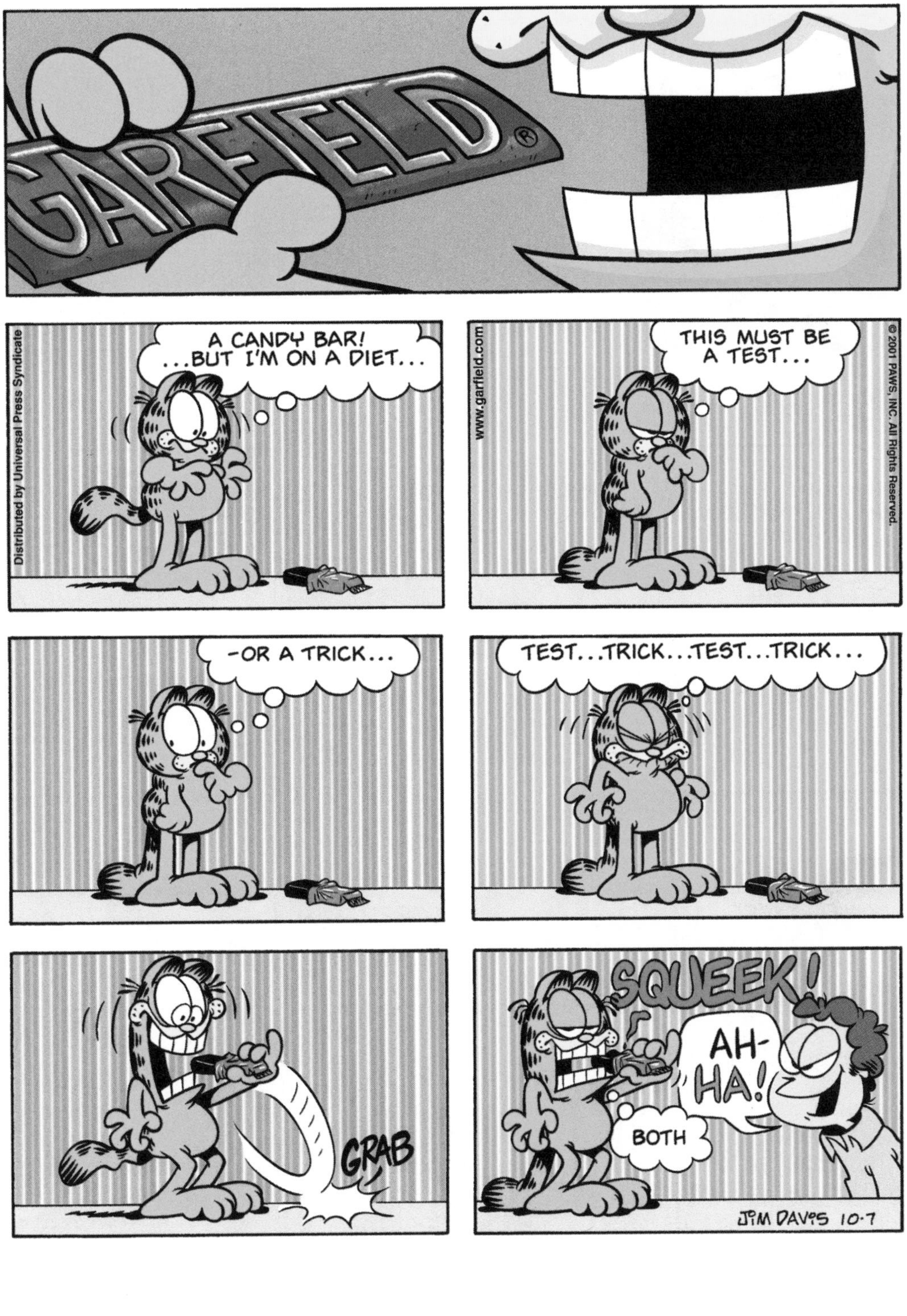
GARFIELD®
Distributed by Universal Press Syndicate
A CANDY BAR! ...BUT I'M ON A DIET...
www.garfield.com
THIS MUST BE A TEST...
© 2001 PAWS, INC. All Rights Reserved.
-OR A TRICK...
TEST...TRICK...TEST...TRICK...
GRAB
SQUEEK!
AH-HA!
BOTH
JIM DAVIS 10-7

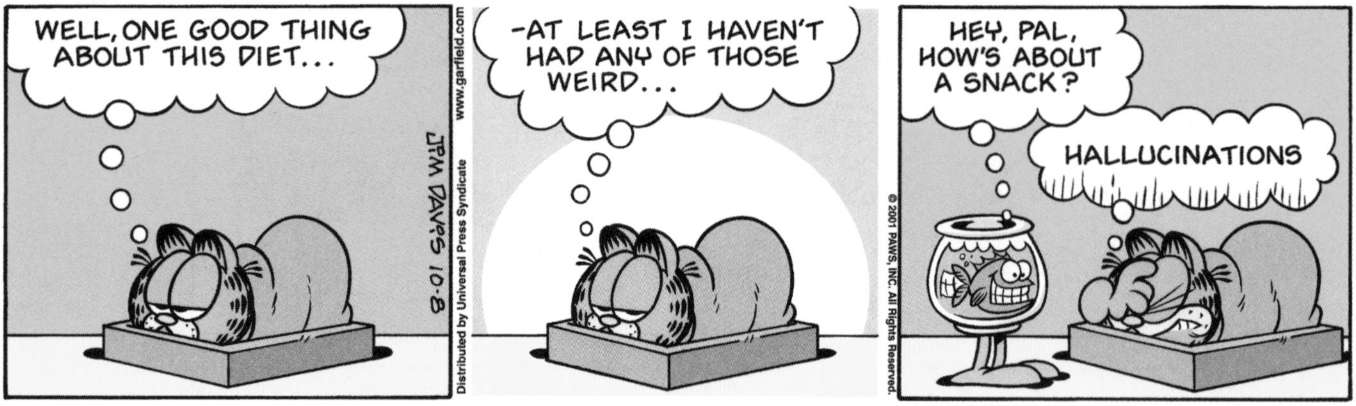
WELL, ONE GOOD THING ABOUT THIS DIET...
JIM DAVIS 10-8
Distributed by Universal Press Syndicate www.garfield.com
-AT LEAST I HAVEN'T HAD ANY OF THOSE WEIRD...
HEY, PAL, HOW'S ABOUT A SNACK?
HALLUCINATIONS
© 2001 PAWS, INC. All Rights Reserved.

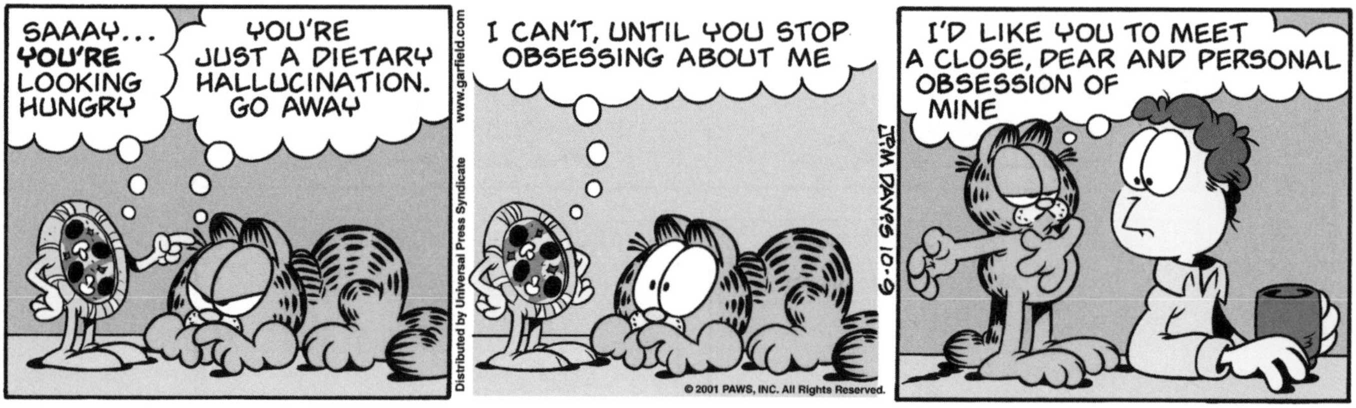
SAAAY... YOU'RE LOOKING HUNGRY
YOU'RE JUST A DIETARY HALLUCINATION. GO AWAY
Distributed by Universal Press Syndicate www.garfield.com
I CAN'T, UNTIL YOU STOP OBSESSING ABOUT ME
JIM DAVIS 10-9
© 2001 PAWS, INC. All Rights Reserved.
I'D LIKE YOU TO MEET A CLOSE, DEAR AND PERSONAL OBSESSION OF MINE

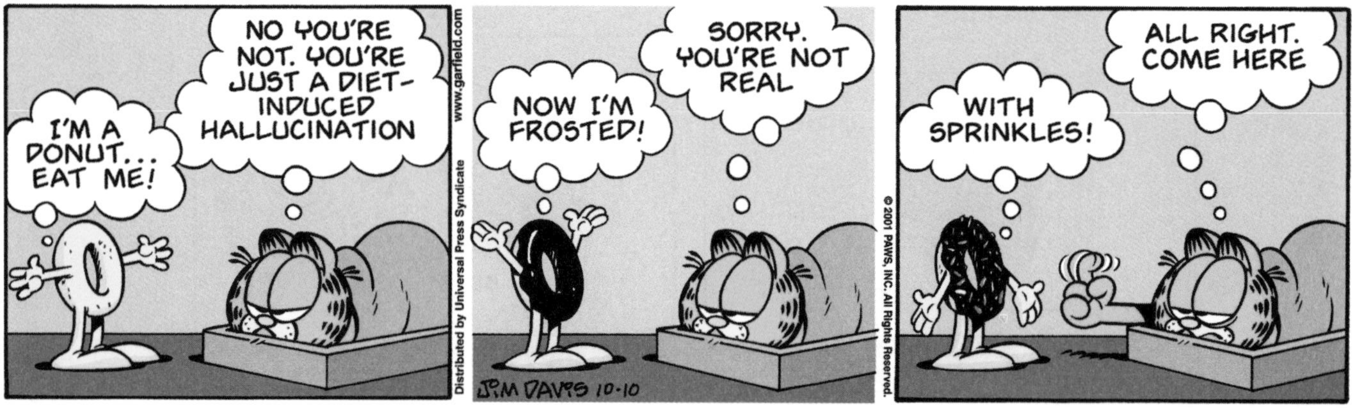
I'M A DONUT... EAT ME!
NO YOU'RE NOT. YOU'RE JUST A DIET-INDUCED HALLUCINATION
Distributed by Universal Press Syndicate www.garfield.com
NOW I'M FROSTED!
SORRY. YOU'RE NOT REAL
JIM DAVIS 10-10
WITH SPRINKLES!
ALL RIGHT. COME HERE
© 2001 PAWS, INC. All Rights Reserved.

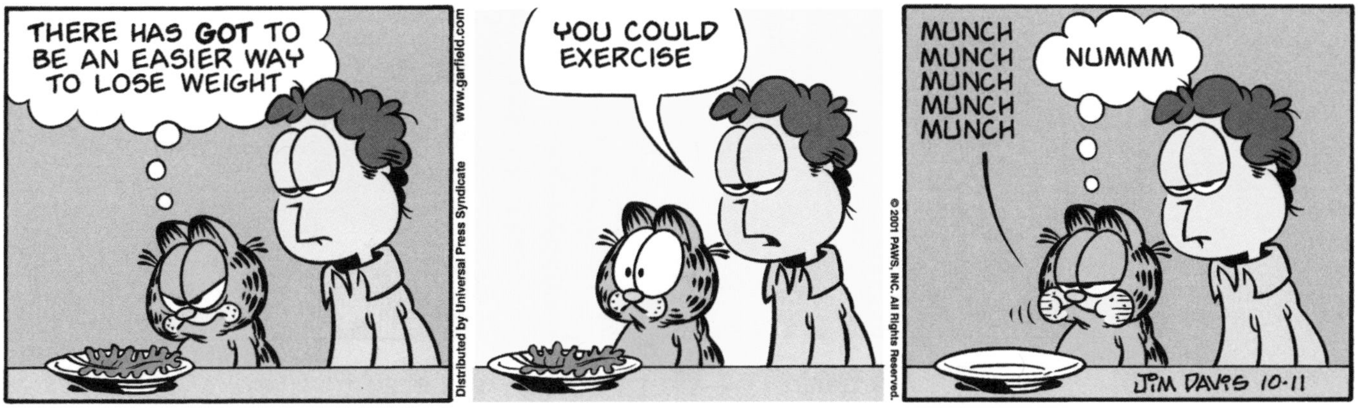
THERE HAS GOT TO BE AN EASIER WAY TO LOSE WEIGHT
YOU COULD EXERCISE
MUNCH MUNCH MUNCH MUNCH MUNCH
NUMMM
JIM DAVIS 10-11
www.garfield.com Distributed by Universal Press Syndicate
© 2001 PAWS, INC. All Rights Reserved.

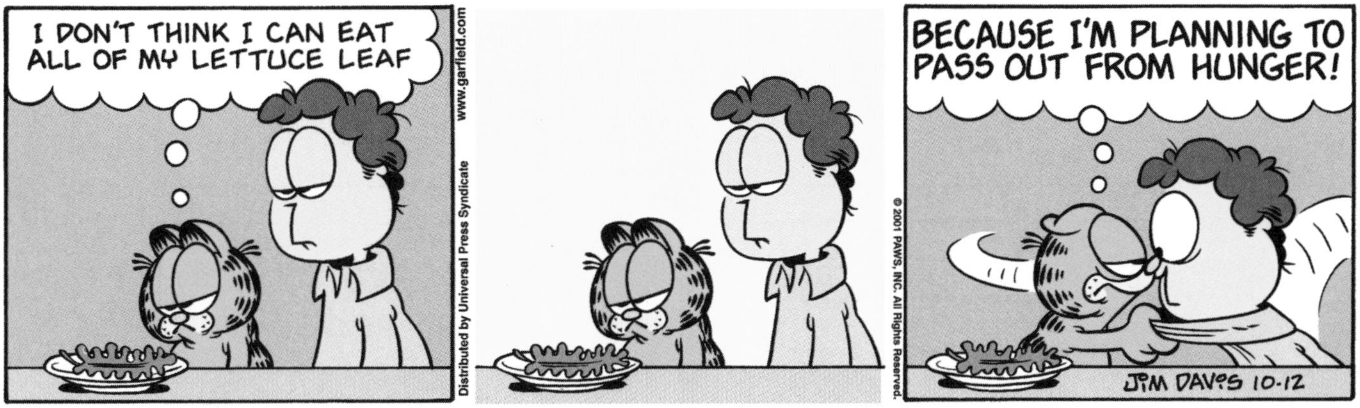
I DON'T THINK I CAN EAT ALL OF MY LETTUCE LEAF
BECAUSE I'M PLANNING TO PASS OUT FROM HUNGER!
JIM DAVIS 10-12
www.garfield.com Distributed by Universal Press Syndicate
© 2001 PAWS, INC. All Rights Reserved.

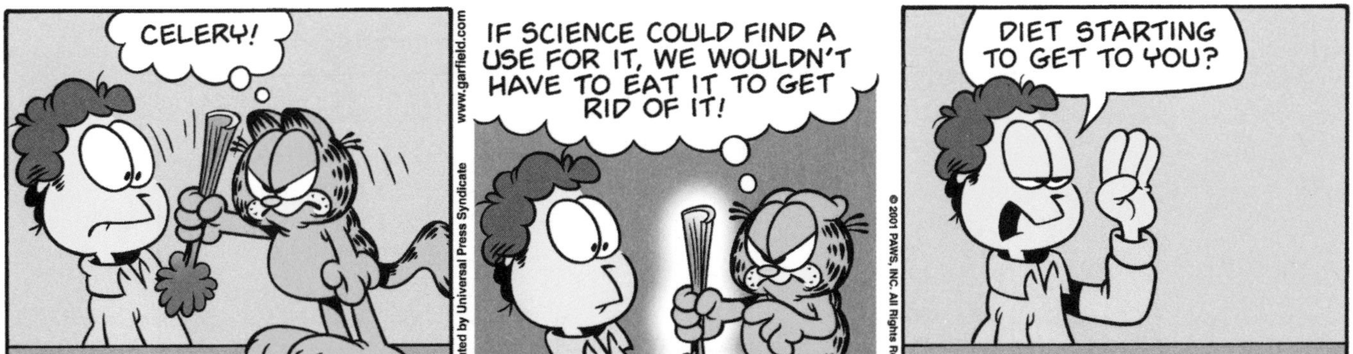
CELERY!
IF SCIENCE COULD FIND A USE FOR IT, WE WOULDN'T HAVE TO EAT IT TO GET RID OF IT!
DIET STARTING TO GET TO YOU?
JIM DAVIS 10-13
www.garfield.com Distributed by Universal Press Syndicate
© 2001 PAWS, INC. All Rights Reserved.

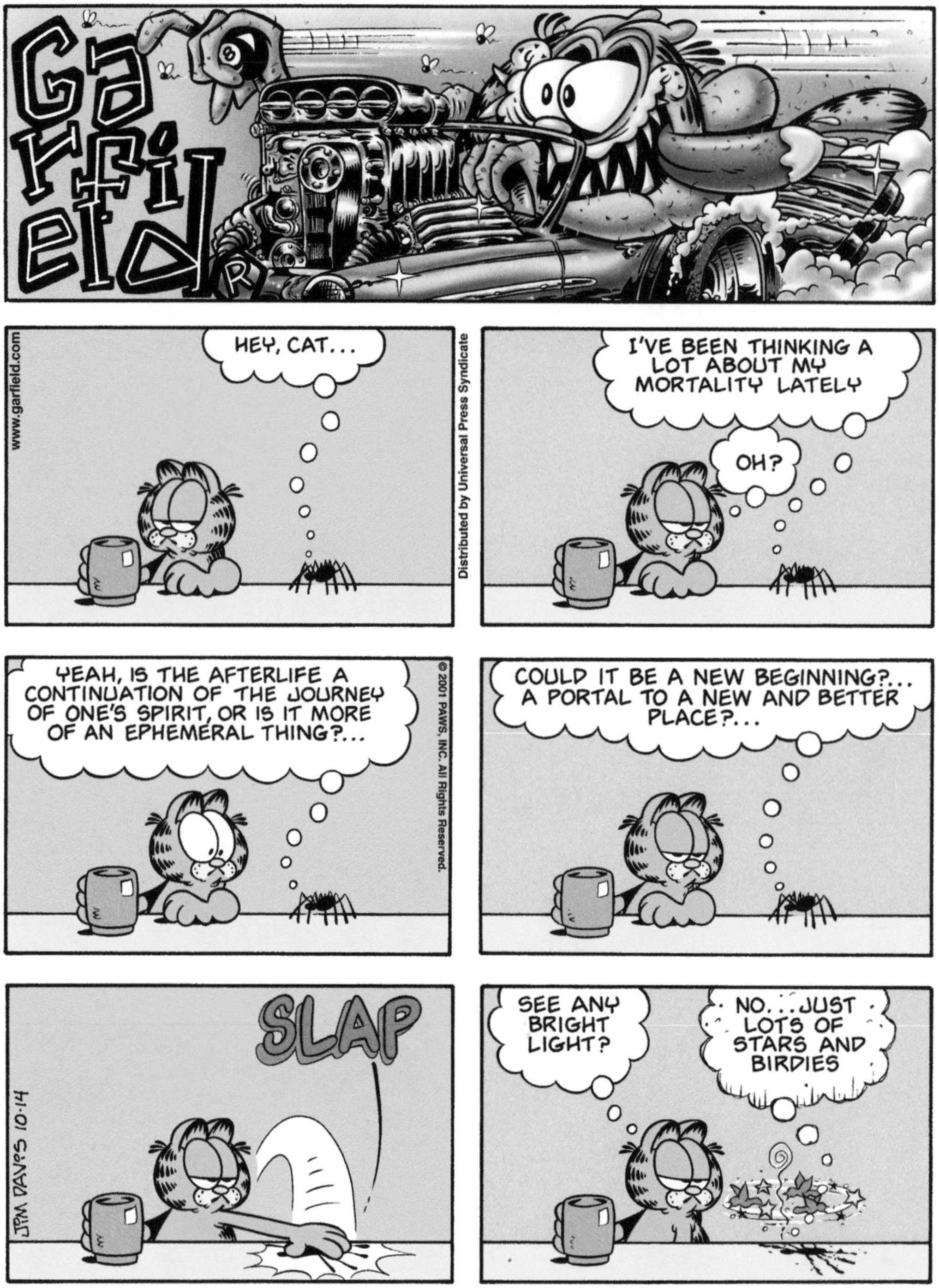
GARFIELD
www.garfield.com
HEY, CAT...
Distributed by Universal Press Syndicate
I'VE BEEN THINKING A LOT ABOUT MY MORTALITY LATELY
OH?
YEAH, IS THE AFTERLIFE A CONTINUATION OF THE JOURNEY OF ONE'S SPIRIT, OR IS IT MORE OF AN EPHEMERAL THING?...
© 2001 PAWS, INC. All Rights Reserved.
COULD IT BE A NEW BEGINNING?... A PORTAL TO A NEW AND BETTER PLACE?...
JPM DAVIS 10·14
SLAP
SEE ANY BRIGHT LIGHT?
NO...JUST LOTS OF STARS AND BIRDIES

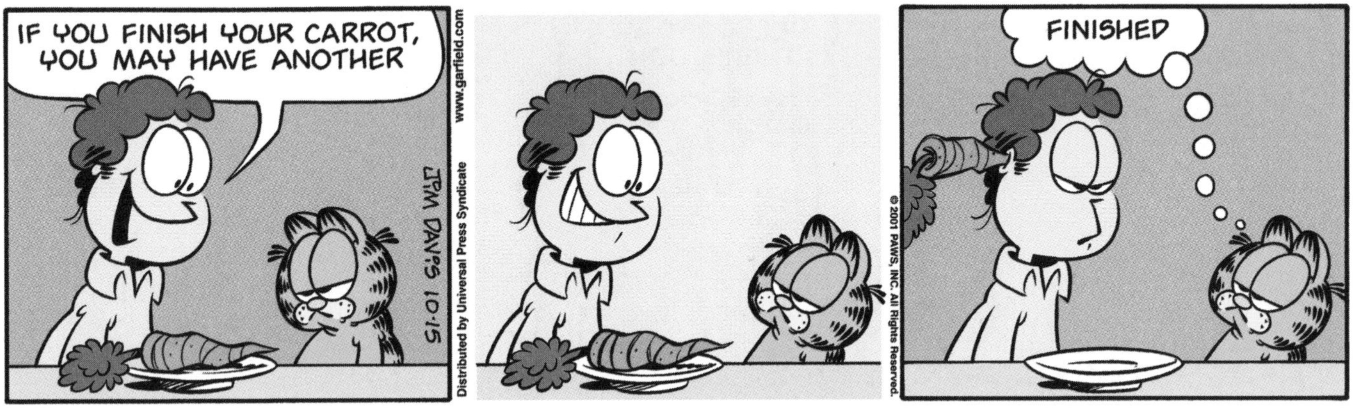
IF YOU FINISH YOUR CARROT, YOU MAY HAVE ANOTHER
JIM DAVIS 10-15
www.garfield.com
Distributed by Universal Press Syndicate
FINISHED
© 2001 PAWS, INC. All Rights Reserved.

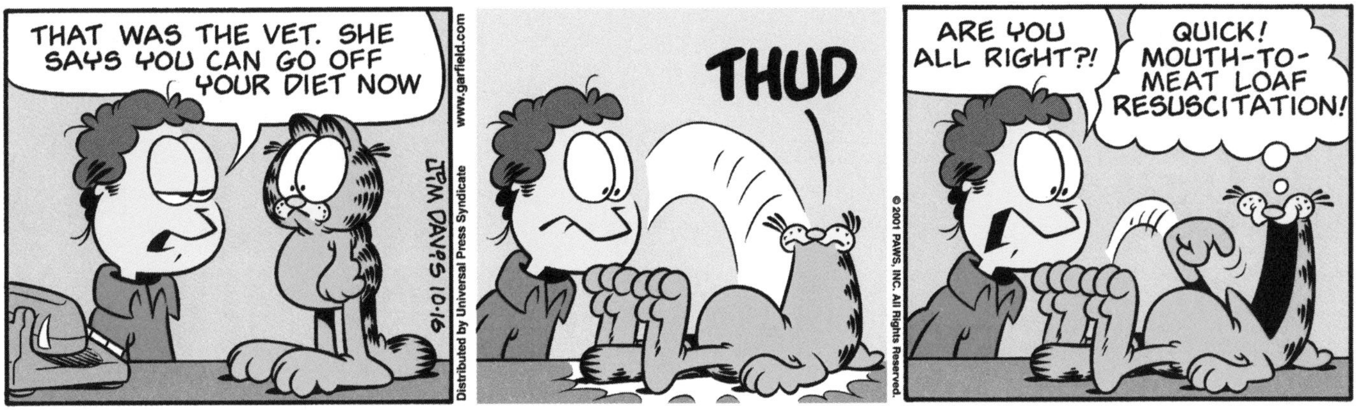
THAT WAS THE VET. SHE SAYS YOU CAN GO OFF YOUR DIET NOW
JIM DAVIS 10-16
www.garfield.com
Distributed by Universal Press Syndicate
THUD
ARE YOU ALL RIGHT?!
QUICK! MOUTH-TO-MEAT LOAF RESUSCITATION!
© 2001 PAWS, INC. All Rights Reserved.

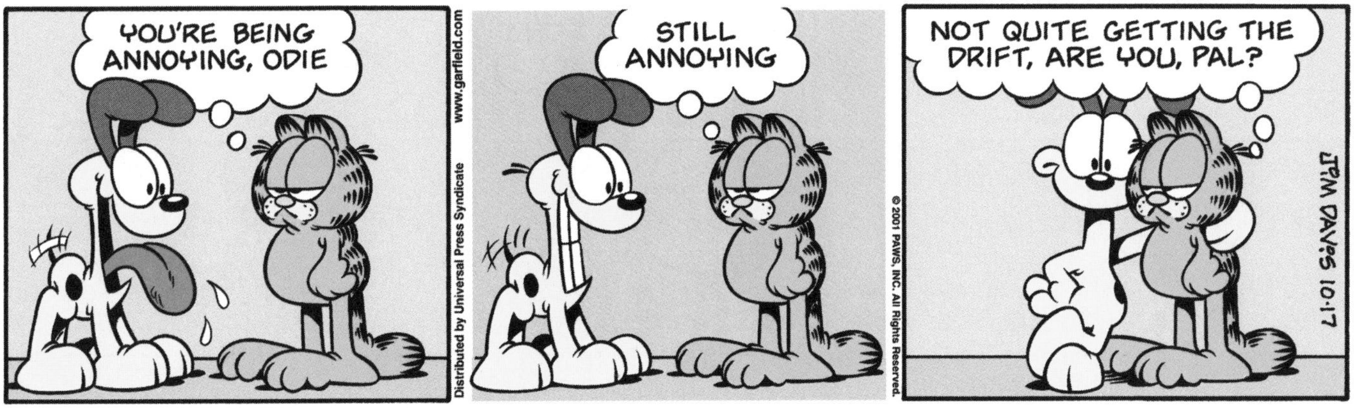
YOU'RE BEING ANNOYING, ODIE
www.garfield.com
Distributed by Universal Press Syndicate
STILL ANNOYING
© 2001 PAWS, INC. All Rights Reserved.
NOT QUITE GETTING THE DRIFT, ARE YOU, PAL?
JIM DAVIS 10-17

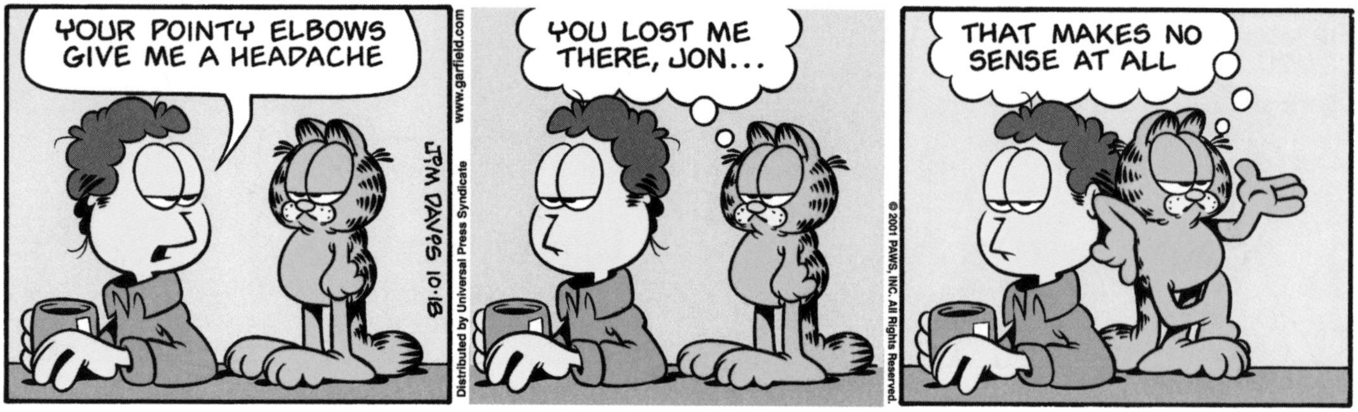
YOUR POINTY ELBOWS GIVE ME A HEADACHE
JIM DAVIS 10-18
www.garfield.com
Distributed by Universal Press Syndicate
YOU LOST ME THERE, JON...
© 2001 PAWS, INC. All Rights Reserved.
THAT MAKES NO SENSE AT ALL

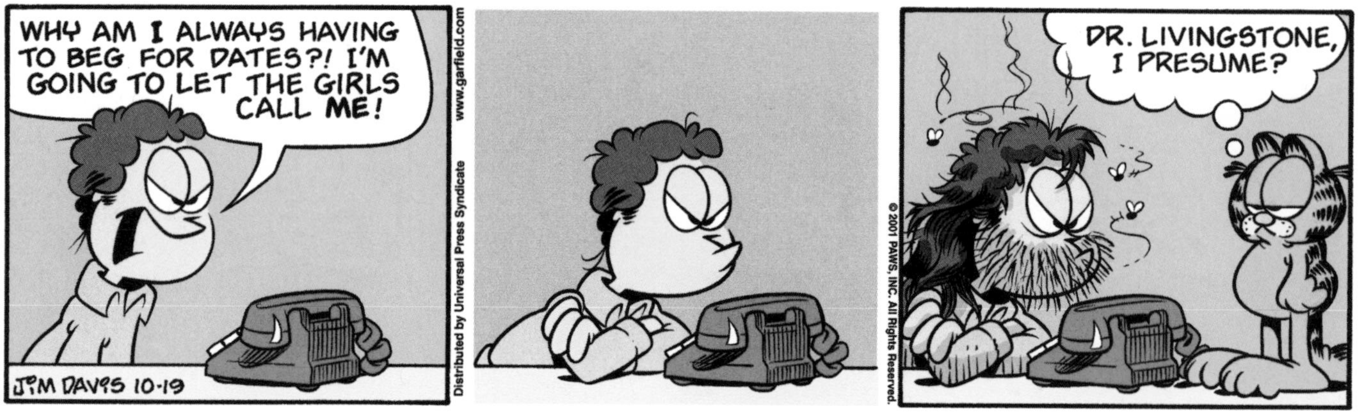
WHY AM I ALWAYS HAVING TO BEG FOR DATES?! I'M GOING TO LET THE GIRLS CALL ME!
JIM DAVIS 10-19
www.garfield.com
Distributed by Universal Press Syndicate
© 2001 PAWS, INC. All Rights Reserved.
DR. LIVINGSTONE, I PRESUME?

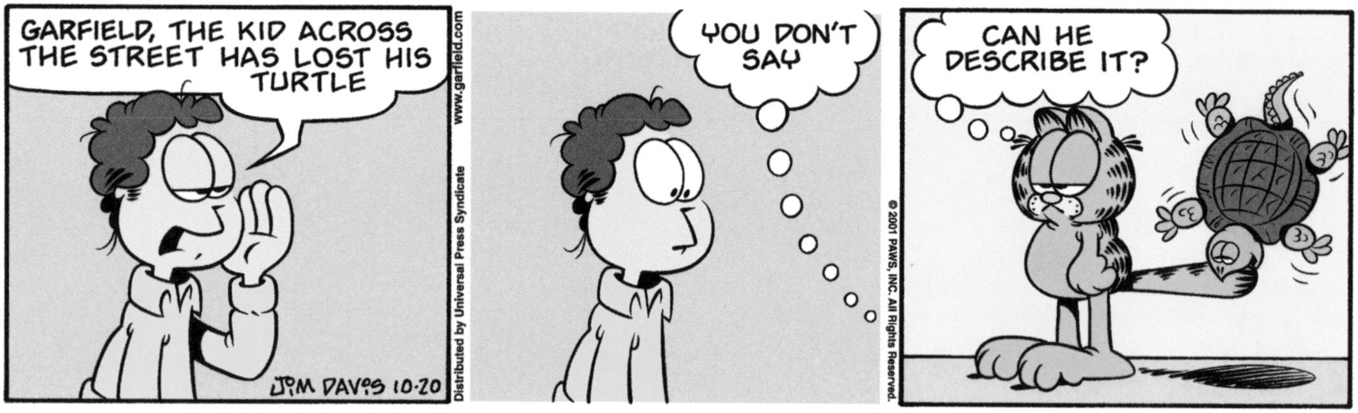
GARFIELD, THE KID ACROSS THE STREET HAS LOST HIS TURTLE
JIM DAVIS 10-20
www.garfield.com
Distributed by Universal Press Syndicate
YOU DON'T SAY
© 2001 PAWS, INC. All Rights Reserved.
CAN HE DESCRIBE IT?

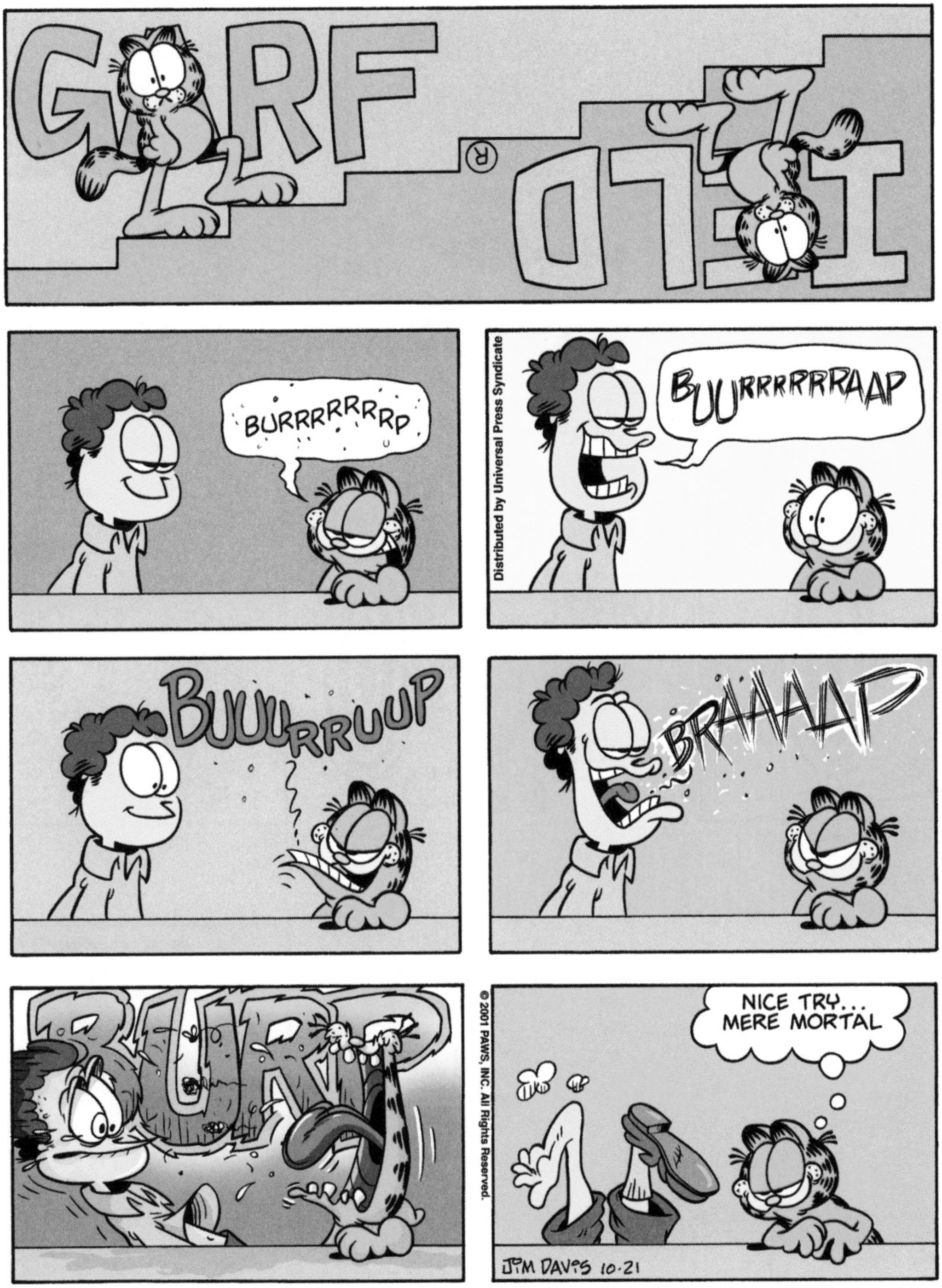
GARFIELD
BURRRRRRRRP
BUURRRRRRRAAP
Distributed by Universal Press Syndicate
BUUURRUUP
BRAAAAP
BURP
© 2001 PAWS, INC. All Rights Reserved.
NICE TRY... MERE MORTAL
JIM DAVIS 10-21

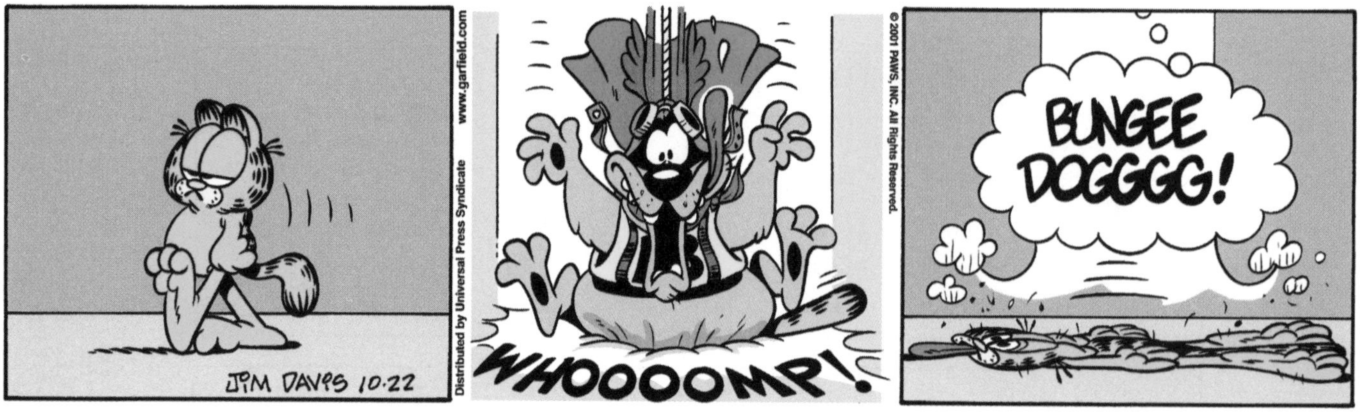
JIM DAVIS 10-22
Distributed by Universal Press Syndicate www.garfield.com
WHOOOOMP!
© 2001 PAWS, INC. All Rights Reserved.
BUNGEE DOGGGG!

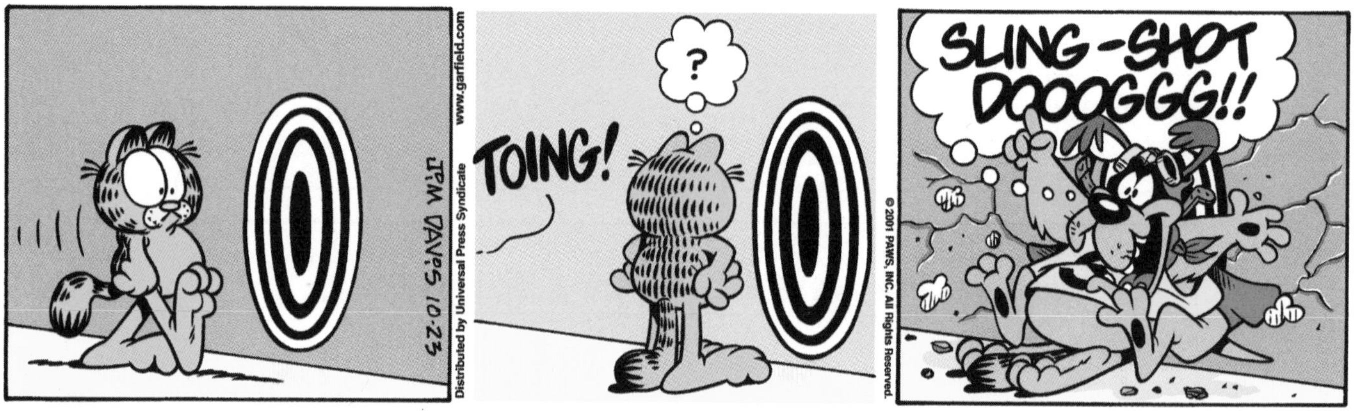
JIM DAVIS 10-23
Distributed by Universal Press Syndicate www.garfield.com
TOING!
?
© 2001 PAWS, INC. All Rights Reserved.
SLING-SHOT DOOOGGG!!

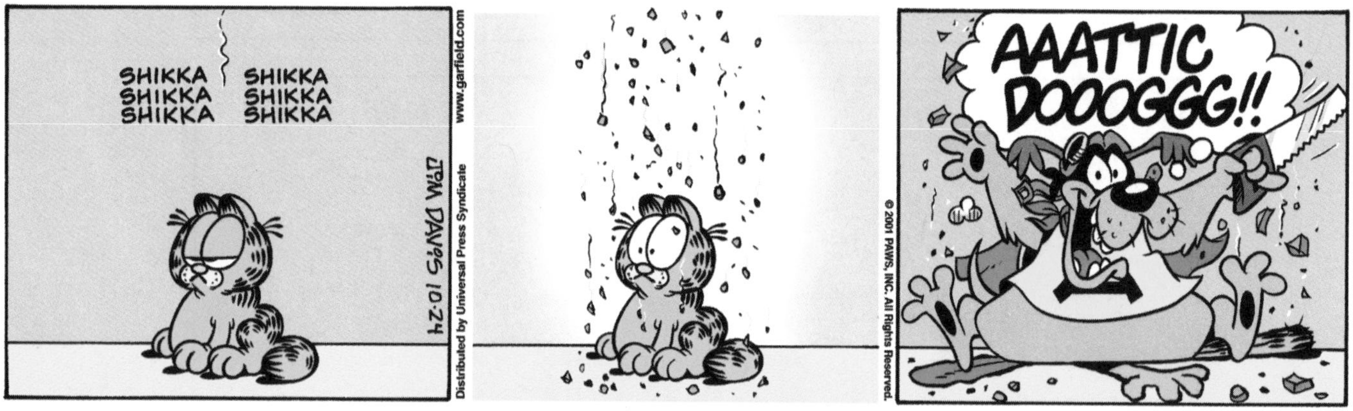
SHIKKA SHIKKA SHIKKA
SHIKKA SHIKKA SHIKKA
JIM DAVIS 10-24
Distributed by Universal Press Syndicate www.garfield.com
© 2001 PAWS, INC. All Rights Reserved.
AAATTIC DOOOGGG!!

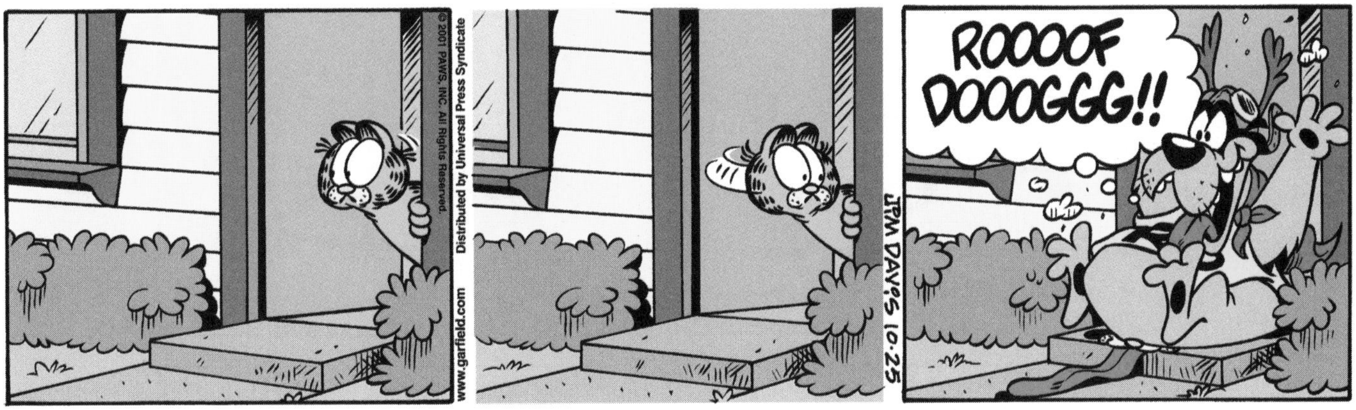
© 2001 PAWS, INC. All Rights Reserved.
Distributed by Universal Press Syndicate
www.garfield.com
JIM DAVIS 10-25
ROOOOF DOOOGGG!!

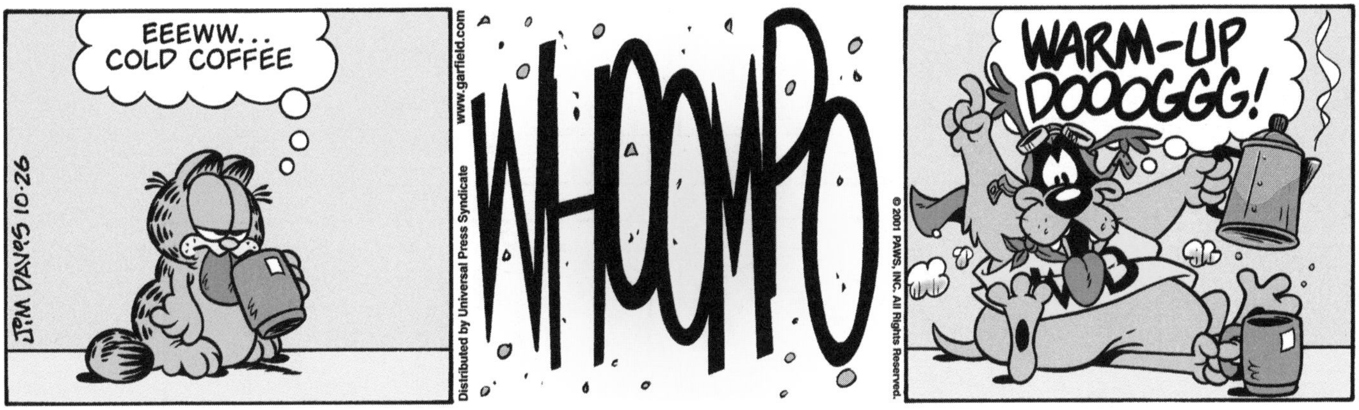
EEEWW... COLD COFFEE
JIM DAVIS 10-26
Distributed by Universal Press Syndicate
www.garfield.com
WHOOMPO
© 2001 PAWS, INC. All Rights Reserved.
WARM-UP DOOOGGG!

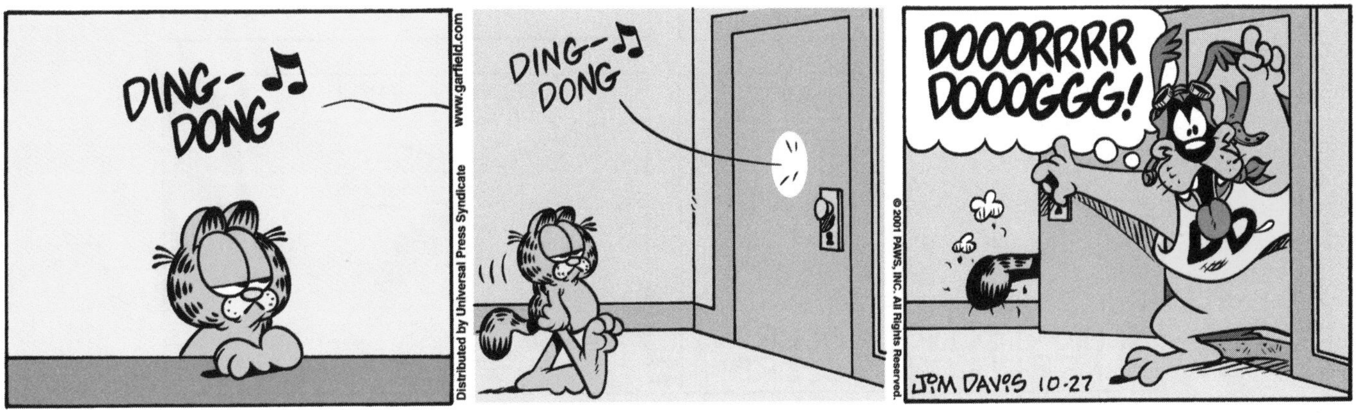
DING-DONG
Distributed by Universal Press Syndicate
www.garfield.com
DING-DONG
© 2001 PAWS, INC. All Rights Reserved.
DOOORRRR DOOOGGG!
JIM DAVIS 10-27

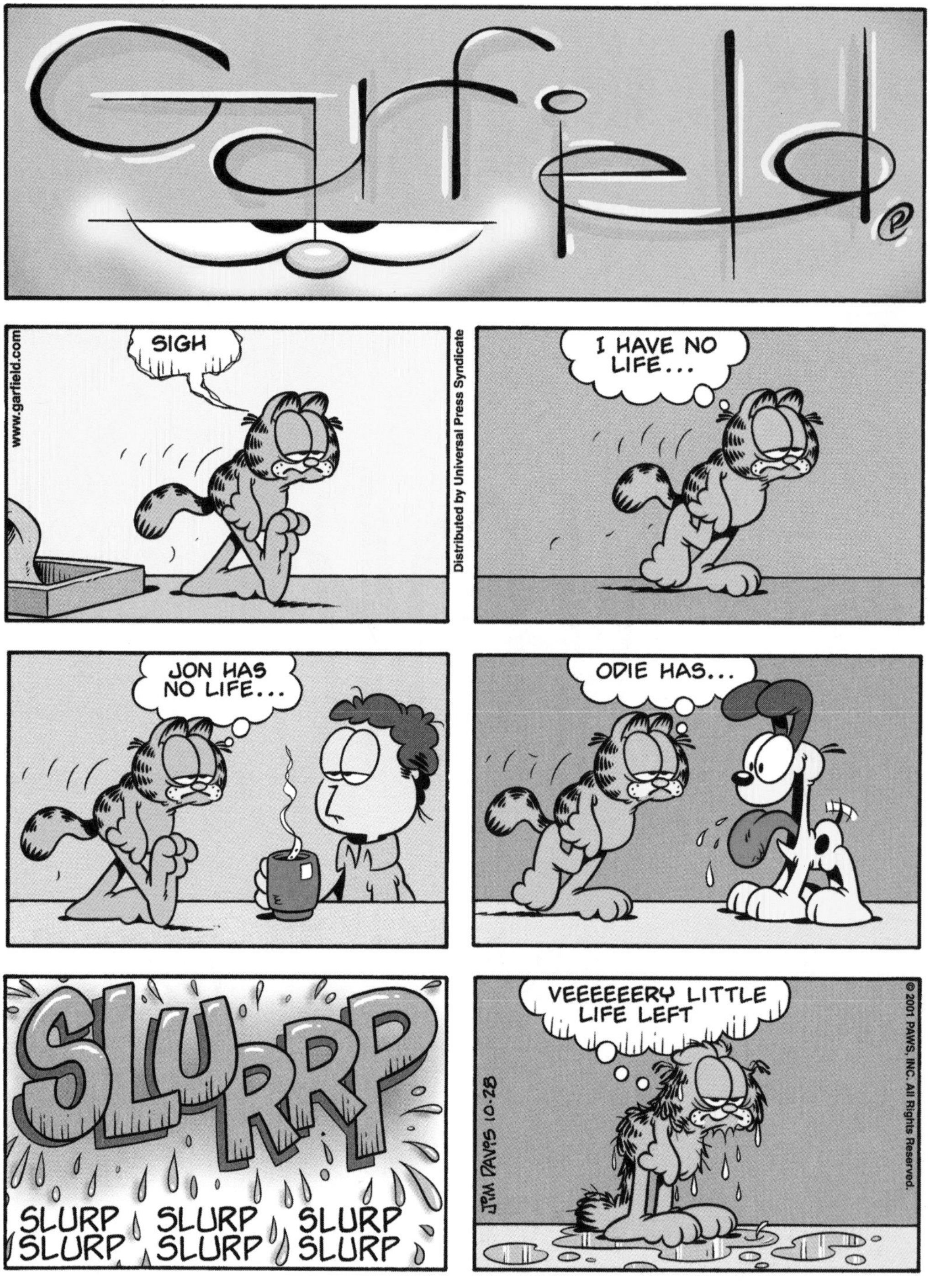
Garfield
www.garfield.com
SIGH
Distributed by Universal Press Syndicate
I HAVE NO LIFE...
JON HAS NO LIFE...
ODIE HAS...
SLURRP
SLURP SLURP
SLURP SLURP
SLURP SLURP
VEEEEEERY LITTLE LIFE LEFT
JPM DAVIS 10-28
© 2001 PAWS, INC. All Rights Reserved.

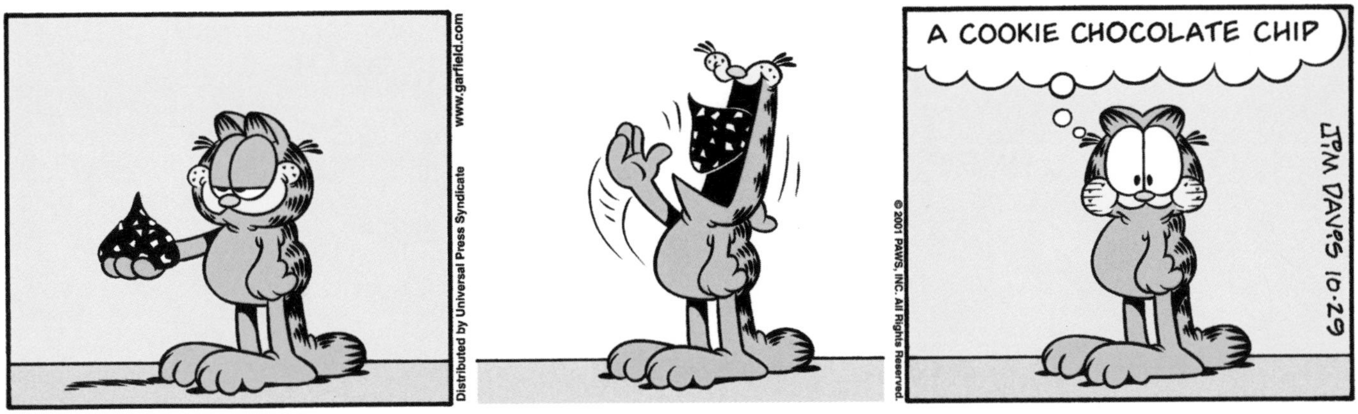
A COOKIE CHOCOLATE CHIP
JIM DAVIS 10-29
www.garfield.com
Distributed by Universal Press Syndicate
© 2001 PAWS, INC. All Rights Reserved.

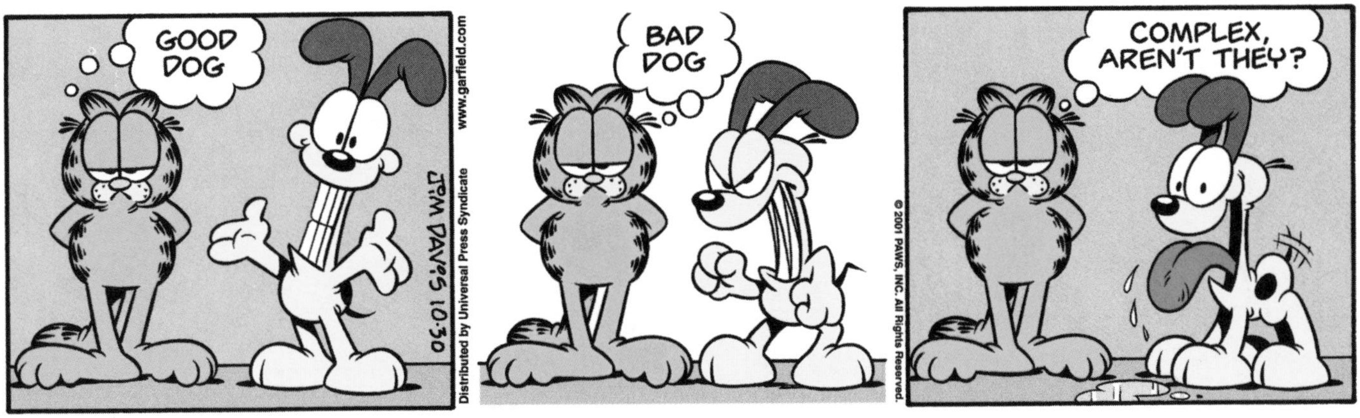
GOOD DOG
BAD DOG
COMPLEX, AREN'T THEY?
JIM DAVIS 10-30
www.garfield.com
Distributed by Universal Press Syndicate
© 2001 PAWS, INC. All Rights Reserved.

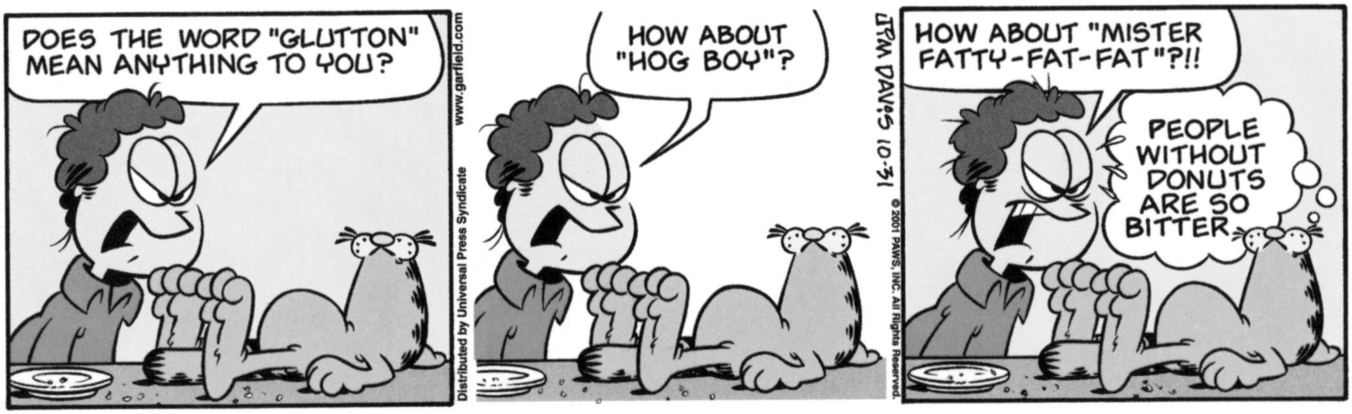
DOES THE WORD "GLUTTON" MEAN ANYTHING TO YOU?
HOW ABOUT "HOG BOY"?
HOW ABOUT "MISTER FATTY-FAT-FAT"?!!
PEOPLE WITHOUT DONUTS ARE SO BITTER
JIM DAVIS 10-31
www.garfield.com
Distributed by Universal Press Syndicate
© 2001 PAWS, INC. All Rights Reserved.

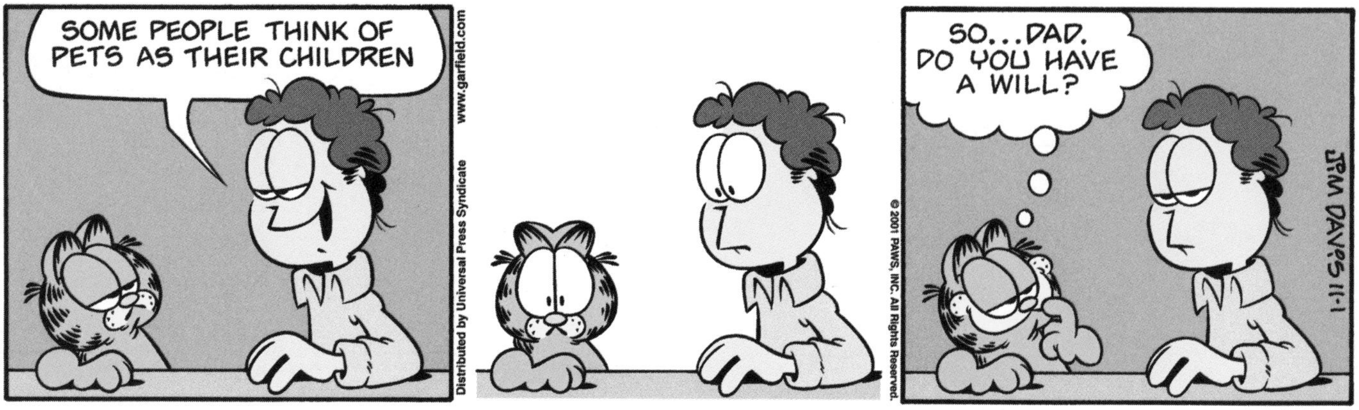
SOME PEOPLE THINK OF PETS AS THEIR CHILDREN
SO...DAD. DO YOU HAVE A WILL?
JPM DAVPS 11-1
Distributed by Universal Press Syndicate www.garfield.com
© 2001 PAWS, INC. All Rights Reserved.

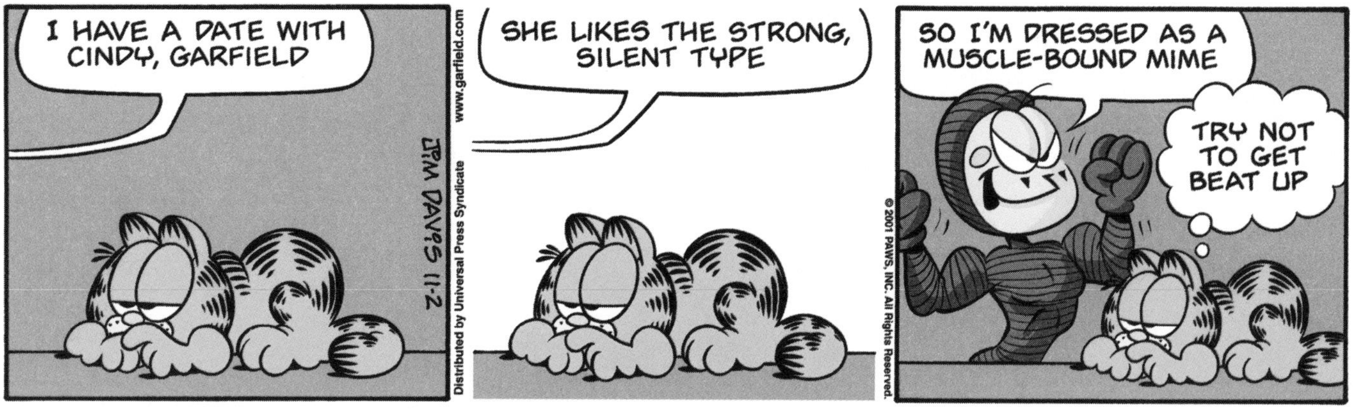
I HAVE A DATE WITH CINDY, GARFIELD
SHE LIKES THE STRONG, SILENT TYPE
SO I'M DRESSED AS A MUSCLE-BOUND MIME
TRY NOT TO GET BEAT UP
JPM DAVPS 11-2
Distributed by Universal Press Syndicate www.garfield.com
© 2001 PAWS, INC. All Rights Reserved.

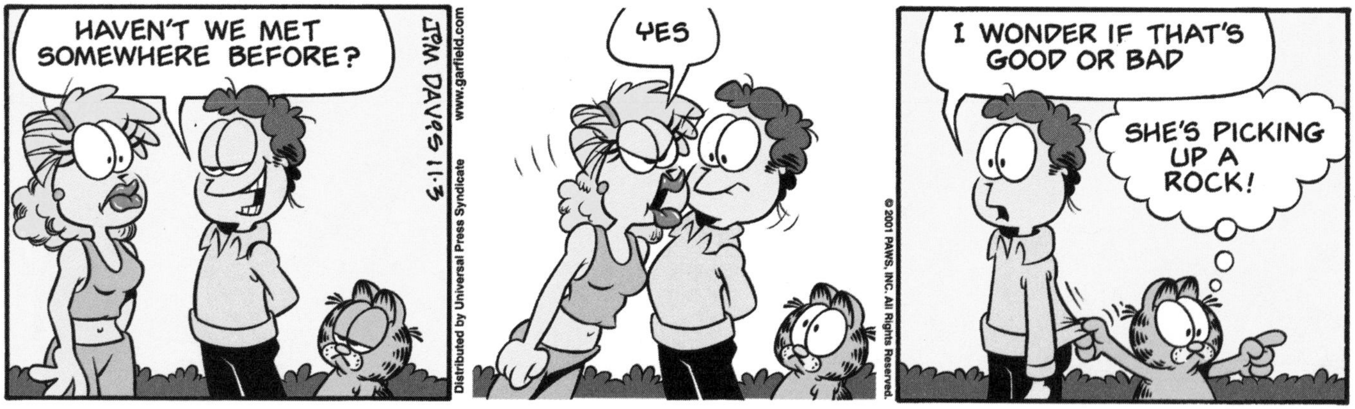
HAVEN'T WE MET SOMEWHERE BEFORE?
YES
I WONDER IF THAT'S GOOD OR BAD
SHE'S PICKING UP A ROCK!
JPM DAVPS 11-3
Distributed by Universal Press Syndicate www.garfield.com
© 2001 PAWS, INC. All Rights Reserved.

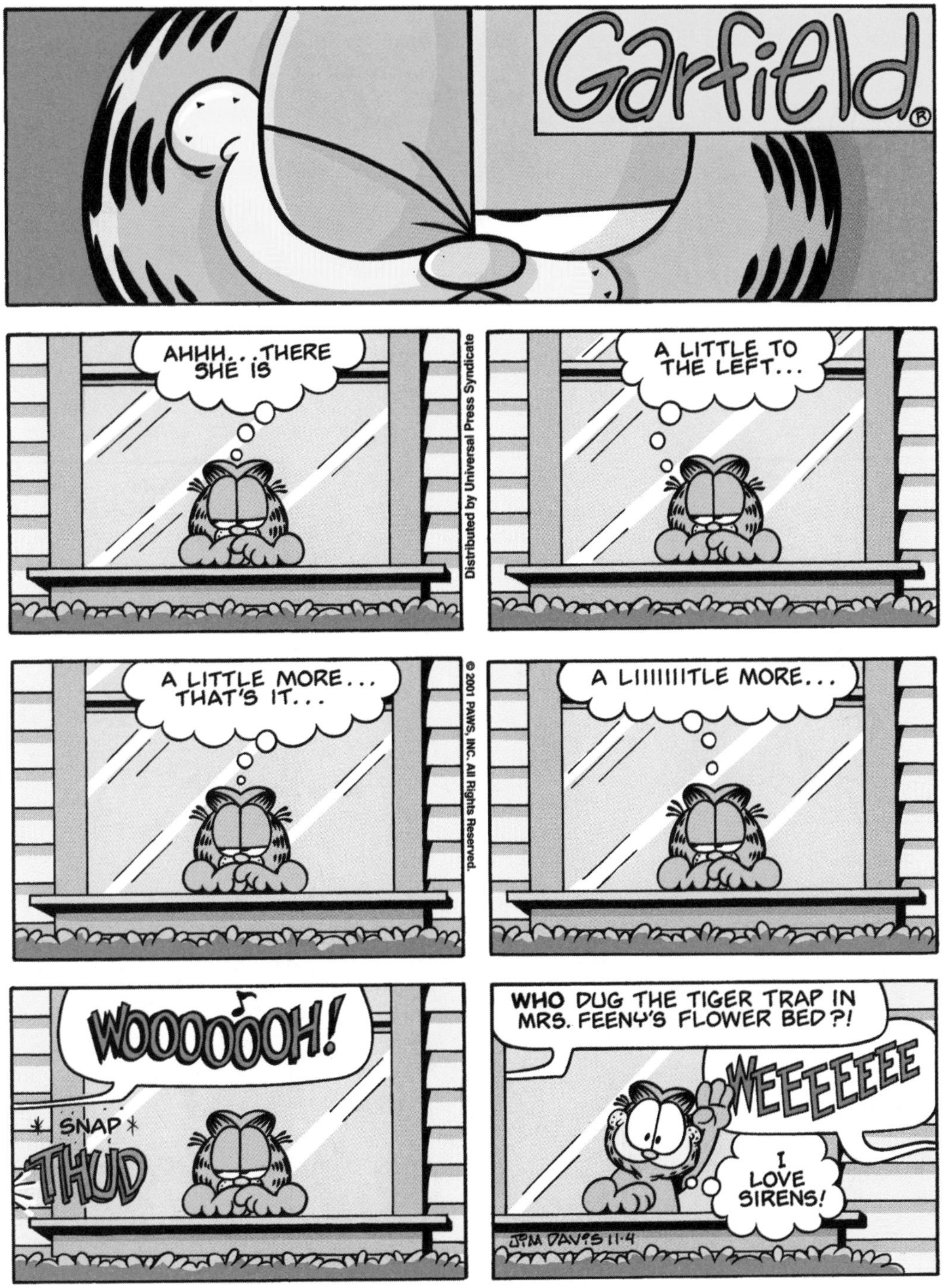
Garfield®
AHHH...THERE SHE IS
Distributed by Universal Press Syndicate
A LITTLE TO THE LEFT...
A LITTLE MORE... THAT'S IT...
© 2001 PAWS, INC. All Rights Reserved.
A LIIIIIIITLE MORE...
WOOOOOOH!
SNAP
THUD
WHO DUG THE TIGER TRAP IN MRS. FEENY'S FLOWER BED?!
WEEEEEEE
I LOVE SIRENS!
JIM DAVIS 11-4

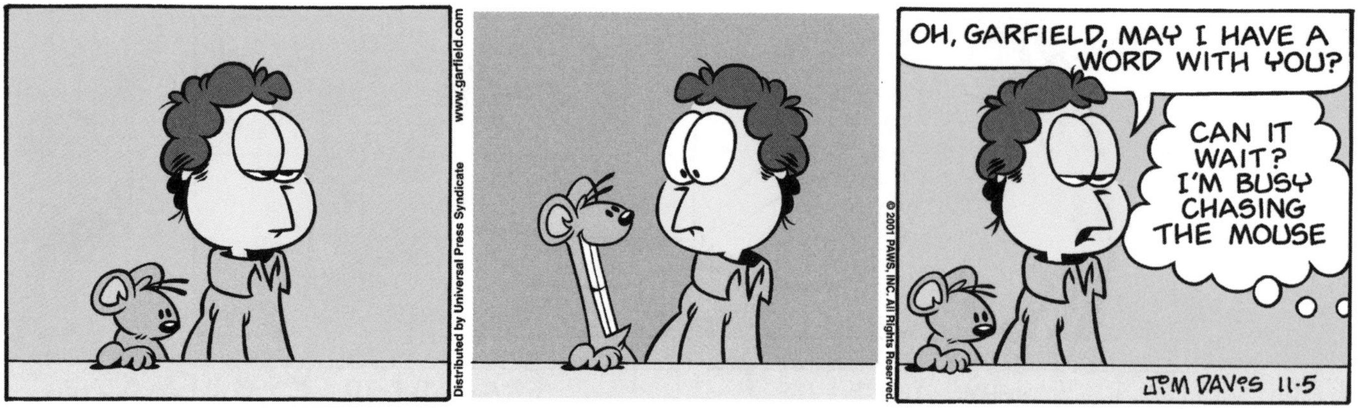
Distributed by Universal Press Syndicate www.garfield.com
© 2001 PAWS, INC. All Rights Reserved.
OH, GARFIELD, MAY I HAVE A WORD WITH YOU?
CAN IT WAIT? I'M BUSY CHASING THE MOUSE
JIM DAVIS 11-5

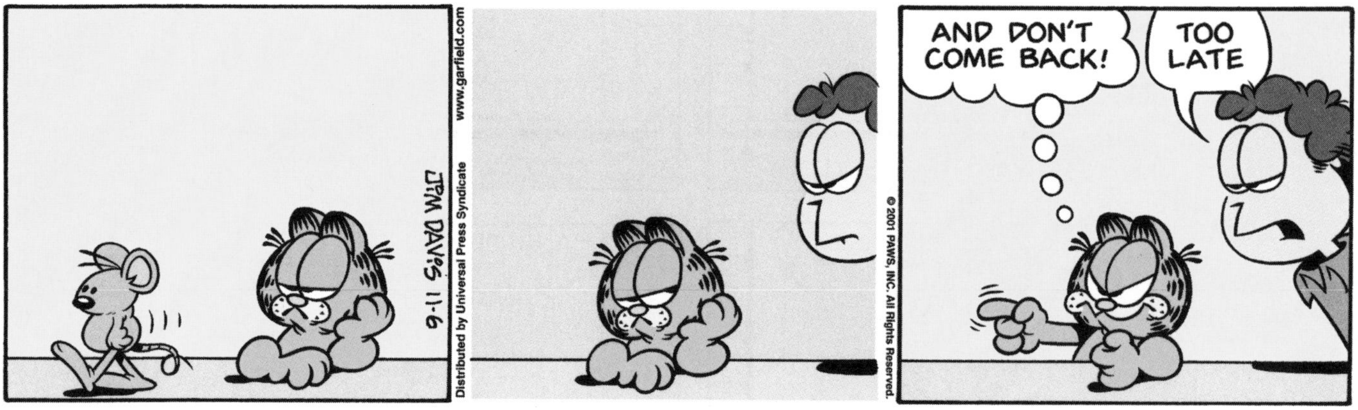
JIM DAVIS 11-6
Distributed by Universal Press Syndicate www.garfield.com
© 2001 PAWS, INC. All Rights Reserved.
AND DON'T COME BACK!
TOO LATE

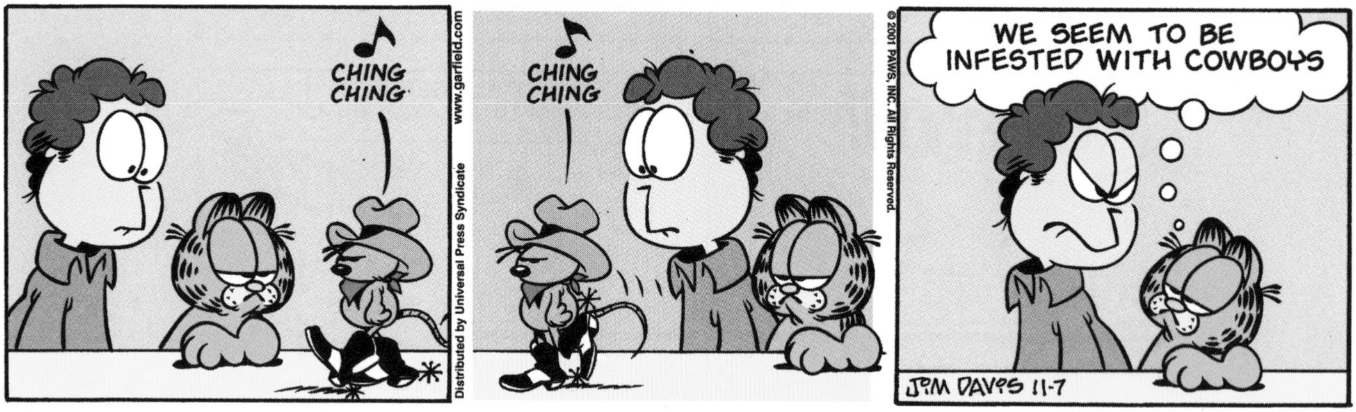
CHING CHING
Distributed by Universal Press Syndicate www.garfield.com
CHING CHING
© 2001 PAWS, INC. All Rights Reserved.
WE SEEM TO BE INFESTED WITH COWBOYS
JIM DAVIS 11-7

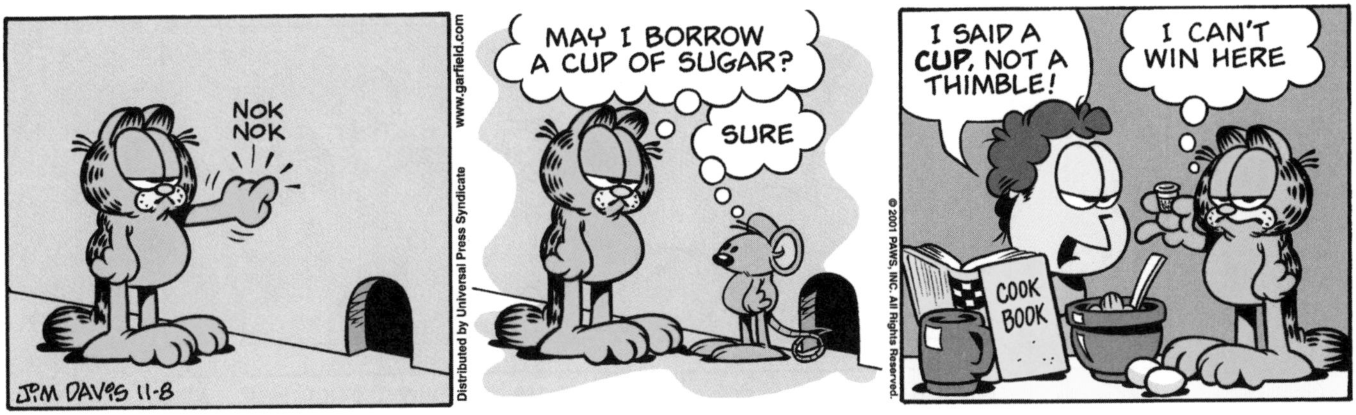
NOK NOK
JIM DAVIS 11-8
www.garfield.com
Distributed by Universal Press Syndicate
MAY I BORROW A CUP OF SUGAR?
SURE
© 2001 PAWS, INC. All Rights Reserved.
I SAID A **CUP**, NOT A THIMBLE!
I CAN'T WIN HERE
COOK BOOK

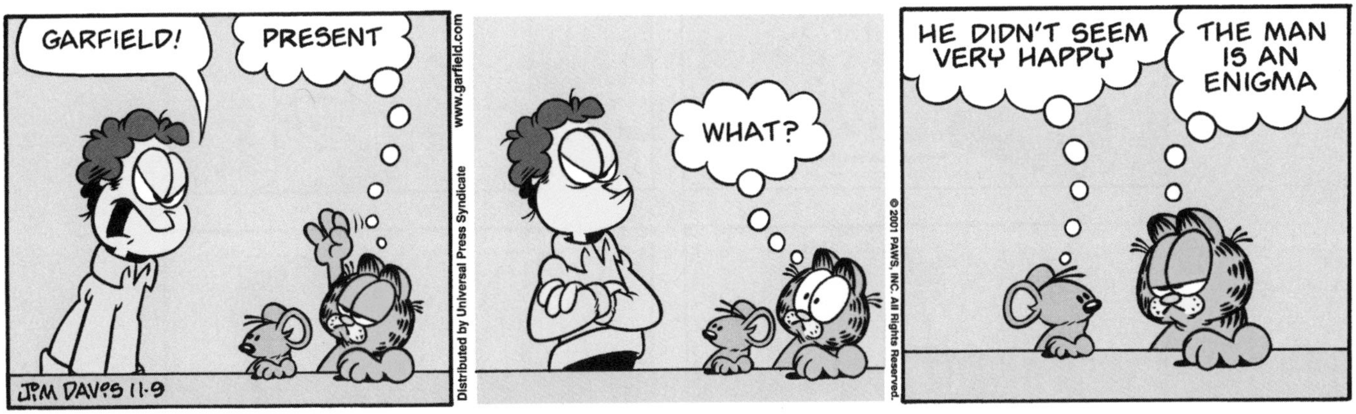
GARFIELD!
PRESENT
JIM DAVIS 11-9
www.garfield.com
Distributed by Universal Press Syndicate
WHAT?
© 2001 PAWS, INC. All Rights Reserved.
HE DIDN'T SEEM VERY HAPPY
THE MAN IS AN ENIGMA

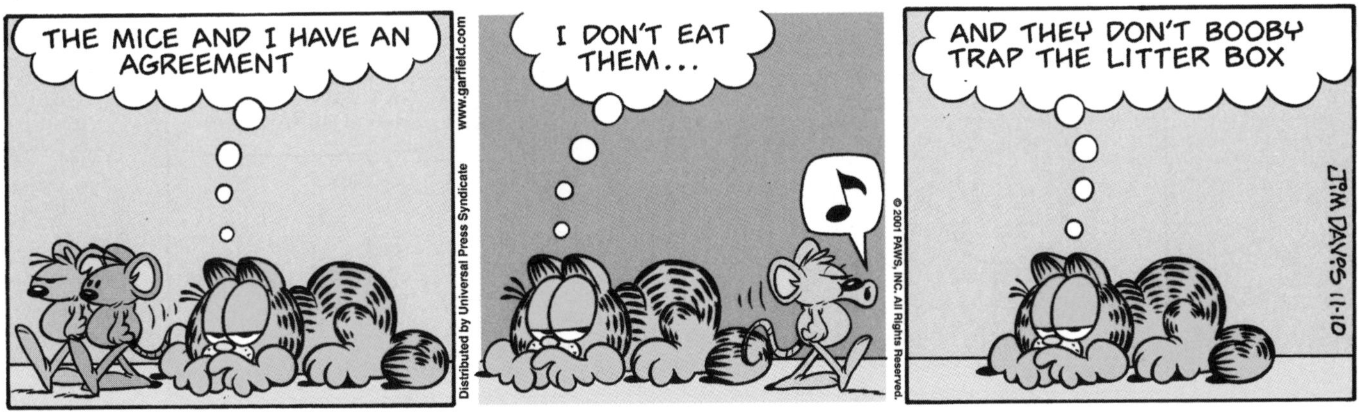
THE MICE AND I HAVE AN AGREEMENT
www.garfield.com
Distributed by Universal Press Syndicate
I DON'T EAT THEM...
© 2001 PAWS, INC. All Rights Reserved.
AND THEY DON'T BOOBY TRAP THE LITTER BOX
JIM DAVIS 11-10

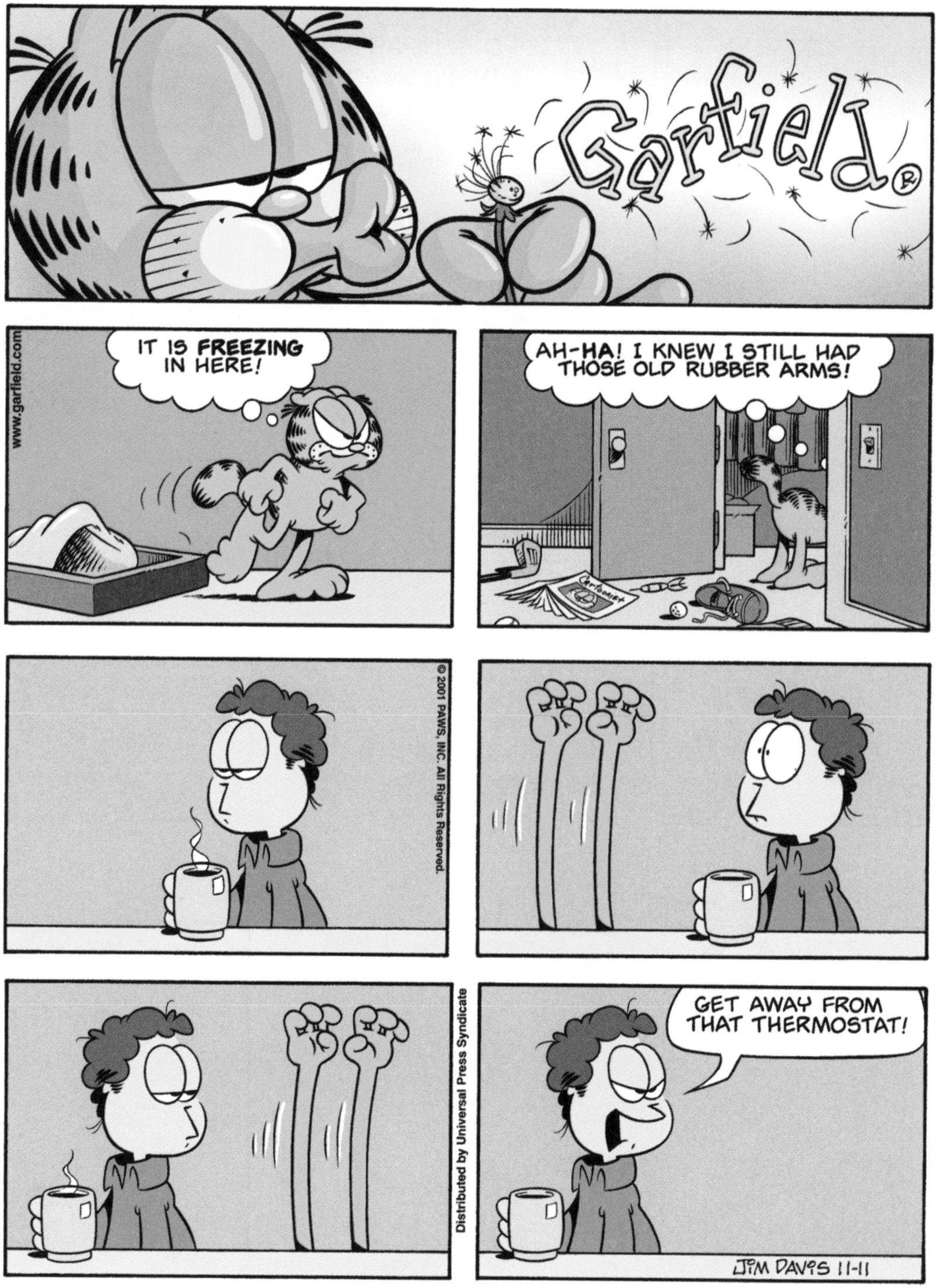
Garfield
www.garfield.com
IT IS FREEZING IN HERE!
AH-HA! I KNEW I STILL HAD THOSE OLD RUBBER ARMS!
© 2001 PAWS, INC. All Rights Reserved.
Distributed by Universal Press Syndicate
GET AWAY FROM THAT THERMOSTAT!
JIM DAVIS 11-11

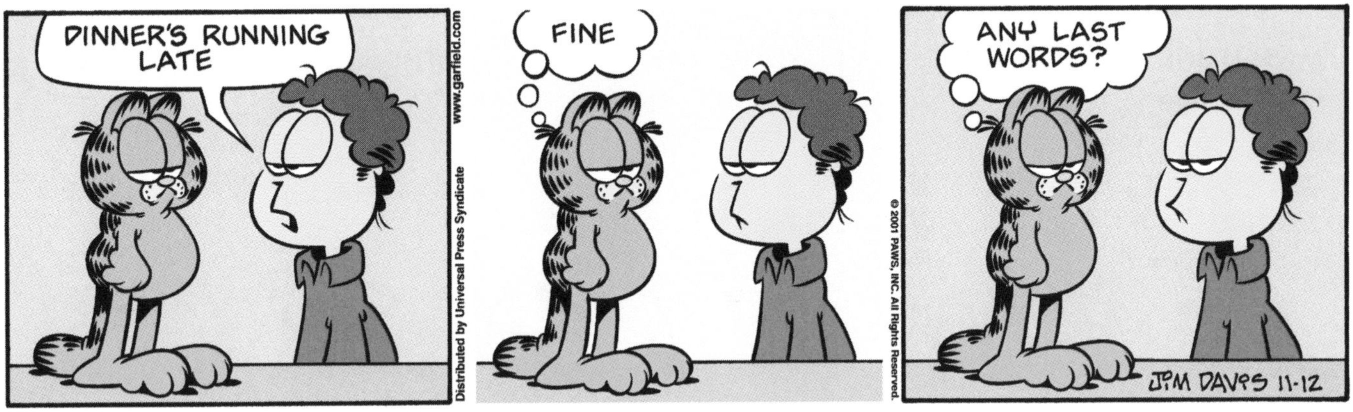
DINNER'S RUNNING LATE
www.garfield.com
Distributed by Universal Press Syndicate
FINE
© 2001 PAWS, INC. All Rights Reserved.
ANY LAST WORDS?
JIM DAVIS 11-12

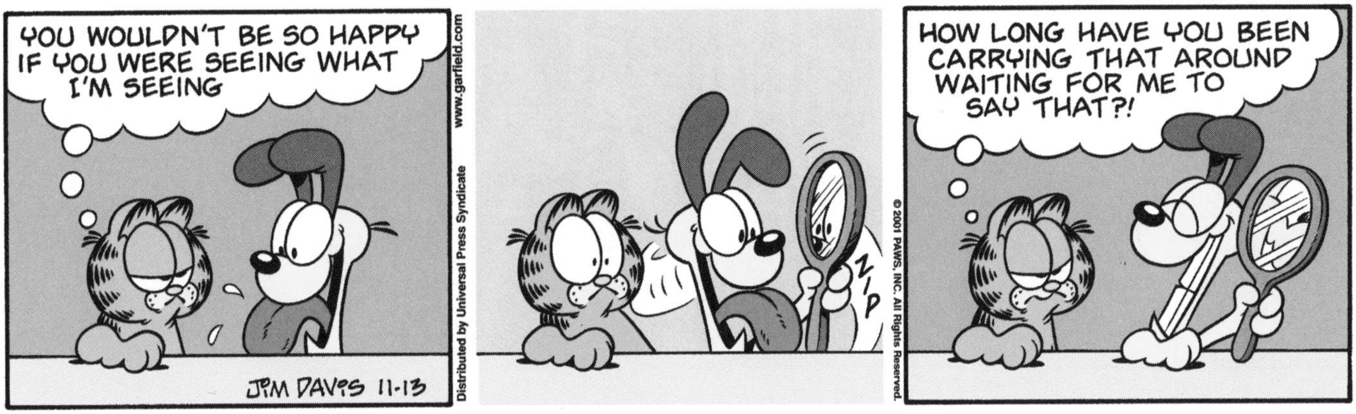
YOU WOULDN'T BE SO HAPPY IF YOU WERE SEEING WHAT I'M SEEING
JIM DAVIS 11-13
www.garfield.com
Distributed by Universal Press Syndicate
ZIP
© 2001 PAWS, INC. All Rights Reserved.
HOW LONG HAVE YOU BEEN CARRYING THAT AROUND WAITING FOR ME TO SAY THAT?!

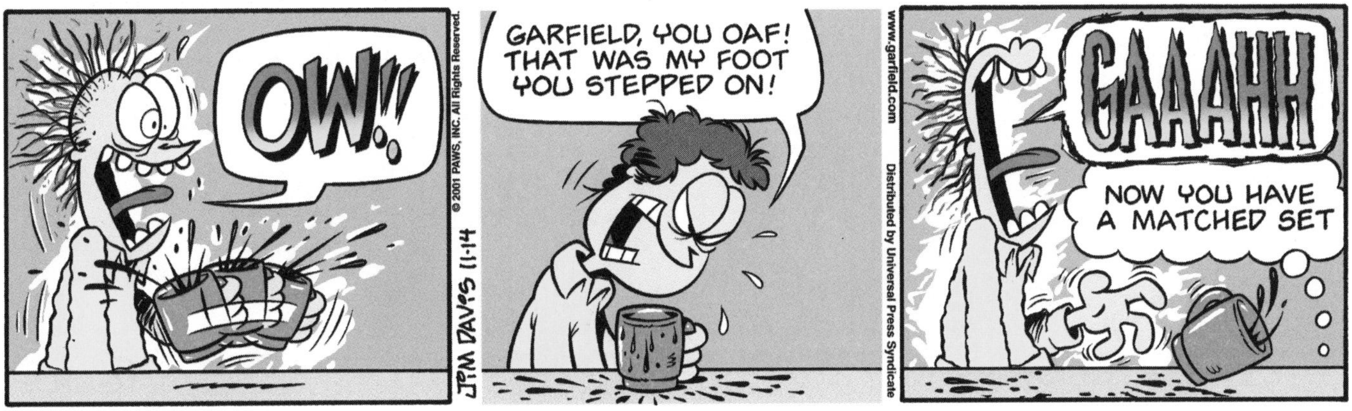
OW!!
© 2001 PAWS, INC. All Rights Reserved.
JIM DAVIS 11-14
GARFIELD, YOU OAF! THAT WAS MY FOOT YOU STEPPED ON!
www.garfield.com
Distributed by Universal Press Syndicate
GAAAHH
NOW YOU HAVE A MATCHED SET

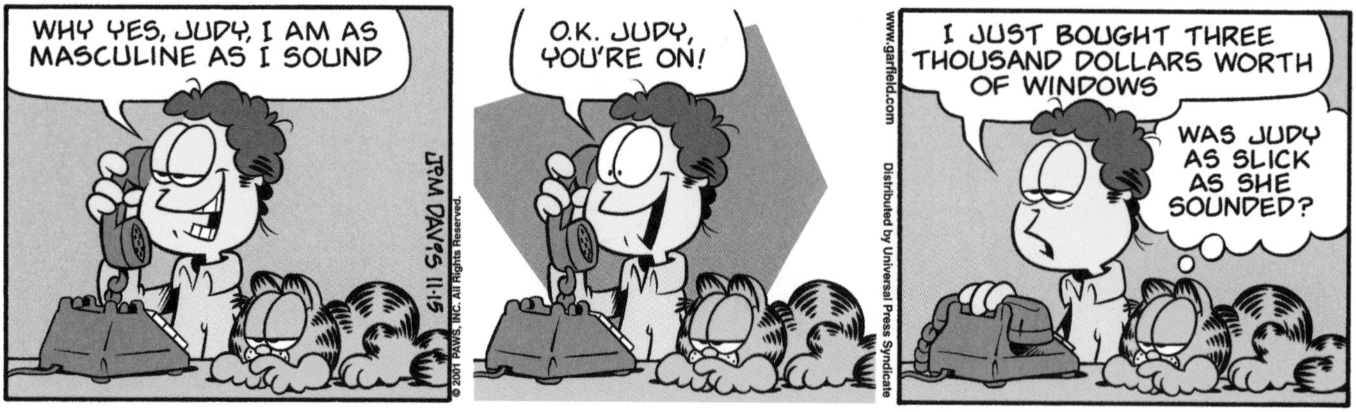
WHY YES, JUDY, I AM AS MASCULINE AS I SOUND
JIM DAVIS 11-15
© 2001 PAWS, INC. All Rights Reserved.
O.K. JUDY, YOU'RE ON!
www.garfield.com
Distributed by Universal Press Syndicate
I JUST BOUGHT THREE THOUSAND DOLLARS WORTH OF WINDOWS
WAS JUDY AS SLICK AS SHE SOUNDED?

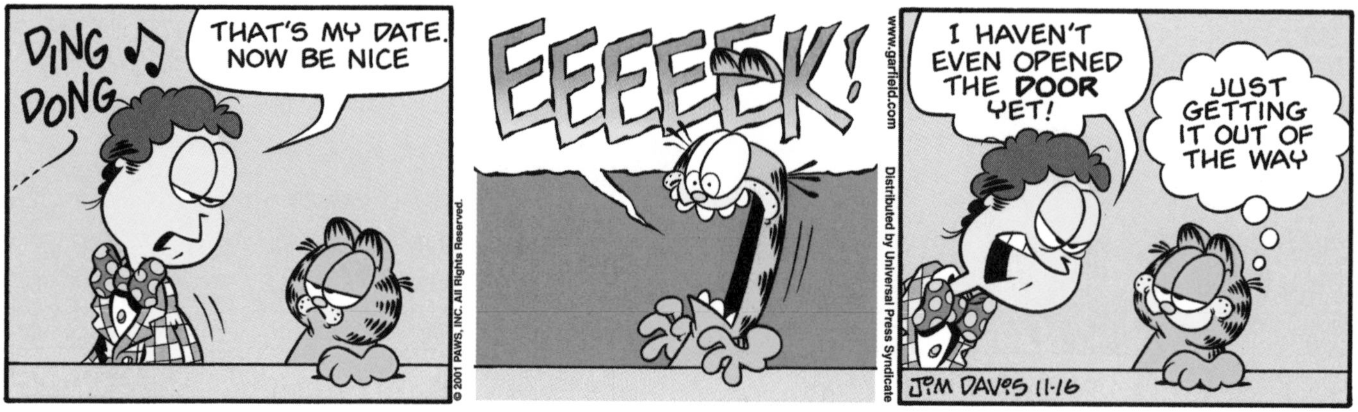
DING ♫ DONG
THAT'S MY DATE. NOW BE NICE
© 2001 PAWS, INC. All Rights Reserved.
EEEEEEK!
www.garfield.com
Distributed by Universal Press Syndicate
I HAVEN'T EVEN OPENED THE **DOOR** YET!
JUST GETTING IT OUT OF THE WAY
JIM DAVIS 11-16

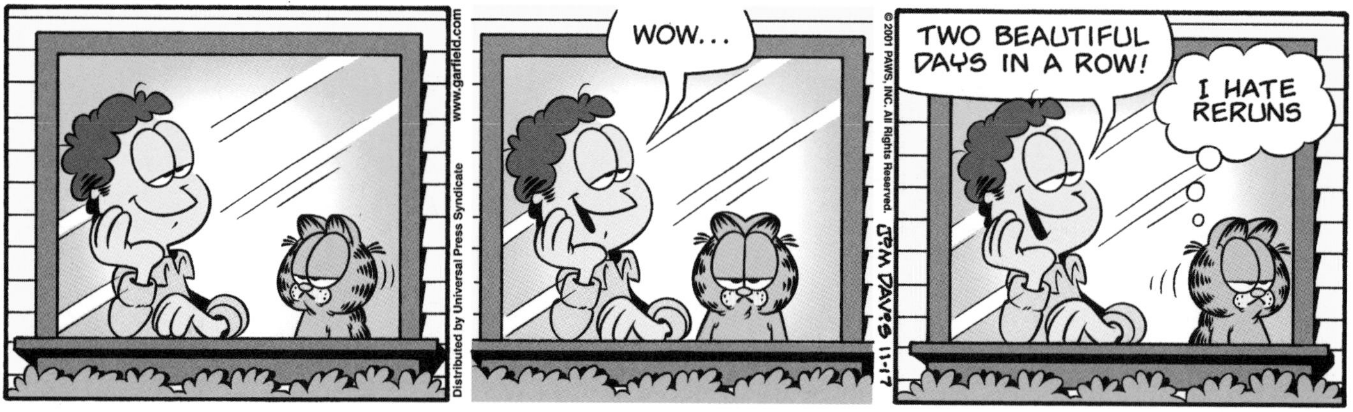
www.garfield.com
Distributed by Universal Press Syndicate
WOW...
© 2001 PAWS, INC. All Rights Reserved.
JIM DAVIS 11-17
TWO BEAUTIFUL DAYS IN A ROW!
I HATE RERUNS

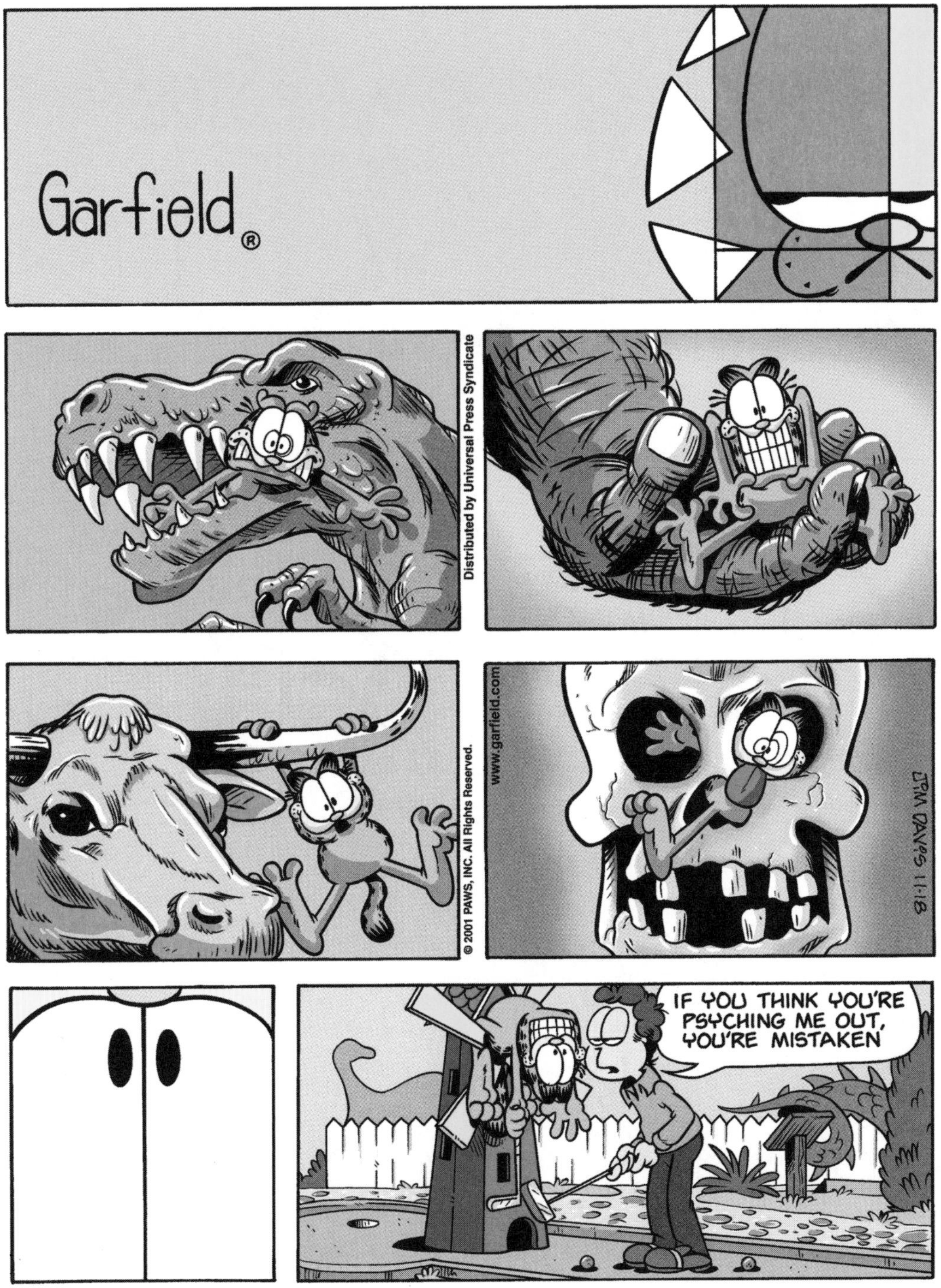
Garfield®
Distributed by Universal Press Syndicate
© 2001 PAWS, INC. All Rights Reserved.
www.garfield.com
JPM DAVPS 11-18
IF YOU THINK YOU'RE PSYCHING ME OUT, YOU'RE MISTAKEN

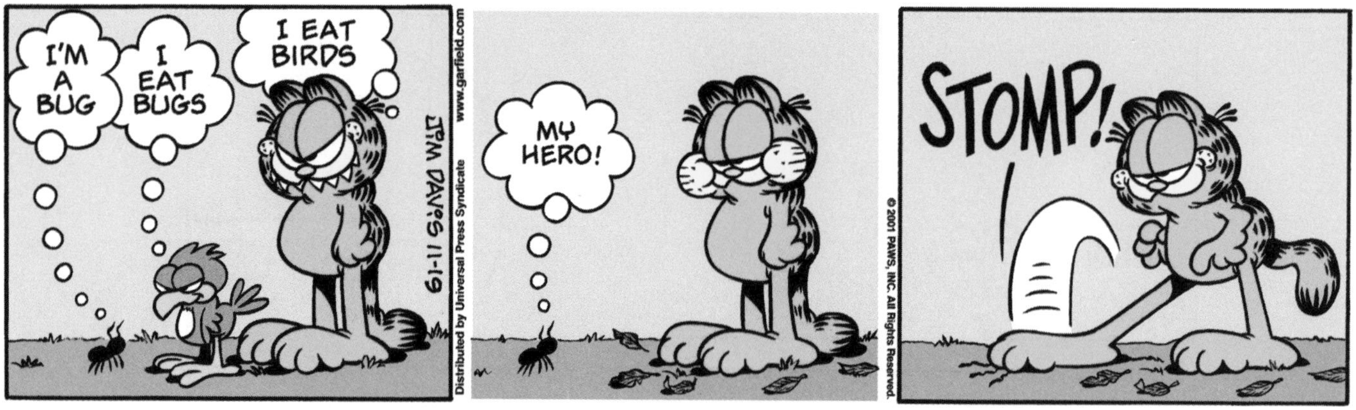
I'M A BUG
I EAT BUGS
I EAT BIRDS
JIM DAVIS 11-19
www.garfield.com
Distributed by Universal Press Syndicate
MY HERO!
© 2001 PAWS, INC. All Rights Reserved.
STOMP!

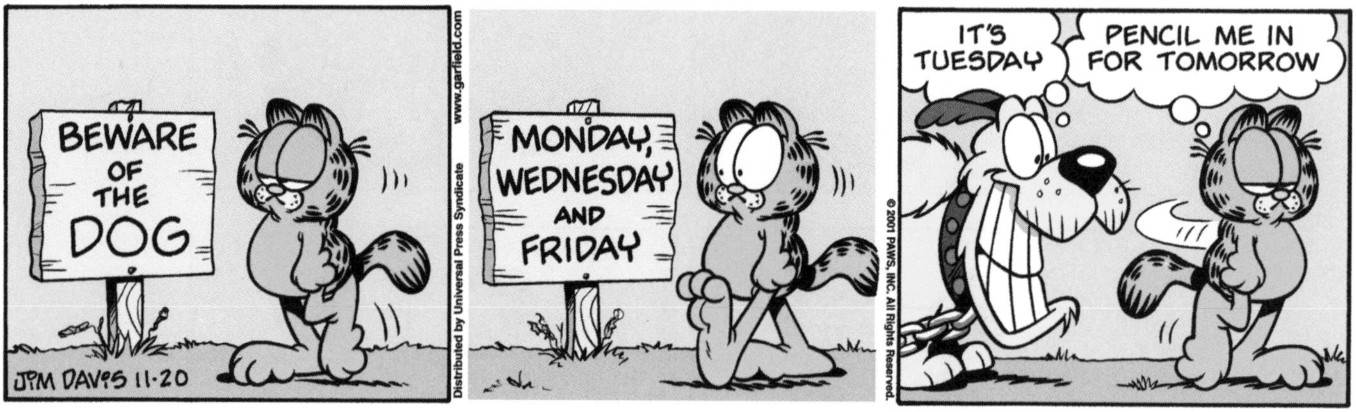
BEWARE OF THE DOG
JIM DAVIS 11-20
www.garfield.com
Distributed by Universal Press Syndicate
MONDAY, WEDNESDAY AND FRIDAY
© 2001 PAWS, INC. All Rights Reserved.
IT'S TUESDAY
PENCIL ME IN FOR TOMORROW

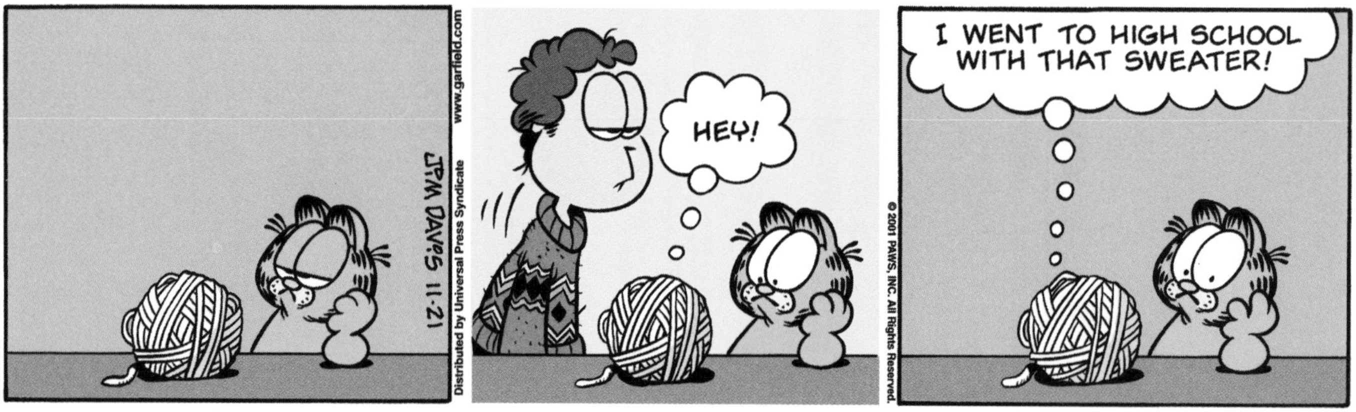
JIM DAVIS 11-21
www.garfield.com
Distributed by Universal Press Syndicate
HEY!
© 2001 PAWS, INC. All Rights Reserved.
I WENT TO HIGH SCHOOL WITH THAT SWEATER!

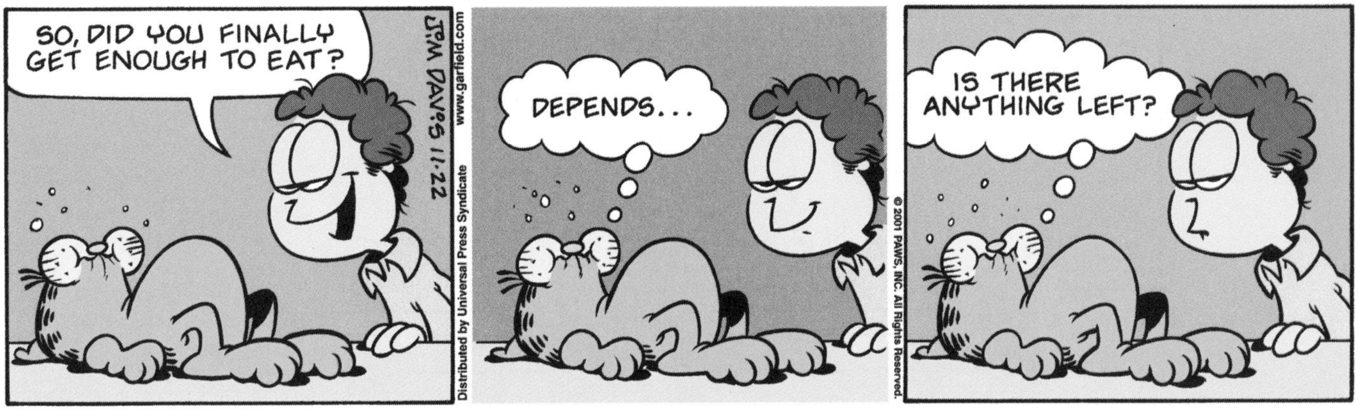
SO, DID YOU FINALLY GET ENOUGH TO EAT?
JIM DAVIS 11-22
www.garfield.com
Distributed by Universal Press Syndicate
DEPENDS...
© 2001 PAWS, INC. All Rights Reserved.
IS THERE ANYTHING LEFT?

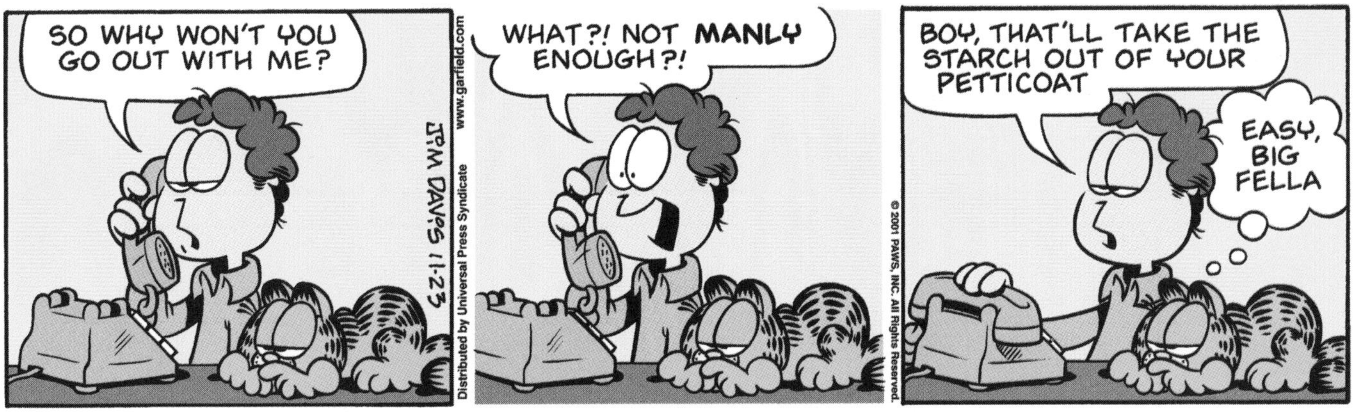
SO WHY WON'T YOU GO OUT WITH ME?
JIM DAVIS 11-23
www.garfield.com
Distributed by Universal Press Syndicate
WHAT?! NOT **MANLY** ENOUGH?!
© 2001 PAWS, INC. All Rights Reserved.
BOY, THAT'LL TAKE THE STARCH OUT OF YOUR PETTICOAT
EASY, BIG FELLA

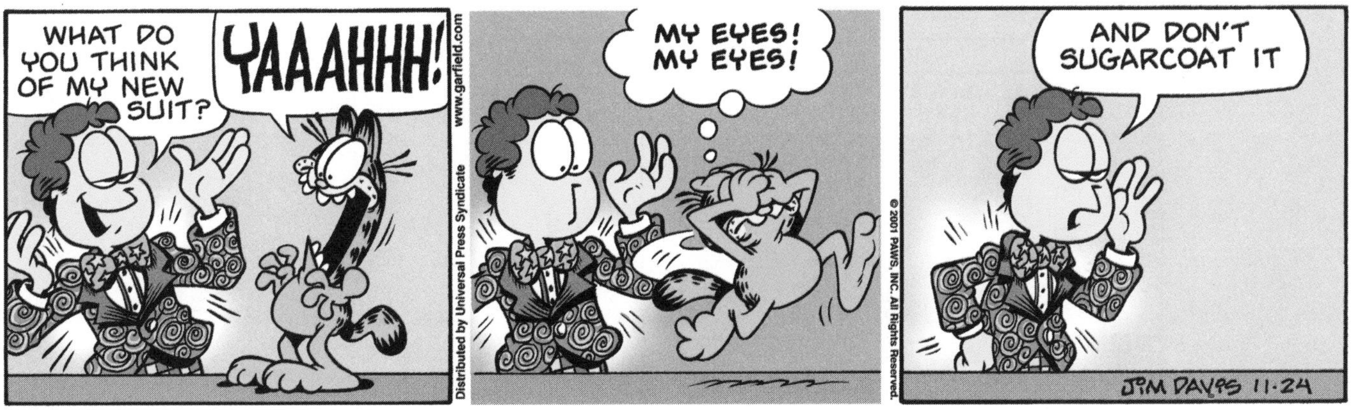
WHAT DO YOU THINK OF MY NEW SUIT?
YAAAHHH!
www.garfield.com
Distributed by Universal Press Syndicate
MY EYES! MY EYES!
© 2001 PAWS, INC. All Rights Reserved.
AND DON'T SUGARCOAT IT
JIM DAVIS 11-24

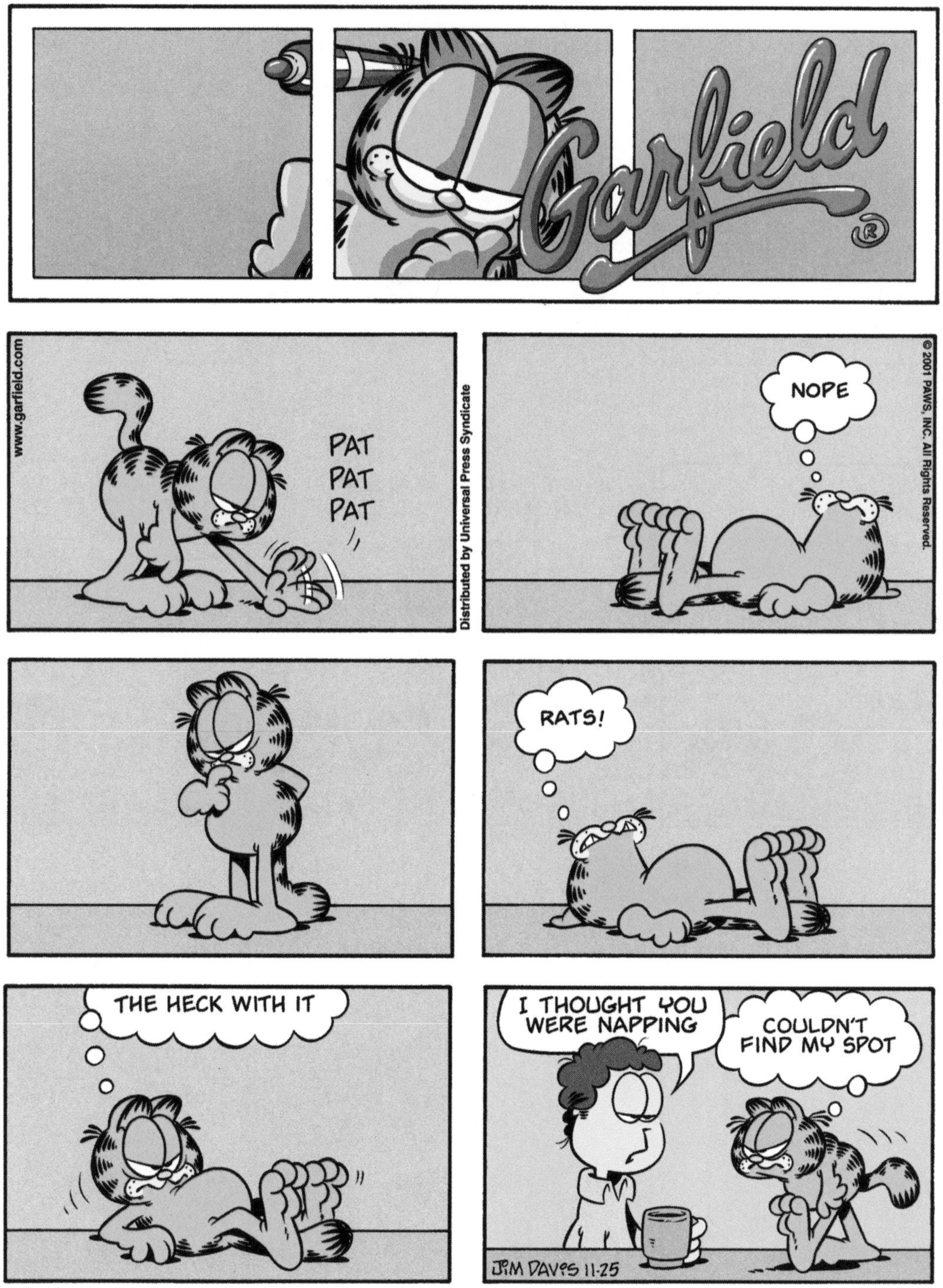
Garfield®
www.garfield.com
Distributed by Universal Press Syndicate
© 2001 PAWS, INC. All Rights Reserved.
PAT PAT PAT
NOPE
RATS!
THE HECK WITH IT
I THOUGHT YOU WERE NAPPING
COULDN'T FIND MY SPOT
JIM DAVIS 11-25

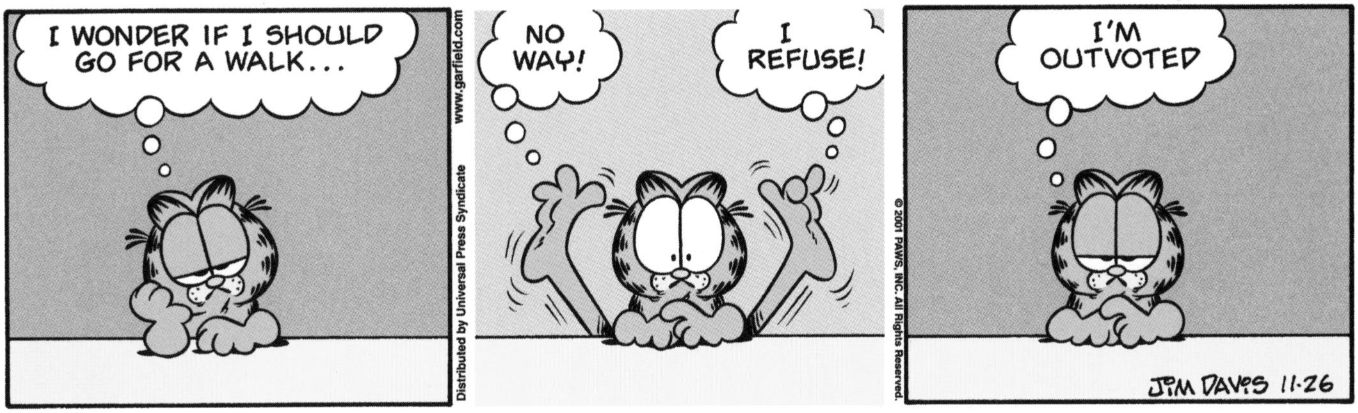
I WONDER IF I SHOULD GO FOR A WALK...
NO WAY!
I REFUSE!
I'M OUTVOTED
JIM DAVIS 11-26
www.garfield.com
Distributed by Universal Press Syndicate
© 2001 PAWS, INC. All Rights Reserved.

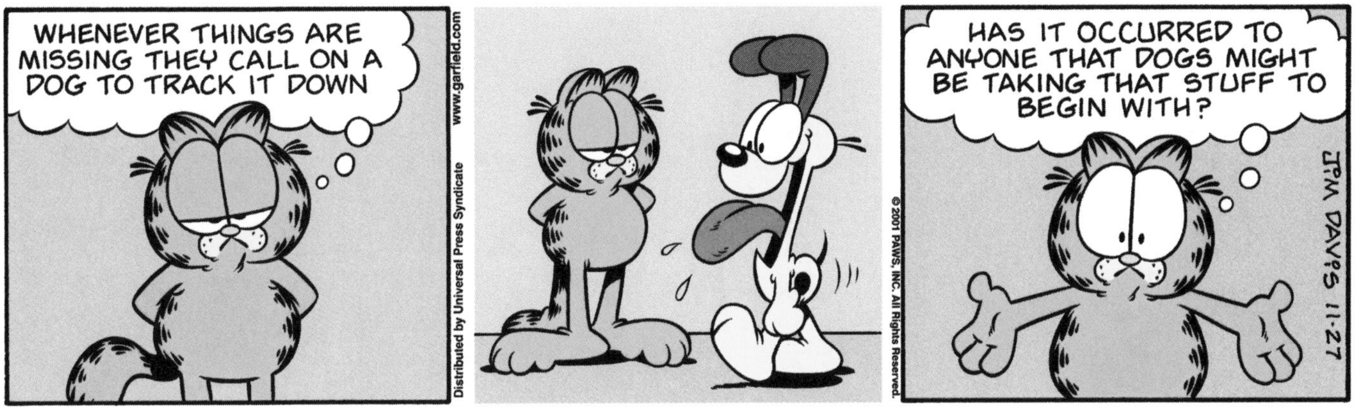
WHENEVER THINGS ARE MISSING THEY CALL ON A DOG TO TRACK IT DOWN
HAS IT OCCURRED TO ANYONE THAT DOGS MIGHT BE TAKING THAT STUFF TO BEGIN WITH?
JIM DAVIS 11-27
www.garfield.com
Distributed by Universal Press Syndicate
© 2001 PAWS, INC. All Rights Reserved.

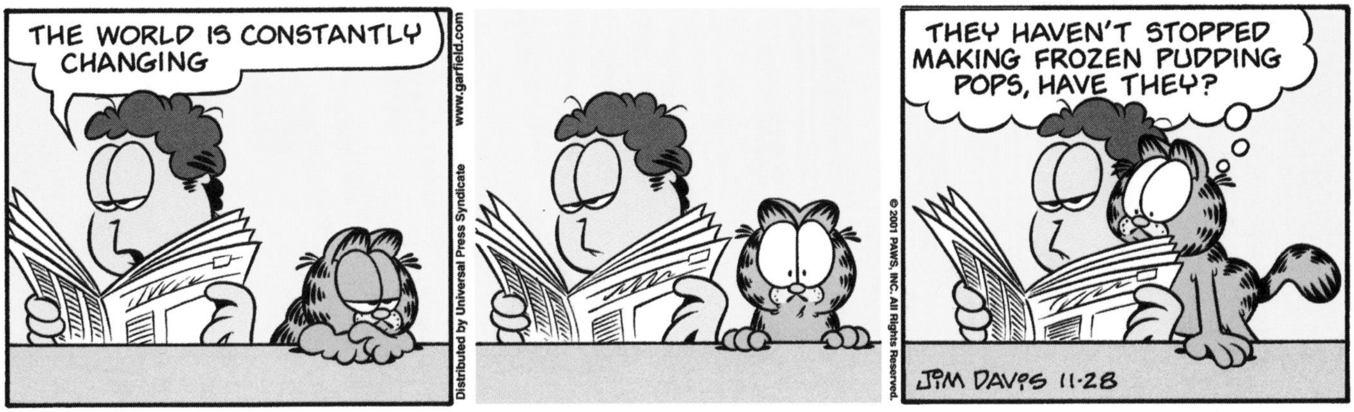
THE WORLD IS CONSTANTLY CHANGING
THEY HAVEN'T STOPPED MAKING FROZEN PUDDING POPS, HAVE THEY?
JIM DAVIS 11-28
www.garfield.com
Distributed by Universal Press Syndicate
© 2001 PAWS, INC. All Rights Reserved.

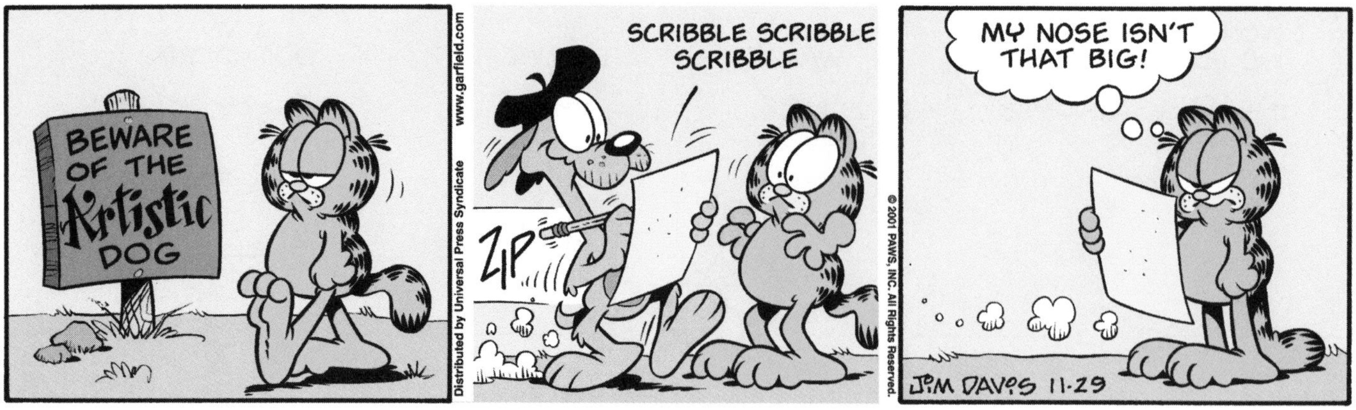
BEWARE OF THE Artistic DOG
SCRIBBLE SCRIBBLE SCRIBBLE
ZIP
MY NOSE ISN'T THAT BIG!
JIM DAVIS 11-29
Distributed by Universal Press Syndicate www.garfield.com
© 2001 PAWS, INC. All Rights Reserved.

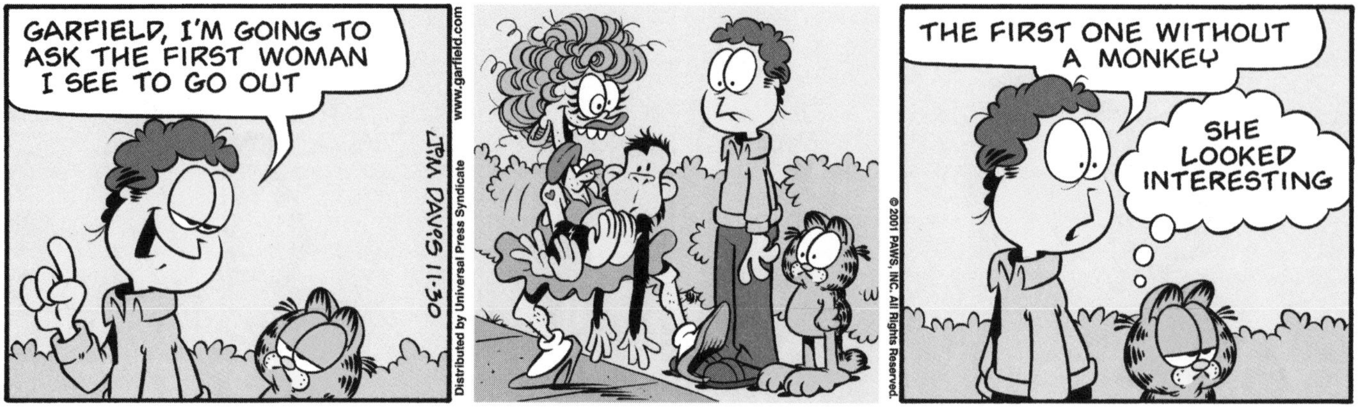
GARFIELD, I'M GOING TO ASK THE FIRST WOMAN I SEE TO GO OUT
JIM DAVIS 11-30
THE FIRST ONE WITHOUT A MONKEY
SHE LOOKED INTERESTING
Distributed by Universal Press Syndicate www.garfield.com
© 2001 PAWS, INC. All Rights Reserved.

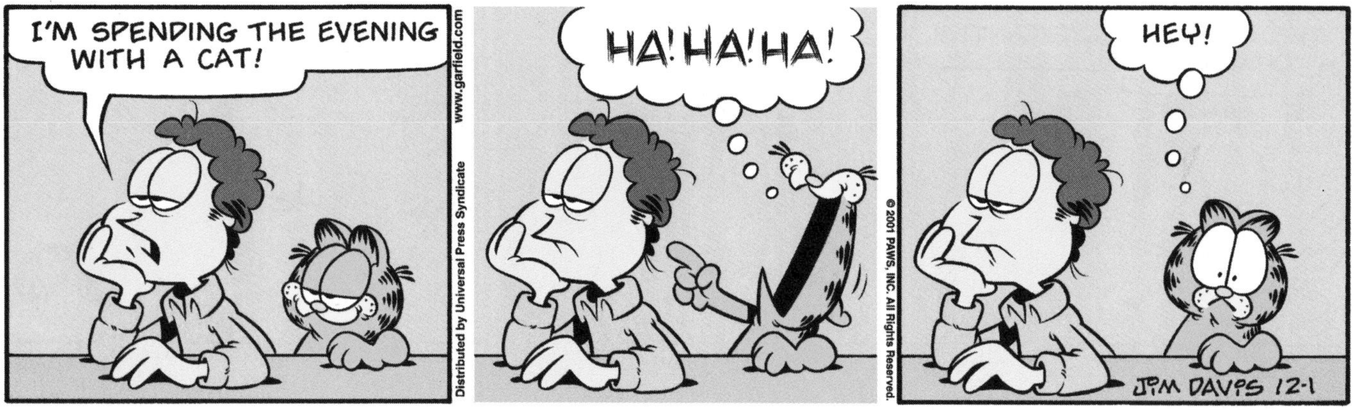
I'M SPENDING THE EVENING WITH A CAT!
HA! HA! HA!
HEY!
JIM DAVIS 12-1
Distributed by Universal Press Syndicate www.garfield.com
© 2001 PAWS, INC. All Rights Reserved.

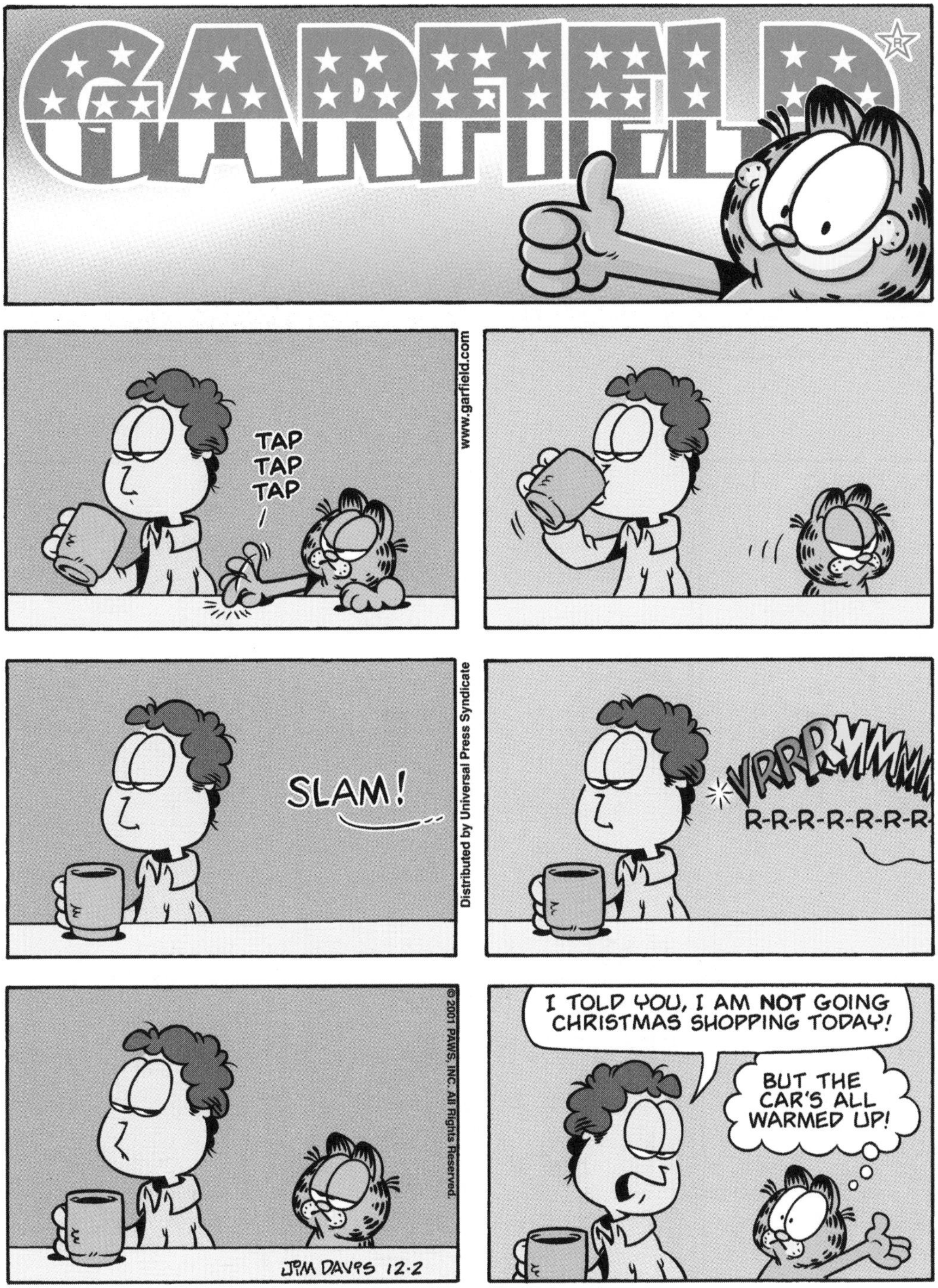
GARFIELD
www.garfield.com
TAP TAP TAP
SLAM!
Distributed by Universal Press Syndicate
VRRRMMMM
R-R-R-R-R-R-R-
© 2001 PAWS, INC. All Rights Reserved.
JIM DAVIS 12-2
I TOLD YOU, I AM **NOT** GOING CHRISTMAS SHOPPING TODAY!
BUT THE CAR'S ALL WARMED UP!

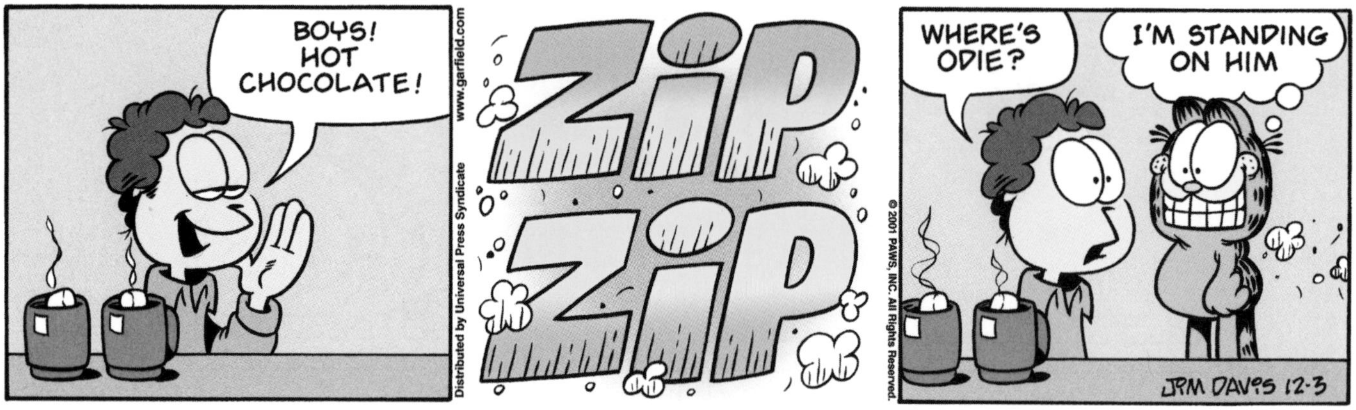
BOYS! HOT CHOCOLATE!
ZIP ZIP
WHERE'S ODIE?
I'M STANDING ON HIM
JIM DAVIS 12-3
Distributed by Universal Press Syndicate www.garfield.com
© 2001 PAWS, INC. All Rights Reserved.

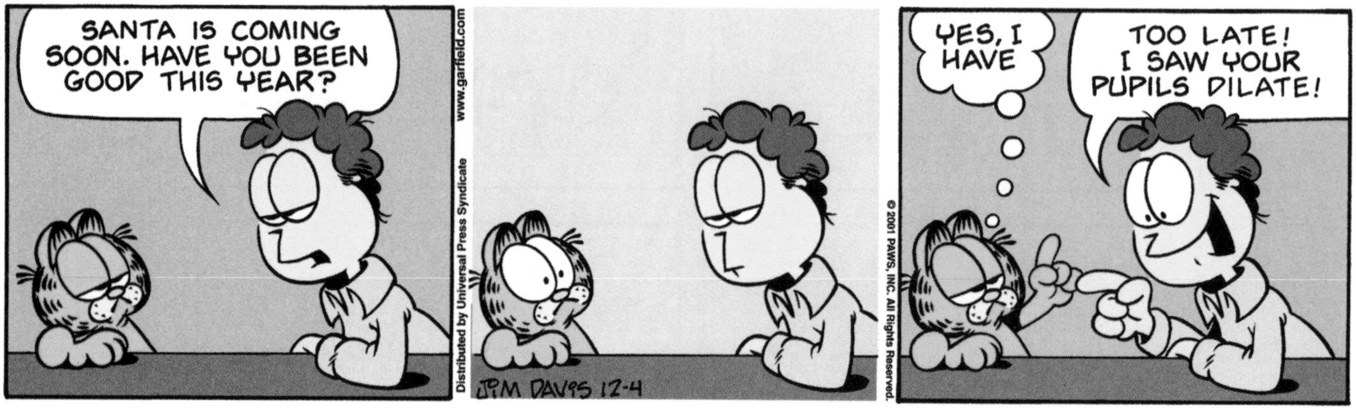
SANTA IS COMING SOON. HAVE YOU BEEN GOOD THIS YEAR?
YES, I HAVE
TOO LATE! I SAW YOUR PUPILS DILATE!
JIM DAVIS 12-4
Distributed by Universal Press Syndicate www.garfield.com
© 2001 PAWS, INC. All Rights Reserved.

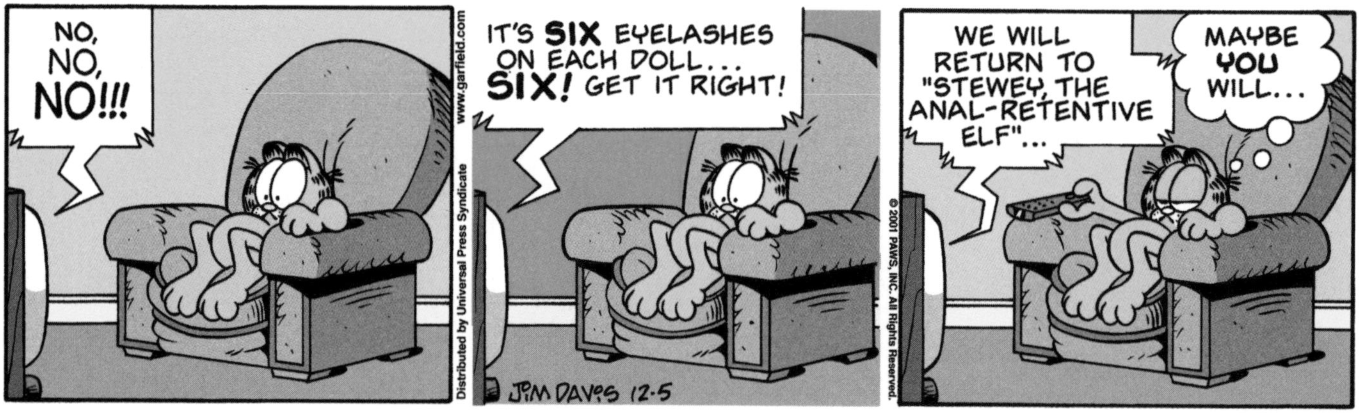
NO, NO, NO!!!
IT'S SIX EYELASHES ON EACH DOLL... SIX! GET IT RIGHT!
WE WILL RETURN TO "STEWEY, THE ANAL-RETENTIVE ELF"...
MAYBE YOU WILL...
JIM DAVIS 12-5
Distributed by Universal Press Syndicate www.garfield.com
© 2001 PAWS, INC. All Rights Reserved.

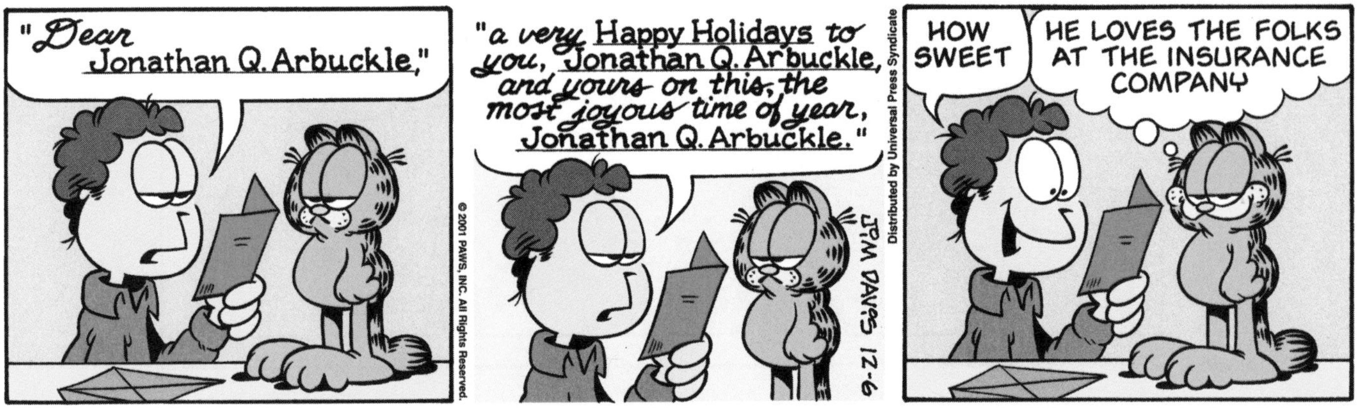
"Dear
Jonathan Q. Arbuckle,"
"a very Happy Holidays to you, Jonathan Q. Arbuckle, and yours on this, the most joyous time of year, Jonathan Q. Arbuckle."
JIM DAVIS 12-6
© 2001 PAWS, INC. All Rights Reserved.
Distributed by Universal Press Syndicate
HOW SWEET
HE LOVES THE FOLKS AT THE INSURANCE COMPANY

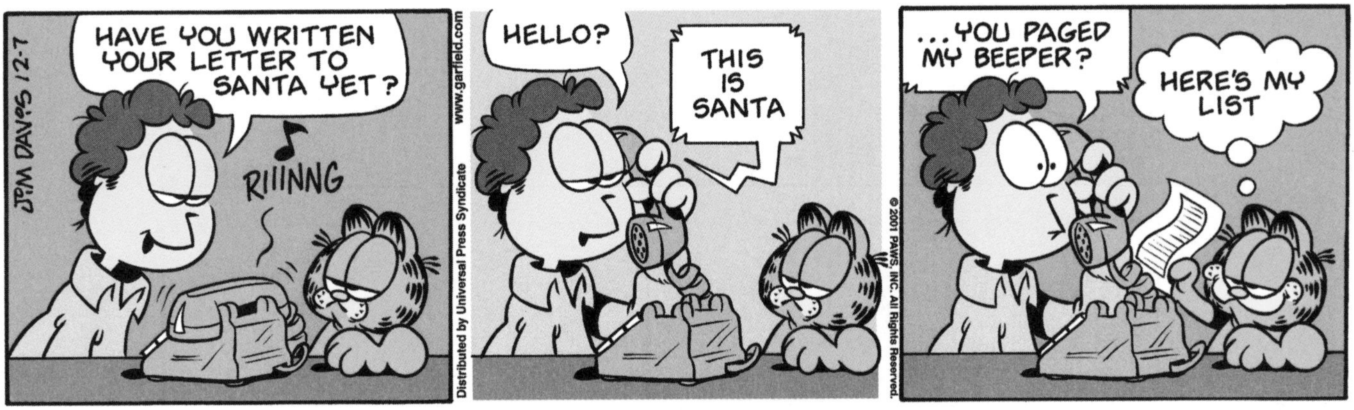
JIM DAVIS 12-7
HAVE YOU WRITTEN YOUR LETTER TO SANTA YET?
RIIINNG
www.garfield.com
Distributed by Universal Press Syndicate
HELLO?
THIS IS SANTA
© 2001 PAWS, INC. All Rights Reserved.
...YOU PAGED MY BEEPER?
HERE'S MY LIST

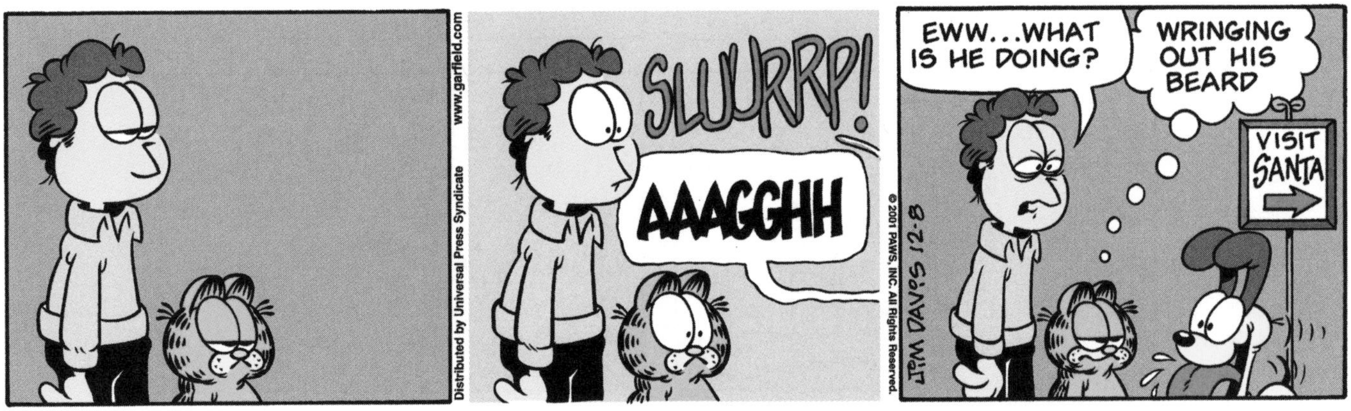
www.garfield.com
Distributed by Universal Press Syndicate
SLUURRP!
AAAGGHH
© 2001 PAWS, INC. All Rights Reserved.
JIM DAVIS 12-8
EWW...WHAT IS HE DOING?
WRINGING OUT HIS BEARD
VISIT SANTA

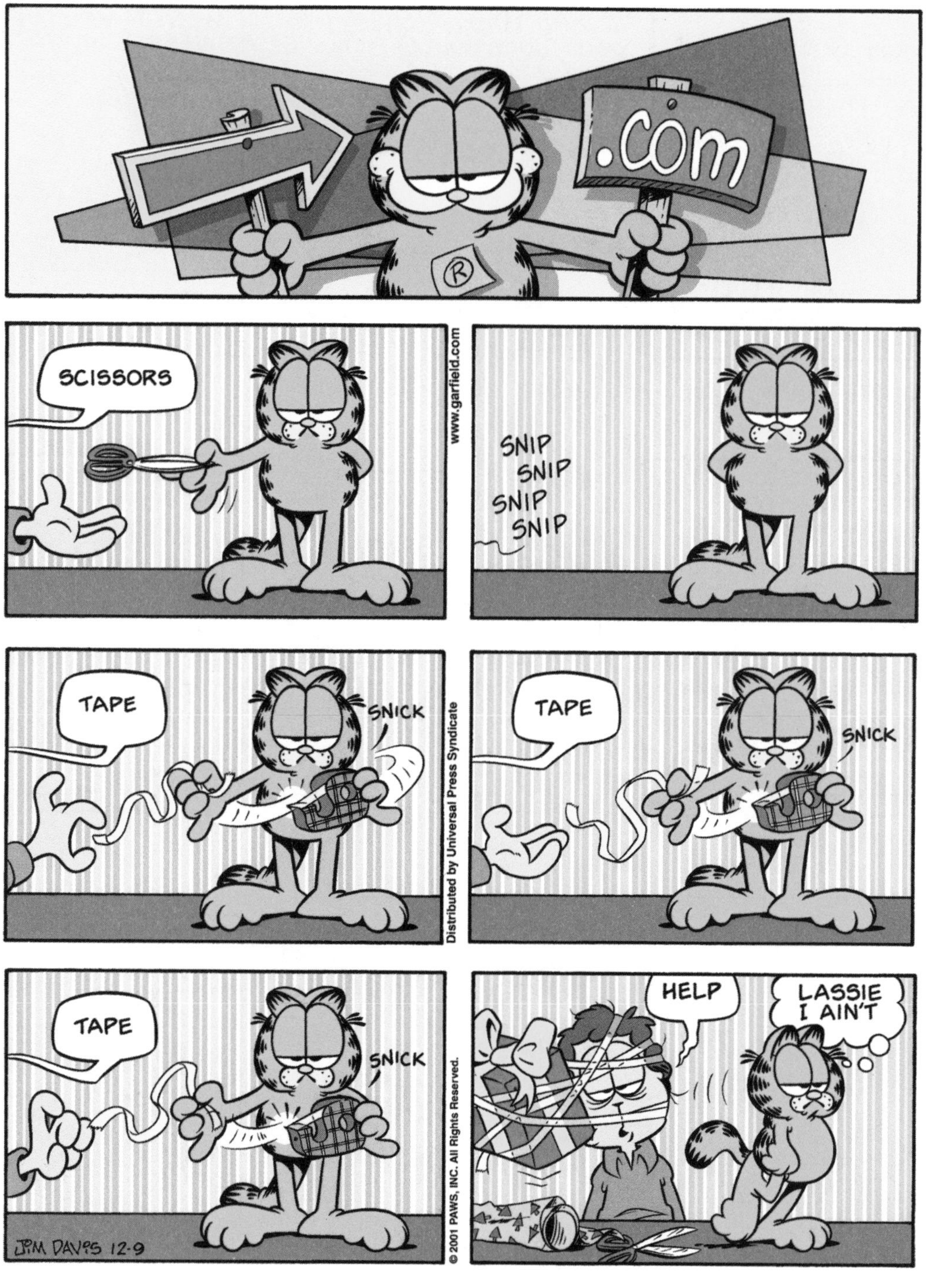
.com
SCISSORS
SNIP
SNIP
SNIP
SNIP
TAPE
SNICK
TAPE
SNICK
TAPE
SNICK
HELP
LASSIE I AIN'T
JIM DAVIS 12-9
www.garfield.com
Distributed by Universal Press Syndicate
© 2001 PAWS, INC. All Rights Reserved.

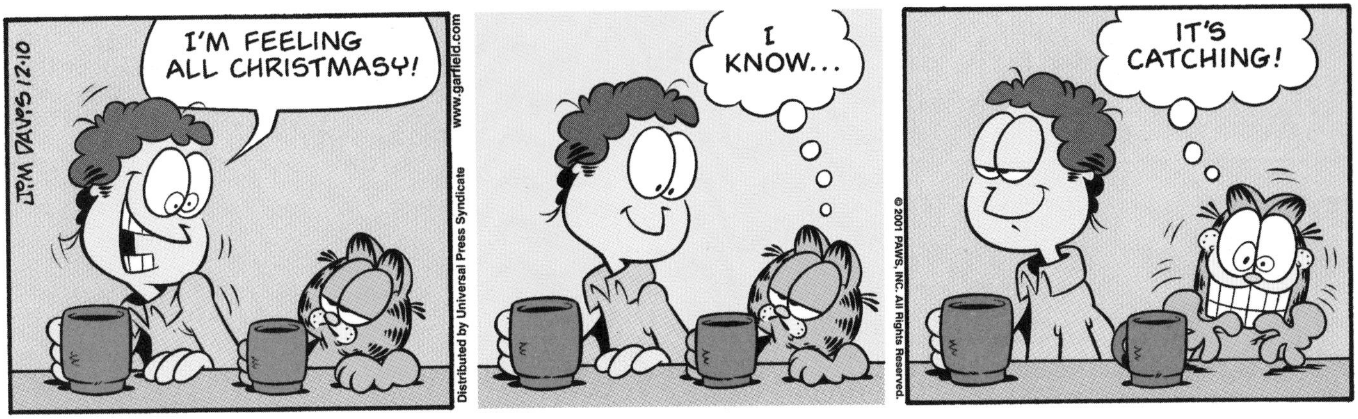
JIM DAVIS 12-10
I'M FEELING ALL CHRISTMASY!
www.garfield.com
Distributed by Universal Press Syndicate
I KNOW...
© 2001 PAWS, INC. All Rights Reserved.
IT'S CATCHING!

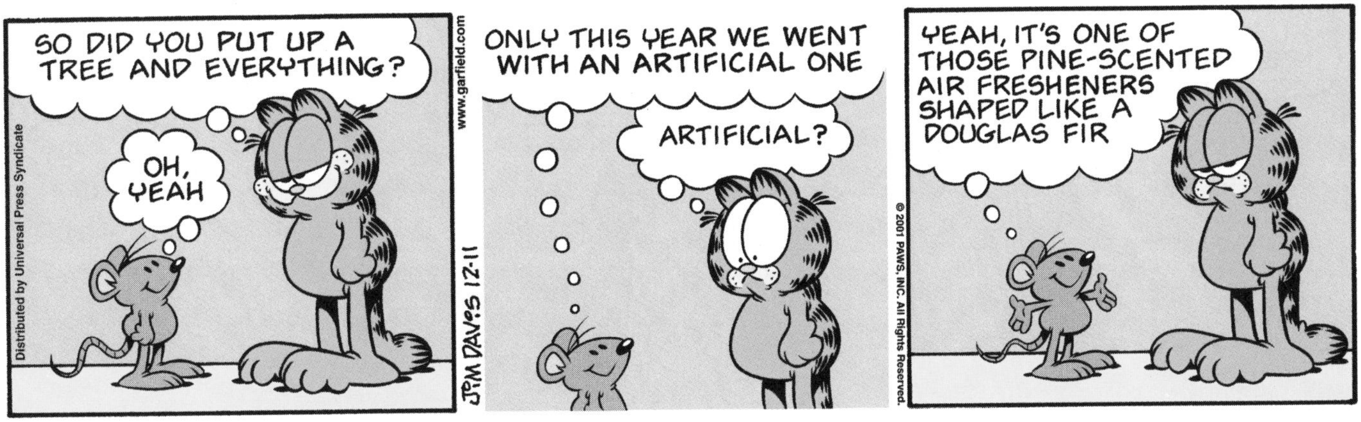
SO DID YOU PUT UP A TREE AND EVERYTHING?
OH, YEAH
Distributed by Universal Press Syndicate
www.garfield.com
JIM DAVIS 12-11
ONLY THIS YEAR WE WENT WITH AN ARTIFICIAL ONE
ARTIFICIAL?
© 2001 PAWS, INC. All Rights Reserved.
YEAH, IT'S ONE OF THOSE PINE-SCENTED AIR FRESHENERS SHAPED LIKE A DOUGLAS FIR

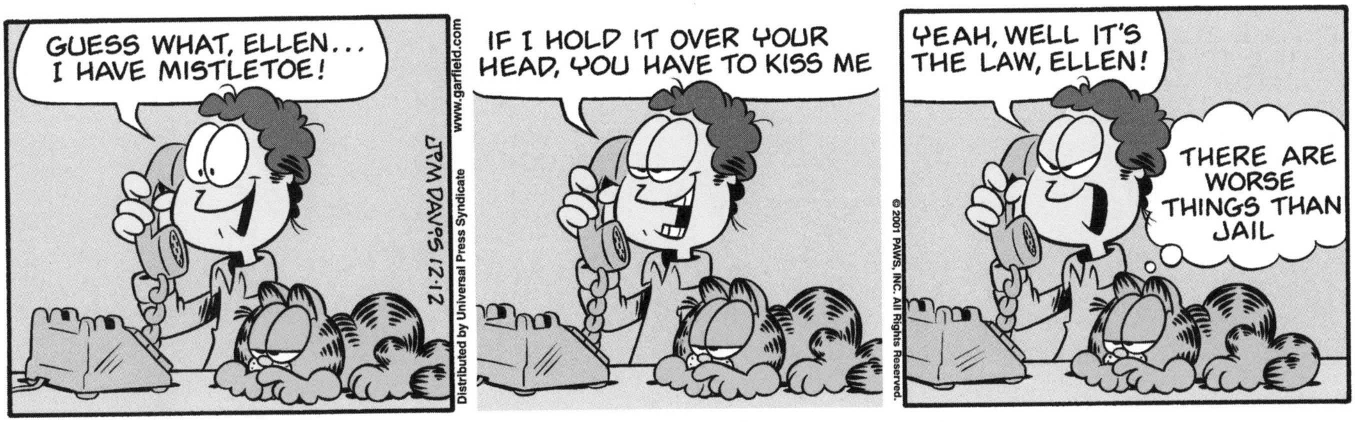
GUESS WHAT, ELLEN... I HAVE MISTLETOE!
JIM DAVIS 12-12
www.garfield.com
Distributed by Universal Press Syndicate
IF I HOLD IT OVER YOUR HEAD, YOU HAVE TO KISS ME
© 2001 PAWS, INC. All Rights Reserved.
YEAH, WELL IT'S THE LAW, ELLEN!
THERE ARE WORSE THINGS THAN JAIL

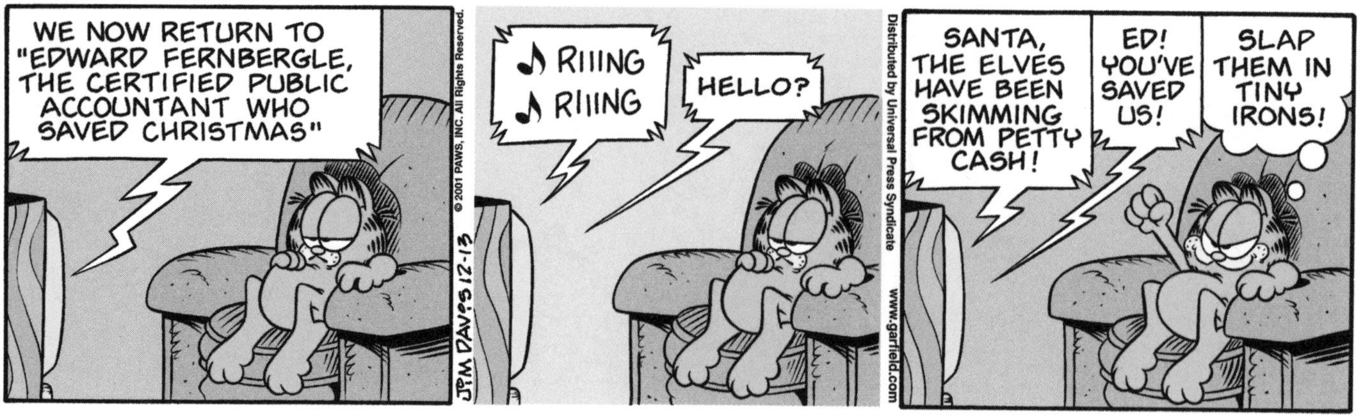
WE NOW RETURN TO "EDWARD FERNBERGLE, THE CERTIFIED PUBLIC ACCOUNTANT WHO SAVED CHRISTMAS"
♪ RIIING ♪ RIIING
HELLO?
SANTA, THE ELVES HAVE BEEN SKIMMING FROM PETTY CASH!
ED! YOU'VE SAVED US!
SLAP THEM IN TINY IRONS!
JIM DAVIS 12-13
© 2001 PAWS, INC. All Rights Reserved.
Distributed by Universal Press Syndicate
www.garfield.com

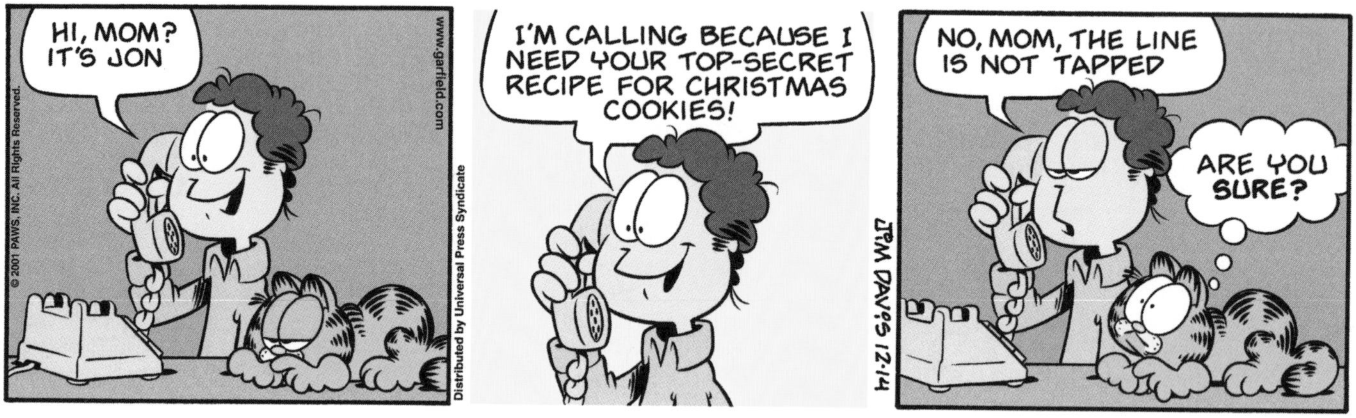
HI, MOM? IT'S JON
I'M CALLING BECAUSE I NEED YOUR TOP-SECRET RECIPE FOR CHRISTMAS COOKIES!
NO, MOM, THE LINE IS NOT TAPPED
ARE YOU SURE?
JIM DAVIS 12-14
© 2001 PAWS, INC. All Rights Reserved.
Distributed by Universal Press Syndicate
www.garfield.com

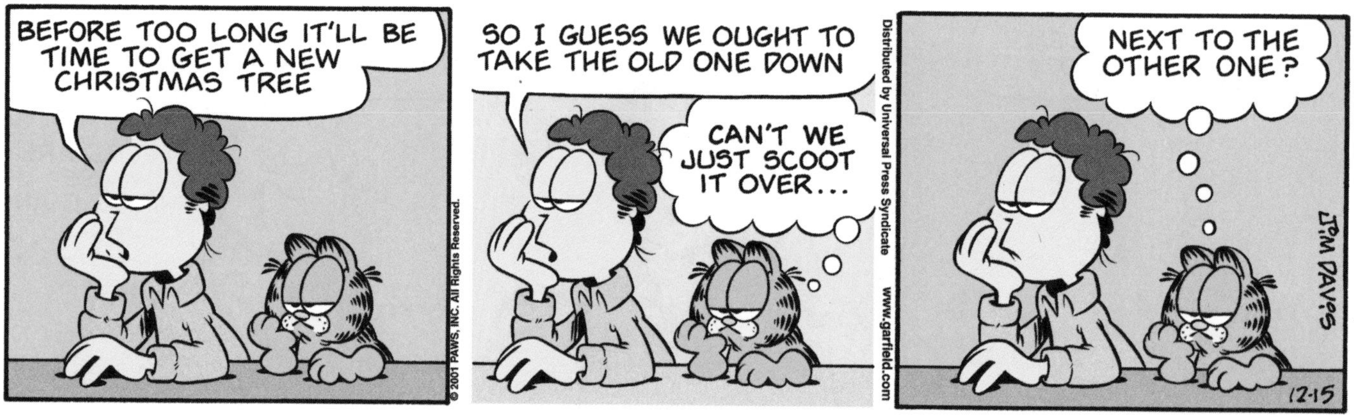
BEFORE TOO LONG IT'LL BE TIME TO GET A NEW CHRISTMAS TREE
SO I GUESS WE OUGHT TO TAKE THE OLD ONE DOWN
CAN'T WE JUST SCOOT IT OVER...
NEXT TO THE OTHER ONE?
JIM DAVIS
12-15
© 2001 PAWS, INC. All Rights Reserved.
Distributed by Universal Press Syndicate
www.garfield.com

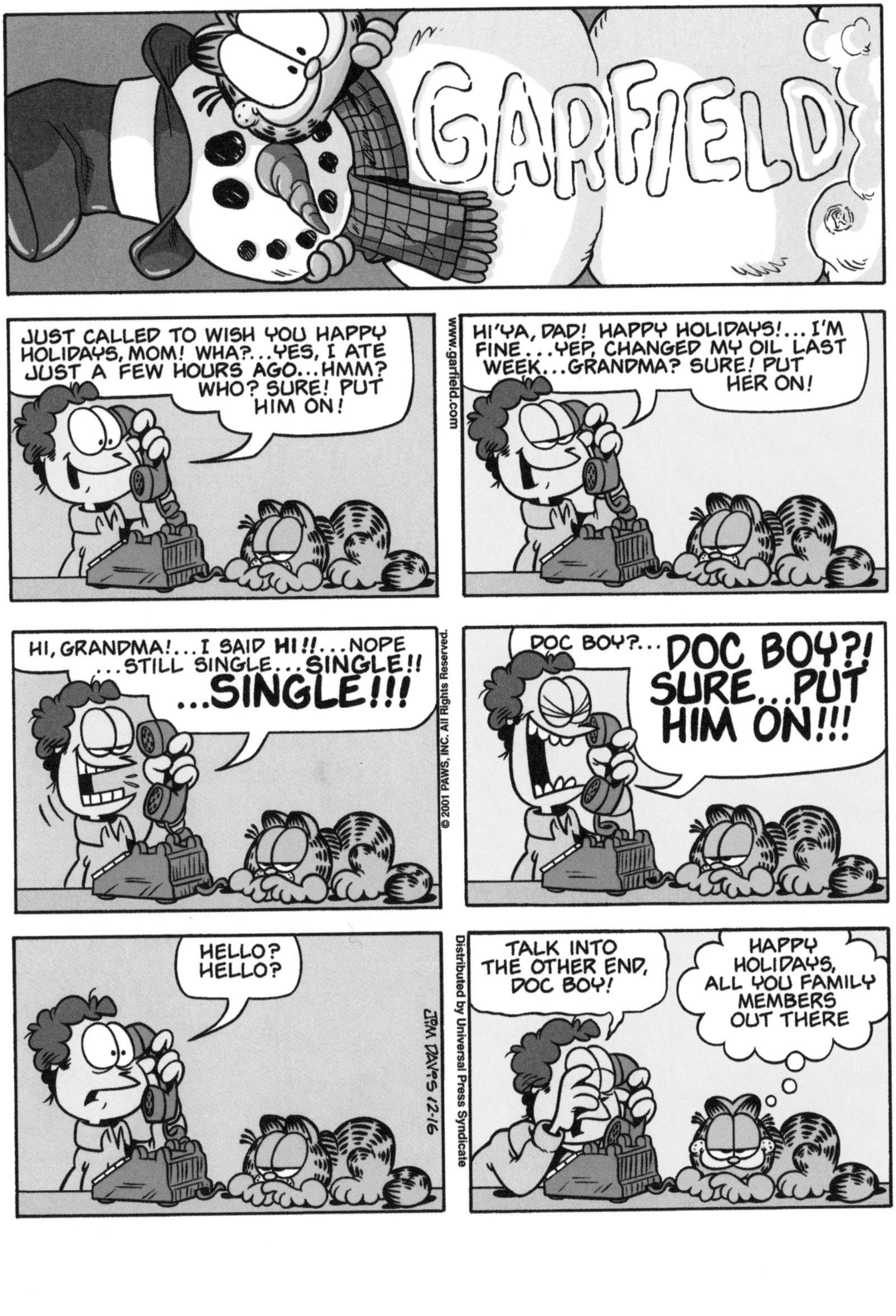
GARFIELD
JUST CALLED TO WISH YOU HAPPY HOLIDAYS, MOM! WHA?...YES, I ATE JUST A FEW HOURS AGO...HMM? WHO? SURE! PUT HIM ON!
www.garfield.com
HI'YA, DAD! HAPPY HOLIDAYS!... I'M FINE...YEP, CHANGED MY OIL LAST WEEK...GRANDMA? SURE! PUT HER ON!
HI, GRANDMA!...I SAID HI!!...NOPE ...STILL SINGLE...SINGLE!! ...SINGLE!!!
© 2001 PAWS, INC. All Rights Reserved.
DOC BOY?... DOC BOY?! SURE...PUT HIM ON!!!
HELLO? HELLO?
JIM DAVIS 12-16
Distributed by Universal Press Syndicate
TALK INTO THE OTHER END, DOC BOY!
HAPPY HOLIDAYS, ALL YOU FAMILY MEMBERS OUT THERE

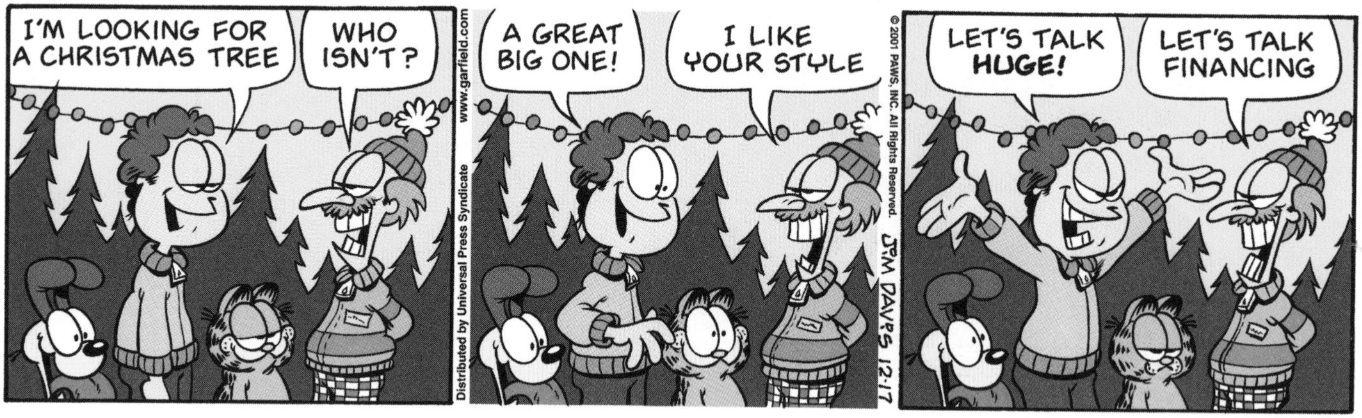
I'M LOOKING FOR A CHRISTMAS TREE
WHO ISN'T?
www.garfield.com
Distributed by Universal Press Syndicate
A GREAT BIG ONE!
I LIKE YOUR STYLE
© 2001 PAWS, INC. All Rights Reserved.
JIM DAVIS 12·17
LET'S TALK **HUGE!**
LET'S TALK FINANCING

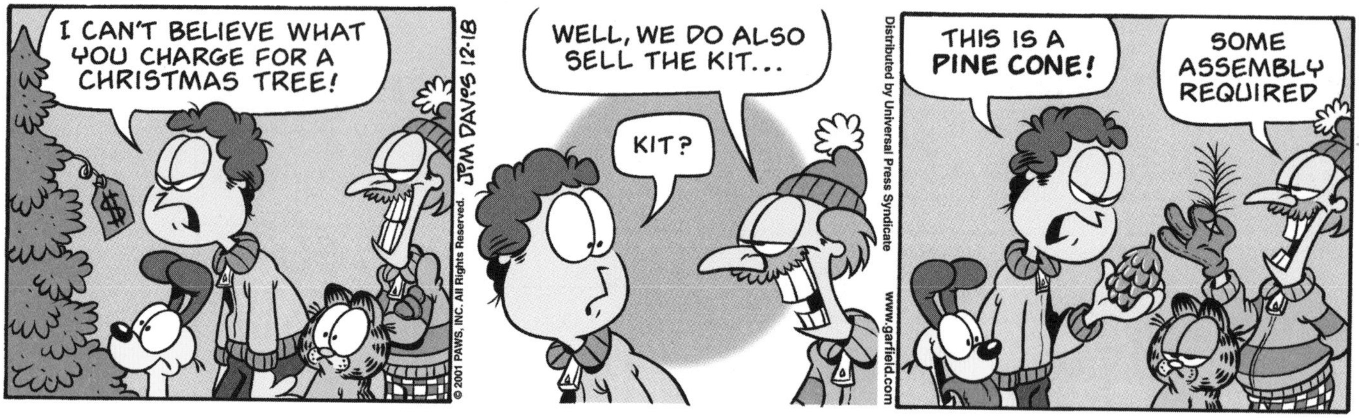
I CAN'T BELIEVE WHAT YOU CHARGE FOR A CHRISTMAS TREE!
$
JIM DAVIS 12·18
© 2001 PAWS, INC. All Rights Reserved.
WELL, WE DO ALSO SELL THE KIT...
KIT?
Distributed by Universal Press Syndicate
www.garfield.com
THIS IS A **PINE CONE!**
SOME ASSEMBLY REQUIRED

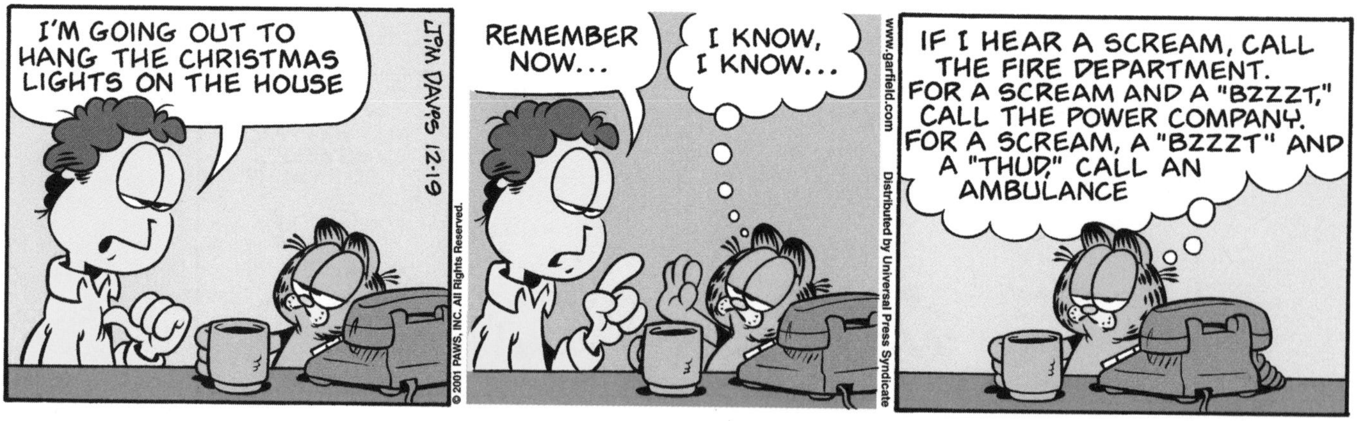
I'M GOING OUT TO HANG THE CHRISTMAS LIGHTS ON THE HOUSE
JIM DAVIS 12·19
© 2001 PAWS, INC. All Rights Reserved.
REMEMBER NOW...
I KNOW, I KNOW...
www.garfield.com
Distributed by Universal Press Syndicate
IF I HEAR A SCREAM, CALL THE FIRE DEPARTMENT. FOR A SCREAM AND A "BZZZT," CALL THE POWER COMPANY. FOR A SCREAM, A "BZZZT" AND A "THUD," CALL AN AMBULANCE

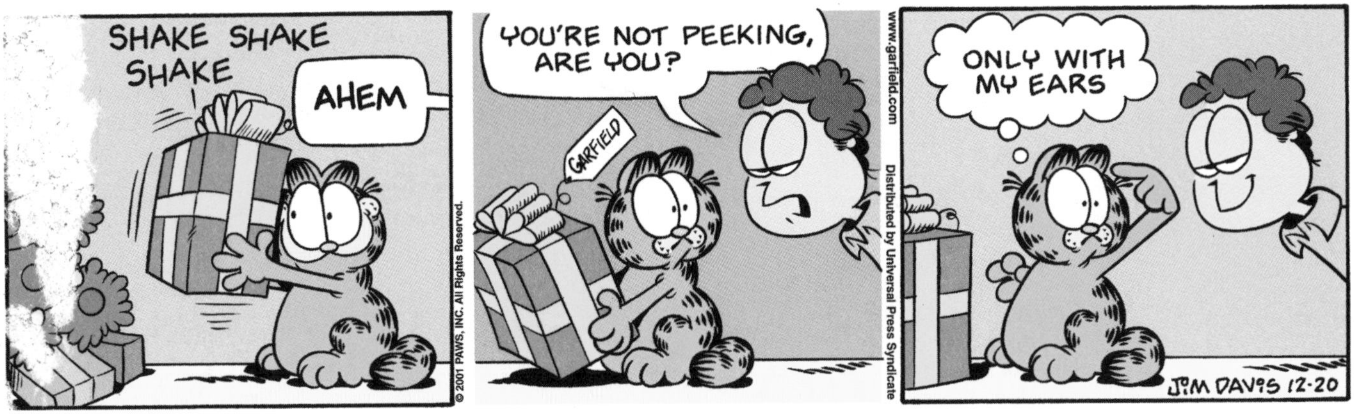
SHAKE SHAKE SHAKE
AHEM
© 2001 PAWS, INC. All Rights Reserved.
YOU'RE NOT PEEKING, ARE YOU?
GARFIELD
www.garfield.com
Distributed by Universal Press Syndicate
ONLY WITH MY EARS
JIM DAVIS 12-20

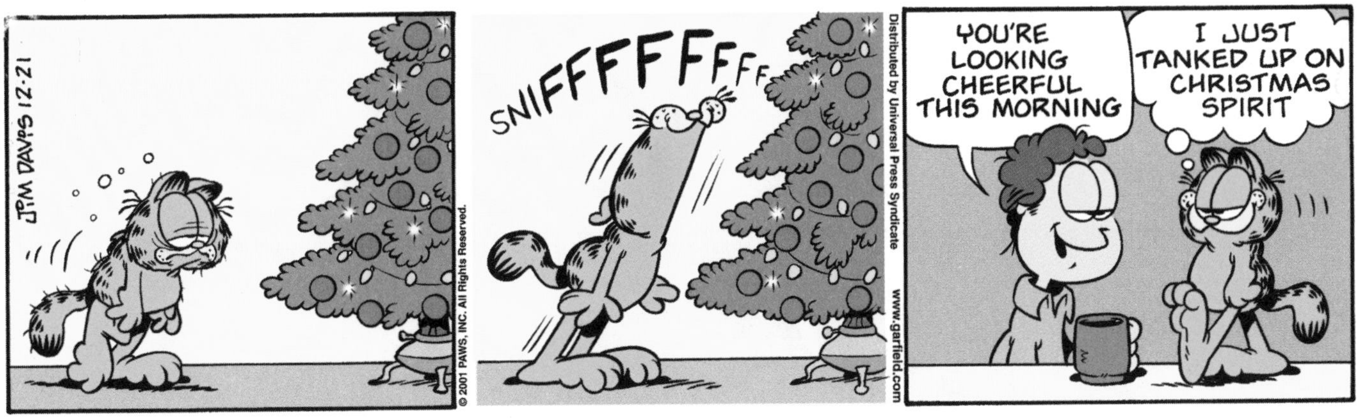
JIM DAVIS 12-21
© 2001 PAWS, INC. All Rights Reserved.
SNIFFFFFFFFF
Distributed by Universal Press Syndicate
www.garfield.com
YOU'RE LOOKING CHEERFUL THIS MORNING
I JUST TANKED UP ON CHRISTMAS SPIRIT

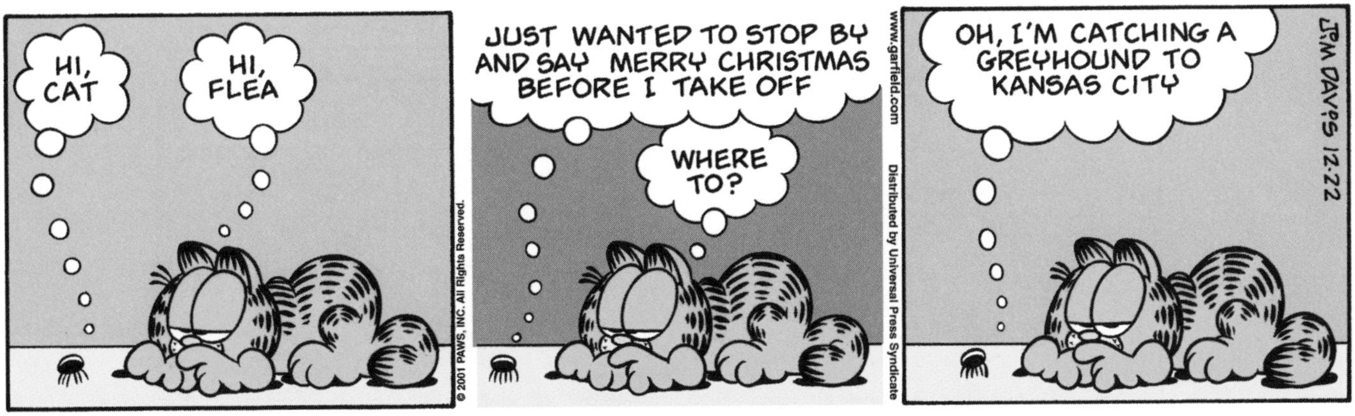
HI, CAT
HI, FLEA
© 2001 PAWS, INC. All Rights Reserved.
JUST WANTED TO STOP BY AND SAY MERRY CHRISTMAS BEFORE I TAKE OFF
WHERE TO?
www.garfield.com
Distributed by Universal Press Syndicate
OH, I'M CATCHING A GREYHOUND TO KANSAS CITY
JIM DAVIS 12-22

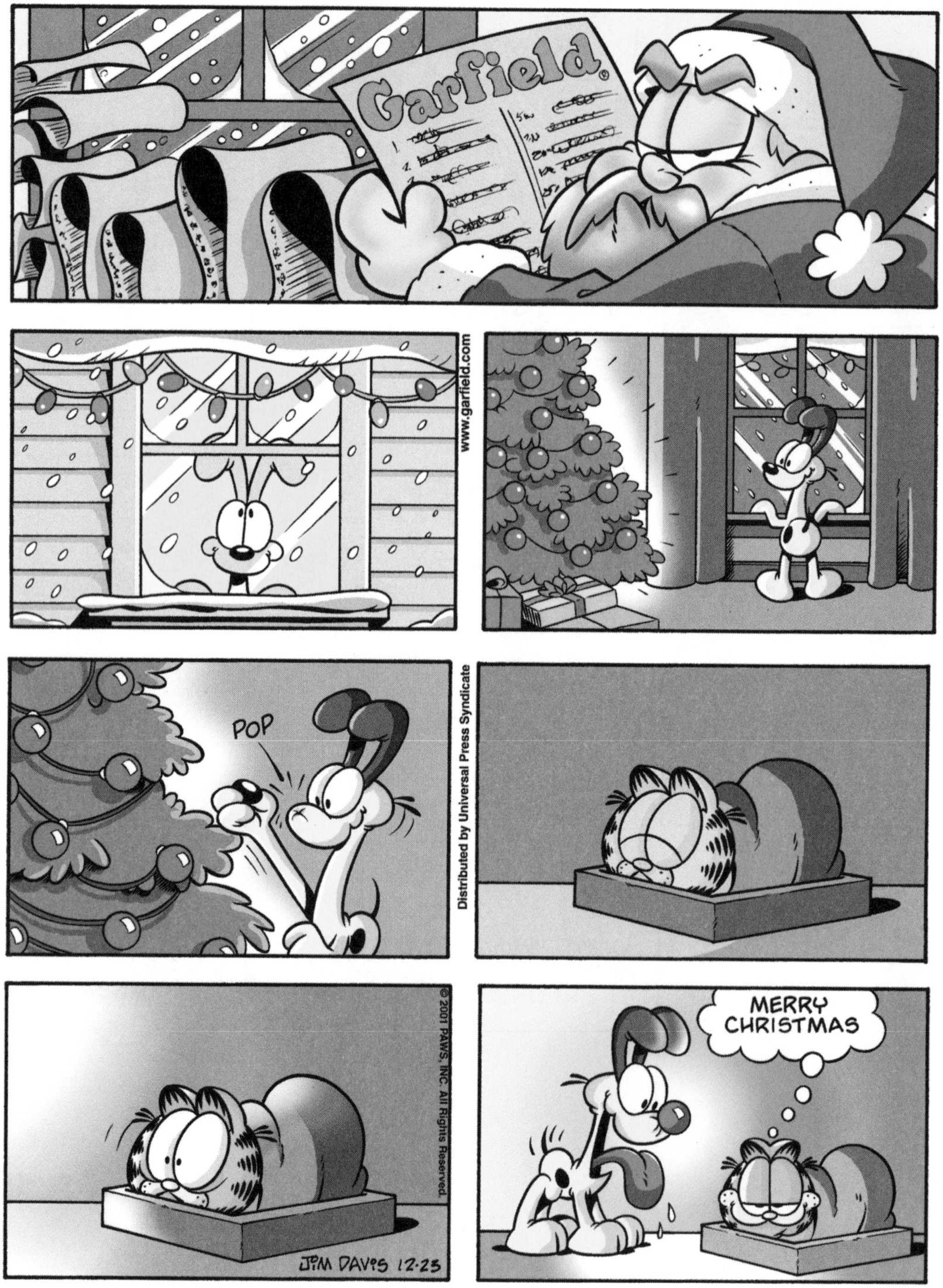
Garfield
POP
MERRY CHRISTMAS
www.garfield.com
Distributed by Universal Press Syndicate
© 2001 PAWS, INC. All Rights Reserved.
JIM DAVIS 12-23

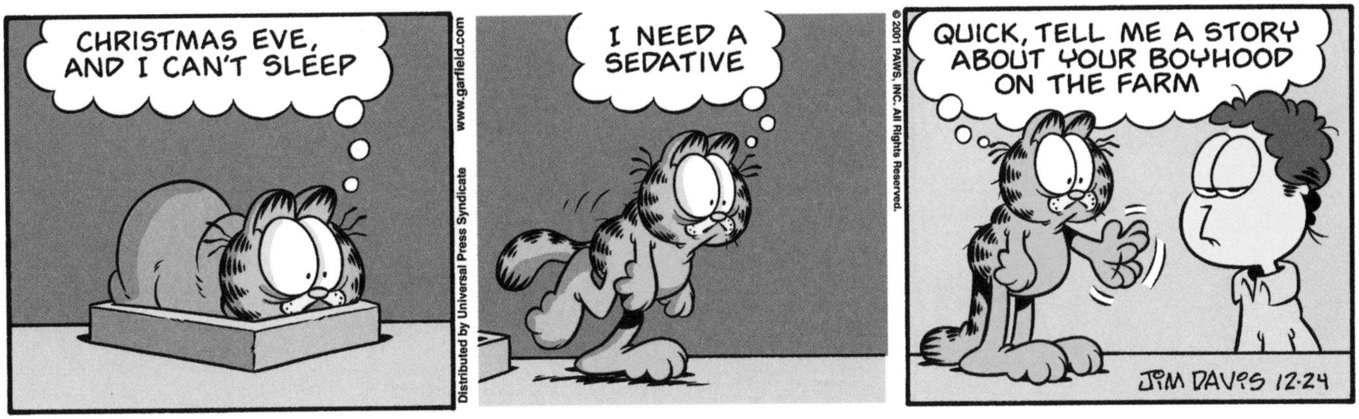
CHRISTMAS EVE, AND I CAN'T SLEEP
I NEED A SEDATIVE
QUICK, TELL ME A STORY ABOUT YOUR BOYHOOD ON THE FARM
JIM DAVIS 12-24
Distributed by Universal Press Syndicate www.garfield.com
© 2001 PAWS, INC. All Rights Reserved.

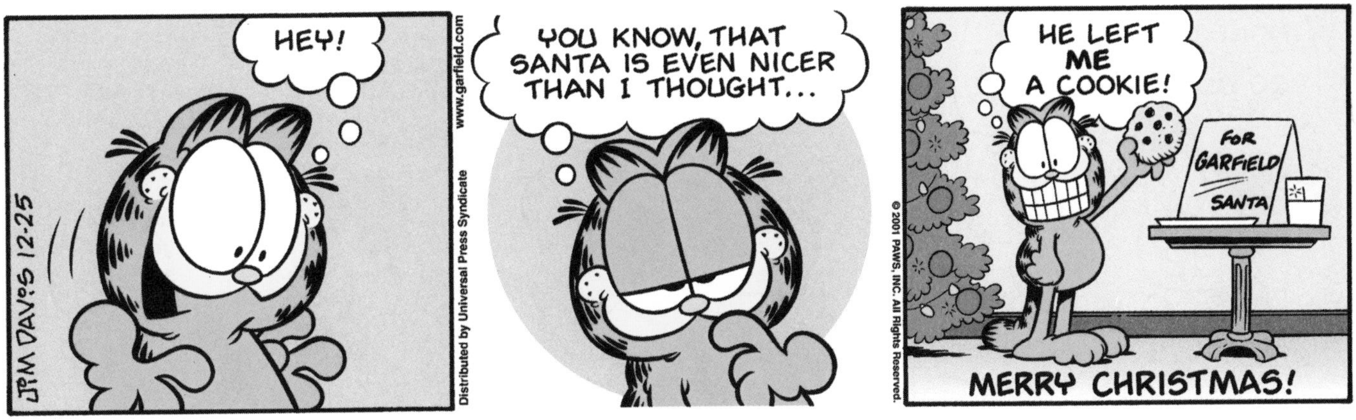
HEY!
JIM DAVIS 12-25
YOU KNOW, THAT SANTA IS EVEN NICER THAN I THOUGHT...
HE LEFT **ME** A COOKIE!
FOR GARFIELD
SANTA
MERRY CHRISTMAS!
Distributed by Universal Press Syndicate www.garfield.com
© 2001 PAWS, INC. All Rights Reserved.

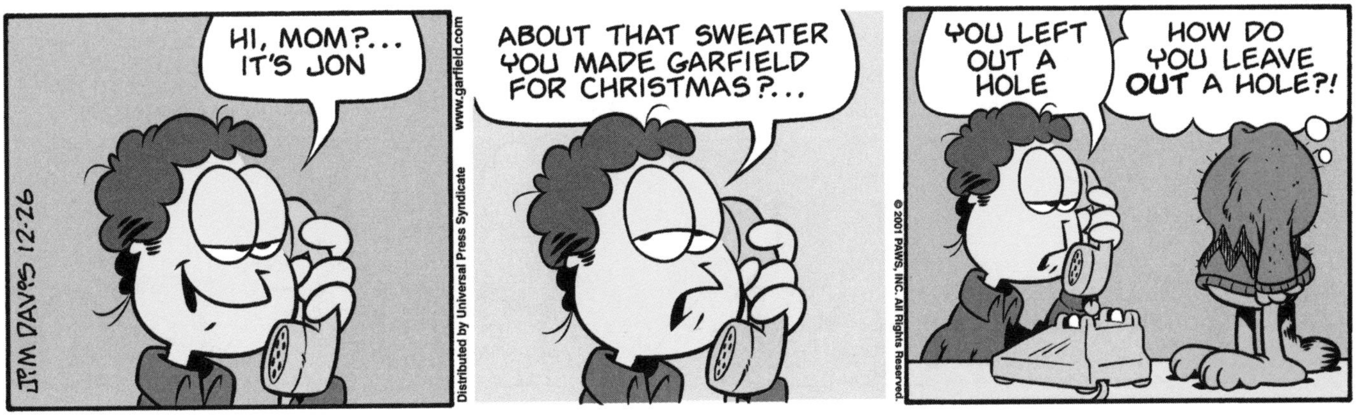
HI, MOM?... IT'S JON
JIM DAVIS 12-26
ABOUT THAT SWEATER YOU MADE GARFIELD FOR CHRISTMAS?...
YOU LEFT OUT A HOLE
HOW DO YOU LEAVE **OUT** A HOLE?!
Distributed by Universal Press Syndicate www.garfield.com
© 2001 PAWS, INC. All Rights Reserved.

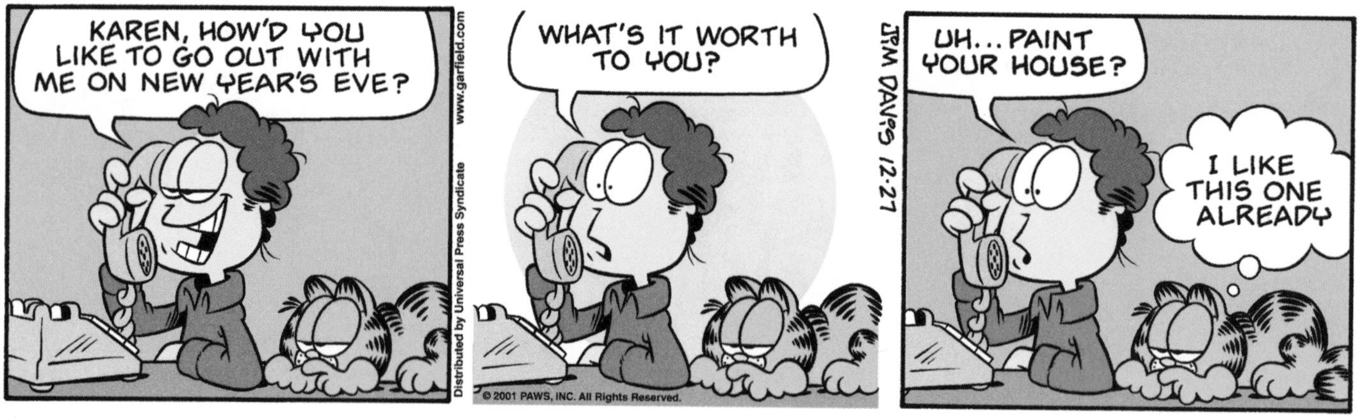
KAREN, HOW'D YOU LIKE TO GO OUT WITH ME ON NEW YEAR'S EVE?
WHAT'S IT WORTH TO YOU?
UH... PAINT YOUR HOUSE?
I LIKE THIS ONE ALREADY

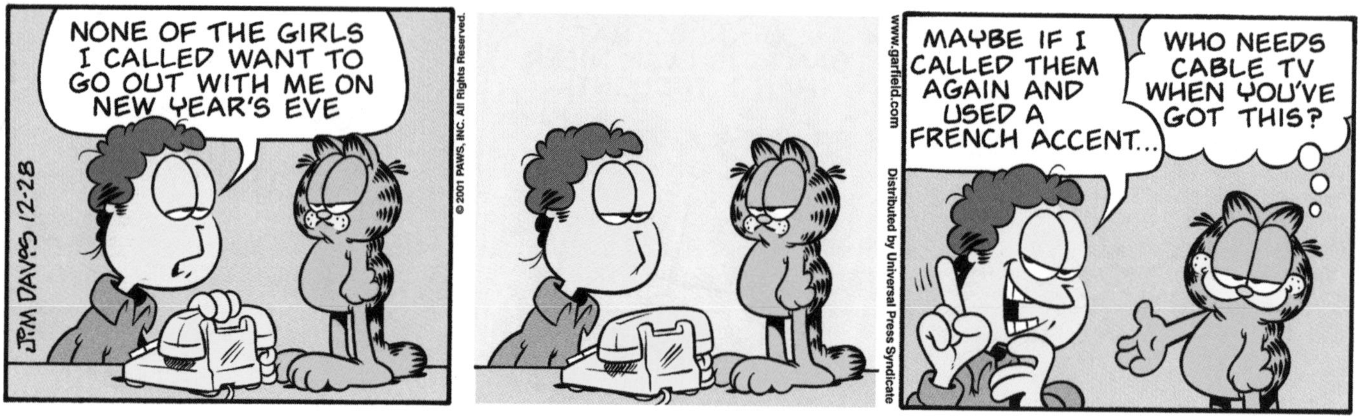
NONE OF THE GIRLS I CALLED WANT TO GO OUT WITH ME ON NEW YEAR'S EVE
MAYBE IF I CALLED THEM AGAIN AND USED A FRENCH ACCENT...
WHO NEEDS CABLE TV WHEN YOU'VE GOT THIS?

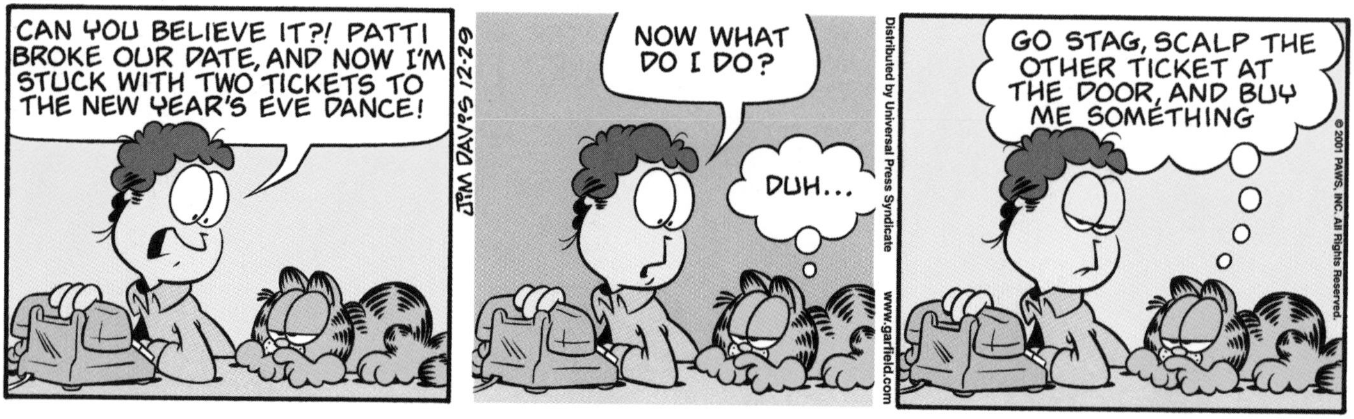
CAN YOU BELIEVE IT?! PATTI BROKE OUR DATE, AND NOW I'M STUCK WITH TWO TICKETS TO THE NEW YEAR'S EVE DANCE!
NOW WHAT DO I DO?
DUH...
GO STAG, SCALP THE OTHER TICKET AT THE DOOR, AND BUY ME SOMETHING

Outrageous Outtakes Part Deux

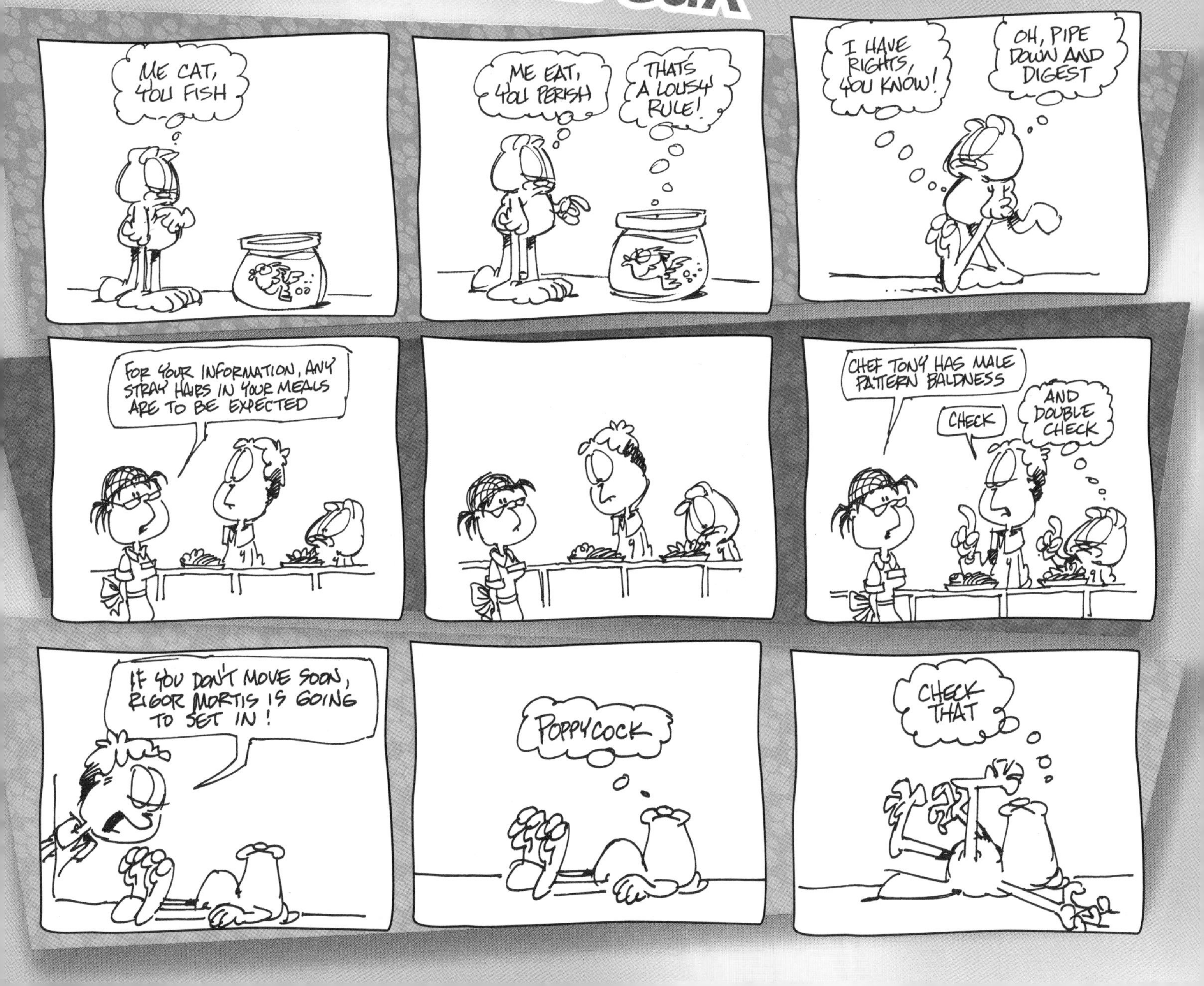

ME CAT, YOU FISH
ME EAT, YOU PERISH
THATS A LOUSY RULE!
I HAVE RIGHTS, YOU KNOW!
OH, PIPE DOWN AND DIGEST
FOR YOUR INFORMATION, ANY STRAY HAIRS IN YOUR MEALS ARE TO BE EXPECTED
CHEF TONY HAS MALE PATTERN BALDNESS
CHECK
AND DOUBLE CHECK
IF YOU DON'T MOVE SOON, RIGOR MORTIS IS GOING TO SET IN!
POPPYCOCK
CHECK THAT

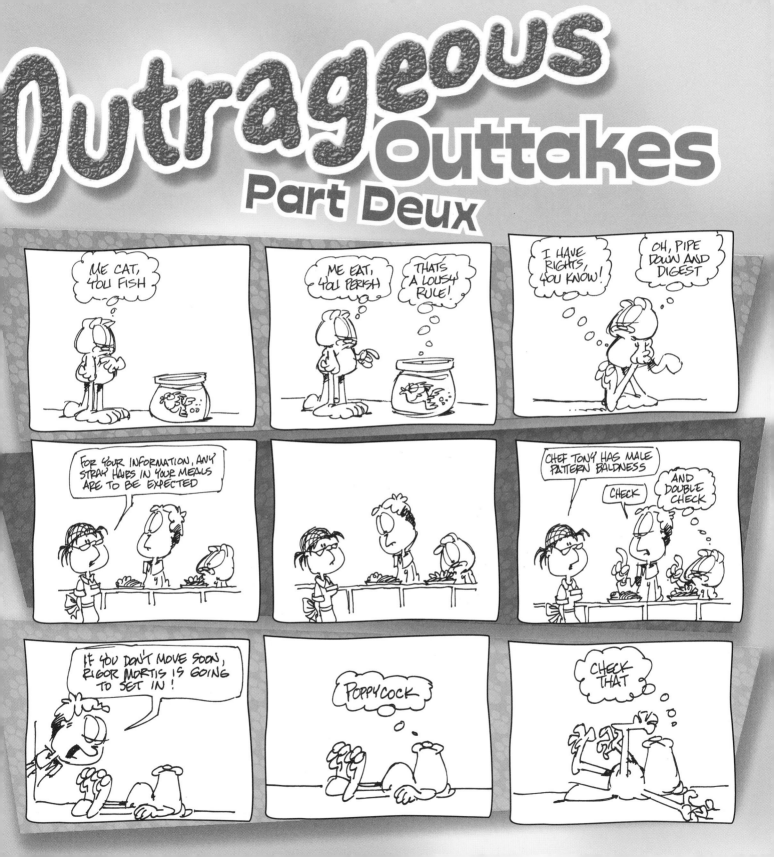

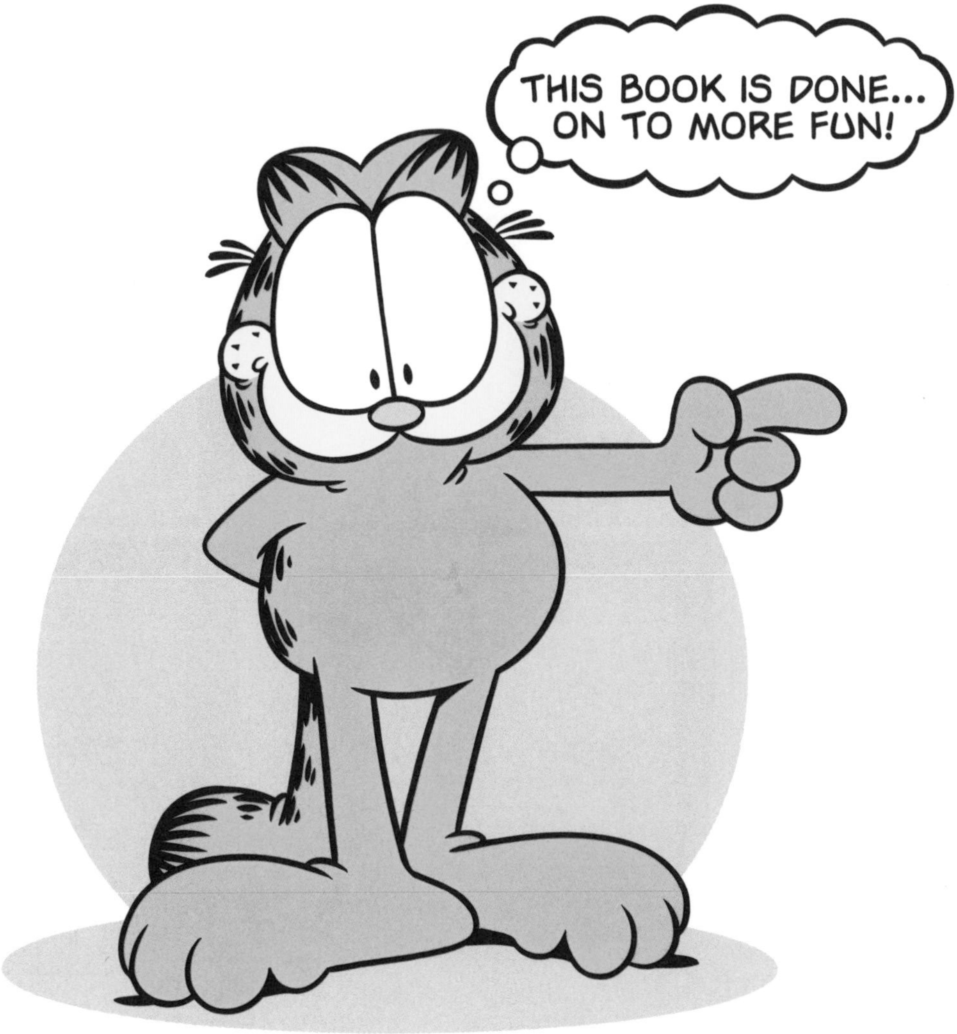
THIS BOOK IS DONE...
ON TO MORE FUN!

Garfield
OLDER & WIDER

BY JIM DAVIS

Ballantine Books • New York

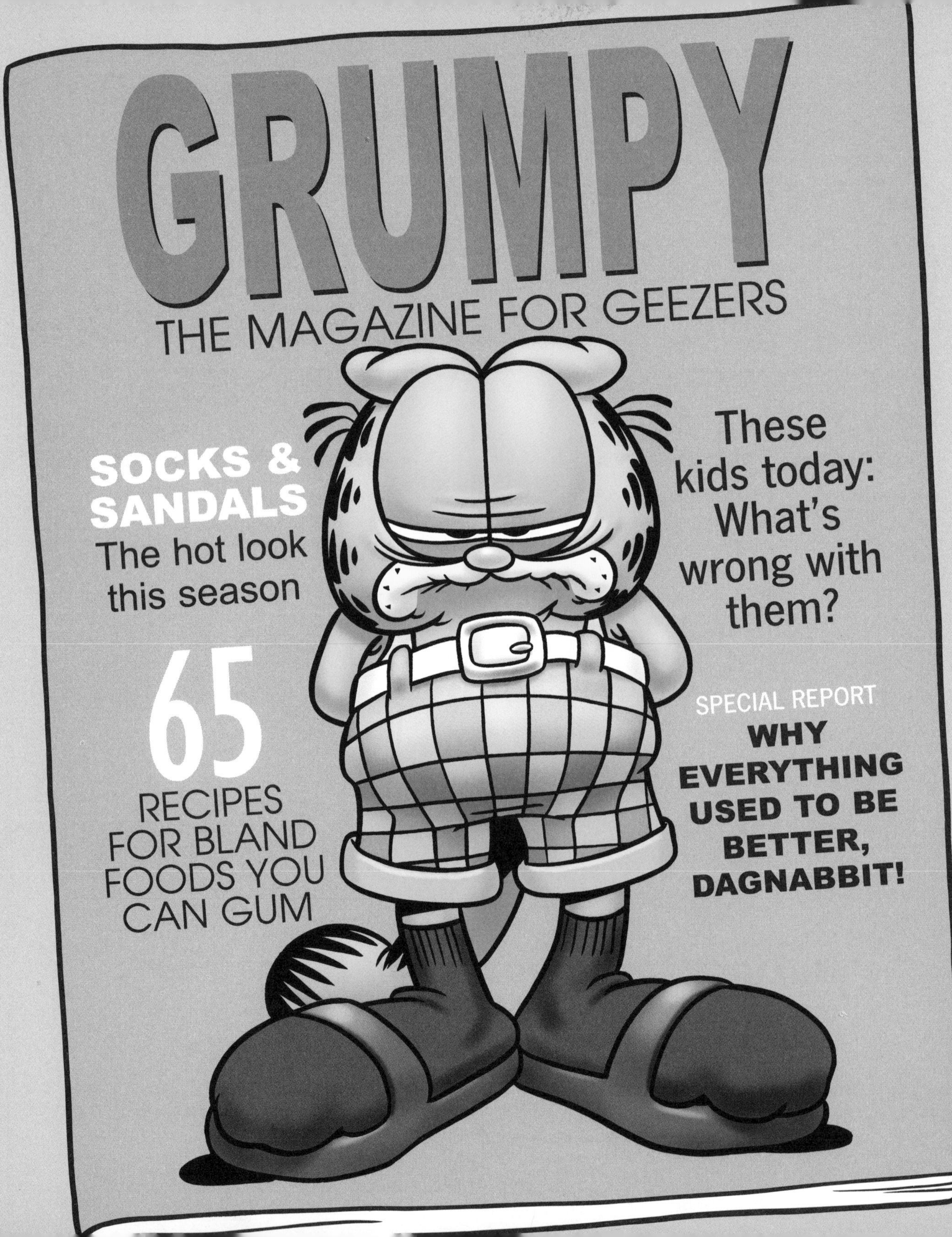
GRUMPY
THE MAGAZINE FOR GEEZERS
SOCKS & SANDALS
The hot look this season
65
RECIPES FOR BLAND FOODS YOU CAN GUM
These kids today: What's wrong with them?
SPECIAL REPORT
WHY EVERYTHING USED TO BE BETTER, DAGNABBIT!

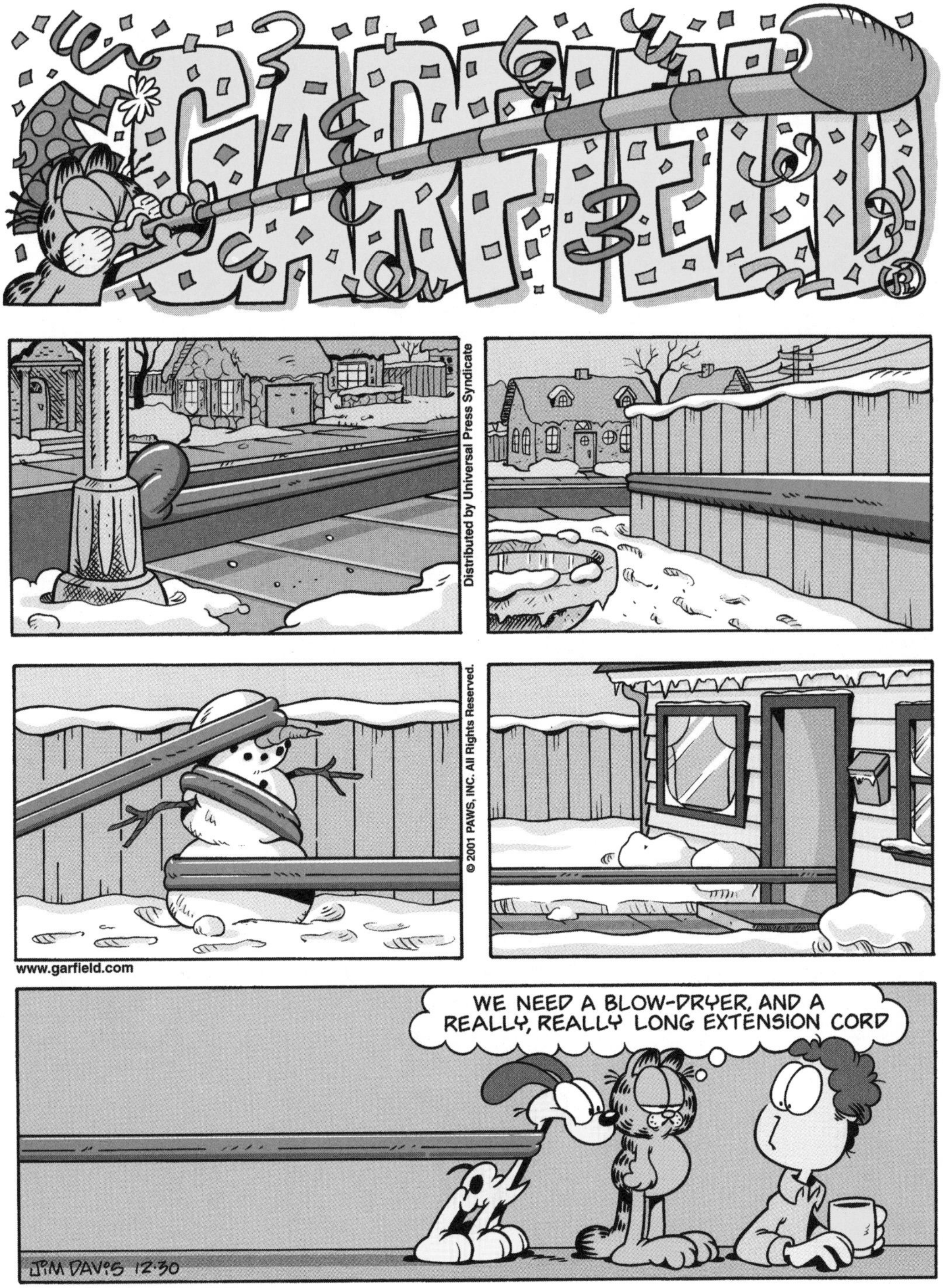
GARFIELD
Distributed by Universal Press Syndicate
© 2001 PAWS, INC. All Rights Reserved.
www.garfield.com
WE NEED A BLOW-DRYER, AND A REALLY, REALLY LONG EXTENSION CORD
JIM DAVIS 12·30

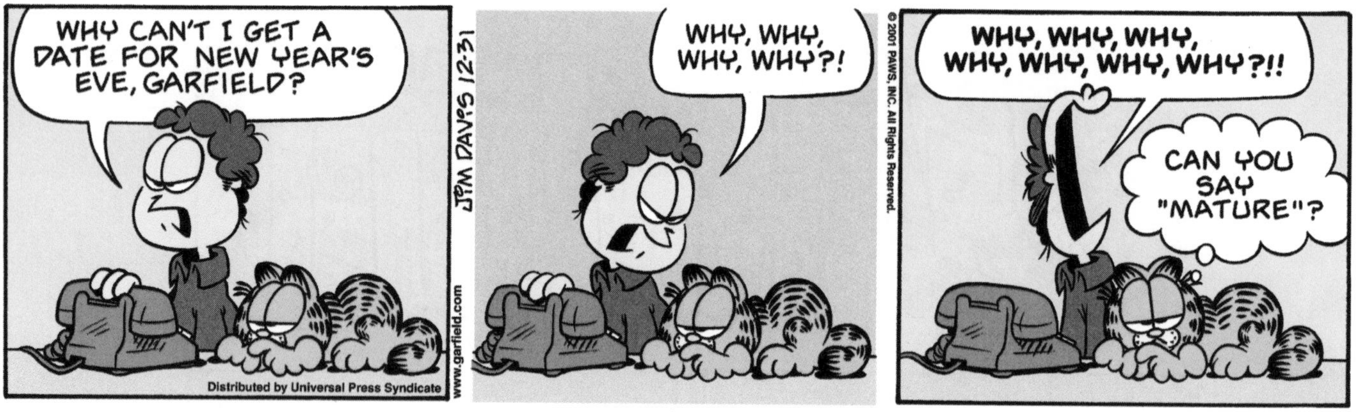
WHY CAN'T I GET A DATE FOR NEW YEAR'S EVE, GARFIELD?
WHY, WHY, WHY, WHY?!
WHY, WHY, WHY, WHY, WHY, WHY, WHY?!!
CAN YOU SAY "MATURE"?
JPM DAVPS 12-31
Distributed by Universal Press Syndicate
www.garfield.com
© 2001 PAWS, INC. All Rights Reserved.

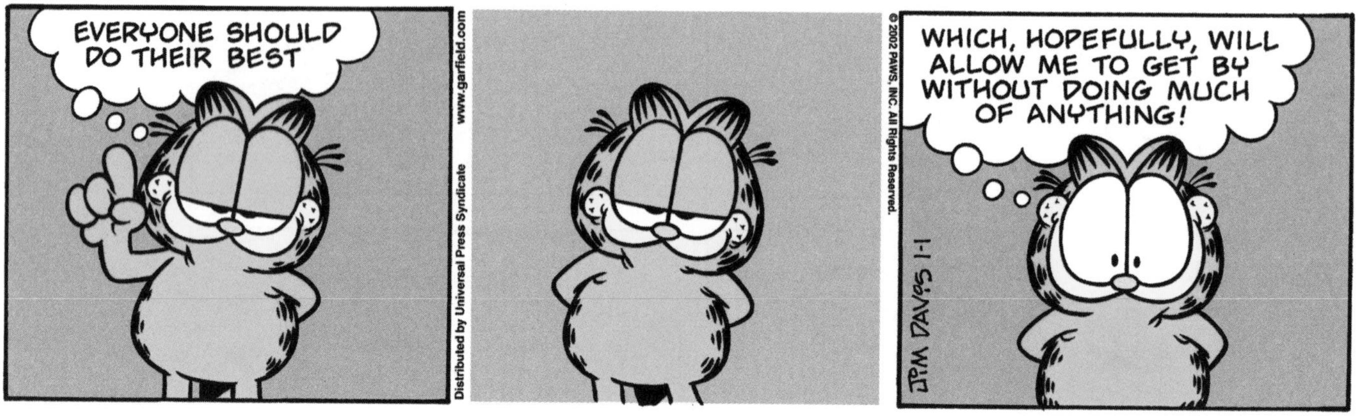
EVERYONE SHOULD DO THEIR BEST
WHICH, HOPEFULLY, WILL ALLOW ME TO GET BY WITHOUT DOING MUCH OF ANYTHING!
JPM DAVPS 1-1
www.garfield.com
Distributed by Universal Press Syndicate
© 2002 PAWS, INC. All Rights Reserved.

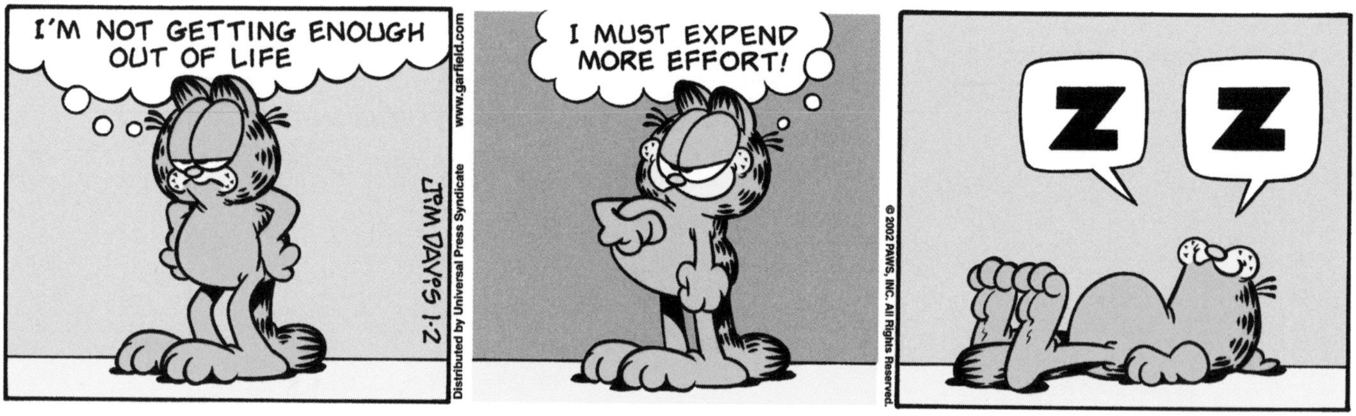
I'M NOT GETTING ENOUGH OUT OF LIFE
I MUST EXPEND MORE EFFORT!
Z
Z
JPM DAVPS 1-2
www.garfield.com
Distributed by Universal Press Syndicate
© 2002 PAWS, INC. All Rights Reserved.

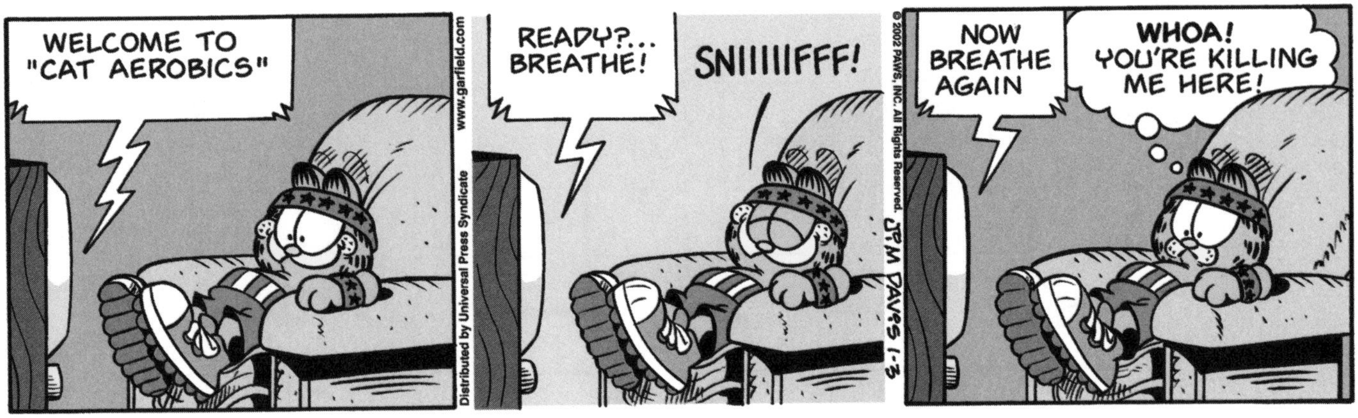
WELCOME TO "CAT AEROBICS"
READY?... BREATHE!
SNIIIIIFFF!
NOW BREATHE AGAIN
WHOA! YOU'RE KILLING ME HERE!
www.garfield.com
Distributed by Universal Press Syndicate
© 2002 PAWS, INC. All Rights Reserved.
JIM DAVIS 1-3

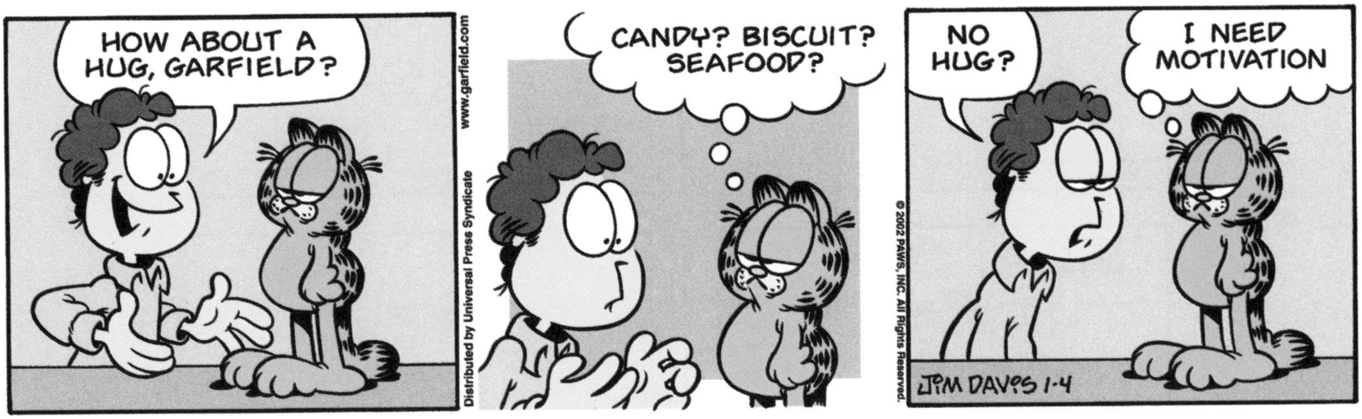
HOW ABOUT A HUG, GARFIELD?
CANDY? BISCUIT? SEAFOOD?
NO HUG?
I NEED MOTIVATION
www.garfield.com
Distributed by Universal Press Syndicate
© 2002 PAWS, INC. All Rights Reserved.
JIM DAVIS 1-4

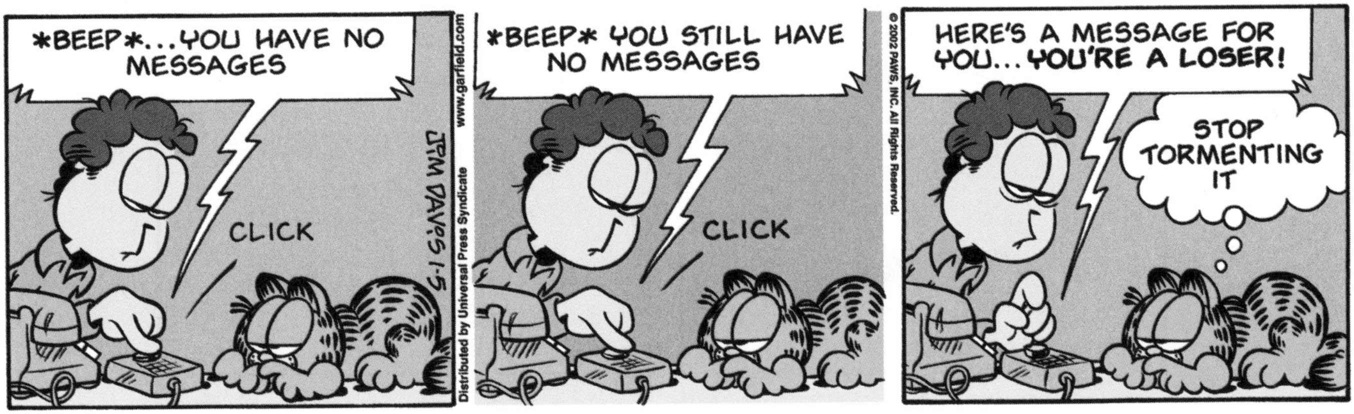
BEEP...YOU HAVE NO MESSAGES
CLICK
BEEP YOU STILL HAVE NO MESSAGES
CLICK
HERE'S A MESSAGE FOR YOU... YOU'RE A LOSER!
STOP TORMENTING IT
JIM DAVIS 1-5
www.garfield.com
Distributed by Universal Press Syndicate
© 2002 PAWS, INC. All Rights Reserved.

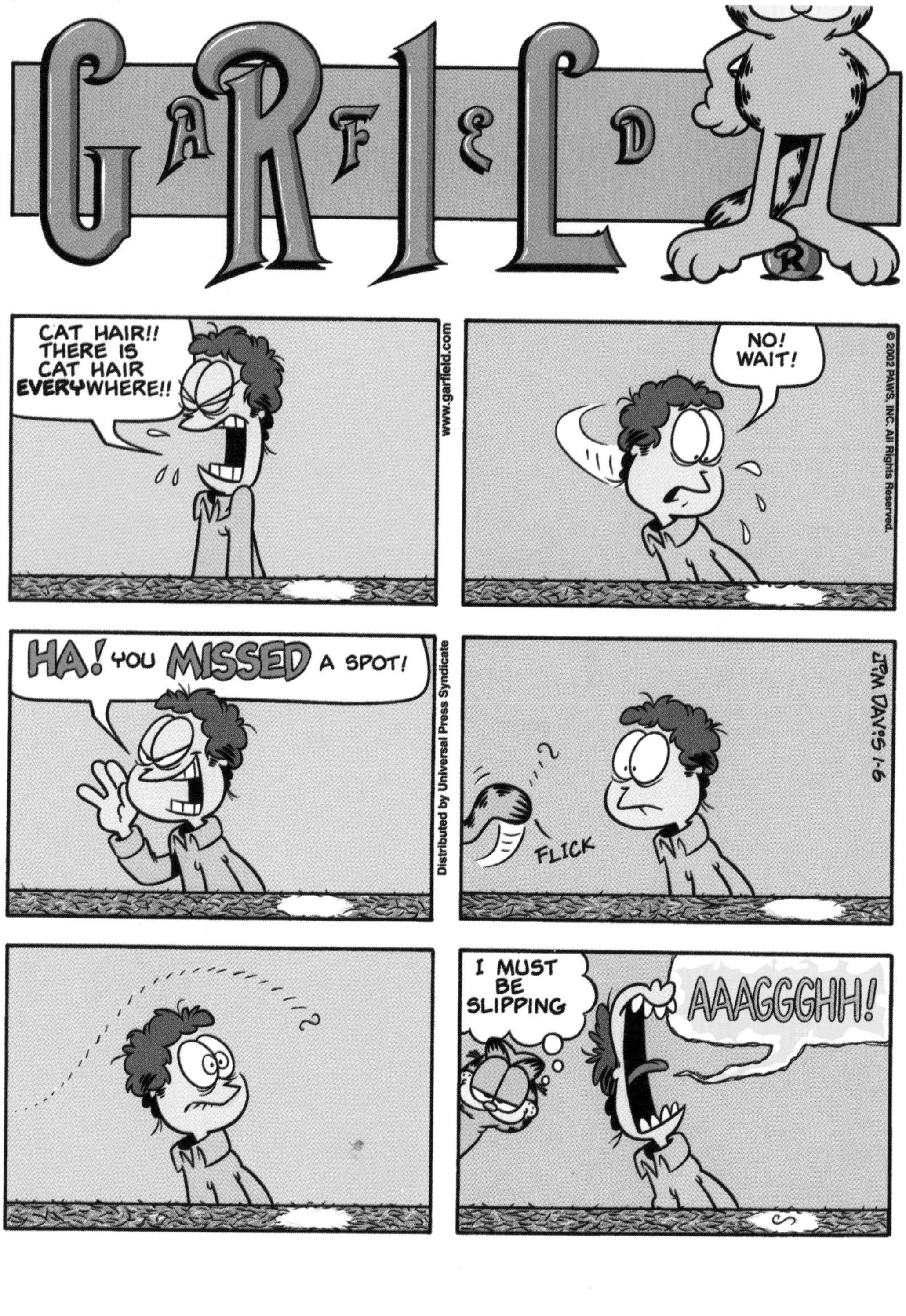
GARFIELD
CAT HAIR!! THERE IS CAT HAIR EVERYWHERE!!
www.garfield.com
NO! WAIT!
© 2002 PAWS, INC. All Rights Reserved.
HA! YOU MISSED A SPOT!
Distributed by Universal Press Syndicate
FLICK
JIM DAVIS 1-6
I MUST BE SLIPPING
AAAGGGHH!

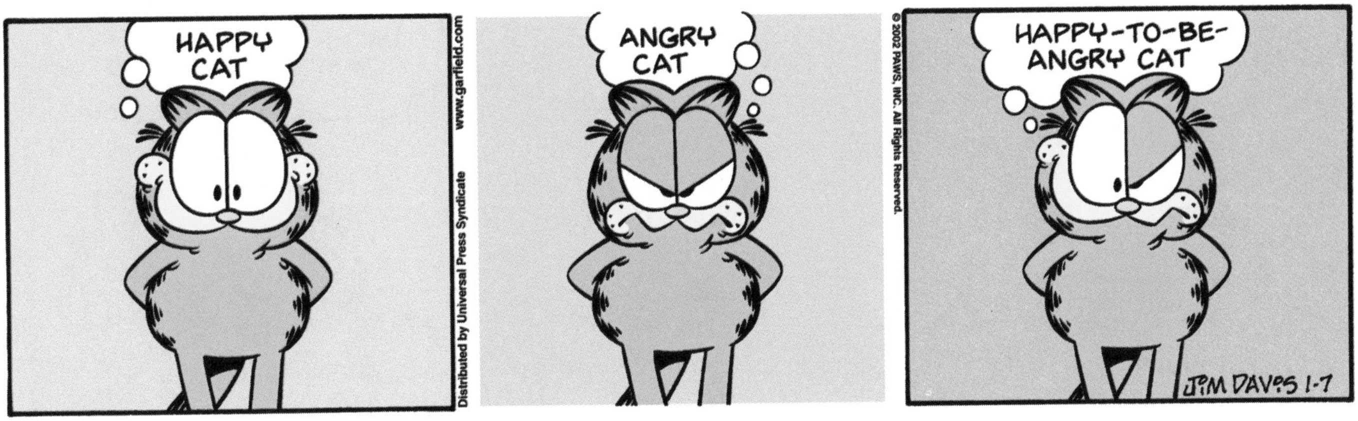
HAPPY CAT
ANGRY CAT
HAPPY-TO-BE-ANGRY CAT
JIM DAVIS 1-7
Distributed by Universal Press Syndicate www.garfield.com
© 2002 PAWS, INC. All Rights Reserved.

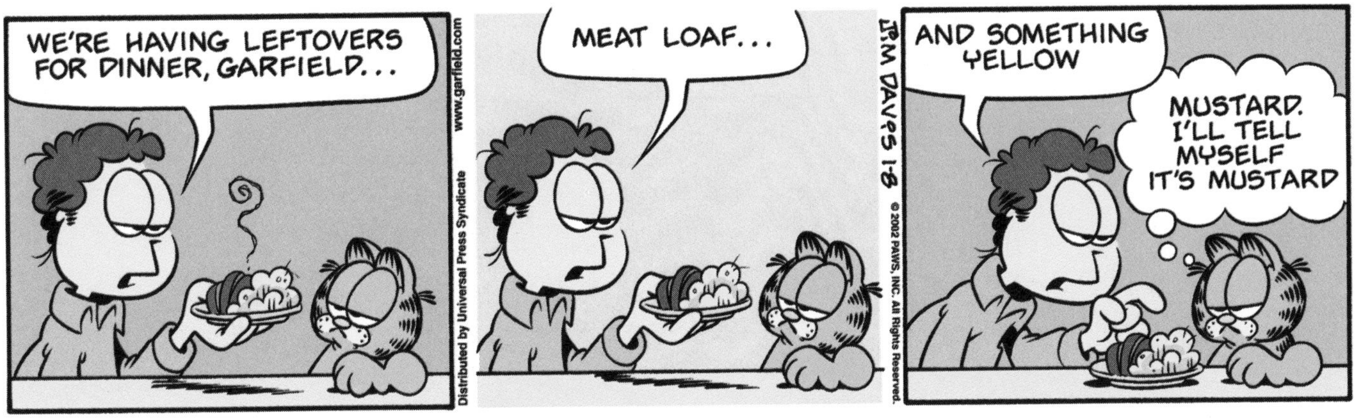
WE'RE HAVING LEFTOVERS FOR DINNER, GARFIELD...
MEAT LOAF...
AND SOMETHING YELLOW
MUSTARD. I'LL TELL MYSELF IT'S MUSTARD
JIM DAVIS 1-8
Distributed by Universal Press Syndicate www.garfield.com
© 2002 PAWS, INC. All Rights Reserved.

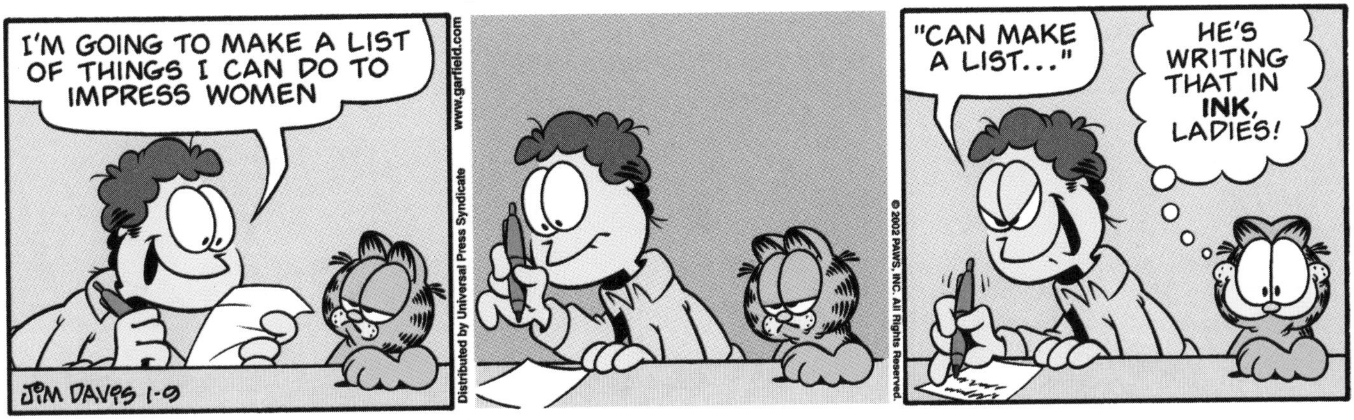
I'M GOING TO MAKE A LIST OF THINGS I CAN DO TO IMPRESS WOMEN
"CAN MAKE A LIST..."
HE'S WRITING THAT IN **INK**, LADIES!
JIM DAVIS 1-9
Distributed by Universal Press Syndicate www.garfield.com
© 2002 PAWS, INC. All Rights Reserved.

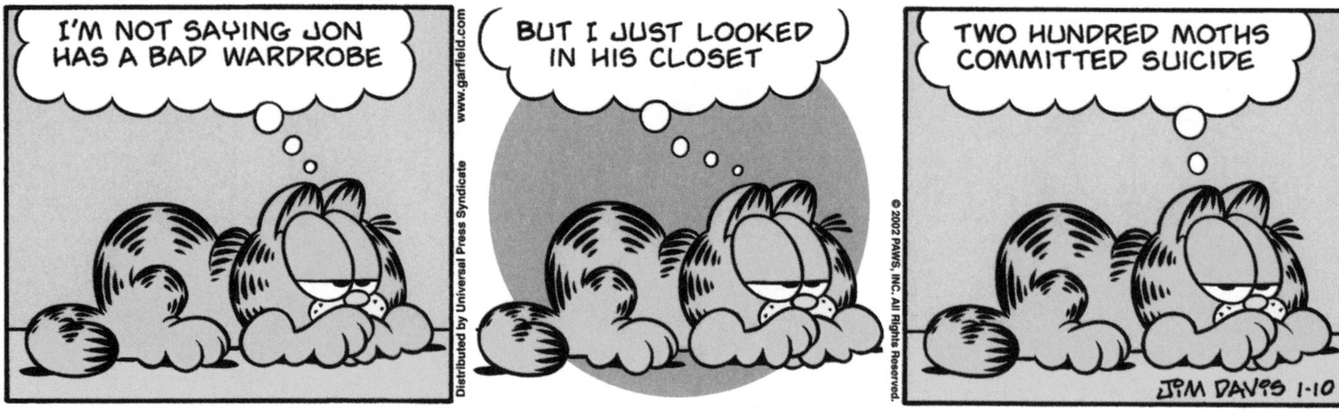
I'M NOT SAYING JON HAS A BAD WARDROBE
BUT I JUST LOOKED IN HIS CLOSET
TWO HUNDRED MOTHS COMMITTED SUICIDE
JIM DAVIS 1-10
Distributed by Universal Press Syndicate www.garfield.com
© 2002 PAWS, INC. All Rights Reserved.

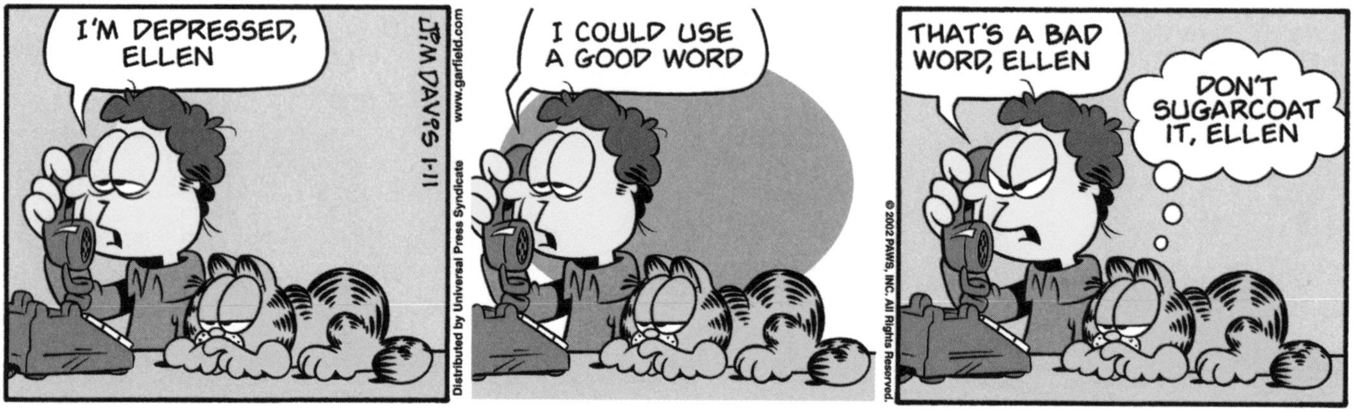
I'M DEPRESSED, ELLEN
JIM DAVIS 1-11
I COULD USE A GOOD WORD
THAT'S A BAD WORD, ELLEN
DON'T SUGARCOAT IT, ELLEN
Distributed by Universal Press Syndicate www.garfield.com
© 2002 PAWS, INC. All Rights Reserved.

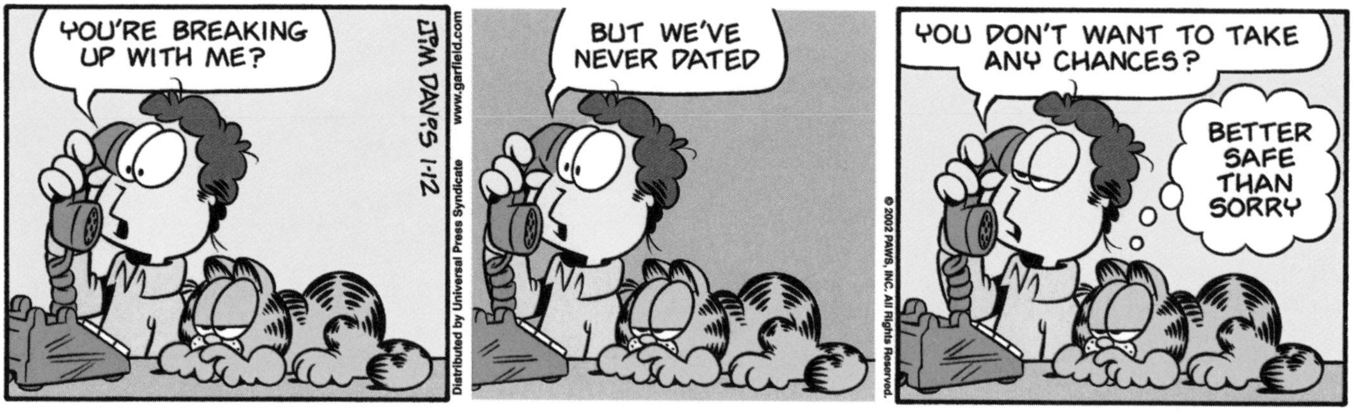
YOU'RE BREAKING UP WITH ME?
JIM DAVIS 1-12
BUT WE'VE NEVER DATED
YOU DON'T WANT TO TAKE ANY CHANCES?
BETTER SAFE THAN SORRY
Distributed by Universal Press Syndicate www.garfield.com
© 2002 PAWS, INC. All Rights Reserved.

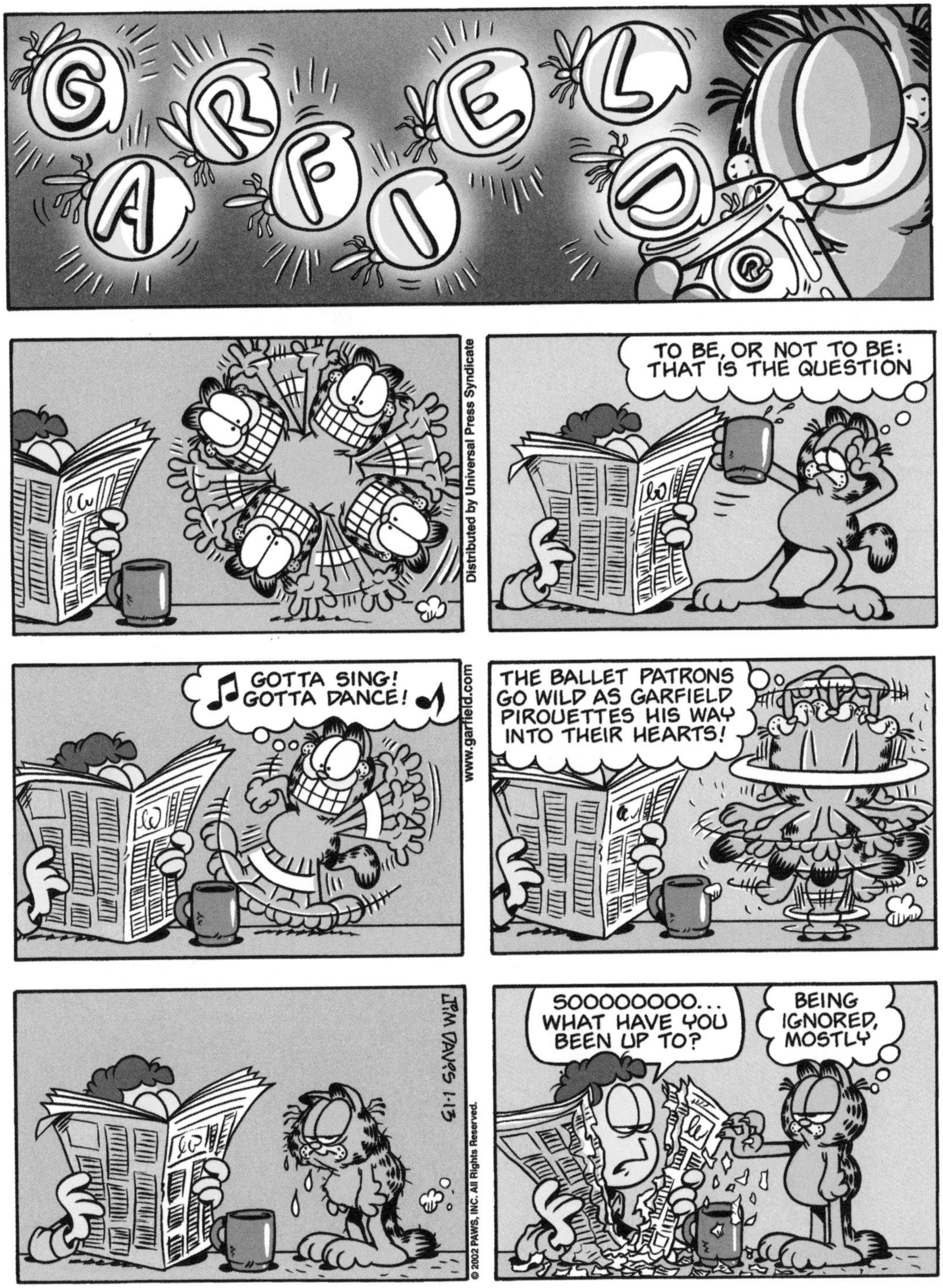
GARFIELD
Distributed by Universal Press Syndicate
TO BE, OR NOT TO BE: THAT IS THE QUESTION
GOTTA SING! GOTTA DANCE!
www.garfield.com
THE BALLET PATRONS GO WILD AS GARFIELD PIROUETTES HIS WAY INTO THEIR HEARTS!
JIM DAVIS 1-13
© 2002 PAWS, INC. All Rights Reserved.
SOOOOOOOO... WHAT HAVE YOU BEEN UP TO?
BEING IGNORED, MOSTLY

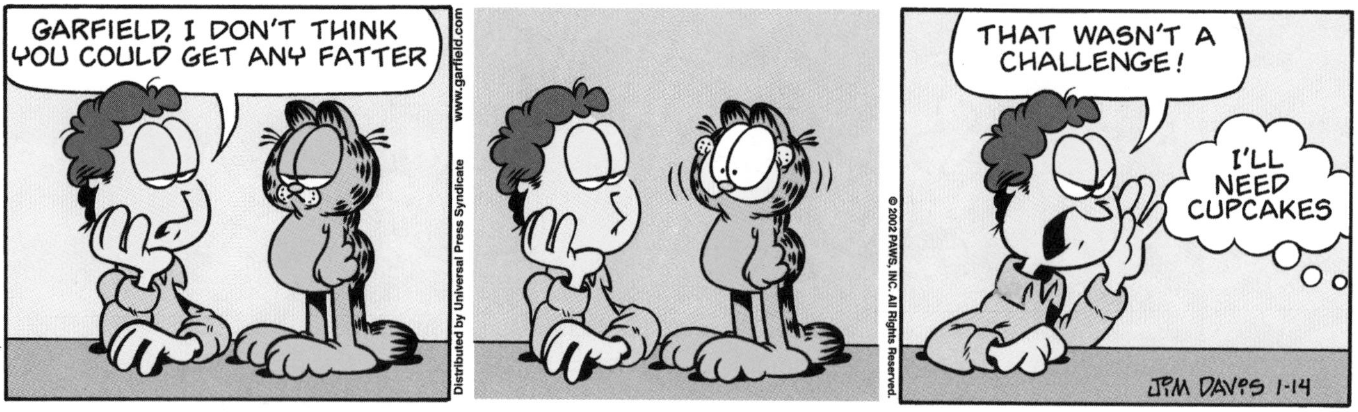
GARFIELD, I DON'T THINK YOU COULD GET ANY FATTER
Distributed by Universal Press Syndicate www.garfield.com
THAT WASN'T A CHALLENGE!
I'LL NEED CUPCAKES
© 2002 PAWS, INC. All Rights Reserved.
JIM DAVIS 1-14

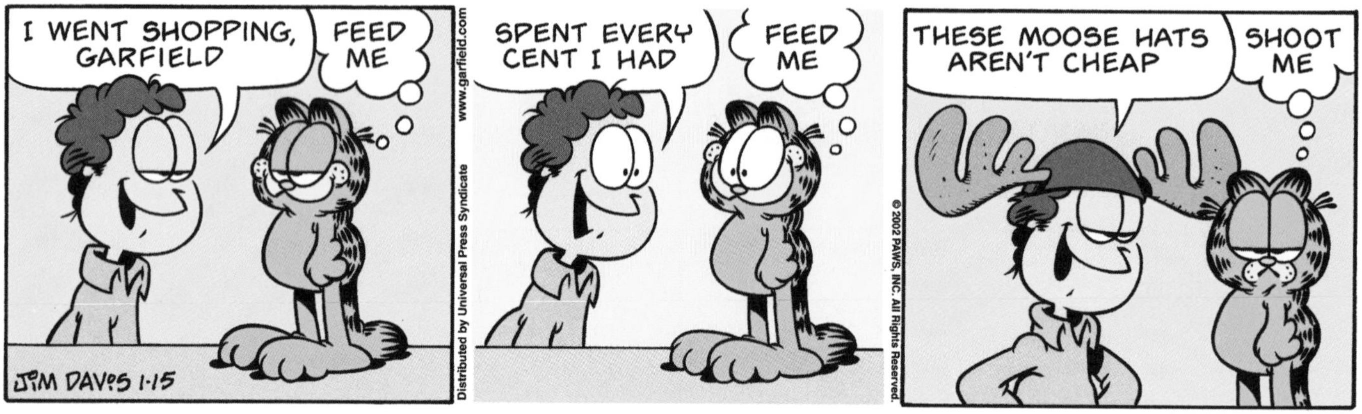
I WENT SHOPPING, GARFIELD
FEED ME
JIM DAVIS 1-15
Distributed by Universal Press Syndicate www.garfield.com
SPENT EVERY CENT I HAD
FEED ME
THESE MOOSE HATS AREN'T CHEAP
SHOOT ME
© 2002 PAWS, INC. All Rights Reserved.

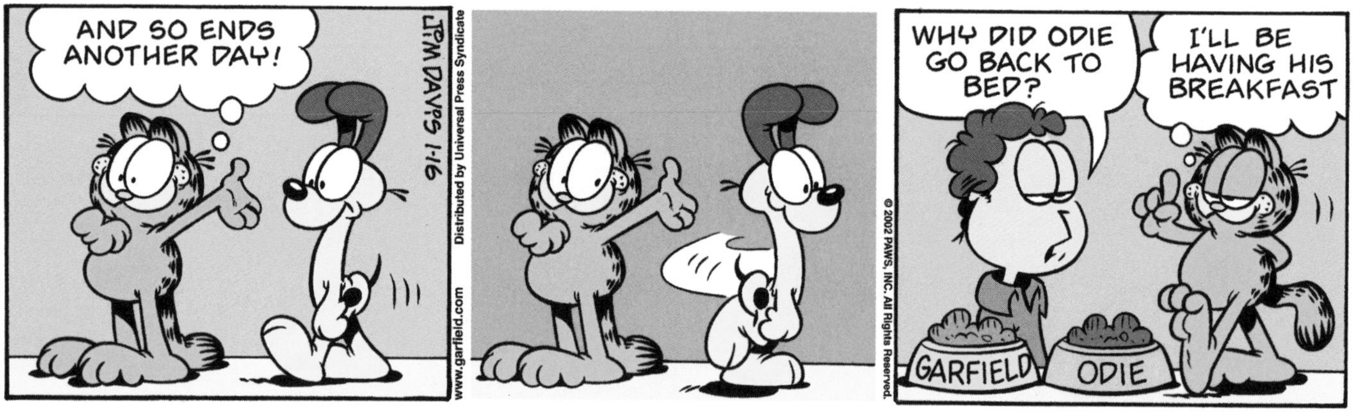
AND SO ENDS ANOTHER DAY!
JIM DAVIS 1-16
Distributed by Universal Press Syndicate www.garfield.com
WHY DID ODIE GO BACK TO BED?
I'LL BE HAVING HIS BREAKFAST
GARFIELD
ODIE
© 2002 PAWS, INC. All Rights Reserved.

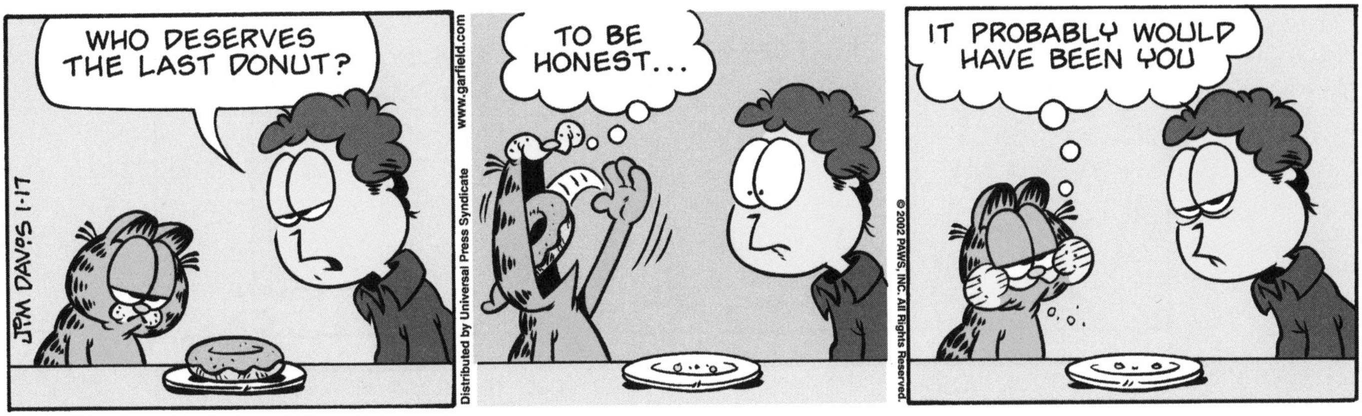
JPM DAVPS 1-17
WHO DESERVES THE LAST DONUT?
www.garfield.com
Distributed by Universal Press Syndicate
TO BE HONEST...
© 2002 PAWS, INC. All Rights Reserved.
IT PROBABLY WOULD HAVE BEEN YOU

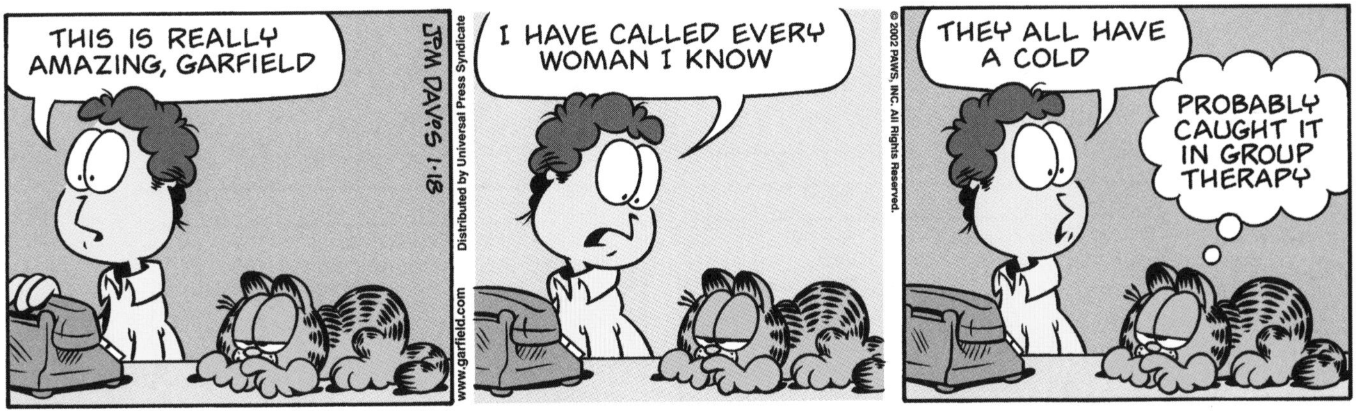
THIS IS REALLY AMAZING, GARFIELD
JPM DAVPS 1-18
Distributed by Universal Press Syndicate
www.garfield.com
I HAVE CALLED EVERY WOMAN I KNOW
© 2002 PAWS, INC. All Rights Reserved.
THEY ALL HAVE A COLD
PROBABLY CAUGHT IT IN GROUP THERAPY

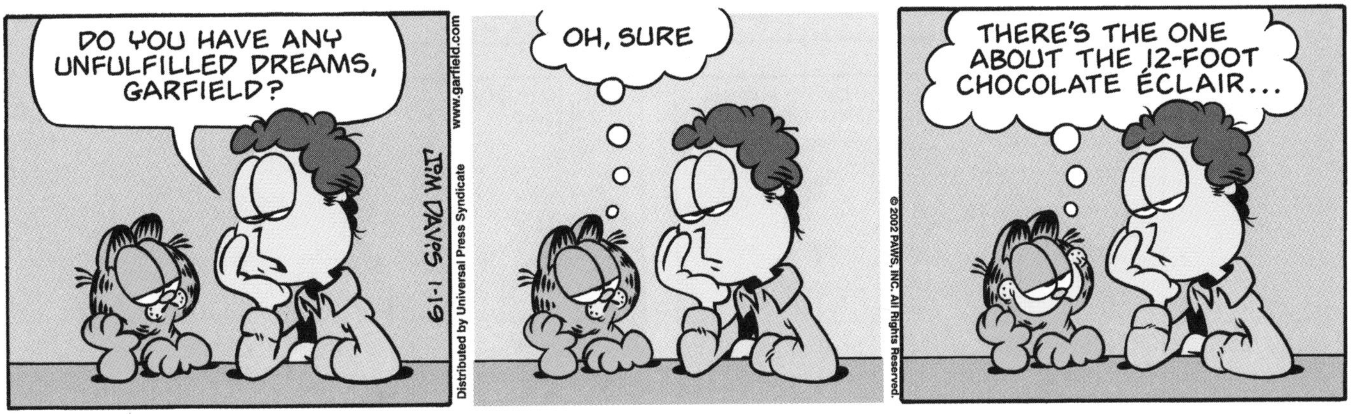
DO YOU HAVE ANY UNFULFILLED DREAMS, GARFIELD?
JPM DAVPS 1-19
www.garfield.com
Distributed by Universal Press Syndicate
OH, SURE
© 2002 PAWS, INC. All Rights Reserved.
THERE'S THE ONE ABOUT THE 12-FOOT CHOCOLATE ÉCLAIR...

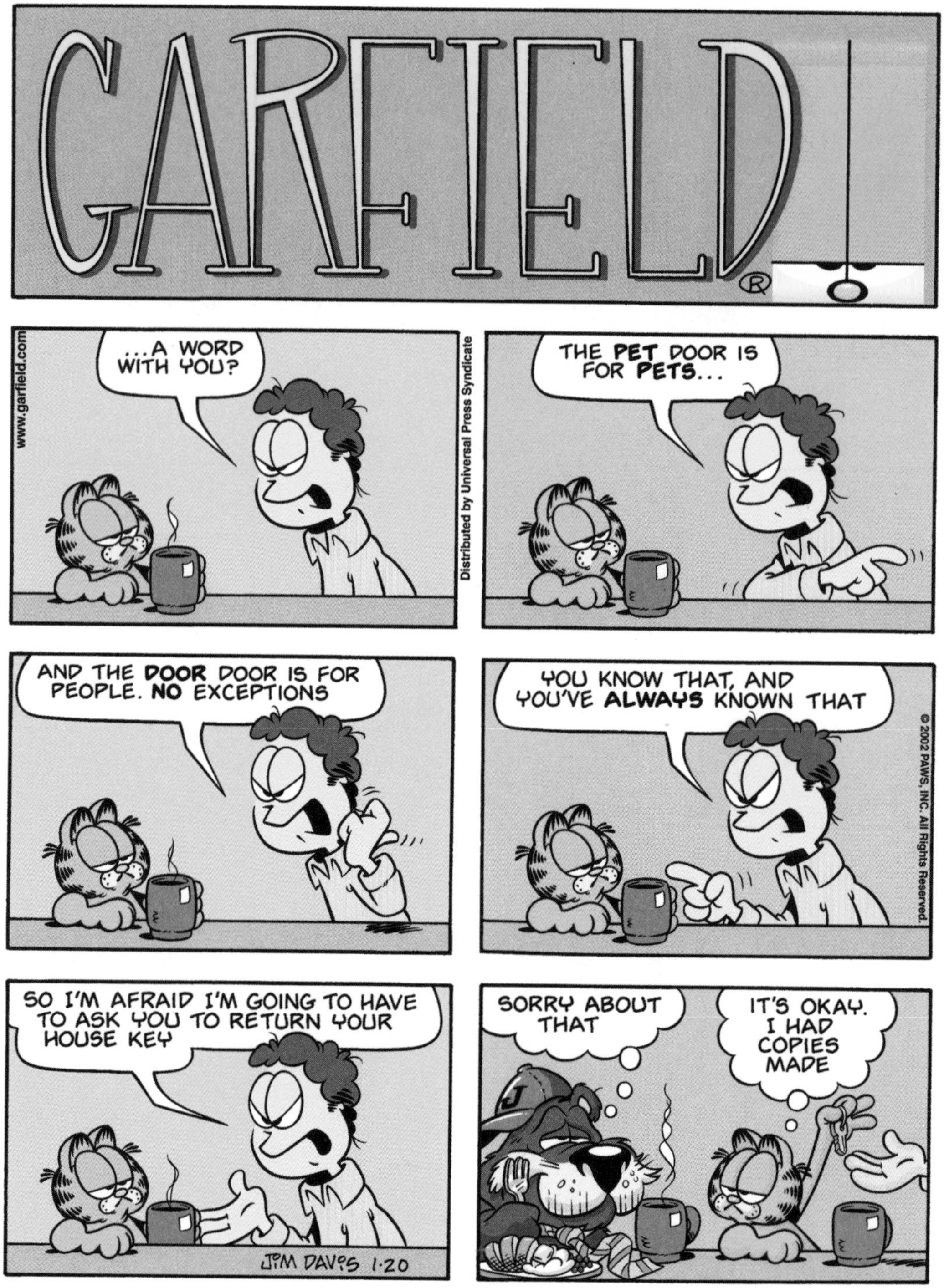
GARFIELD®
www.garfield.com
...A WORD WITH YOU?
Distributed by Universal Press Syndicate
THE PET DOOR IS FOR PETS...
AND THE DOOR DOOR IS FOR PEOPLE. NO EXCEPTIONS
YOU KNOW THAT, AND YOU'VE ALWAYS KNOWN THAT
© 2002 PAWS, INC. All Rights Reserved.
SO I'M AFRAID I'M GOING TO HAVE TO ASK YOU TO RETURN YOUR HOUSE KEY
JIM DAVIS 1-20
SORRY ABOUT THAT
IT'S OKAY. I HAD COPIES MADE

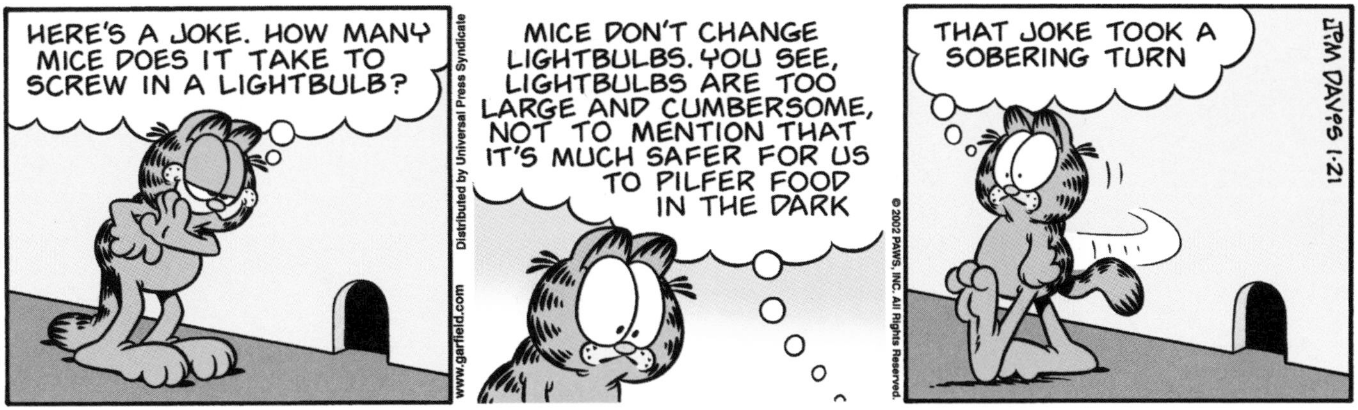
HERE'S A JOKE. HOW MANY MICE DOES IT TAKE TO SCREW IN A LIGHTBULB?
MICE DON'T CHANGE LIGHTBULBS. YOU SEE, LIGHTBULBS ARE TOO LARGE AND CUMBERSOME, NOT TO MENTION THAT IT'S MUCH SAFER FOR US TO PILFER FOOD IN THE DARK
THAT JOKE TOOK A SOBERING TURN
JIM DAVIS 1·21
Distributed by Universal Press Syndicate
www.garfield.com
© 2002 PAWS, INC. All Rights Reserved.

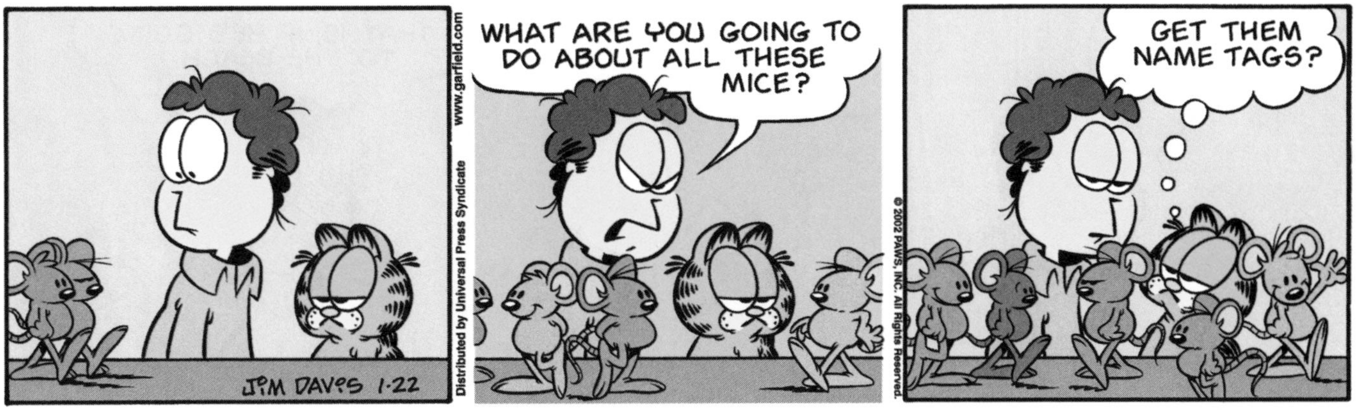
JIM DAVIS 1·22
WHAT ARE YOU GOING TO DO ABOUT ALL THESE MICE?
GET THEM NAME TAGS?
Distributed by Universal Press Syndicate
www.garfield.com
© 2002 PAWS, INC. All Rights Reserved.

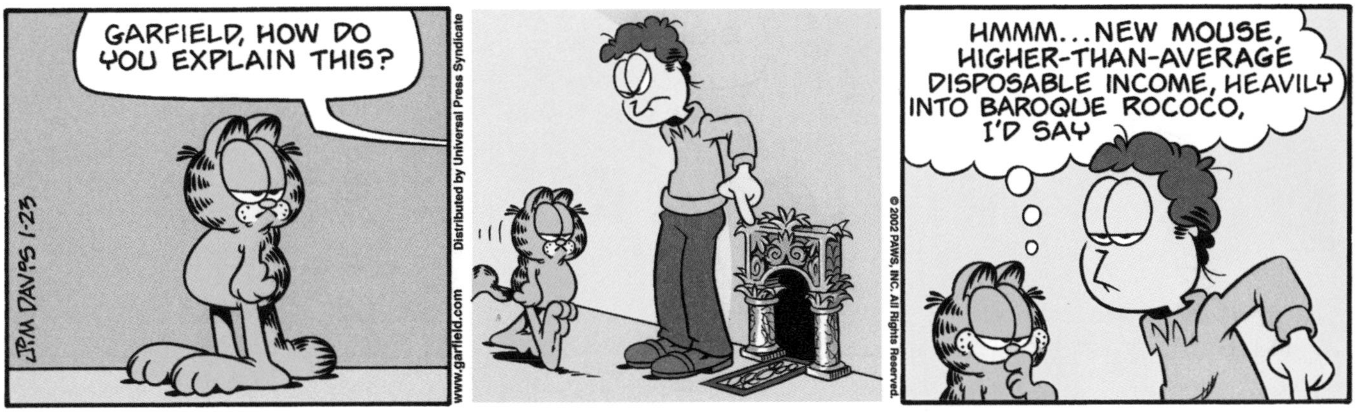
GARFIELD, HOW DO YOU EXPLAIN THIS?
JIM DAVIS 1·23
HMMM...NEW MOUSE, HIGHER-THAN-AVERAGE DISPOSABLE INCOME, HEAVILY INTO BAROQUE ROCOCO, I'D SAY
Distributed by Universal Press Syndicate
www.garfield.com
© 2002 PAWS, INC. All Rights Reserved.

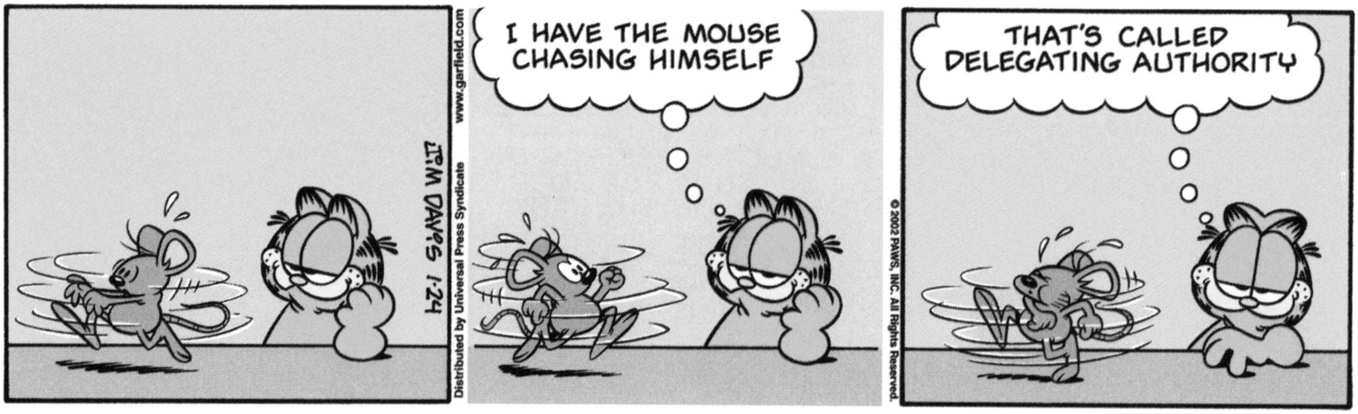
JIM DAVIS 1·24
Distributed by Universal Press Syndicate www.garfield.com
I HAVE THE MOUSE CHASING HIMSELF
© 2002 PAWS, INC. All Rights Reserved.
THAT'S CALLED DELEGATING AUTHORITY

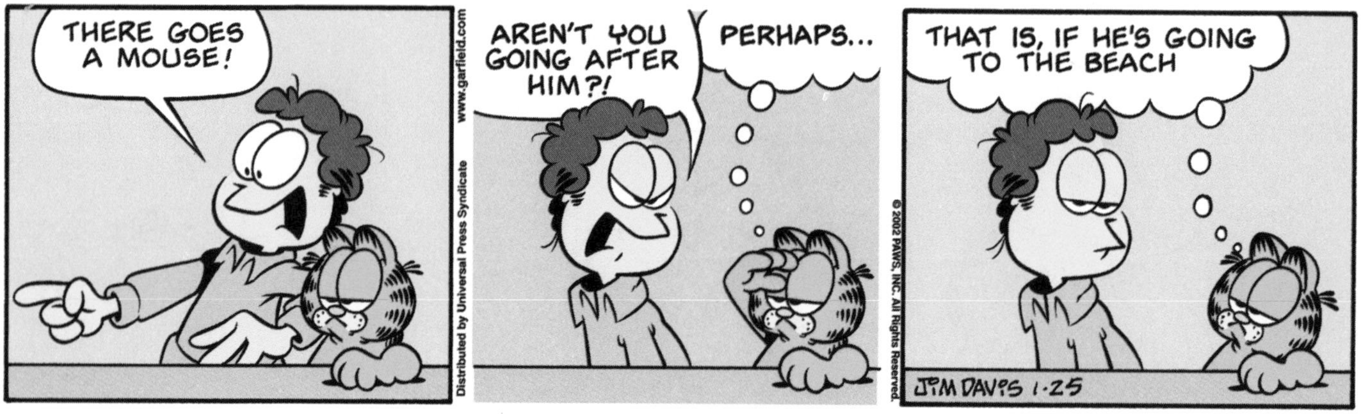
THERE GOES A MOUSE!
Distributed by Universal Press Syndicate www.garfield.com
AREN'T YOU GOING AFTER HIM?!
PERHAPS...
© 2002 PAWS, INC. All Rights Reserved.
THAT IS, IF HE'S GOING TO THE BEACH
JIM DAVIS 1·25

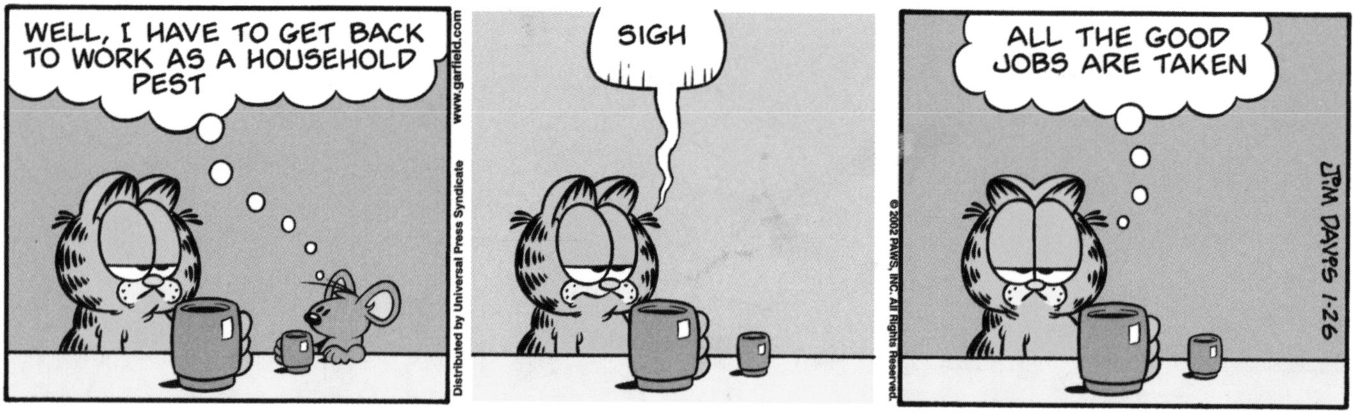
WELL, I HAVE TO GET BACK TO WORK AS A HOUSEHOLD PEST
Distributed by Universal Press Syndicate www.garfield.com
SIGH
© 2002 PAWS, INC. All Rights Reserved.
ALL THE GOOD JOBS ARE TAKEN
JIM DAVIS 1·26

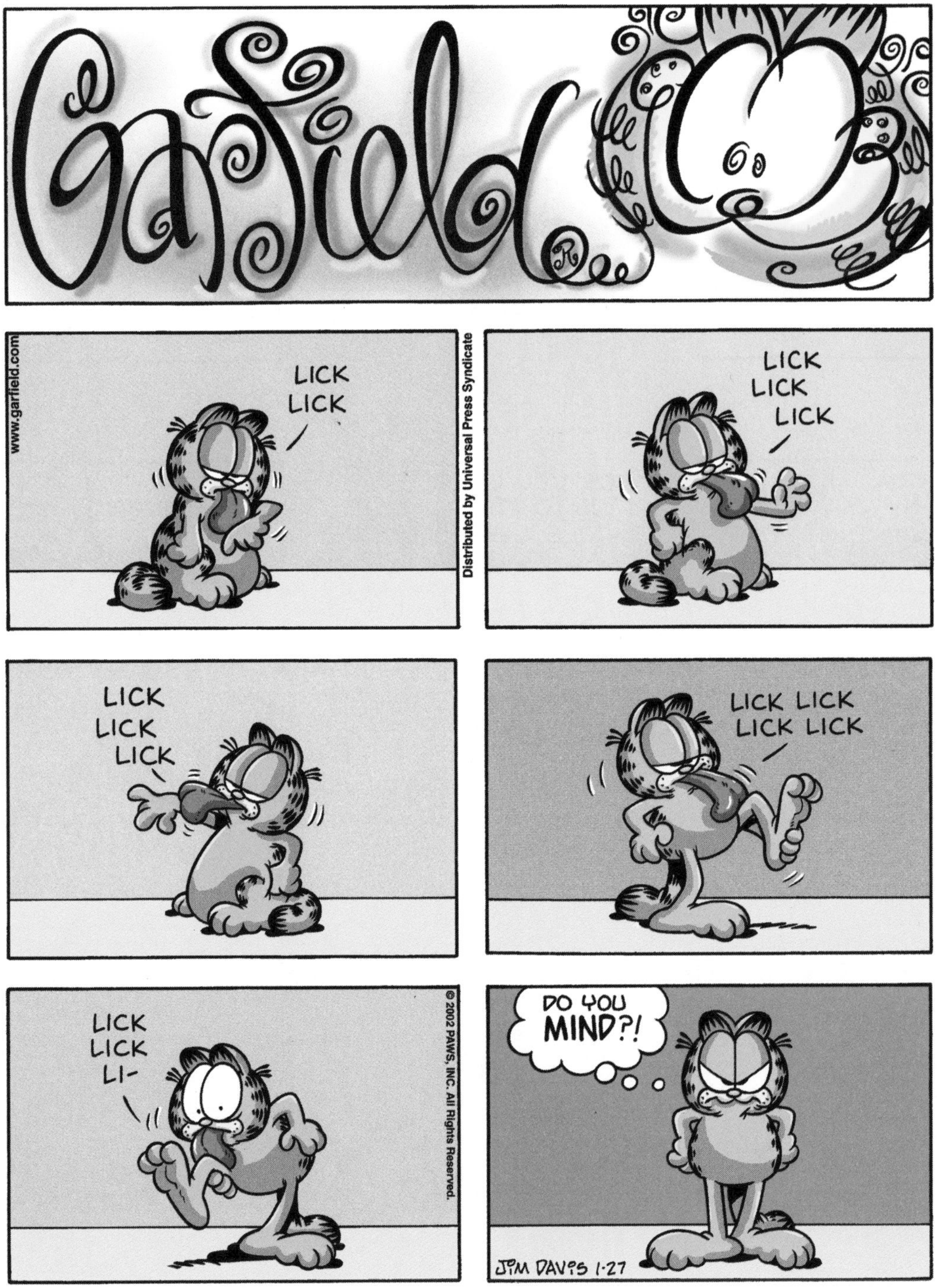
Garfield
www.garfield.com
LICK LICK
Distributed by Universal Press Syndicate
LICK LICK LICK
LICK LICK LICK
LICK LICK LICK LICK
LICK LICK LI-
© 2002 PAWS, INC. All Rights Reserved.
DO YOU MIND?!
JIM DAVIS 1-27

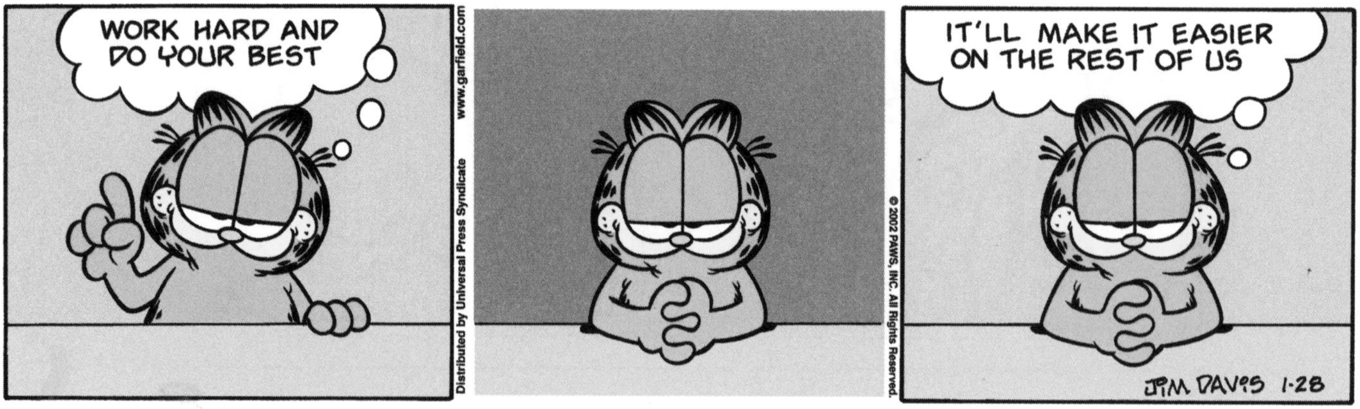
WORK HARD AND DO YOUR BEST
IT'LL MAKE IT EASIER ON THE REST OF US
JIM DAVIS 1-28
Distributed by Universal Press Syndicate www.garfield.com
© 2002 PAWS, INC. All Rights Reserved.

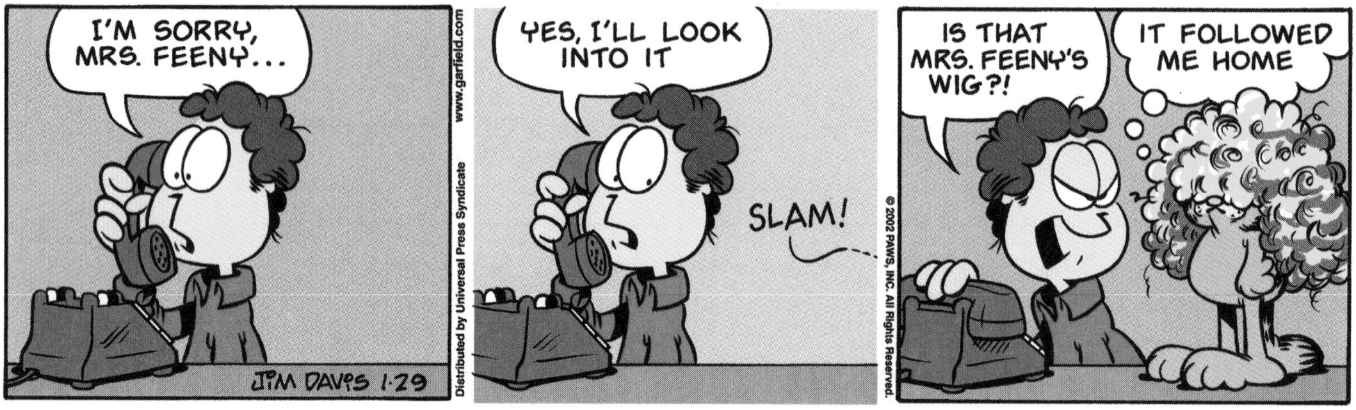
I'M SORRY, MRS. FEENY...
JIM DAVIS 1-29
YES, I'LL LOOK INTO IT
SLAM!
IS THAT MRS. FEENY'S WIG?!
IT FOLLOWED ME HOME
Distributed by Universal Press Syndicate www.garfield.com
© 2002 PAWS, INC. All Rights Reserved.

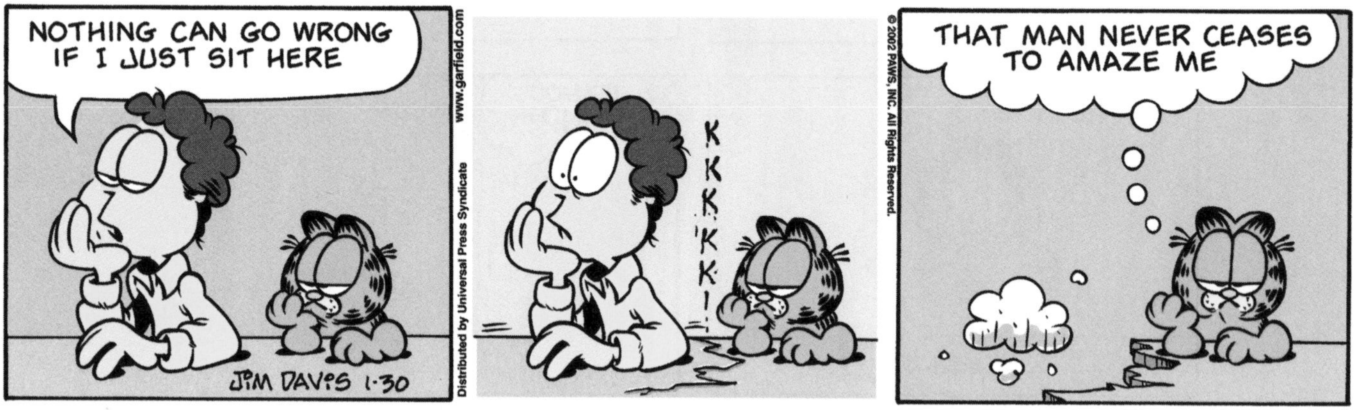
NOTHING CAN GO WRONG IF I JUST SIT HERE
JIM DAVIS 1-30
KKKKK!
THAT MAN NEVER CEASES TO AMAZE ME
Distributed by Universal Press Syndicate www.garfield.com
© 2002 PAWS, INC. All Rights Reserved.

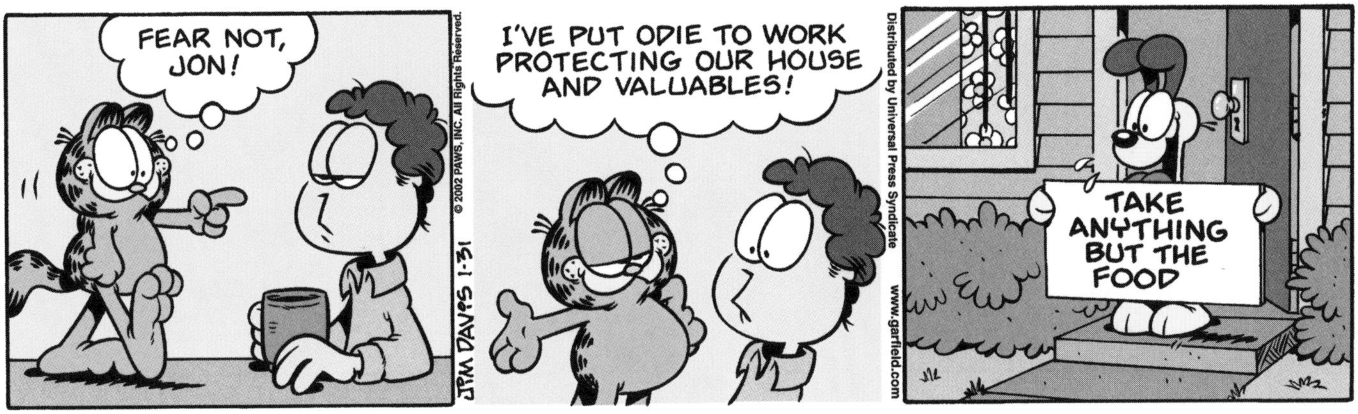
FEAR NOT, JON!
© 2002 PAWS, INC. All Rights Reserved.
JIM DAVIS 1-31
I'VE PUT ODIE TO WORK PROTECTING OUR HOUSE AND VALUABLES!
Distributed by Universal Press Syndicate
www.garfield.com
TAKE ANYTHING BUT THE FOOD

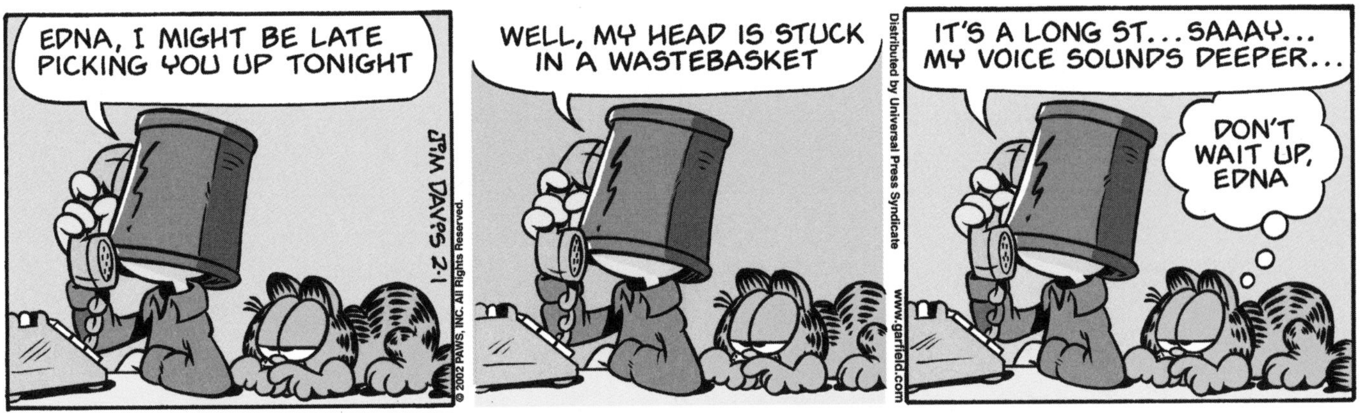
EDNA, I MIGHT BE LATE PICKING YOU UP TONIGHT
JIM DAVIS 2-1
© 2002 PAWS, INC. All Rights Reserved.
WELL, MY HEAD IS STUCK IN A WASTEBASKET
Distributed by Universal Press Syndicate
www.garfield.com
IT'S A LONG ST... SAAAY... MY VOICE SOUNDS DEEPER...
DON'T WAIT UP, EDNA

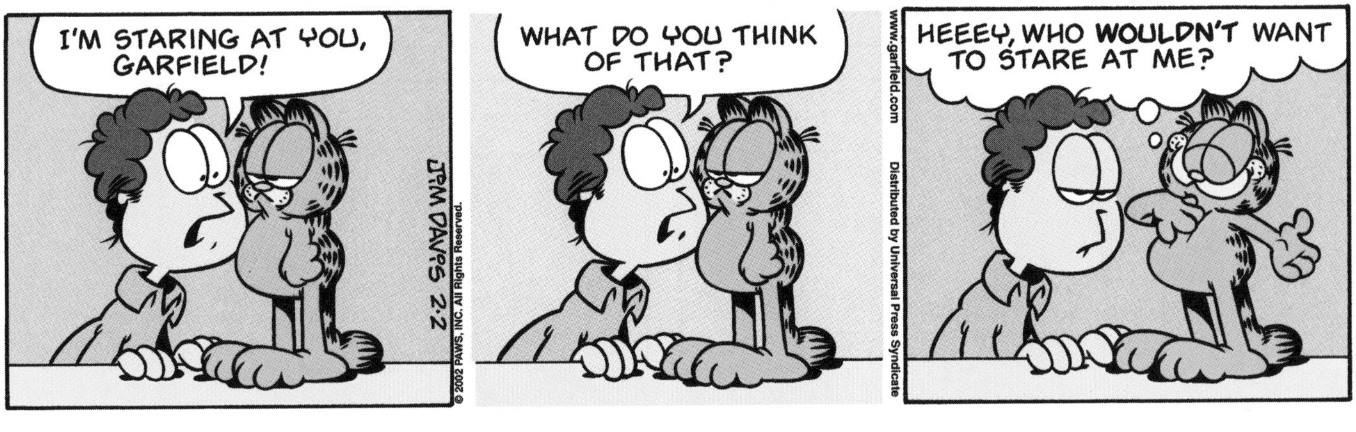
I'M STARING AT YOU, GARFIELD!
JIM DAVIS 2-2
© 2002 PAWS, INC. All Rights Reserved.
WHAT DO YOU THINK OF THAT?
www.garfield.com
Distributed by Universal Press Syndicate
HEEEY, WHO **WOULDN'T** WANT TO STARE AT ME?

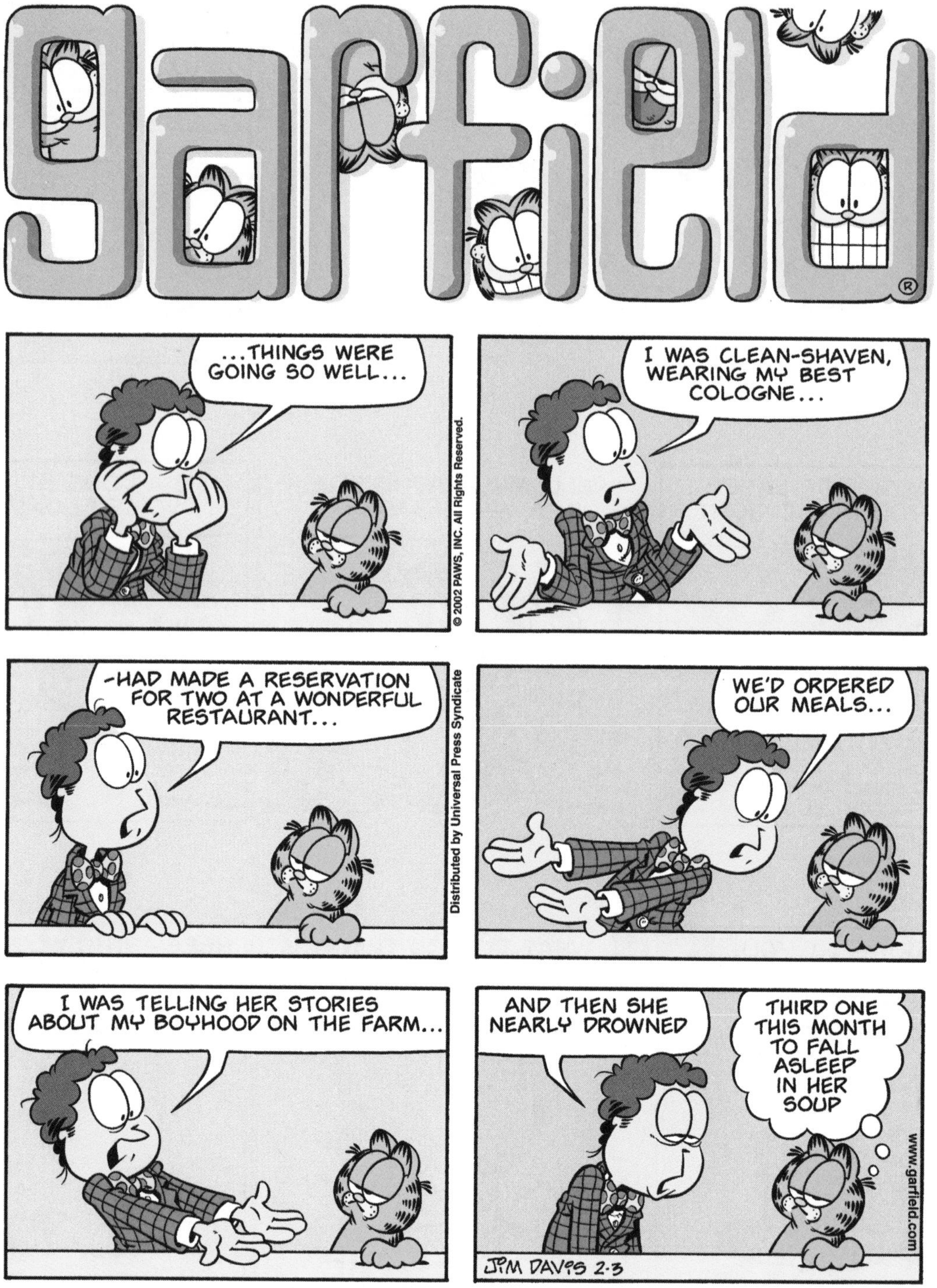
garfield®
...THINGS WERE GOING SO WELL...
I WAS CLEAN-SHAVEN, WEARING MY BEST COLOGNE...
-HAD MADE A RESERVATION FOR TWO AT A WONDERFUL RESTAURANT...
WE'D ORDERED OUR MEALS...
I WAS TELLING HER STORIES ABOUT MY BOYHOOD ON THE FARM...
AND THEN SHE NEARLY DROWNED
THIRD ONE THIS MONTH TO FALL ASLEEP IN HER SOUP
JIM DAVIS 2-3
www.garfield.com
© 2002 PAWS, INC. All Rights Reserved.
Distributed by Universal Press Syndicate

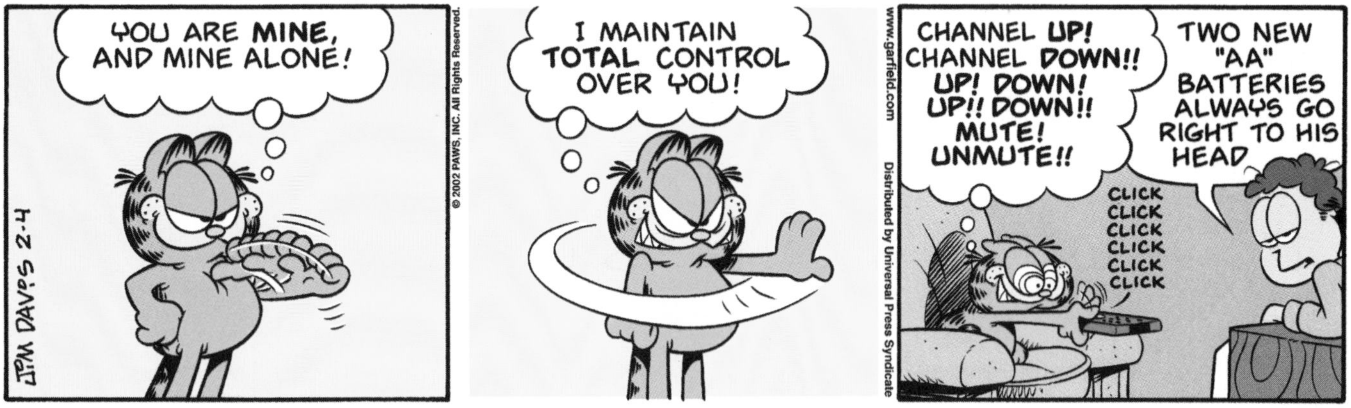
YOU ARE **MINE**, AND MINE ALONE!
JIM DAVIS 2-4
© 2002 PAWS, INC. All Rights Reserved.
I MAINTAIN **TOTAL** CONTROL OVER YOU!
www.garfield.com
Distributed by Universal Press Syndicate
CHANNEL **UP!** CHANNEL **DOWN!!** **UP! DOWN! UP!! DOWN!!** **MUTE! UNMUTE!!**
CLICK CLICK CLICK CLICK CLICK CLICK
TWO NEW "AA" BATTERIES ALWAYS GO RIGHT TO HIS HEAD

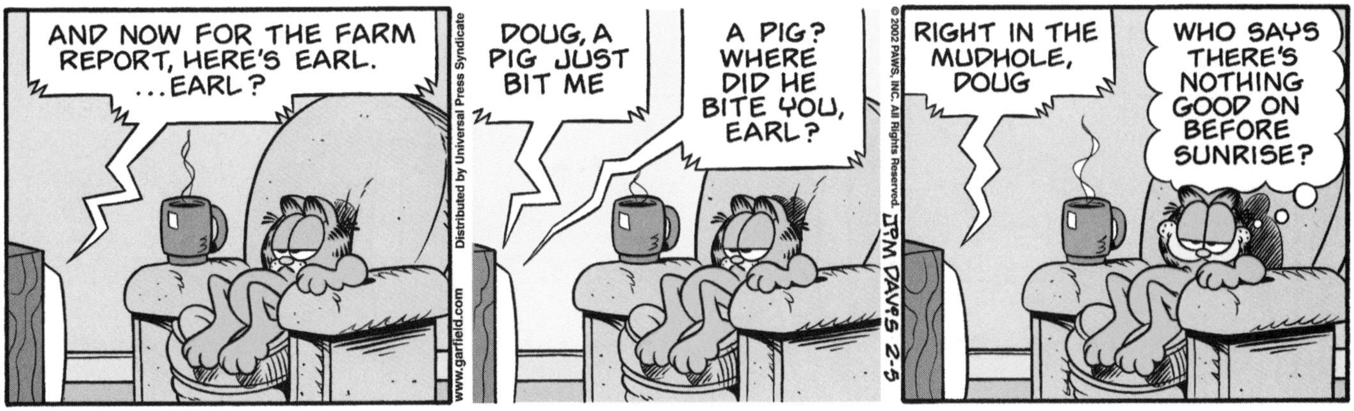
AND NOW FOR THE FARM REPORT, HERE'S EARL. ...EARL?
Distributed by Universal Press Syndicate
www.garfield.com
DOUG, A PIG JUST BIT ME
A PIG? WHERE DID HE BITE YOU, EARL?
JIM DAVIS 2-5
© 2002 PAWS, INC. All Rights Reserved.
RIGHT IN THE MUDHOLE, DOUG
WHO SAYS THERE'S NOTHING GOOD ON BEFORE SUNRISE?

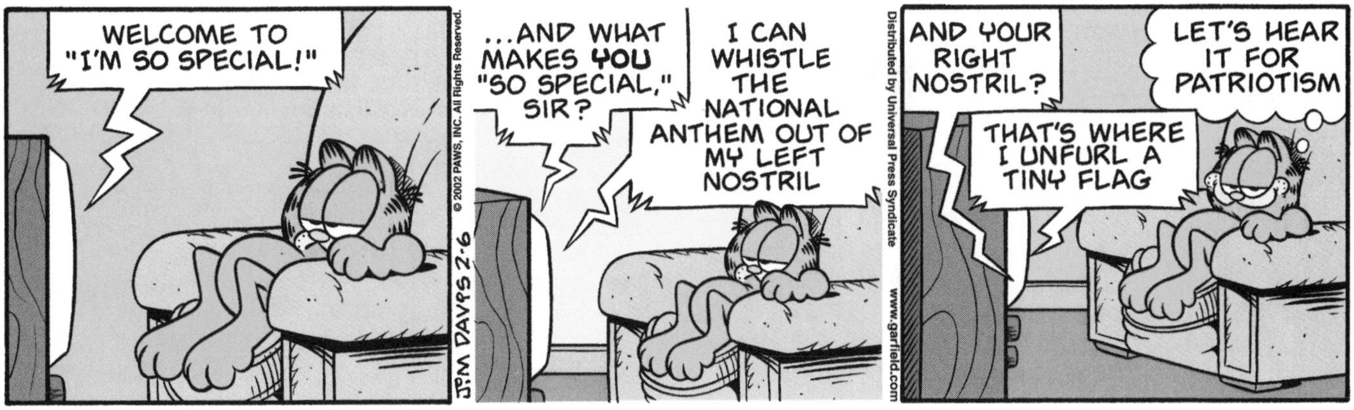
WELCOME TO "I'M SO SPECIAL!"
JIM DAVIS 2-6
© 2002 PAWS, INC. All Rights Reserved.
...AND WHAT MAKES **YOU** "SO SPECIAL," SIR?
I CAN WHISTLE THE NATIONAL ANTHEM OUT OF MY LEFT NOSTRIL
Distributed by Universal Press Syndicate
www.garfield.com
AND YOUR RIGHT NOSTRIL?
THAT'S WHERE I UNFURL A TINY FLAG
LET'S HEAR IT FOR PATRIOTISM

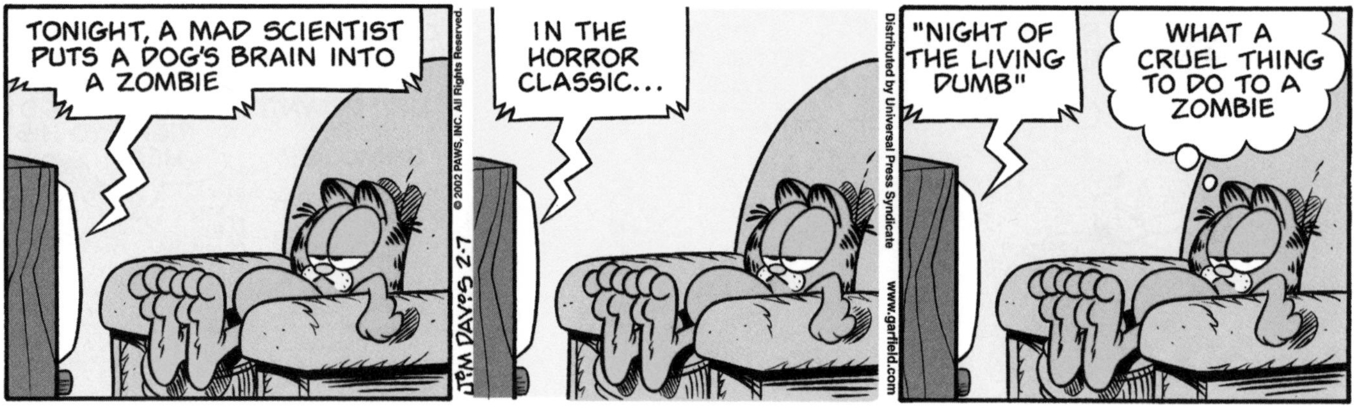
TONIGHT, A MAD SCIENTIST PUTS A DOG'S BRAIN INTO A ZOMBIE
IN THE HORROR CLASSIC...
"NIGHT OF THE LIVING DUMB"
WHAT A CRUEL THING TO DO TO A ZOMBIE
JPM DAVPS 2-7
© 2002 PAWS, INC. All Rights Reserved.
Distributed by Universal Press Syndicate
www.garfield.com

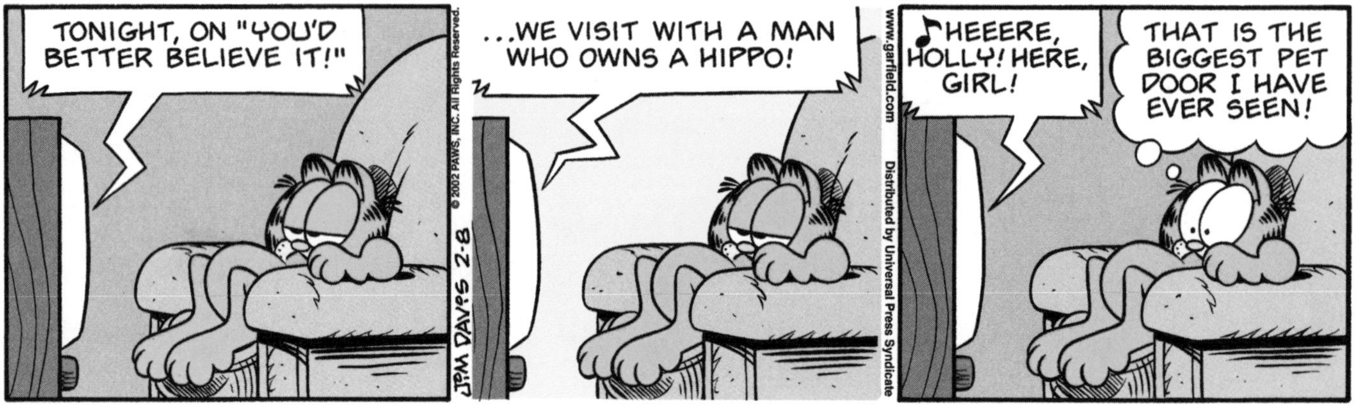
TONIGHT, ON "YOU'D BETTER BELIEVE IT!"
...WE VISIT WITH A MAN WHO OWNS A HIPPO!
♪HEEERE, HOLLY! HERE, GIRL!
THAT IS THE BIGGEST PET DOOR I HAVE EVER SEEN!
JPM DAVPS 2-8
© 2002 PAWS, INC. All Rights Reserved.
www.garfield.com
Distributed by Universal Press Syndicate

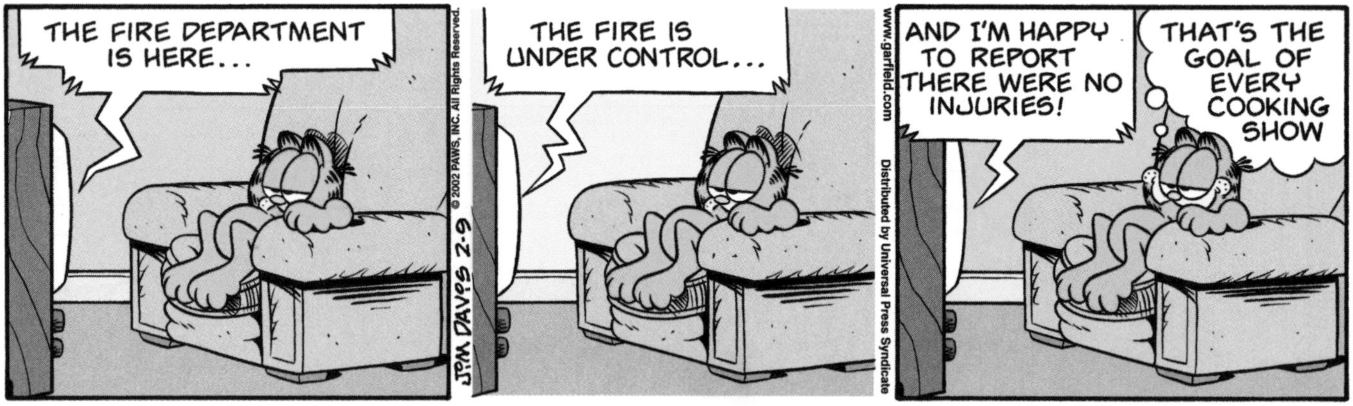
THE FIRE DEPARTMENT IS HERE...
THE FIRE IS UNDER CONTROL...
AND I'M HAPPY TO REPORT THERE WERE NO INJURIES!
THAT'S THE GOAL OF EVERY COOKING SHOW
JPM DAVPS 2-9
© 2002 PAWS, INC. All Rights Reserved.
www.garfield.com
Distributed by Universal Press Syndicate

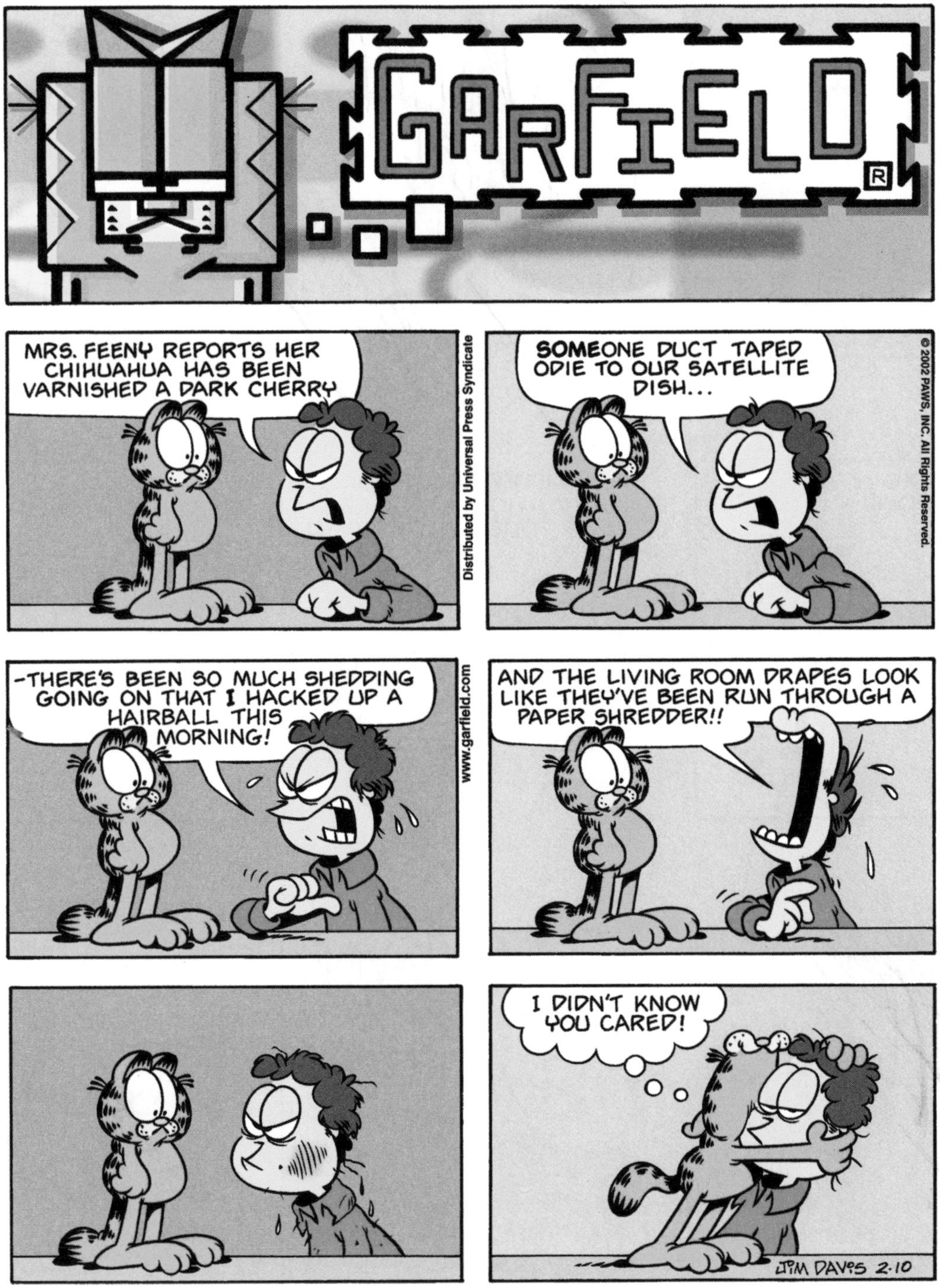
GARFIELD®
MRS. FEENY REPORTS HER CHIHUAHUA HAS BEEN VARNISHED A DARK CHERRY
Distributed by Universal Press Syndicate
SOMEONE DUCT TAPED ODIE TO OUR SATELLITE DISH...
© 2002 PAWS, INC. All Rights Reserved.
-THERE'S BEEN SO MUCH SHEDDING GOING ON THAT I HACKED UP A HAIRBALL THIS MORNING!
www.garfield.com
AND THE LIVING ROOM DRAPES LOOK LIKE THEY'VE BEEN RUN THROUGH A PAPER SHREDDER!!
I DIDN'T KNOW YOU CARED!
JIM DAVIS 2-10

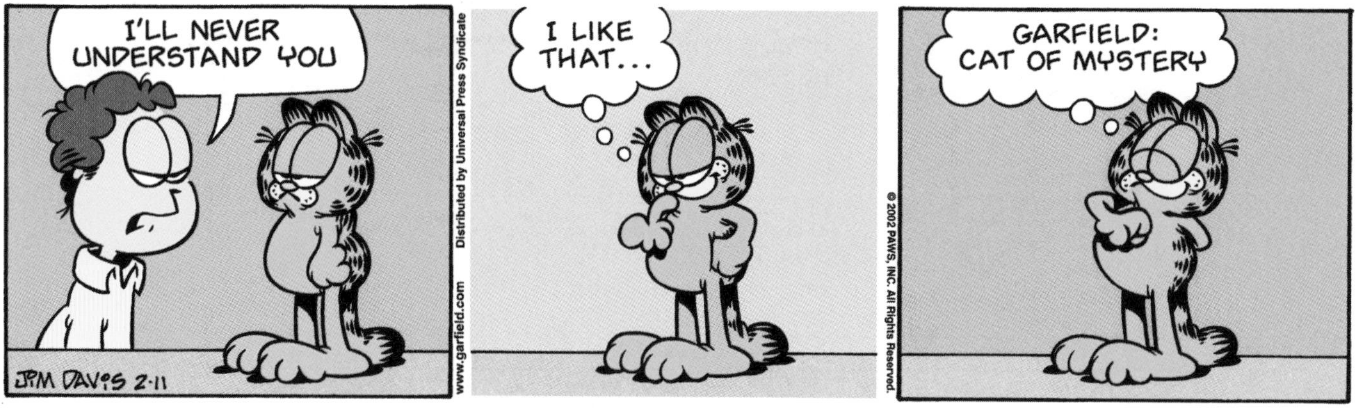
I'LL NEVER UNDERSTAND YOU
JIM DAVIS 2-11
Distributed by Universal Press Syndicate
www.garfield.com
I LIKE THAT...
© 2002 PAWS, INC. All Rights Reserved.
GARFIELD: CAT OF MYSTERY

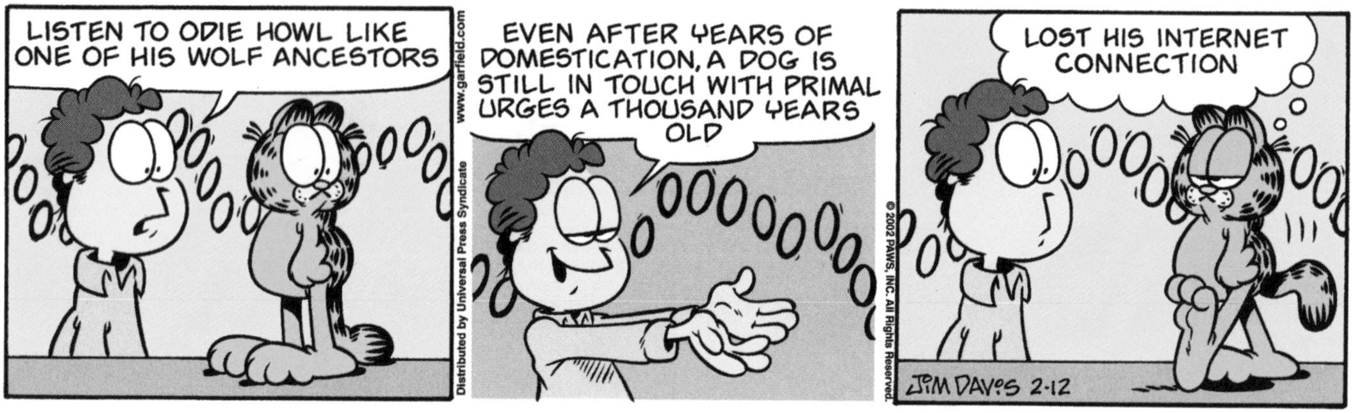
LISTEN TO ODIE HOWL LIKE ONE OF HIS WOLF ANCESTORS
www.garfield.com
Distributed by Universal Press Syndicate
EVEN AFTER YEARS OF DOMESTICATION, A DOG IS STILL IN TOUCH WITH PRIMAL URGES A THOUSAND YEARS OLD
© 2002 PAWS, INC. All Rights Reserved.
LOST HIS INTERNET CONNECTION
JIM DAVIS 2-12

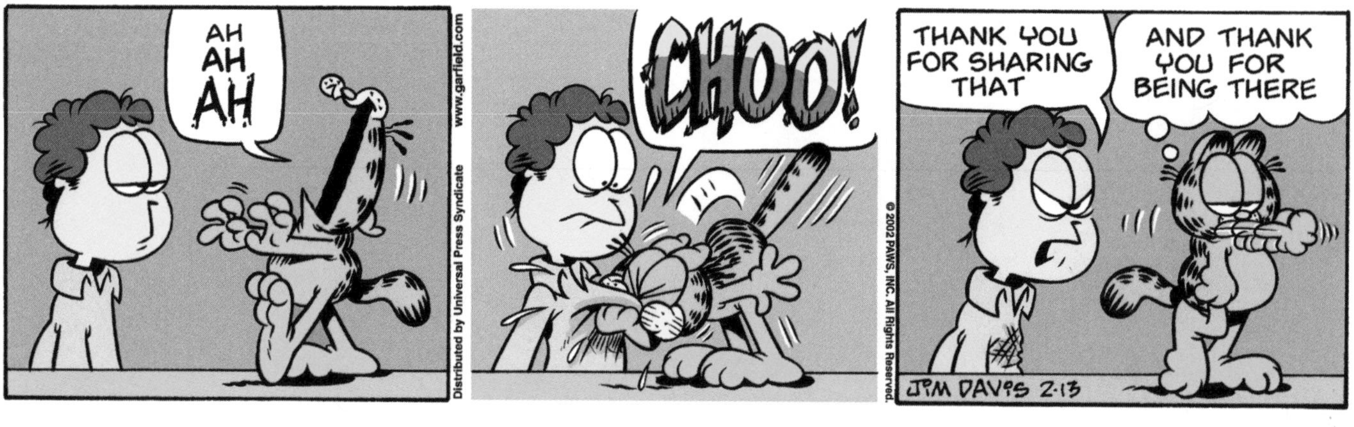
AH
AH
AH
www.garfield.com
Distributed by Universal Press Syndicate
CHOO!
© 2002 PAWS, INC. All Rights Reserved.
THANK YOU FOR SHARING THAT
AND THANK YOU FOR BEING THERE
JIM DAVIS 2-13

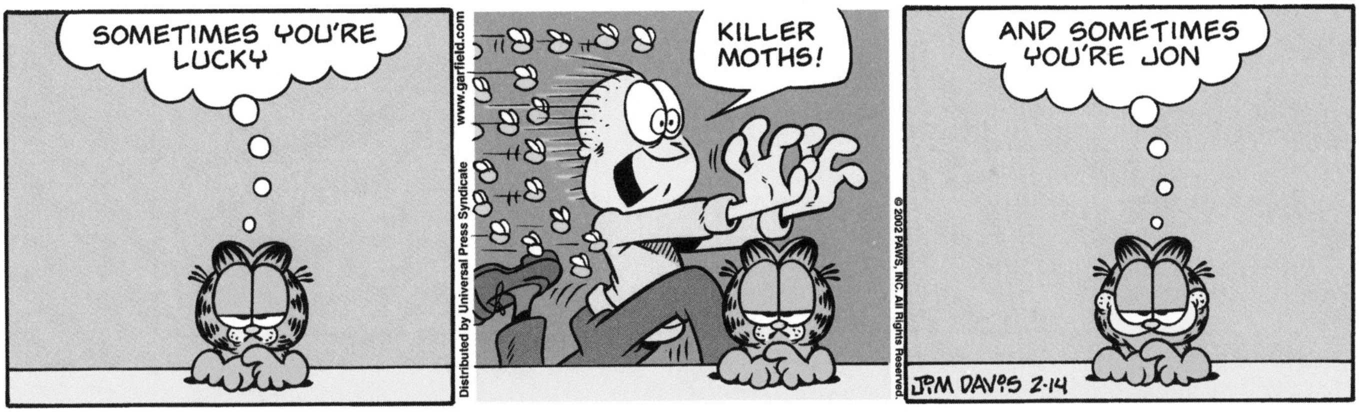
SOMETIMES YOU'RE LUCKY
KILLER MOTHS!
AND SOMETIMES YOU'RE JON
JIM DAVIS 2-14
www.garfield.com
Distributed by Universal Press Syndicate
© 2002 PAWS, INC. All Rights Reserved.

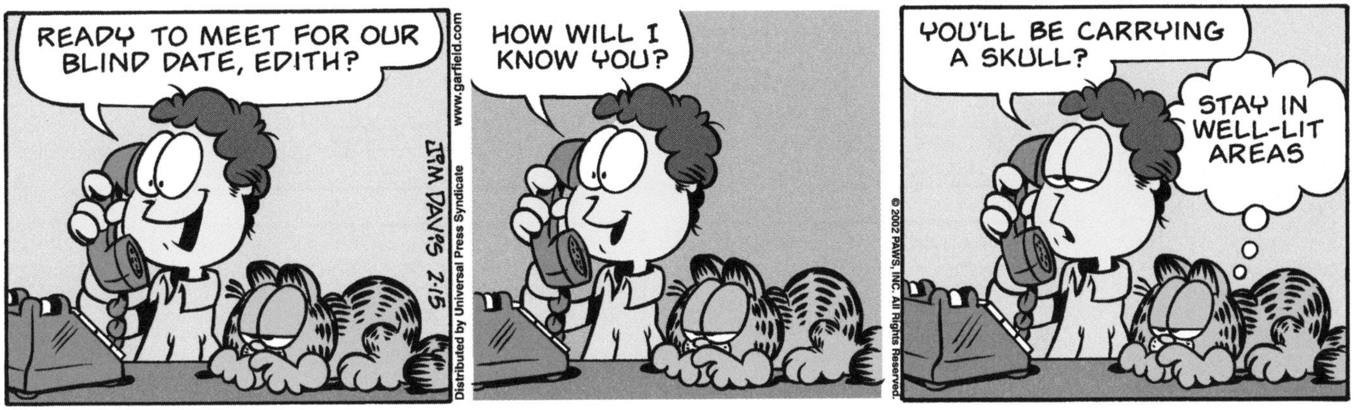
READY TO MEET FOR OUR BLIND DATE, EDITH?
HOW WILL I KNOW YOU?
YOU'LL BE CARRYING A SKULL?
STAY IN WELL-LIT AREAS
JIM DAVIS 2-15
www.garfield.com
Distributed by Universal Press Syndicate
© 2002 PAWS, INC. All Rights Reserved.

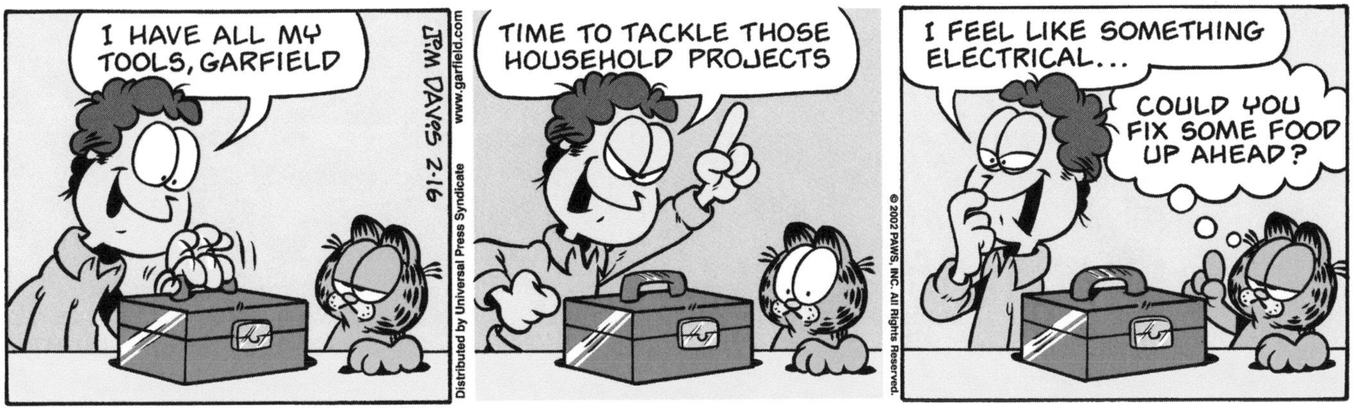
I HAVE ALL MY TOOLS, GARFIELD
TIME TO TACKLE THOSE HOUSEHOLD PROJECTS
I FEEL LIKE SOMETHING ELECTRICAL...
COULD YOU FIX SOME FOOD UP AHEAD?
JIM DAVIS 2-16
www.garfield.com
Distributed by Universal Press Syndicate
© 2002 PAWS, INC. All Rights Reserved.

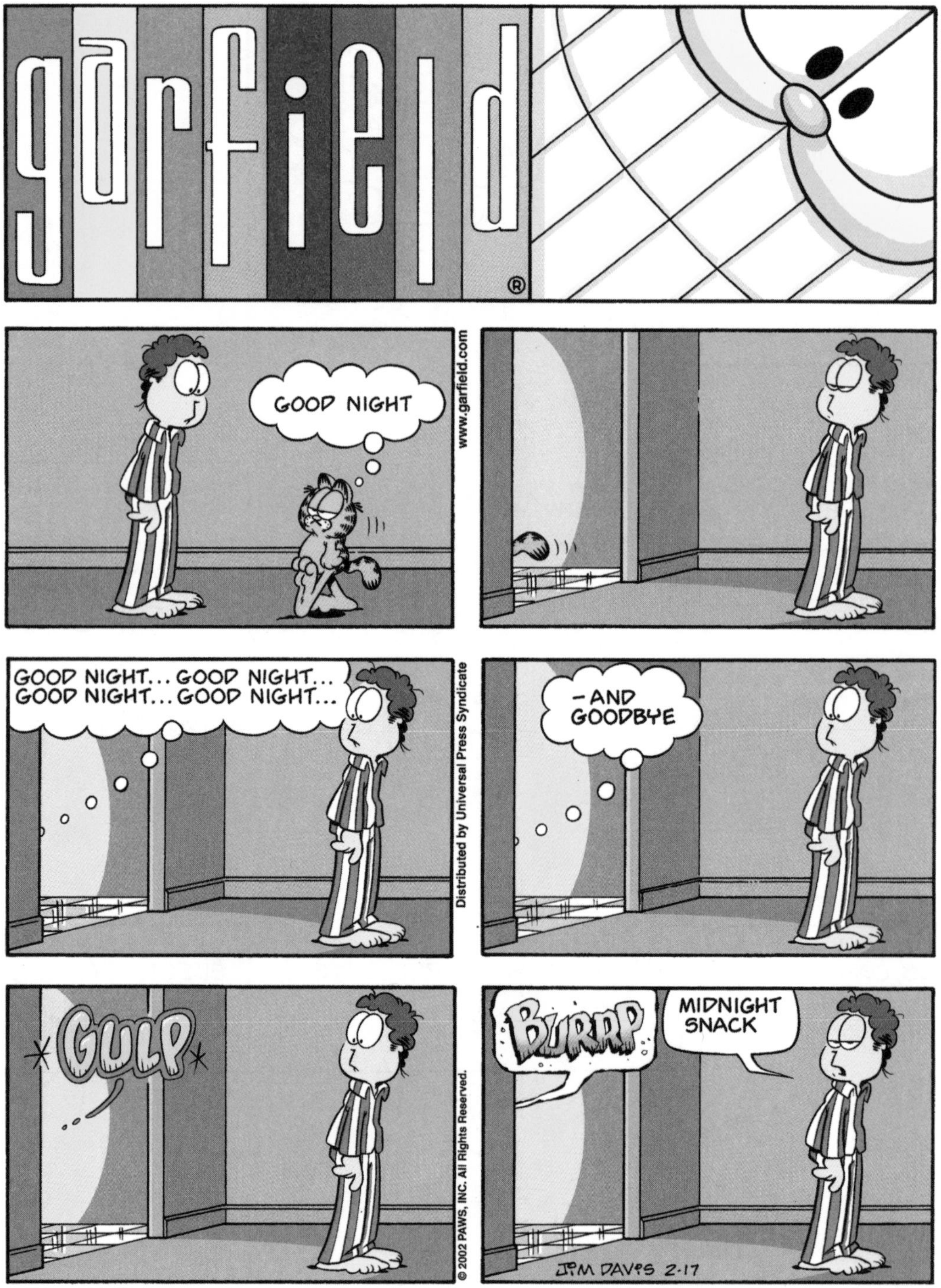
garfield®
www.garfield.com
GOOD NIGHT
GOOD NIGHT... GOOD NIGHT... GOOD NIGHT... GOOD NIGHT...
Distributed by Universal Press Syndicate
-AND GOODBYE
GULP
© 2002 PAWS, INC. All Rights Reserved.
BURRP
MIDNIGHT SNACK
JIM DAVIS 2-17

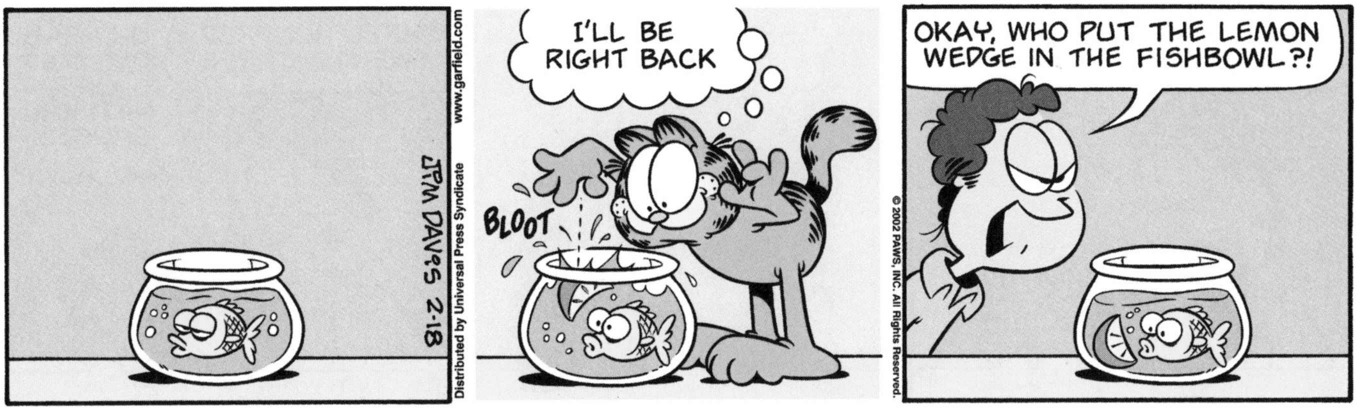
JIM DAVIS 2-18
www.garfield.com
Distributed by Universal Press Syndicate
I'LL BE RIGHT BACK
BLOOT
OKAY, WHO PUT THE LEMON WEDGE IN THE FISHBOWL?!
© 2002 PAWS, INC. All Rights Reserved.

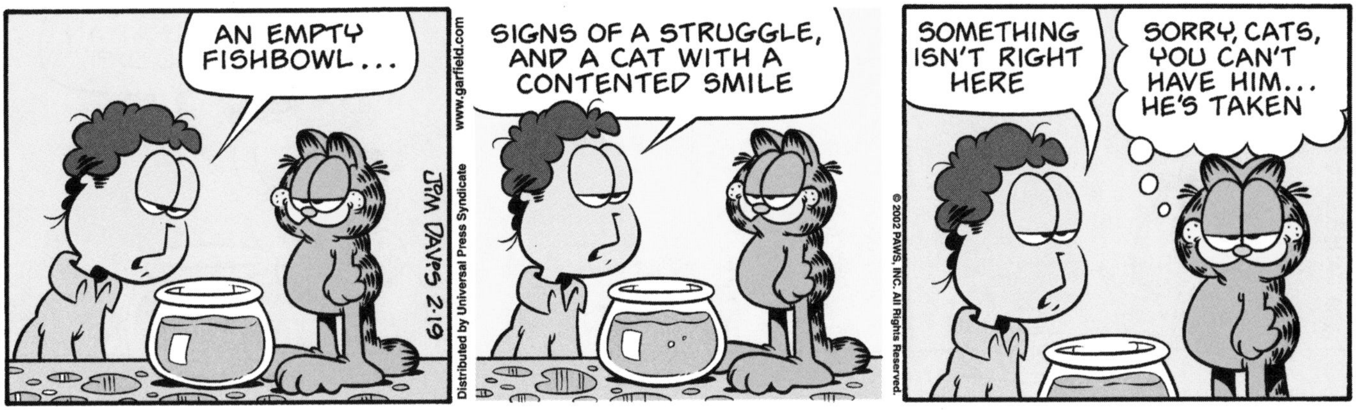
AN EMPTY FISHBOWL...
JIM DAVIS 2-19
www.garfield.com
Distributed by Universal Press Syndicate
SIGNS OF A STRUGGLE, AND A CAT WITH A CONTENTED SMILE
© 2002 PAWS, INC. All Rights Reserved.
SOMETHING ISN'T RIGHT HERE
SORRY, CATS, YOU CAN'T HAVE HIM... HE'S TAKEN

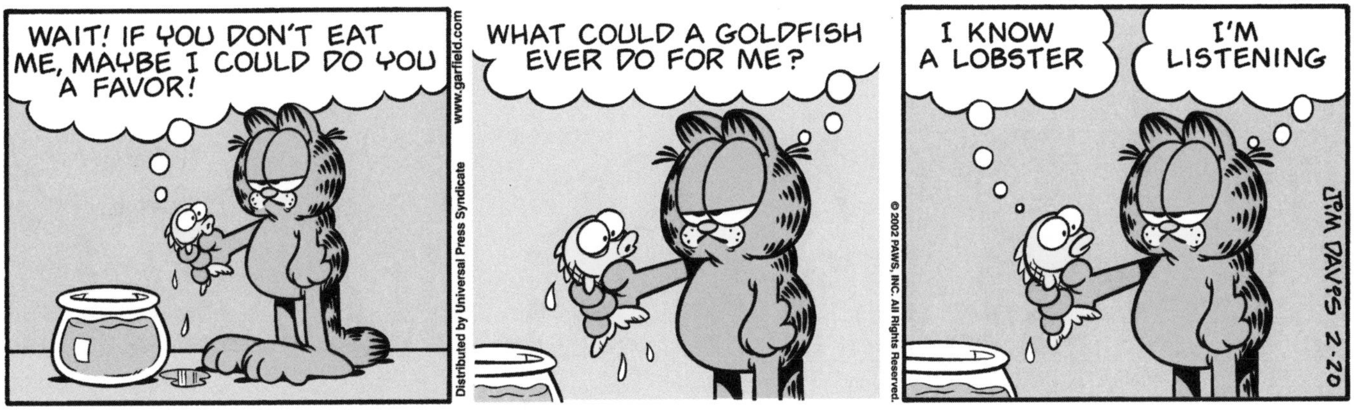
WAIT! IF YOU DON'T EAT ME, MAYBE I COULD DO YOU A FAVOR!
www.garfield.com
Distributed by Universal Press Syndicate
WHAT COULD A GOLDFISH EVER DO FOR ME?
© 2002 PAWS, INC. All Rights Reserved.
I KNOW A LOBSTER
I'M LISTENING
JIM DAVIS 2-20

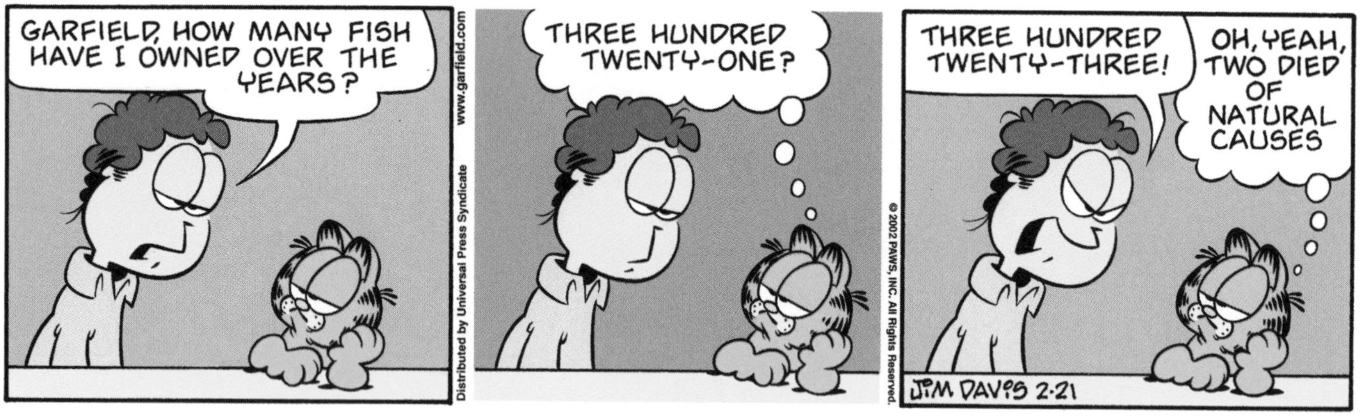
GARFIELD, HOW MANY FISH HAVE I OWNED OVER THE YEARS?
THREE HUNDRED TWENTY-ONE?
THREE HUNDRED TWENTY-THREE!
OH, YEAH, TWO DIED OF NATURAL CAUSES
JIM DAVIS 2-21
www.garfield.com
Distributed by Universal Press Syndicate
© 2002 PAWS, INC. All Rights Reserved.

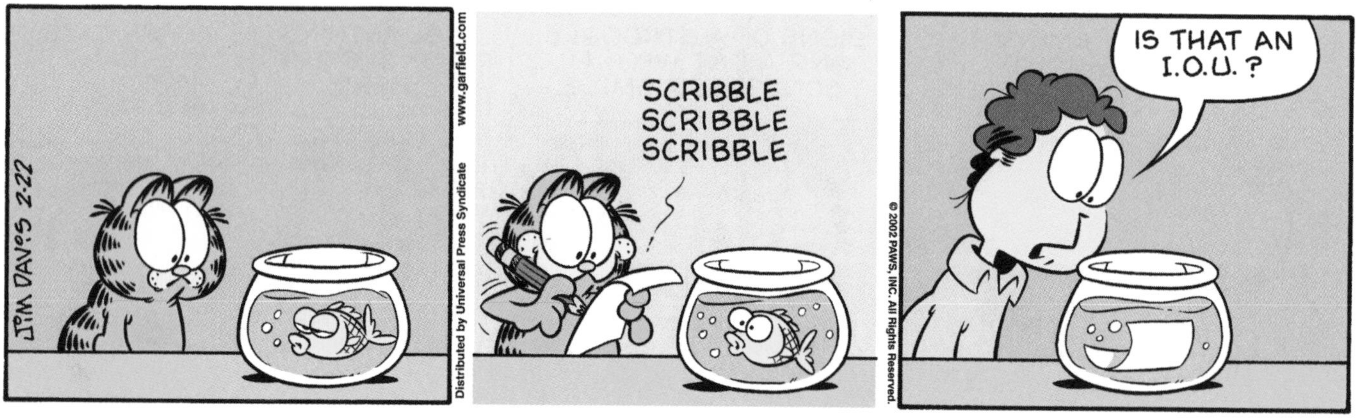
JIM DAVIS 2-22
SCRIBBLE SCRIBBLE SCRIBBLE
IS THAT AN I.O.U.?
www.garfield.com
Distributed by Universal Press Syndicate
© 2002 PAWS, INC. All Rights Reserved.

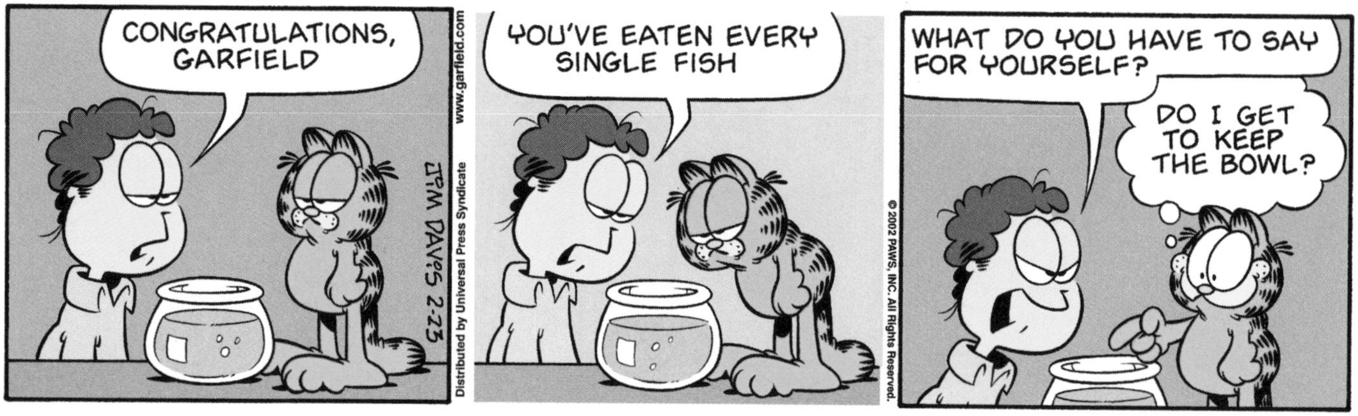
CONGRATULATIONS, GARFIELD
JIM DAVIS 2-23
YOU'VE EATEN EVERY SINGLE FISH
WHAT DO YOU HAVE TO SAY FOR YOURSELF?
DO I GET TO KEEP THE BOWL?
www.garfield.com
Distributed by Universal Press Syndicate
© 2002 PAWS, INC. All Rights Reserved.

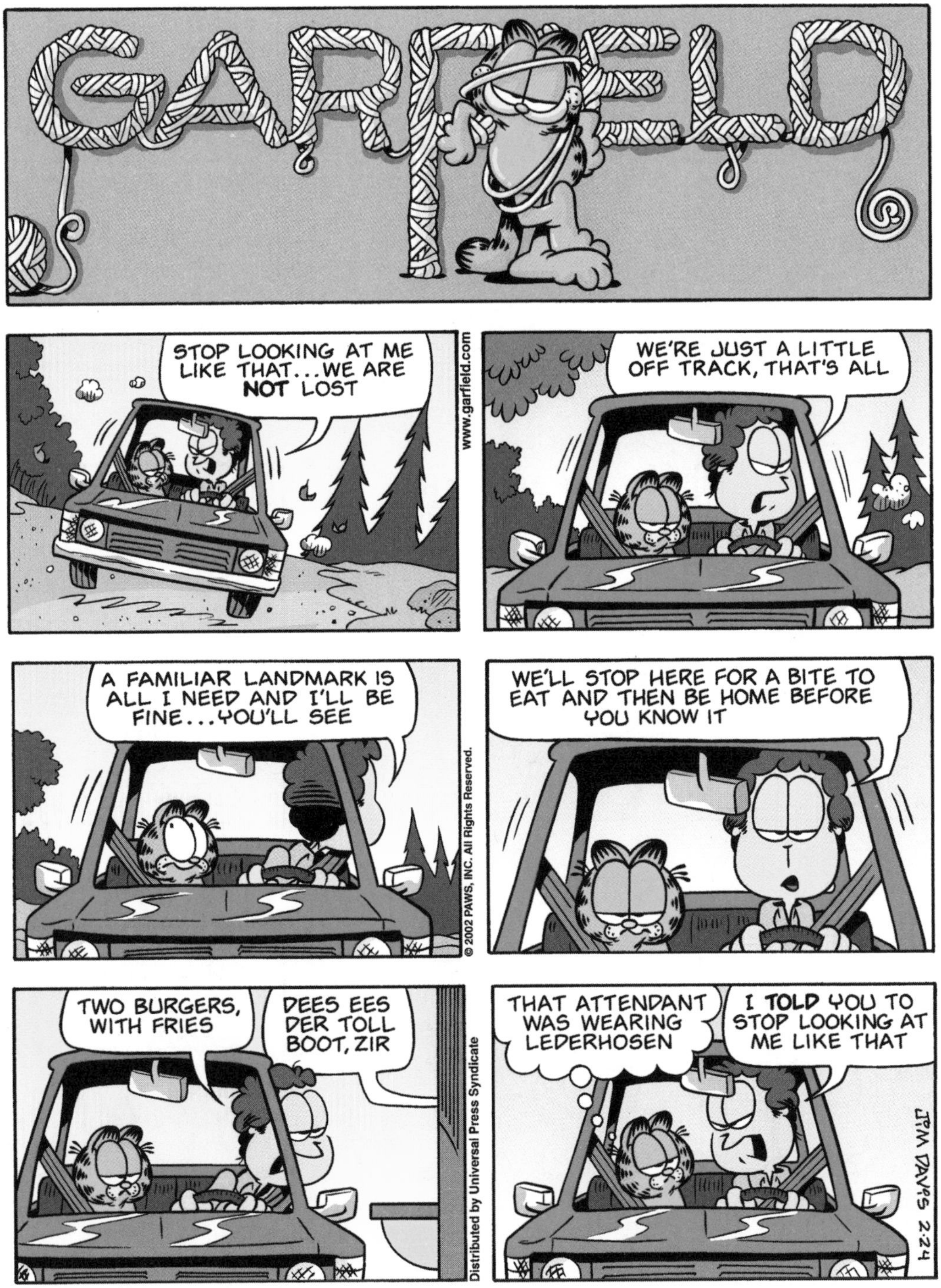
GARFIELD
STOP LOOKING AT ME LIKE THAT...WE ARE NOT LOST
WE'RE JUST A LITTLE OFF TRACK, THAT'S ALL
A FAMILIAR LANDMARK IS ALL I NEED AND I'LL BE FINE...YOU'LL SEE
WE'LL STOP HERE FOR A BITE TO EAT AND THEN BE HOME BEFORE YOU KNOW IT
TWO BURGERS, WITH FRIES
DEES EES DER TOLL BOOT, ZIR
THAT ATTENDANT WAS WEARING LEDERHOSEN
I TOLD YOU TO STOP LOOKING AT ME LIKE THAT
JIM DAVIS 2-24

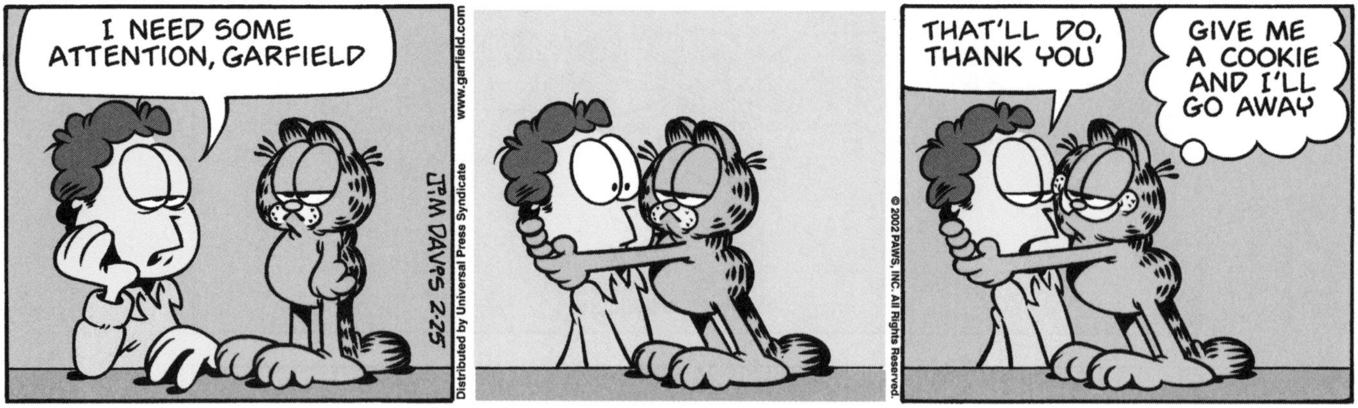
I NEED SOME ATTENTION, GARFIELD
JIM DAVIS 2-25
www.garfield.com
Distributed by Universal Press Syndicate
THAT'LL DO, THANK YOU
GIVE ME A COOKIE AND I'LL GO AWAY
© 2002 PAWS, INC. All Rights Reserved.

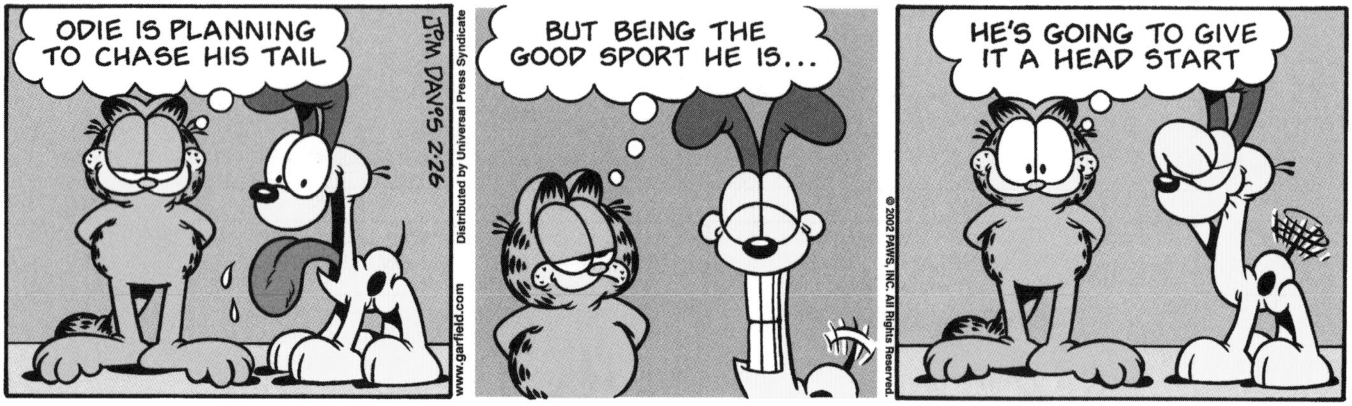
ODIE IS PLANNING TO CHASE HIS TAIL
JIM DAVIS 2-26
Distributed by Universal Press Syndicate
www.garfield.com
BUT BEING THE GOOD SPORT HE IS...
HE'S GOING TO GIVE IT A HEAD START
© 2002 PAWS, INC. All Rights Reserved.

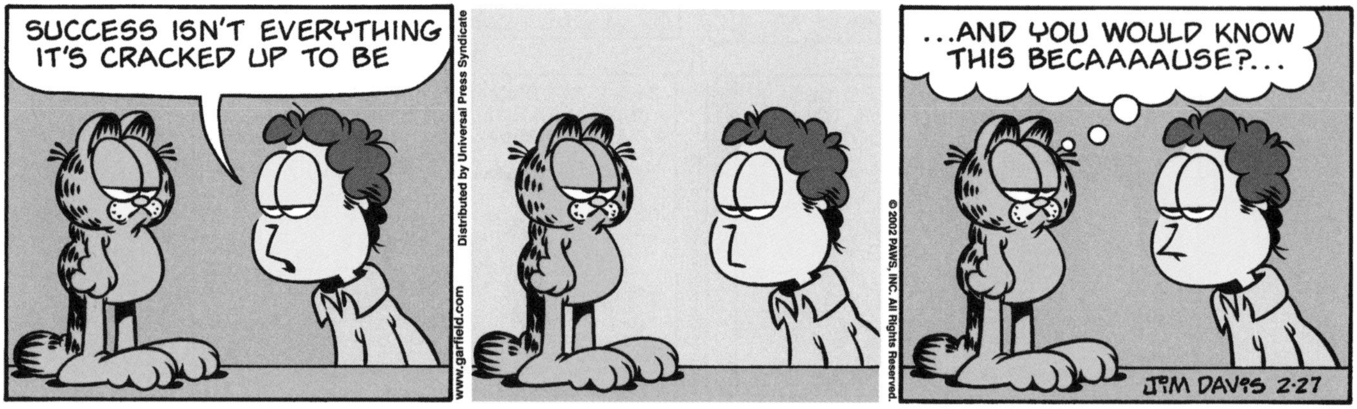
SUCCESS ISN'T EVERYTHING IT'S CRACKED UP TO BE
Distributed by Universal Press Syndicate
www.garfield.com
...AND YOU WOULD KNOW THIS BECAAAAUSE?...
© 2002 PAWS, INC. All Rights Reserved.
JIM DAVIS 2-27

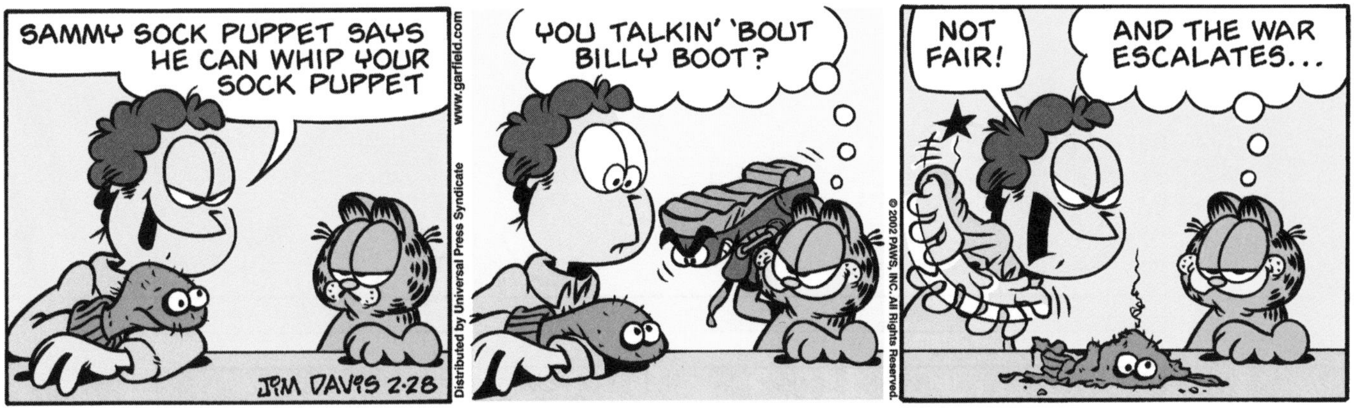
SAMMY SOCK PUPPET SAYS HE CAN WHIP YOUR SOCK PUPPET
JIM DAVIS 2-28
Distributed by Universal Press Syndicate www.garfield.com
YOU TALKIN' 'BOUT BILLY BOOT?
© 2002 PAWS, INC. All Rights Reserved.
NOT FAIR!
AND THE WAR ESCALATES...

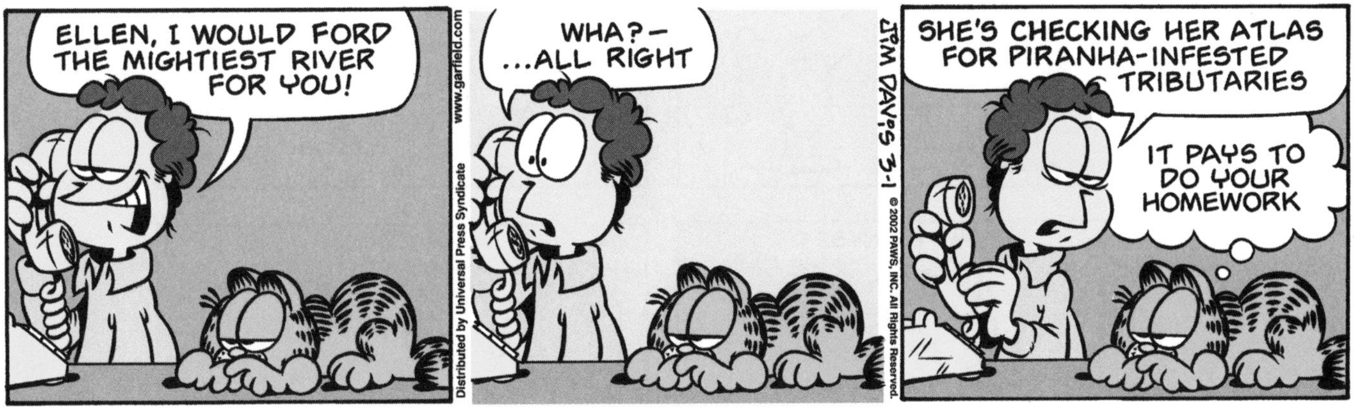
ELLEN, I WOULD FORD THE MIGHTIEST RIVER FOR YOU!
Distributed by Universal Press Syndicate www.garfield.com
WHA?– ...ALL RIGHT
JIM DAVIS 3-1
© 2002 PAWS, INC. All Rights Reserved.
SHE'S CHECKING HER ATLAS FOR PIRANHA-INFESTED TRIBUTARIES
IT PAYS TO DO YOUR HOMEWORK

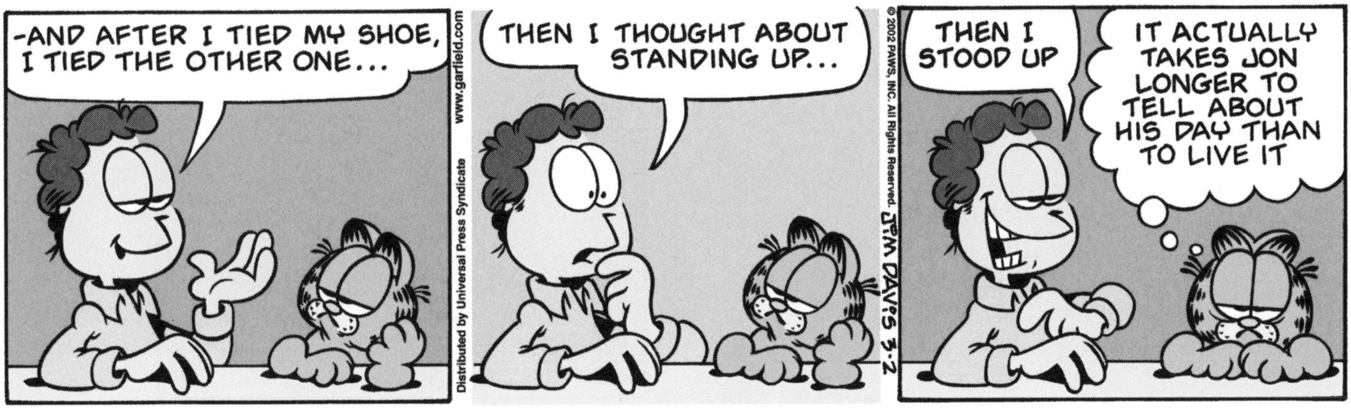
-AND AFTER I TIED MY SHOE, I TIED THE OTHER ONE...
Distributed by Universal Press Syndicate www.garfield.com
THEN I THOUGHT ABOUT STANDING UP...
© 2002 PAWS, INC. All Rights Reserved.
JIM DAVIS 3-2
THEN I STOOD UP
IT ACTUALLY TAKES JON LONGER TO TELL ABOUT HIS DAY THAN TO LIVE IT

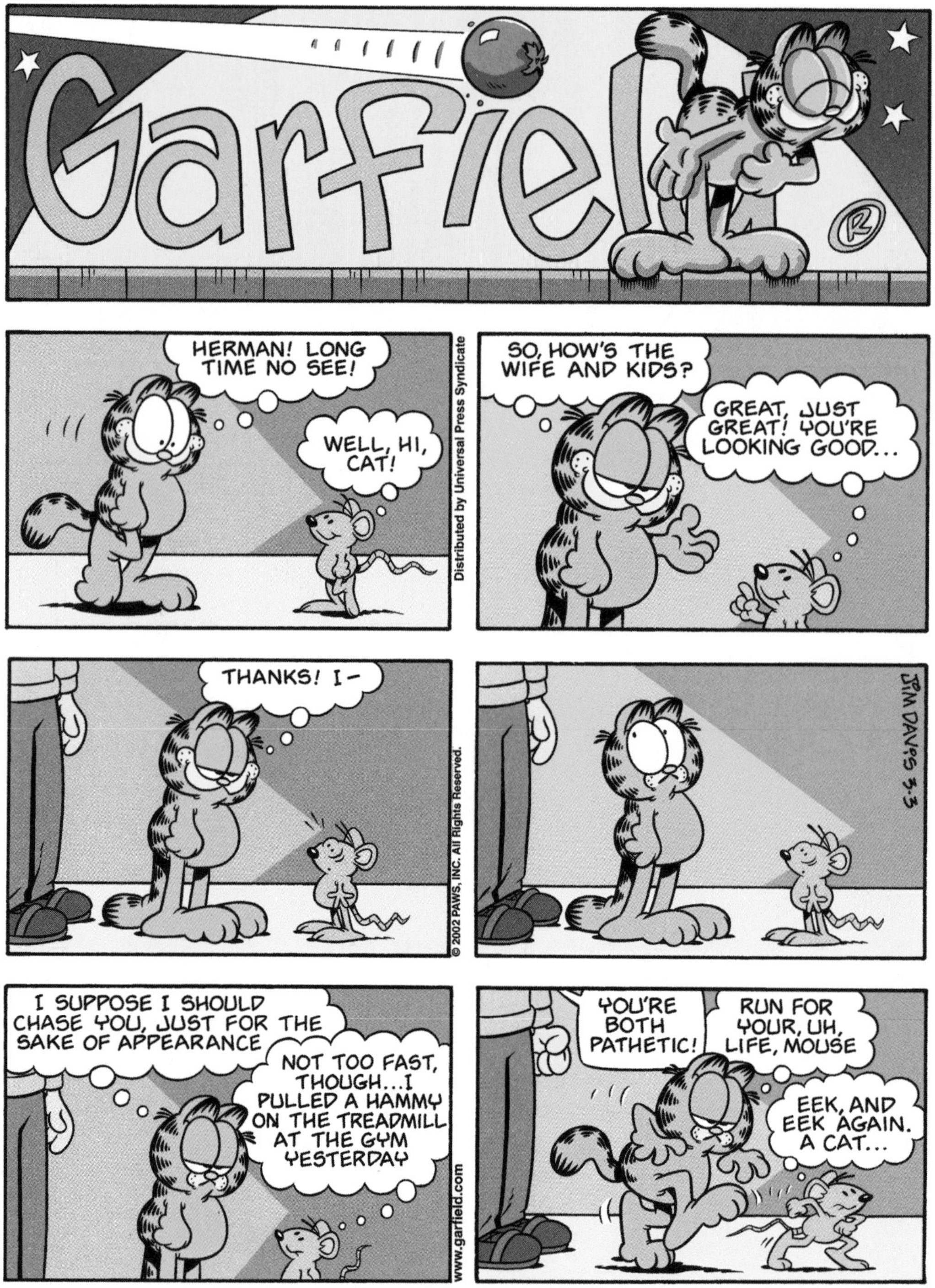
Garfield®
HERMAN! LONG TIME NO SEE!
WELL, HI, CAT!
Distributed by Universal Press Syndicate
SO, HOW'S THE WIFE AND KIDS?
GREAT, JUST GREAT! YOU'RE LOOKING GOOD...
THANKS! I–
© 2002 PAWS, INC. All Rights Reserved.
JIM DAVIS 3-3
I SUPPOSE I SHOULD CHASE YOU, JUST FOR THE SAKE OF APPEARANCE
NOT TOO FAST, THOUGH...I PULLED A HAMMY ON THE TREADMILL AT THE GYM YESTERDAY
www.garfield.com
YOU'RE BOTH PATHETIC!
RUN FOR YOUR, UH, LIFE, MOUSE
EEK, AND EEK AGAIN. A CAT...

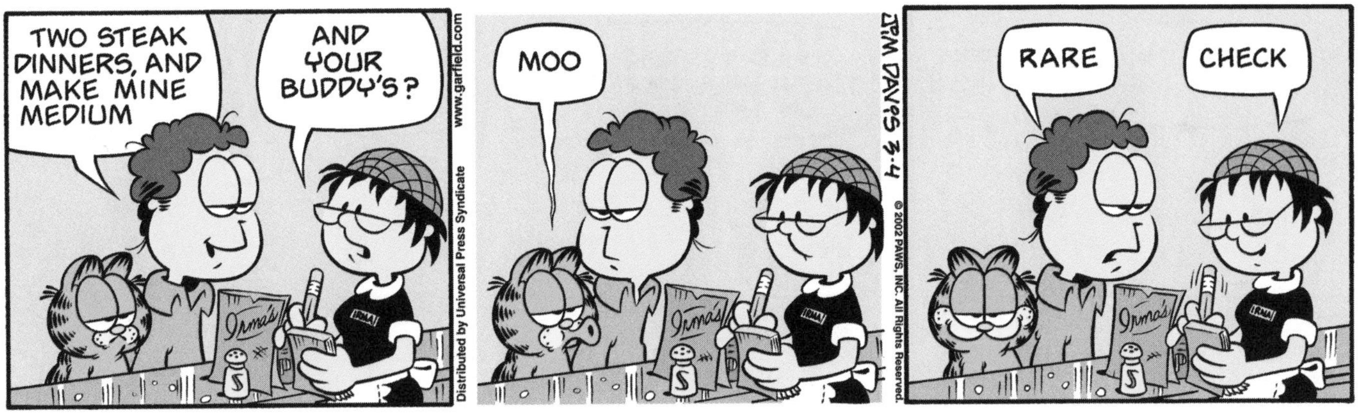
TWO STEAK DINNERS, AND MAKE MINE MEDIUM
AND YOUR BUDDY'S?
www.garfield.com
Distributed by Universal Press Syndicate
MOO
JIM DAVIS 3-4
© 2002 PAWS, INC. All Rights Reserved.
RARE
CHECK

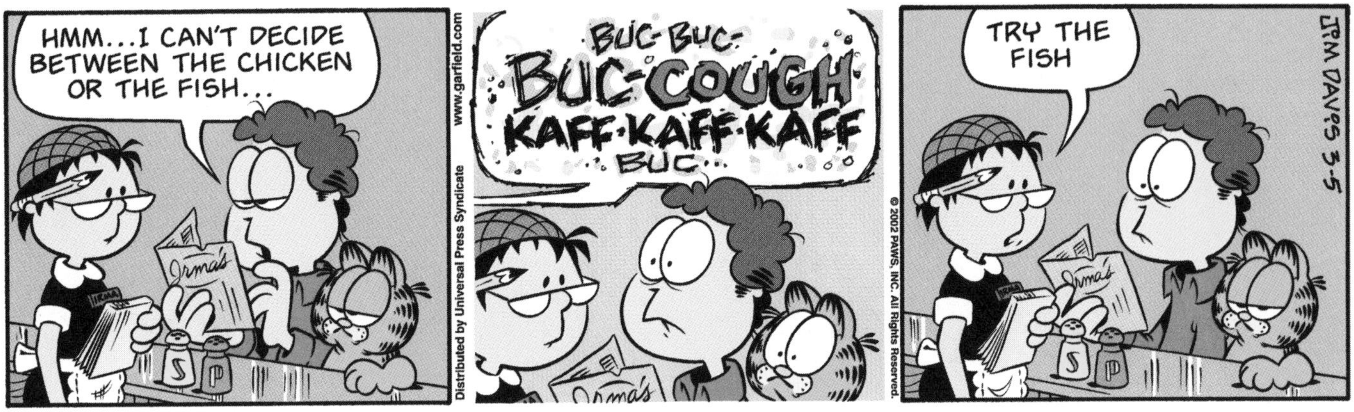
HMM...I CAN'T DECIDE BETWEEN THE CHICKEN OR THE FISH...
www.garfield.com
Distributed by Universal Press Syndicate
BUC-BUC-
BUC-COUGH
KAFF-KAFF-KAFF
BUC
© 2002 PAWS, INC. All Rights Reserved.
JIM DAVIS 3-5
TRY THE FISH

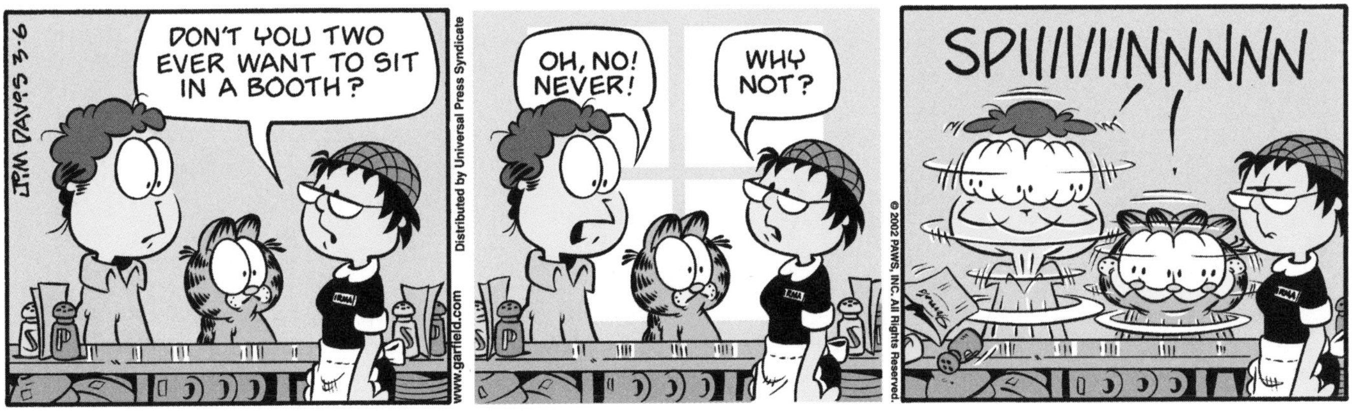
JIM DAVIS 3-6
DON'T YOU TWO EVER WANT TO SIT IN A BOOTH?
Distributed by Universal Press Syndicate
www.garfield.com
OH, NO! NEVER!
WHY NOT?
© 2002 PAWS, INC. All Rights Reserved.
SPIIIIIINNNNN

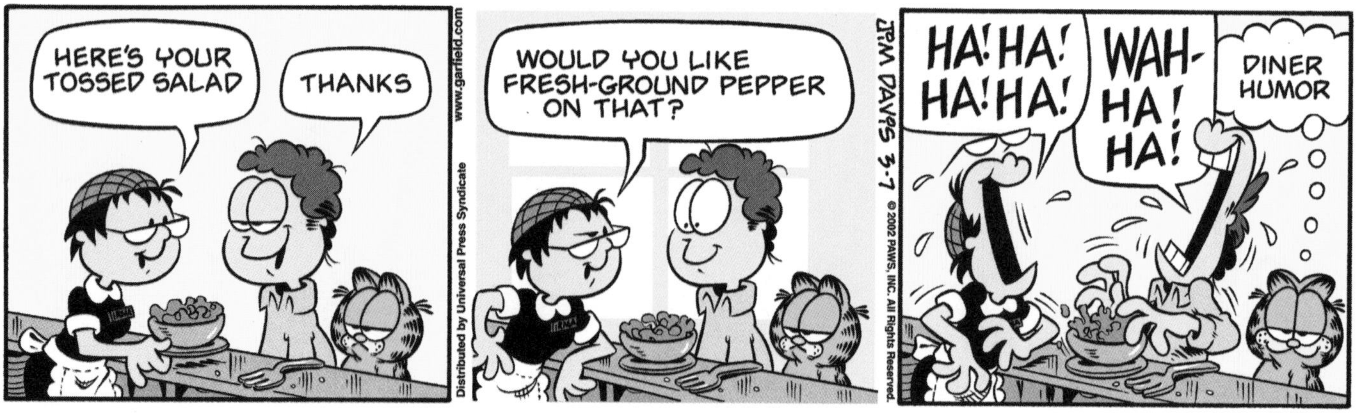
HERE'S YOUR TOSSED SALAD
THANKS
WOULD YOU LIKE FRESH-GROUND PEPPER ON THAT?
HA! HA! HA! HA!
WAH-HA! HA!
DINER HUMOR
JPM DAVIS 3-7
www.garfield.com
Distributed by Universal Press Syndicate
© 2002 PAWS, INC. All Rights Reserved.

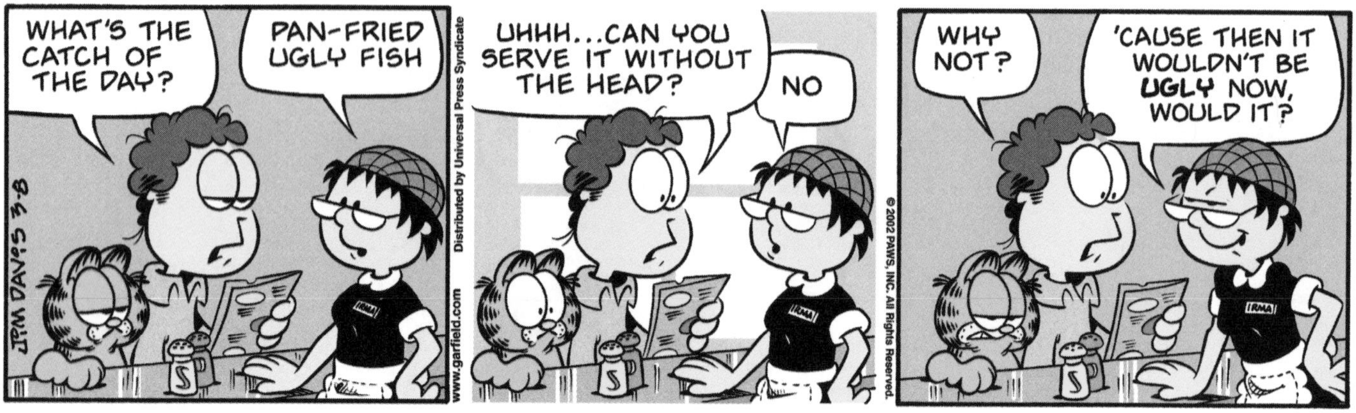
WHAT'S THE CATCH OF THE DAY?
PAN-FRIED UGLY FISH
UHHH...CAN YOU SERVE IT WITHOUT THE HEAD?
NO
WHY NOT?
'CAUSE THEN IT WOULDN'T BE **UGLY** NOW, WOULD IT?
JPM DAVIS 3-8
Distributed by Universal Press Syndicate
www.garfield.com
© 2002 PAWS, INC. All Rights Reserved.

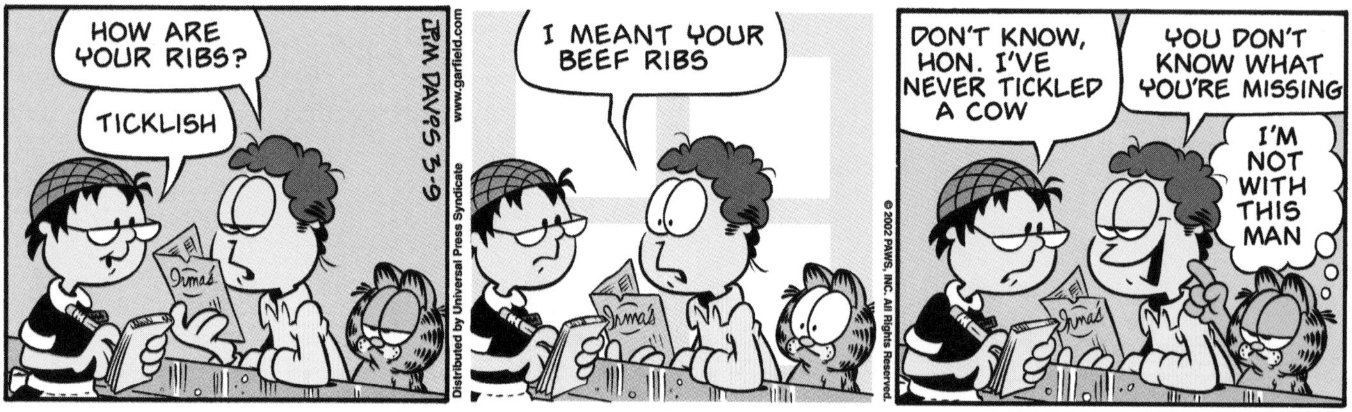
HOW ARE YOUR RIBS?
TICKLISH
I MEANT YOUR BEEF RIBS
DON'T KNOW, HON. I'VE NEVER TICKLED A COW
YOU DON'T KNOW WHAT YOU'RE MISSING
I'M NOT WITH THIS MAN
JPM DAVIS 3-9
www.garfield.com
Distributed by Universal Press Syndicate
© 2002 PAWS, INC. All Rights Reserved.

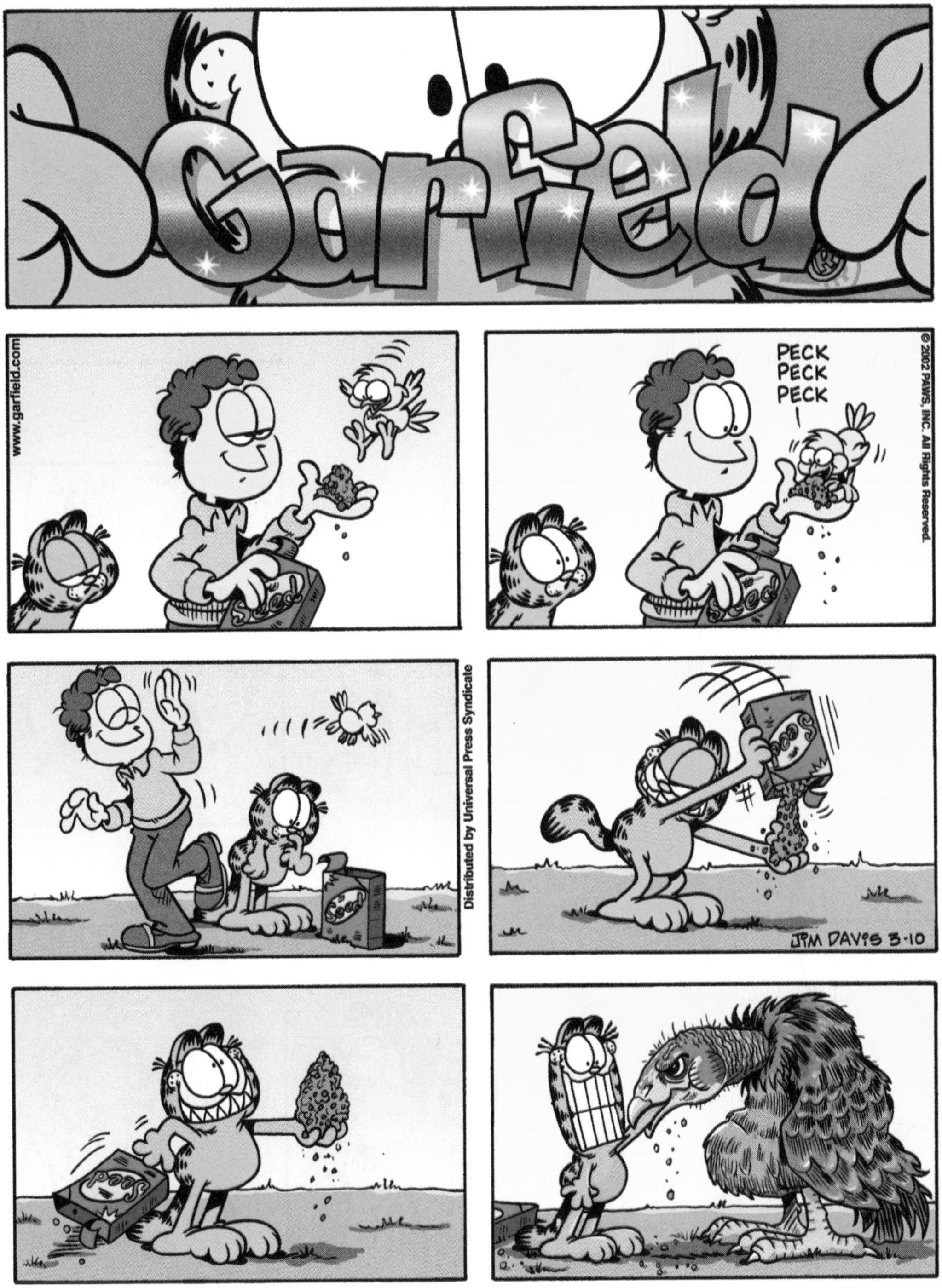
Garfield
www.garfield.com
PECK
PECK
PECK
© 2002 PAWS, INC. All Rights Reserved.
Distributed by Universal Press Syndicate
JIM DAVIS 3-10

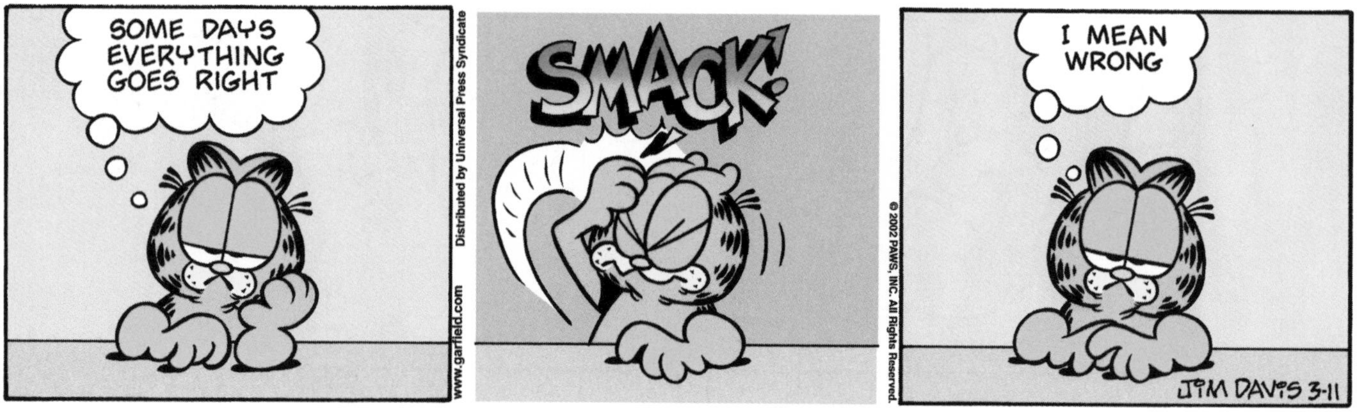
SOME DAYS EVERYTHING GOES RIGHT
SMACK!
I MEAN WRONG
JIM DAVIS 3-11
Distributed by Universal Press Syndicate
www.garfield.com
© 2002 PAWS, INC. All Rights Reserved.

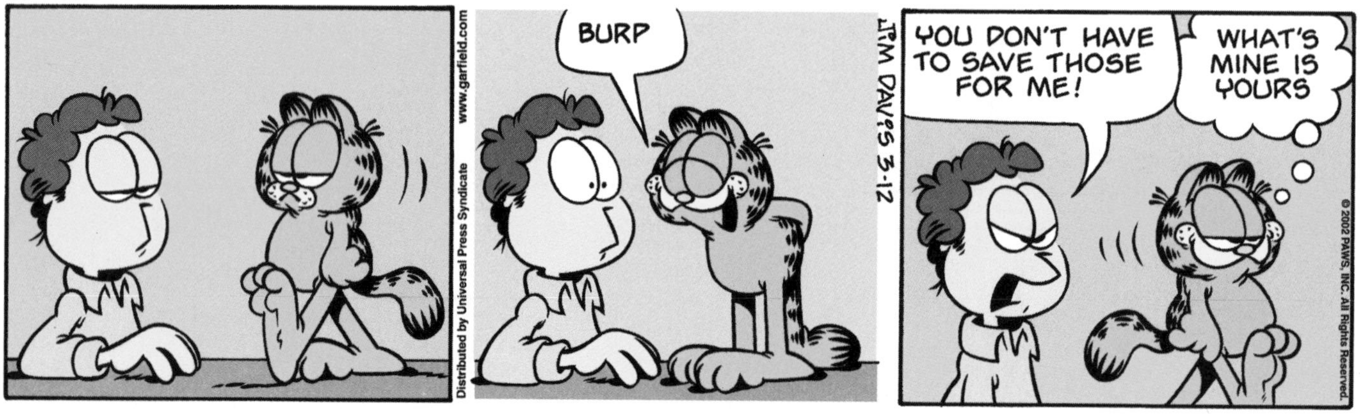
BURP
YOU DON'T HAVE TO SAVE THOSE FOR ME!
WHAT'S MINE IS YOURS
JIM DAVIS 3-12
Distributed by Universal Press Syndicate
www.garfield.com
© 2002 PAWS, INC. All Rights Reserved.

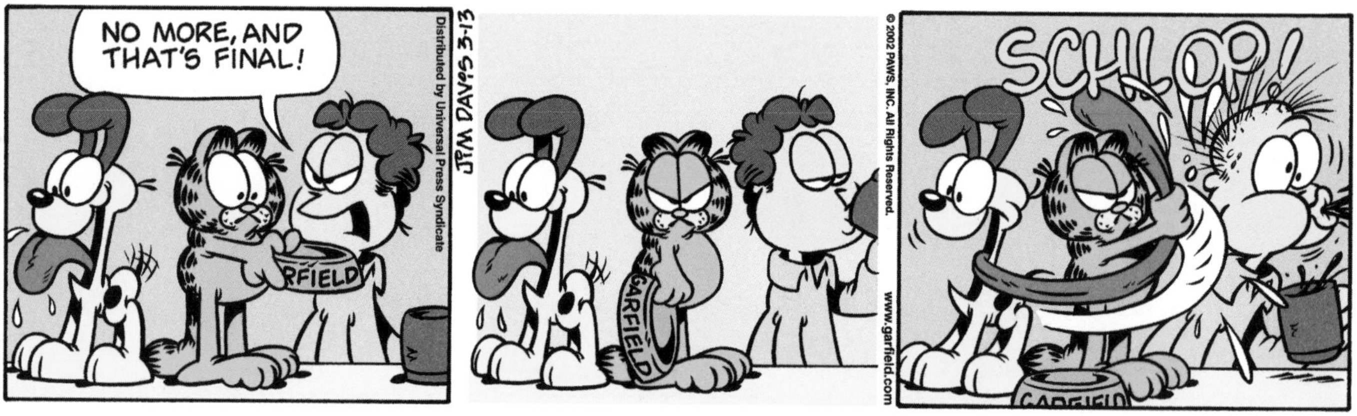
NO MORE, AND THAT'S FINAL!
GARFIELD
SCHLOP!
JIM DAVIS 3-13
Distributed by Universal Press Syndicate
© 2002 PAWS, INC. All Rights Reserved.
www.garfield.com

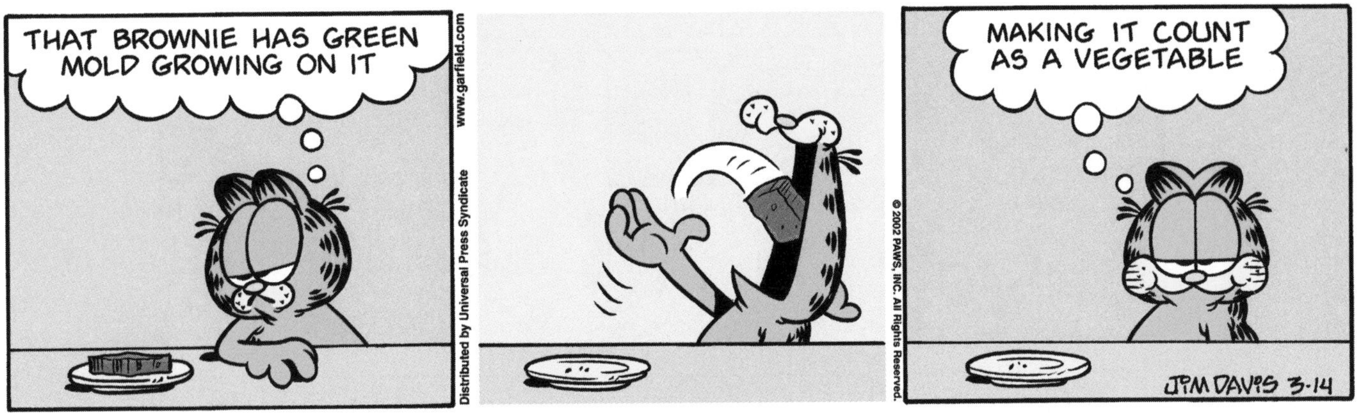
THAT BROWNIE HAS GREEN MOLD GROWING ON IT
MAKING IT COUNT AS A VEGETABLE
JIM DAVIS 3-14
www.garfield.com
Distributed by Universal Press Syndicate
© 2002 PAWS, INC. All Rights Reserved.

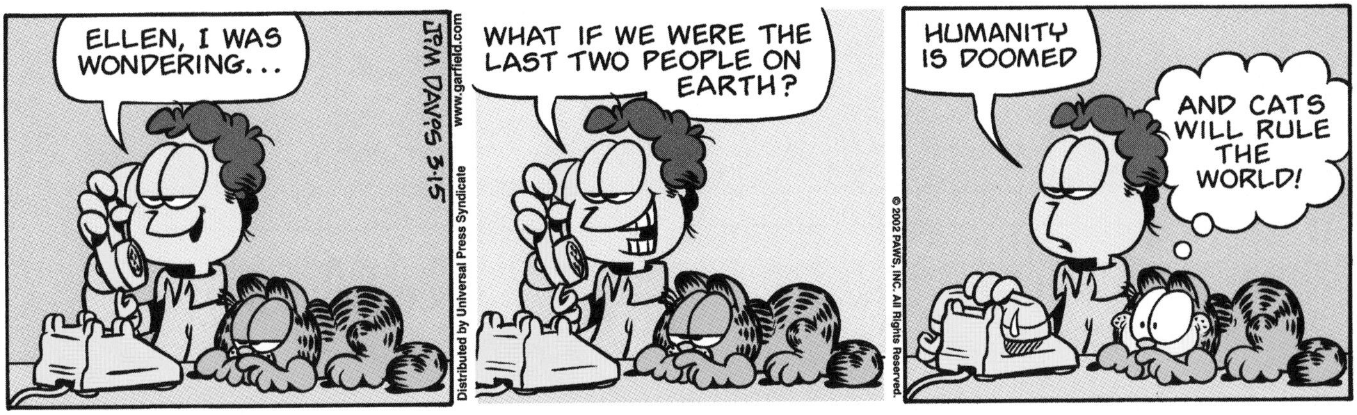
ELLEN, I WAS WONDERING...
JIM DAVIS 3-15
www.garfield.com
Distributed by Universal Press Syndicate
WHAT IF WE WERE THE LAST TWO PEOPLE ON EARTH?
© 2002 PAWS, INC. All Rights Reserved.
HUMANITY IS DOOMED
AND CATS WILL RULE THE WORLD!

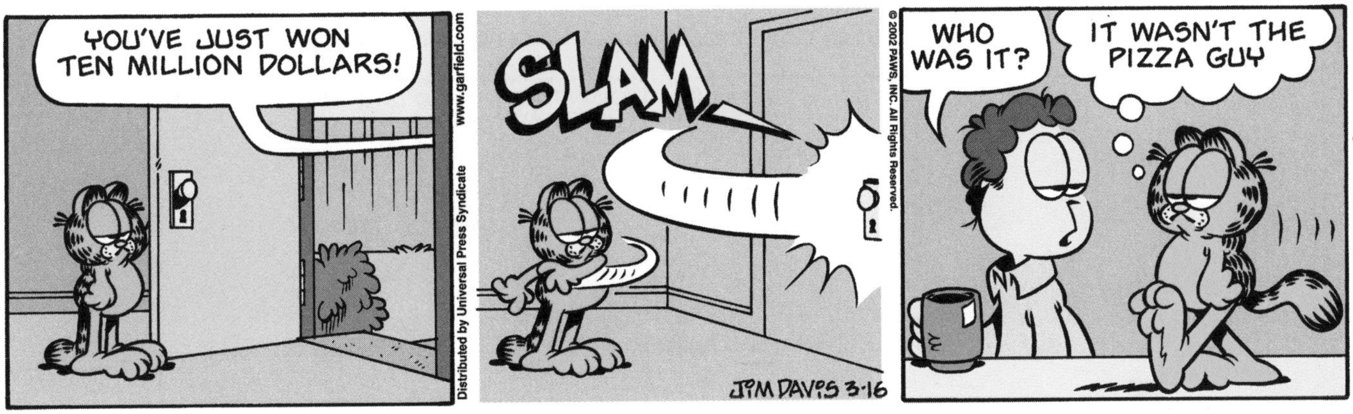
YOU'VE JUST WON TEN MILLION DOLLARS!
www.garfield.com
Distributed by Universal Press Syndicate
SLAM
JIM DAVIS 3-16
© 2002 PAWS, INC. All Rights Reserved.
WHO WAS IT?
IT WASN'T THE PIZZA GUY

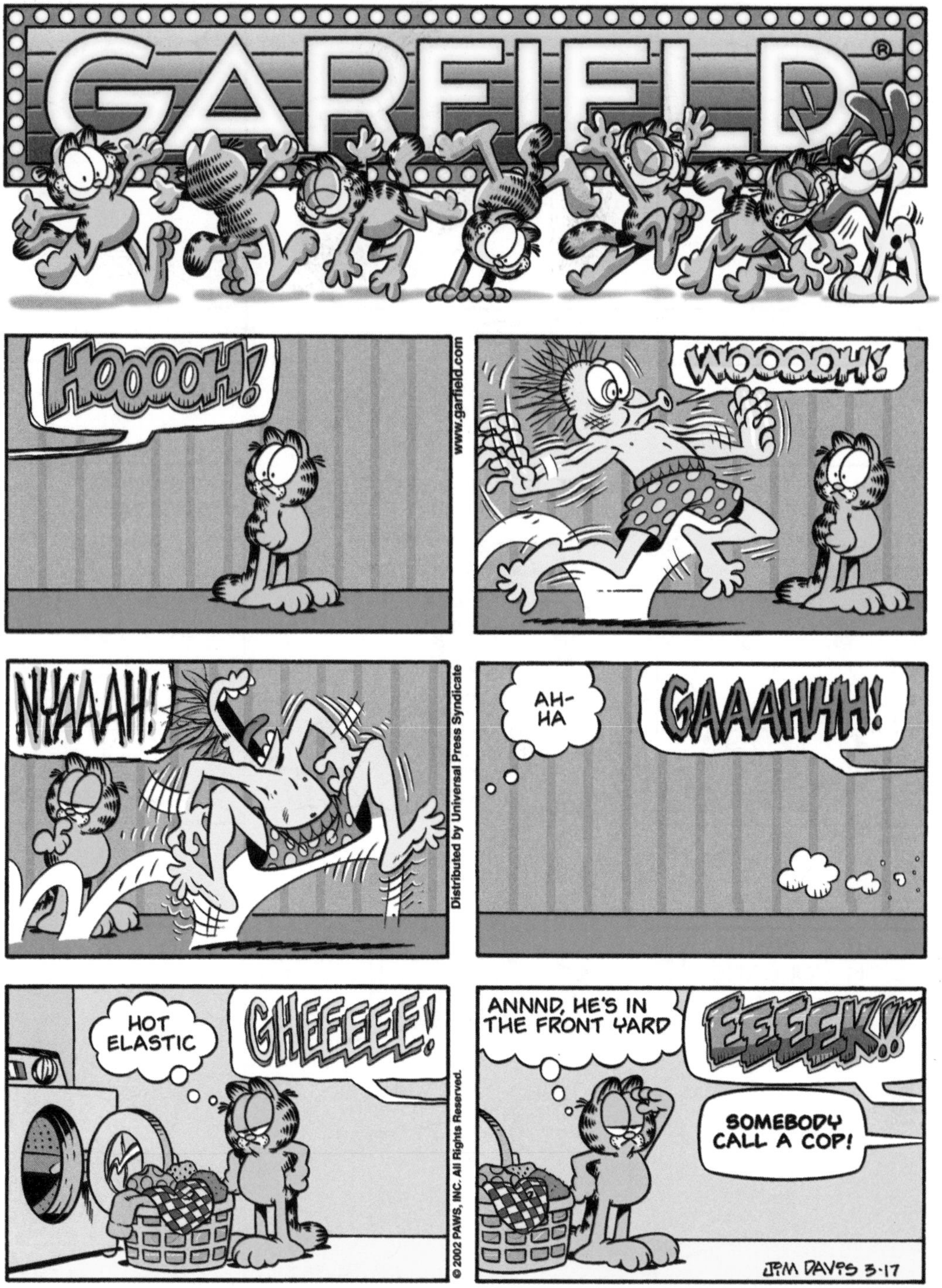
GARFIELD
HOOOOH!
WOOOOH!
NYAAAH!
AH-HA
GAAAHHH!
HOT ELASTIC
GHEEEEE!
ANNND, HE'S IN THE FRONT YARD
EEEEK!!
SOMEBODY CALL A COP!
JIM DAVIS 3-17

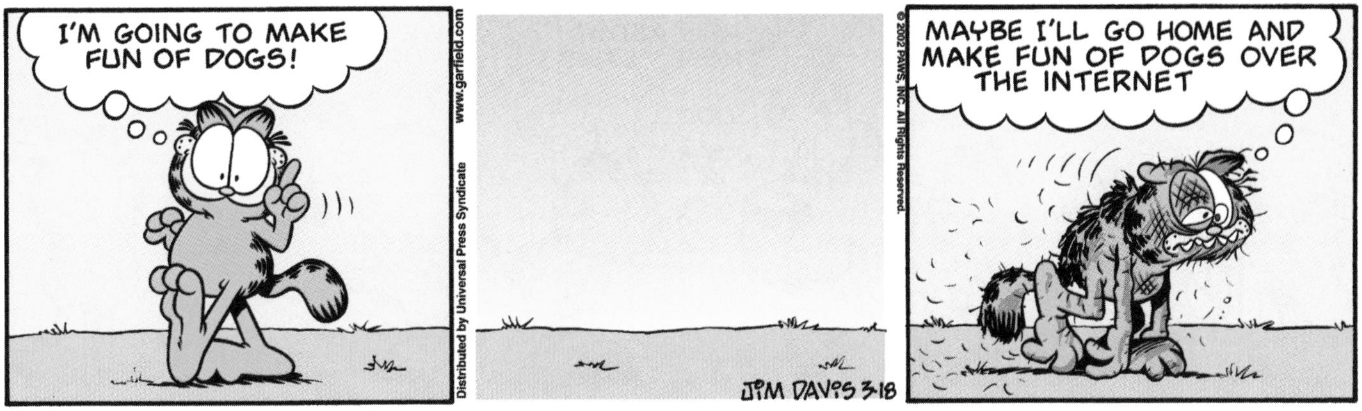
I'M GOING TO MAKE FUN OF DOGS!
MAYBE I'LL GO HOME AND MAKE FUN OF DOGS OVER THE INTERNET
JIM DAVIS 3-18
Distributed by Universal Press Syndicate www.garfield.com
© 2002 PAWS, INC. All Rights Reserved.

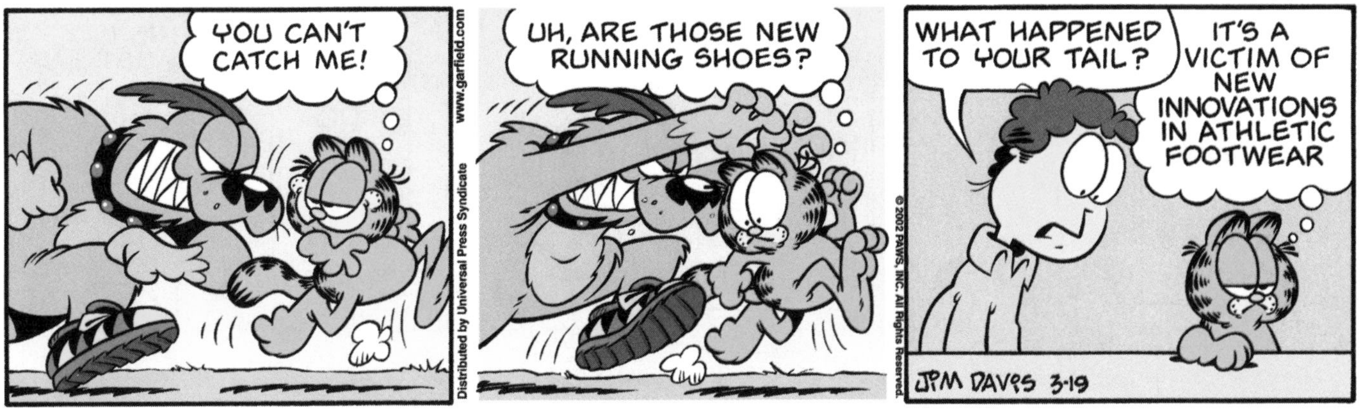
YOU CAN'T CATCH ME!
UH, ARE THOSE NEW RUNNING SHOES?
WHAT HAPPENED TO YOUR TAIL?
IT'S A VICTIM OF NEW INNOVATIONS IN ATHLETIC FOOTWEAR
JIM DAVIS 3-19
Distributed by Universal Press Syndicate www.garfield.com
© 2002 PAWS, INC. All Rights Reserved.

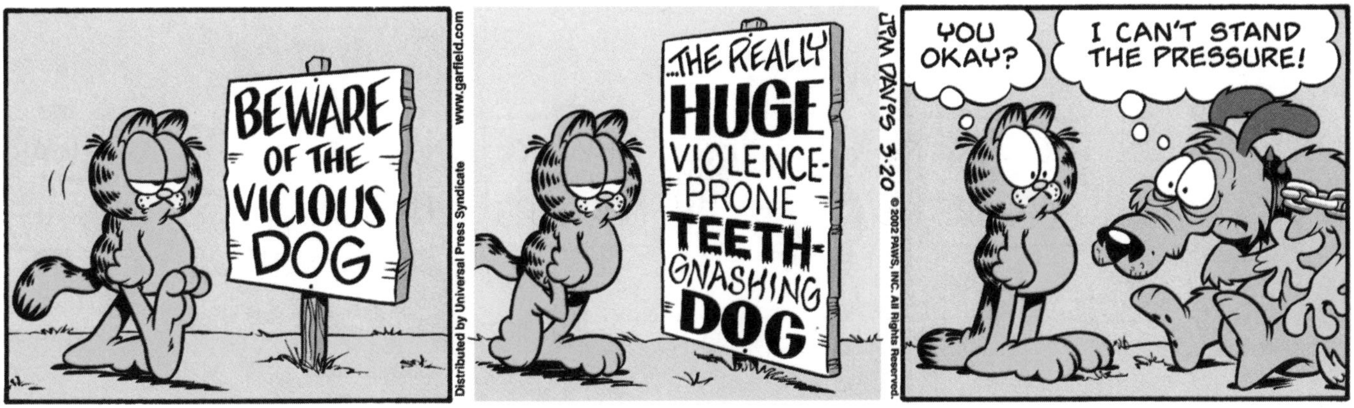
BEWARE OF THE VICIOUS DOG
...THE REALLY HUGE VIOLENCE-PRONE TEETH-GNASHING DOG
YOU OKAY?
I CAN'T STAND THE PRESSURE!
JIM DAVIS 3-20
Distributed by Universal Press Syndicate www.garfield.com
© 2002 PAWS, INC. All Rights Reserved.

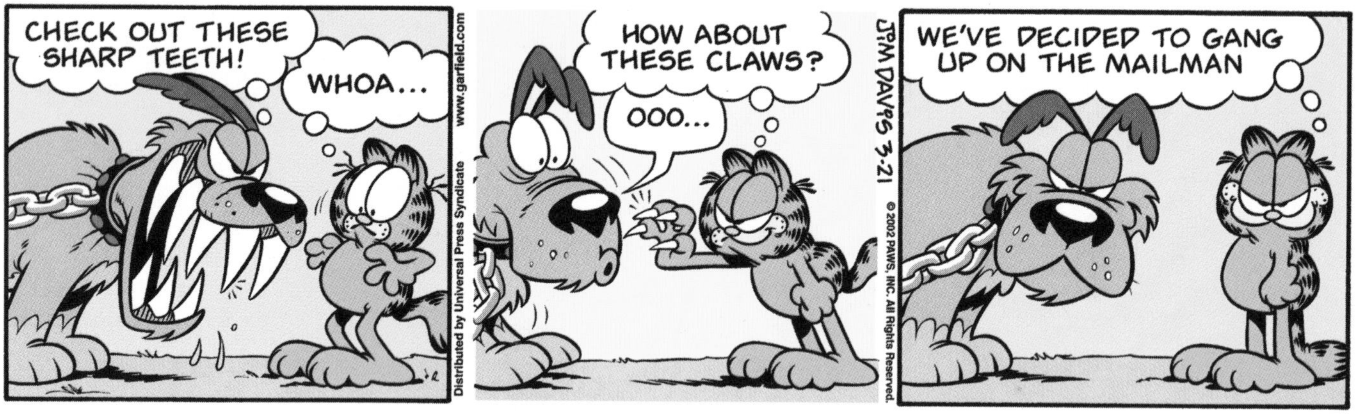
CHECK OUT THESE SHARP TEETH!
WHOA...
HOW ABOUT THESE CLAWS?
OOO...
WE'VE DECIDED TO GANG UP ON THE MAILMAN
JIM DAVIS 3-21
Distributed by Universal Press Syndicate www.garfield.com
© 2002 PAWS, INC. All Rights Reserved.

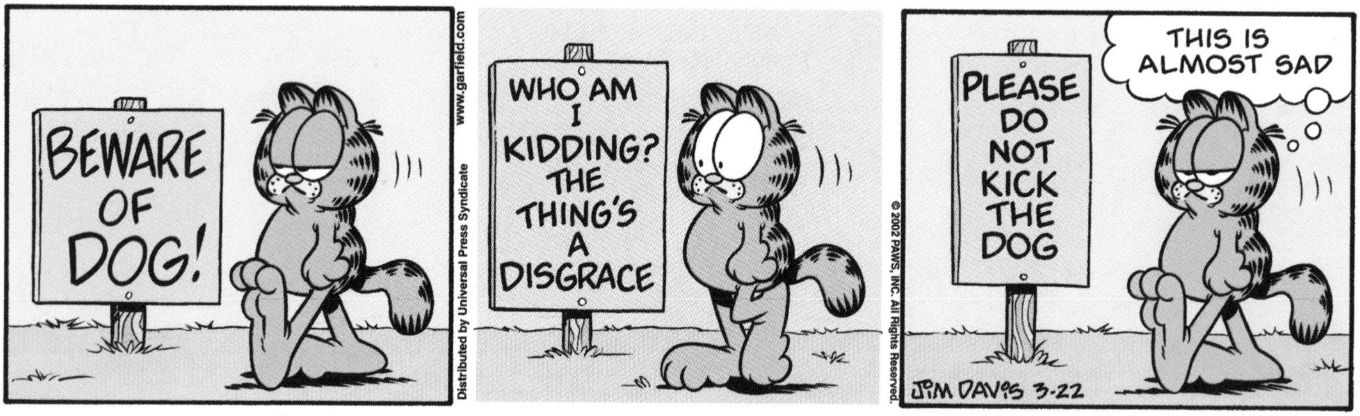
BEWARE OF DOG!
WHO AM I KIDDING? THE THING'S A DISGRACE
PLEASE DO NOT KICK THE DOG
THIS IS ALMOST SAD
JIM DAVIS 3-22
Distributed by Universal Press Syndicate www.garfield.com
© 2002 PAWS, INC. All Rights Reserved.

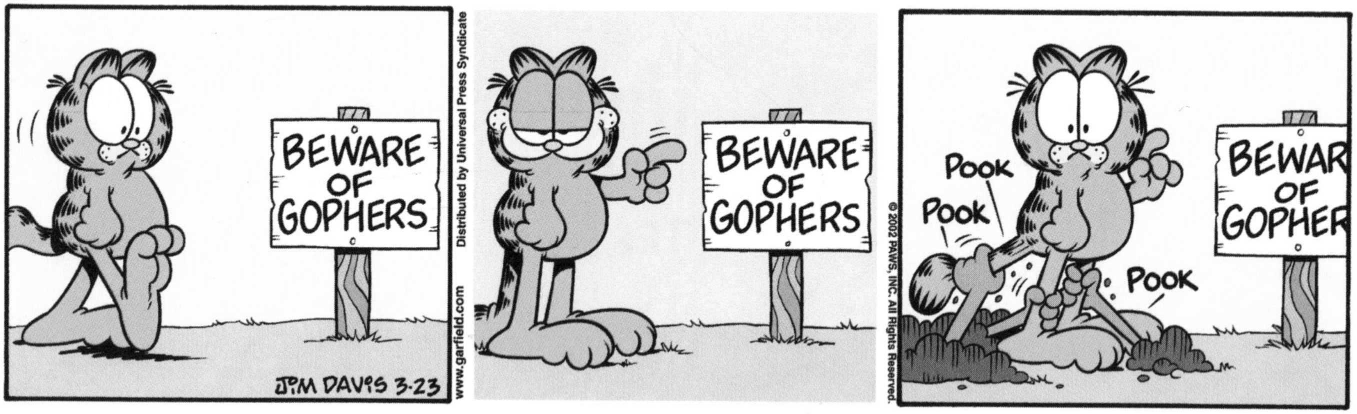
BEWARE OF GOPHERS
JIM DAVIS 3-23
BEWARE OF GOPHERS
POOK
POOK
POOK
BEWAR OF GOPHER
Distributed by Universal Press Syndicate www.garfield.com
© 2002 PAWS, INC. All Rights Reserved.

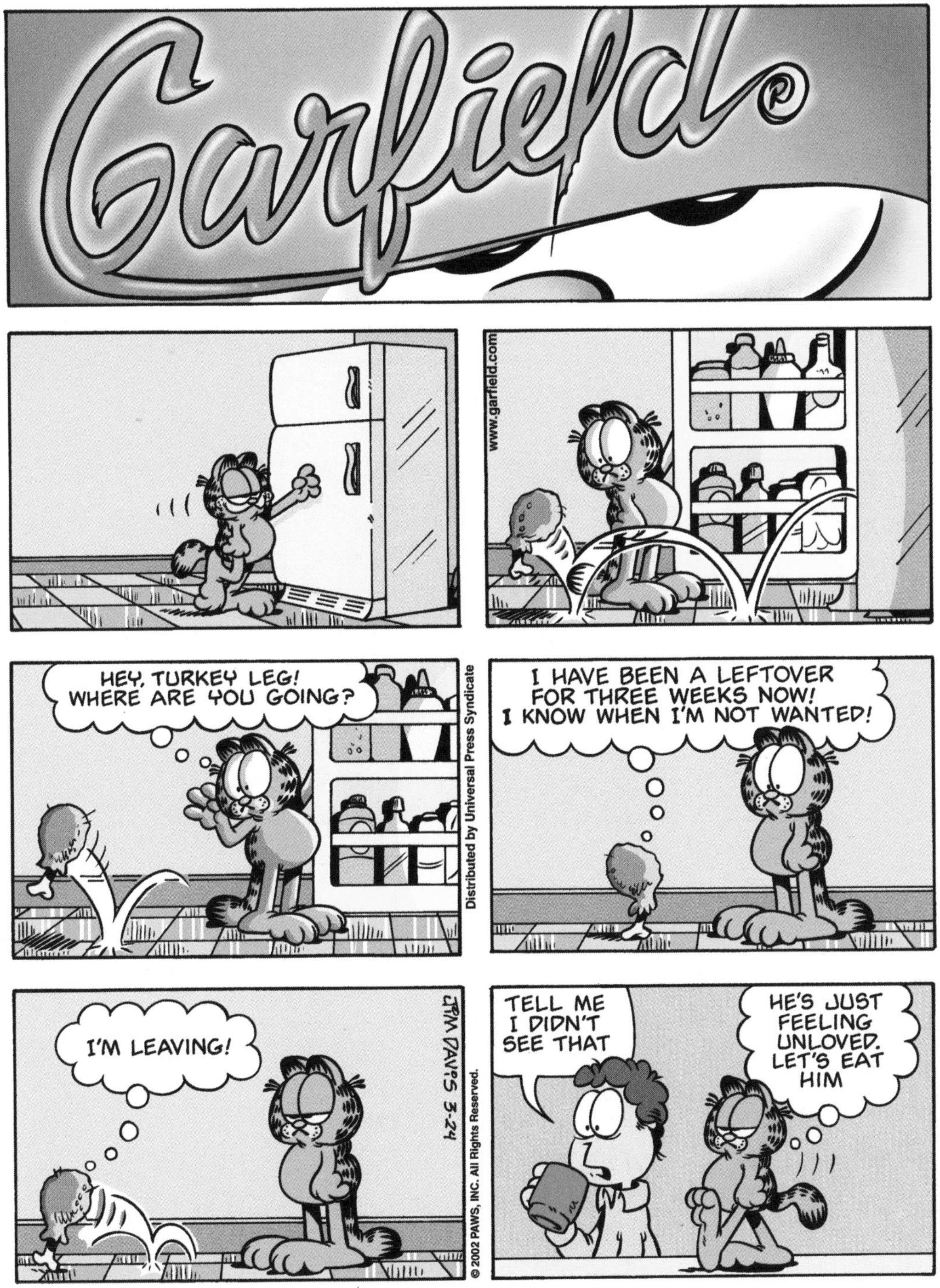
Garfield
www.garfield.com
HEY, TURKEY LEG! WHERE ARE YOU GOING?
Distributed by Universal Press Syndicate
I HAVE BEEN A LEFTOVER FOR THREE WEEKS NOW! I KNOW WHEN I'M NOT WANTED!
I'M LEAVING!
JIM DAVIS 3-24
© 2002 PAWS, INC. All Rights Reserved.
TELL ME I DIDN'T SEE THAT
HE'S JUST FEELING UNLOVED. LET'S EAT HIM

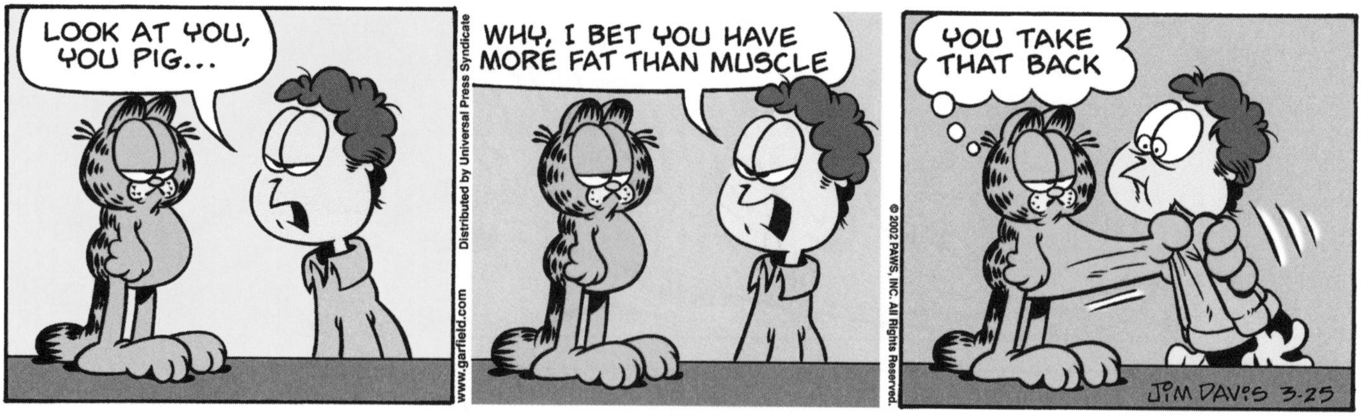
LOOK AT YOU, YOU PIG...
WHY, I BET YOU HAVE MORE FAT THAN MUSCLE
YOU TAKE THAT BACK
www.garfield.com Distributed by Universal Press Syndicate
© 2002 PAWS, INC. All Rights Reserved.
JIM DAVIS 3-25

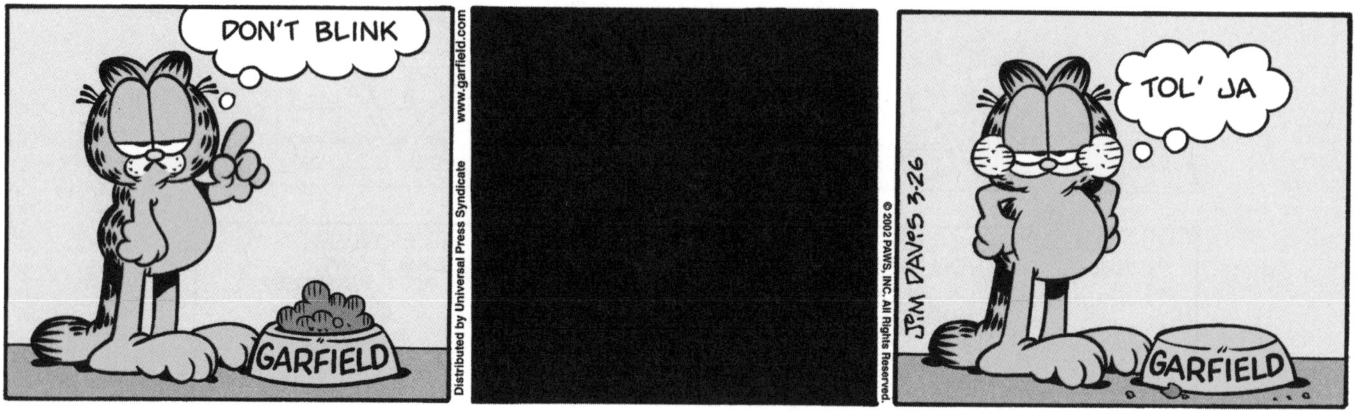
DON'T BLINK
GARFIELD
TOL' JA
GARFIELD
Distributed by Universal Press Syndicate www.garfield.com
© 2002 PAWS, INC. All Rights Reserved.
JIM DAVIS 3-26

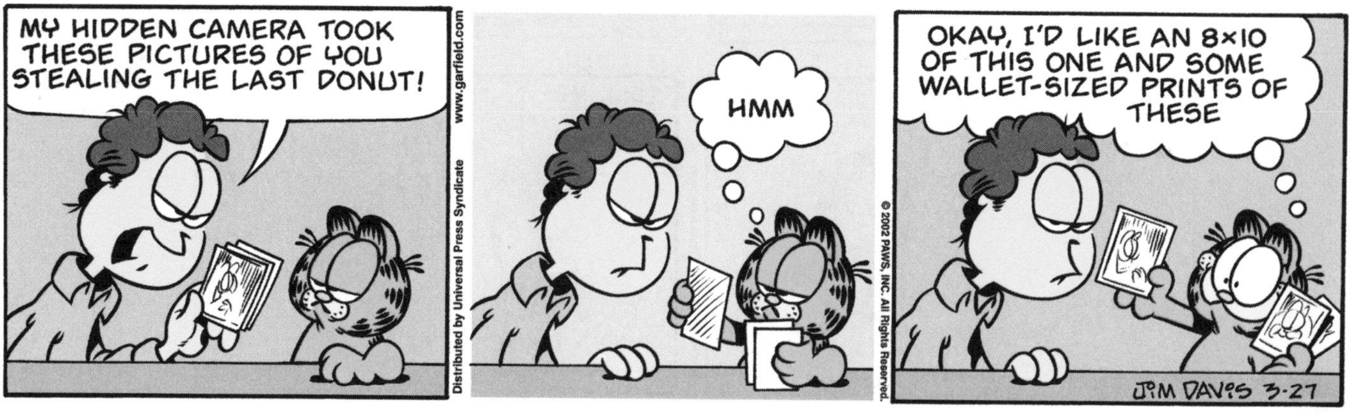
MY HIDDEN CAMERA TOOK THESE PICTURES OF YOU STEALING THE LAST DONUT!
HMM
OKAY, I'D LIKE AN 8×10 OF THIS ONE AND SOME WALLET-SIZED PRINTS OF THESE
Distributed by Universal Press Syndicate www.garfield.com
© 2002 PAWS, INC. All Rights Reserved.
JIM DAVIS 3-27

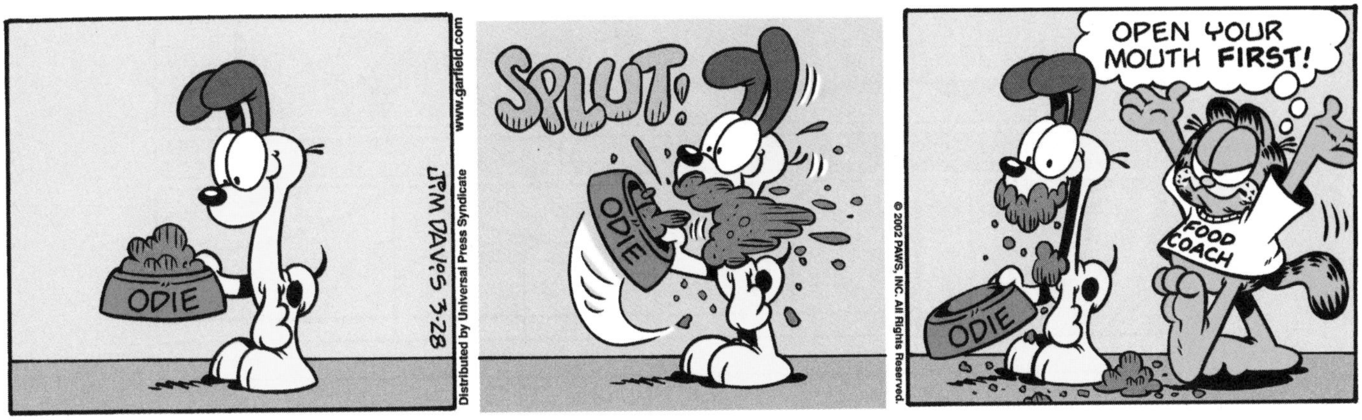
JIM DAVIS 3-28
www.garfield.com
Distributed by Universal Press Syndicate
ODIE
SPLUT!
© 2002 PAWS, INC. All Rights Reserved.
OPEN YOUR MOUTH **FIRST!**
FOOD COACH

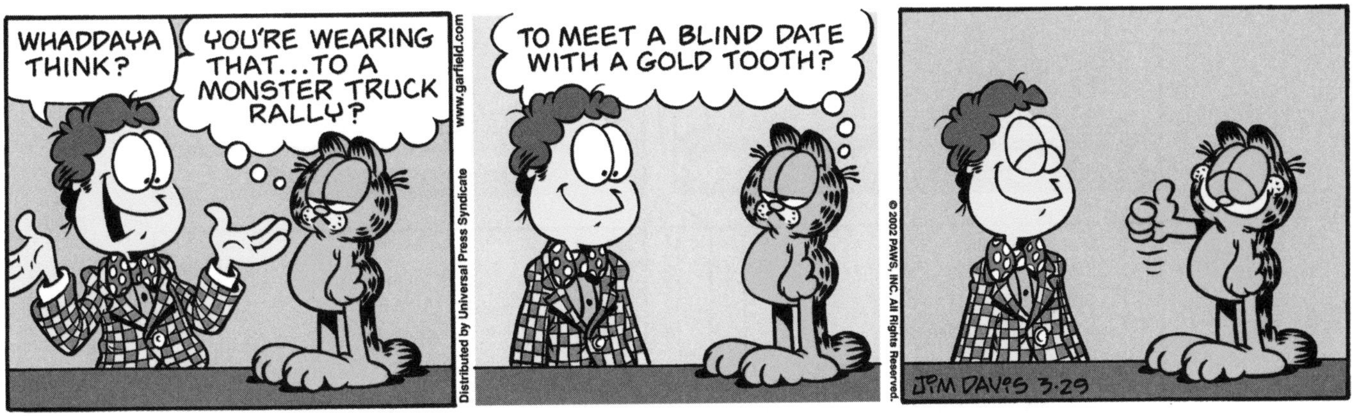
WHADDAYA THINK?
YOU'RE WEARING THAT...TO A MONSTER TRUCK RALLY?
www.garfield.com
Distributed by Universal Press Syndicate
TO MEET A BLIND DATE WITH A GOLD TOOTH?
© 2002 PAWS, INC. All Rights Reserved.
JIM DAVIS 3-29

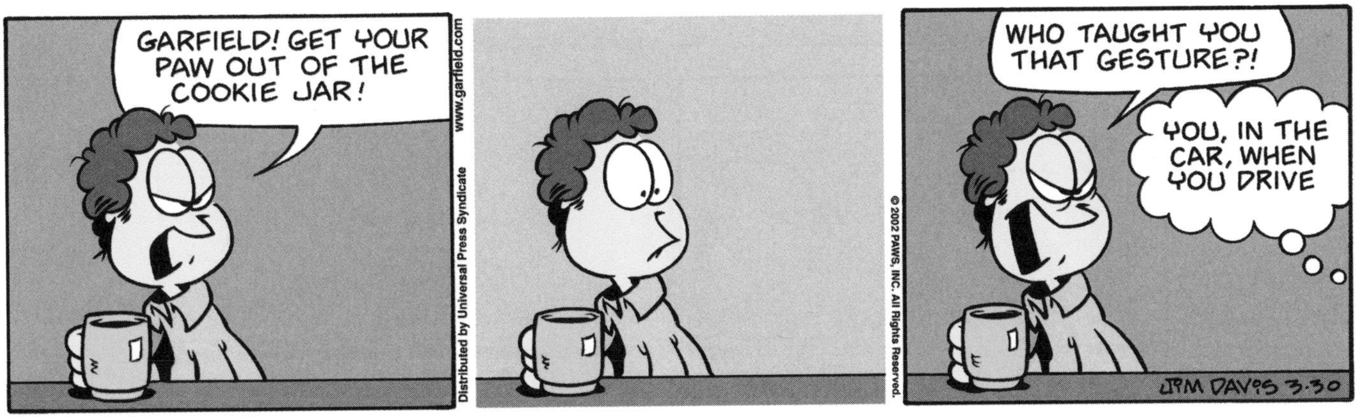
GARFIELD! GET YOUR PAW OUT OF THE COOKIE JAR!
www.garfield.com
Distributed by Universal Press Syndicate
© 2002 PAWS, INC. All Rights Reserved.
WHO TAUGHT YOU THAT GESTURE?!
YOU, IN THE CAR, WHEN YOU DRIVE
JIM DAVIS 3-30

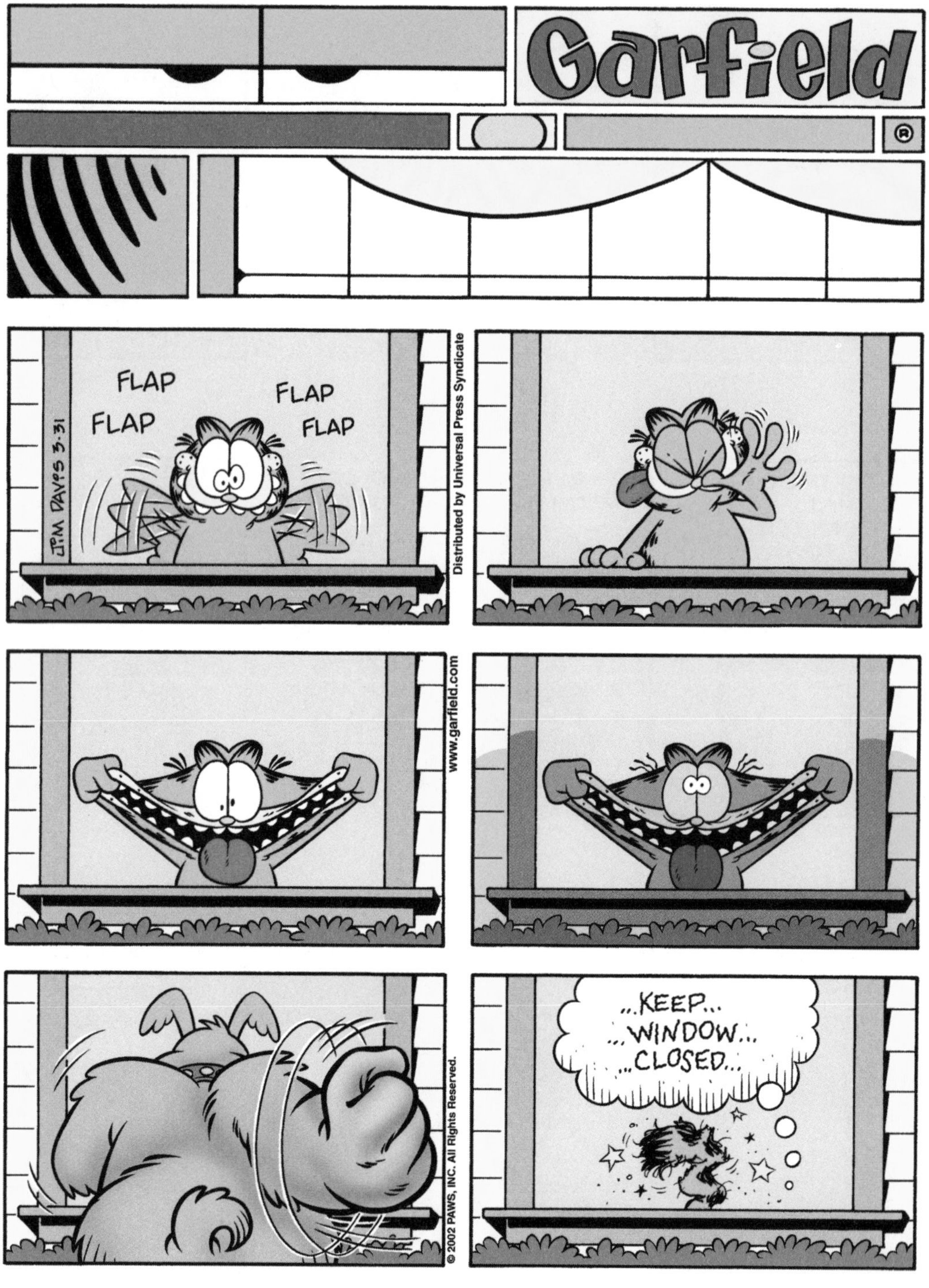
Garfield
FLAP
FLAP
FLAP
FLAP
JIM DAVIS 3-31
Distributed by Universal Press Syndicate
www.garfield.com
© 2002 PAWS, INC. All Rights Reserved.
...KEEP...
...WINDOW...
...CLOSED...

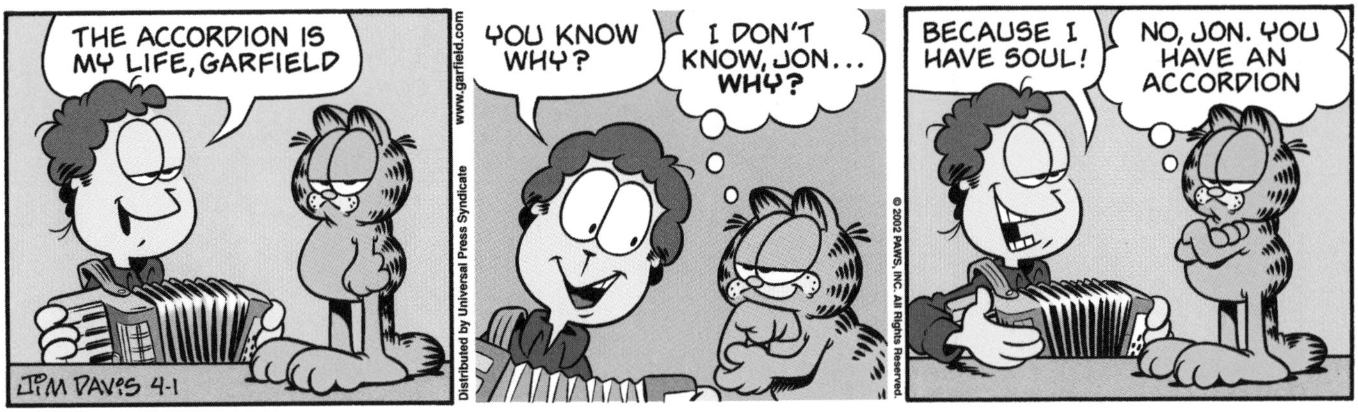
THE ACCORDION IS MY LIFE, GARFIELD
JIM DAVIS 4-1
Distributed by Universal Press Syndicate www.garfield.com
YOU KNOW WHY?
I DON'T KNOW, JON... WHY?
© 2002 PAWS, INC. All Rights Reserved.
BECAUSE I HAVE SOUL!
NO, JON. YOU HAVE AN ACCORDION

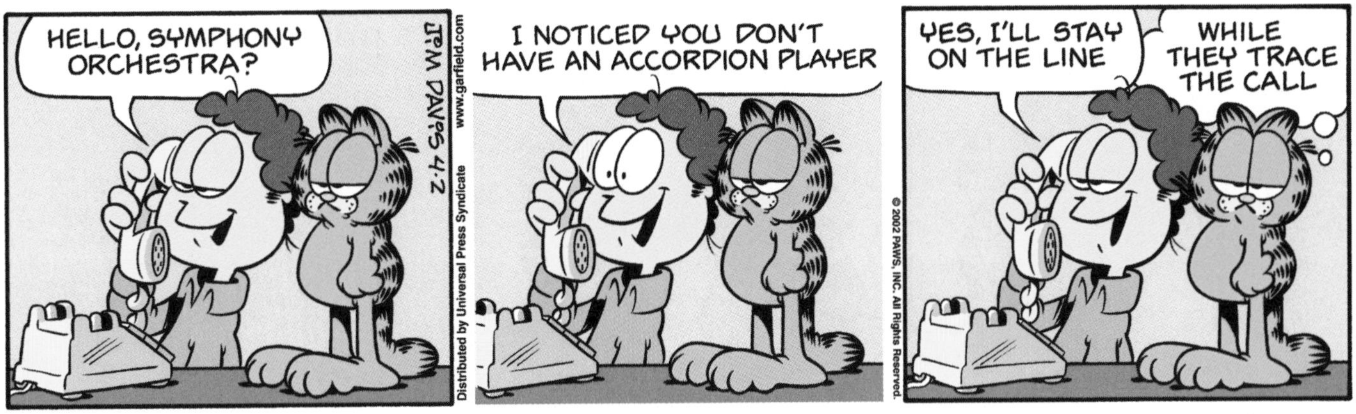
HELLO, SYMPHONY ORCHESTRA?
JIM DAVIS 4-2
Distributed by Universal Press Syndicate www.garfield.com
I NOTICED YOU DON'T HAVE AN ACCORDION PLAYER
© 2002 PAWS, INC. All Rights Reserved.
YES, I'LL STAY ON THE LINE
WHILE THEY TRACE THE CALL

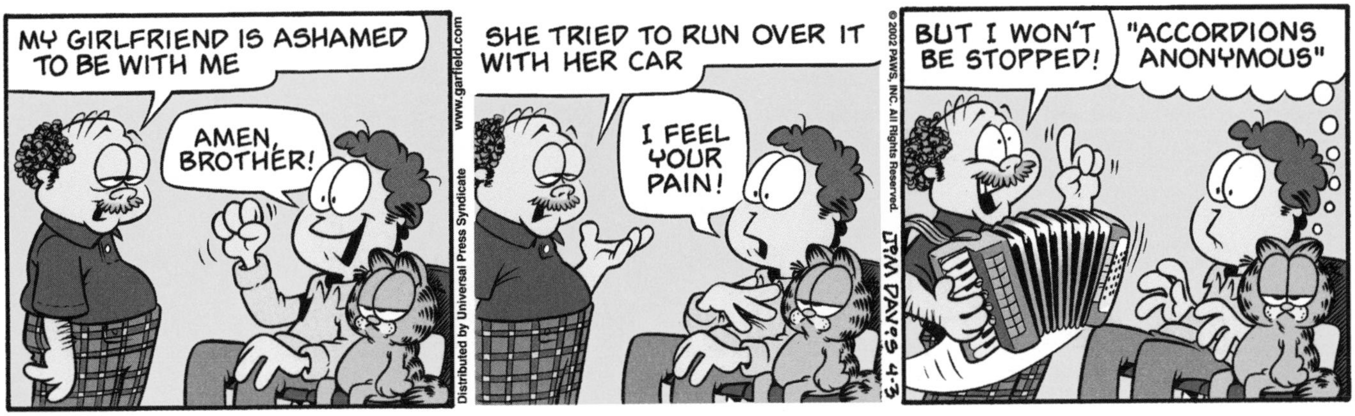
MY GIRLFRIEND IS ASHAMED TO BE WITH ME
AMEN, BROTHER!
Distributed by Universal Press Syndicate www.garfield.com
SHE TRIED TO RUN OVER IT WITH HER CAR
I FEEL YOUR PAIN!
© 2002 PAWS, INC. All Rights Reserved.
JIM DAVIS 4-3
BUT I WON'T BE STOPPED!
"ACCORDIONS ANONYMOUS"

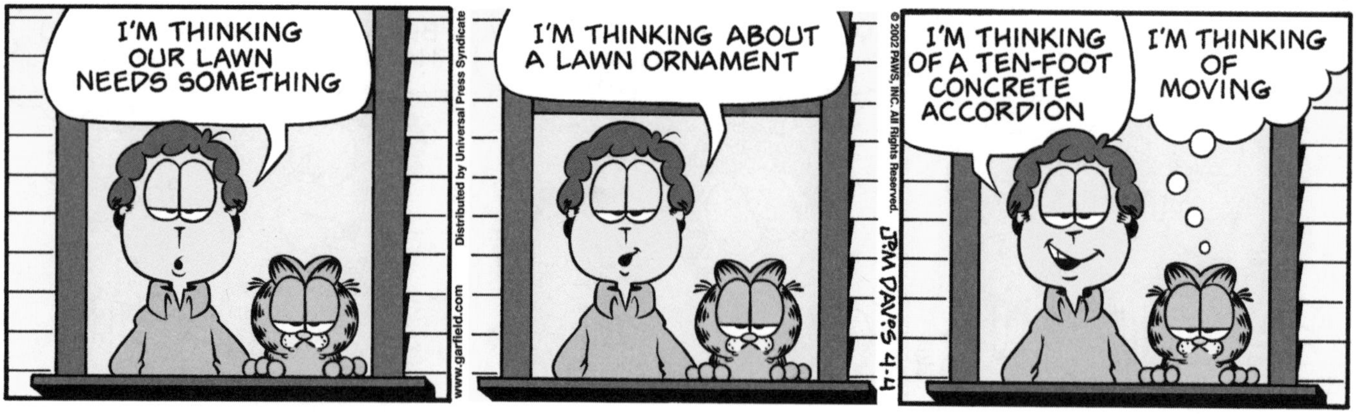
I'M THINKING OUR LAWN NEEDS SOMETHING
Distributed by Universal Press Syndicate
www.garfield.com
I'M THINKING ABOUT A LAWN ORNAMENT
© 2002 PAWS, INC. All Rights Reserved.
JIM DAVIS 4-4
I'M THINKING OF A TEN-FOOT CONCRETE ACCORDION
I'M THINKING OF MOVING

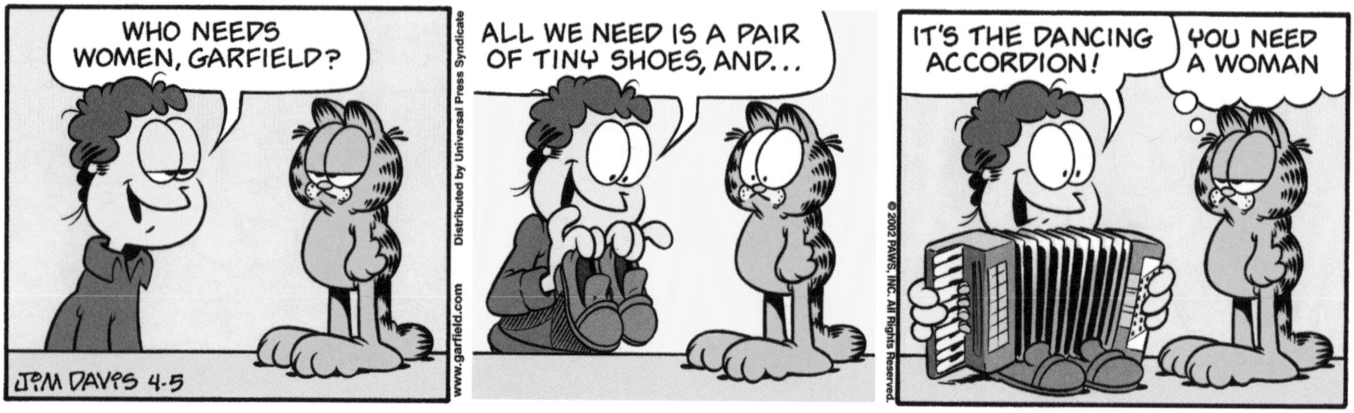
WHO NEEDS WOMEN, GARFIELD?
JIM DAVIS 4-5
Distributed by Universal Press Syndicate
www.garfield.com
ALL WE NEED IS A PAIR OF TINY SHOES, AND...
© 2002 PAWS, INC. All Rights Reserved.
IT'S THE DANCING ACCORDION!
YOU NEED A WOMAN

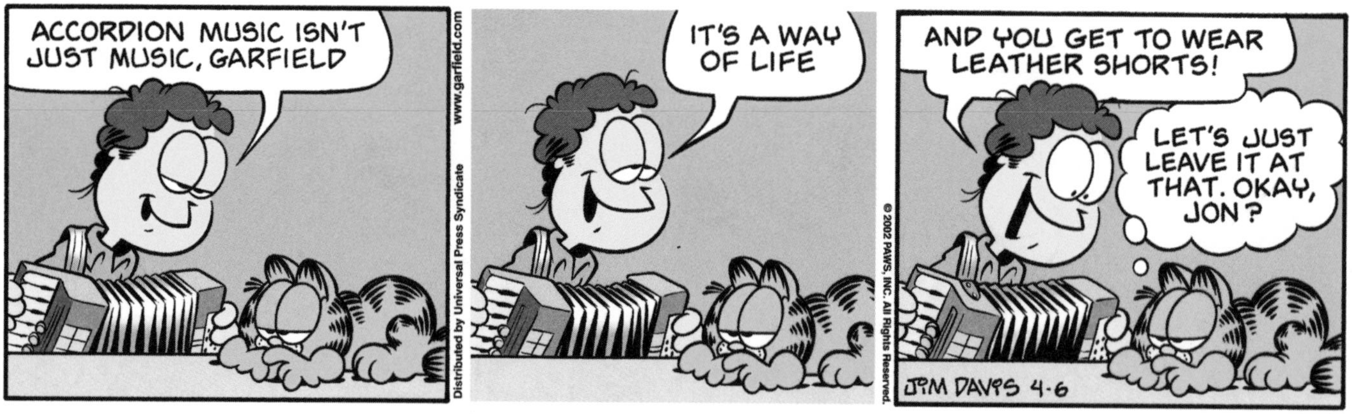
ACCORDION MUSIC ISN'T JUST MUSIC, GARFIELD
www.garfield.com
Distributed by Universal Press Syndicate
IT'S A WAY OF LIFE
© 2002 PAWS, INC. All Rights Reserved.
AND YOU GET TO WEAR LEATHER SHORTS!
LET'S JUST LEAVE IT AT THAT. OKAY, JON?
JIM DAVIS 4-6

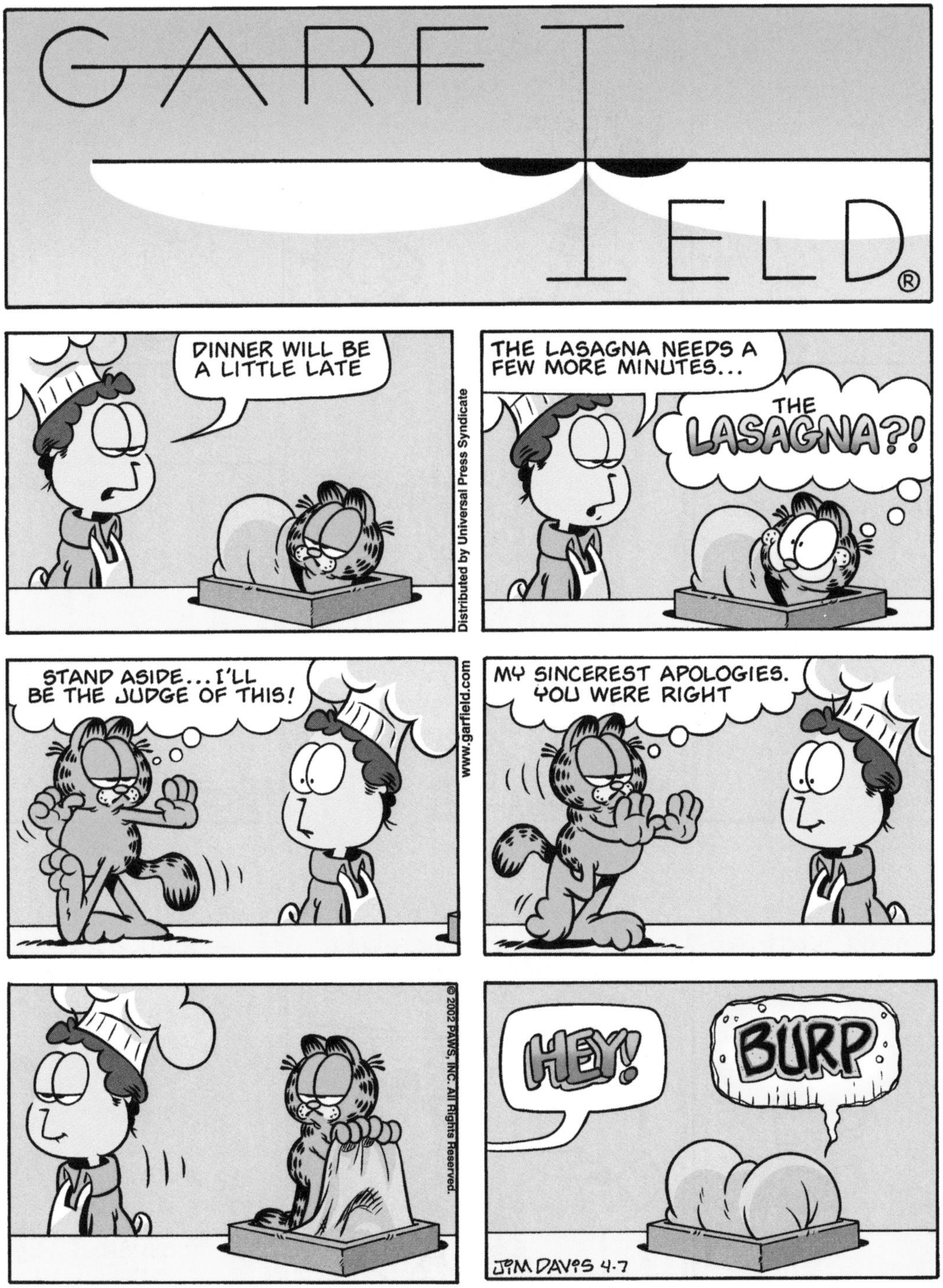
GARFIELD®
DINNER WILL BE A LITTLE LATE
Distributed by Universal Press Syndicate
THE LASAGNA NEEDS A FEW MORE MINUTES...
THE LASAGNA?!
STAND ASIDE... I'LL BE THE JUDGE OF THIS!
www.garfield.com
MY SINCEREST APOLOGIES. YOU WERE RIGHT
© 2002 PAWS, INC. All Rights Reserved.
HEY!
BURP
JIM DAVIS 4-7

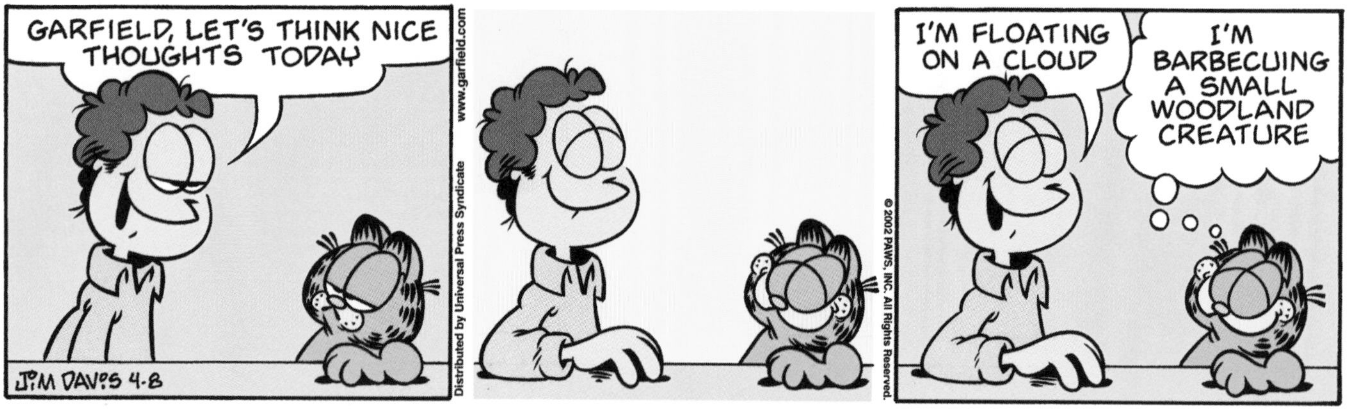
GARFIELD, LET'S THINK NICE THOUGHTS TODAY
JIM DAVIS 4-8
Distributed by Universal Press Syndicate www.garfield.com
I'M FLOATING ON A CLOUD
I'M BARBECUING A SMALL WOODLAND CREATURE
© 2002 PAWS, INC. All Rights Reserved.

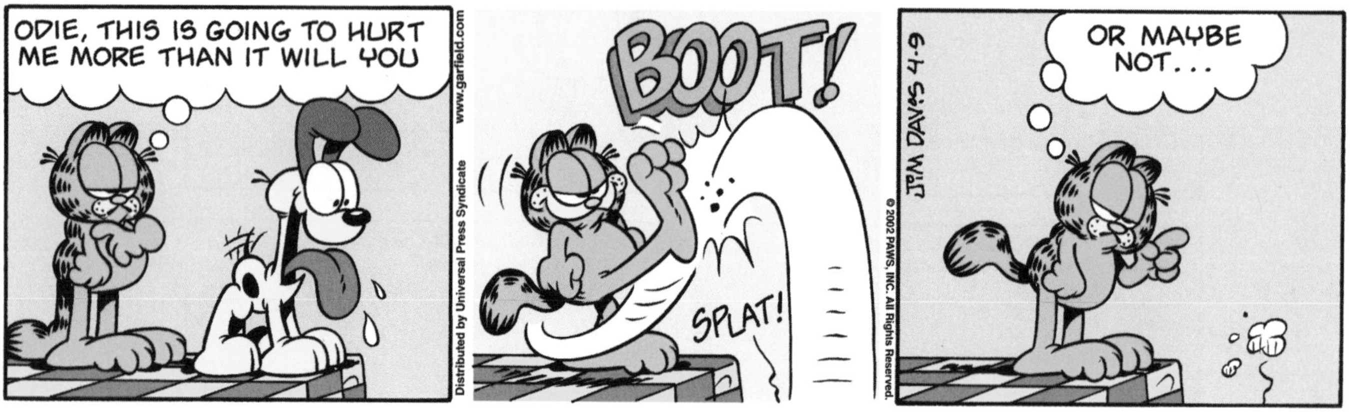
ODIE, THIS IS GOING TO HURT ME MORE THAN IT WILL YOU
Distributed by Universal Press Syndicate www.garfield.com
BOOT!
SPLAT!
© 2002 PAWS, INC. All Rights Reserved.
JIM DAVIS 4-9
OR MAYBE NOT...

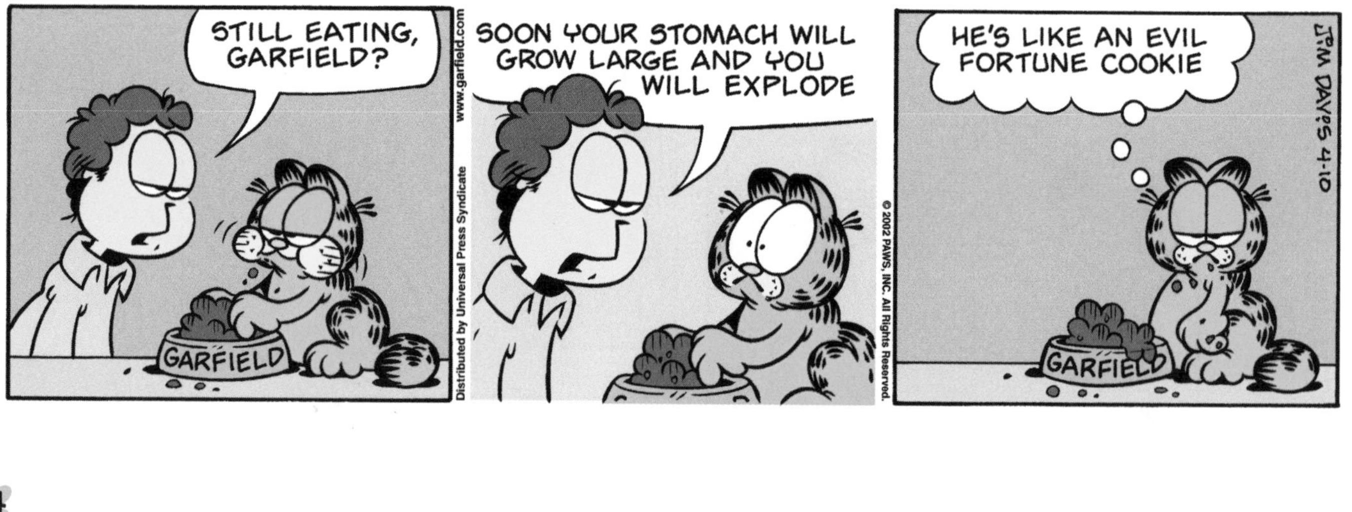
STILL EATING, GARFIELD?
GARFIELD
Distributed by Universal Press Syndicate www.garfield.com
SOON YOUR STOMACH WILL GROW LARGE AND YOU WILL EXPLODE
© 2002 PAWS, INC. All Rights Reserved.
HE'S LIKE AN EVIL FORTUNE COOKIE
JIM DAVIS 4-10
GARFIELD

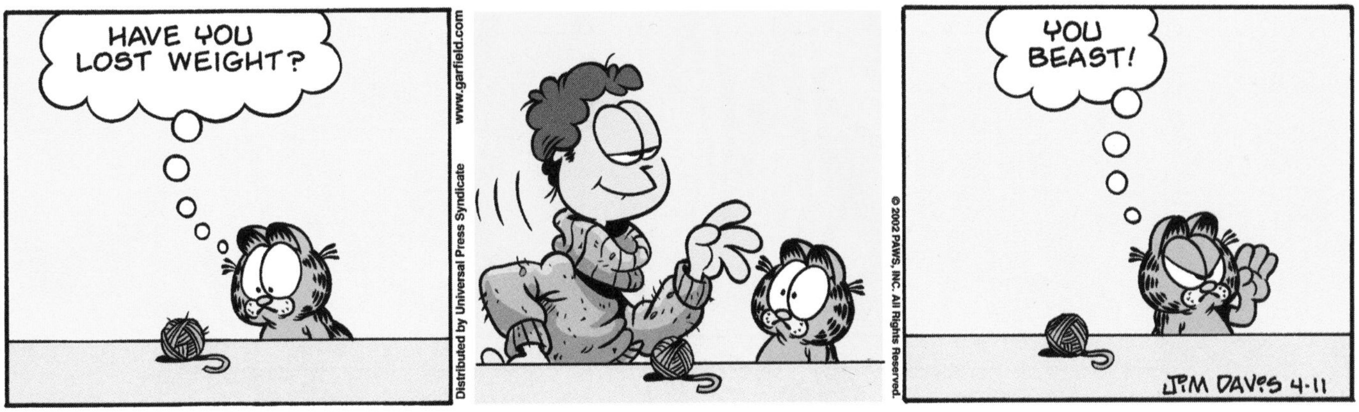
HAVE YOU LOST WEIGHT?
YOU BEAST!
JIM DAVIS 4-11
Distributed by Universal Press Syndicate
www.garfield.com
© 2002 PAWS, INC. All Rights Reserved.

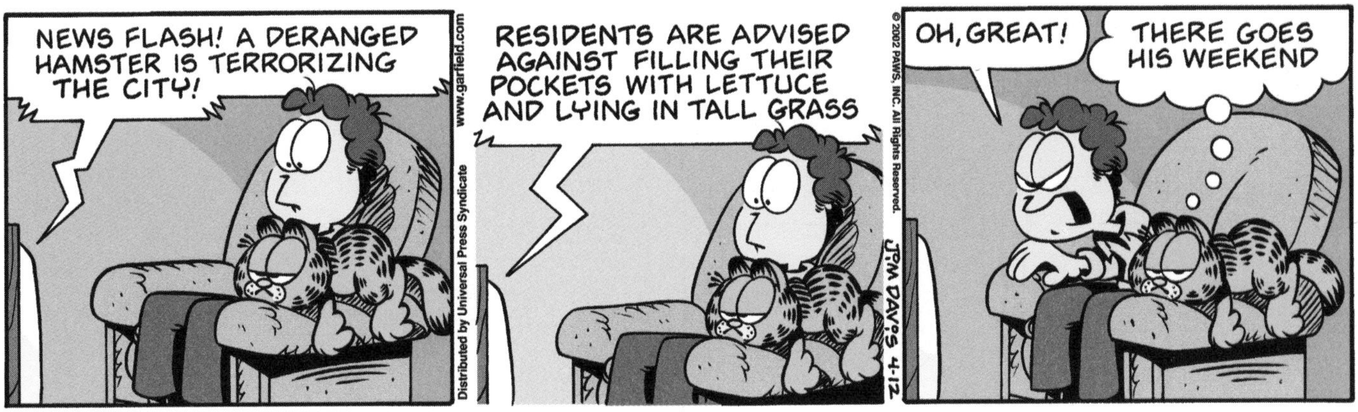
NEWS FLASH! A DERANGED HAMSTER IS TERRORIZING THE CITY!
RESIDENTS ARE ADVISED AGAINST FILLING THEIR POCKETS WITH LETTUCE AND LYING IN TALL GRASS
OH, GREAT!
THERE GOES HIS WEEKEND
JIM DAVIS 4-12
Distributed by Universal Press Syndicate
www.garfield.com
© 2002 PAWS, INC. All Rights Reserved.

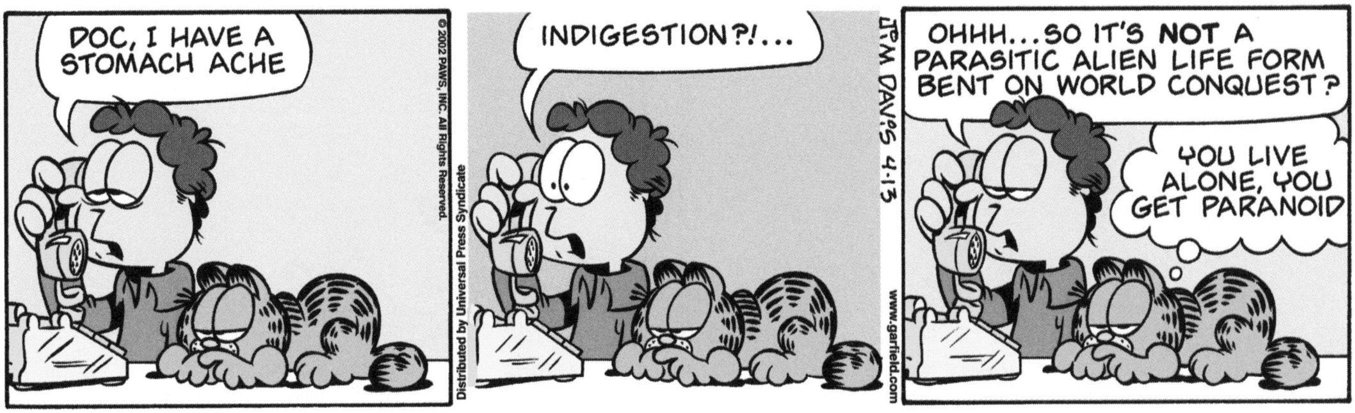
DOC, I HAVE A STOMACH ACHE
INDIGESTION?!...
OHHH...SO IT'S **NOT** A PARASITIC ALIEN LIFE FORM BENT ON WORLD CONQUEST?
YOU LIVE ALONE, YOU GET PARANOID
JIM DAVIS 4-13
© 2002 PAWS, INC. All Rights Reserved.
Distributed by Universal Press Syndicate
www.garfield.com

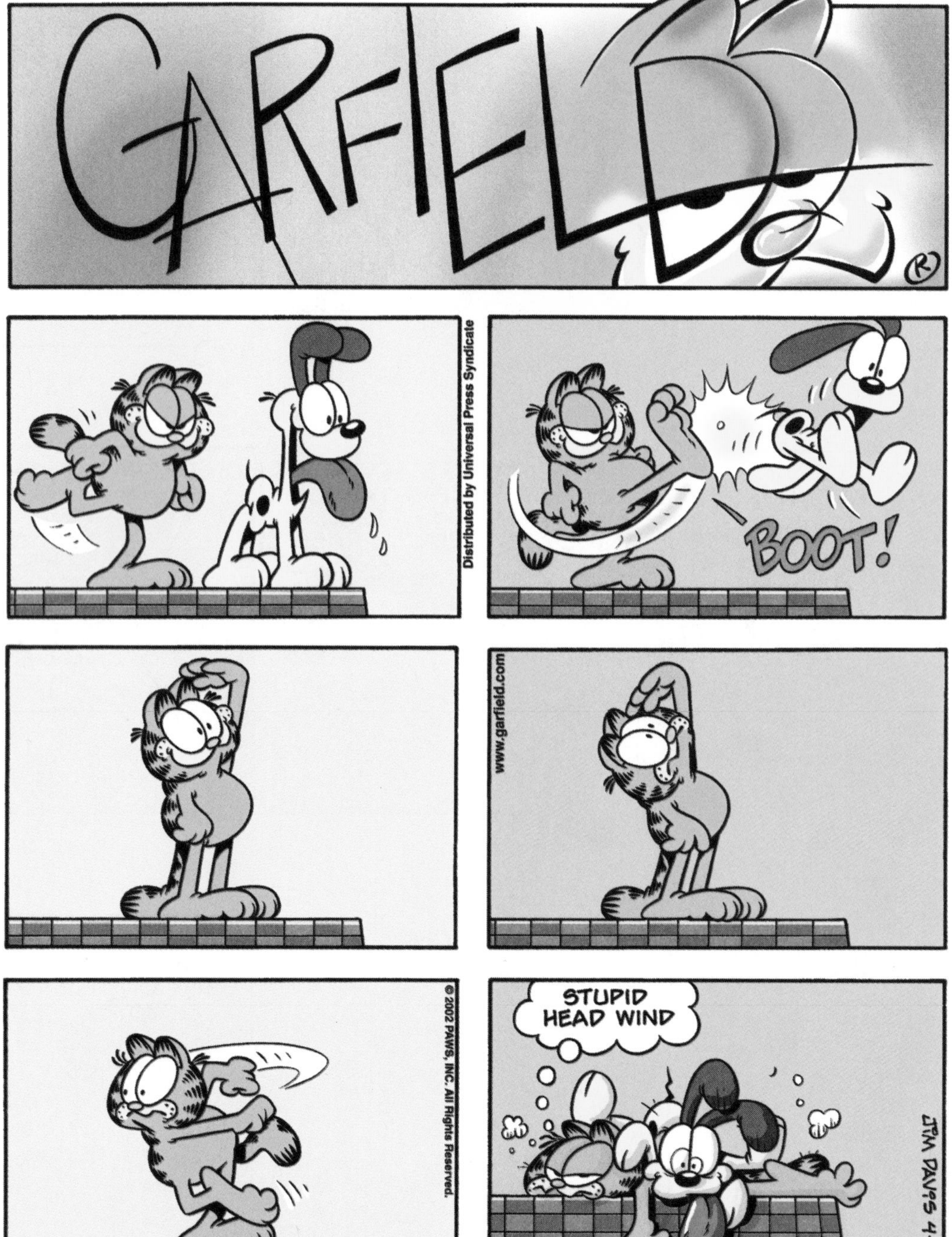
GARFIELD®
Distributed by Universal Press Syndicate
BOOT!
www.garfield.com
© 2002 PAWS, INC. All Rights Reserved.
STUPID HEAD WIND
JIM DAVIS 4-14

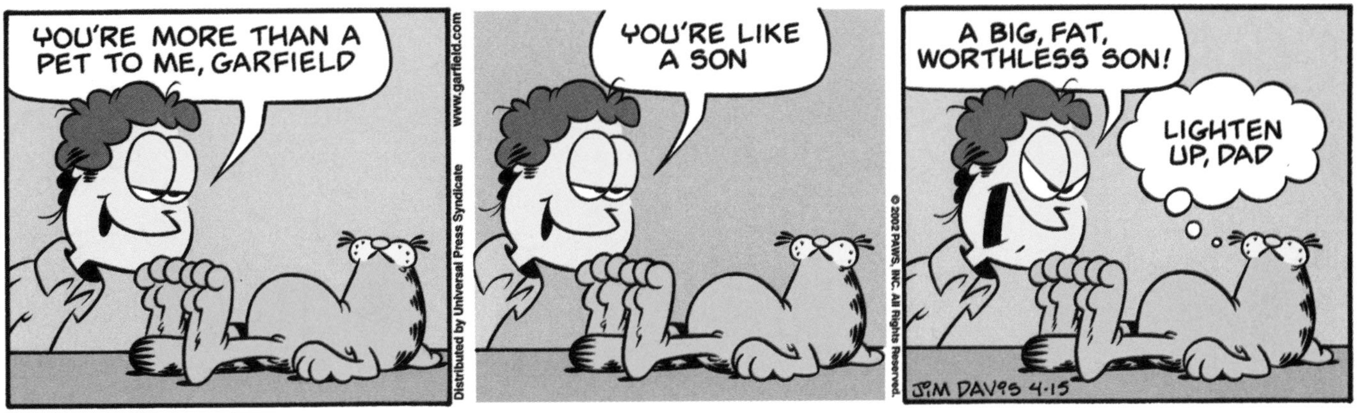
YOU'RE MORE THAN A PET TO ME, GARFIELD
YOU'RE LIKE A SON
A BIG, FAT, WORTHLESS SON!
LIGHTEN UP, DAD
JIM DAVIS 4-15
Distributed by Universal Press Syndicate www.garfield.com
© 2002 PAWS, INC. All Rights Reserved.

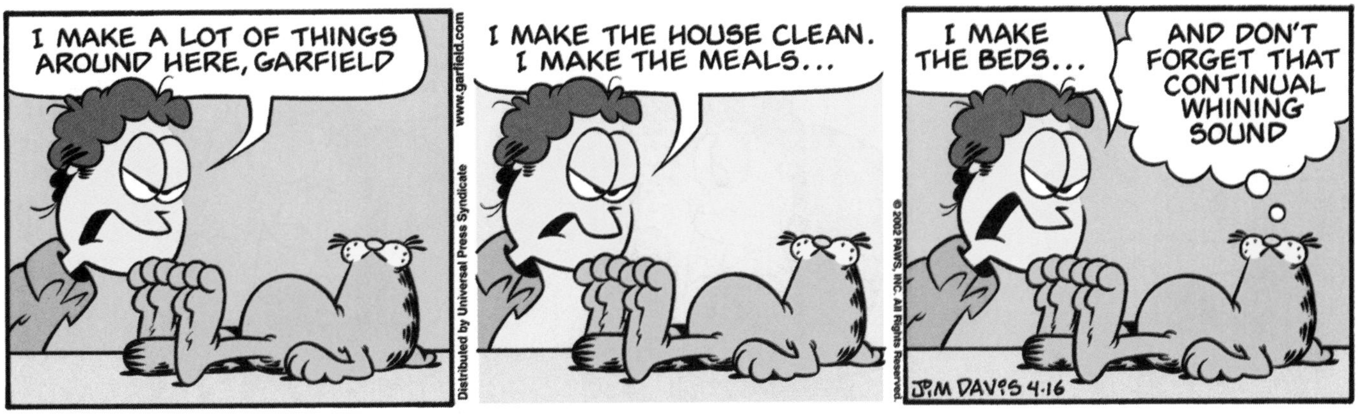
I MAKE A LOT OF THINGS AROUND HERE, GARFIELD
I MAKE THE HOUSE CLEAN. I MAKE THE MEALS...
I MAKE THE BEDS...
AND DON'T FORGET THAT CONTINUAL WHINING SOUND
JIM DAVIS 4-16
Distributed by Universal Press Syndicate www.garfield.com
© 2002 PAWS, INC. All Rights Reserved.

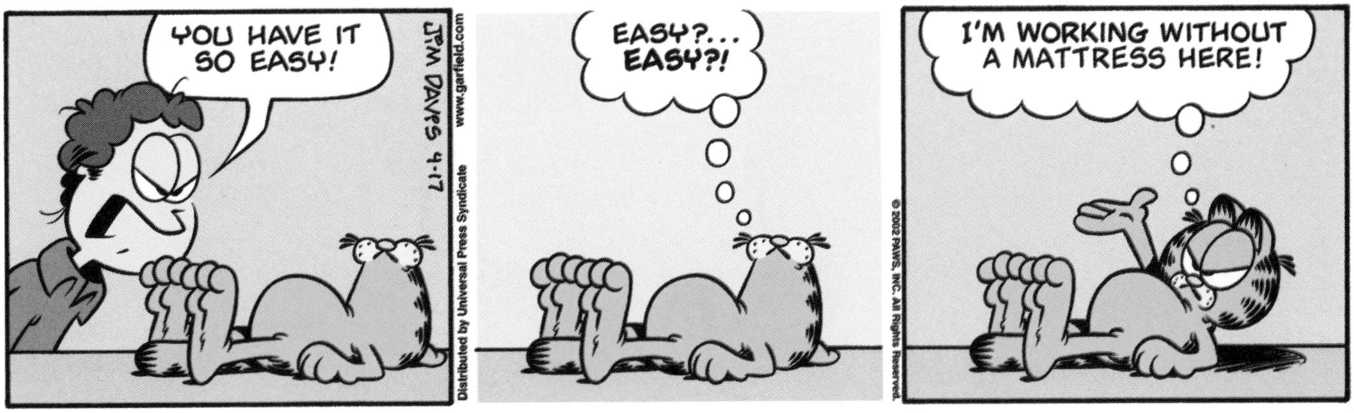
YOU HAVE IT SO EASY!
JIM DAVIS 4-17
EASY?... **EASY?!**
I'M WORKING WITHOUT A MATTRESS HERE!
Distributed by Universal Press Syndicate www.garfield.com
© 2002 PAWS, INC. All Rights Reserved.

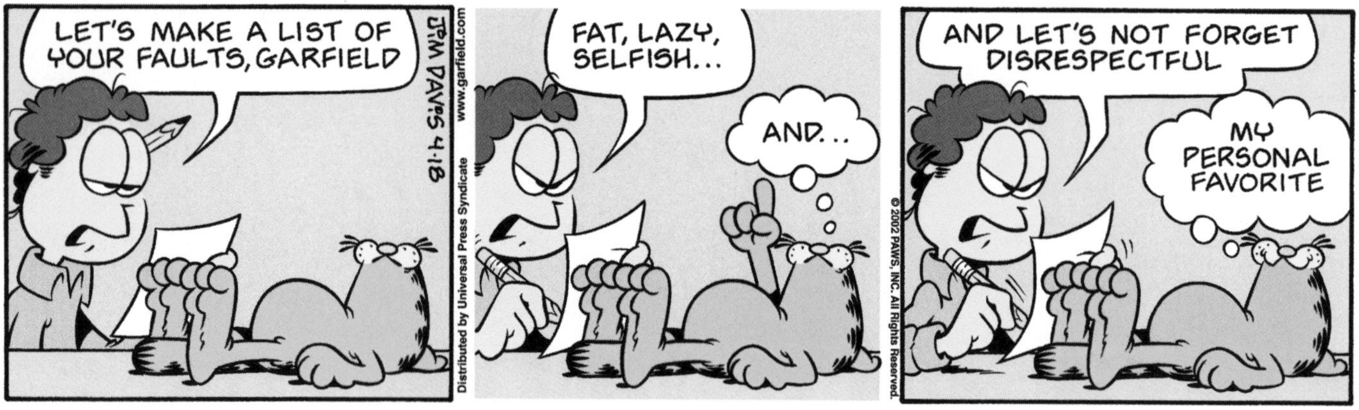
LET'S MAKE A LIST OF YOUR FAULTS, GARFIELD
JIM DAVIS 4-18
FAT, LAZY, SELFISH...
AND...
AND LET'S NOT FORGET DISRESPECTFUL
MY PERSONAL FAVORITE
www.garfield.com
Distributed by Universal Press Syndicate
© 2002 PAWS, INC. All Rights Reserved.

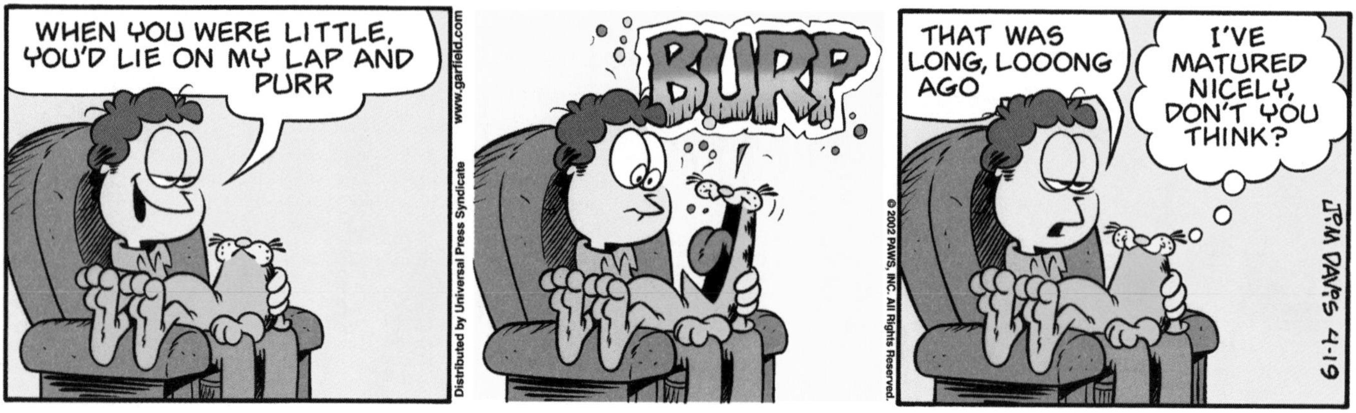
WHEN YOU WERE LITTLE, YOU'D LIE ON MY LAP AND PURR
BURP
THAT WAS LONG, LOOONG AGO
I'VE MATURED NICELY, DON'T YOU THINK?
JIM DAVIS 4-19
www.garfield.com
Distributed by Universal Press Syndicate
© 2002 PAWS, INC. All Rights Reserved.

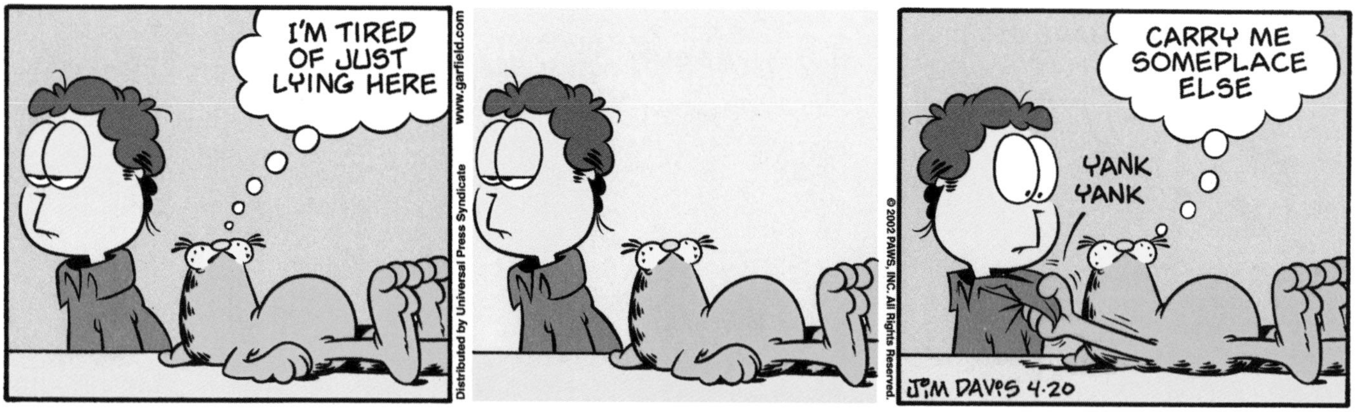
I'M TIRED OF JUST LYING HERE
CARRY ME SOMEPLACE ELSE
YANK YANK
JIM DAVIS 4-20
www.garfield.com
Distributed by Universal Press Syndicate
© 2002 PAWS, INC. All Rights Reserved.

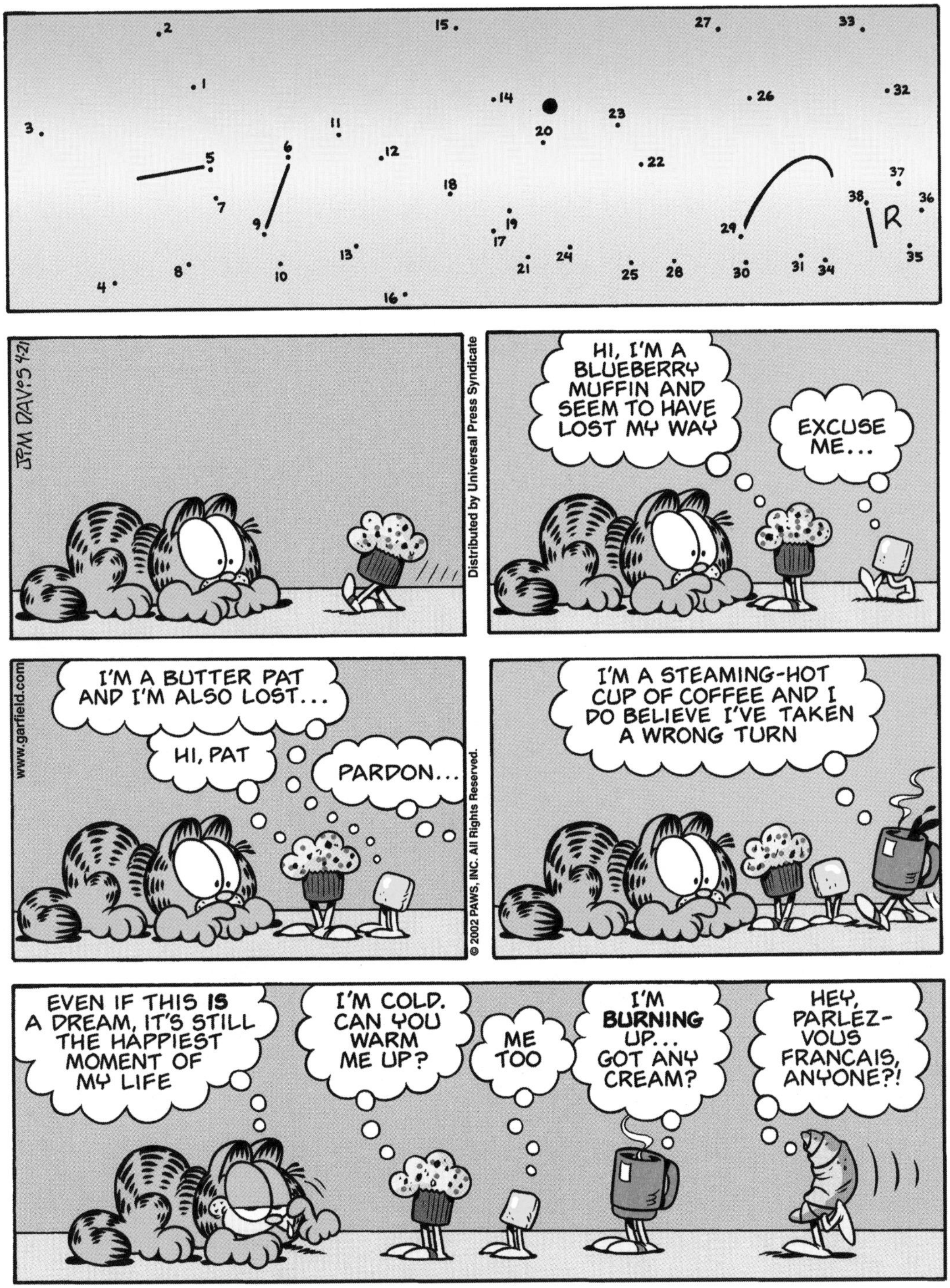
JIM DAVIS 4-21
Distributed by Universal Press Syndicate
HI, I'M A BLUEBERRY MUFFIN AND SEEM TO HAVE LOST MY WAY
EXCUSE ME...
www.garfield.com
I'M A BUTTER PAT AND I'M ALSO LOST...
HI, PAT
PARDON...
© 2002 PAWS, INC. All Rights Reserved.
I'M A STEAMING-HOT CUP OF COFFEE AND I DO BELIEVE I'VE TAKEN A WRONG TURN
EVEN IF THIS **IS** A DREAM, IT'S STILL THE HAPPIEST MOMENT OF MY LIFE
I'M COLD. CAN YOU WARM ME UP?
ME TOO
I'M **BURNING** UP... GOT ANY CREAM?
HEY, PARLEZ-VOUS FRANCAIS, ANYONE?!

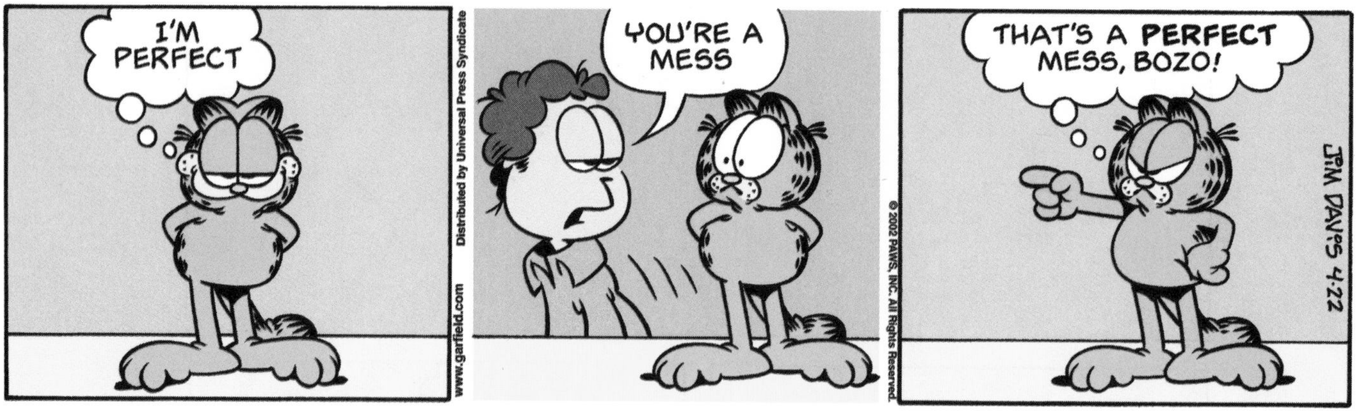
I'M PERFECT
YOU'RE A MESS
THAT'S A **PERFECT** MESS, BOZO!
JIM DAVIS 4-22
www.garfield.com Distributed by Universal Press Syndicate
© 2002 PAWS, INC. All Rights Reserved.

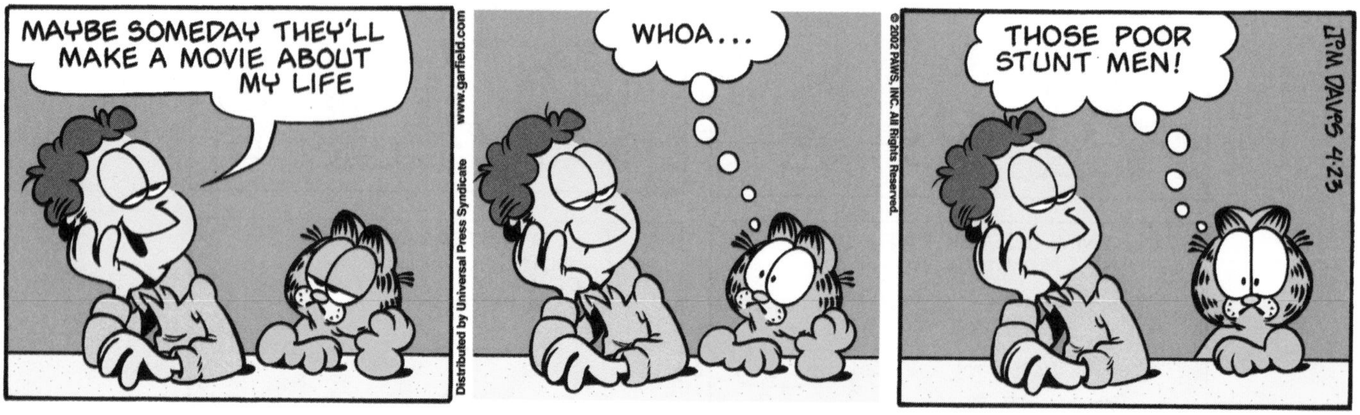
MAYBE SOMEDAY THEY'LL MAKE A MOVIE ABOUT MY LIFE
WHOA...
THOSE POOR STUNT MEN!
JIM DAVIS 4-23
Distributed by Universal Press Syndicate www.garfield.com
© 2002 PAWS, INC. All Rights Reserved.

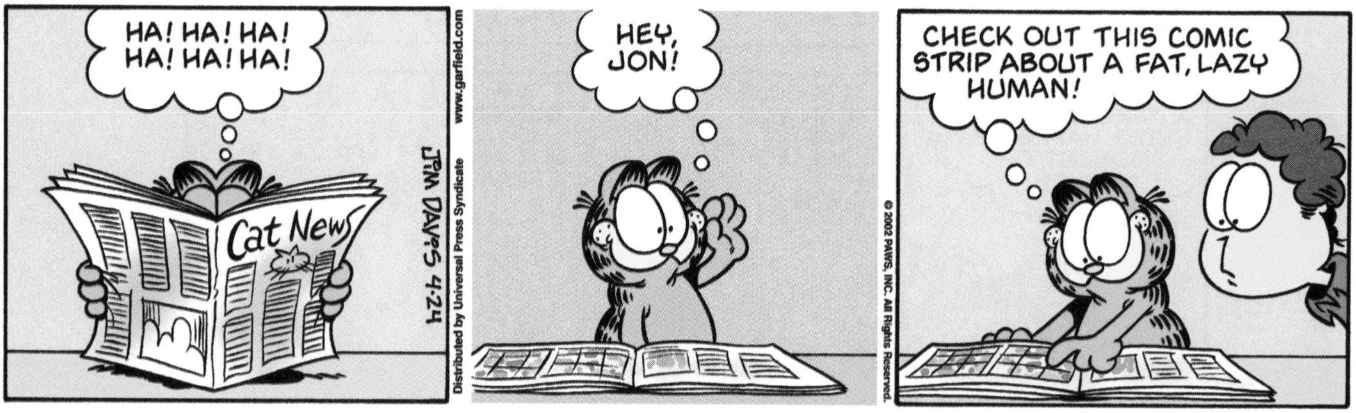
HA! HA! HA! HA! HA! HA!
Cat News
JIM DAVIS 4-24
Distributed by Universal Press Syndicate www.garfield.com
HEY, JON!
CHECK OUT THIS COMIC STRIP ABOUT A FAT, LAZY HUMAN!
© 2002 PAWS, INC. All Rights Reserved.

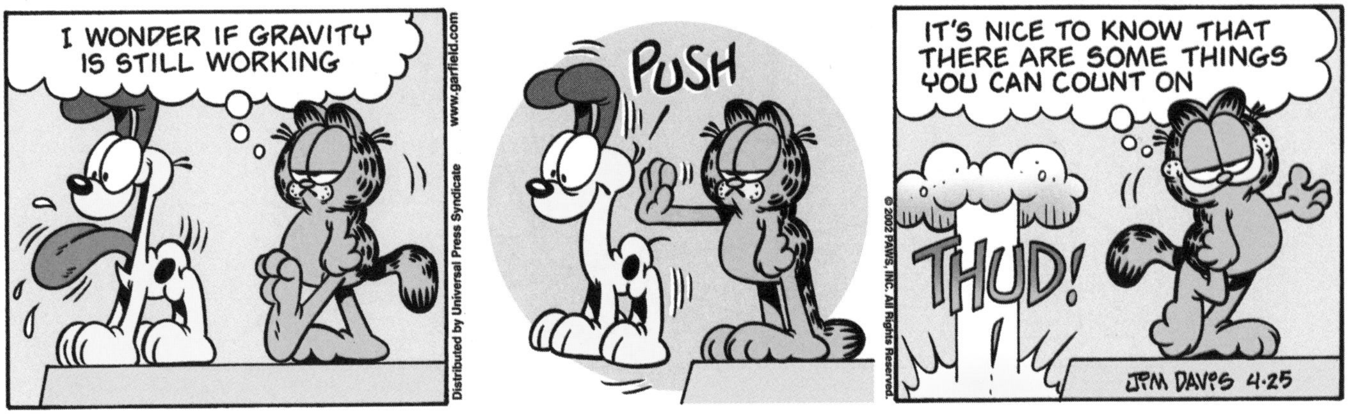
I WONDER IF GRAVITY IS STILL WORKING
PUSH
IT'S NICE TO KNOW THAT THERE ARE SOME THINGS YOU CAN COUNT ON
THUD!
JIM DAVIS 4-25
Distributed by Universal Press Syndicate www.garfield.com
© 2002 PAWS, INC. All Rights Reserved.

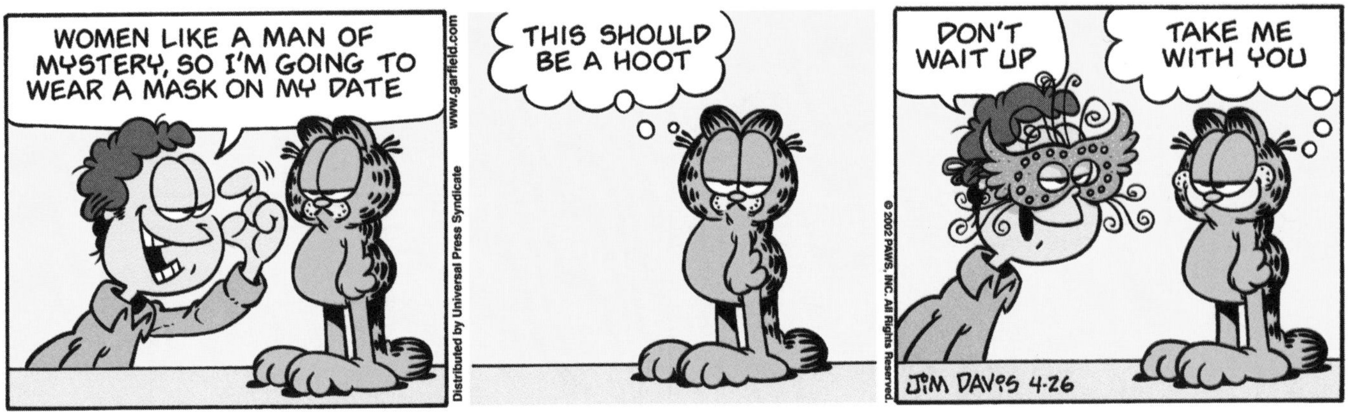
WOMEN LIKE A MAN OF MYSTERY, SO I'M GOING TO WEAR A MASK ON MY DATE
THIS SHOULD BE A HOOT
DON'T WAIT UP
TAKE ME WITH YOU
JIM DAVIS 4-26
Distributed by Universal Press Syndicate www.garfield.com
© 2002 PAWS, INC. All Rights Reserved.

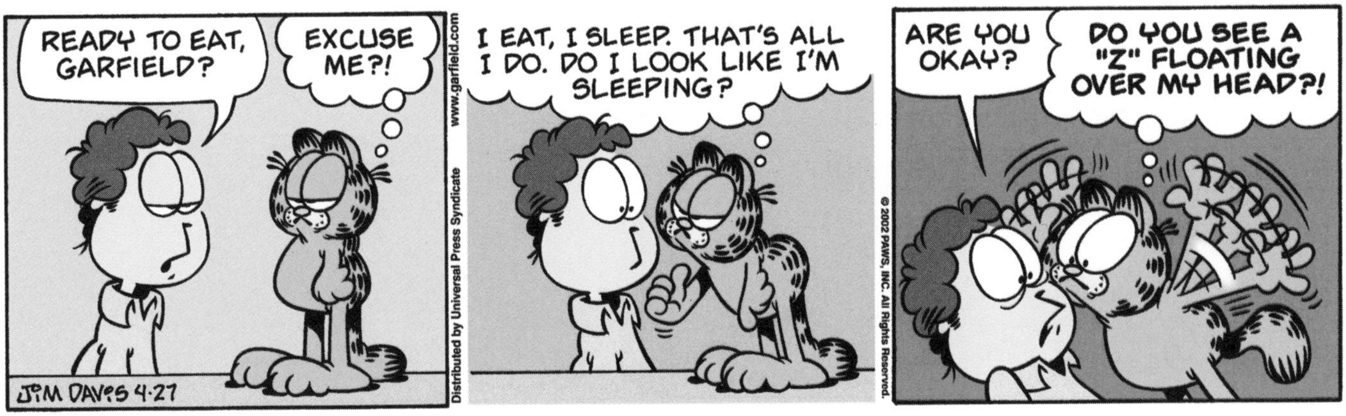
READY TO EAT, GARFIELD?
EXCUSE ME?!
I EAT, I SLEEP. THAT'S ALL I DO. DO I LOOK LIKE I'M SLEEPING?
ARE YOU OKAY?
DO YOU SEE A "Z" FLOATING OVER MY HEAD?!
JIM DAVIS 4-27
Distributed by Universal Press Syndicate www.garfield.com
© 2002 PAWS, INC. All Rights Reserved.

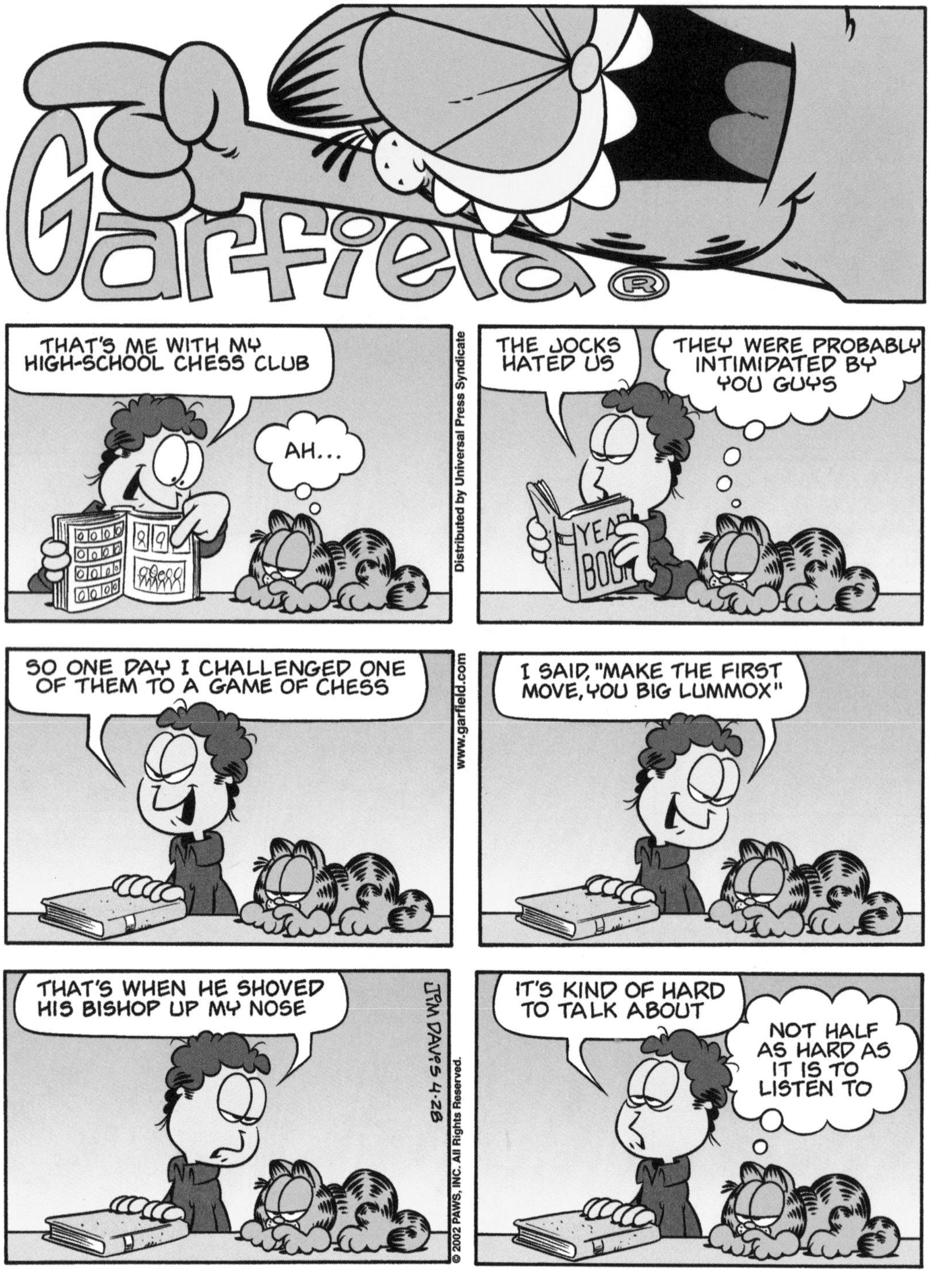
Garfield®
THAT'S ME WITH MY HIGH-SCHOOL CHESS CLUB
AH...
Distributed by Universal Press Syndicate
THE JOCKS HATED US
THEY WERE PROBABLY INTIMIDATED BY YOU GUYS
YEAR BOOK
SO ONE DAY I CHALLENGED ONE OF THEM TO A GAME OF CHESS
www.garfield.com
I SAID, "MAKE THE FIRST MOVE, YOU BIG LUMMOX"
THAT'S WHEN HE SHOVED HIS BISHOP UP MY NOSE
JIM DAVIS 4-28
© 2002 PAWS, INC. All Rights Reserved.
IT'S KIND OF HARD TO TALK ABOUT
NOT HALF AS HARD AS IT IS TO LISTEN TO

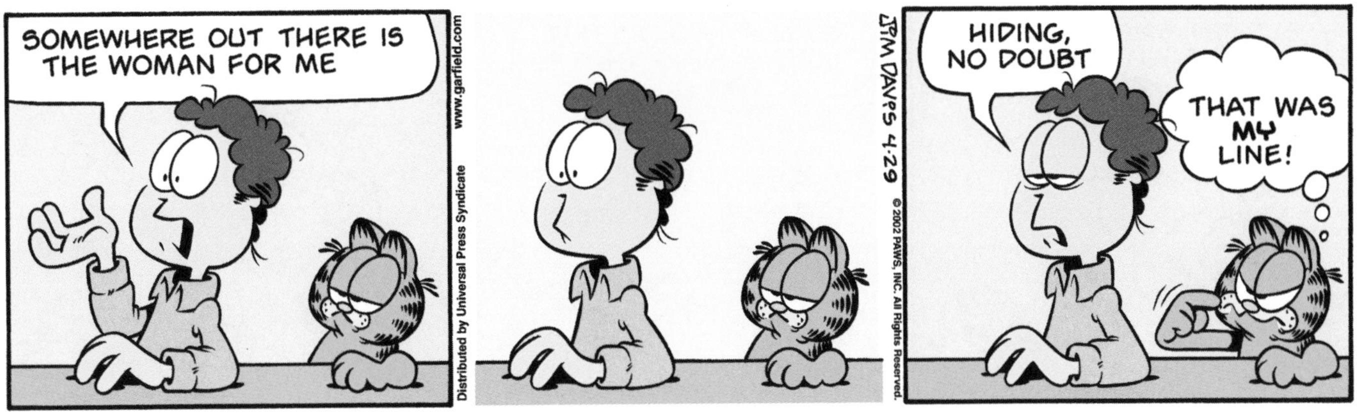
SOMEWHERE OUT THERE IS THE WOMAN FOR ME
www.garfield.com
Distributed by Universal Press Syndicate
JIM DAVIS 4-29
© 2002 PAWS, INC. All Rights Reserved.
HIDING, NO DOUBT
THAT WAS MY LINE!

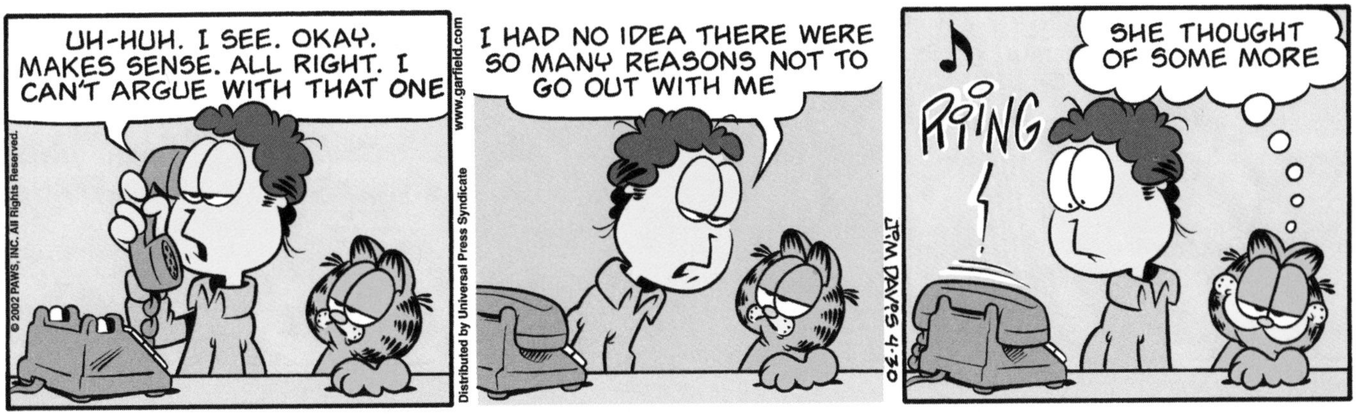
UH-HUH. I SEE. OKAY. MAKES SENSE. ALL RIGHT. I CAN'T ARGUE WITH THAT ONE
© 2002 PAWS, INC. All Rights Reserved.
www.garfield.com
Distributed by Universal Press Syndicate
I HAD NO IDEA THERE WERE SO MANY REASONS NOT TO GO OUT WITH ME
JIM DAVIS 4-30
RING
SHE THOUGHT OF SOME MORE

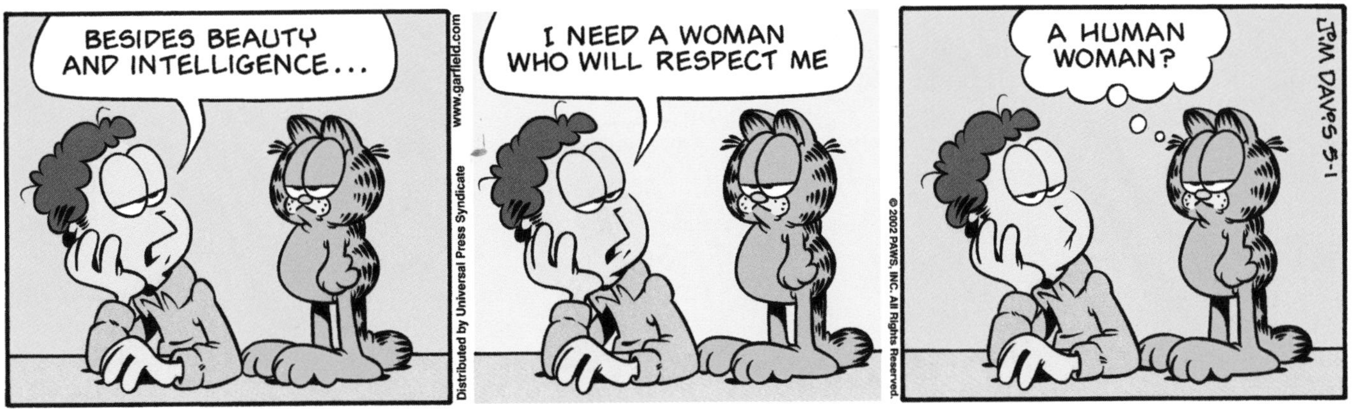
BESIDES BEAUTY AND INTELLIGENCE...
www.garfield.com
Distributed by Universal Press Syndicate
I NEED A WOMAN WHO WILL RESPECT ME
© 2002 PAWS, INC. All Rights Reserved.
A HUMAN WOMAN?
JIM DAVIS 5-1

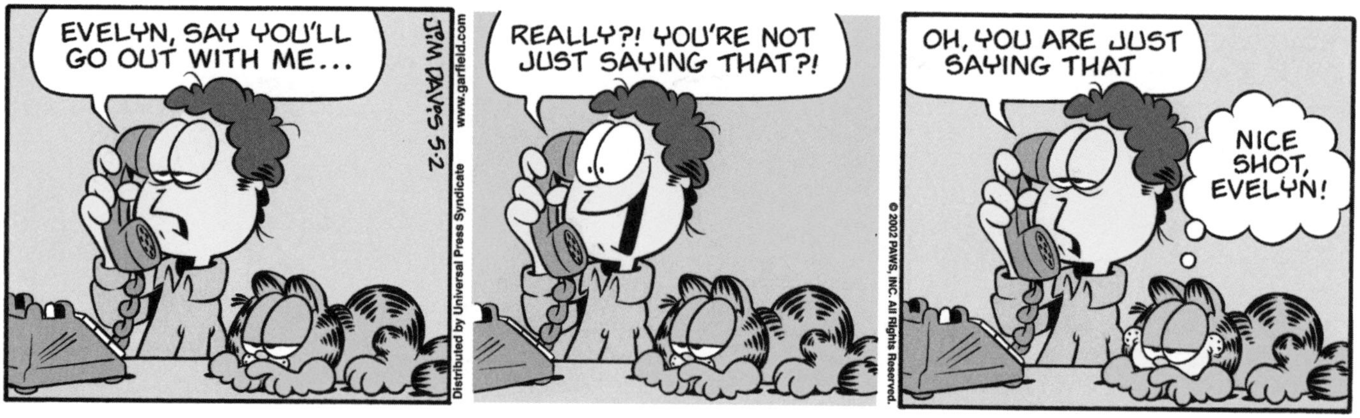
EVELYN, SAY YOU'LL GO OUT WITH ME...
JIM DAVIS 5-2
www.garfield.com
Distributed by Universal Press Syndicate
REALLY?! YOU'RE NOT JUST SAYING THAT?!
© 2002 PAWS, INC. All Rights Reserved.
OH, YOU ARE JUST SAYING THAT
NICE SHOT, EVELYN!

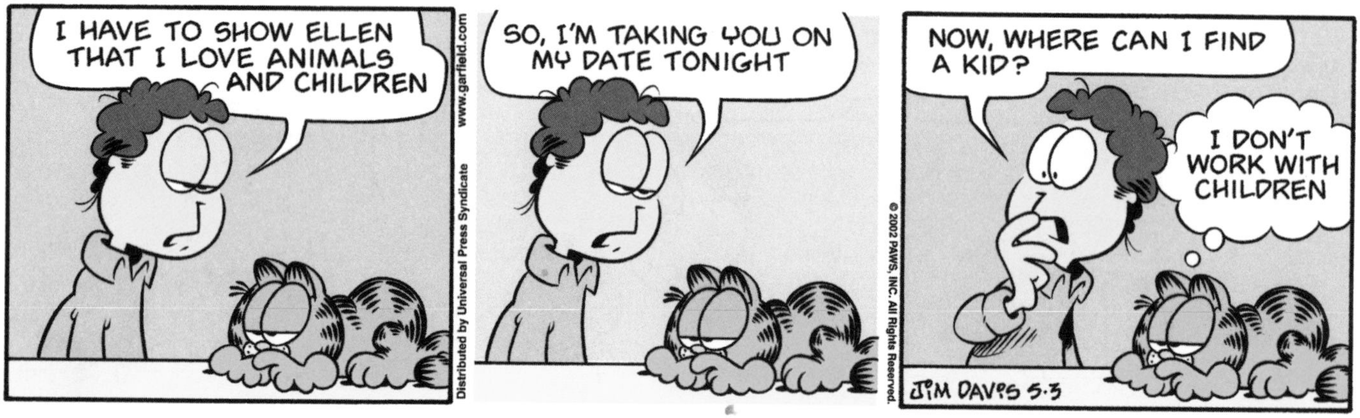
I HAVE TO SHOW ELLEN THAT I LOVE ANIMALS AND CHILDREN
www.garfield.com
Distributed by Universal Press Syndicate
SO, I'M TAKING YOU ON MY DATE TONIGHT
© 2002 PAWS, INC. All Rights Reserved.
NOW, WHERE CAN I FIND A KID?
I DON'T WORK WITH CHILDREN
JIM DAVIS 5-3

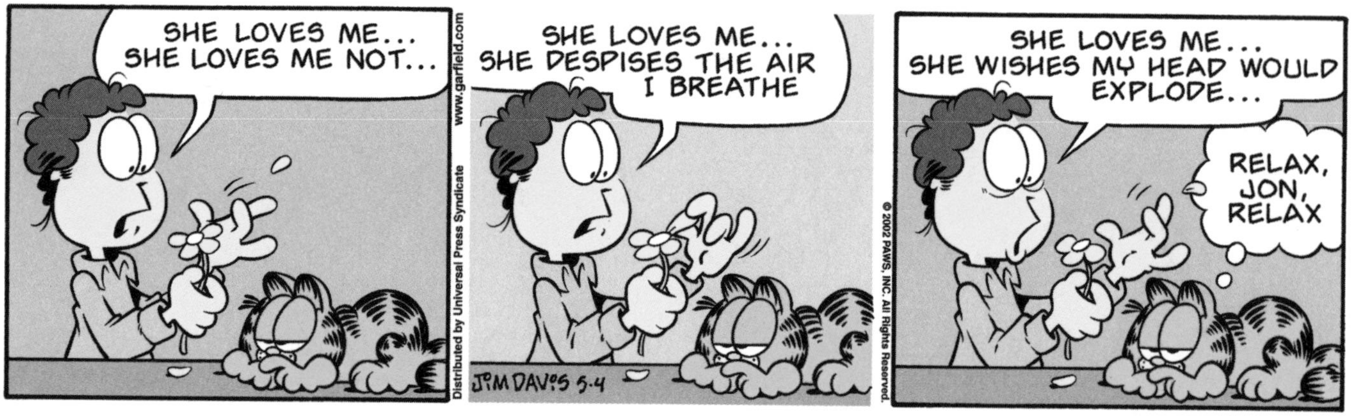
SHE LOVES ME... SHE LOVES ME NOT...
www.garfield.com
Distributed by Universal Press Syndicate
SHE LOVES ME... SHE DESPISES THE AIR I BREATHE
JIM DAVIS 5-4
© 2002 PAWS, INC. All Rights Reserved.
SHE LOVES ME... SHE WISHES MY HEAD WOULD EXPLODE...
RELAX, JON, RELAX

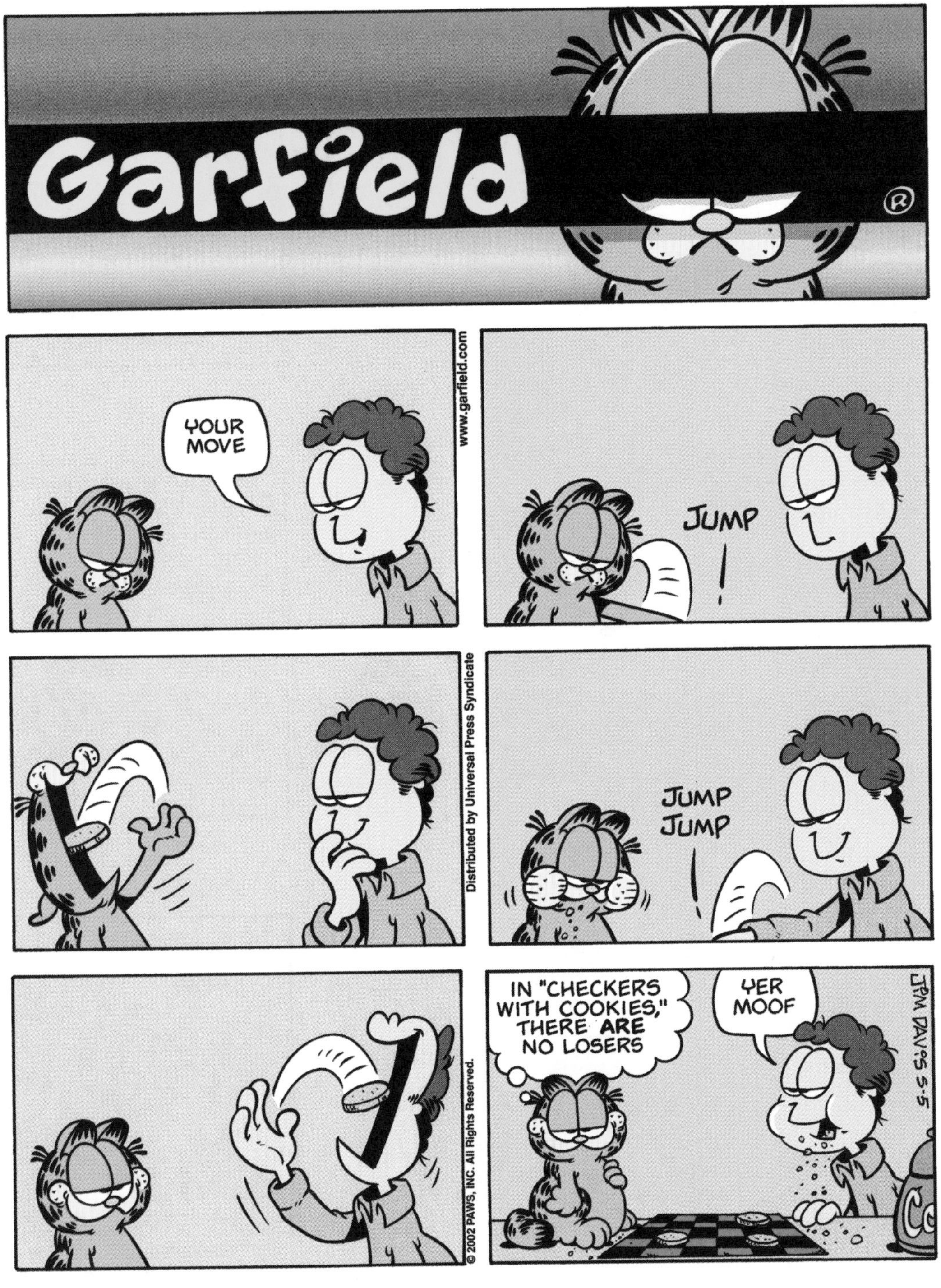
Garfield®
www.garfield.com
YOUR MOVE
JUMP
Distributed by Universal Press Syndicate
JUMP JUMP
© 2002 PAWS, INC. All Rights Reserved.
IN "CHECKERS WITH COOKIES," THERE **ARE** NO LOSERS
YER MOOF
JPM DAVIS 5-5

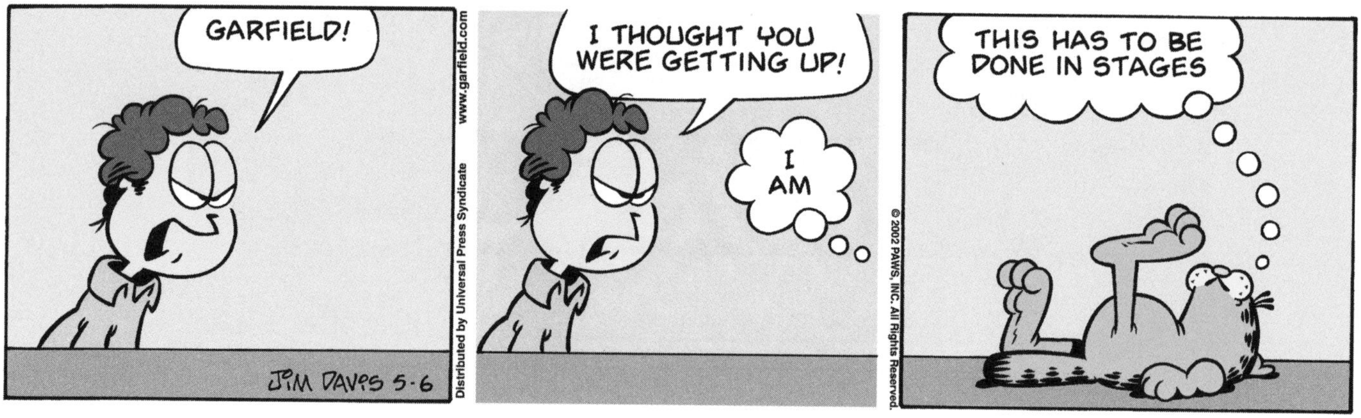
GARFIELD!
I THOUGHT YOU WERE GETTING UP!
I AM
THIS HAS TO BE DONE IN STAGES
JIM DAVIS 5-6
Distributed by Universal Press Syndicate www.garfield.com
© 2002 PAWS, INC. All Rights Reserved.

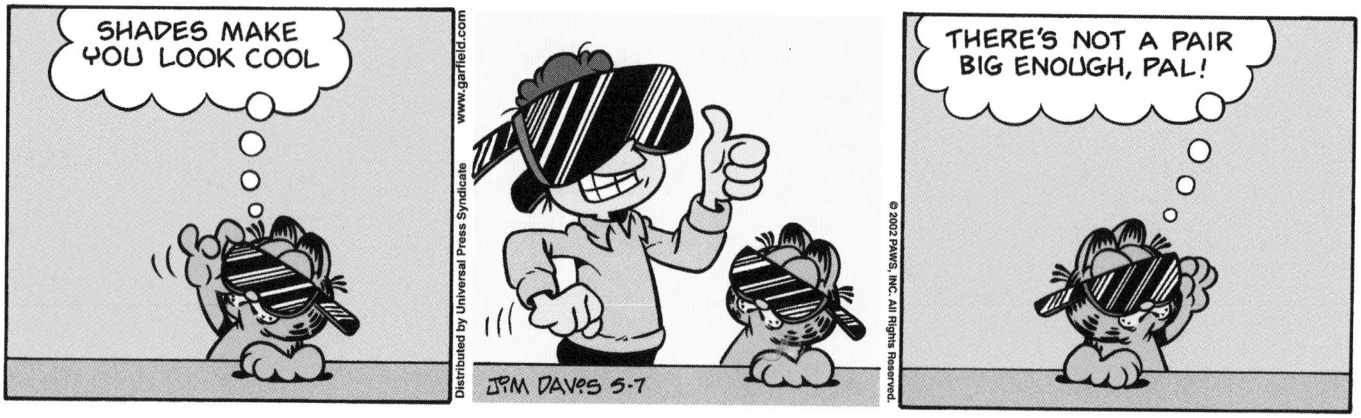
SHADES MAKE YOU LOOK COOL
THERE'S NOT A PAIR BIG ENOUGH, PAL!
JIM DAVIS 5-7
Distributed by Universal Press Syndicate www.garfield.com
© 2002 PAWS, INC. All Rights Reserved.

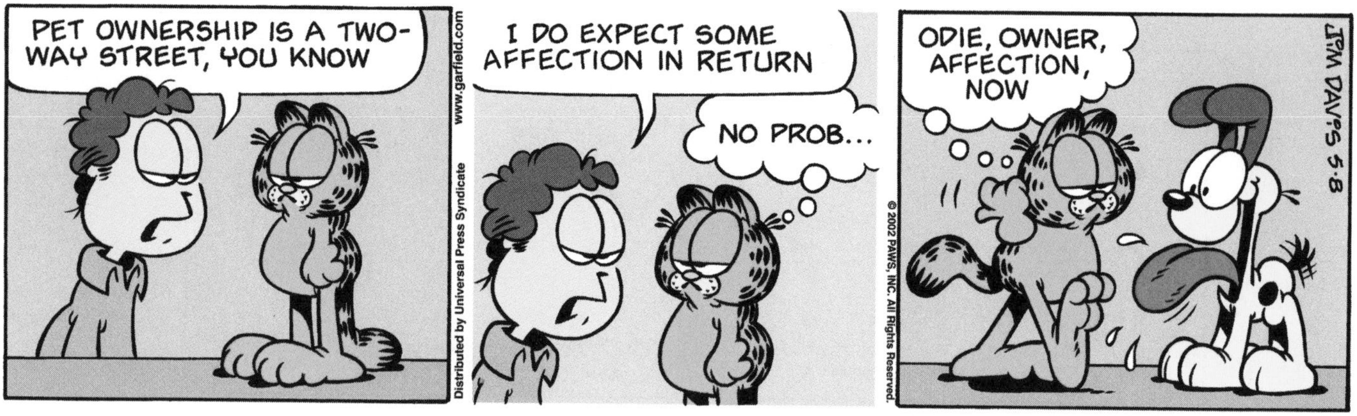
PET OWNERSHIP IS A TWO-WAY STREET, YOU KNOW
I DO EXPECT SOME AFFECTION IN RETURN
NO PROB...
ODIE, OWNER, AFFECTION, NOW
JIM DAVIS 5-8
Distributed by Universal Press Syndicate www.garfield.com
© 2002 PAWS, INC. All Rights Reserved.

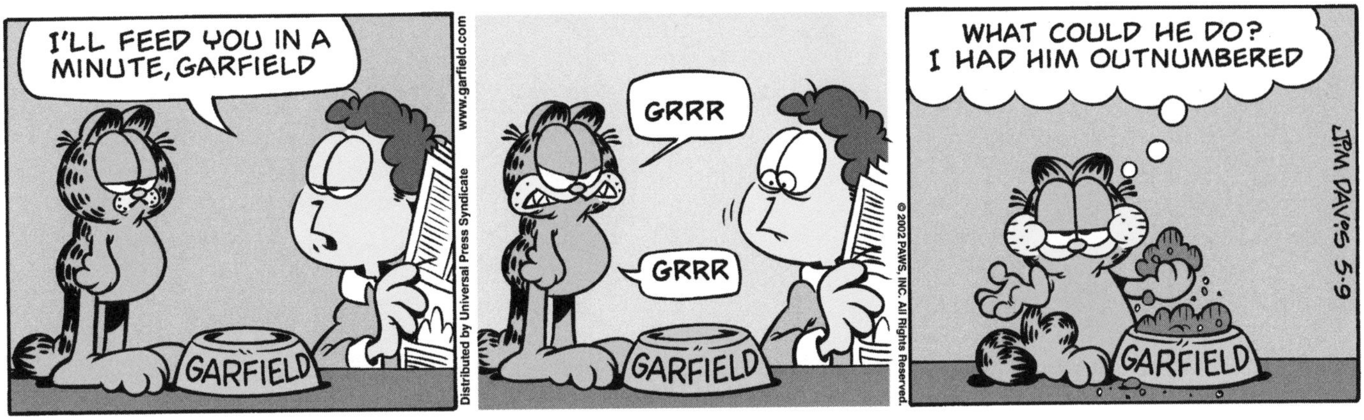
I'LL FEED YOU IN A MINUTE, GARFIELD
GRRR
GRRR
WHAT COULD HE DO? I HAD HIM OUTNUMBERED
GARFIELD
GARFIELD
GARFIELD
JIM DAVIS 5-9
Distributed by Universal Press Syndicate www.garfield.com
© 2002 PAWS, INC. All Rights Reserved.

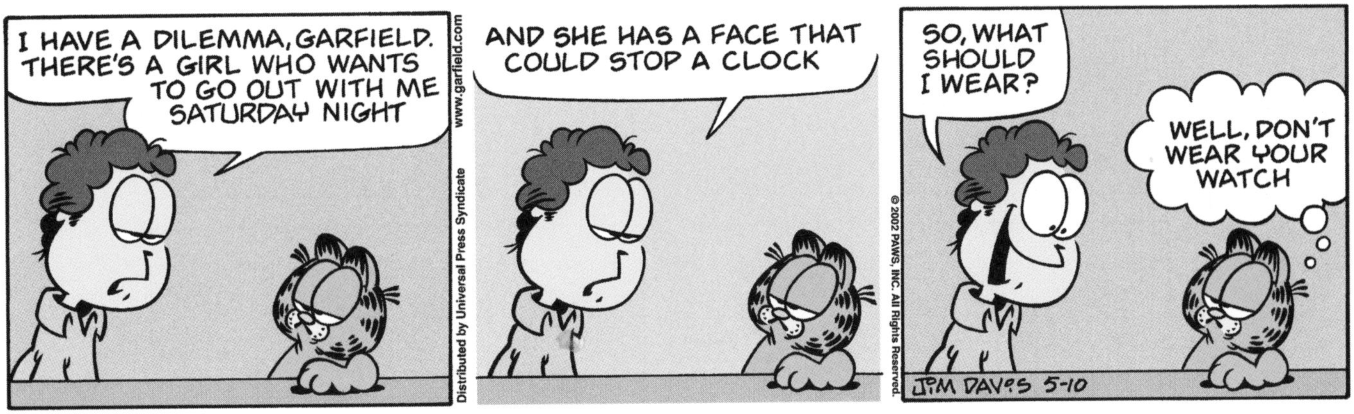
I HAVE A DILEMMA, GARFIELD. THERE'S A GIRL WHO WANTS TO GO OUT WITH ME SATURDAY NIGHT
AND SHE HAS A FACE THAT COULD STOP A CLOCK
SO, WHAT SHOULD I WEAR?
WELL, DON'T WEAR YOUR WATCH
JIM DAVIS 5-10
Distributed by Universal Press Syndicate www.garfield.com
© 2002 PAWS, INC. All Rights Reserved.

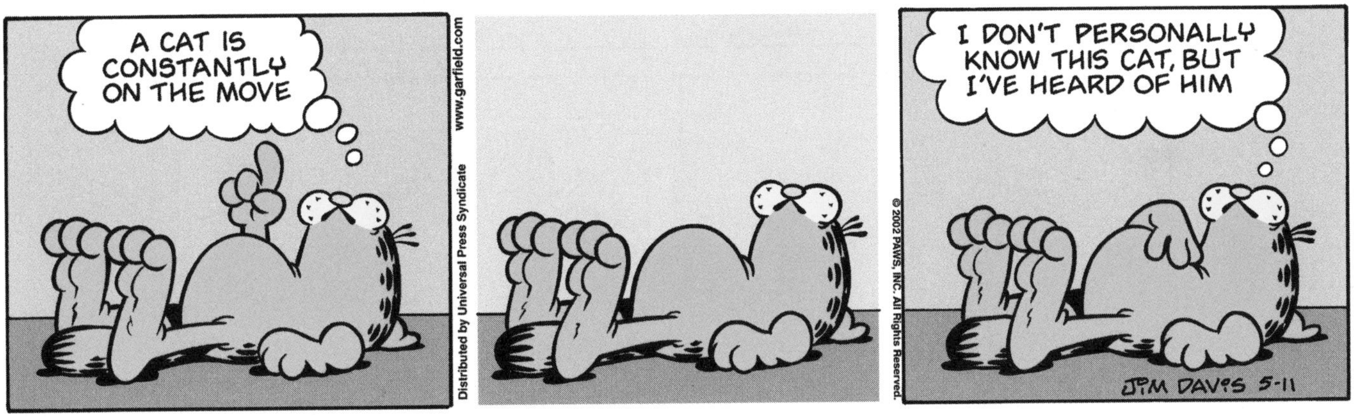
A CAT IS CONSTANTLY ON THE MOVE
I DON'T PERSONALLY KNOW THIS CAT, BUT I'VE HEARD OF HIM
JIM DAVIS 5-11
Distributed by Universal Press Syndicate www.garfield.com
© 2002 PAWS, INC. All Rights Reserved.

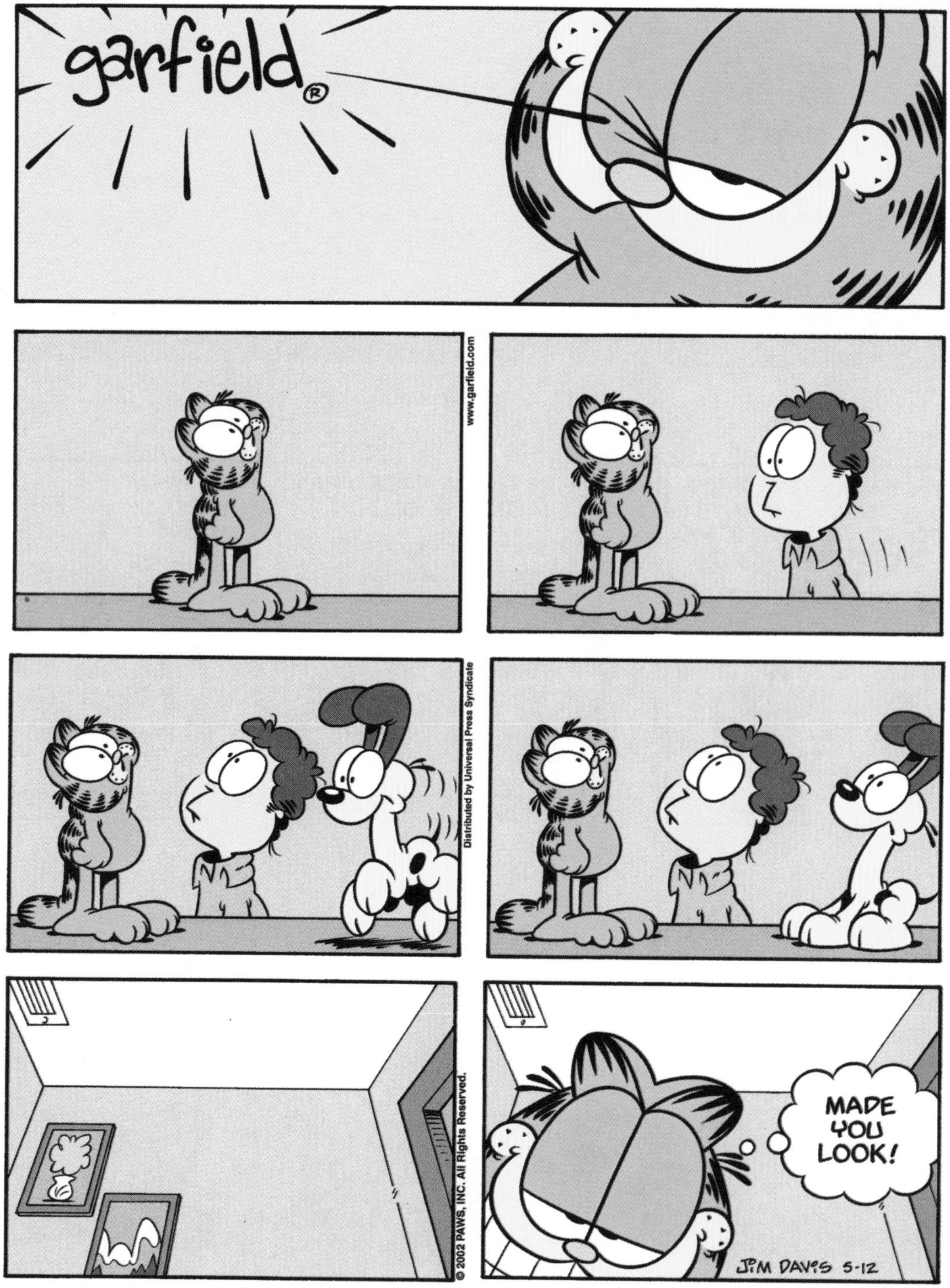
garfield®
www.garfield.com
Distributed by Universal Press Syndicate
© 2002 PAWS, INC. All Rights Reserved.
MADE YOU LOOK!
JIM DAVIS 5-12

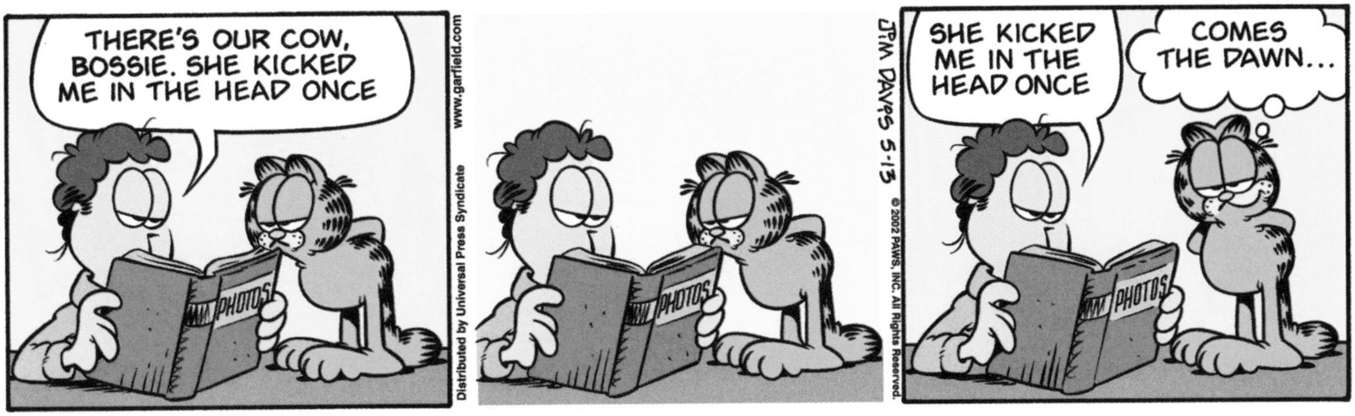
THERE'S OUR COW, BOSSIE. SHE KICKED ME IN THE HEAD ONCE
PHOTOS
Distributed by Universal Press Syndicate www.garfield.com
JIM DAVIS 5-13
© 2002 PAWS, INC. All Rights Reserved.
SHE KICKED ME IN THE HEAD ONCE
COMES THE DAWN...

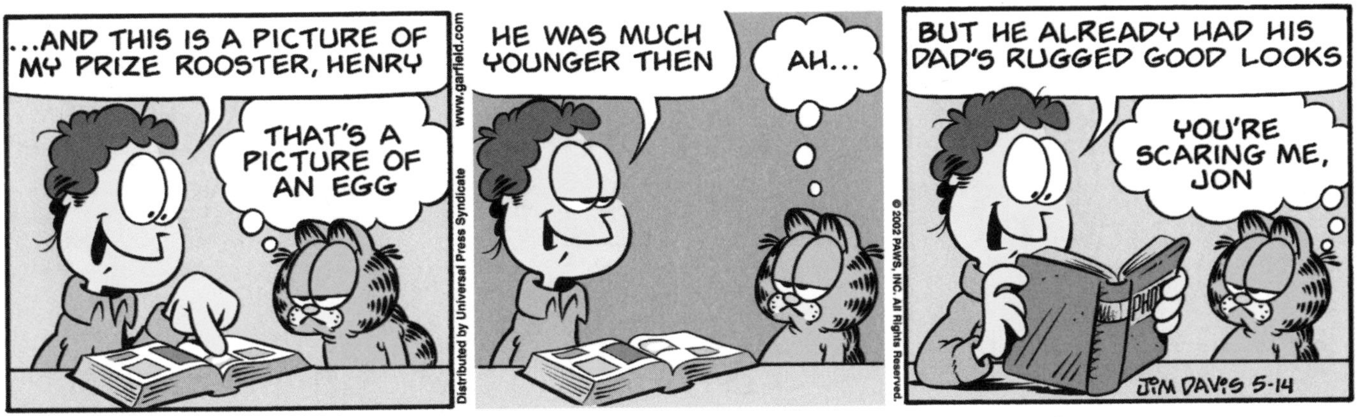
...AND THIS IS A PICTURE OF MY PRIZE ROOSTER, HENRY
THAT'S A PICTURE OF AN EGG
Distributed by Universal Press Syndicate www.garfield.com
HE WAS MUCH YOUNGER THEN
AH...
© 2002 PAWS, INC. All Rights Reserved.
BUT HE ALREADY HAD HIS DAD'S RUGGED GOOD LOOKS
YOU'RE SCARING ME, JON
JIM DAVIS 5-14

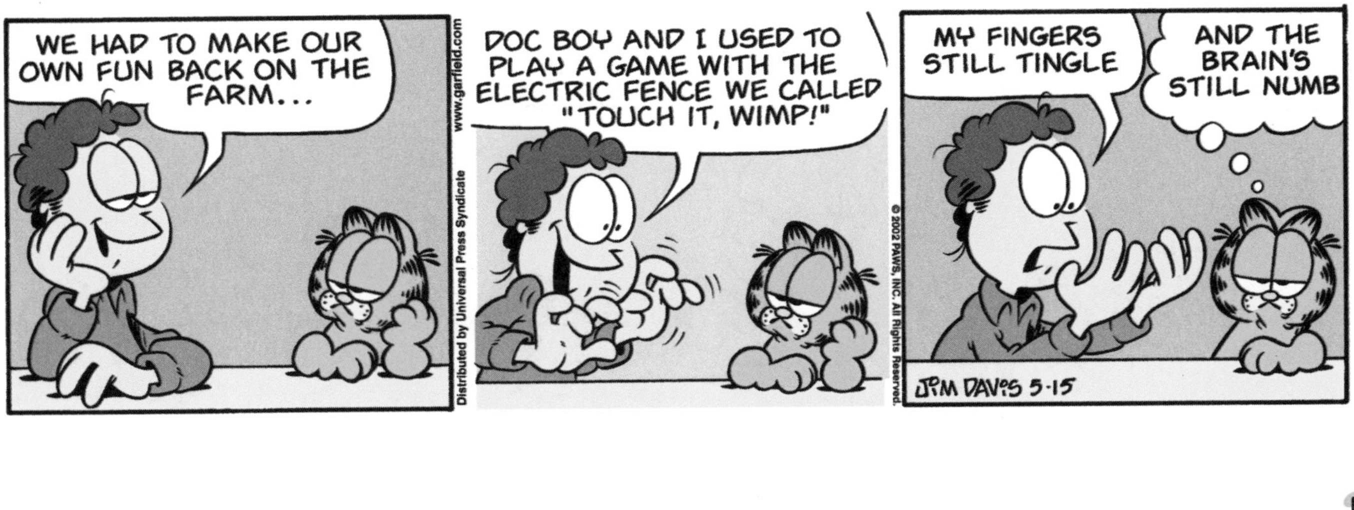
WE HAD TO MAKE OUR OWN FUN BACK ON THE FARM...
Distributed by Universal Press Syndicate www.garfield.com
DOC BOY AND I USED TO PLAY A GAME WITH THE ELECTRIC FENCE WE CALLED "TOUCH IT, WIMP!"
© 2002 PAWS, INC. All Rights Reserved.
MY FINGERS STILL TINGLE
AND THE BRAIN'S STILL NUMB
JIM DAVIS 5-15

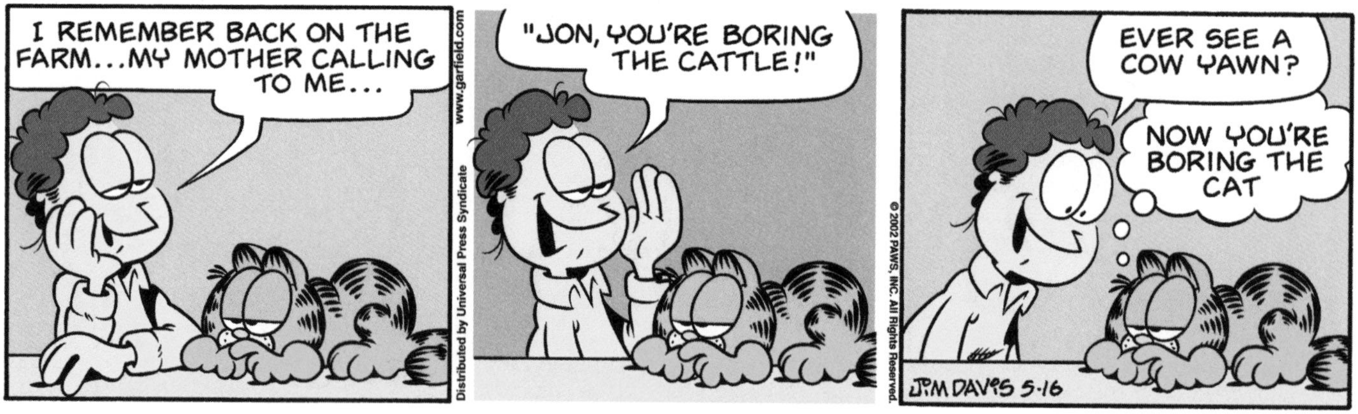
I REMEMBER BACK ON THE FARM...MY MOTHER CALLING TO ME...
"JON, YOU'RE BORING THE CATTLE!"
EVER SEE A COW YAWN?
NOW YOU'RE BORING THE CAT
JIM DAVIS 5-16
www.garfield.com
Distributed by Universal Press Syndicate
© 2002 PAWS, INC. All Rights Reserved.

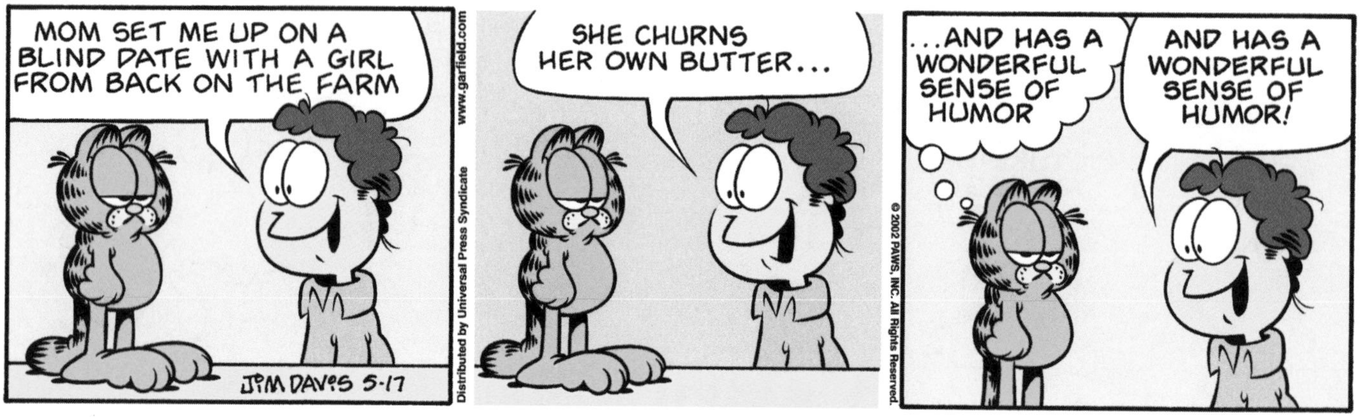
MOM SET ME UP ON A BLIND DATE WITH A GIRL FROM BACK ON THE FARM
SHE CHURNS HER OWN BUTTER...
...AND HAS A WONDERFUL SENSE OF HUMOR
AND HAS A WONDERFUL SENSE OF HUMOR!
JIM DAVIS 5-17
www.garfield.com
Distributed by Universal Press Syndicate
© 2002 PAWS, INC. All Rights Reserved.

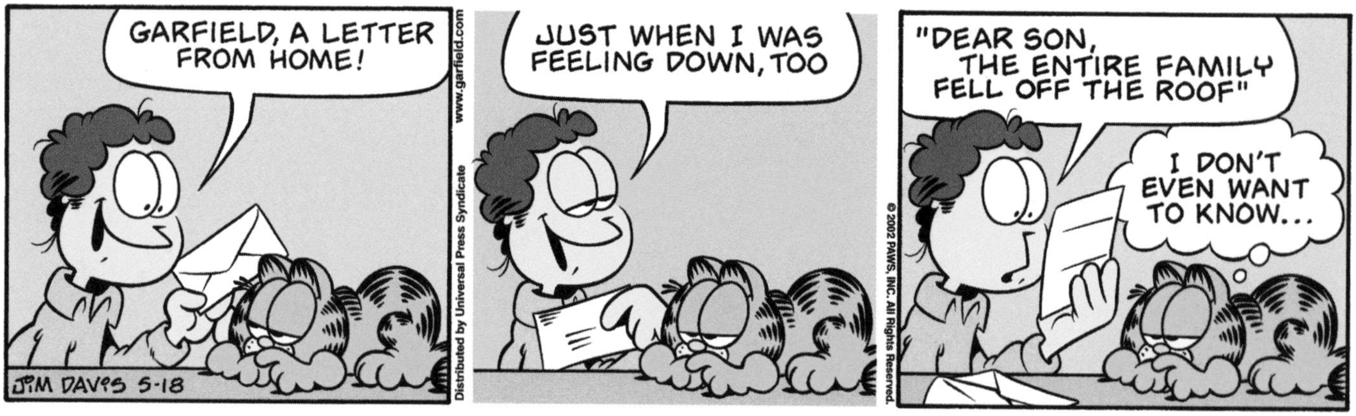
GARFIELD, A LETTER FROM HOME!
JUST WHEN I WAS FEELING DOWN, TOO
"DEAR SON, THE ENTIRE FAMILY FELL OFF THE ROOF"
I DON'T EVEN WANT TO KNOW...
JIM DAVIS 5-18
www.garfield.com
Distributed by Universal Press Syndicate
© 2002 PAWS, INC. All Rights Reserved.

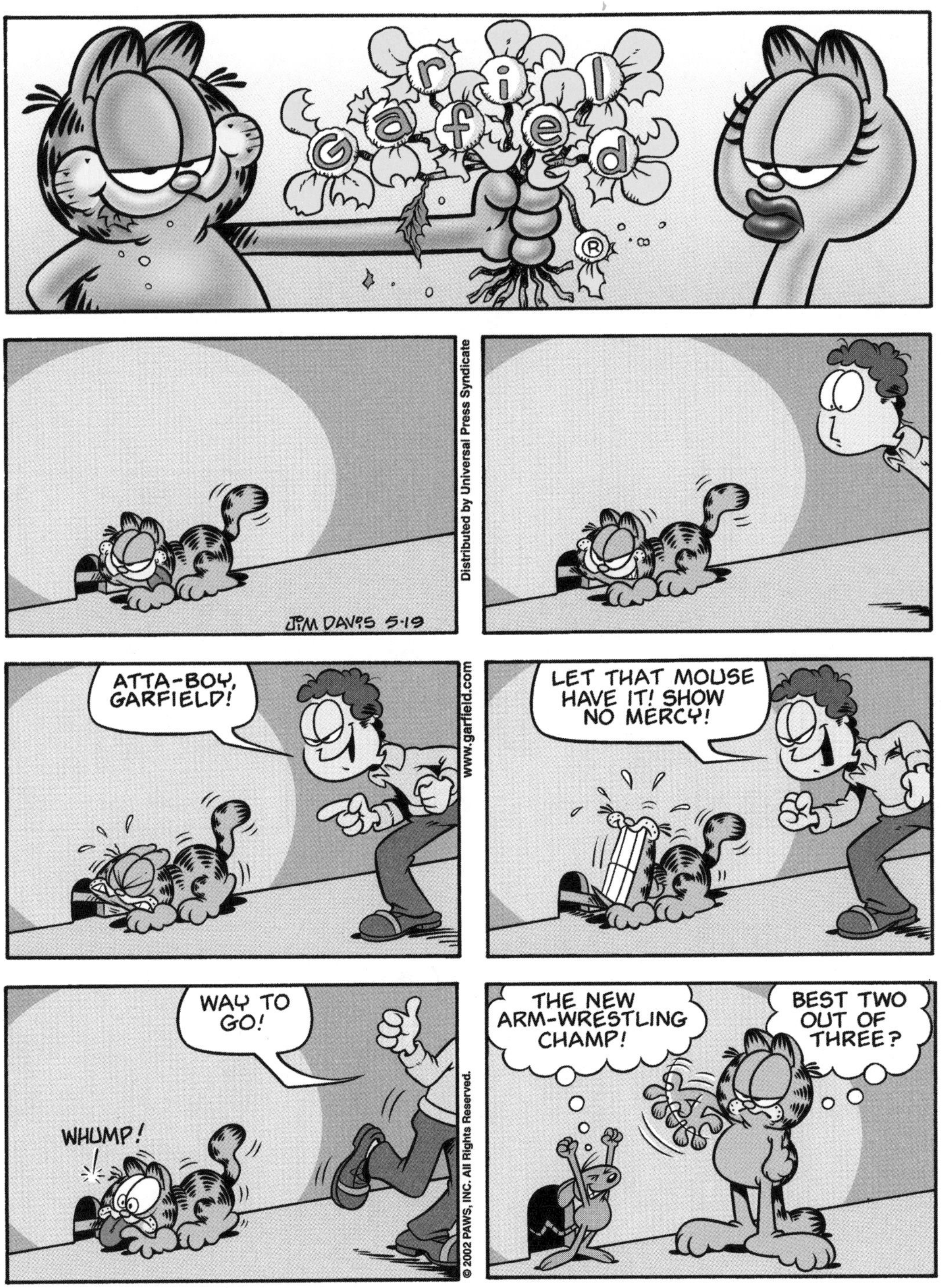
Garfield
JIM DAVIS 5-19
Distributed by Universal Press Syndicate
ATTA-BOY, GARFIELD!
www.garfield.com
LET THAT MOUSE HAVE IT! SHOW NO MERCY!
WAY TO GO!
WHUMP!
© 2002 PAWS, INC. All Rights Reserved.
THE NEW ARM-WRESTLING CHAMP!
BEST TWO OUT OF THREE?

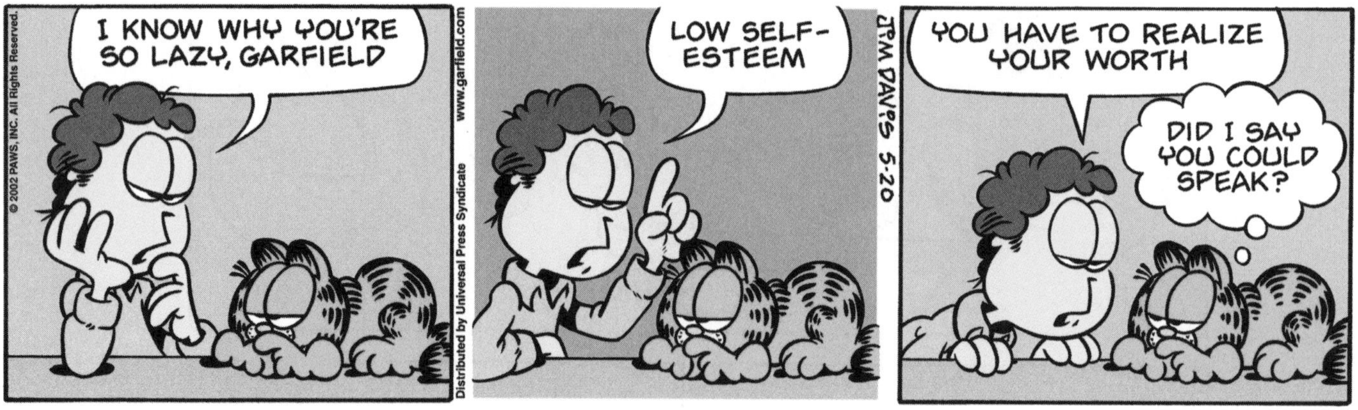
© 2002 PAWS, INC. All Rights Reserved.
I KNOW WHY YOU'RE SO LAZY, GARFIELD
www.garfield.com
Distributed by Universal Press Syndicate
LOW SELF-ESTEEM
JIM DAVIS 5-20
YOU HAVE TO REALIZE YOUR WORTH
DID I SAY YOU COULD SPEAK?

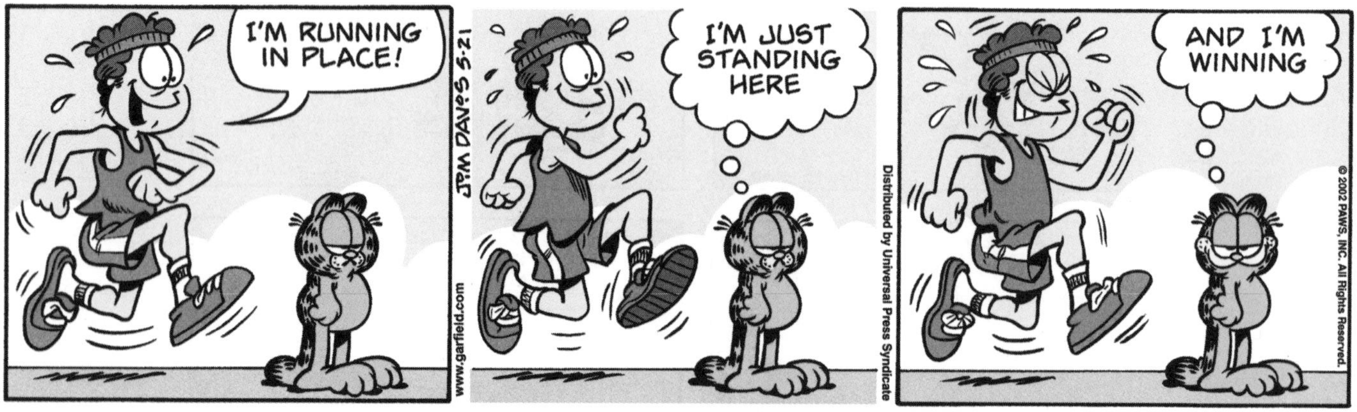
I'M RUNNING IN PLACE!
JIM DAVIS 5-21
www.garfield.com
I'M JUST STANDING HERE
Distributed by Universal Press Syndicate
AND I'M WINNING
© 2002 PAWS, INC. All Rights Reserved.

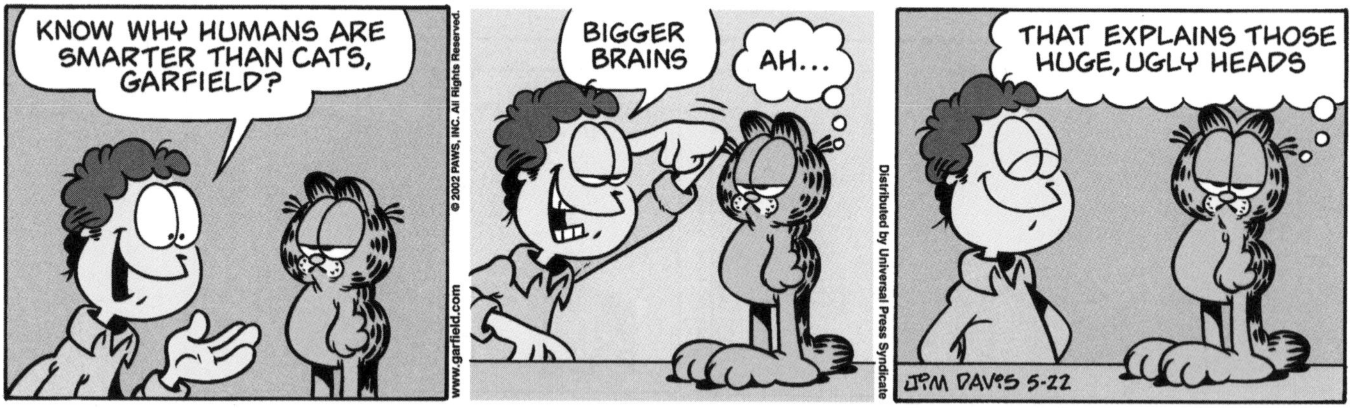
KNOW WHY HUMANS ARE SMARTER THAN CATS, GARFIELD?
© 2002 PAWS, INC. All Rights Reserved.
www.garfield.com
BIGGER BRAINS
AH...
Distributed by Universal Press Syndicate
THAT EXPLAINS THOSE HUGE, UGLY HEADS
JIM DAVIS 5-22

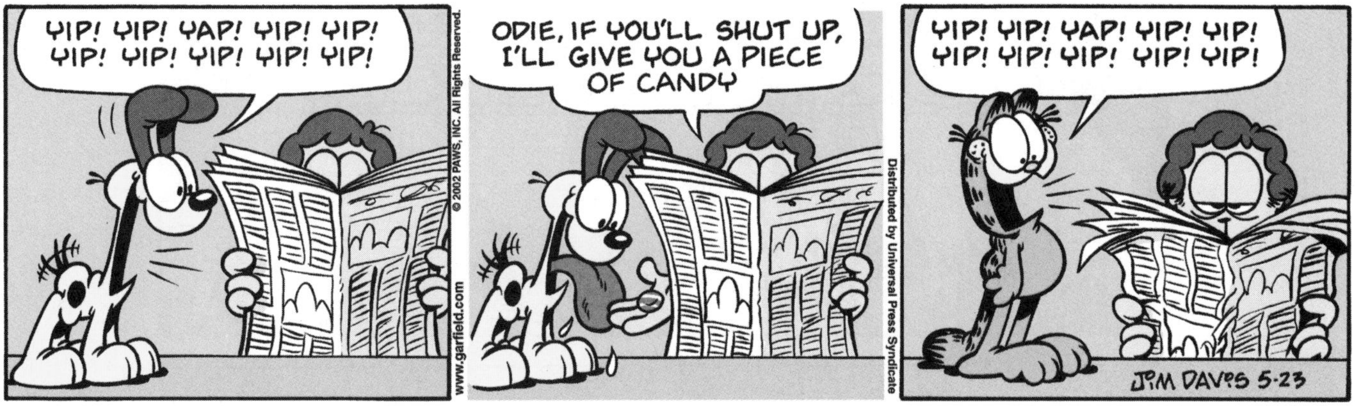
YIP! YIP! YAP! YIP! YIP! YIP! YIP! YIP! YIP! YIP!
© 2002 PAWS, INC. All Rights Reserved.
www.garfield.com
ODIE, IF YOU'LL SHUT UP, I'LL GIVE YOU A PIECE OF CANDY
Distributed by Universal Press Syndicate
YIP! YIP! YAP! YIP! YIP! YIP! YIP! YIP! YIP! YIP!
JIM DAVIS 5-23

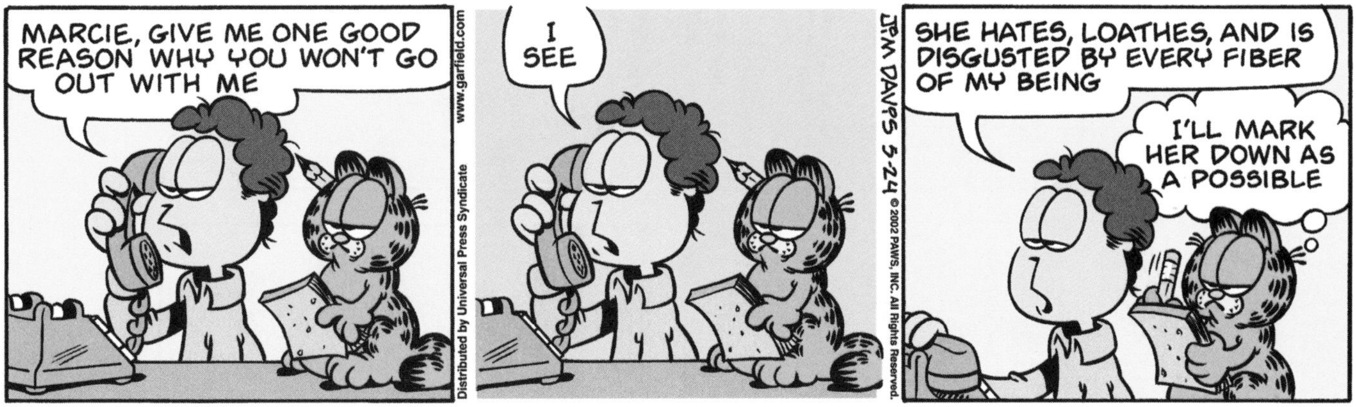
MARCIE, GIVE ME ONE GOOD REASON WHY YOU WON'T GO OUT WITH ME
www.garfield.com
Distributed by Universal Press Syndicate
I SEE
JIM DAVIS 5-24
© 2002 PAWS, INC. All Rights Reserved.
SHE HATES, LOATHES, AND IS DISGUSTED BY EVERY FIBER OF MY BEING
I'LL MARK HER DOWN AS A POSSIBLE

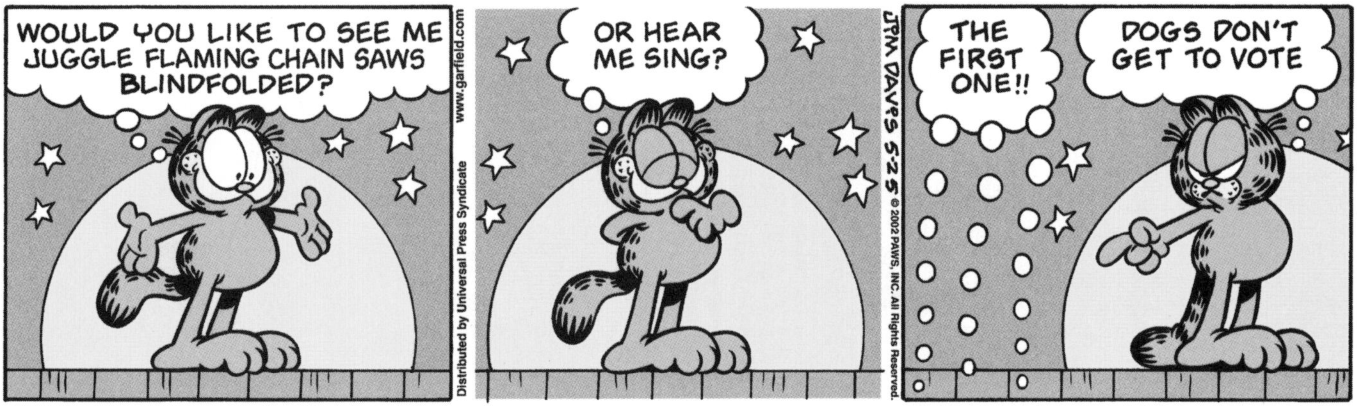
WOULD YOU LIKE TO SEE ME JUGGLE FLAMING CHAIN SAWS BLINDFOLDED?
www.garfield.com
Distributed by Universal Press Syndicate
OR HEAR ME SING?
JIM DAVIS 5-25
© 2002 PAWS, INC. All Rights Reserved.
THE FIRST ONE!!
DOGS DON'T GET TO VOTE

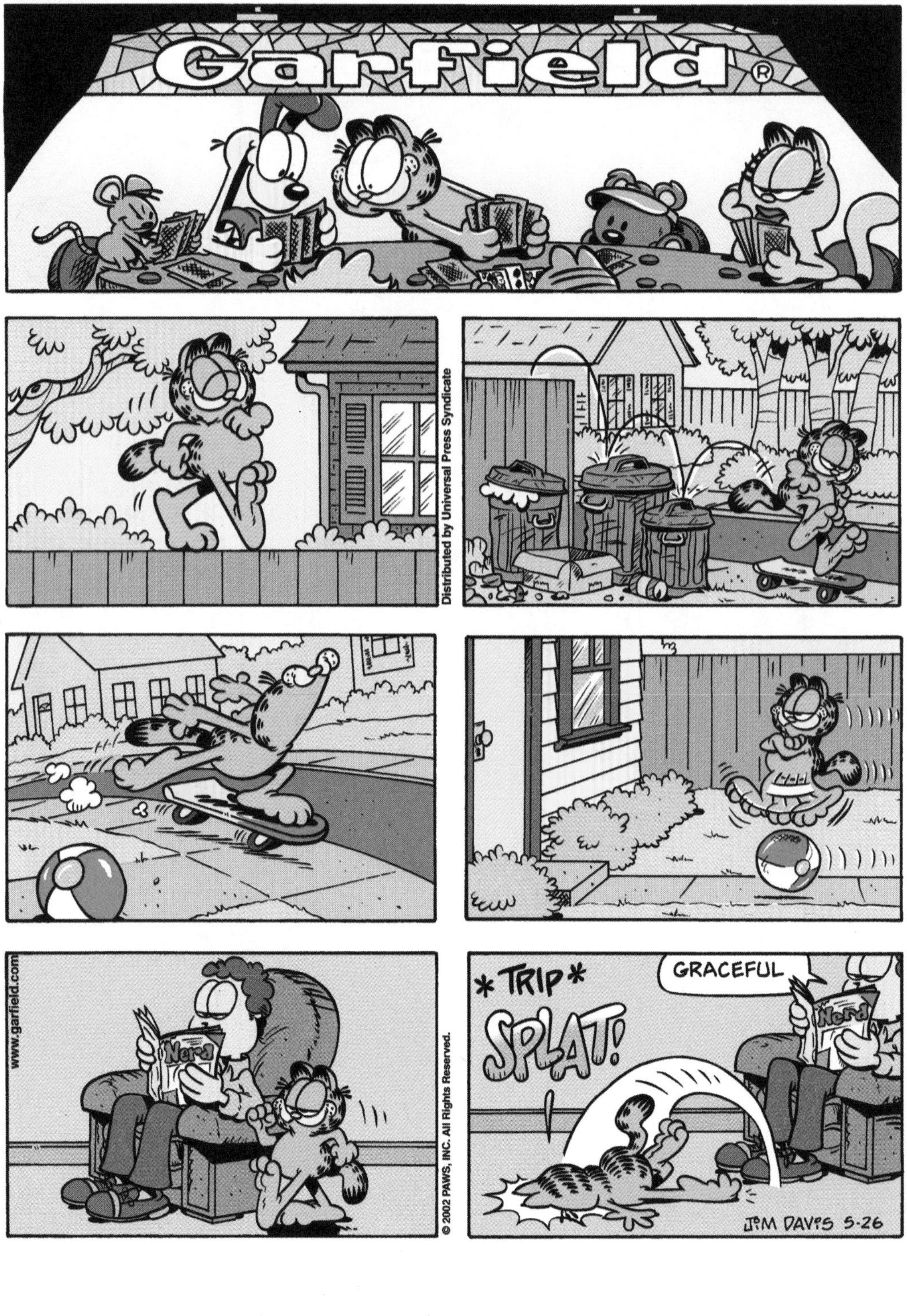
Garfield®
Distributed by Universal Press Syndicate
www.garfield.com
© 2002 PAWS, INC. All Rights Reserved.
TRIP
SPLAT!
GRACEFUL
JIM DAVIS 5-26

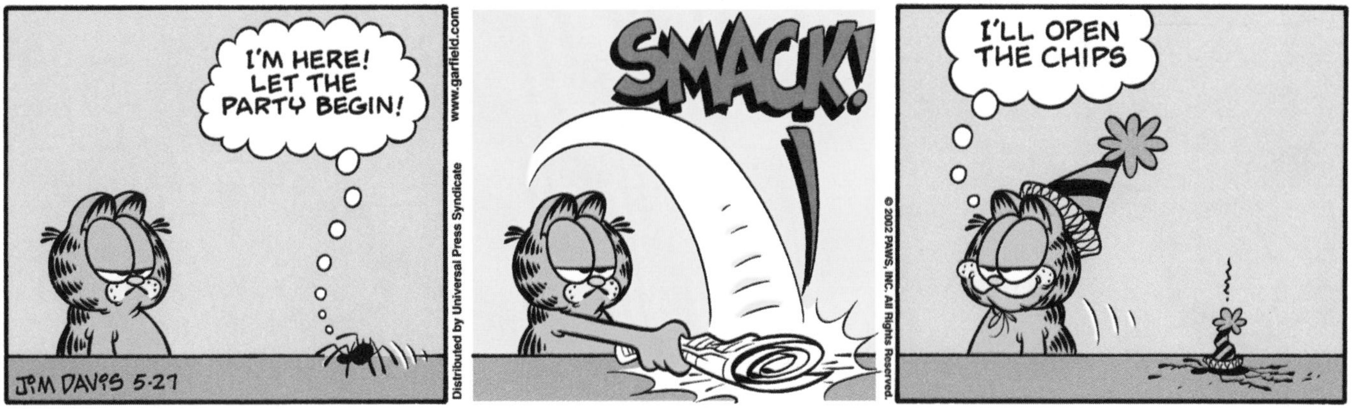
I'M HERE! LET THE PARTY BEGIN!
JIM DAVIS 5-27
www.garfield.com
Distributed by Universal Press Syndicate
SMACK!
© 2002 PAWS, INC. All Rights Reserved.
I'LL OPEN THE CHIPS

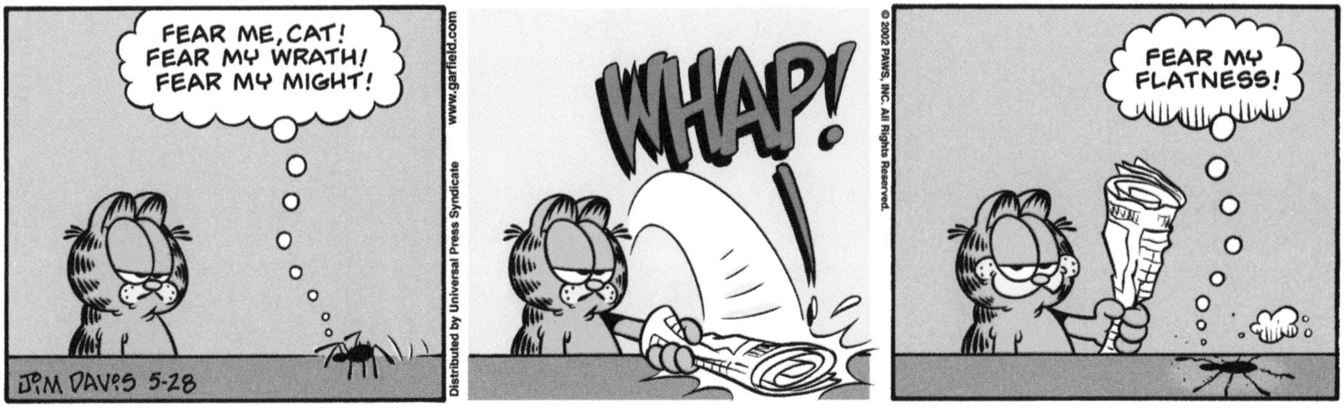
FEAR ME, CAT! FEAR MY WRATH! FEAR MY MIGHT!
JIM DAVIS 5-28
www.garfield.com
Distributed by Universal Press Syndicate
WHAP!
© 2002 PAWS, INC. All Rights Reserved.
FEAR MY FLATNESS!

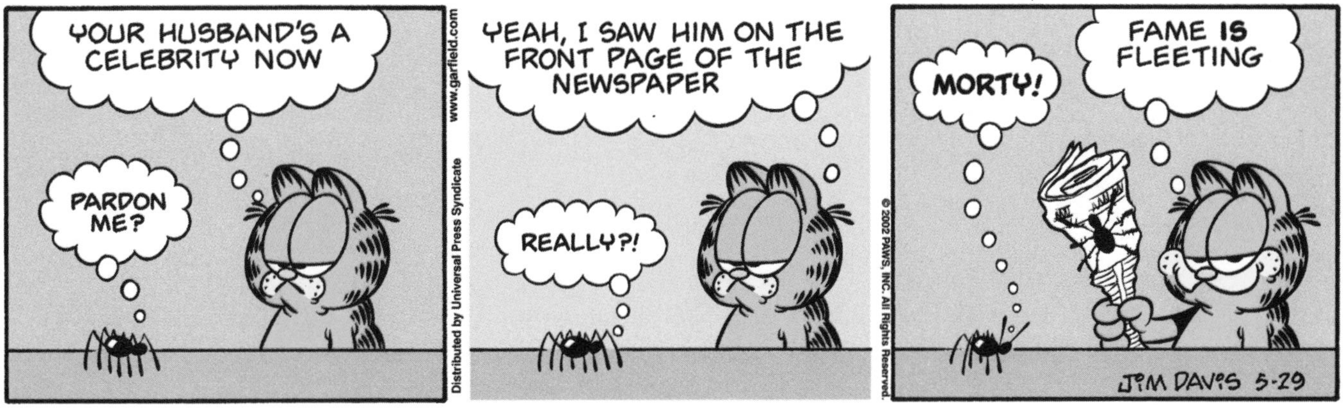
YOUR HUSBAND'S A CELEBRITY NOW
PARDON ME?
www.garfield.com
Distributed by Universal Press Syndicate
YEAH, I SAW HIM ON THE FRONT PAGE OF THE NEWSPAPER
REALLY?!
© 2002 PAWS, INC. All Rights Reserved.
MORTY!
FAME IS FLEETING
JIM DAVIS 5-29

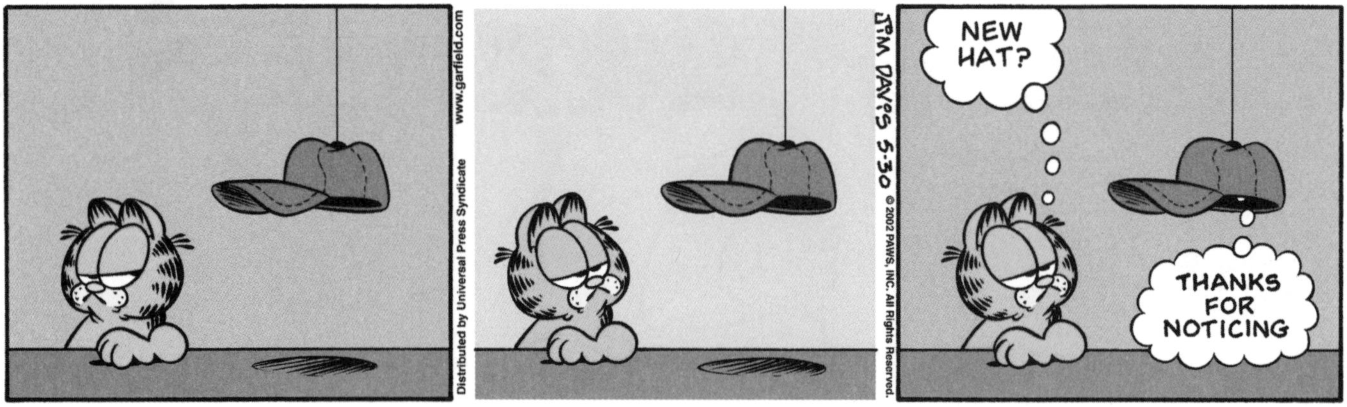
Distributed by Universal Press Syndicate www.garfield.com
JIM DAVIS 5-30
© 2002 PAWS, INC. All Rights Reserved.
NEW HAT?
THANKS FOR NOTICING

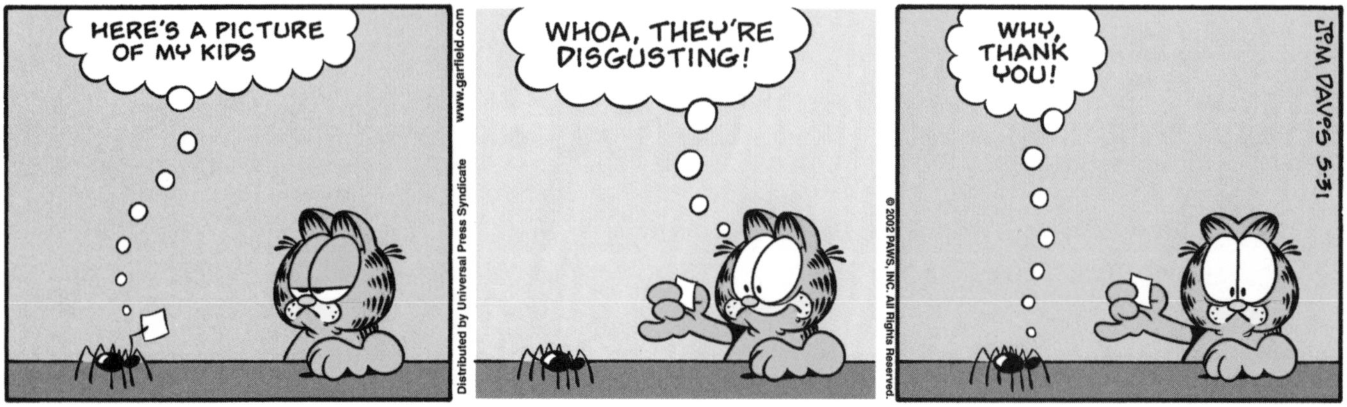
HERE'S A PICTURE OF MY KIDS
Distributed by Universal Press Syndicate www.garfield.com
WHOA, THEY'RE DISGUSTING!
© 2002 PAWS, INC. All Rights Reserved.
WHY, THANK YOU!
JIM DAVIS 5-31

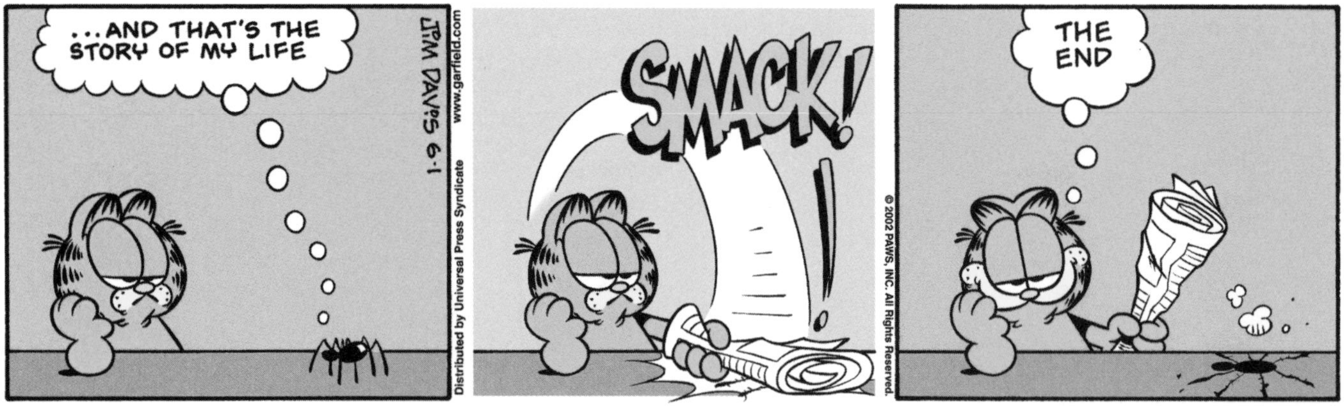
...AND THAT'S THE STORY OF MY LIFE
JIM DAVIS 6-1
Distributed by Universal Press Syndicate www.garfield.com
SMACK!
© 2002 PAWS, INC. All Rights Reserved.
THE END

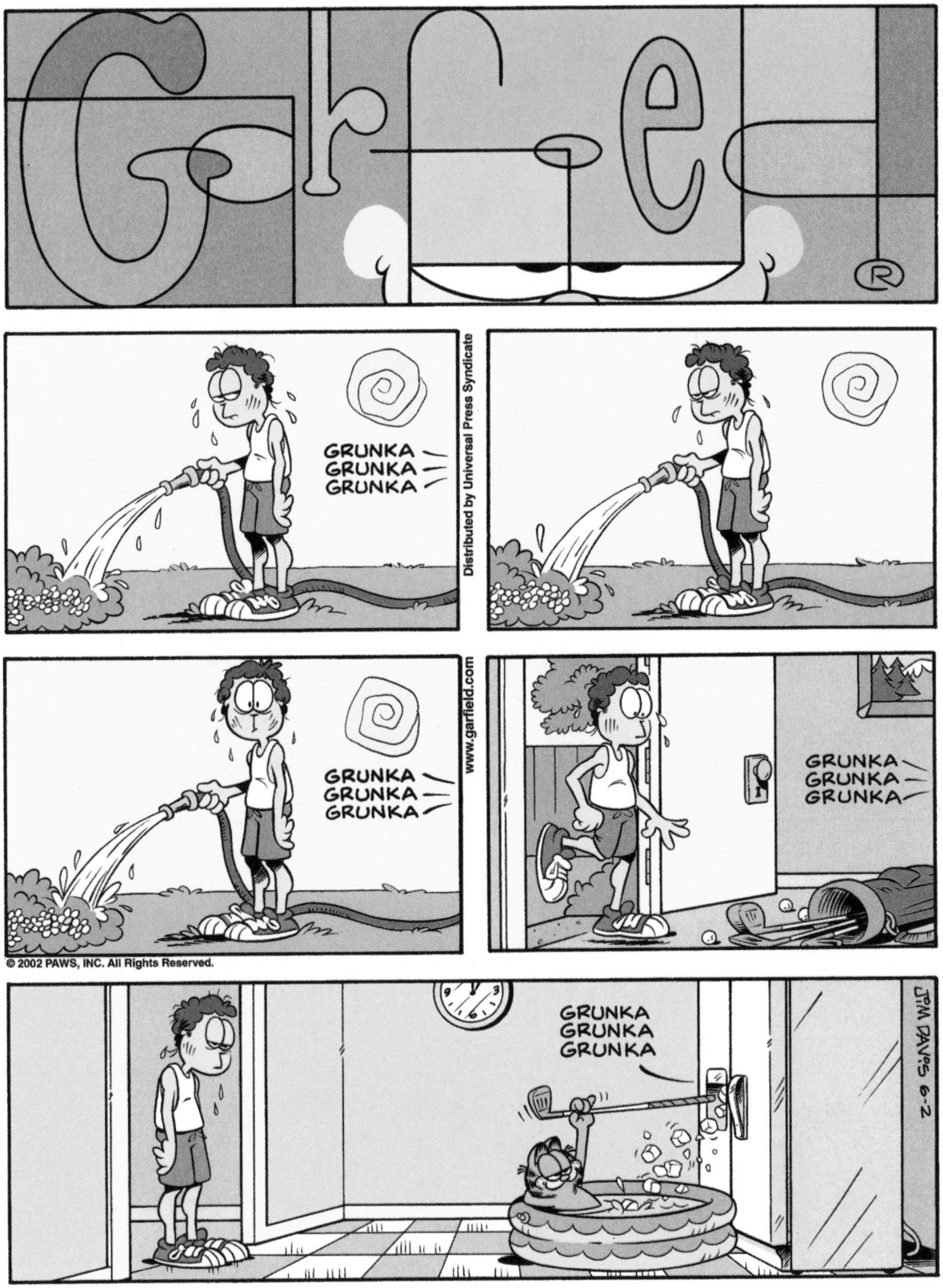
Garfield
Distributed by Universal Press Syndicate
GRUNKA
GRUNKA
GRUNKA
GRUNKA
GRUNKA
GRUNKA
www.garfield.com
GRUNKA
GRUNKA
GRUNKA
GRUNKA
GRUNKA
GRUNKA
GRUNKA
GRUNKA
GRUNKA
JIM DAVIS 6-2

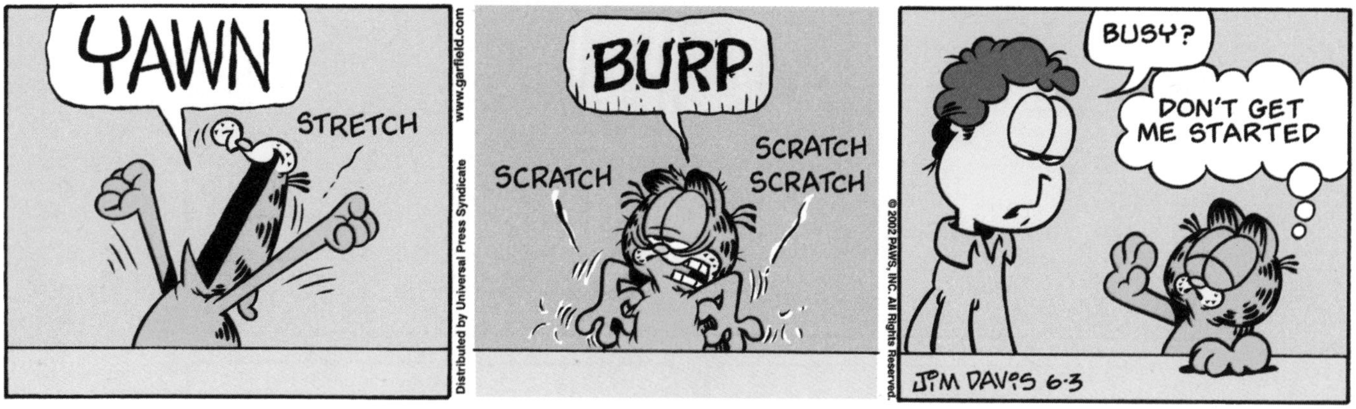
YAWN
STRETCH
BURP
SCRATCH
SCRATCH
SCRATCH
BUSY?
DON'T GET ME STARTED
JIM DAVIS 6-3
Distributed by Universal Press Syndicate www.garfield.com
© 2002 PAWS, INC. All Rights Reserved.

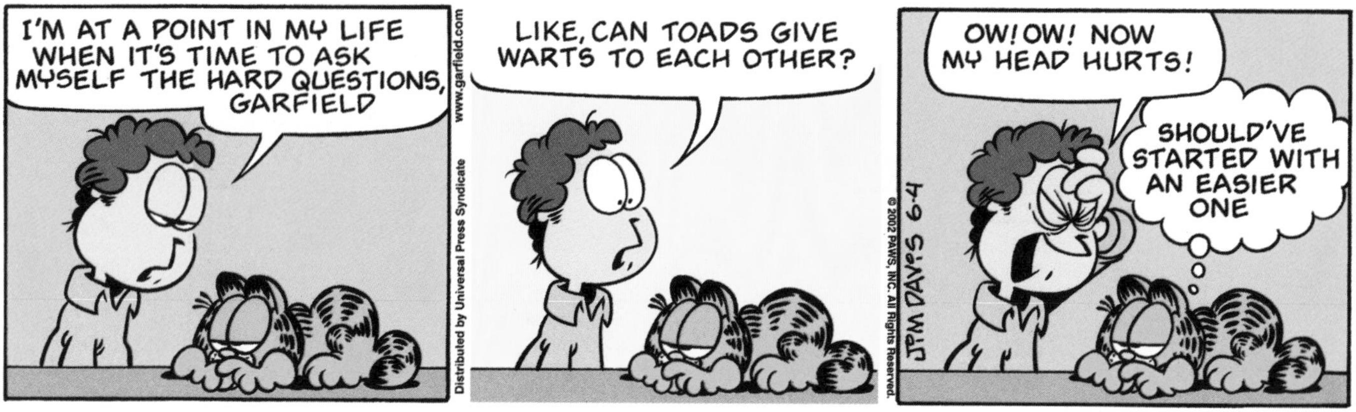
I'M AT A POINT IN MY LIFE WHEN IT'S TIME TO ASK MYSELF THE HARD QUESTIONS, GARFIELD
LIKE, CAN TOADS GIVE WARTS TO EACH OTHER?
OW! OW! NOW MY HEAD HURTS!
SHOULD'VE STARTED WITH AN EASIER ONE
JIM DAVIS 6-4
Distributed by Universal Press Syndicate www.garfield.com
© 2002 PAWS, INC. All Rights Reserved.

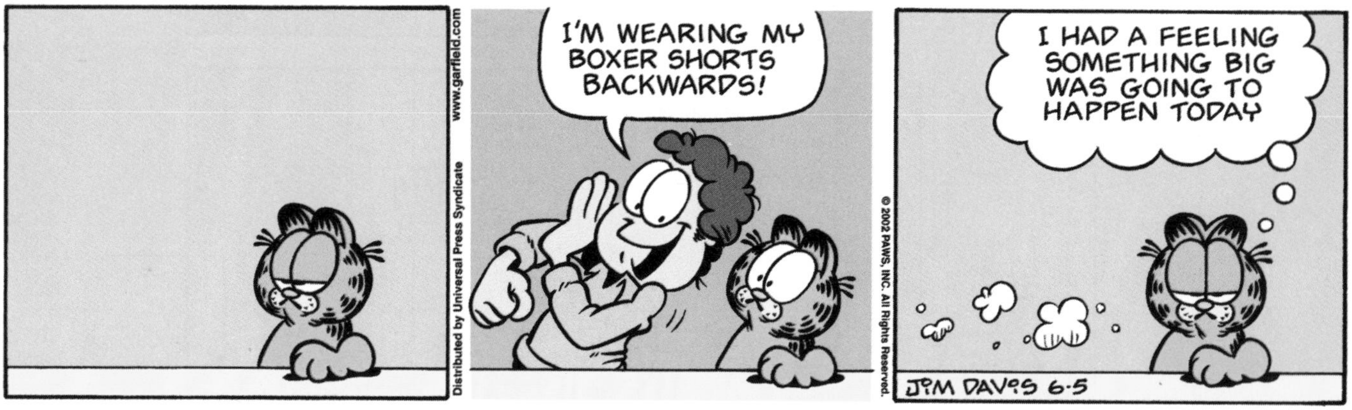
I'M WEARING MY BOXER SHORTS BACKWARDS!
I HAD A FEELING SOMETHING BIG WAS GOING TO HAPPEN TODAY
JIM DAVIS 6-5
Distributed by Universal Press Syndicate www.garfield.com
© 2002 PAWS, INC. All Rights Reserved.

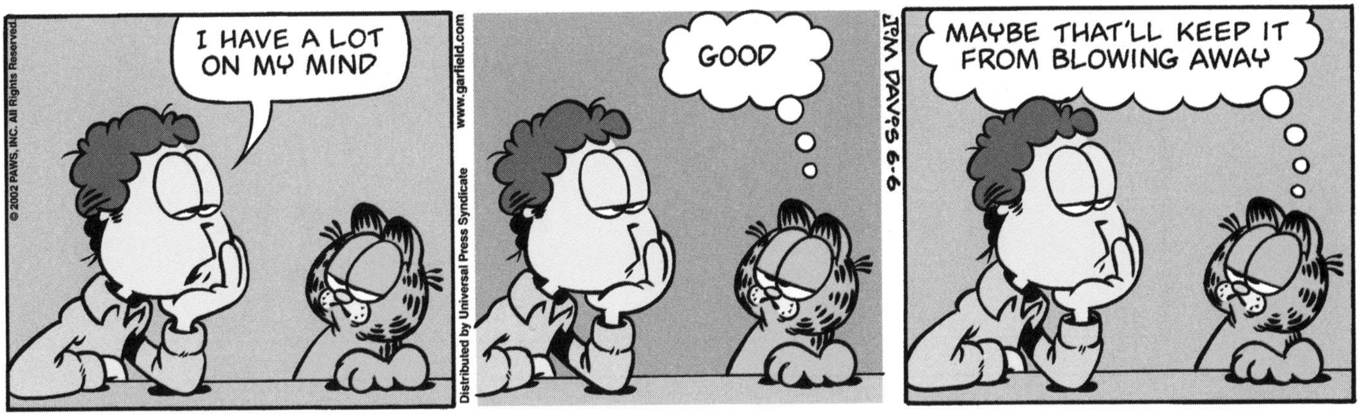
© 2002 PAWS, INC. All Rights Reserved
I HAVE A LOT ON MY MIND
Distributed by Universal Press Syndicate www.garfield.com
GOOD
JIM DAVIS 6-6
MAYBE THAT'LL KEEP IT FROM BLOWING AWAY

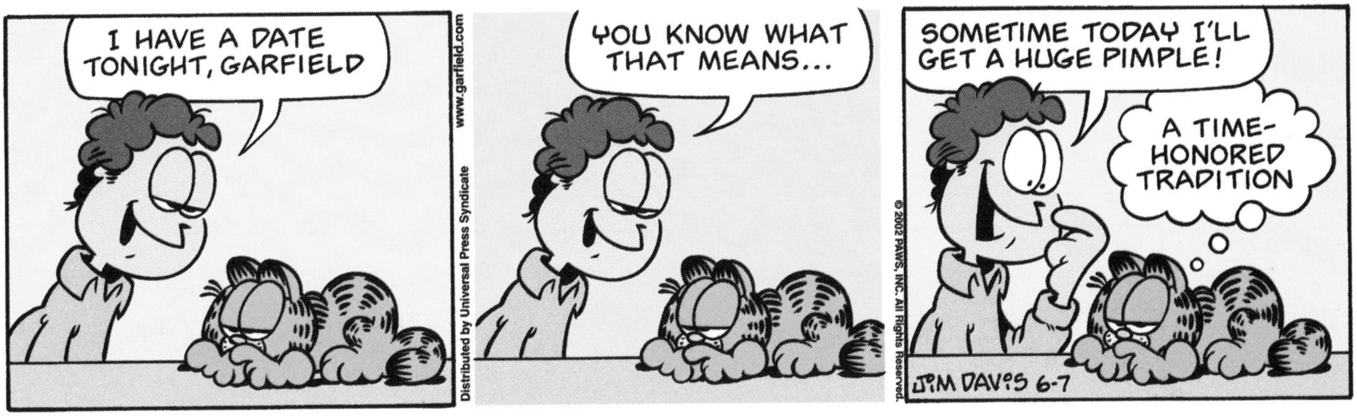
I HAVE A DATE TONIGHT, GARFIELD
Distributed by Universal Press Syndicate www.garfield.com
YOU KNOW WHAT THAT MEANS...
© 2002 PAWS, INC. All Rights Reserved.
SOMETIME TODAY I'LL GET A HUGE PIMPLE!
A TIME-HONORED TRADITION
JIM DAVIS 6-7

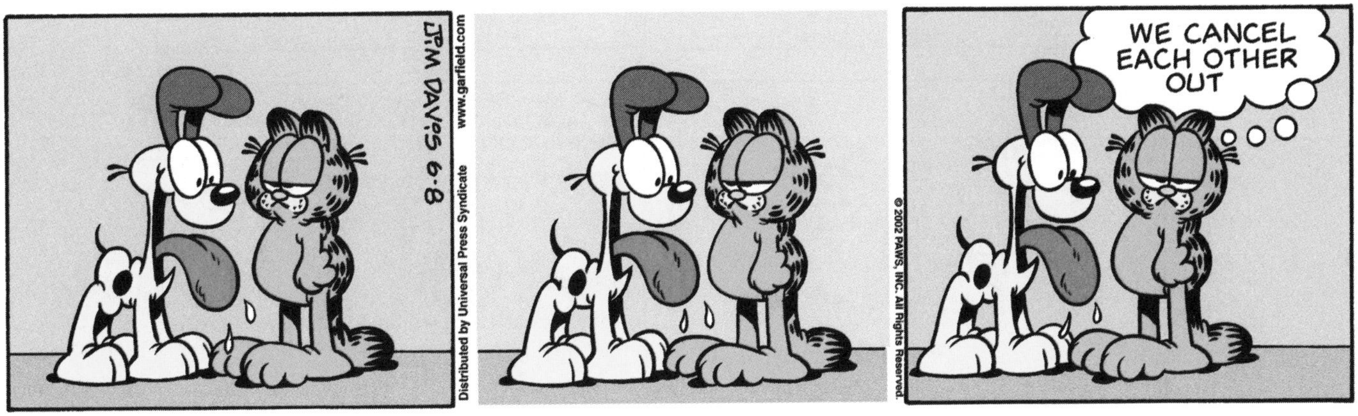
JIM DAVIS 6-8
Distributed by Universal Press Syndicate www.garfield.com
© 2002 PAWS, INC. All Rights Reserved.
WE CANCEL EACH OTHER OUT

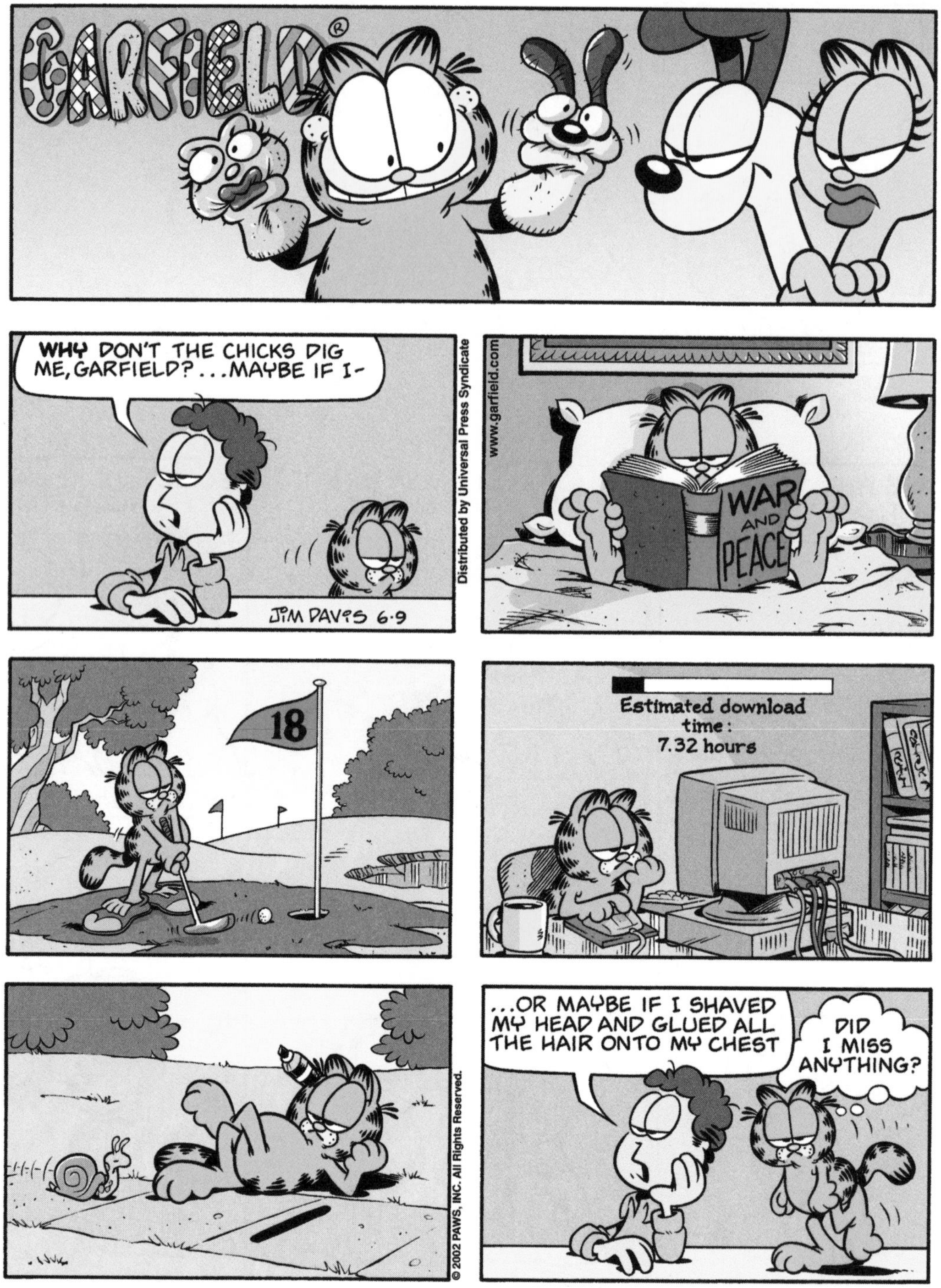

GARFIELD®
WHY DON'T THE CHICKS DIG ME, GARFIELD? . . . MAYBE IF I-
JIM DAVIS 6-9
Distributed by Universal Press Syndicate
www.garfield.com
WAR AND PEACE
18
Estimated download time : 7.32 hours
© 2002 PAWS, INC. All Rights Reserved.
. . .OR MAYBE IF I SHAVED MY HEAD AND GLUED ALL THE HAIR ONTO MY CHEST
DID I MISS ANYTHING?

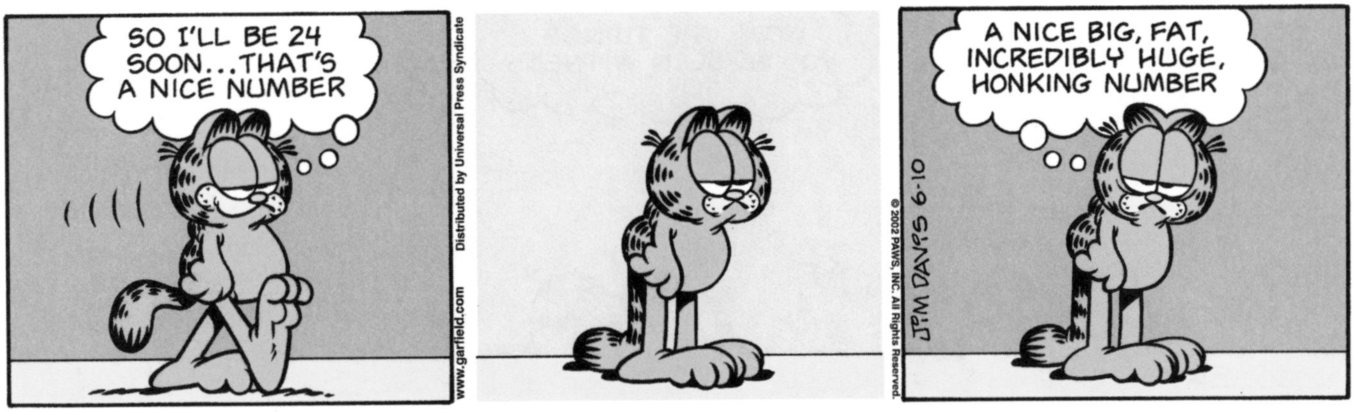
SO I'LL BE 24 SOON...THAT'S A NICE NUMBER
A NICE BIG, FAT, INCREDIBLY HUGE, HONKING NUMBER
www.garfield.com Distributed by Universal Press Syndicate
© 2002 PAWS, INC. All Rights Reserved.
JIM DAVIS 6-10

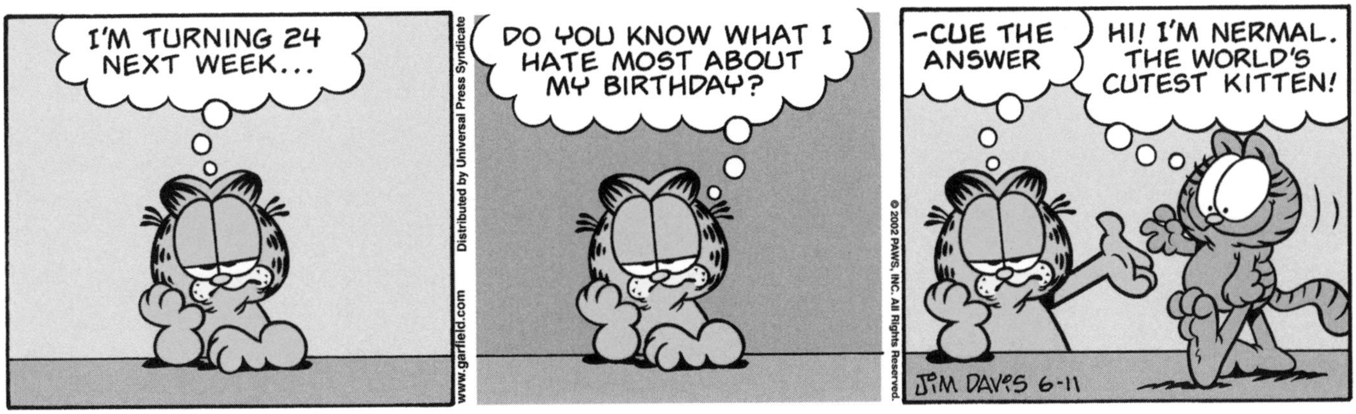
I'M TURNING 24 NEXT WEEK...
DO YOU KNOW WHAT I HATE MOST ABOUT MY BIRTHDAY?
-CUE THE ANSWER
HI! I'M NERMAL. THE WORLD'S CUTEST KITTEN!
www.garfield.com Distributed by Universal Press Syndicate
© 2002 PAWS, INC. All Rights Reserved.
JIM DAVIS 6-11

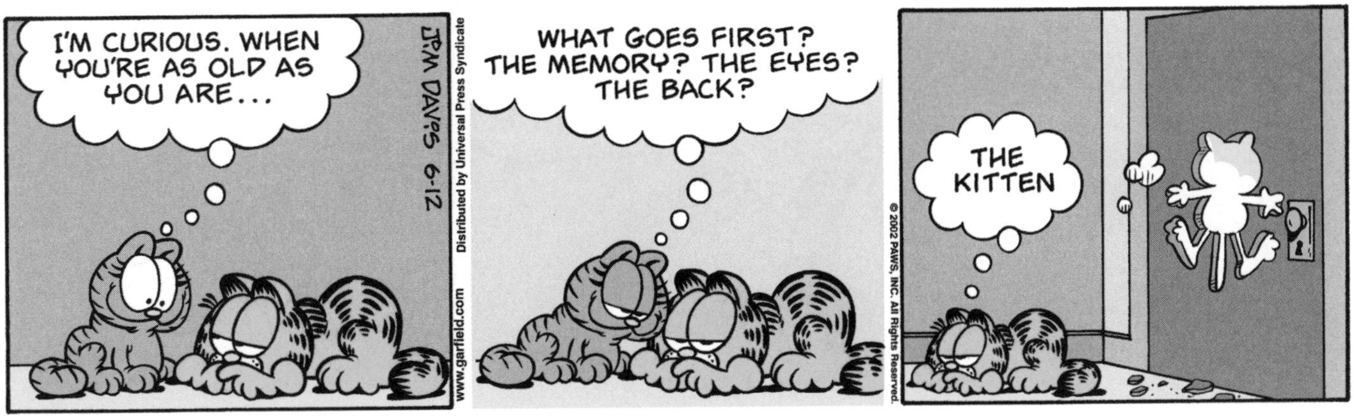
I'M CURIOUS. WHEN YOU'RE AS OLD AS YOU ARE...
WHAT GOES FIRST? THE MEMORY? THE EYES? THE BACK?
THE KITTEN
JIM DAVIS 6-12
www.garfield.com Distributed by Universal Press Syndicate
© 2002 PAWS, INC. All Rights Reserved.

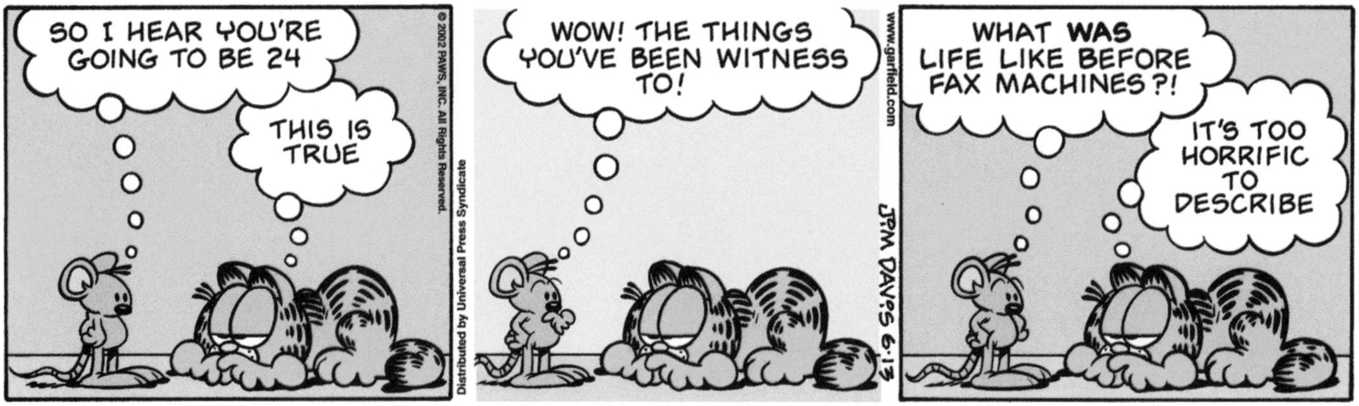
SO I HEAR YOU'RE GOING TO BE 24
THIS IS TRUE
WOW! THE THINGS YOU'VE BEEN WITNESS TO!
WHAT WAS LIFE LIKE BEFORE FAX MACHINES?!
IT'S TOO HORRIFIC TO DESCRIBE

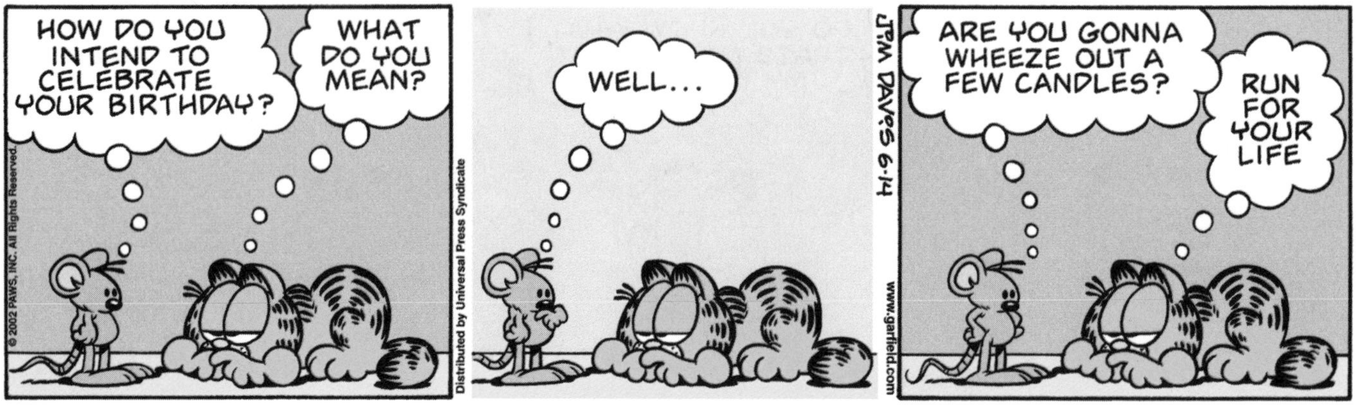
HOW DO YOU INTEND TO CELEBRATE YOUR BIRTHDAY?
WHAT DO YOU MEAN?
WELL...
ARE YOU GONNA WHEEZE OUT A FEW CANDLES?
RUN FOR YOUR LIFE

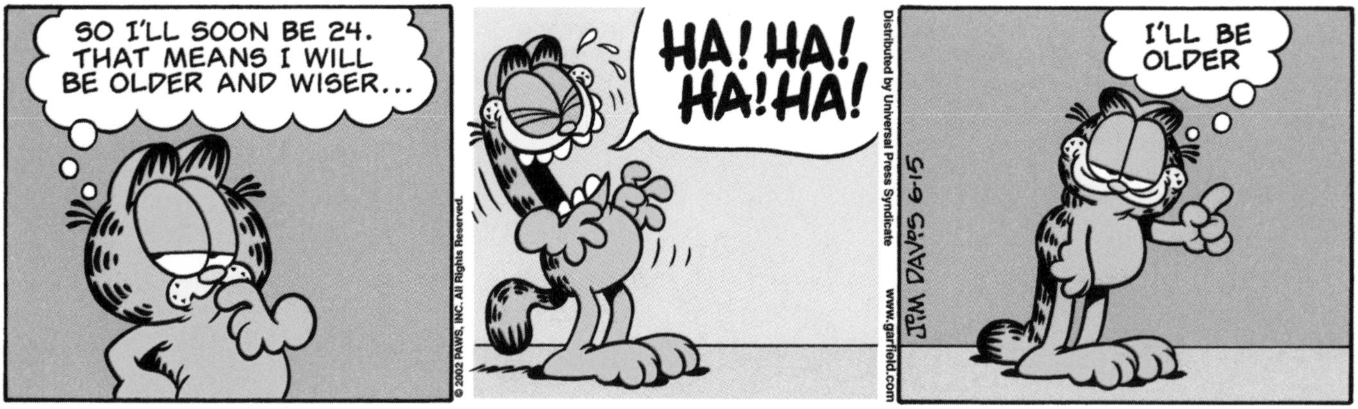
SO I'LL SOON BE 24. THAT MEANS I WILL BE OLDER AND WISER...
HA! HA! HA! HA!
I'LL BE OLDER

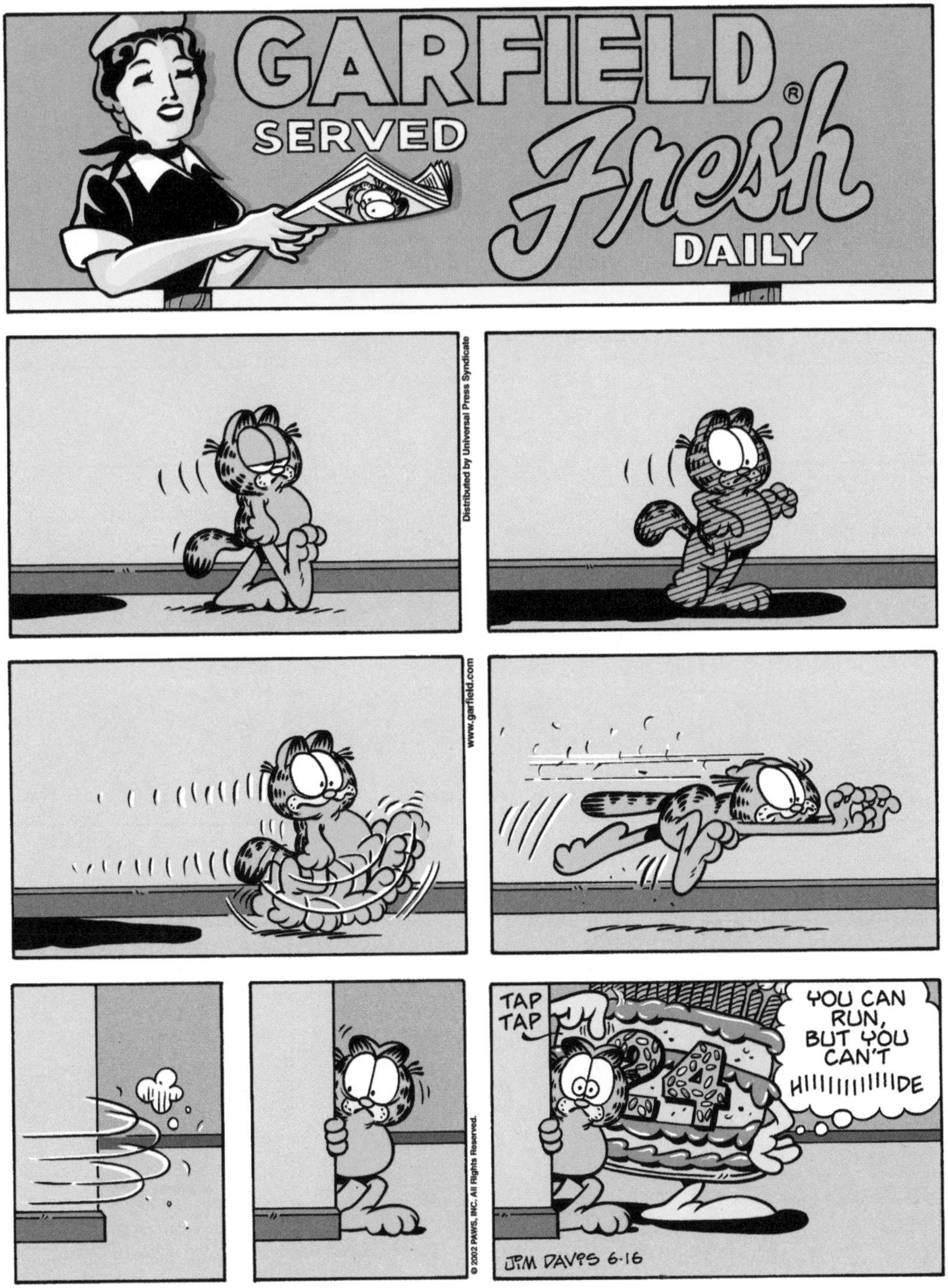
GARFIELD®
SERVED
Fresh
DAILY
Distributed by Universal Press Syndicate
www.garfield.com
© 2002 PAWS, INC. All Rights Reserved.
TAP TAP
YOU CAN RUN, BUT YOU CAN'T HIIIIIIIIIIIDE
JIM DAVIS 6-16

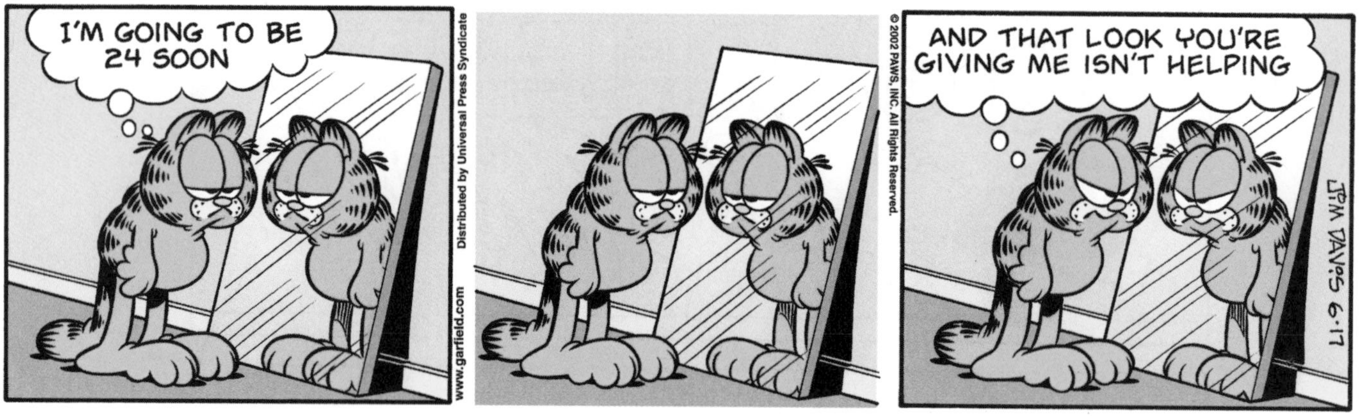
I'M GOING TO BE 24 SOON
AND THAT LOOK YOU'RE GIVING ME ISN'T HELPING
JIM DAVIS 6-17
Distributed by Universal Press Syndicate
www.garfield.com
© 2002 PAWS, INC. All Rights Reserved.

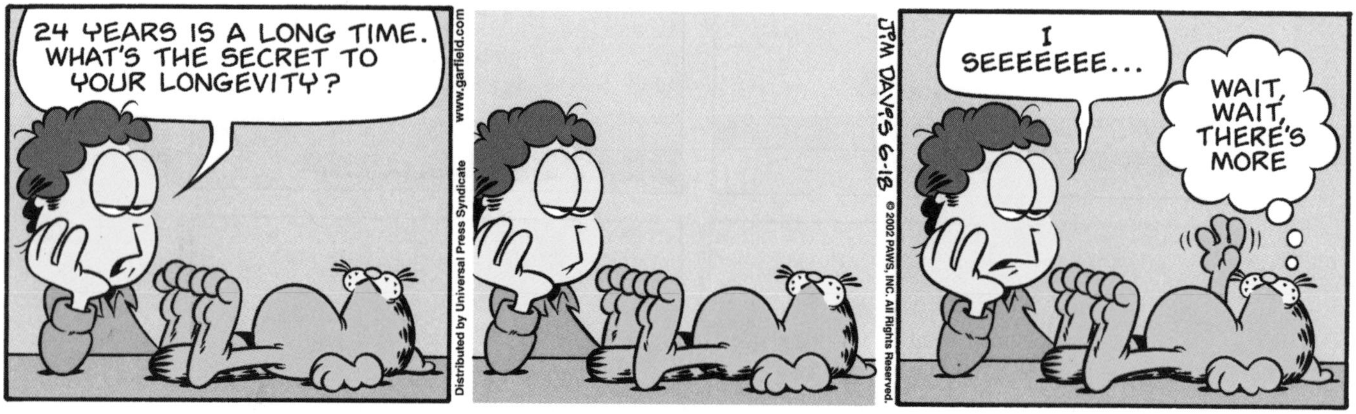
24 YEARS IS A LONG TIME. WHAT'S THE SECRET TO YOUR LONGEVITY?
I SEEEEEEE...
WAIT, WAIT, THERE'S MORE
JIM DAVIS 6-18
Distributed by Universal Press Syndicate
www.garfield.com
© 2002 PAWS, INC. All Rights Reserved.

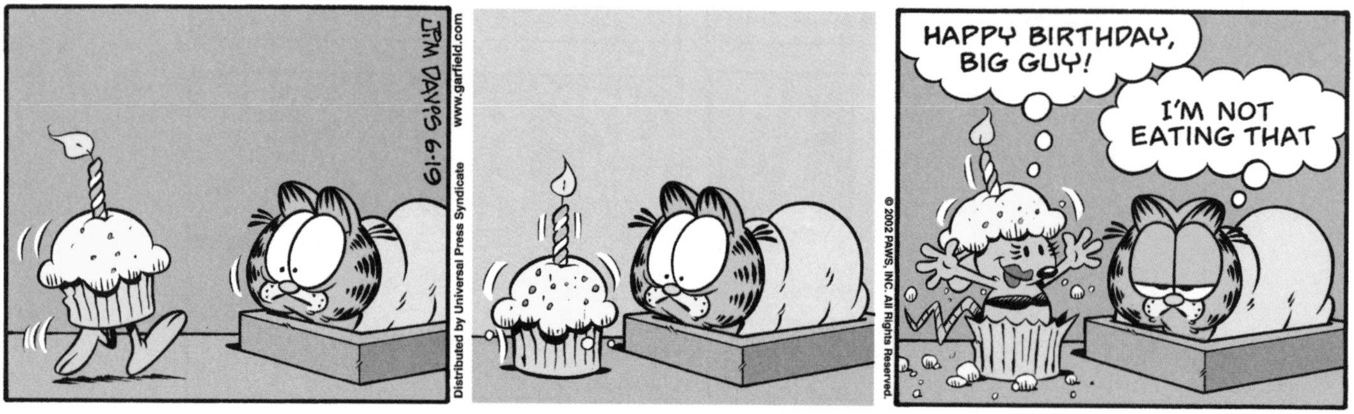
HAPPY BIRTHDAY, BIG GUY!
I'M NOT EATING THAT
JIM DAVIS 6-19
Distributed by Universal Press Syndicate
www.garfield.com
© 2002 PAWS, INC. All Rights Reserved.

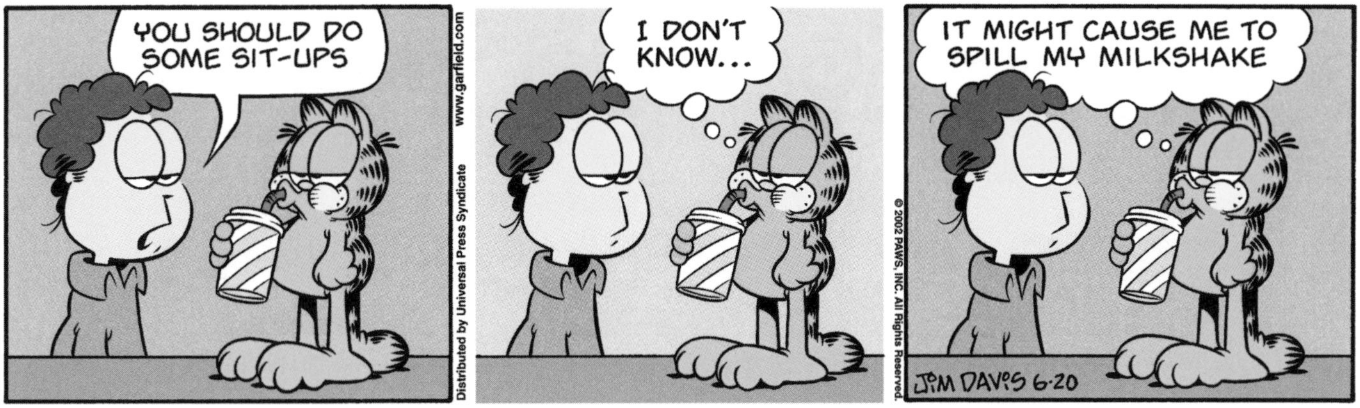
YOU SHOULD DO SOME SIT-UPS
www.garfield.com
Distributed by Universal Press Syndicate
I DON'T KNOW...
© 2002 PAWS, INC. All Rights Reserved.
IT MIGHT CAUSE ME TO SPILL MY MILKSHAKE
JIM DAVIS 6-20

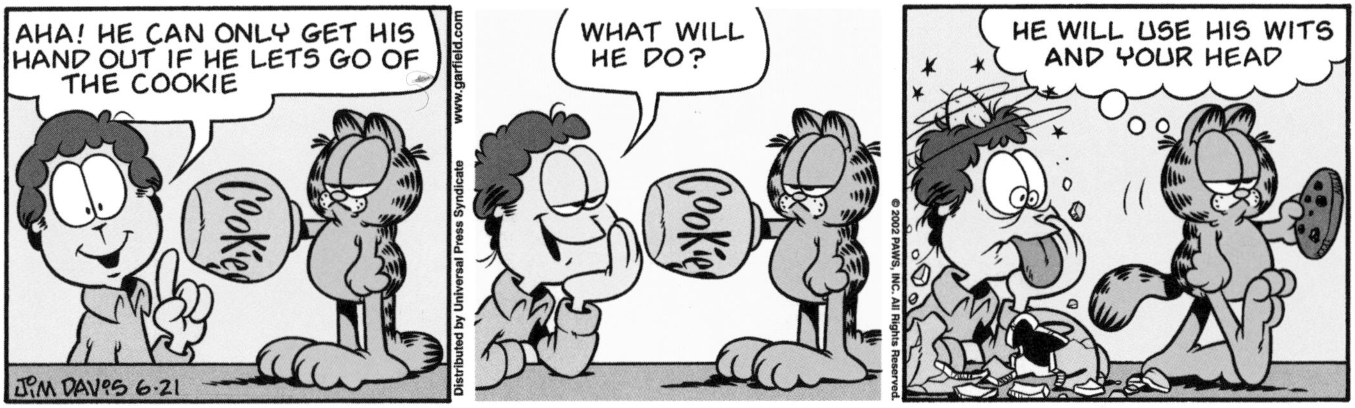
AHA! HE CAN ONLY GET HIS HAND OUT IF HE LETS GO OF THE COOKIE
COOKIES
JIM DAVIS 6-21
www.garfield.com
Distributed by Universal Press Syndicate
WHAT WILL HE DO?
© 2002 PAWS, INC. All Rights Reserved.
HE WILL USE HIS WITS AND YOUR HEAD

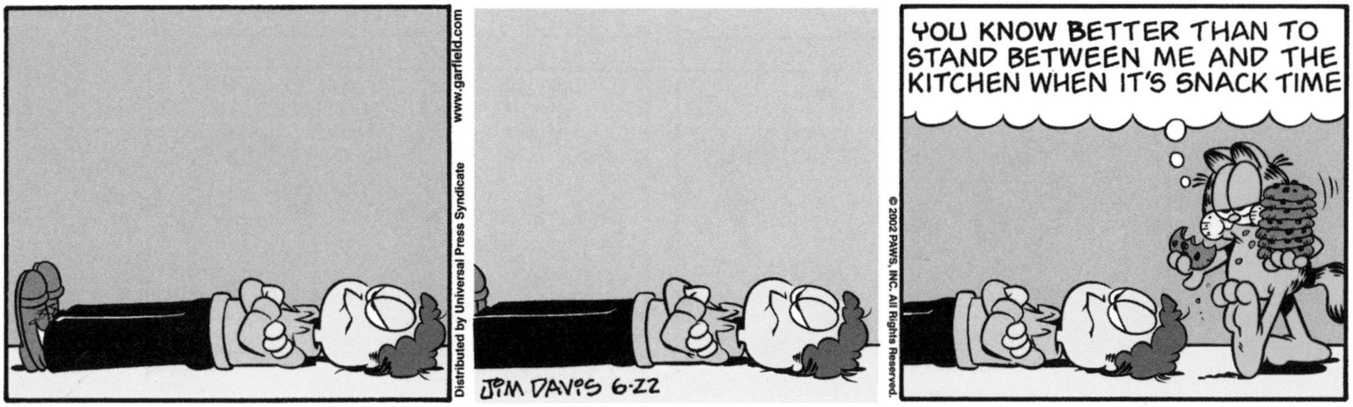
www.garfield.com
Distributed by Universal Press Syndicate
JIM DAVIS 6-22
© 2002 PAWS, INC. All Rights Reserved.
YOU KNOW BETTER THAN TO STAND BETWEEN ME AND THE KITCHEN WHEN IT'S SNACK TIME

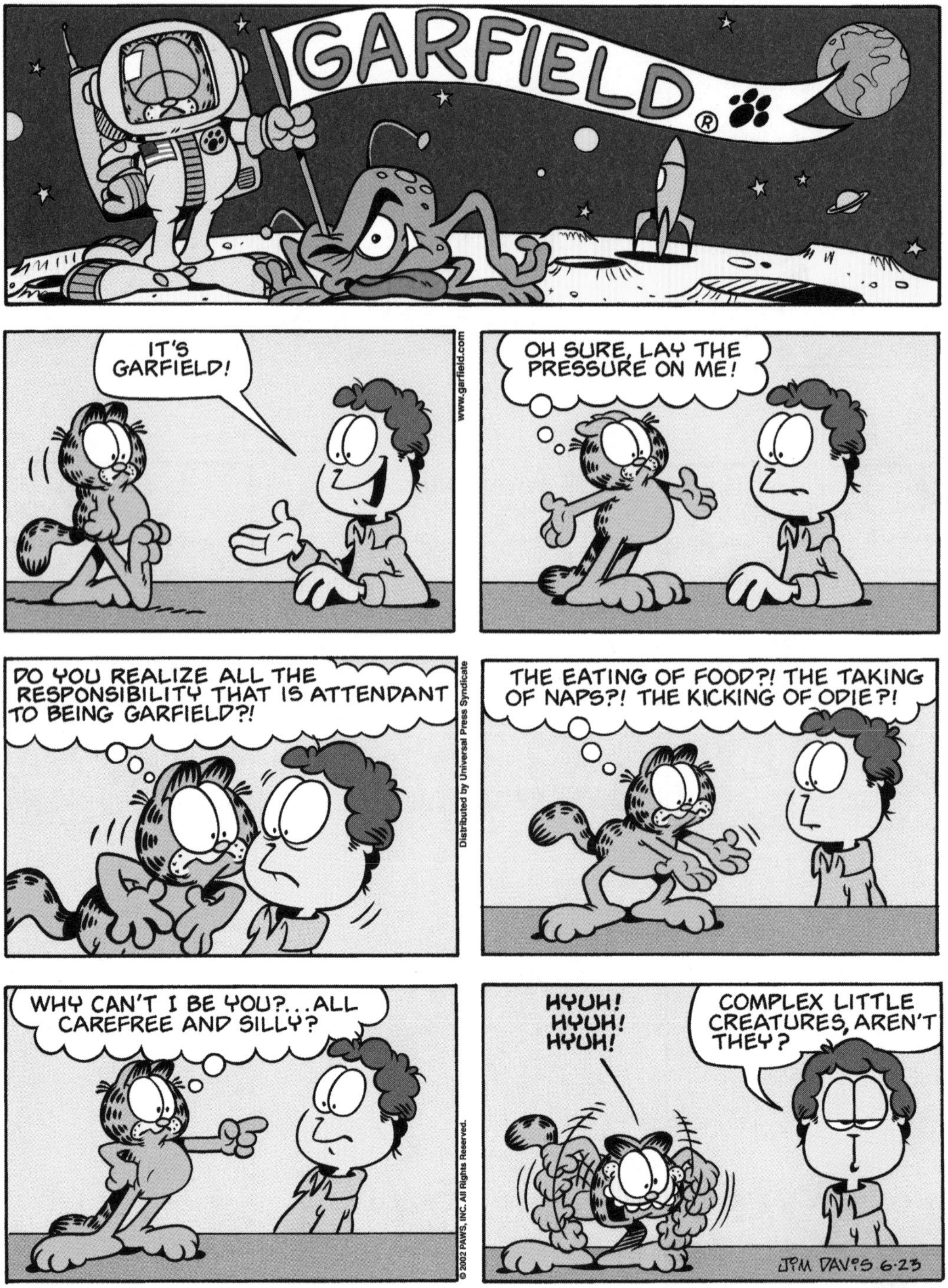
GARFIELD®
IT'S GARFIELD!
OH SURE, LAY THE PRESSURE ON ME!
DO YOU REALIZE ALL THE RESPONSIBILITY THAT IS ATTENDANT TO BEING GARFIELD?!
THE EATING OF FOOD?! THE TAKING OF NAPS?! THE KICKING OF ODIE?!
WHY CAN'T I BE YOU?...ALL CAREFREE AND SILLY?
HYUH! HYUH! HYUH!
COMPLEX LITTLE CREATURES, AREN'T THEY?
JIM DAVIS 6-23
www.garfield.com
Distributed by Universal Press Syndicate
© 2002 PAWS, INC. All Rights Reserved.

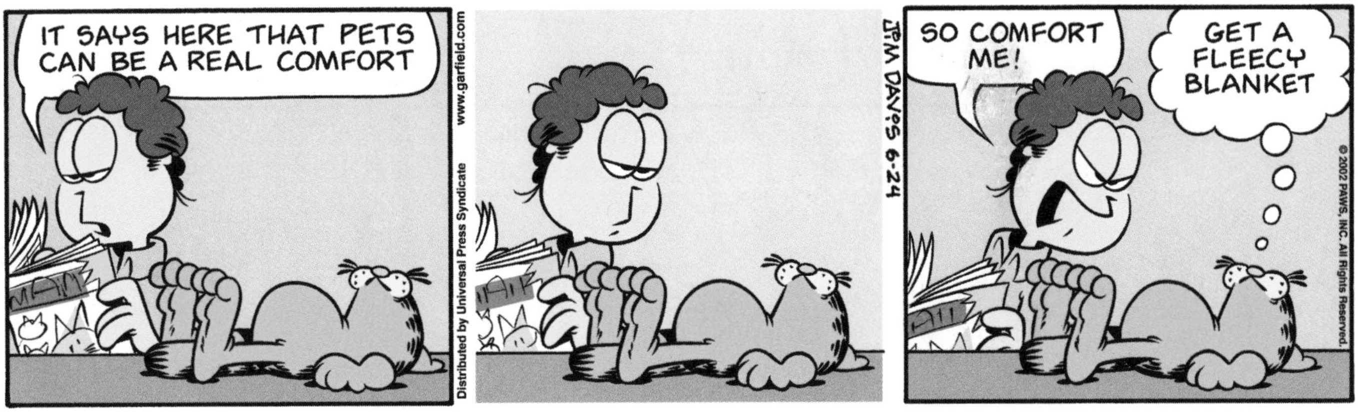
IT SAYS HERE THAT PETS CAN BE A REAL COMFORT
www.garfield.com
Distributed by Universal Press Syndicate
JIM DAVIS 6-24
SO COMFORT ME!
GET A FLEECY BLANKET
© 2002 PAWS, INC. All Rights Reserved.

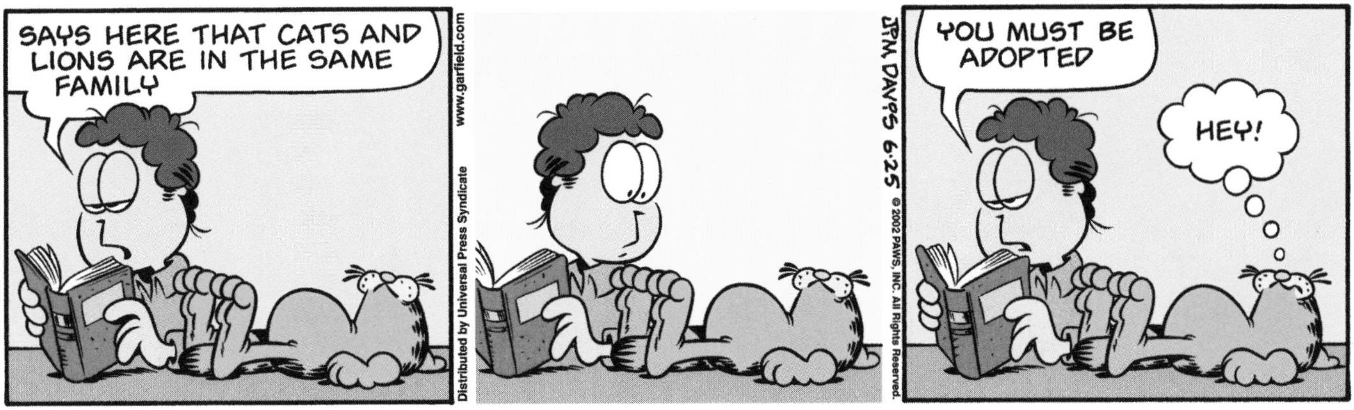
SAYS HERE THAT CATS AND LIONS ARE IN THE SAME FAMILY
www.garfield.com
Distributed by Universal Press Syndicate
JIM DAVIS 6-25
© 2002 PAWS, INC. All Rights Reserved.
YOU MUST BE ADOPTED
HEY!

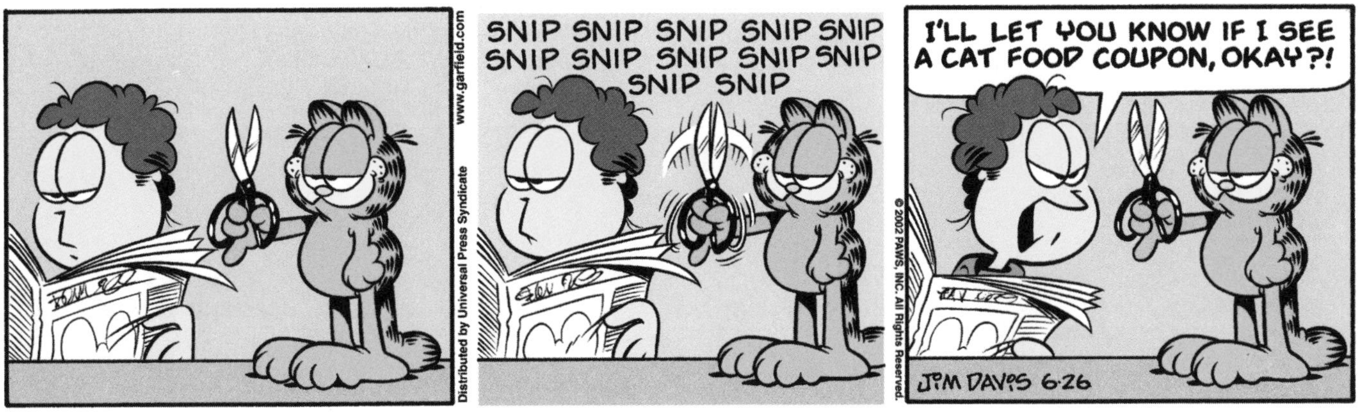
www.garfield.com
Distributed by Universal Press Syndicate
SNIP SNIP SNIP SNIP SNIP SNIP SNIP SNIP SNIP SNIP SNIP SNIP
© 2002 PAWS, INC. All Rights Reserved.
I'LL LET YOU KNOW IF I SEE A CAT FOOD COUPON, OKAY?!
JIM DAVIS 6-26

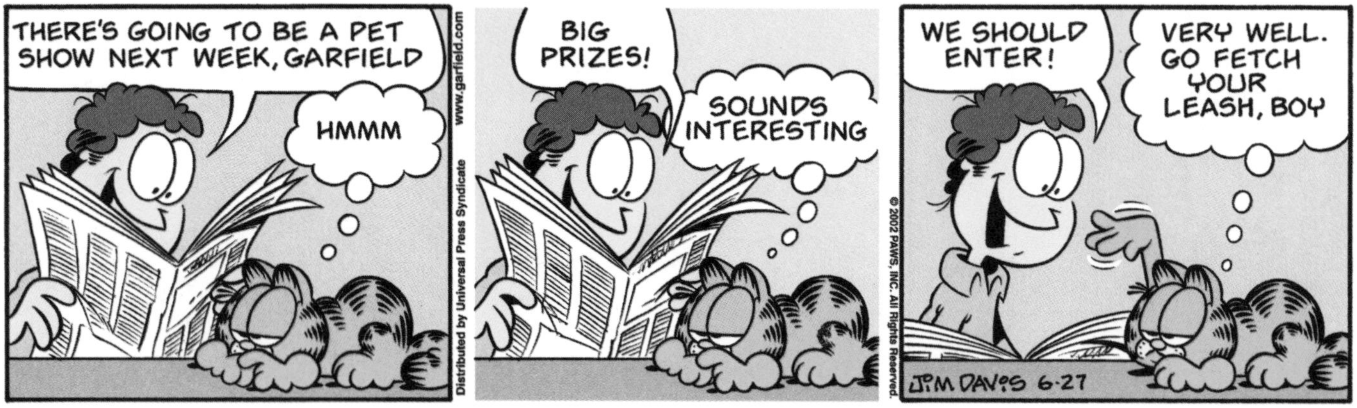
THERE'S GOING TO BE A PET SHOW NEXT WEEK, GARFIELD
HMMM
BIG PRIZES!
SOUNDS INTERESTING
WE SHOULD ENTER!
VERY WELL. GO FETCH YOUR LEASH, BOY
JIM DAVIS 6-27
www.garfield.com
Distributed by Universal Press Syndicate
© 2002 PAWS, INC. All Rights Reserved.

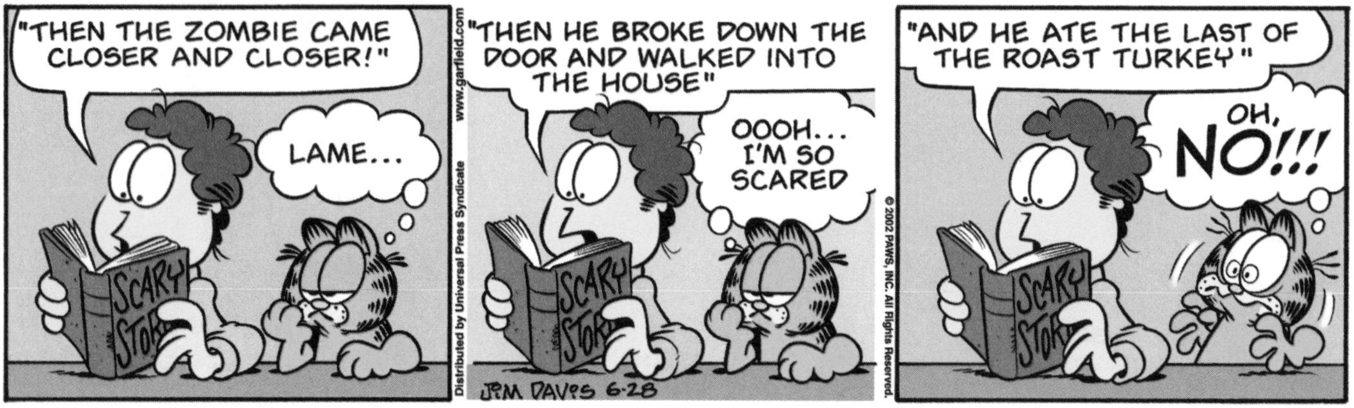
"THEN THE ZOMBIE CAME CLOSER AND CLOSER!"
LAME...
SCARY STORIES
"THEN HE BROKE DOWN THE DOOR AND WALKED INTO THE HOUSE"
OOOH... I'M SO SCARED
"AND HE ATE THE LAST OF THE ROAST TURKEY"
OH, NO!!!
JIM DAVIS 6-28
www.garfield.com
Distributed by Universal Press Syndicate
© 2002 PAWS, INC. All Rights Reserved.

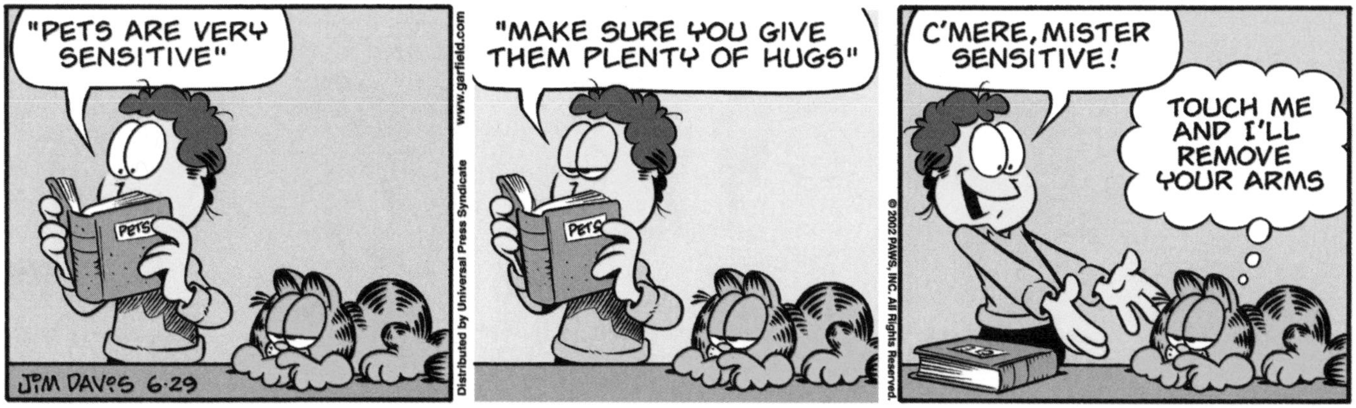
"PETS ARE VERY SENSITIVE"
PETS
"MAKE SURE YOU GIVE THEM PLENTY OF HUGS"
C'MERE, MISTER SENSITIVE!
TOUCH ME AND I'LL REMOVE YOUR ARMS
JIM DAVIS 6-29
www.garfield.com
Distributed by Universal Press Syndicate
© 2002 PAWS, INC. All Rights Reserved.

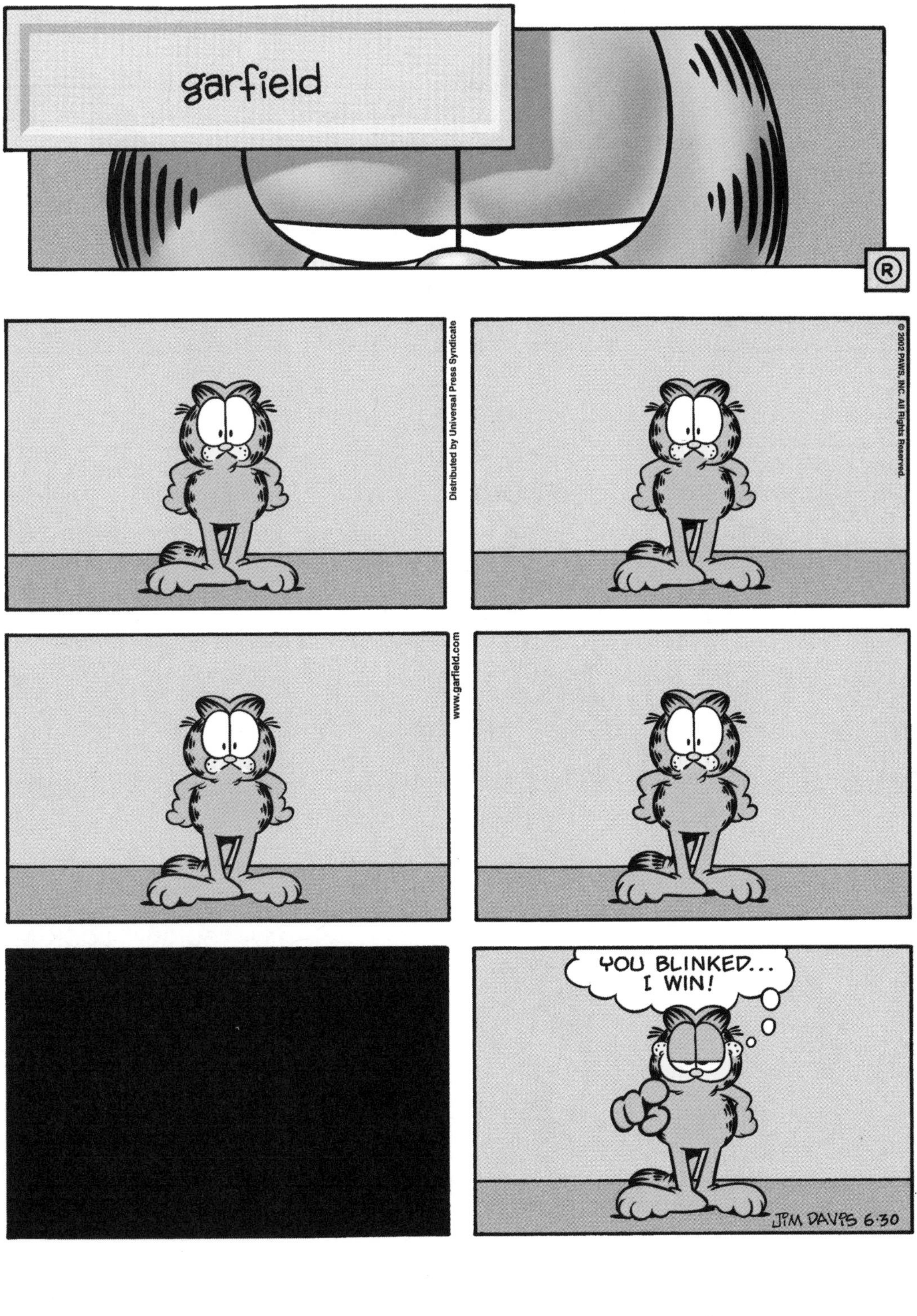
garfield
Distributed by Universal Press Syndicate
© 2002 PAWS, INC. All Rights Reserved.
www.garfield.com
YOU BLINKED... I WIN!
JIM DAVIS 6·30

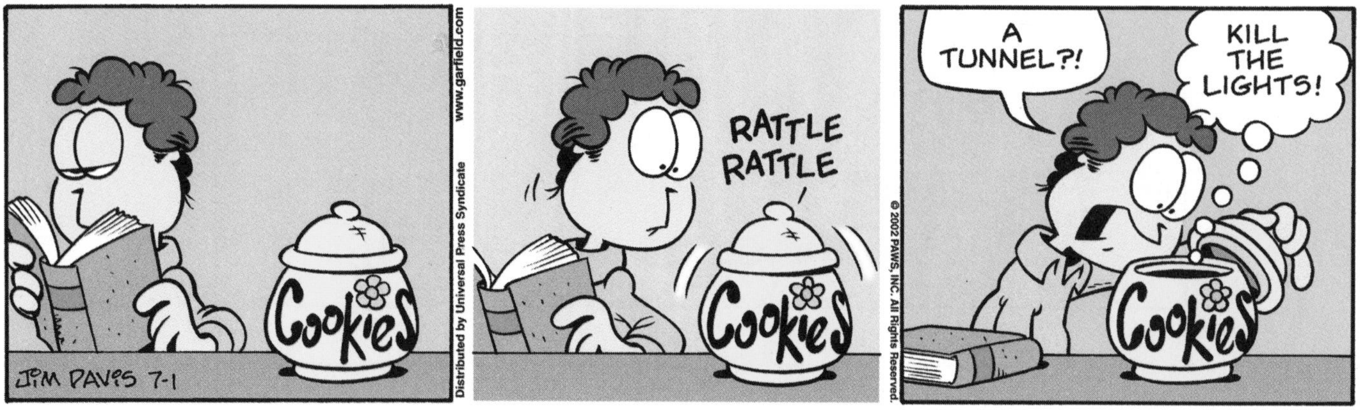
JIM DAVIS 7-1
www.garfield.com
Distributed by Universal Press Syndicate
RATTLE RATTLE
© 2002 PAWS, INC. All Rights Reserved.
A TUNNEL?!
KILL THE LIGHTS!

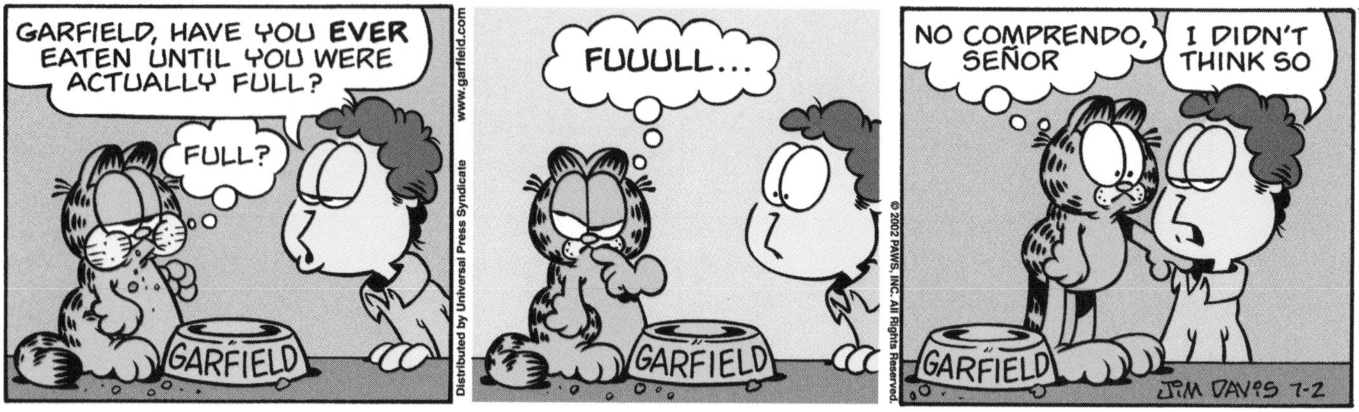
GARFIELD, HAVE YOU **EVER** EATEN UNTIL YOU WERE ACTUALLY FULL?
FULL?
GARFIELD
www.garfield.com
Distributed by Universal Press Syndicate
FUUULL...
GARFIELD
© 2002 PAWS, INC. All Rights Reserved.
NO COMPRENDO, SEÑOR
I DIDN'T THINK SO
GARFIELD
JIM DAVIS 7-2

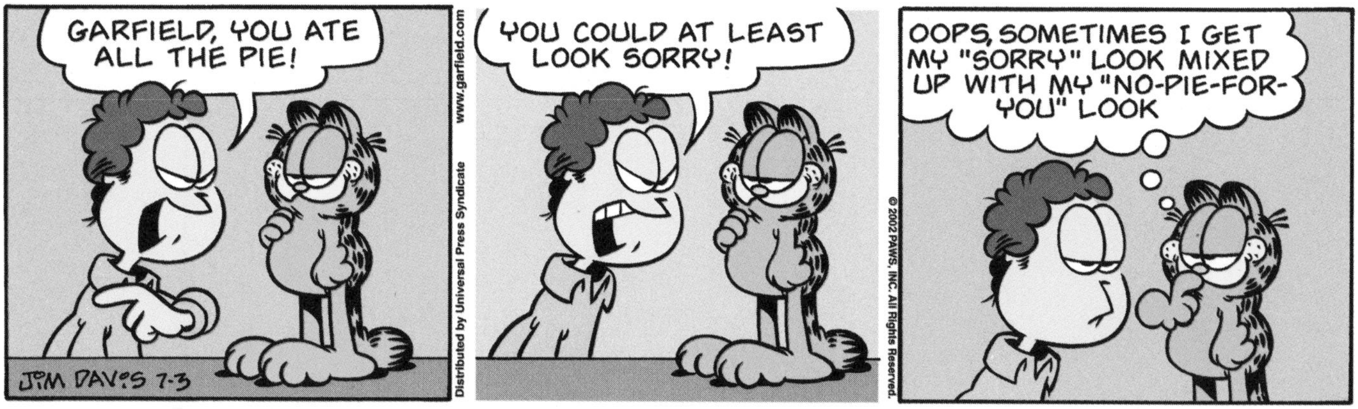
GARFIELD, YOU ATE ALL THE PIE!
JIM DAVIS 7-3
www.garfield.com
Distributed by Universal Press Syndicate
YOU COULD AT LEAST LOOK SORRY!
© 2002 PAWS, INC. All Rights Reserved.
OOPS, SOMETIMES I GET MY "SORRY" LOOK MIXED UP WITH MY "NO-PIE-FOR-YOU" LOOK

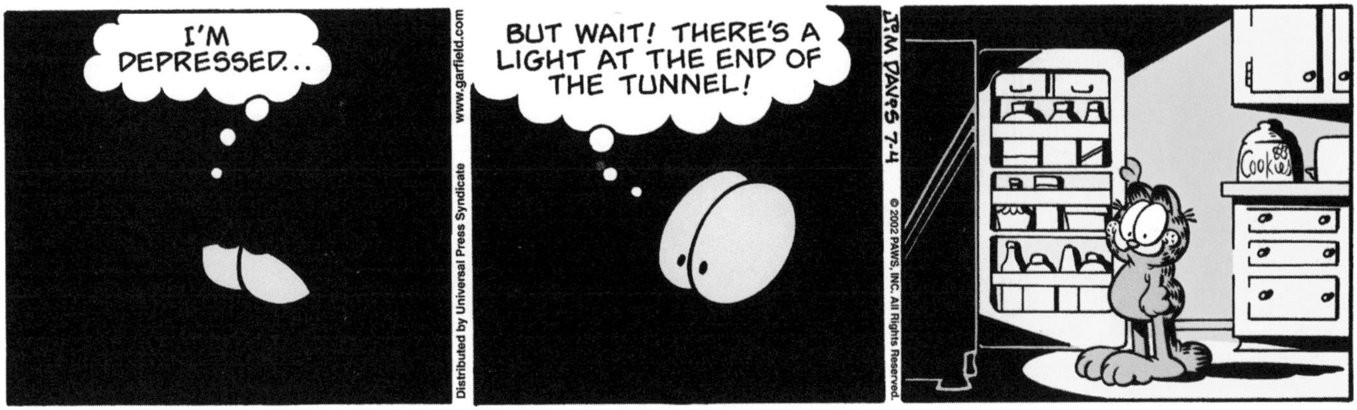
I'M DEPRESSED...
www.garfield.com
Distributed by Universal Press Syndicate
BUT WAIT! THERE'S A LIGHT AT THE END OF THE TUNNEL!
JIM DAVIS 7-4
© 2002 PAWS, INC. All Rights Reserved.
Cookies

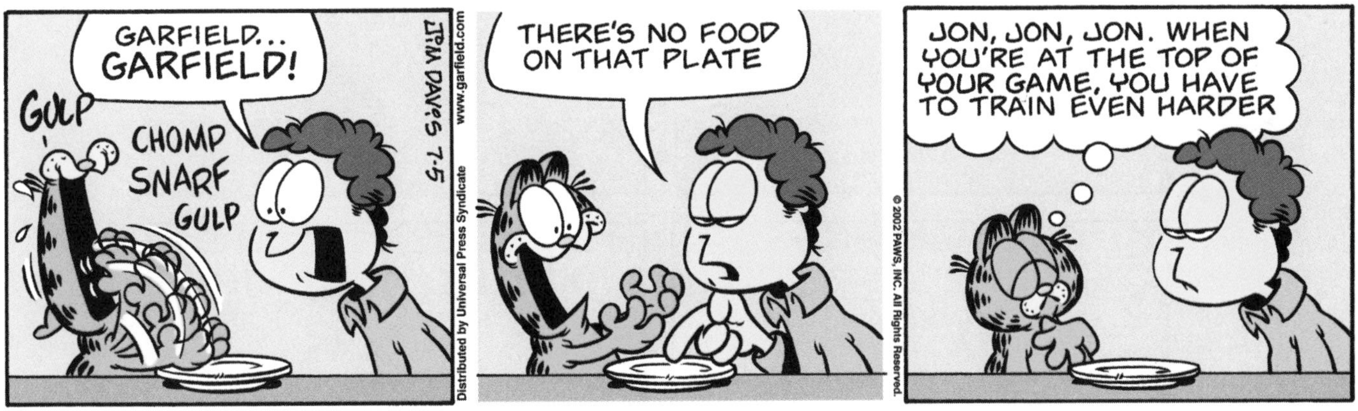
GARFIELD... GARFIELD!
GULP
CHOMP
SNARF
GULP
JIM DAVIS 7-5
www.garfield.com
Distributed by Universal Press Syndicate
THERE'S NO FOOD ON THAT PLATE
© 2002 PAWS, INC. All Rights Reserved.
JON, JON, JON. WHEN YOU'RE AT THE TOP OF YOUR GAME, YOU HAVE TO TRAIN EVEN HARDER

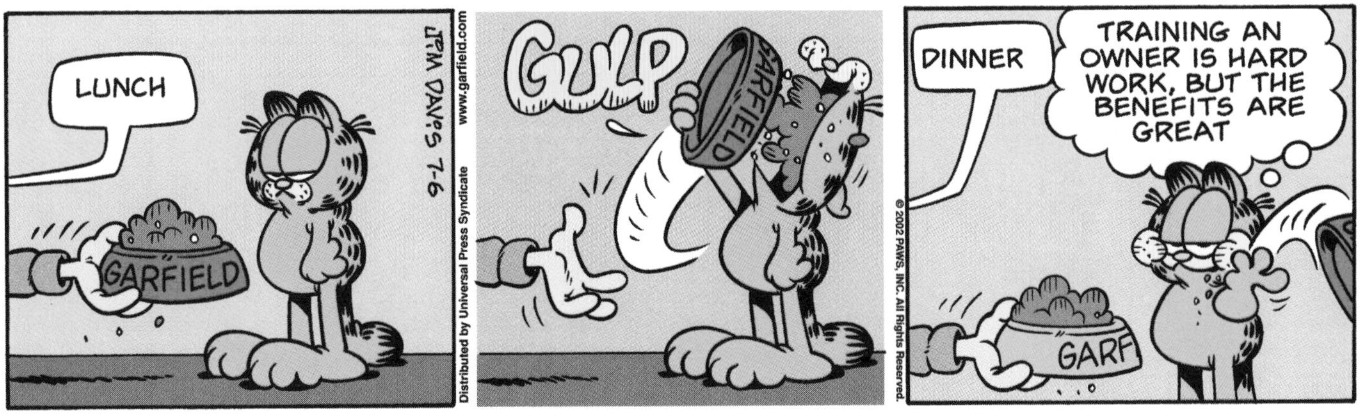
LUNCH
GARFIELD
JIM DAVIS 7-6
www.garfield.com
Distributed by Universal Press Syndicate
GULP
GARFIELD
© 2002 PAWS, INC. All Rights Reserved.
DINNER
TRAINING AN OWNER IS HARD WORK, BUT THE BENEFITS ARE GREAT
GARF

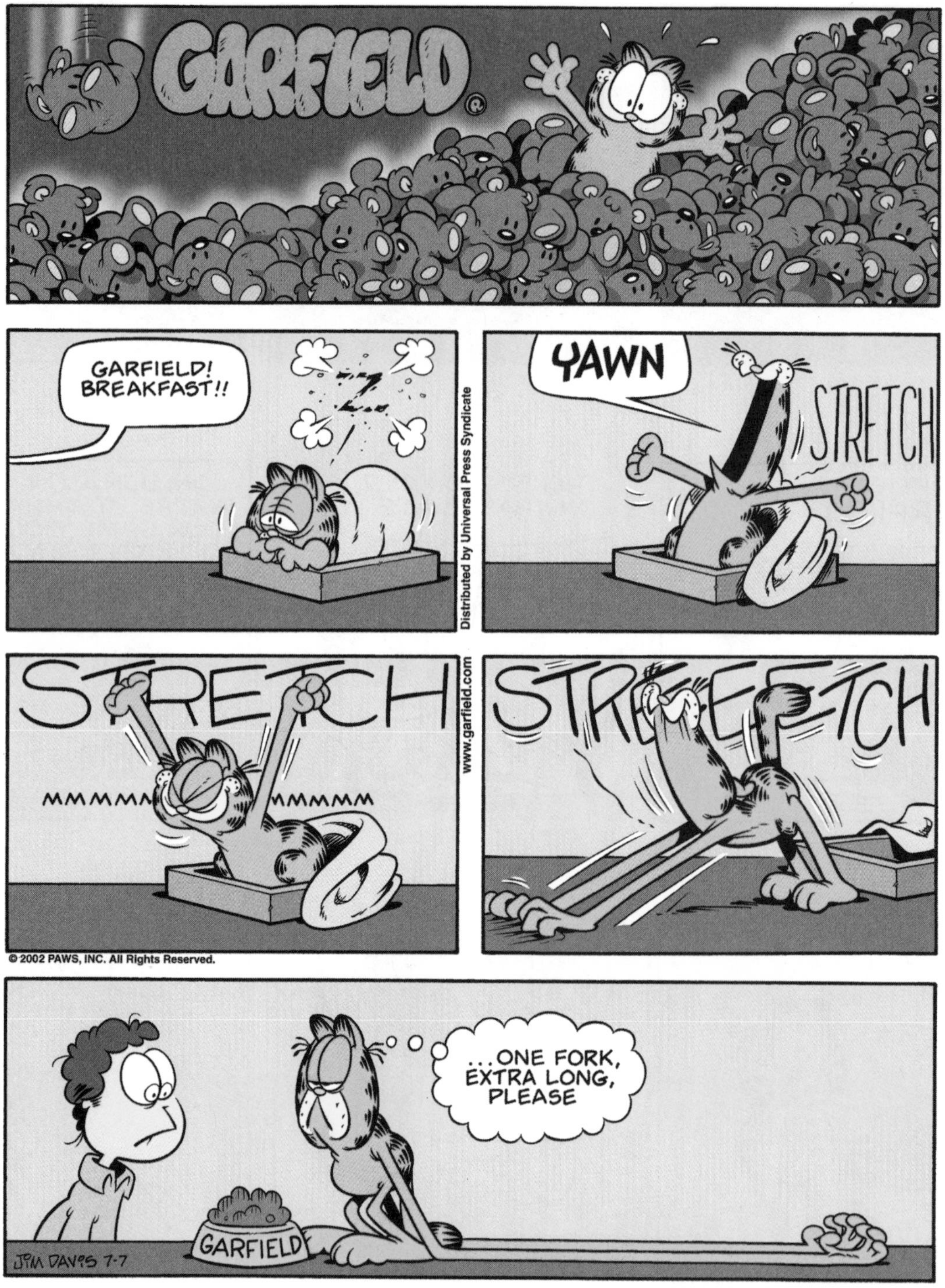
GARFIELD
GARFIELD! BREAKFAST!!
Z
Distributed by Universal Press Syndicate
YAWN
STRETCH
STRETCH
MMMMM MMMMM
www.garfield.com
STREEEETCH
© 2002 PAWS, INC. All Rights Reserved.
...ONE FORK, EXTRA LONG, PLEASE
GARFIELD
JIM DAVIS 7-7

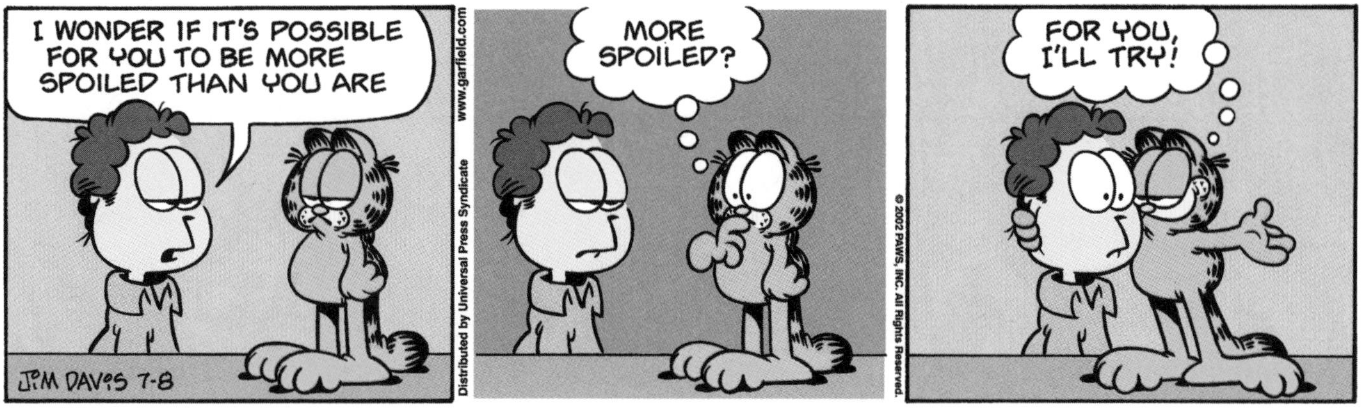
I WONDER IF IT'S POSSIBLE FOR YOU TO BE MORE SPOILED THAN YOU ARE
MORE SPOILED?
FOR YOU, I'LL TRY!
JIM DAVIS 7-8
www.garfield.com
Distributed by Universal Press Syndicate
© 2002 PAWS, INC. All Rights Reserved.

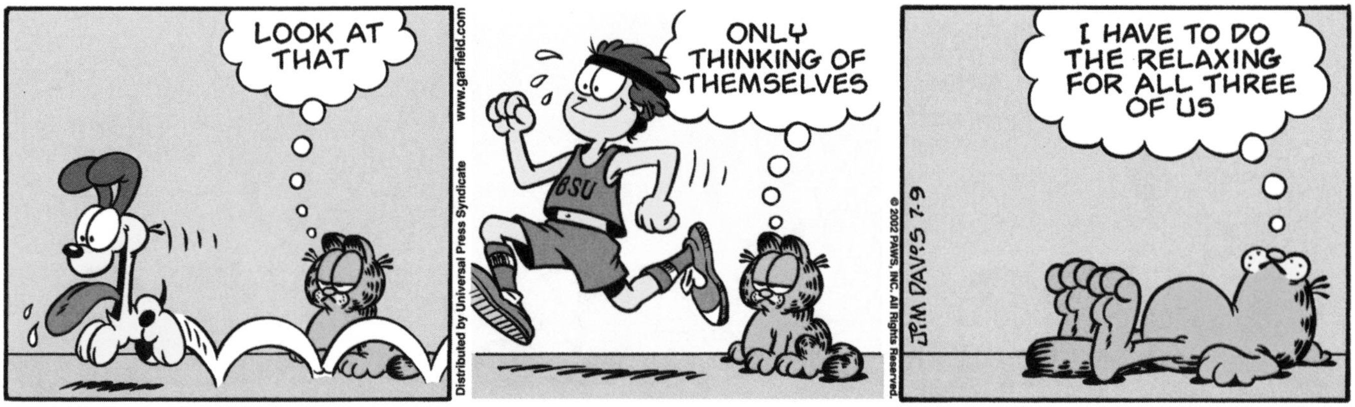
LOOK AT THAT
ONLY THINKING OF THEMSELVES
I HAVE TO DO THE RELAXING FOR ALL THREE OF US
BSU
JIM DAVIS 7-9
www.garfield.com
Distributed by Universal Press Syndicate
© 2002 PAWS, INC. All Rights Reserved.

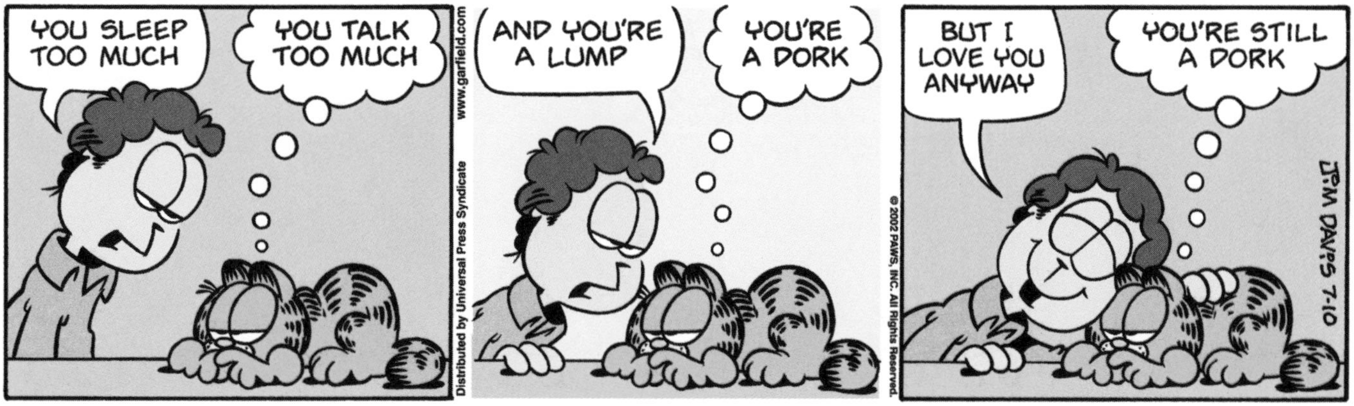
YOU SLEEP TOO MUCH
YOU TALK TOO MUCH
AND YOU'RE A LUMP
YOU'RE A DORK
BUT I LOVE YOU ANYWAY
YOU'RE STILL A DORK
JIM DAVIS 7-10
www.garfield.com
Distributed by Universal Press Syndicate
© 2002 PAWS, INC. All Rights Reserved.

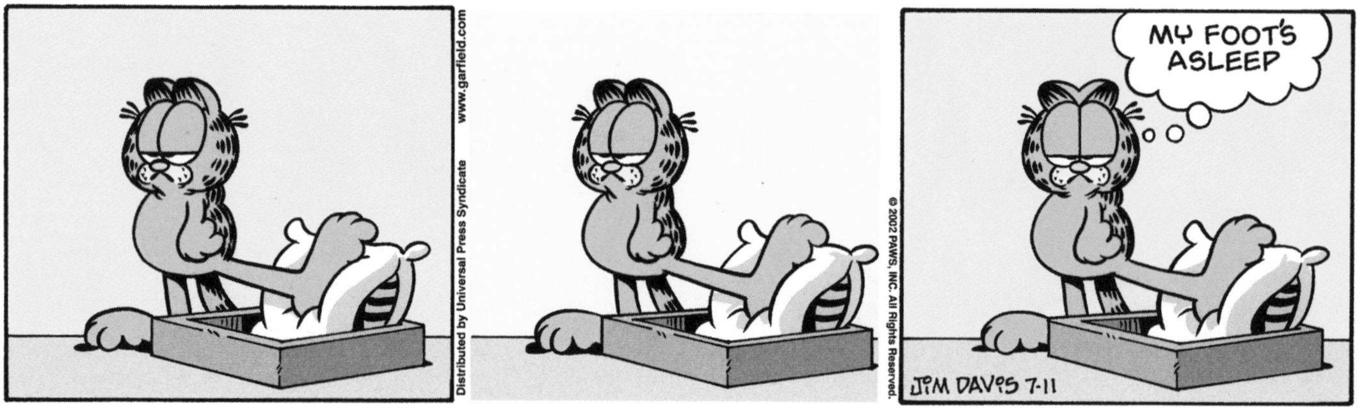
MY FOOT'S ASLEEP
www.garfield.com
Distributed by Universal Press Syndicate
© 2002 PAWS, INC. All Rights Reserved.
JIM DAVIS 7-11

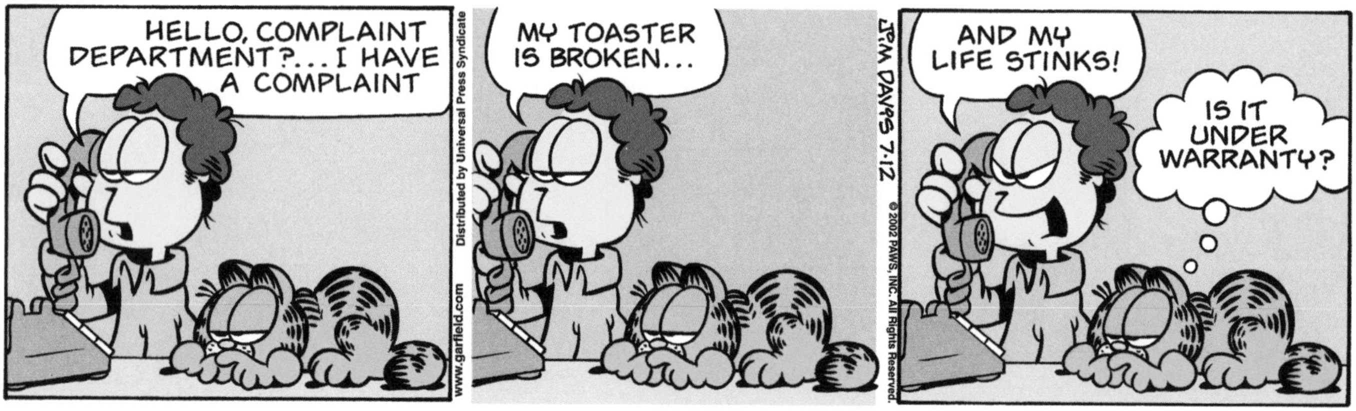
HELLO, COMPLAINT DEPARTMENT?... I HAVE A COMPLAINT
MY TOASTER IS BROKEN...
AND MY LIFE STINKS!
IS IT UNDER WARRANTY?
Distributed by Universal Press Syndicate
www.garfield.com
JIM DAVIS 7-12
© 2002 PAWS, INC. All Rights Reserved.

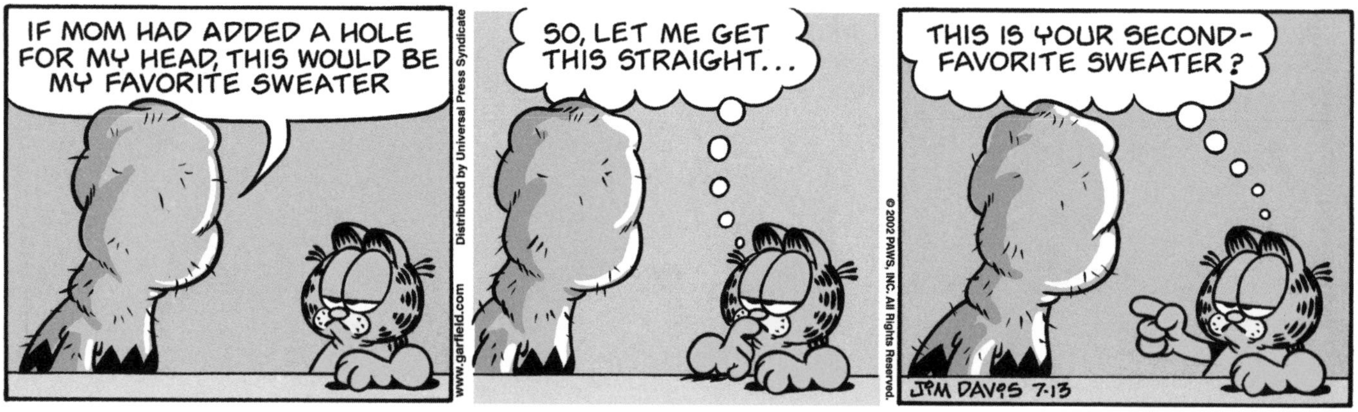
IF MOM HAD ADDED A HOLE FOR MY HEAD, THIS WOULD BE MY FAVORITE SWEATER
SO, LET ME GET THIS STRAIGHT...
THIS IS YOUR SECOND-FAVORITE SWEATER?
Distributed by Universal Press Syndicate
www.garfield.com
© 2002 PAWS, INC. All Rights Reserved.
JIM DAVIS 7-13

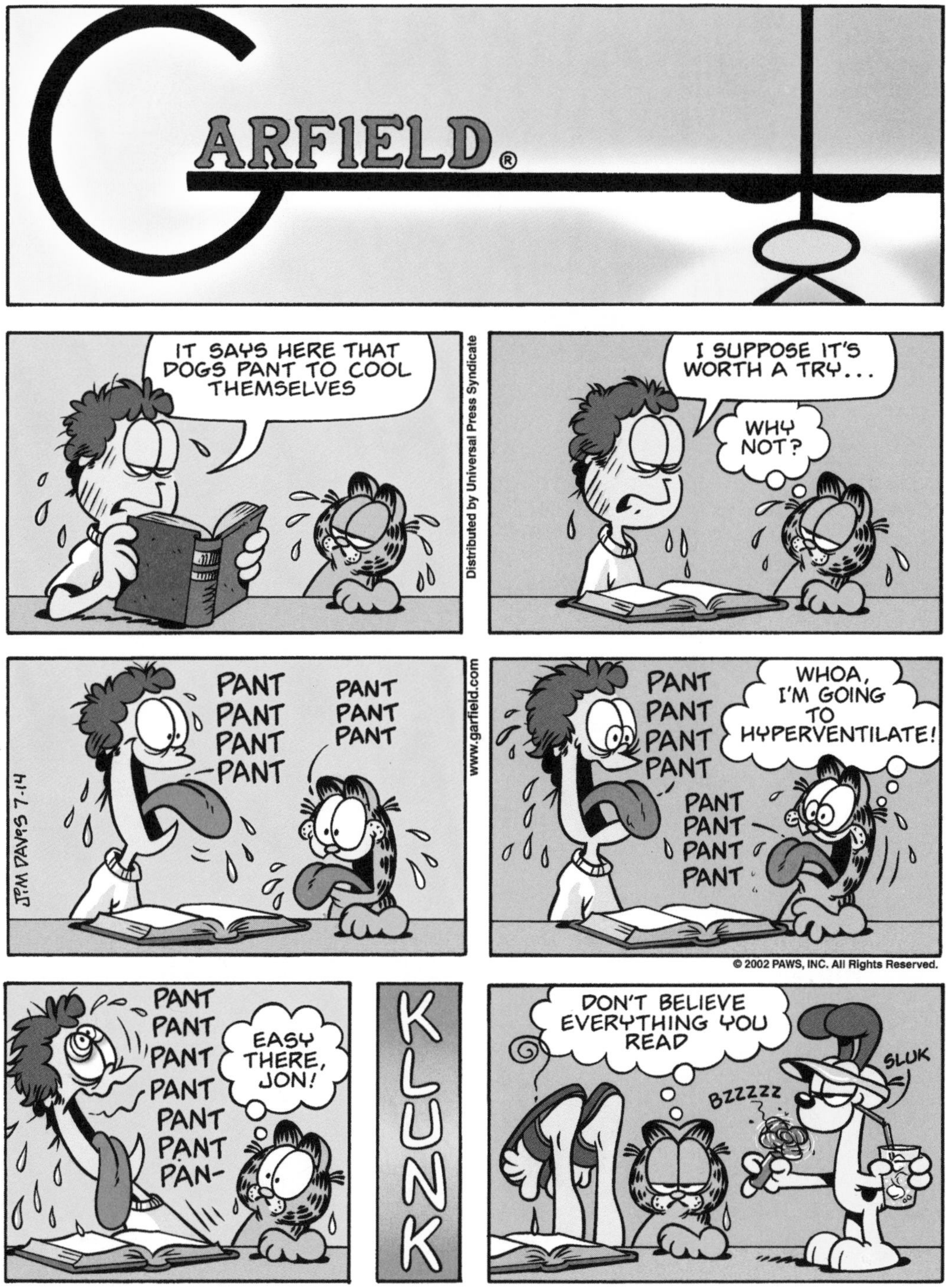
GARFIELD®
IT SAYS HERE THAT DOGS PANT TO COOL THEMSELVES
Distributed by Universal Press Syndicate
I SUPPOSE IT'S WORTH A TRY...
WHY NOT?
PANT PANT PANT PANT
PANT PANT PANT
JPM DAVPS 7·14
www.garfield.com
PANT PANT PANT PANT
WHOA, I'M GOING TO HYPERVENTILATE!
PANT PANT PANT PANT
© 2002 PAWS, INC. All Rights Reserved.
PANT PANT PANT PANT PANT PANT PAN-
EASY THERE, JON!
KLUNK
DON'T BELIEVE EVERYTHING YOU READ
BZZZZZ
SLUK

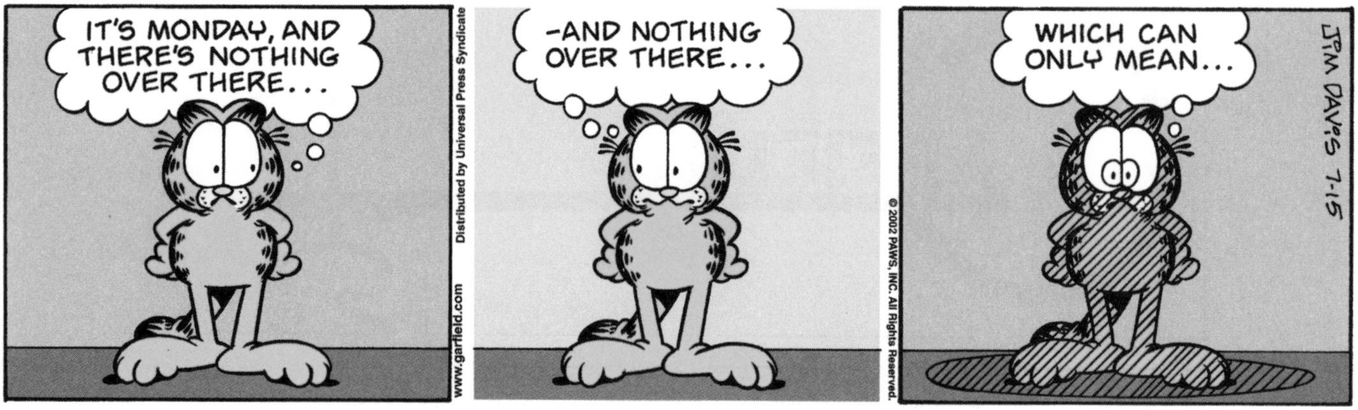
IT'S MONDAY, AND THERE'S NOTHING OVER THERE...
-AND NOTHING OVER THERE...
WHICH CAN ONLY MEAN...
JIM DAVIS 7-15
www.garfield.com Distributed by Universal Press Syndicate
© 2002 PAWS, INC. All Rights Reserved.

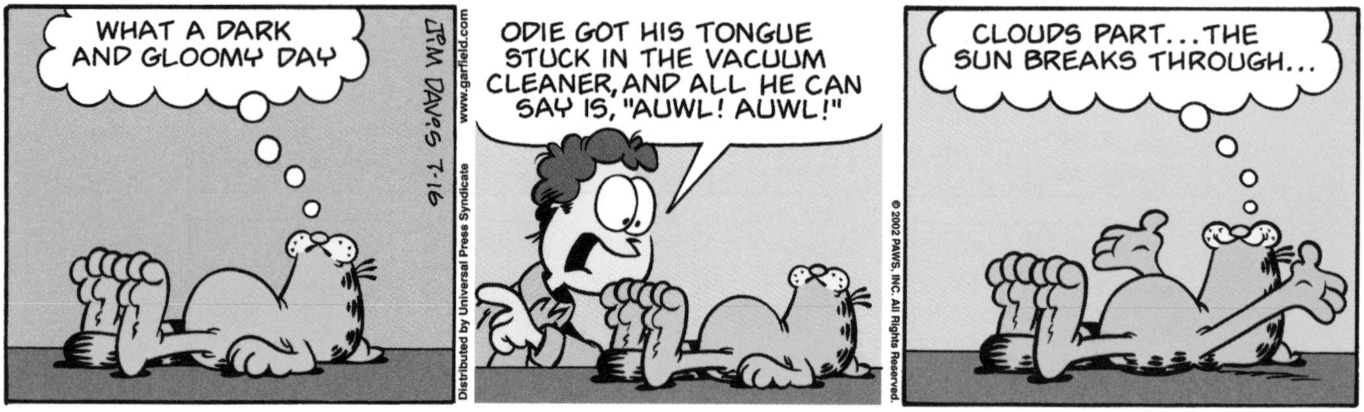
WHAT A DARK AND GLOOMY DAY
JIM DAVIS 7-16
www.garfield.com Distributed by Universal Press Syndicate
ODIE GOT HIS TONGUE STUCK IN THE VACUUM CLEANER, AND ALL HE CAN SAY IS, "AUWL! AUWL!"
© 2002 PAWS, INC. All Rights Reserved.
CLOUDS PART...THE SUN BREAKS THROUGH...

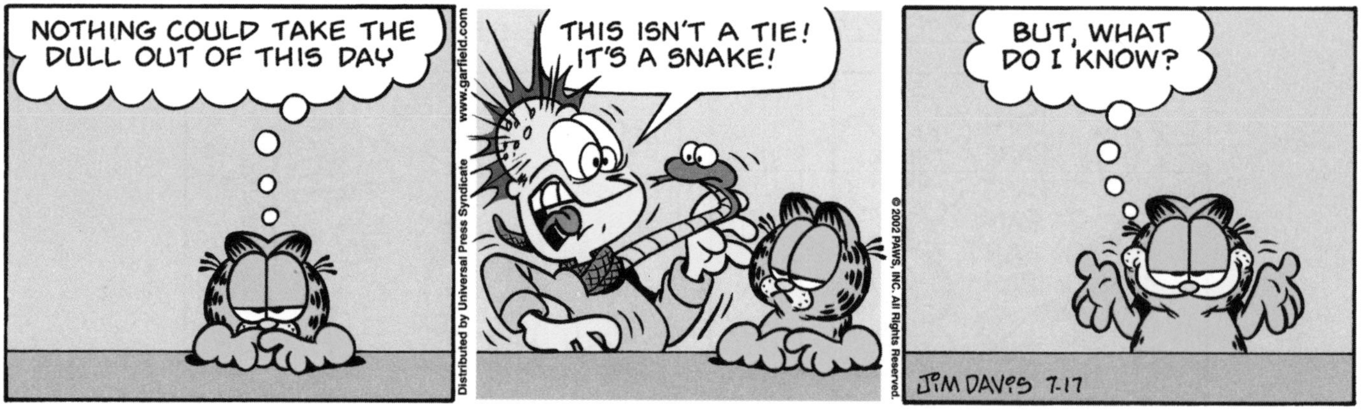
NOTHING COULD TAKE THE DULL OUT OF THIS DAY
www.garfield.com Distributed by Universal Press Syndicate
THIS ISN'T A TIE! IT'S A SNAKE!
© 2002 PAWS, INC. All Rights Reserved.
BUT, WHAT DO I KNOW?
JIM DAVIS 7-17

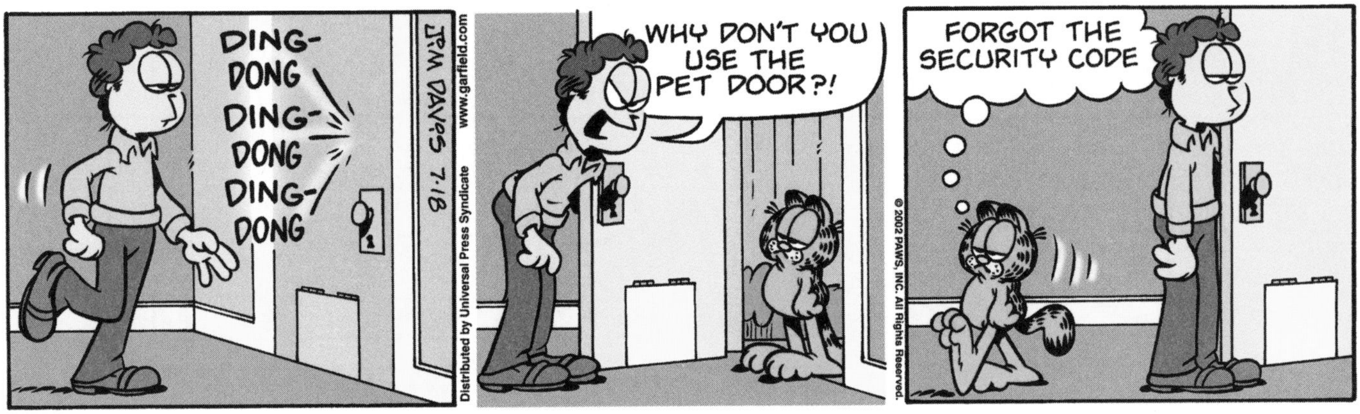
DING-DONG DING-DONG DING-DONG
JIM DAVIS 7-18
www.garfield.com
Distributed by Universal Press Syndicate
WHY DON'T YOU USE THE PET DOOR?!
© 2002 PAWS, INC. All Rights Reserved.
FORGOT THE SECURITY CODE

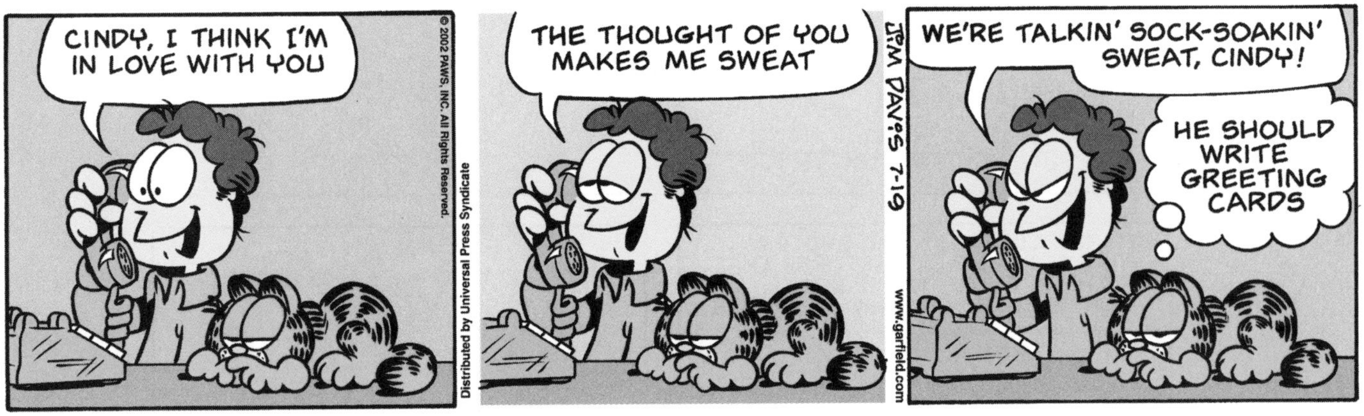
CINDY, I THINK I'M IN LOVE WITH YOU
© 2002 PAWS, INC. All Rights Reserved.
Distributed by Universal Press Syndicate
THE THOUGHT OF YOU MAKES ME SWEAT
JIM DAVIS 7-19
www.garfield.com
WE'RE TALKIN' SOCK-SOAKIN' SWEAT, CINDY!
HE SHOULD WRITE GREETING CARDS

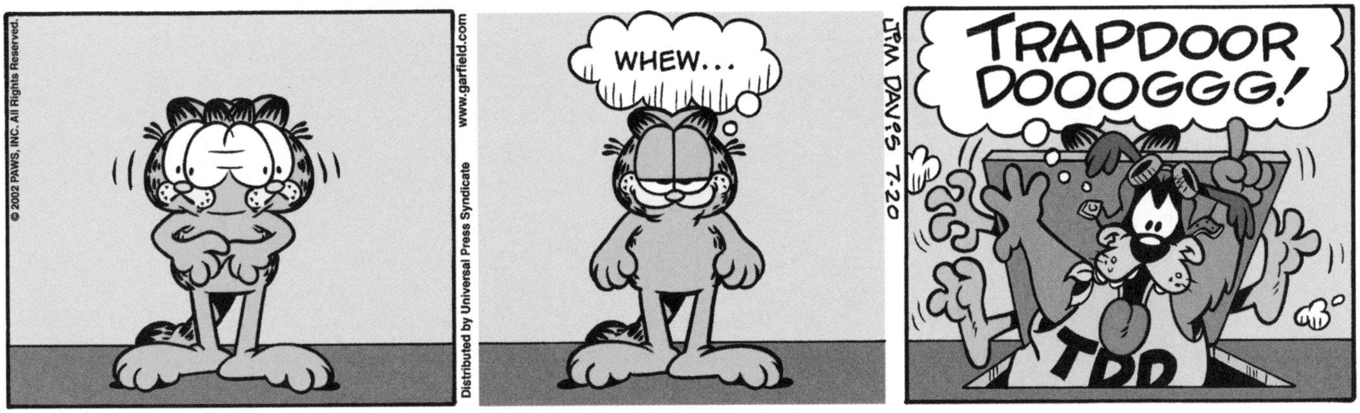
© 2002 PAWS, INC. All Rights Reserved.
www.garfield.com
Distributed by Universal Press Syndicate
WHEW...
JIM DAVIS 7-20
TRAPDOOR DOOOGGG!
TDD

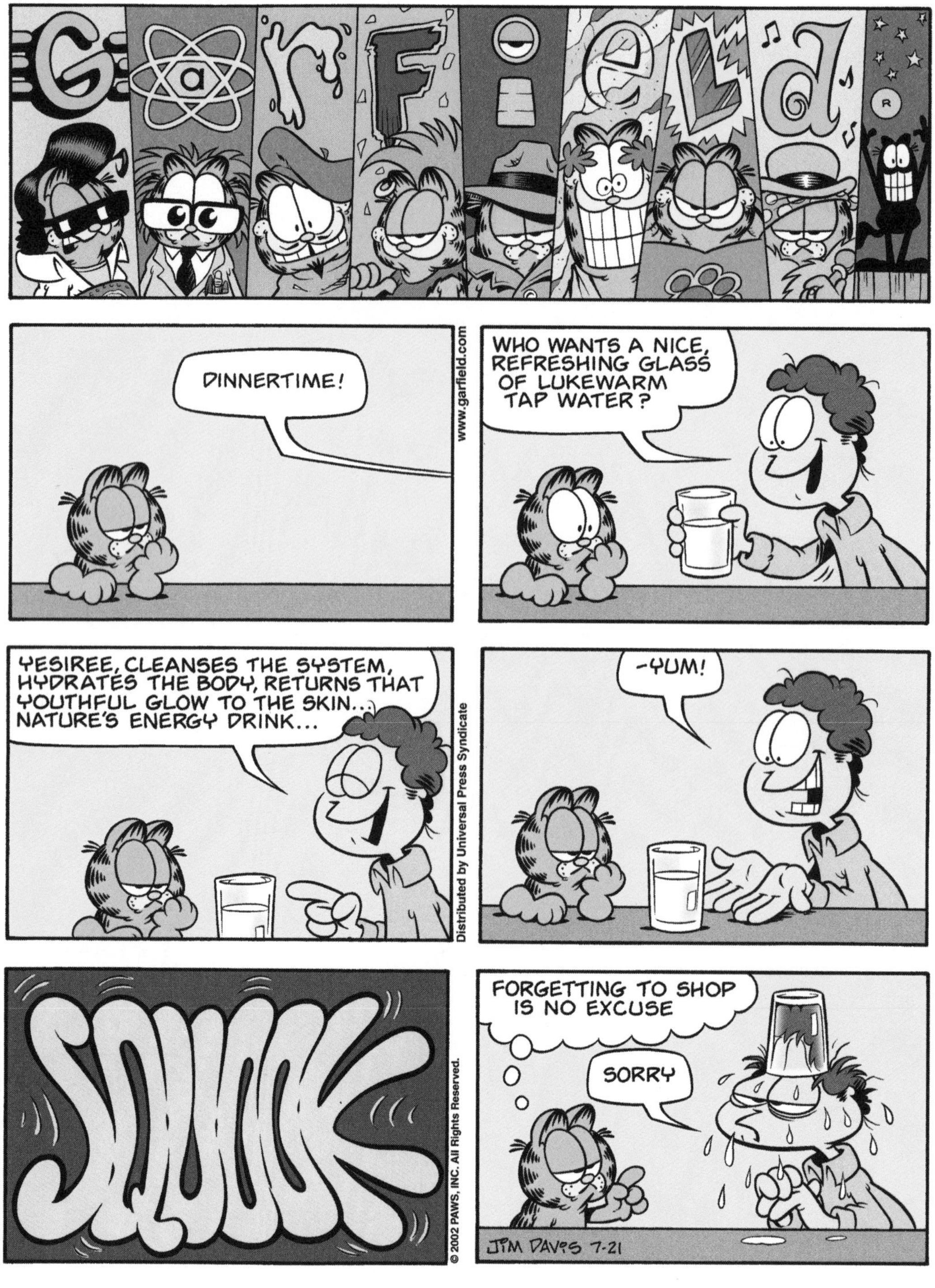
Garfield
DINNERTIME!
www.garfield.com
WHO WANTS A NICE, REFRESHING GLASS OF LUKEWARM TAP WATER?
YESIREE, CLEANSES THE SYSTEM, HYDRATES THE BODY, RETURNS THAT YOUTHFUL GLOW TO THE SKIN... NATURE'S ENERGY DRINK...
Distributed by Universal Press Syndicate
-YUM!
SQUOOK
© 2002 PAWS, INC. All Rights Reserved.
FORGETTING TO SHOP IS NO EXCUSE
SORRY
JIM DAVIS 7-21

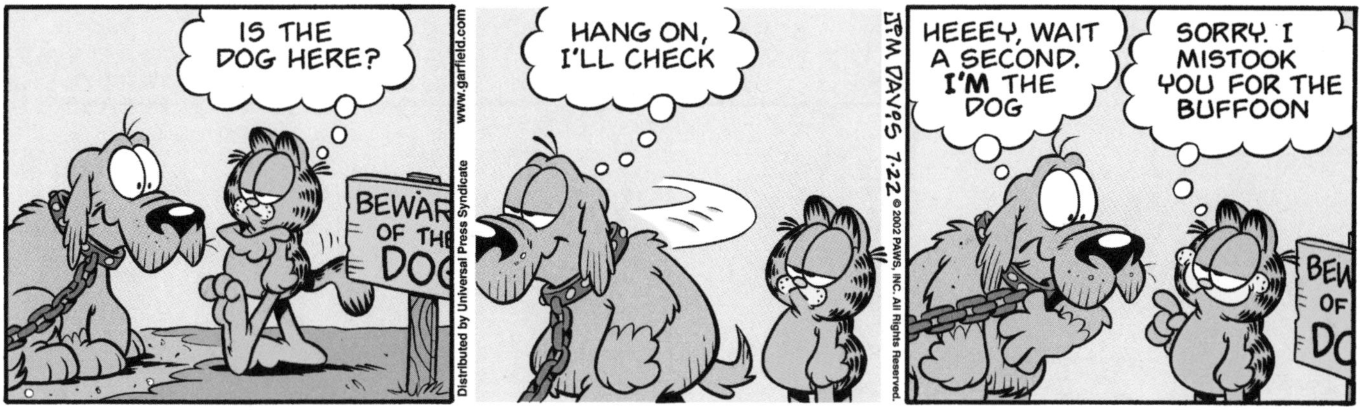
IS THE DOG HERE?
BEWARE OF THE DOG
www.garfield.com
Distributed by Universal Press Syndicate
HANG ON, I'LL CHECK
JIM DAVIS 7-22
© 2002 PAWS, INC. All Rights Reserved.
HEEEY, WAIT A SECOND. **I'M** THE DOG
SORRY. I MISTOOK YOU FOR THE BUFFOON

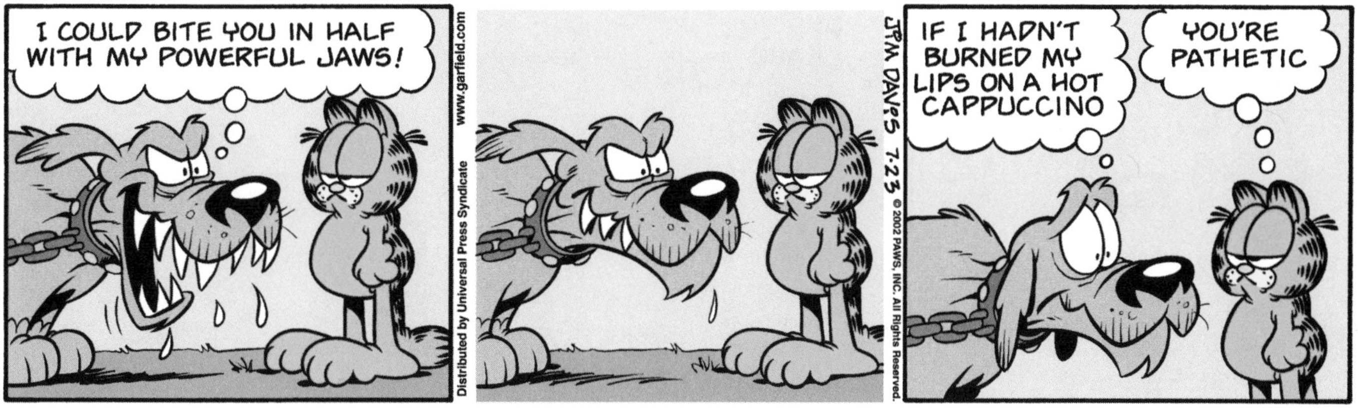
I COULD BITE YOU IN HALF WITH MY POWERFUL JAWS!
www.garfield.com
Distributed by Universal Press Syndicate
JIM DAVIS 7-23
© 2002 PAWS, INC. All Rights Reserved.
IF I HADN'T BURNED MY LIPS ON A HOT CAPPUCCINO
YOU'RE PATHETIC

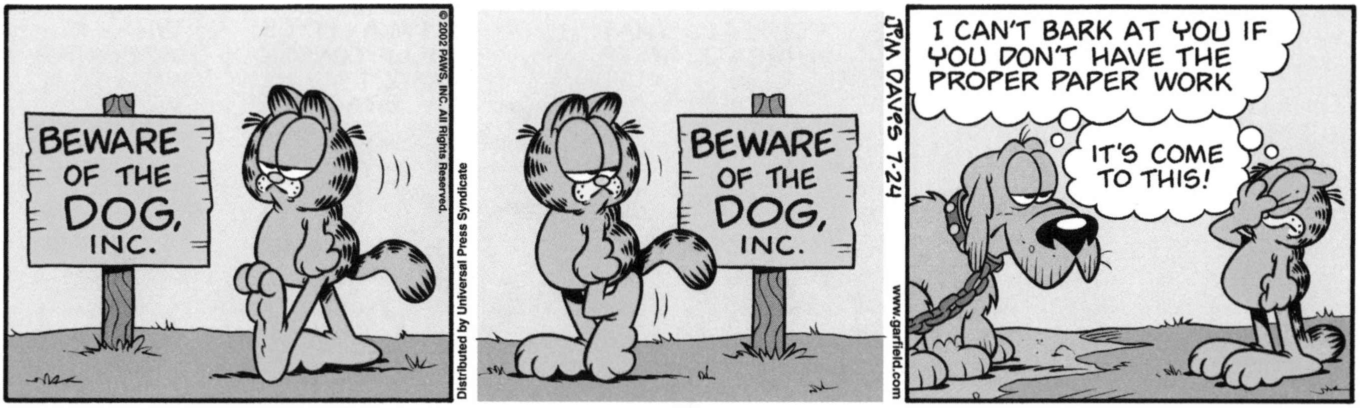
BEWARE OF THE DOG, INC.
© 2002 PAWS, INC. All Rights Reserved.
Distributed by Universal Press Syndicate
BEWARE OF THE DOG, INC.
JIM DAVIS 7-24
www.garfield.com
I CAN'T BARK AT YOU IF YOU DON'T HAVE THE PROPER PAPER WORK
IT'S COME TO THIS!

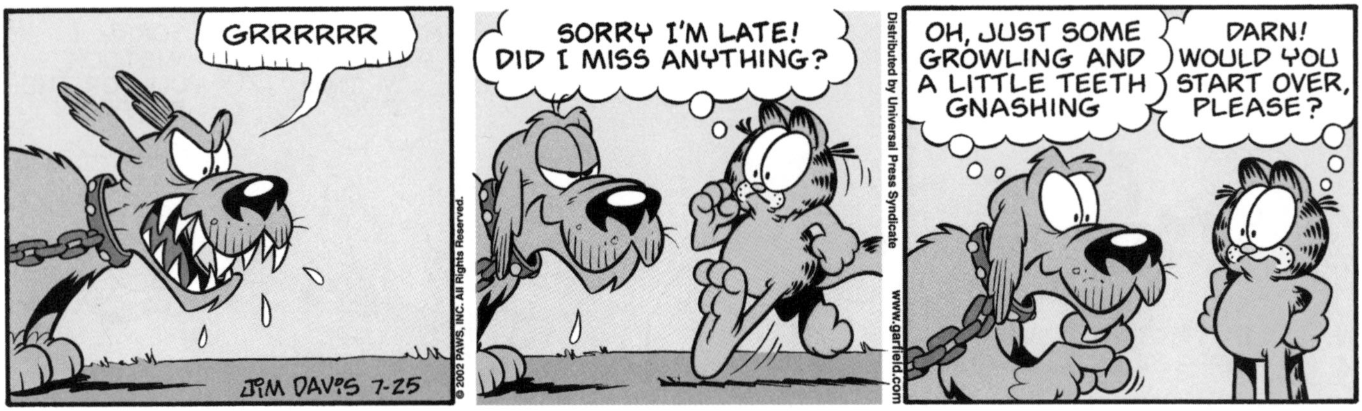
GRRRRRR
JIM DAVIS 7-25
© 2002 PAWS, INC. All Rights Reserved.
SORRY I'M LATE! DID I MISS ANYTHING?
Distributed by Universal Press Syndicate
www.garfield.com
OH, JUST SOME GROWLING AND A LITTLE TEETH GNASHING
DARN! WOULD YOU START OVER, PLEASE?

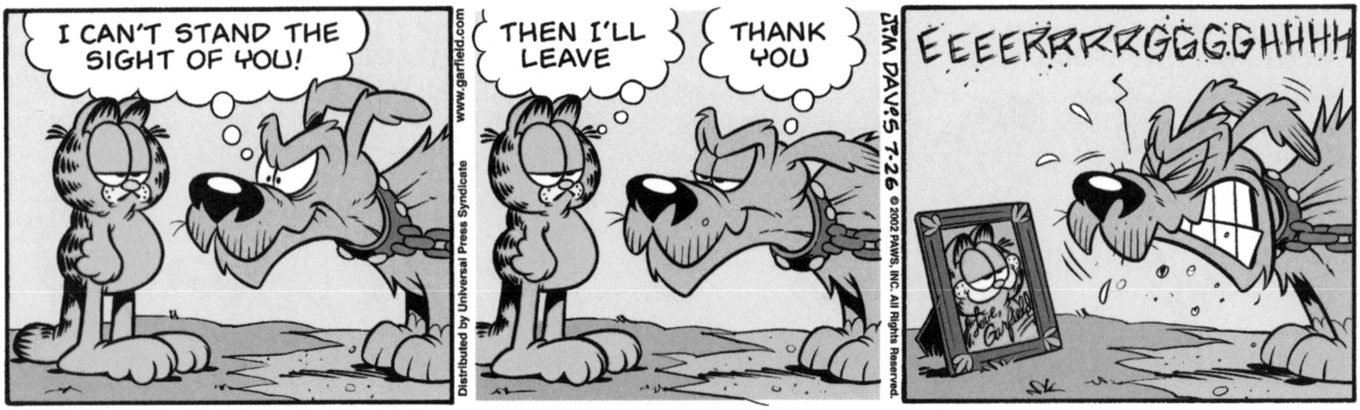
I CAN'T STAND THE SIGHT OF YOU!
Distributed by Universal Press Syndicate
www.garfield.com
THEN I'LL LEAVE
THANK YOU
JIM DAVIS 7-26
© 2002 PAWS, INC. All Rights Reserved.
EEEERRRRGGGGHHHH

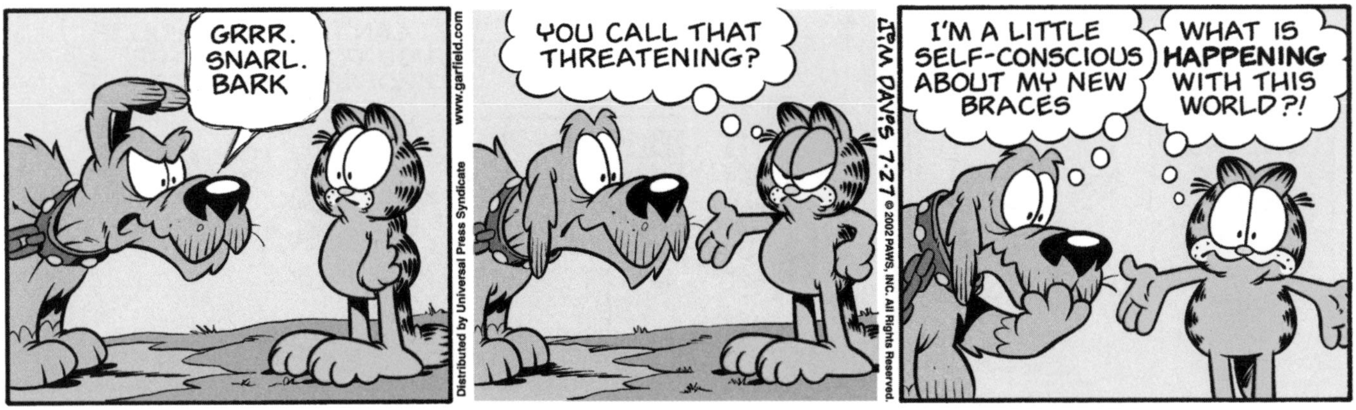
GRRR. SNARL. BARK
Distributed by Universal Press Syndicate
www.garfield.com
YOU CALL THAT THREATENING?
JIM DAVIS 7-27
© 2002 PAWS, INC. All Rights Reserved.
I'M A LITTLE SELF-CONSCIOUS ABOUT MY NEW BRACES
WHAT IS **HAPPENING** WITH THIS WORLD?!

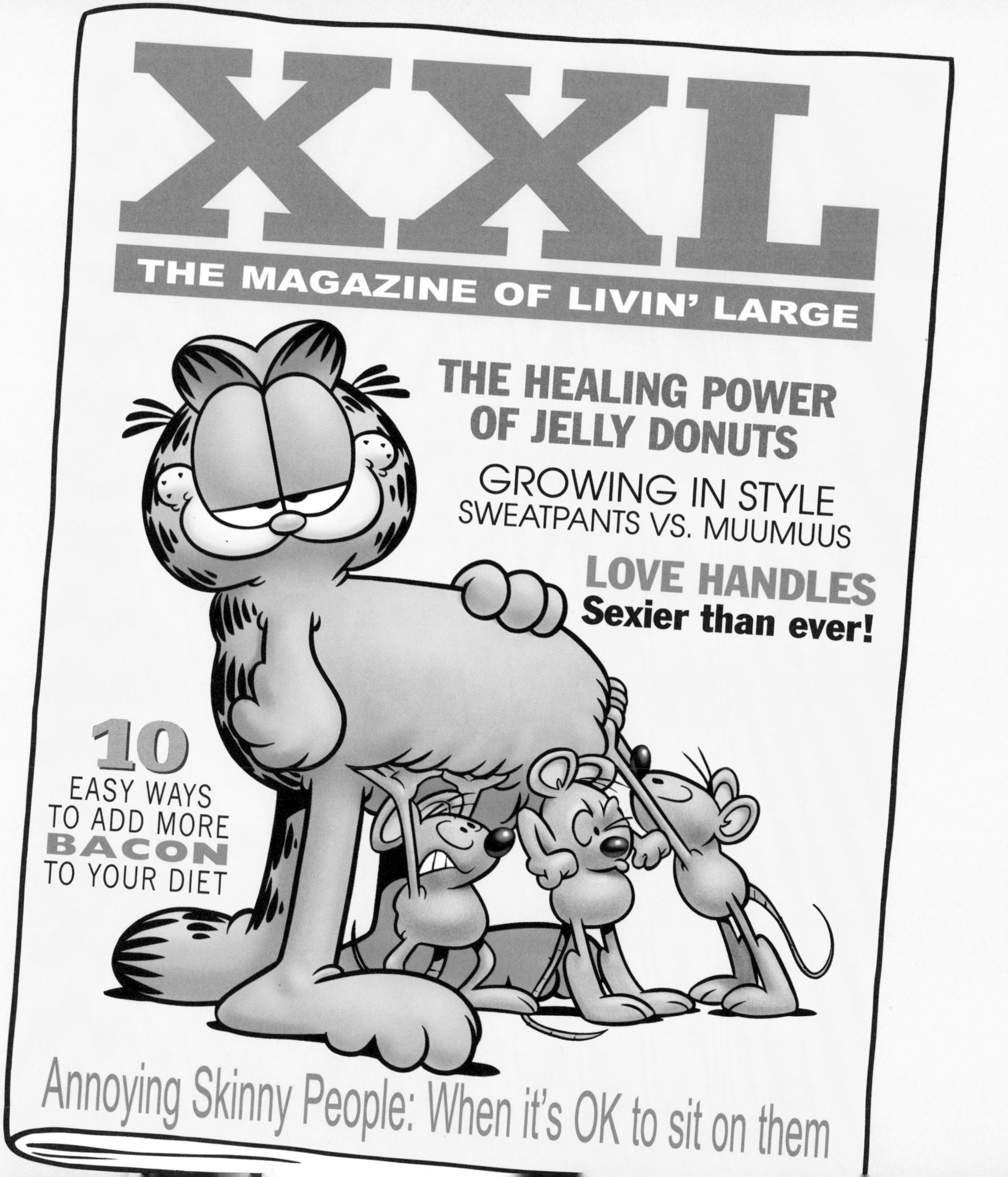
XXL
THE MAGAZINE OF LIVIN' LARGE
THE HEALING POWER OF JELLY DONUTS
GROWING IN STYLE
SWEATPANTS VS. MUUMUUS
LOVE HANDLES
Sexier than ever!
10 EASY WAYS TO ADD MORE BACON TO YOUR DIET
Annoying Skinny People: When it's OK to sit on them

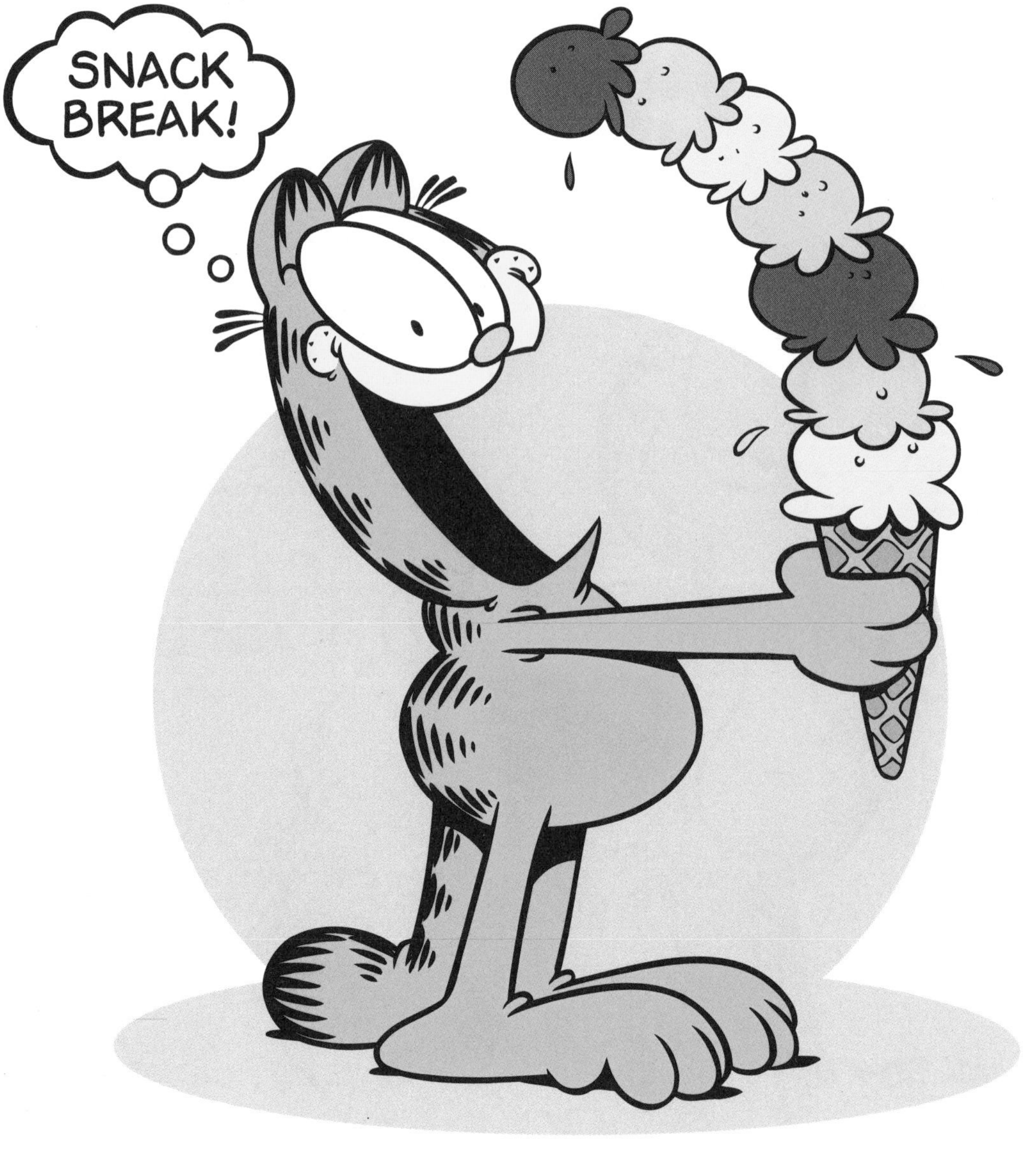
SNACK BREAK!

Garfield PIGS OUT

BY JIM DAVIS

Ballantine Books • New York

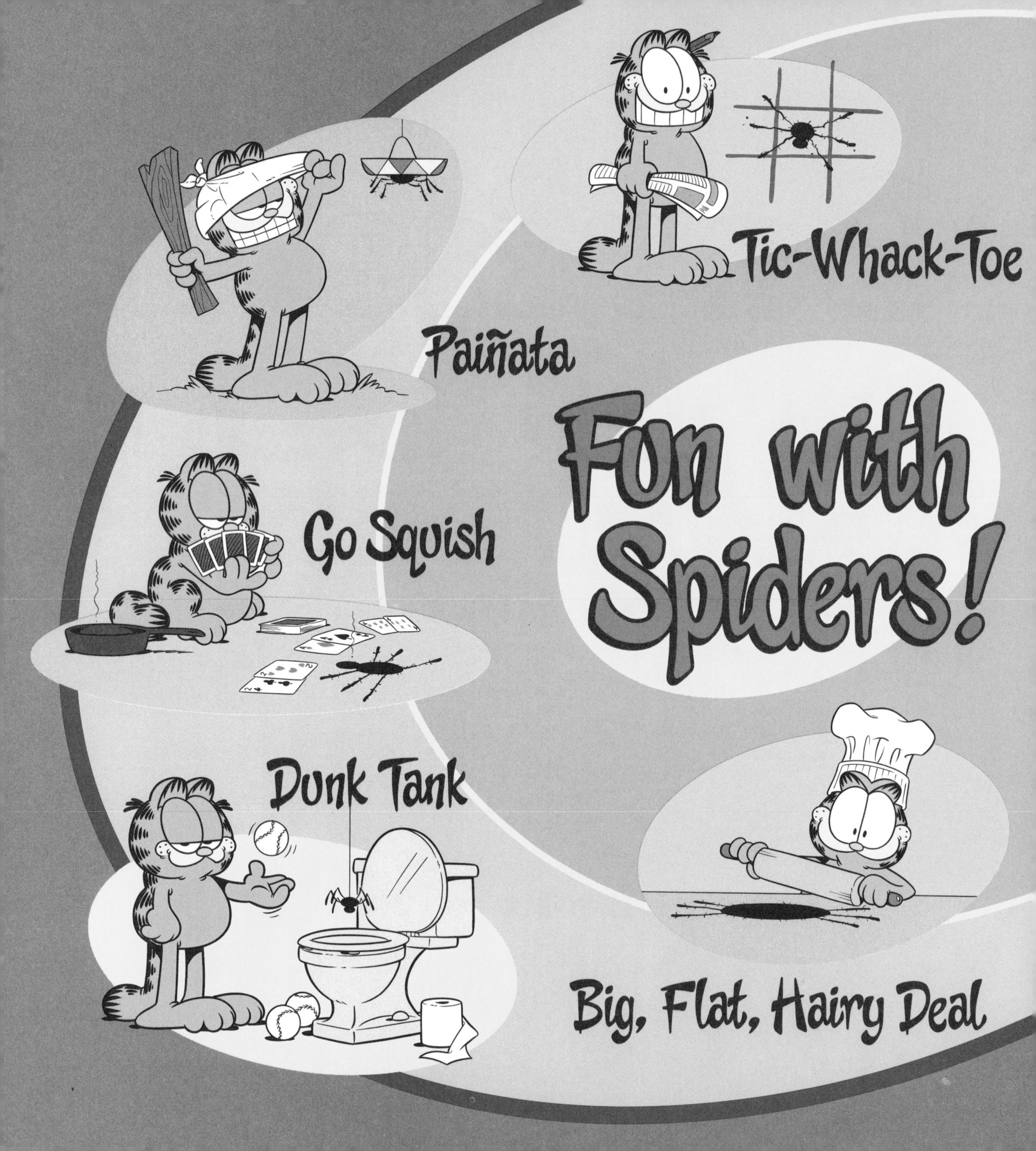
Fun with Spiders!
Tic-Whack-Toe
Paiñata
Go Squish
Dunk Tank
Big, Flat, Hairy Deal

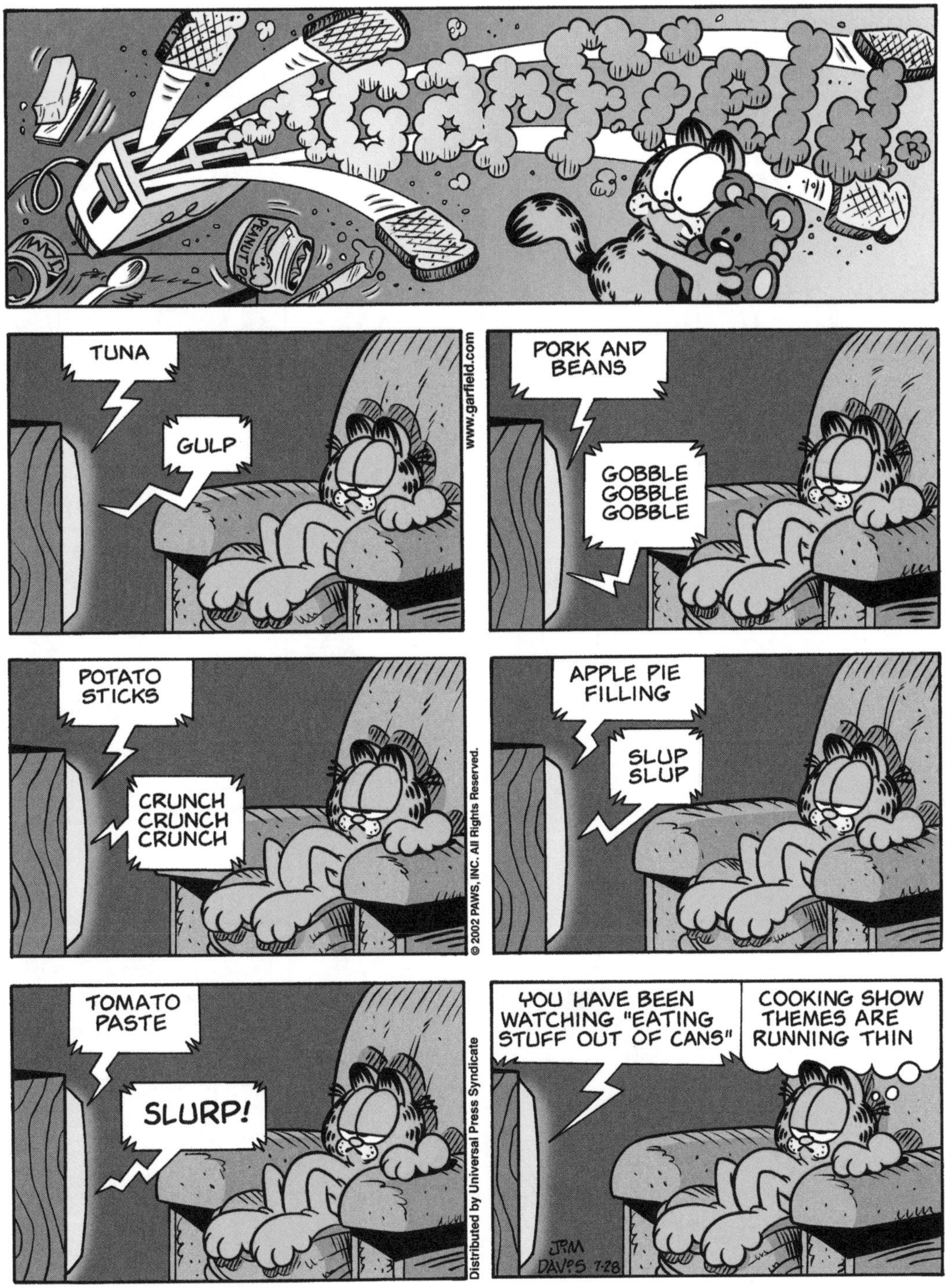

GARFIELD
PEANUT
JAM
TUNA
GULP
PORK AND BEANS
GOBBLE GOBBLE GOBBLE
POTATO STICKS
CRUNCH CRUNCH CRUNCH
APPLE PIE FILLING
SLUP SLUP
TOMATO PASTE
SLURP!
YOU HAVE BEEN WATCHING "EATING STUFF OUT OF CANS"
COOKING SHOW THEMES ARE RUNNING THIN
JIM DAVIS 7-28
www.garfield.com
© 2002 PAWS, INC. All Rights Reserved.
Distributed by Universal Press Syndicate

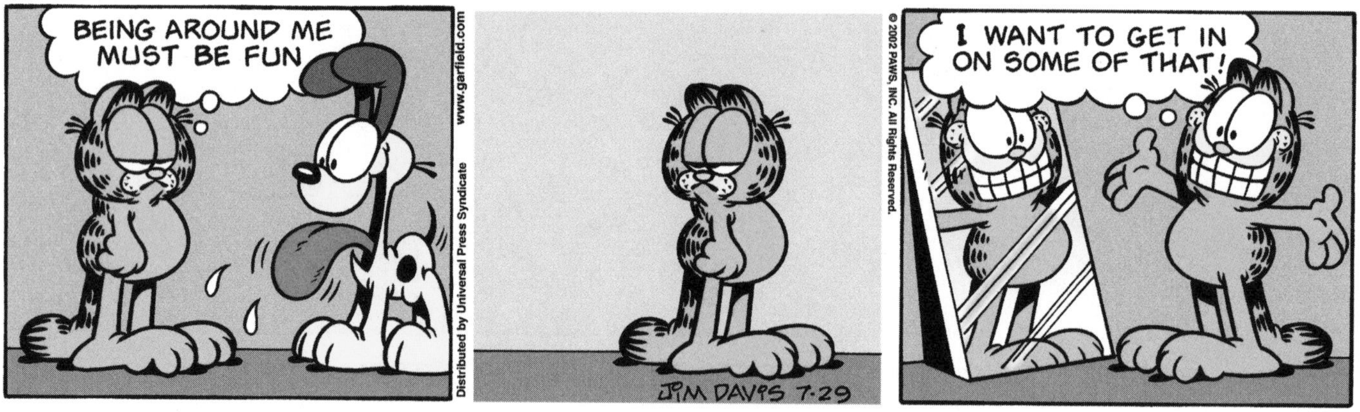
BEING AROUND ME MUST BE FUN
I WANT TO GET IN ON SOME OF THAT!
JIM DAVIS 7-29
www.garfield.com
Distributed by Universal Press Syndicate
© 2002 PAWS, INC. All Rights Reserved.

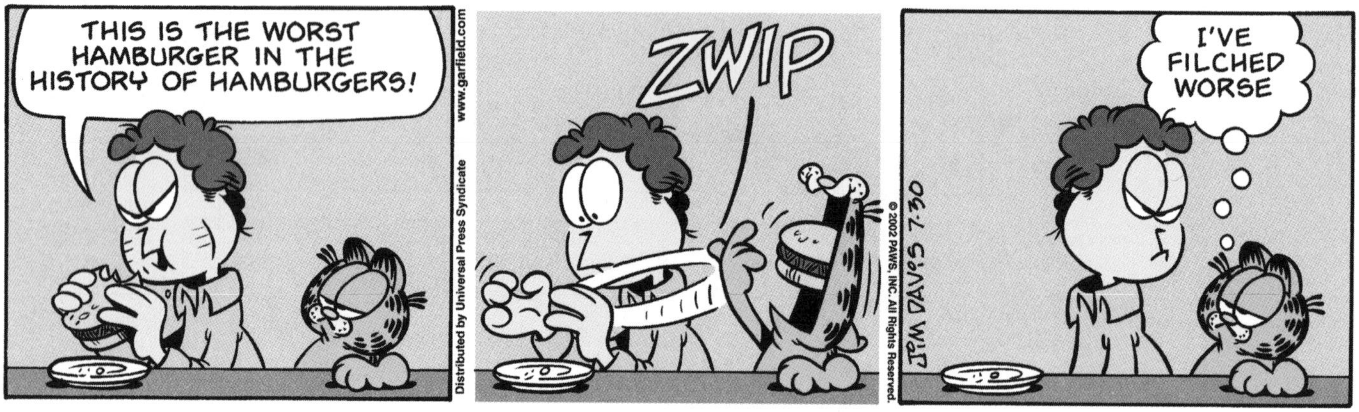
THIS IS THE WORST HAMBURGER IN THE HISTORY OF HAMBURGERS!
ZWIP
I'VE FILCHED WORSE
JIM DAVIS 7-30
www.garfield.com
Distributed by Universal Press Syndicate
© 2002 PAWS, INC. All Rights Reserved.

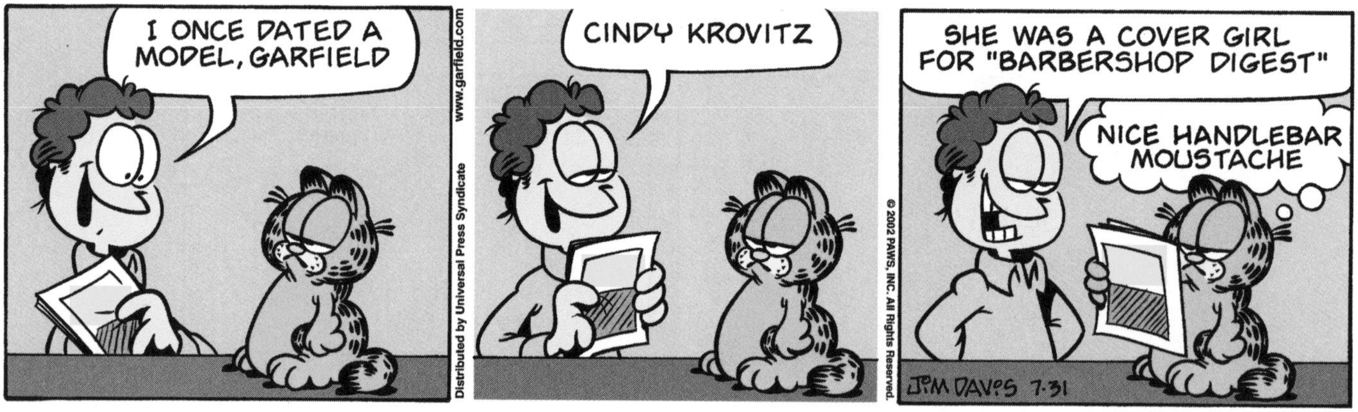
I ONCE DATED A MODEL, GARFIELD
CINDY KROVITZ
SHE WAS A COVER GIRL FOR "BARBERSHOP DIGEST"
NICE HANDLEBAR MOUSTACHE
JIM DAVIS 7-31
www.garfield.com
Distributed by Universal Press Syndicate
© 2002 PAWS, INC. All Rights Reserved.

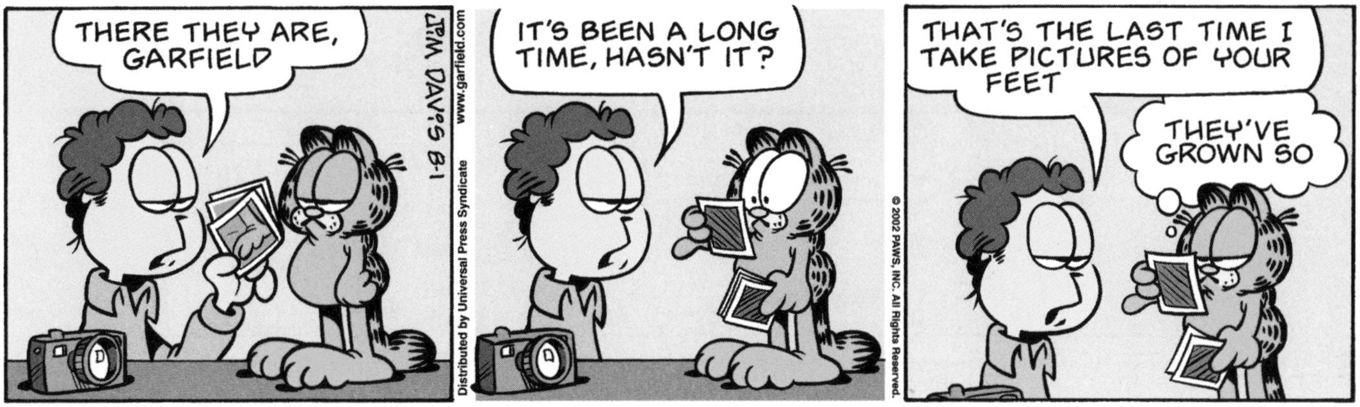
THERE THEY ARE, GARFIELD
JIM DAVIS 8-1
www.garfield.com
Distributed by Universal Press Syndicate
IT'S BEEN A LONG TIME, HASN'T IT?
© 2002 PAWS, INC. All Rights Reserved.
THAT'S THE LAST TIME I TAKE PICTURES OF YOUR FEET
THEY'VE GROWN SO

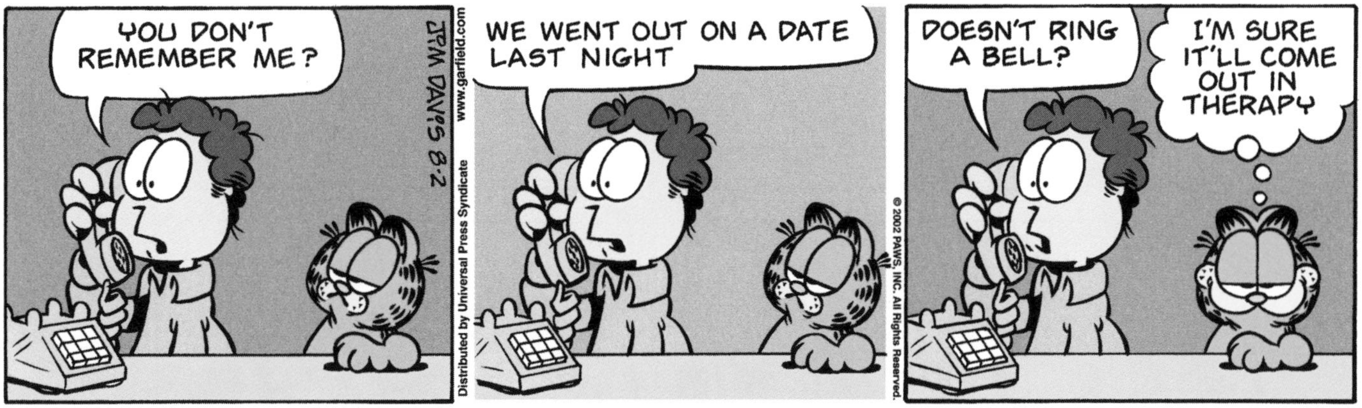
YOU DON'T REMEMBER ME?
JIM DAVIS 8-2
www.garfield.com
Distributed by Universal Press Syndicate
WE WENT OUT ON A DATE LAST NIGHT
© 2002 PAWS, INC. All Rights Reserved.
DOESN'T RING A BELL?
I'M SURE IT'LL COME OUT IN THERAPY

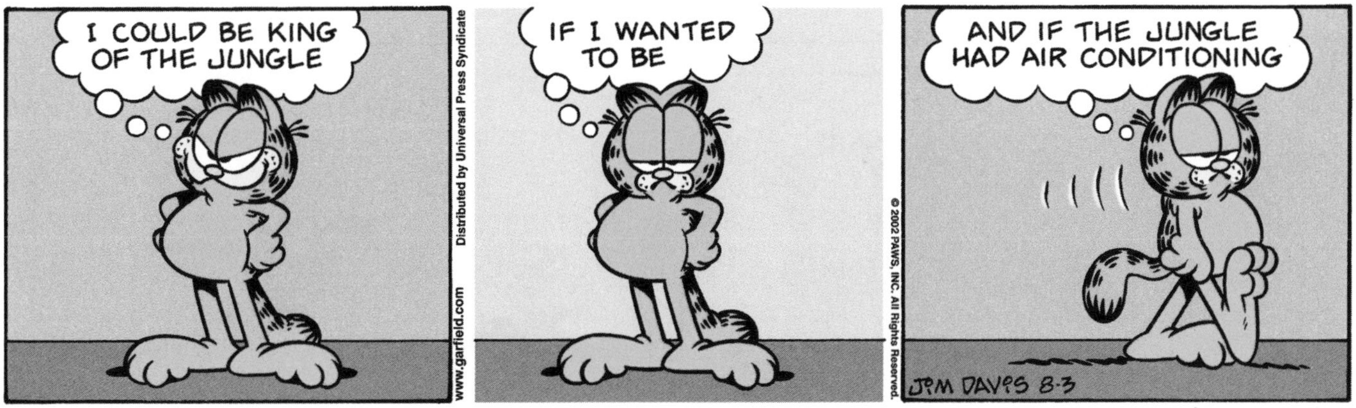
I COULD BE KING OF THE JUNGLE
www.garfield.com
Distributed by Universal Press Syndicate
IF I WANTED TO BE
© 2002 PAWS, INC. All Rights Reserved.
AND IF THE JUNGLE HAD AIR CONDITIONING
JIM DAVIS 8-3

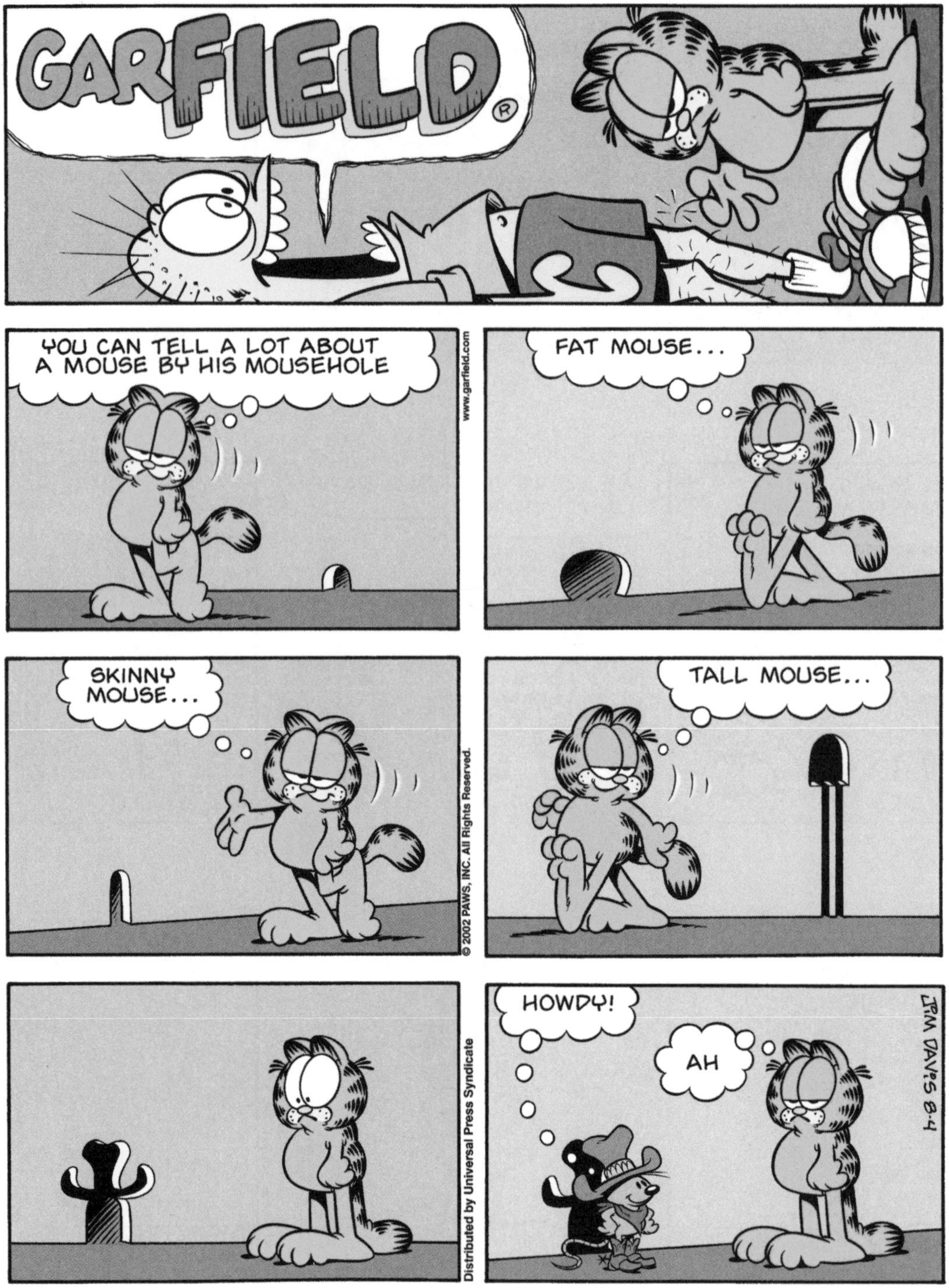
GARFIELD®
YOU CAN TELL A LOT ABOUT A MOUSE BY HIS MOUSEHOLE
FAT MOUSE...
SKINNY MOUSE...
TALL MOUSE...
HOWDY!
AH
JIM DAVIS 8-4
www.garfield.com
© 2002 PAWS, INC. All Rights Reserved.
Distributed by Universal Press Syndicate

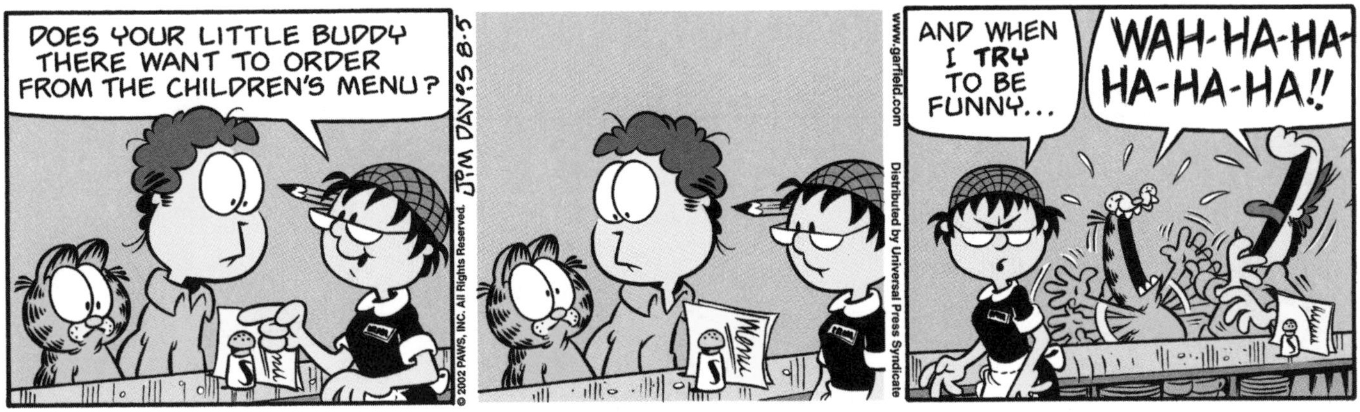
DOES YOUR LITTLE BUDDY THERE WANT TO ORDER FROM THE CHILDREN'S MENU?
JIM DAVIS 8-5
© 2002 PAWS, INC. All Rights Reserved.
www.garfield.com Distributed by Universal Press Syndicate
AND WHEN I **TRY** TO BE FUNNY...
WAH-HA-HA-HA-HA-HA!!

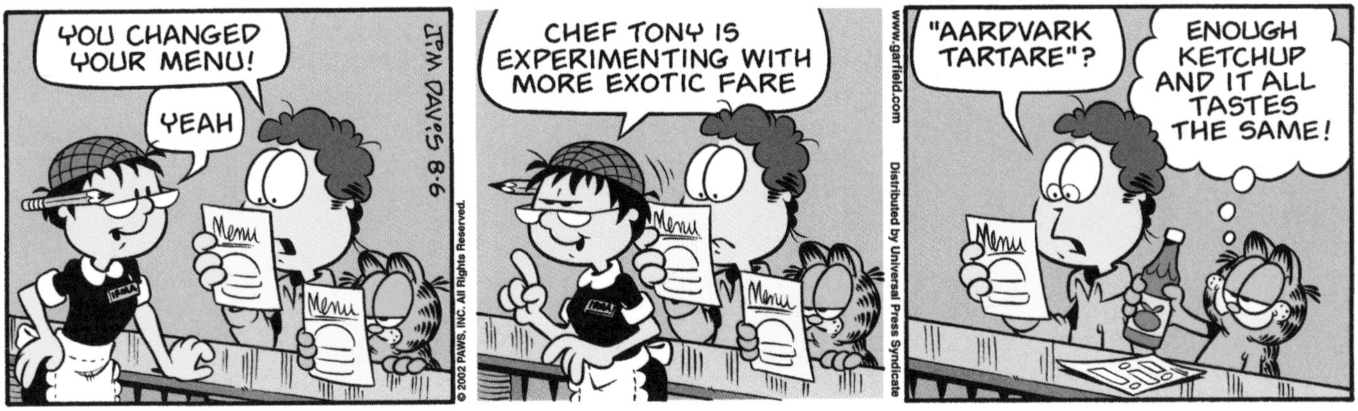
YOU CHANGED YOUR MENU!
YEAH
JIM DAVIS 8-6
© 2002 PAWS, INC. All Rights Reserved.
CHEF TONY IS EXPERIMENTING WITH MORE EXOTIC FARE
www.garfield.com Distributed by Universal Press Syndicate
"AARDVARK TARTARE"?
ENOUGH KETCHUP AND IT ALL TASTES THE SAME!

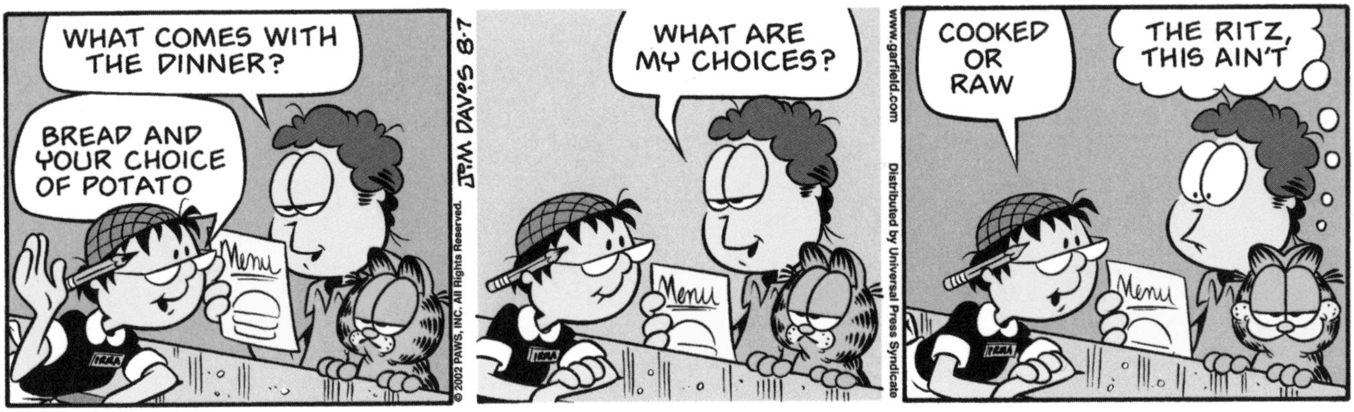
WHAT COMES WITH THE DINNER?
BREAD AND YOUR CHOICE OF POTATO
JIM DAVIS 8-7
© 2002 PAWS, INC. All Rights Reserved.
WHAT ARE MY CHOICES?
www.garfield.com Distributed by Universal Press Syndicate
COOKED OR RAW
THE RITZ, THIS AIN'T

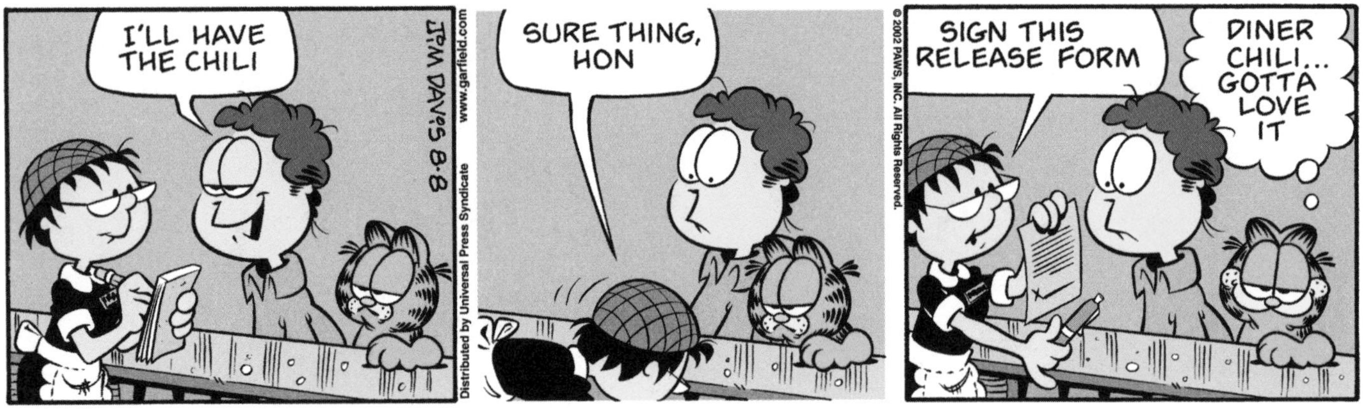
I'LL HAVE THE CHILI
JIM DAVIS 8-8
www.garfield.com
Distributed by Universal Press Syndicate
SURE THING, HON
© 2002 PAWS, INC. All Rights Reserved.
SIGN THIS RELEASE FORM
DINER CHILI... GOTTA LOVE IT

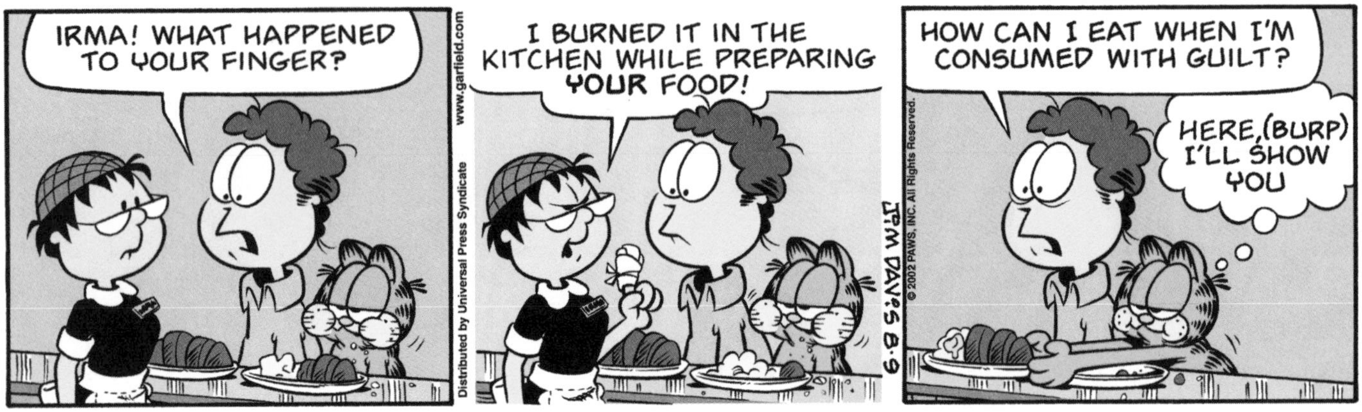
IRMA! WHAT HAPPENED TO YOUR FINGER?
www.garfield.com
Distributed by Universal Press Syndicate
I BURNED IT IN THE KITCHEN WHILE PREPARING **YOUR** FOOD!
JIM DAVIS 8-9
© 2002 PAWS, INC. All Rights Reserved.
HOW CAN I EAT WHEN I'M CONSUMED WITH GUILT?
HERE, (BURP) I'LL SHOW YOU

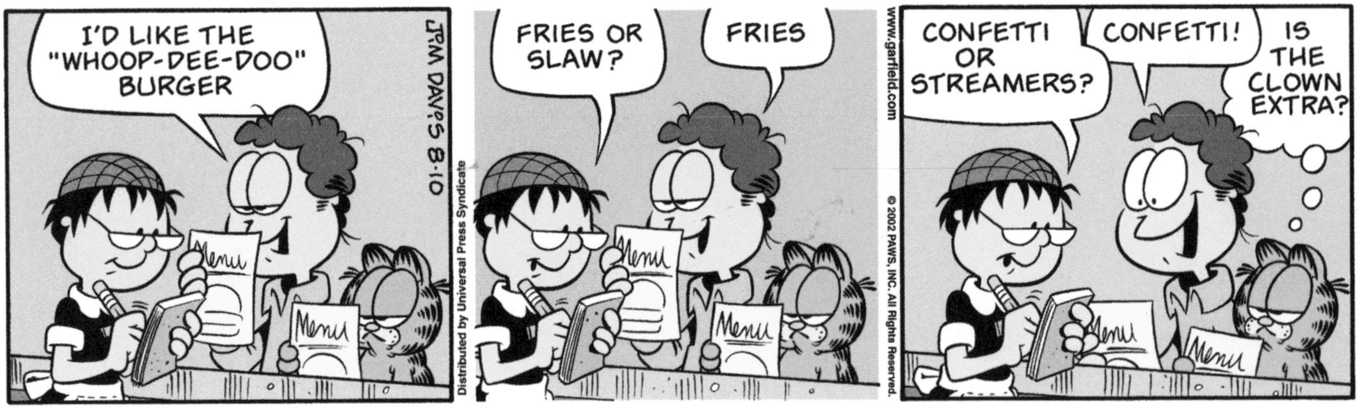
I'D LIKE THE "WHOOP-DEE-DOO" BURGER
JIM DAVIS 8-10
Distributed by Universal Press Syndicate
FRIES OR SLAW?
FRIES
www.garfield.com
© 2002 PAWS, INC. All Rights Reserved.
CONFETTI OR STREAMERS?
CONFETTI!
IS THE CLOWN EXTRA?

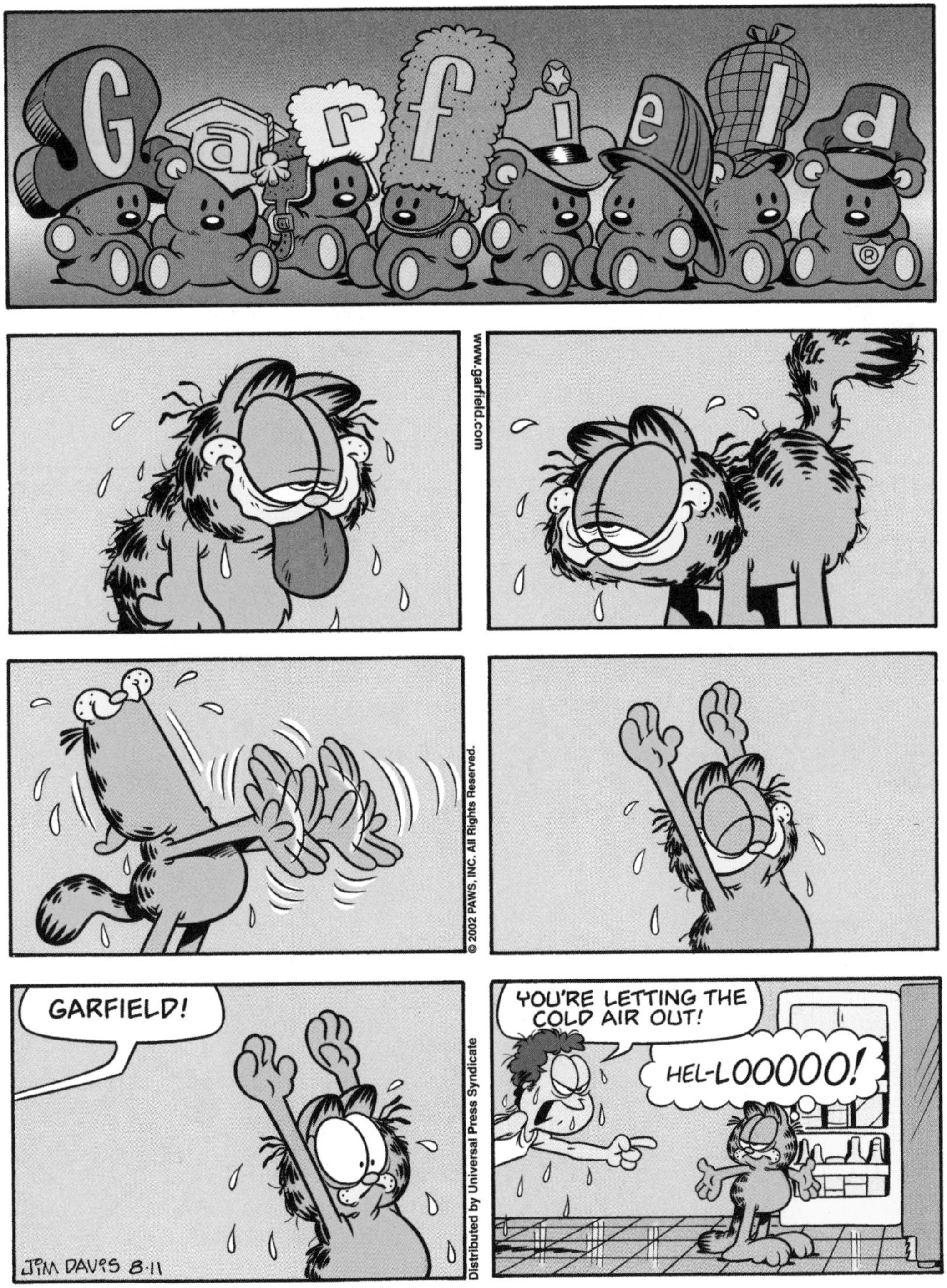
Garfield
www.garfield.com
© 2002 PAWS, INC. All Rights Reserved.
GARFIELD!
JIM DAVIS 8·11
Distributed by Universal Press Syndicate
YOU'RE LETTING THE COLD AIR OUT!
HEL-LOOOOO!

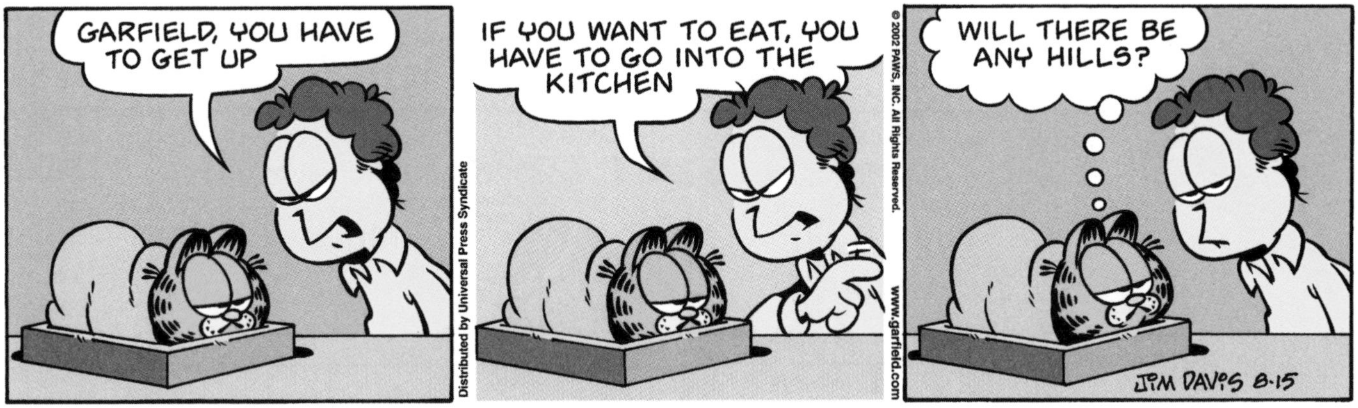
GARFIELD, YOU HAVE TO GET UP
Distributed by Universal Press Syndicate
IF YOU WANT TO EAT, YOU HAVE TO GO INTO THE KITCHEN
www.garfield.com
© 2002 PAWS, INC. All Rights Reserved.
WILL THERE BE ANY HILLS?
JIM DAVIS 8·15

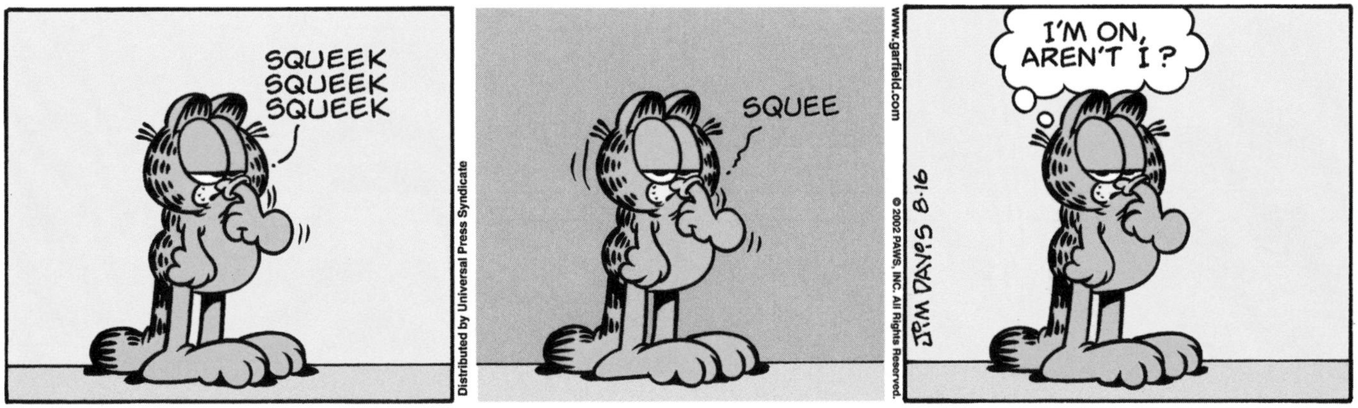
SQUEEK SQUEEK SQUEEK
Distributed by Universal Press Syndicate
SQUEE
www.garfield.com
© 2002 PAWS, INC. All Rights Reserved.
JIM DAVIS 8·16
I'M ON, AREN'T I ?

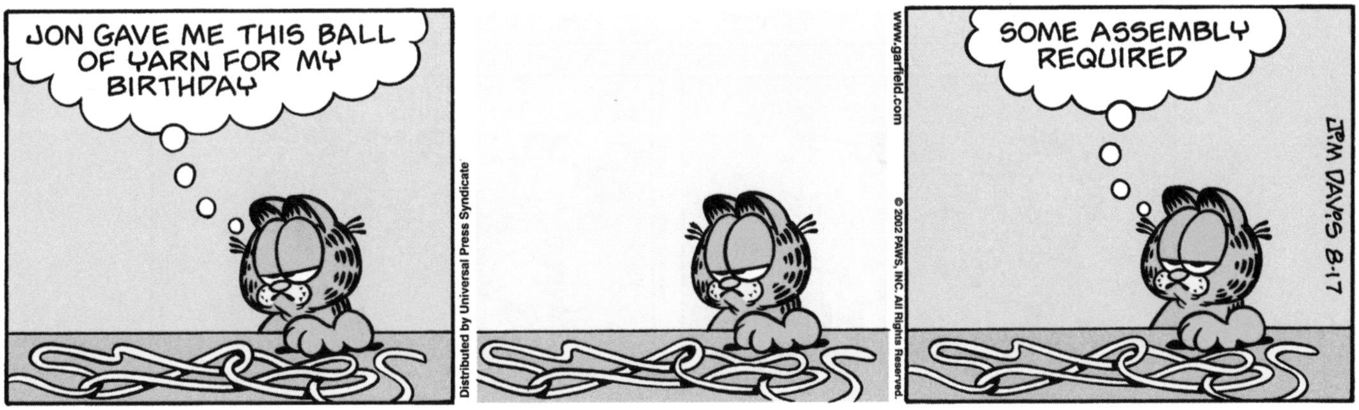
JON GAVE ME THIS BALL OF YARN FOR MY BIRTHDAY
Distributed by Universal Press Syndicate
www.garfield.com
© 2002 PAWS, INC. All Rights Reserved.
SOME ASSEMBLY REQUIRED
JIM DAVIS 8·17

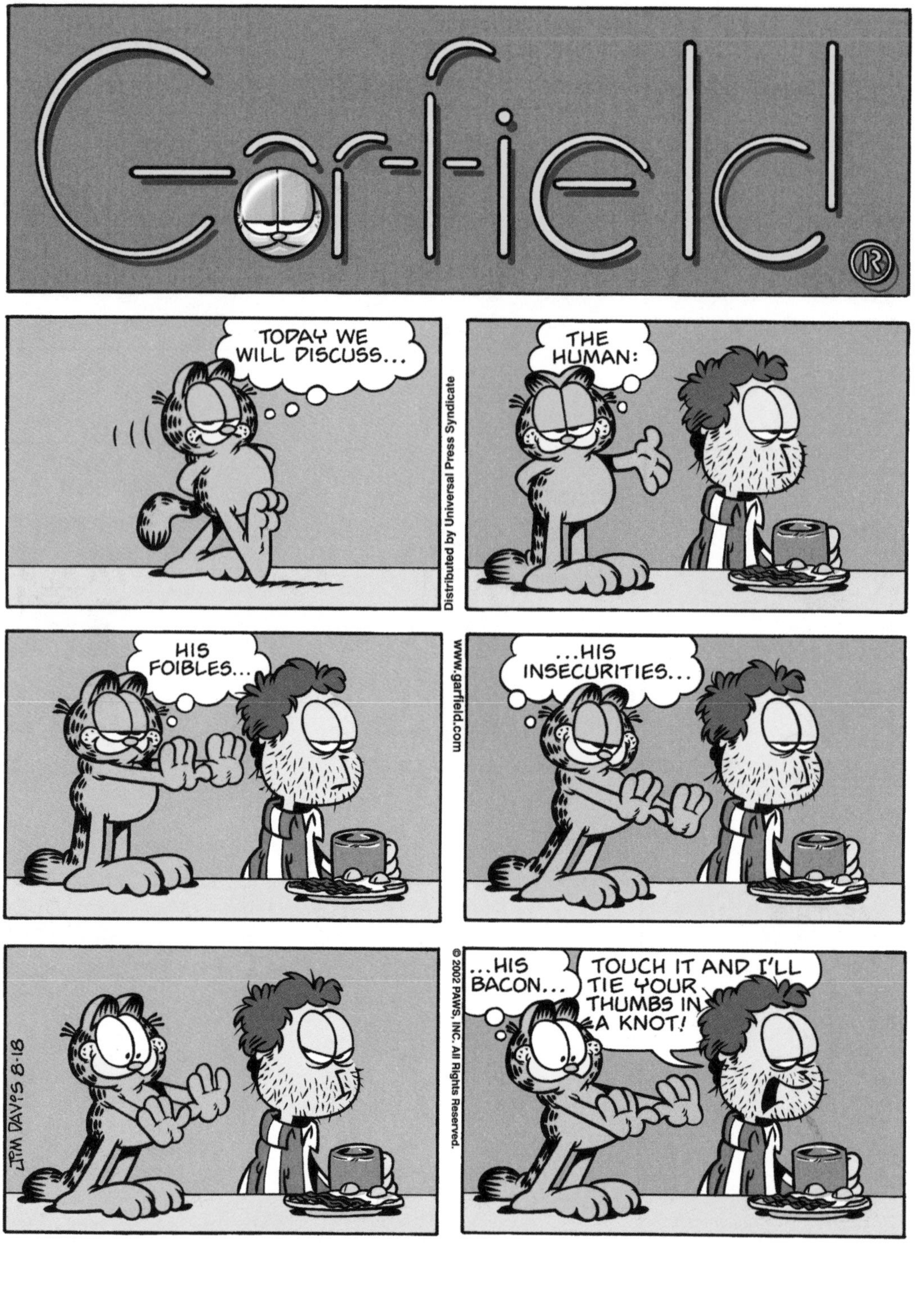
Garfield®
TODAY WE WILL DISCUSS...
THE HUMAN:
HIS FOIBLES...
...HIS INSECURITIES...
JIM DAVIS 8-18
...HIS BACON...
TOUCH IT AND I'LL TIE YOUR THUMBS IN A KNOT!
Distributed by Universal Press Syndicate
www.garfield.com
© 2002 PAWS, INC. All Rights Reserved.

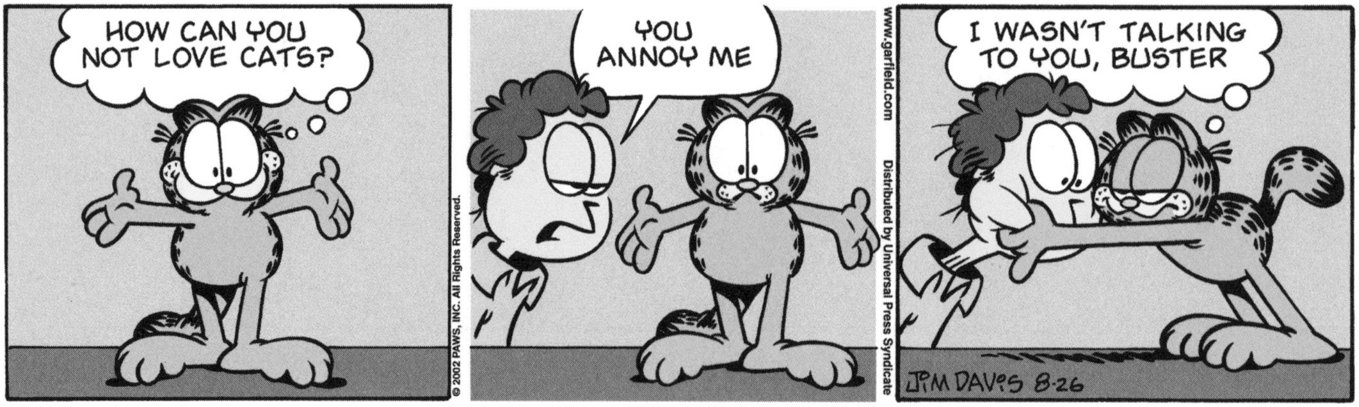
HOW CAN YOU NOT LOVE CATS?
YOU ANNOY ME
I WASN'T TALKING TO YOU, BUSTER
JIM DAVIS 8-26
© 2002 PAWS, INC. All Rights Reserved.
www.garfield.com
Distributed by Universal Press Syndicate

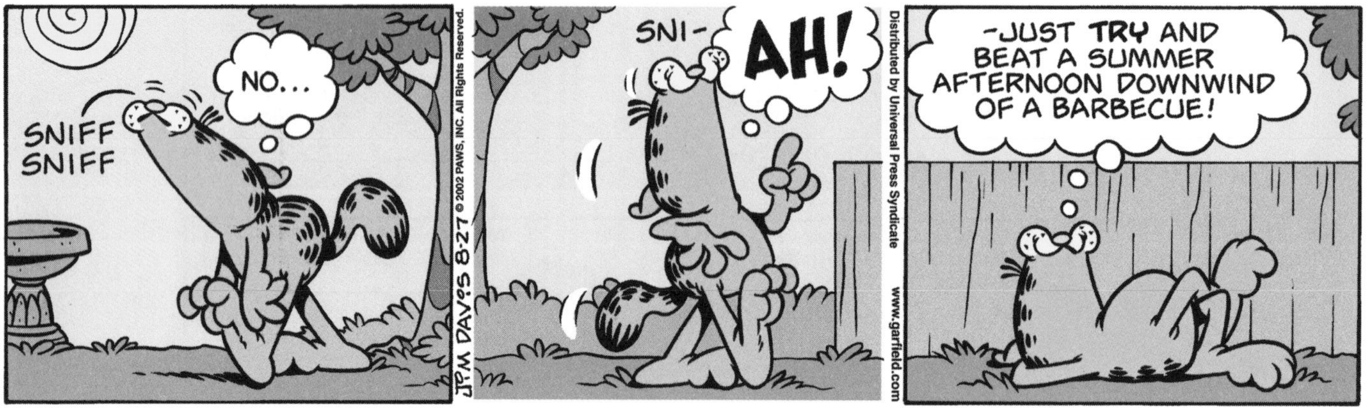
SNIFF SNIFF
NO...
JIM DAVIS 8-27
© 2002 PAWS, INC. All Rights Reserved.
SNI-
AH!
-JUST TRY AND BEAT A SUMMER AFTERNOON DOWNWIND OF A BARBECUE!
Distributed by Universal Press Syndicate
www.garfield.com

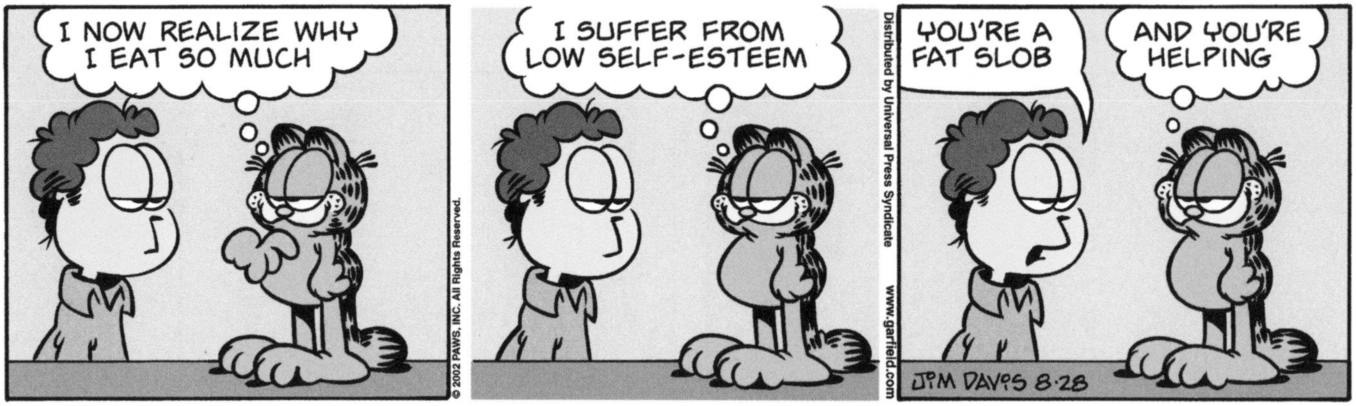
I NOW REALIZE WHY I EAT SO MUCH
© 2002 PAWS, INC. All Rights Reserved.
I SUFFER FROM LOW SELF-ESTEEM
YOU'RE A FAT SLOB
AND YOU'RE HELPING
JIM DAVIS 8-28
Distributed by Universal Press Syndicate
www.garfield.com

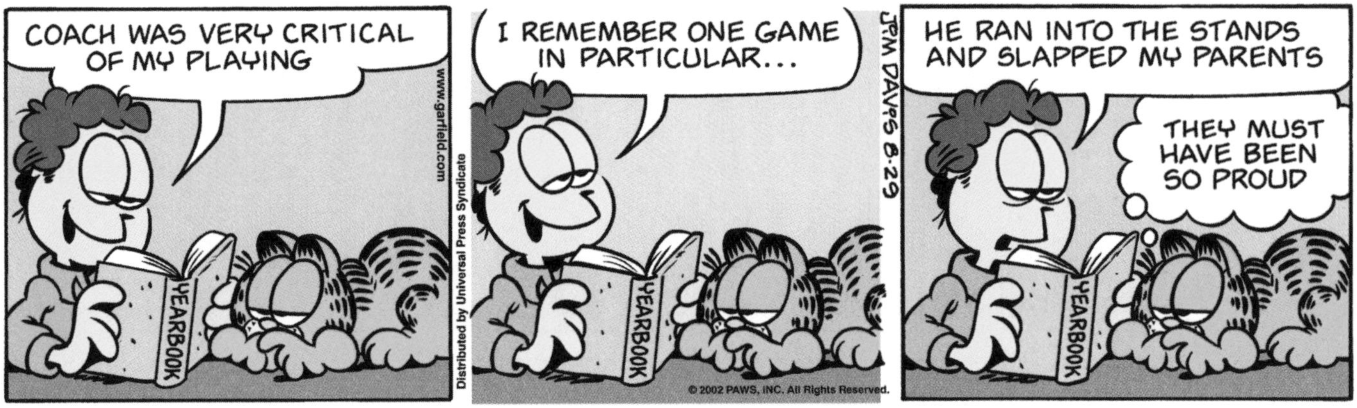
COACH WAS VERY CRITICAL OF MY PLAYING
www.garfield.com
Distributed by Universal Press Syndicate
I REMEMBER ONE GAME IN PARTICULAR...
YEARBOOK
© 2002 PAWS, INC. All Rights Reserved.
JIM DAVIS 8-29
HE RAN INTO THE STANDS AND SLAPPED MY PARENTS
THEY MUST HAVE BEEN SO PROUD

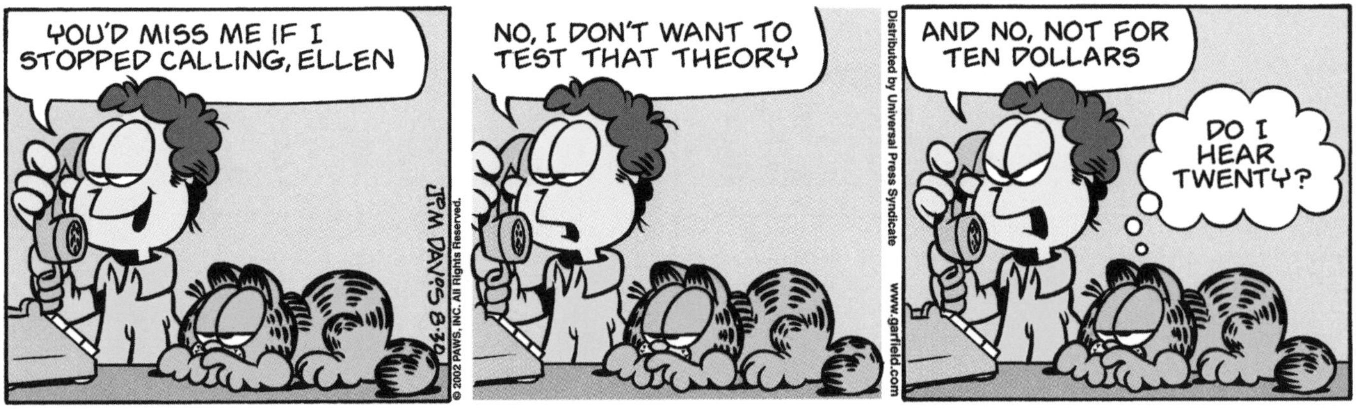
YOU'D MISS ME IF I STOPPED CALLING, ELLEN
JIM DAVIS 8-30
© 2002 PAWS, INC. All Rights Reserved.
NO, I DON'T WANT TO TEST THAT THEORY
Distributed by Universal Press Syndicate
www.garfield.com
AND NO, NOT FOR TEN DOLLARS
DO I HEAR TWENTY?

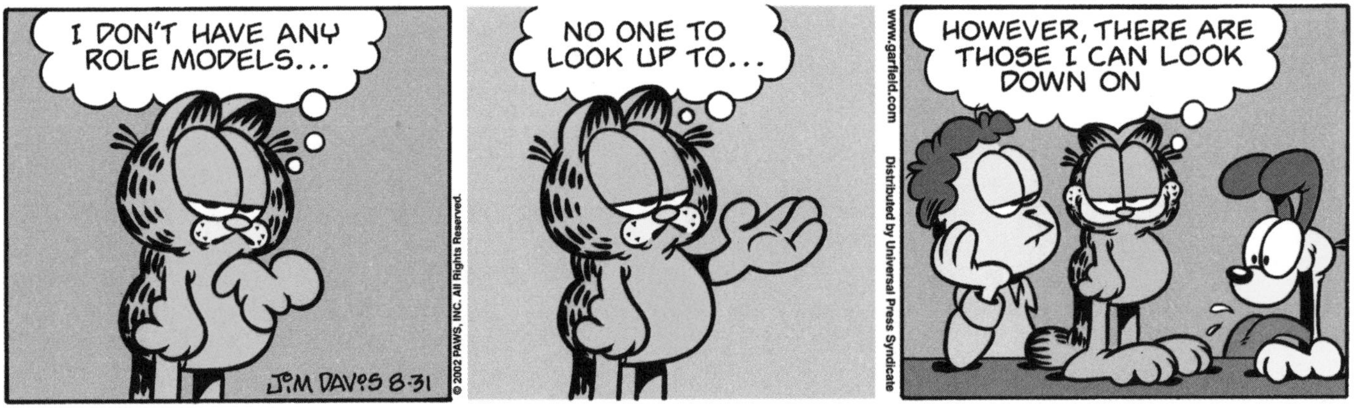
I DON'T HAVE ANY ROLE MODELS...
JIM DAVIS 8-31
© 2002 PAWS, INC. All Rights Reserved.
NO ONE TO LOOK UP TO...
www.garfield.com
Distributed by Universal Press Syndicate
HOWEVER, THERE ARE THOSE I CAN LOOK DOWN ON

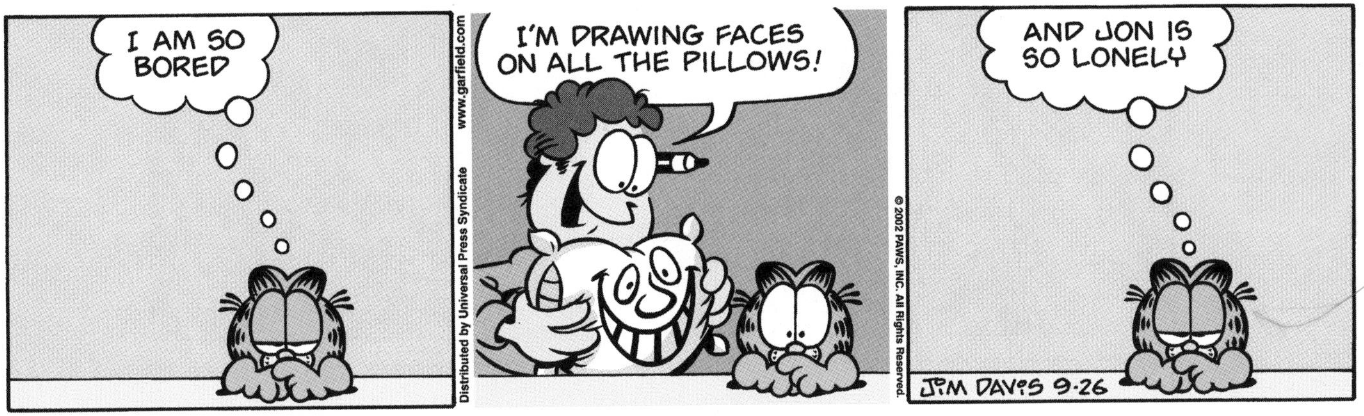
I AM SO BORED
I'M DRAWING FACES ON ALL THE PILLOWS!
AND JON IS SO LONELY
www.garfield.com
Distributed by Universal Press Syndicate
© 2002 PAWS, INC. All Rights Reserved.
JIM DAVIS 9-26

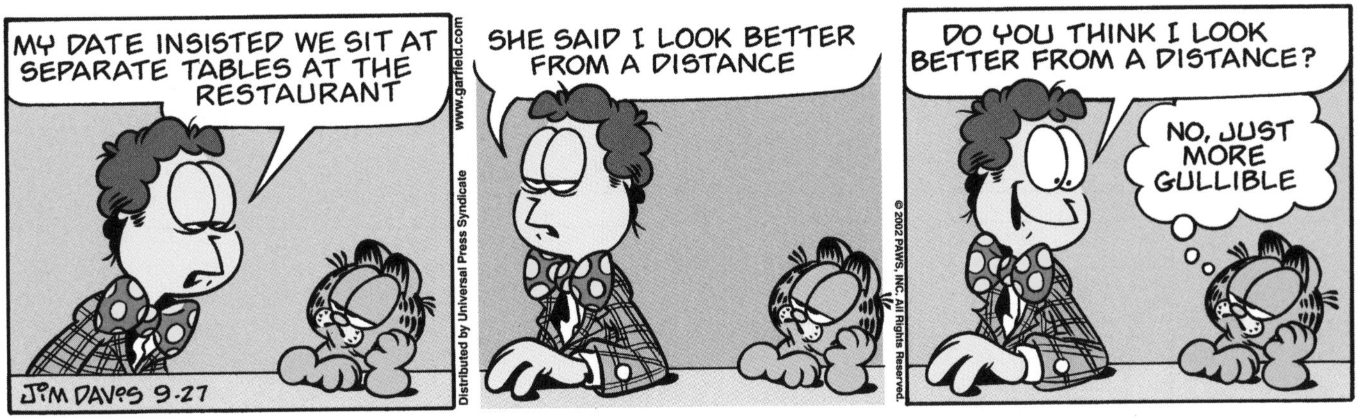
MY DATE INSISTED WE SIT AT SEPARATE TABLES AT THE RESTAURANT
SHE SAID I LOOK BETTER FROM A DISTANCE
DO YOU THINK I LOOK BETTER FROM A DISTANCE?
NO, JUST MORE GULLIBLE
www.garfield.com
Distributed by Universal Press Syndicate
© 2002 PAWS, INC. All Rights Reserved.
JIM DAVIS 9-27

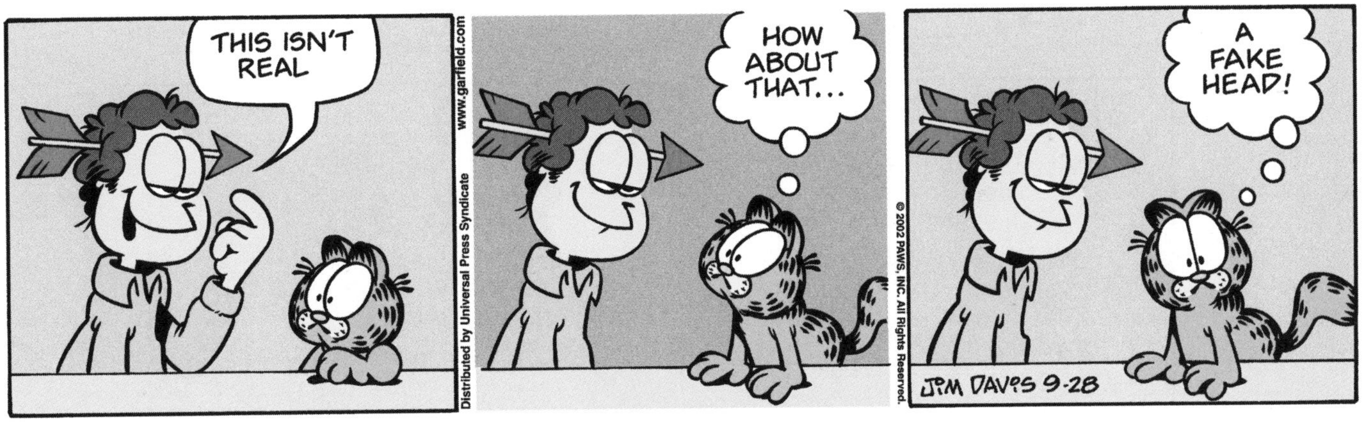
THIS ISN'T REAL
HOW ABOUT THAT...
A FAKE HEAD!
www.garfield.com
Distributed by Universal Press Syndicate
© 2002 PAWS, INC. All Rights Reserved.
JIM DAVIS 9-28

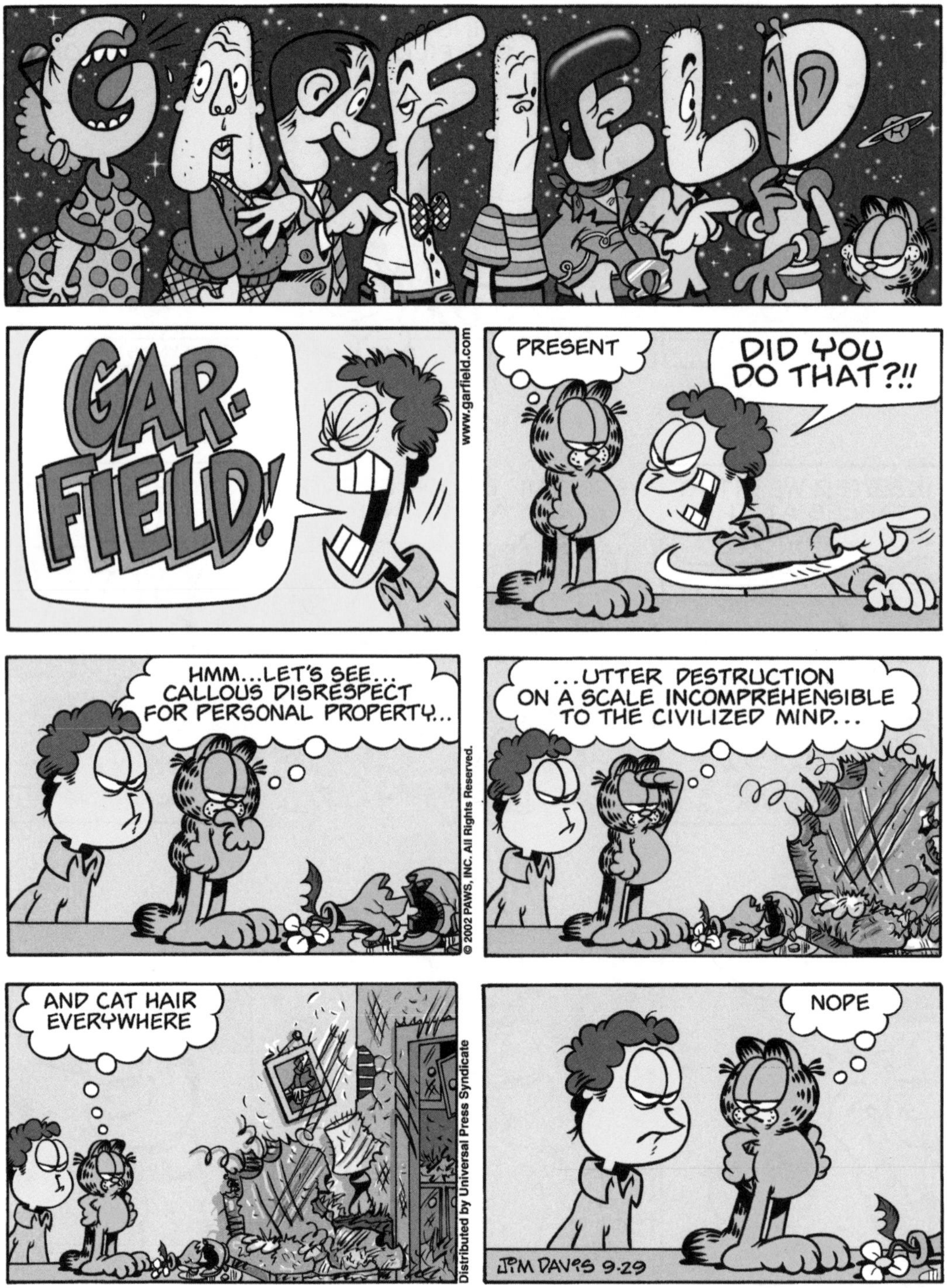
GARFIELD
GAR-FIELD!
PRESENT
DID YOU DO THAT?!!
HMM...LET'S SEE... CALLOUS DISRESPECT FOR PERSONAL PROPERTY...
...UTTER DESTRUCTION ON A SCALE INCOMPREHENSIBLE TO THE CIVILIZED MIND...
AND CAT HAIR EVERYWHERE
NOPE
JIM DAVIS 9-29
www.garfield.com
© 2002 PAWS, INC. All Rights Reserved.
Distributed by Universal Press Syndicate

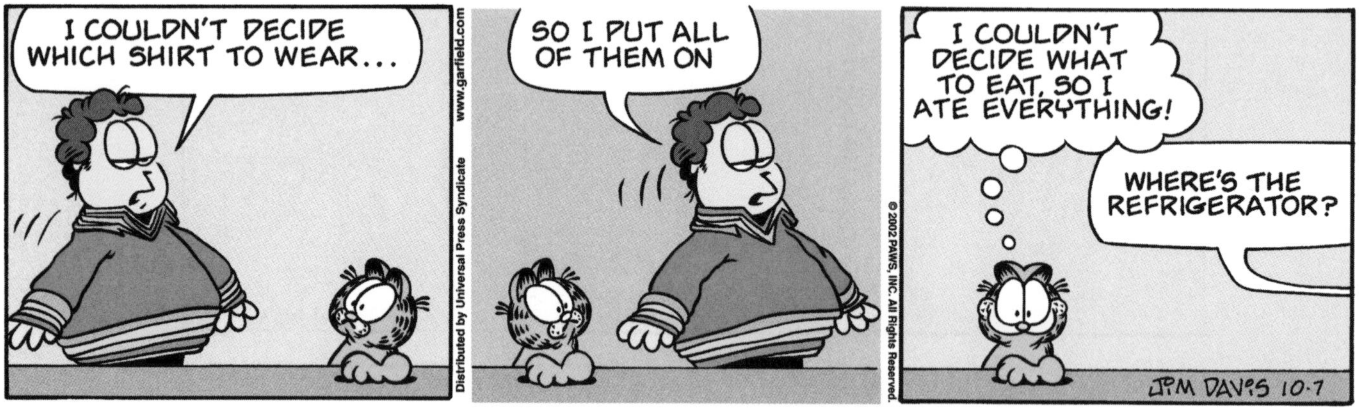
I COULDN'T DECIDE WHICH SHIRT TO WEAR...
SO I PUT ALL OF THEM ON
I COULDN'T DECIDE WHAT TO EAT, SO I ATE EVERYTHING!
WHERE'S THE REFRIGERATOR?
JIM DAVIS 10-7

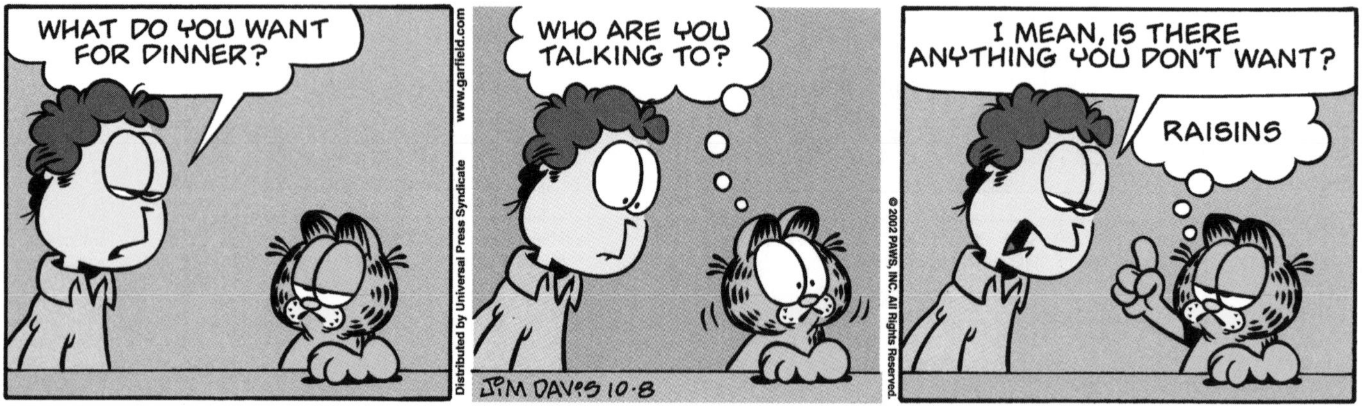
WHAT DO YOU WANT FOR DINNER?
WHO ARE YOU TALKING TO?
I MEAN, IS THERE ANYTHING YOU DON'T WANT?
RAISINS
JIM DAVIS 10-8

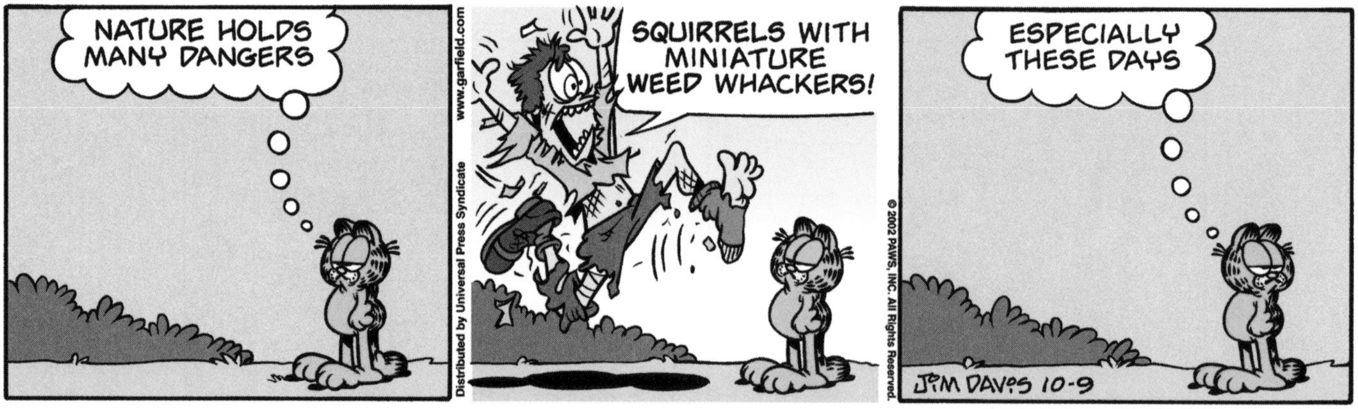
NATURE HOLDS MANY DANGERS
SQUIRRELS WITH MINIATURE WEED WHACKERS!
ESPECIALLY THESE DAYS
JIM DAVIS 10-9

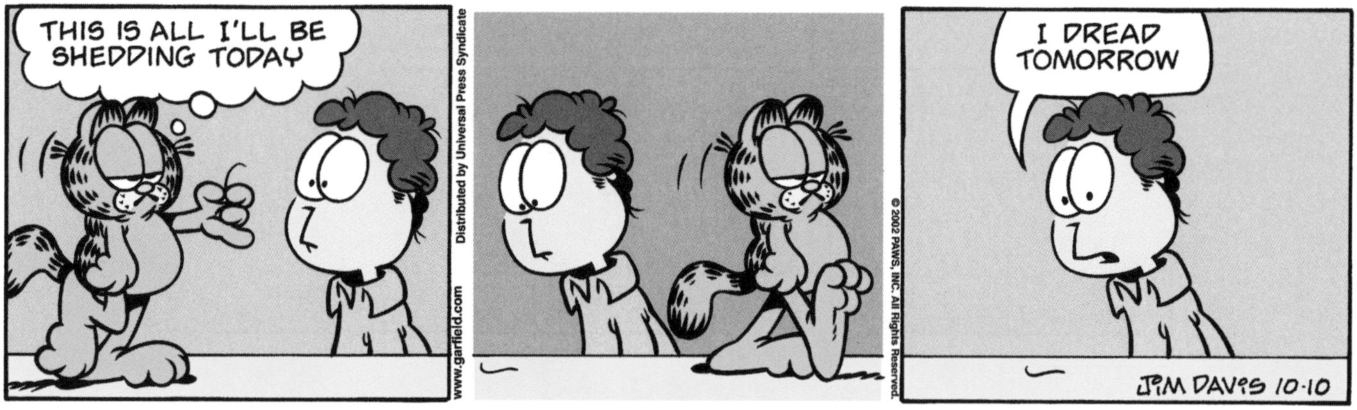
THIS IS ALL I'LL BE SHEDDING TODAY
www.garfield.com Distributed by Universal Press Syndicate
© 2002 PAWS, INC. All Rights Reserved.
I DREAD TOMORROW
JIM DAVIS 10-10

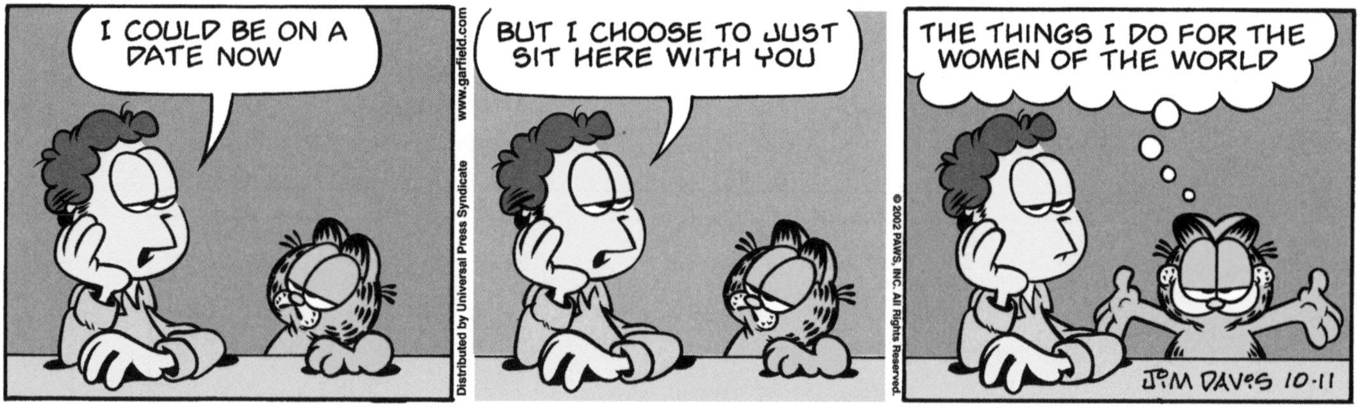
I COULD BE ON A DATE NOW
Distributed by Universal Press Syndicate www.garfield.com
BUT I CHOOSE TO JUST SIT HERE WITH YOU
© 2002 PAWS, INC. All Rights Reserved.
THE THINGS I DO FOR THE WOMEN OF THE WORLD
JIM DAVIS 10-11

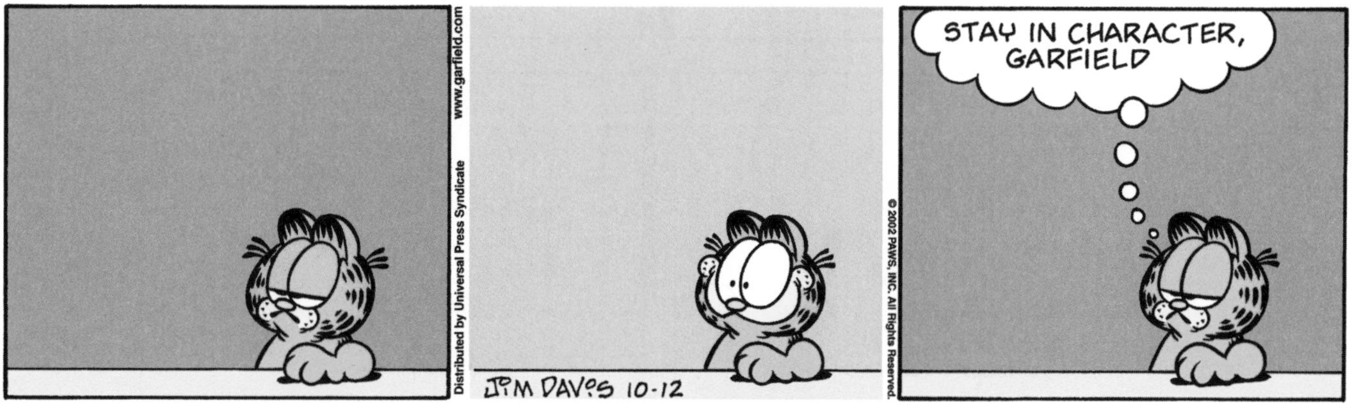
Distributed by Universal Press Syndicate www.garfield.com
JIM DAVIS 10-12
© 2002 PAWS, INC. All Rights Reserved.
STAY IN CHARACTER, GARFIELD

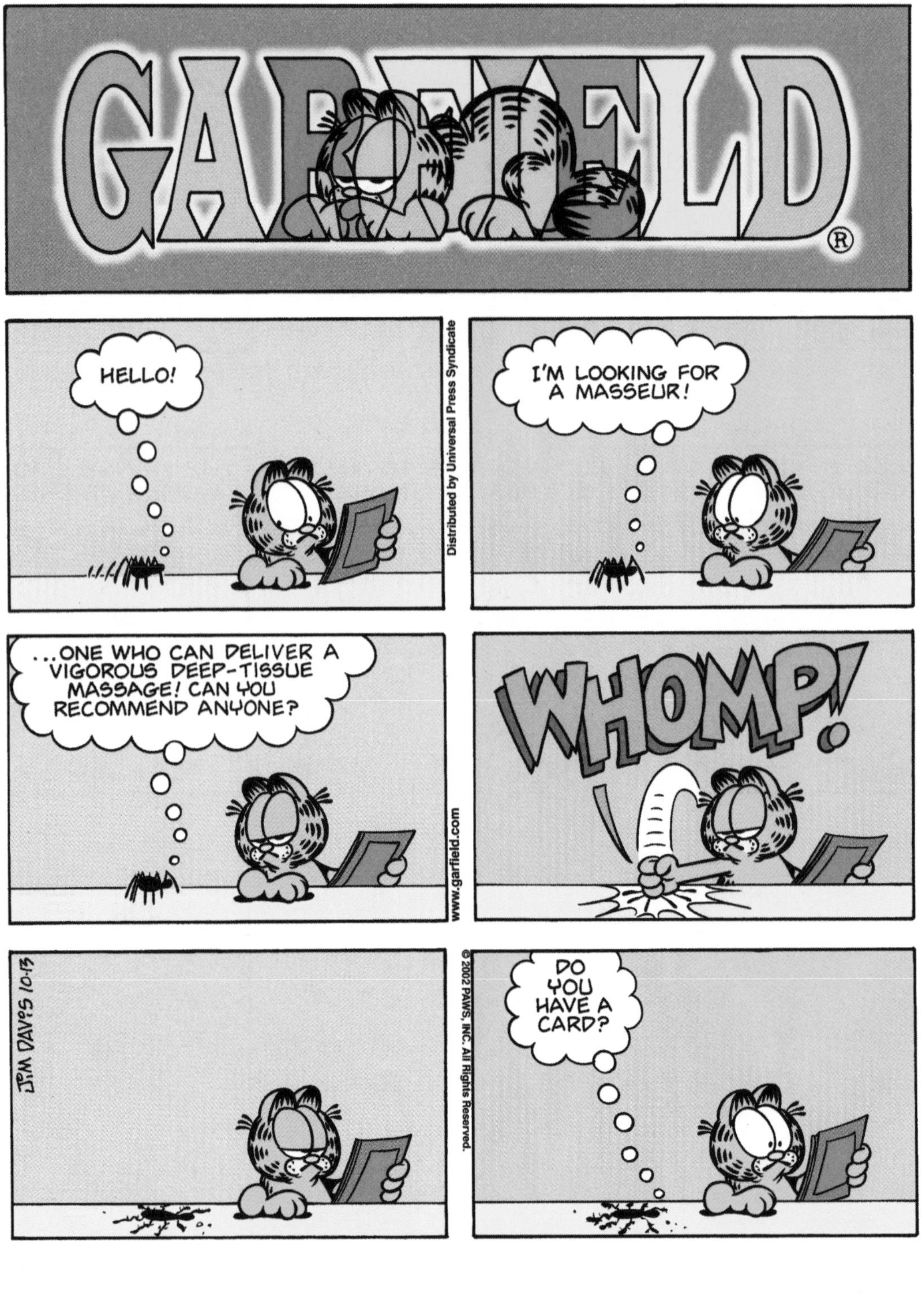
GARFIELD®
HELLO!
I'M LOOKING FOR A MASSEUR!
...ONE WHO CAN DELIVER A VIGOROUS DEEP-TISSUE MASSAGE! CAN YOU RECOMMEND ANYONE?
WHOMP!
JIM DAVIS 10-13
DO YOU HAVE A CARD?
Distributed by Universal Press Syndicate
www.garfield.com
© 2002 PAWS, INC. All Rights Reserved.

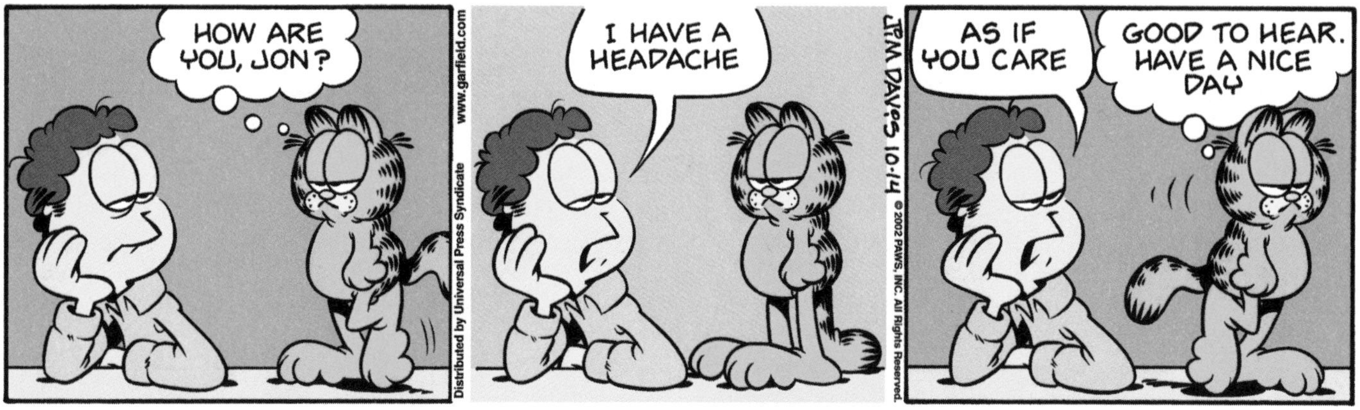
HOW ARE YOU, JON?
www.garfield.com
Distributed by Universal Press Syndicate
I HAVE A HEADACHE
JIM DAVIS 10-14
© 2002 PAWS, INC. All Rights Reserved.
AS IF YOU CARE
GOOD TO HEAR. HAVE A NICE DAY

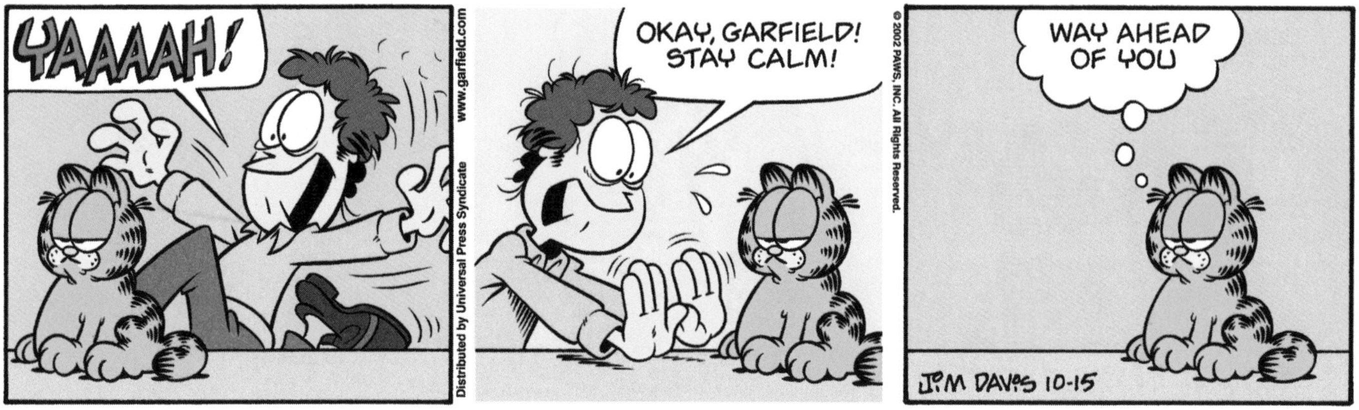
YAAAAH!
www.garfield.com
Distributed by Universal Press Syndicate
OKAY, GARFIELD! STAY CALM!
© 2002 PAWS, INC. All Rights Reserved.
WAY AHEAD OF YOU
JIM DAVIS 10-15

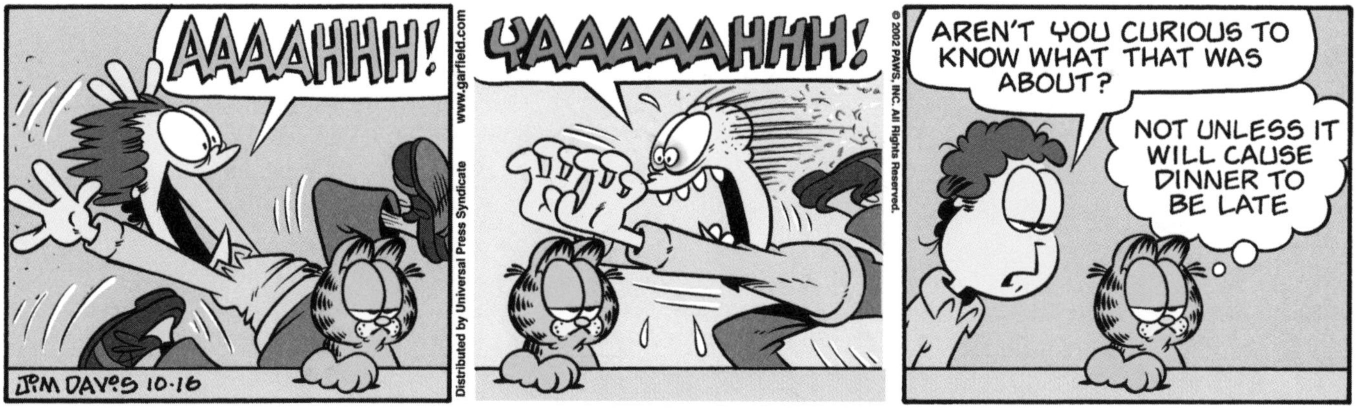
AAAAHHH!
JIM DAVIS 10-16
www.garfield.com
Distributed by Universal Press Syndicate
YAAAAAHHH!
© 2002 PAWS, INC. All Rights Reserved.
AREN'T YOU CURIOUS TO KNOW WHAT THAT WAS ABOUT?
NOT UNLESS IT WILL CAUSE DINNER TO BE LATE

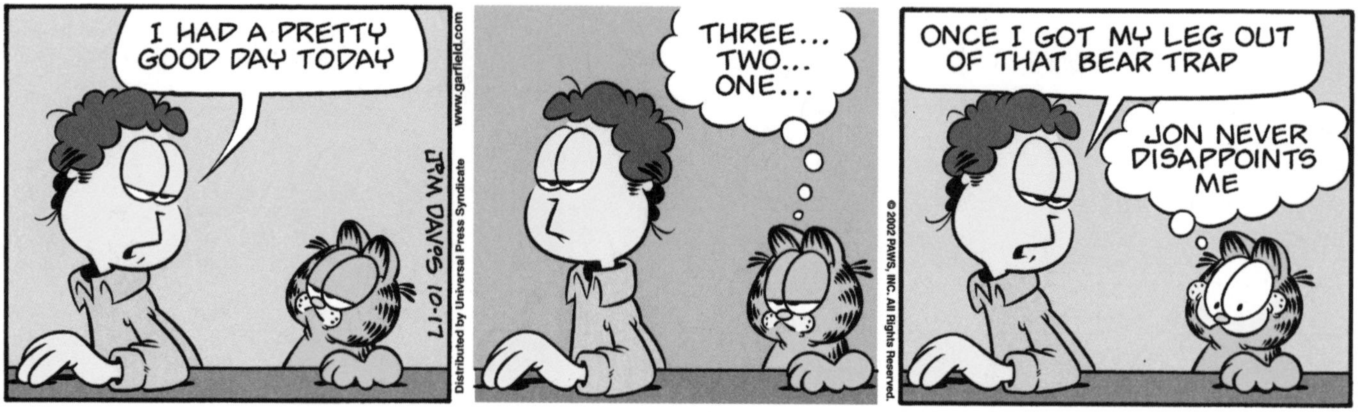
I HAD A PRETTY GOOD DAY TODAY
JIM DAVIS 10-17
Distributed by Universal Press Syndicate www.garfield.com
THREE... TWO... ONE...
© 2002 PAWS, INC. All Rights Reserved.
ONCE I GOT MY LEG OUT OF THAT BEAR TRAP
JON NEVER DISAPPOINTS ME

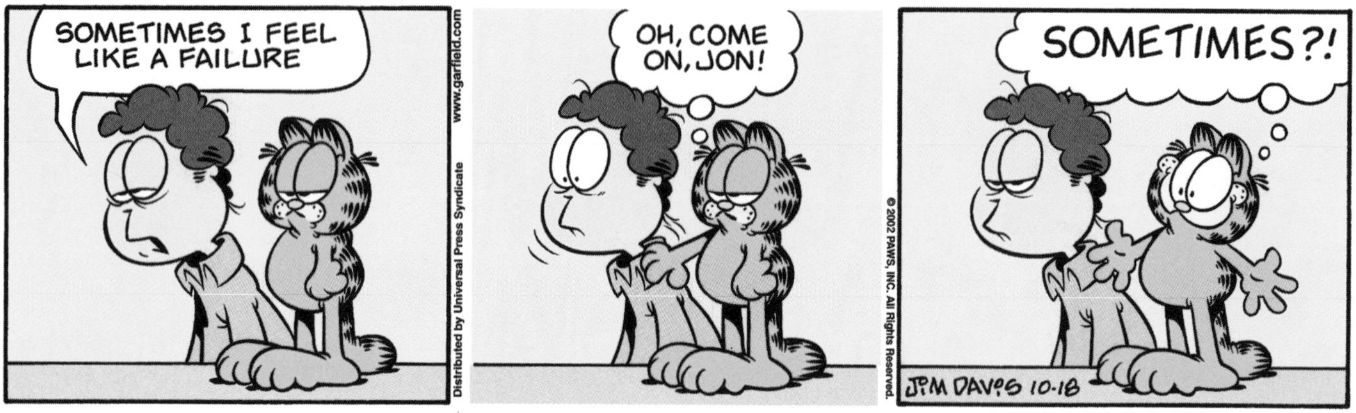
SOMETIMES I FEEL LIKE A FAILURE
Distributed by Universal Press Syndicate www.garfield.com
OH, COME ON, JON!
© 2002 PAWS, INC. All Rights Reserved.
SOMETIMES?!
JIM DAVIS 10-18

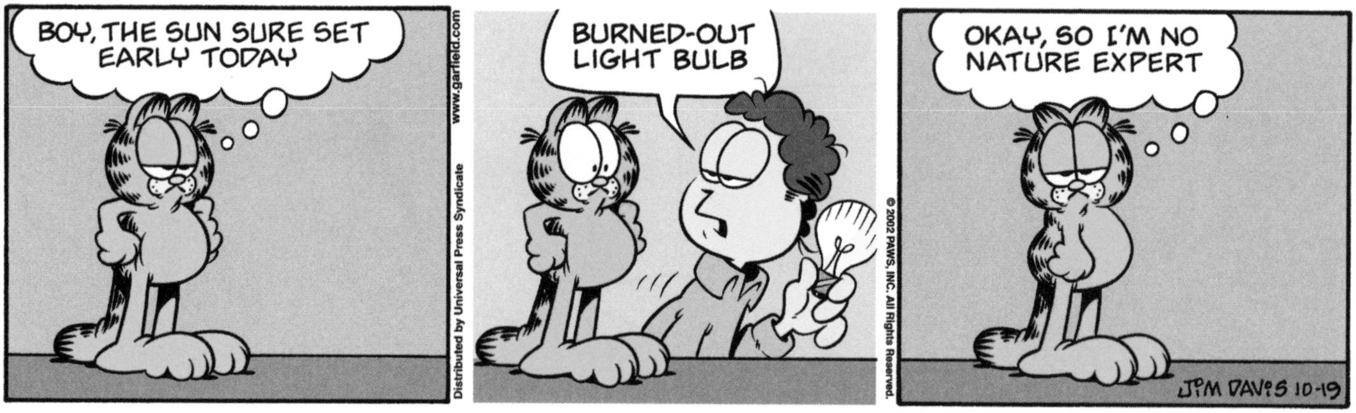
BOY, THE SUN SURE SET EARLY TODAY
Distributed by Universal Press Syndicate www.garfield.com
BURNED-OUT LIGHT BULB
© 2002 PAWS, INC. All Rights Reserved.
OKAY, SO I'M NO NATURE EXPERT
JIM DAVIS 10-19

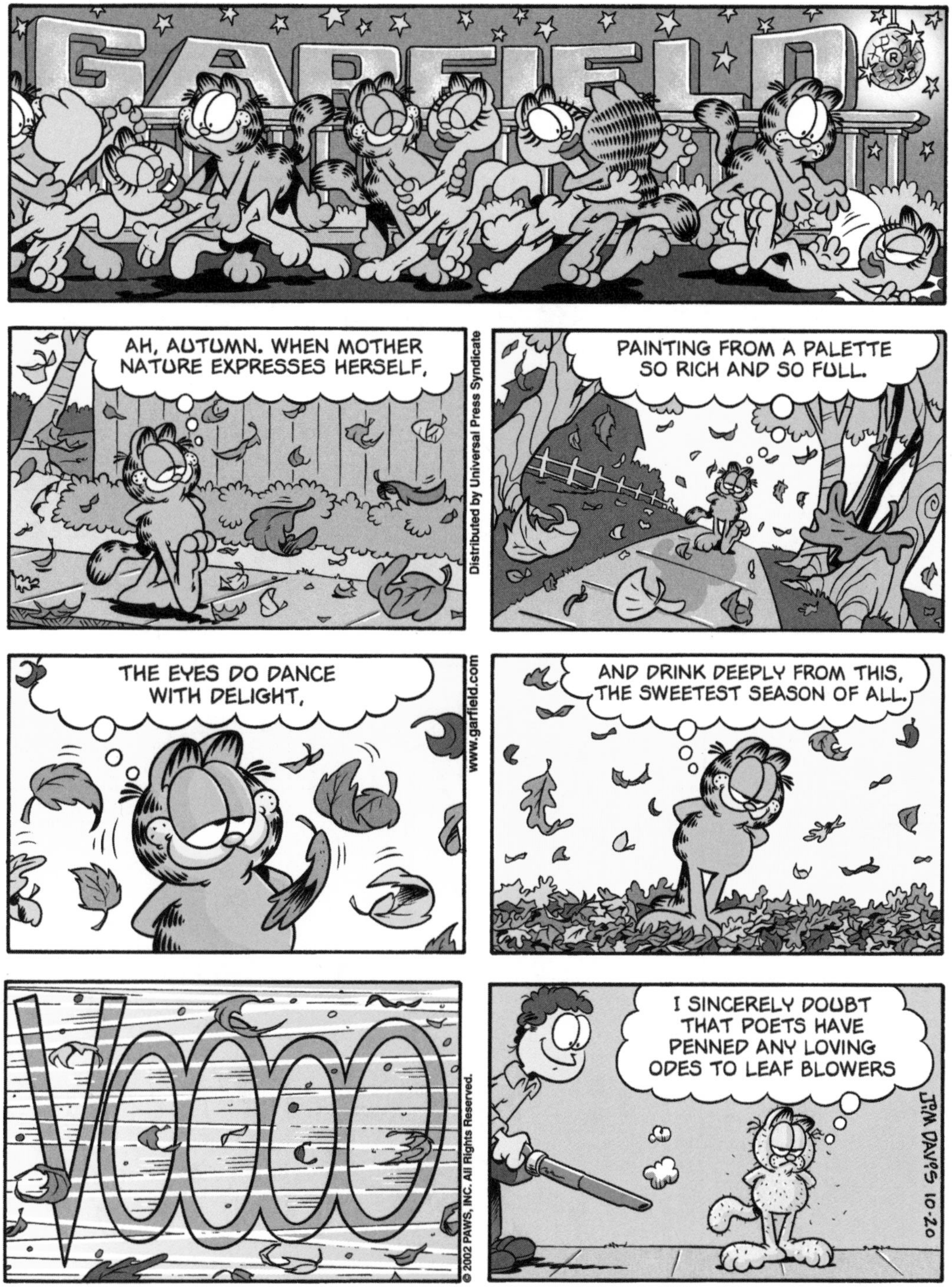
GARFIELD
AH, AUTUMN. WHEN MOTHER NATURE EXPRESSES HERSELF,
Distributed by Universal Press Syndicate
PAINTING FROM A PALETTE SO RICH AND SO FULL.
THE EYES DO DANCE WITH DELIGHT,
www.garfield.com
AND DRINK DEEPLY FROM THIS, THE SWEETEST SEASON OF ALL.
VOOOOO
© 2002 PAWS, INC. All Rights Reserved.
I SINCERELY DOUBT THAT POETS HAVE PENNED ANY LOVING ODES TO LEAF BLOWERS
JIM DAVIS 10-20

233

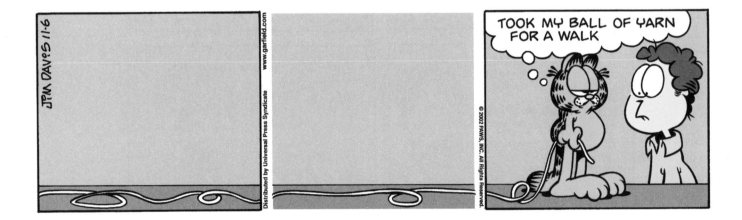

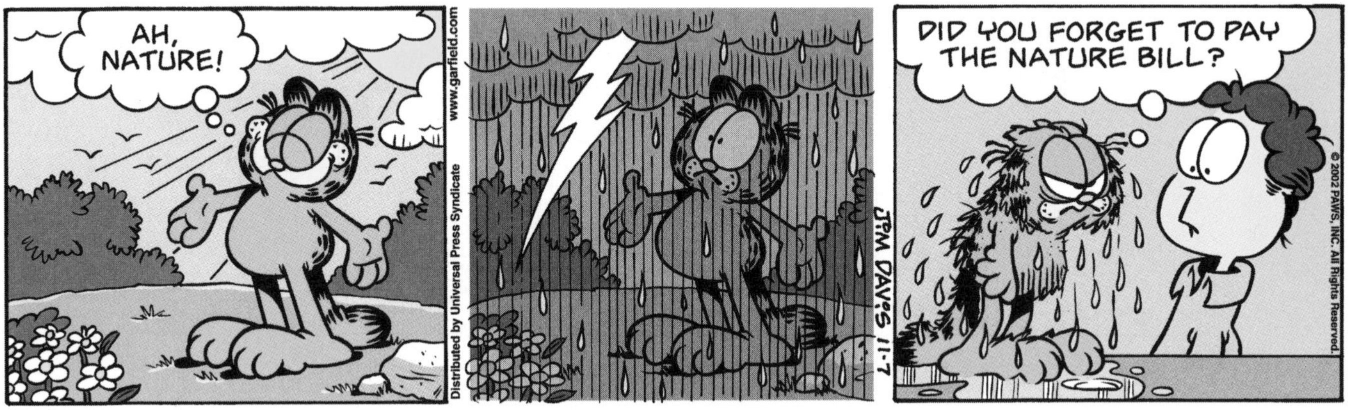
AH, NATURE!
Distributed by Universal Press Syndicate www.garfield.com
JIM DAVIS 11-7
DID YOU FORGET TO PAY THE NATURE BILL?
© 2002 PAWS, INC. All Rights Reserved.

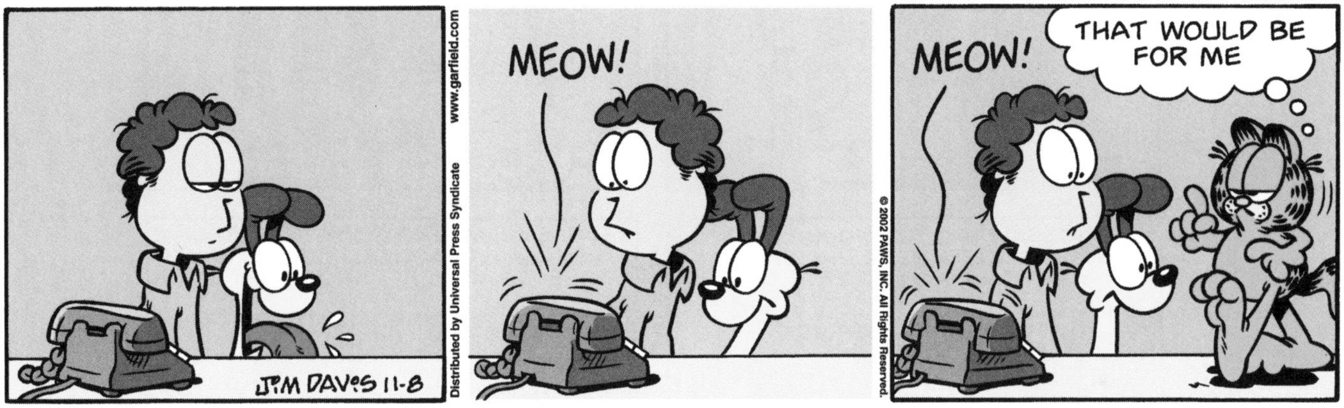
JIM DAVIS 11-8
Distributed by Universal Press Syndicate www.garfield.com
MEOW!
© 2002 PAWS, INC. All Rights Reserved.
MEOW!
THAT WOULD BE FOR ME

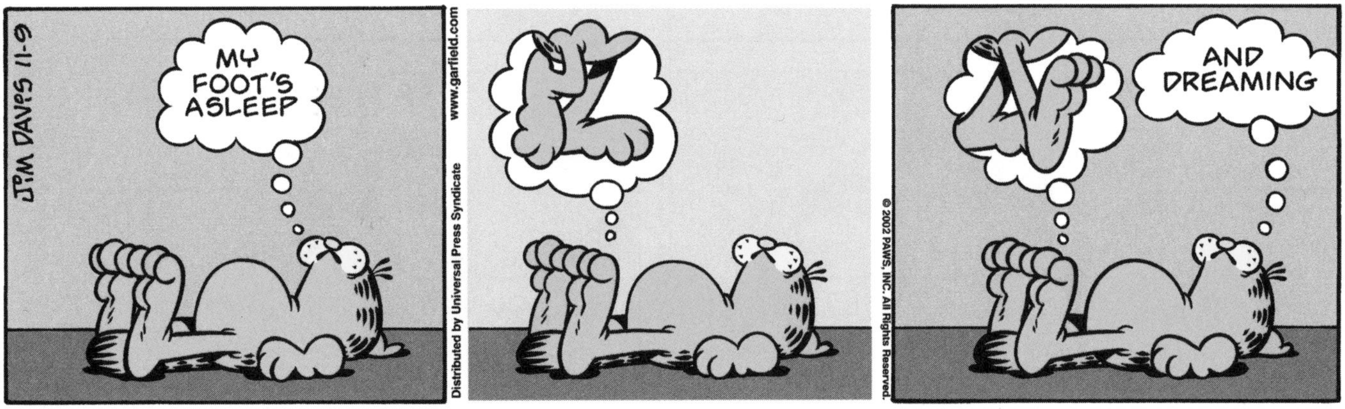
JIM DAVIS 11-9
MY FOOT'S ASLEEP
Distributed by Universal Press Syndicate www.garfield.com
© 2002 PAWS, INC. All Rights Reserved.
AND DREAMING

YOU KNOW, SOME FOLKS WOULDN'T SEE THIS FOR WHAT IT IS

SOME FOLKS WOULDN'T UNDERSTAND THE ASTONISHING RESERVES OF SELF-DISCIPLINE THIS REQUIRES

SOME FOLKS WOULDN'T COMPREHEND THE INTENSE CONCENTRATION INVOLVED

SOME FOLKS WOULDN'T APPRECIATE THE CONDITIONING THAT GOES INTO PRODUCING MUSCLE MEMORY THIS ADVANCED

ARE YOU GOING TO LIE THERE ALL DAY?!

YEEEES. IT'S THE OLD "FEAR-OF-WHAT-YOU-DON'T-UNDERSTAND" SYNDROME

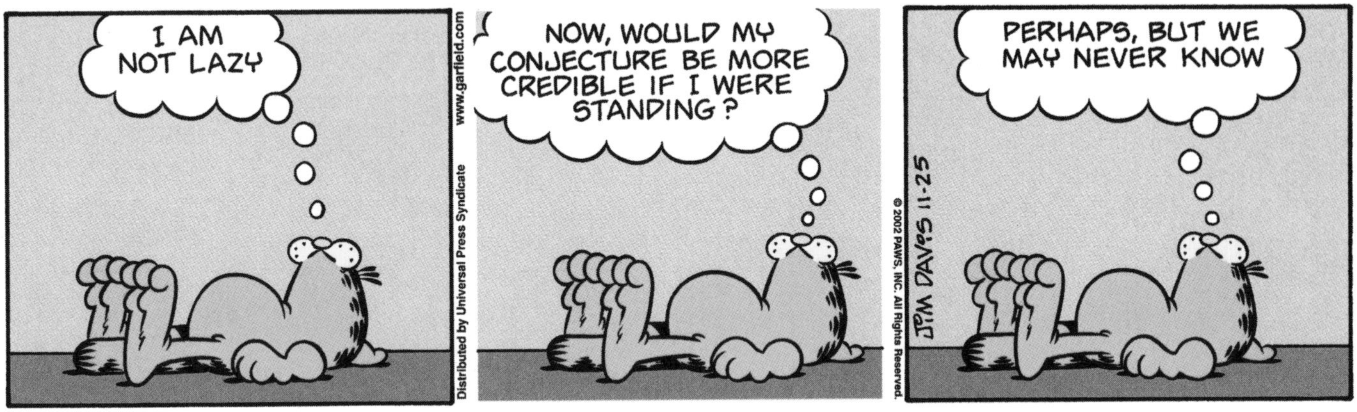
I AM NOT LAZY
www.garfield.com
Distributed by Universal Press Syndicate
NOW, WOULD MY CONJECTURE BE MORE CREDIBLE IF I WERE STANDING?
© 2002 PAWS, INC. All Rights Reserved.
JPM DAVPS 11-25
PERHAPS, BUT WE MAY NEVER KNOW

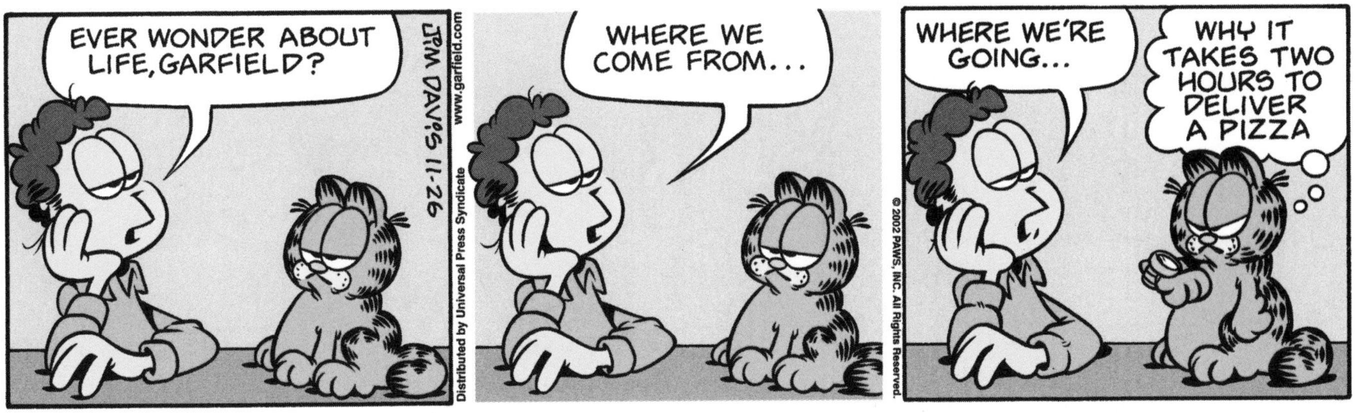
EVER WONDER ABOUT LIFE, GARFIELD?
JPM DAVPS 11-26
www.garfield.com
Distributed by Universal Press Syndicate
WHERE WE COME FROM...
© 2002 PAWS, INC. All Rights Reserved.
WHERE WE'RE GOING...
WHY IT TAKES TWO HOURS TO DELIVER A PIZZA

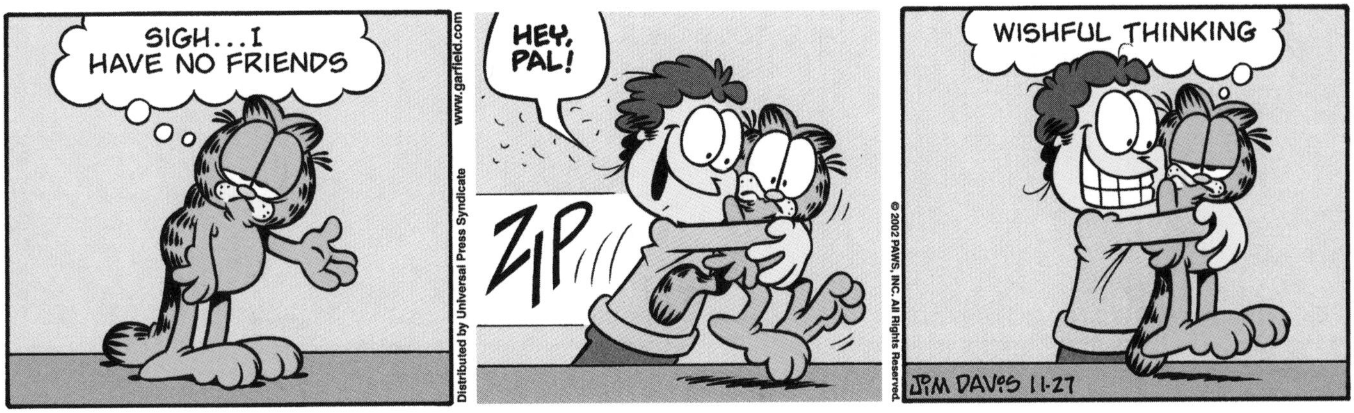
SIGH...I HAVE NO FRIENDS
www.garfield.com
Distributed by Universal Press Syndicate
HEY, PAL!
ZIP
© 2002 PAWS, INC. All Rights Reserved.
WISHFUL THINKING
JPM DAVPS 11-27

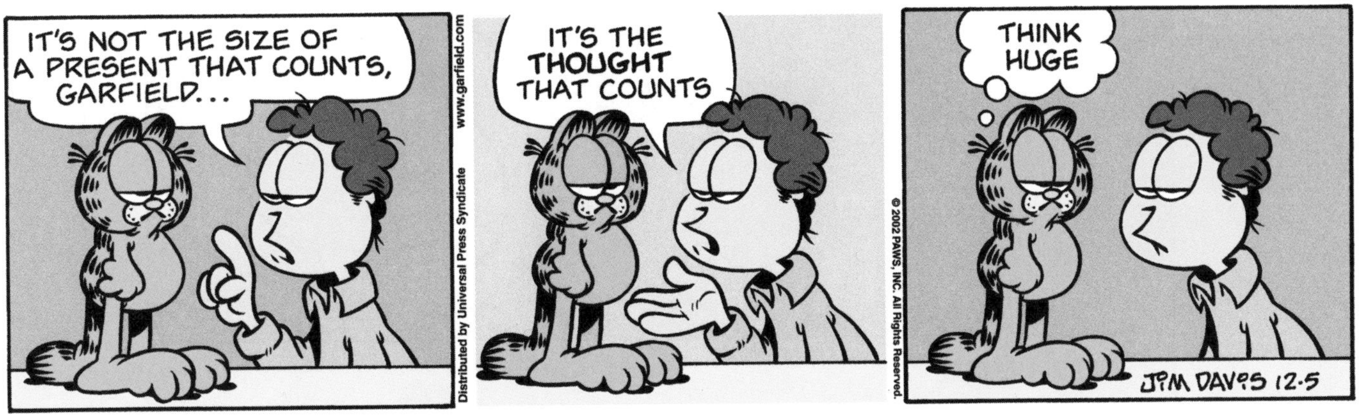
IT'S NOT THE SIZE OF A PRESENT THAT COUNTS, GARFIELD...
IT'S THE THOUGHT THAT COUNTS
THINK HUGE
JIM DAVIS 12-5
Distributed by Universal Press Syndicate www.garfield.com
© 2002 PAWS, INC. All Rights Reserved.

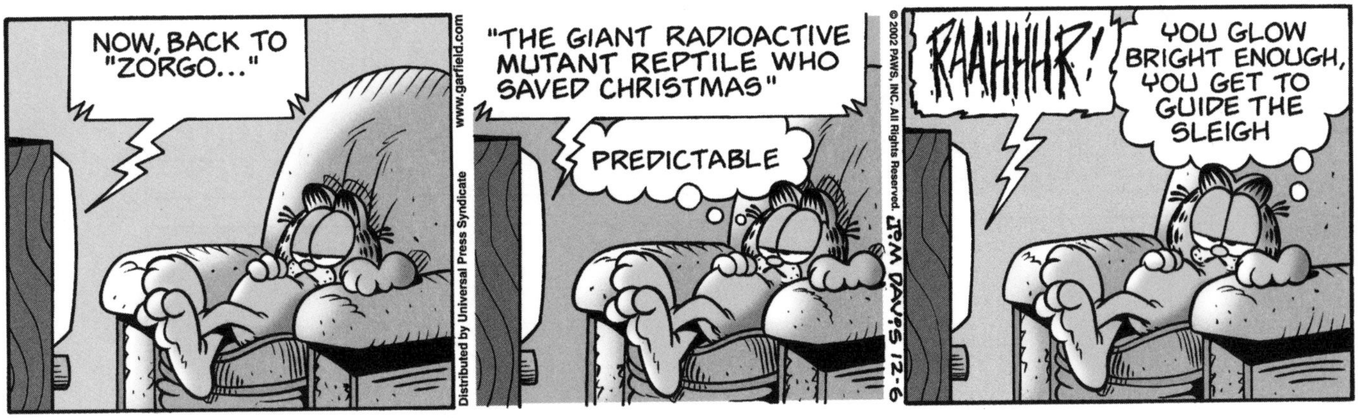
NOW, BACK TO "ZORGO..."
"THE GIANT RADIOACTIVE MUTANT REPTILE WHO SAVED CHRISTMAS"
PREDICTABLE
RAAHHHR!
YOU GLOW BRIGHT ENOUGH, YOU GET TO GUIDE THE SLEIGH
JIM DAVIS 12-6
Distributed by Universal Press Syndicate www.garfield.com
© 2002 PAWS, INC. All Rights Reserved.

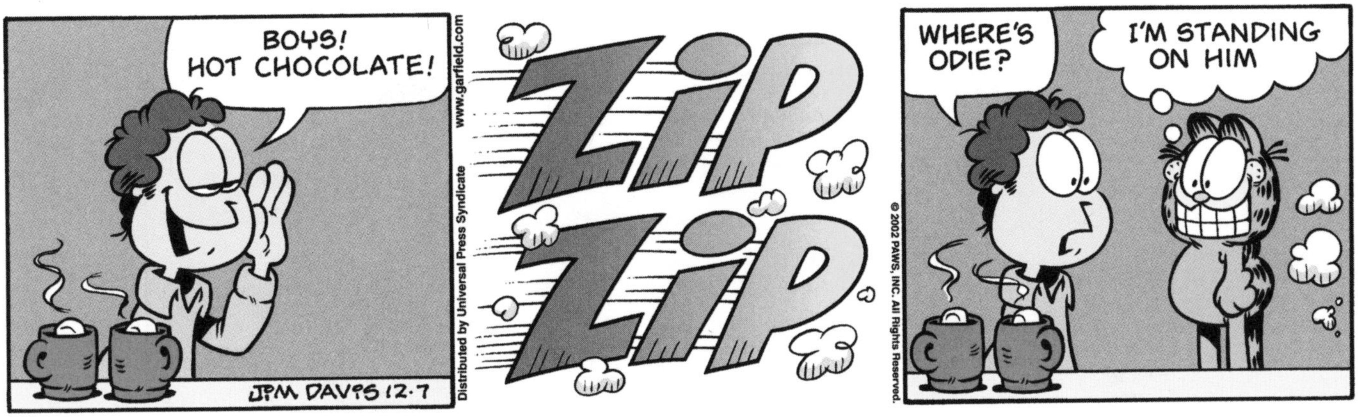
BOYS! HOT CHOCOLATE!
ZIP ZIP
WHERE'S ODIE?
I'M STANDING ON HIM
JIM DAVIS 12-7
Distributed by Universal Press Syndicate www.garfield.com
© 2002 PAWS, INC. All Rights Reserved.

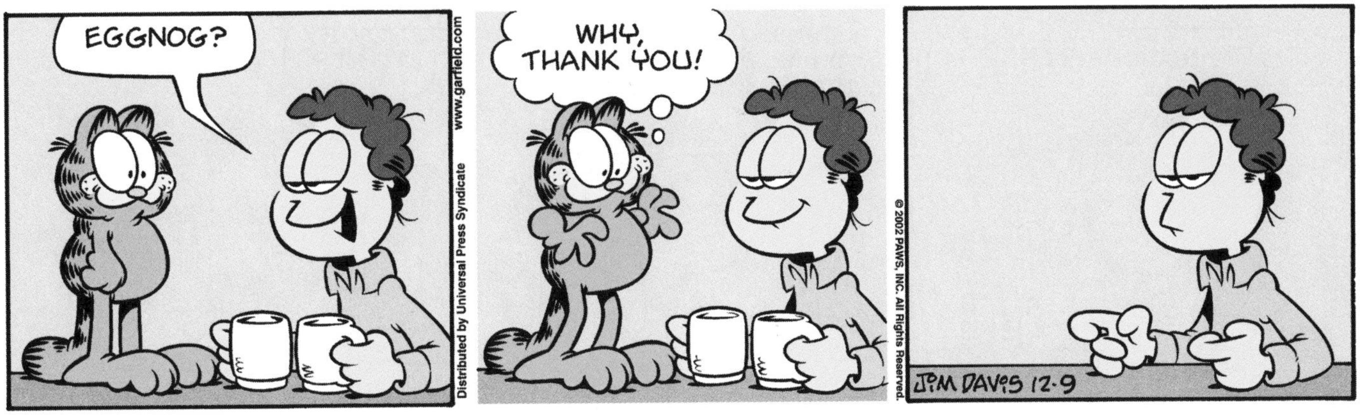
EGGNOG?
WHY, THANK YOU!
JIM DAVIS 12-9
www.garfield.com
Distributed by Universal Press Syndicate
© 2002 PAWS, INC. All Rights Reserved.

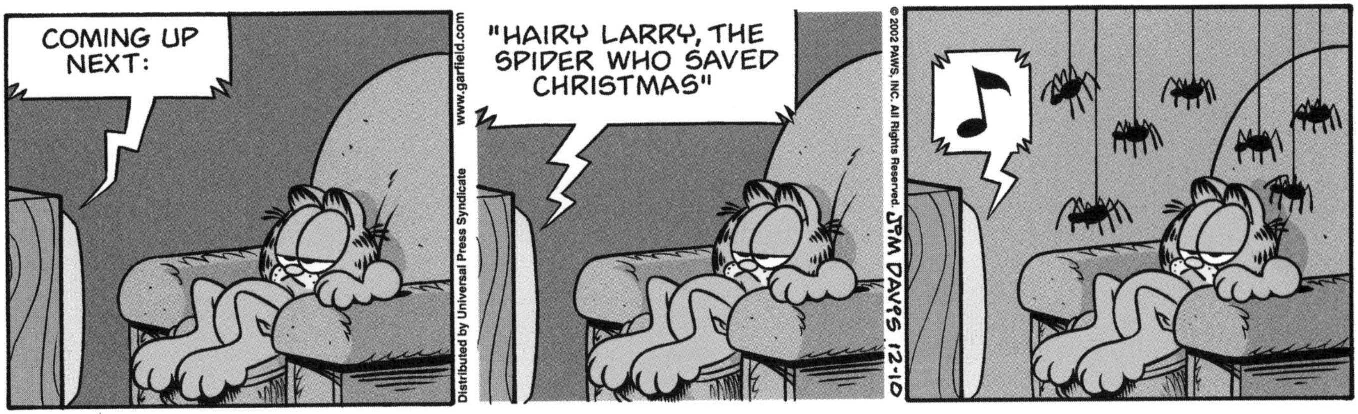
COMING UP NEXT:
"HAIRY LARRY, THE SPIDER WHO SAVED CHRISTMAS"
JIM DAVIS 12-10
www.garfield.com
Distributed by Universal Press Syndicate
© 2002 PAWS, INC. All Rights Reserved.

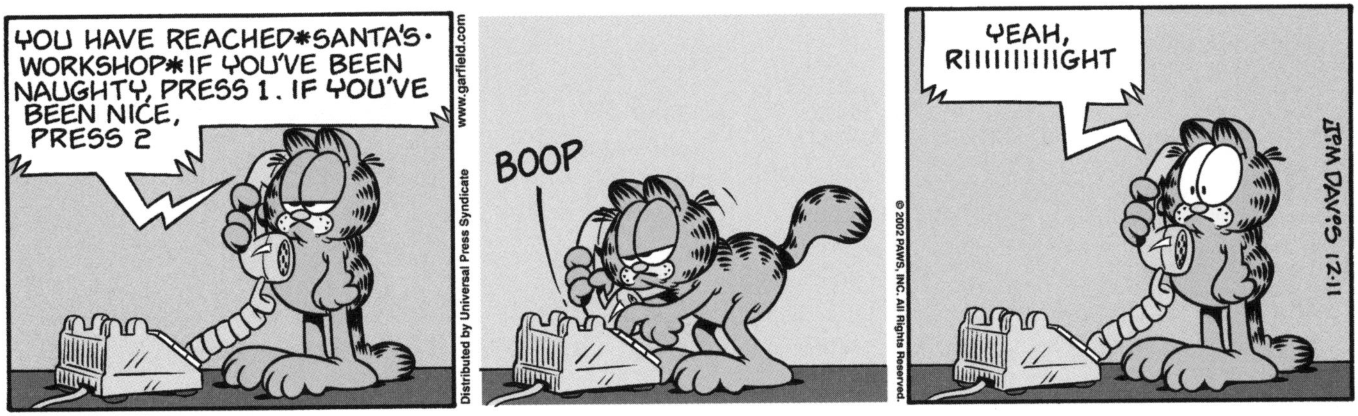
YOU HAVE REACHED*SANTA'S• WORKSHOP*IF YOU'VE BEEN NAUGHTY, PRESS 1. IF YOU'VE BEEN NICE, PRESS 2
BOOP
YEAH, RIIIIIIIIIIGHT
JIM DAVIS 12-11
www.garfield.com
Distributed by Universal Press Syndicate
© 2002 PAWS, INC. All Rights Reserved.

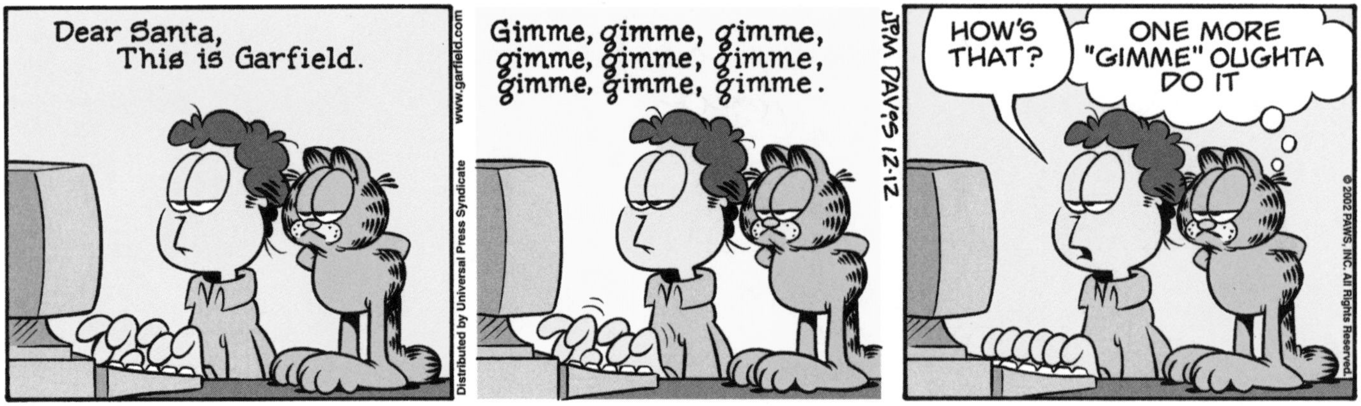
Dear Santa,
This is Garfield.
Distributed by Universal Press Syndicate www.garfield.com
Gimme, gimme, gimme, gimme, gimme, gimme, gimme, gimme, gimme.
JIM DAVIS 12-12
HOW'S THAT?
ONE MORE "GIMME" OUGHTA DO IT
© 2002 PAWS, INC. All Rights Reserved.

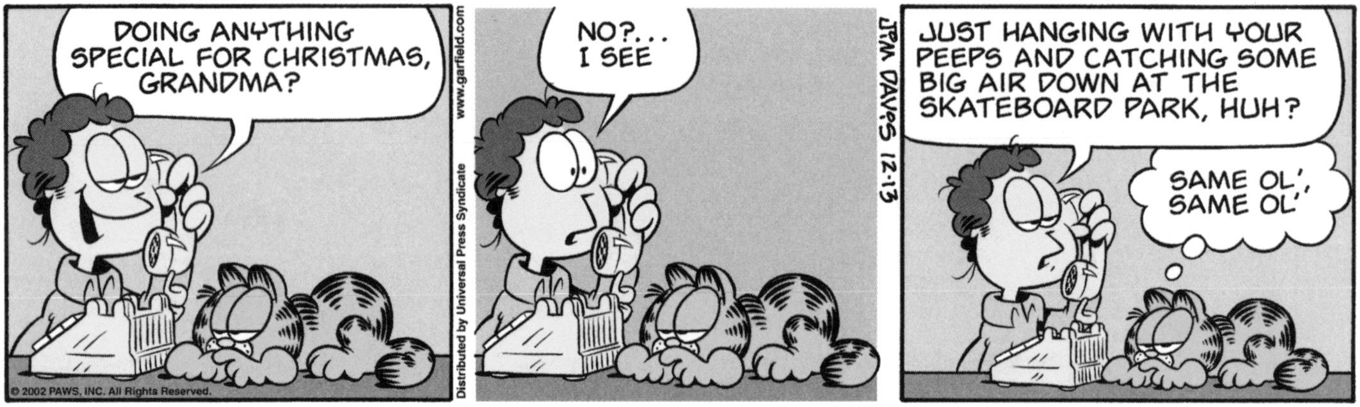
DOING ANYTHING SPECIAL FOR CHRISTMAS, GRANDMA?
© 2002 PAWS, INC. All Rights Reserved.
Distributed by Universal Press Syndicate www.garfield.com
NO?... I SEE
JIM DAVIS 12-13
JUST HANGING WITH YOUR PEEPS AND CATCHING SOME BIG AIR DOWN AT THE SKATEBOARD PARK, HUH?
SAME OL', SAME OL'

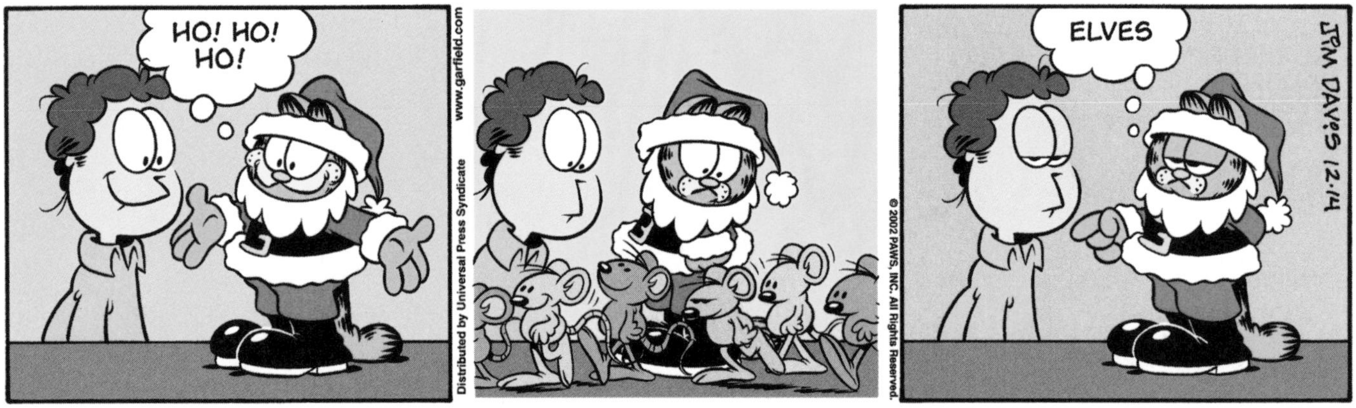
HO! HO! HO!
Distributed by Universal Press Syndicate www.garfield.com
© 2002 PAWS, INC. All Rights Reserved.
ELVES
JIM DAVIS 12-14

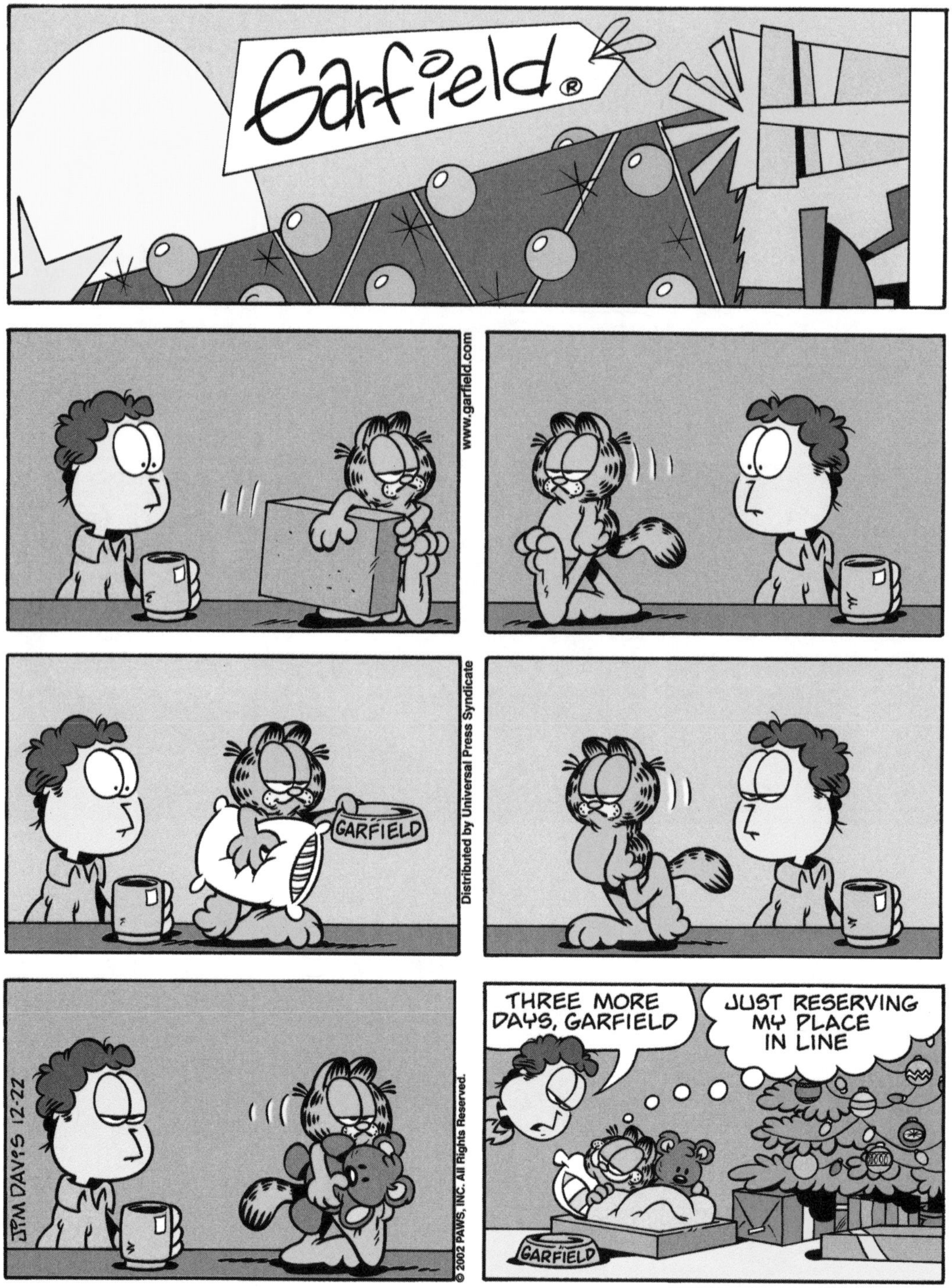
Garfield®
www.garfield.com
GARFIELD
Distributed by Universal Press Syndicate
JIM DAVIS 12-22
© 2002 PAWS, INC. All Rights Reserved.
THREE MORE DAYS, GARFIELD
JUST RESERVING MY PLACE IN LINE
GARFIELD

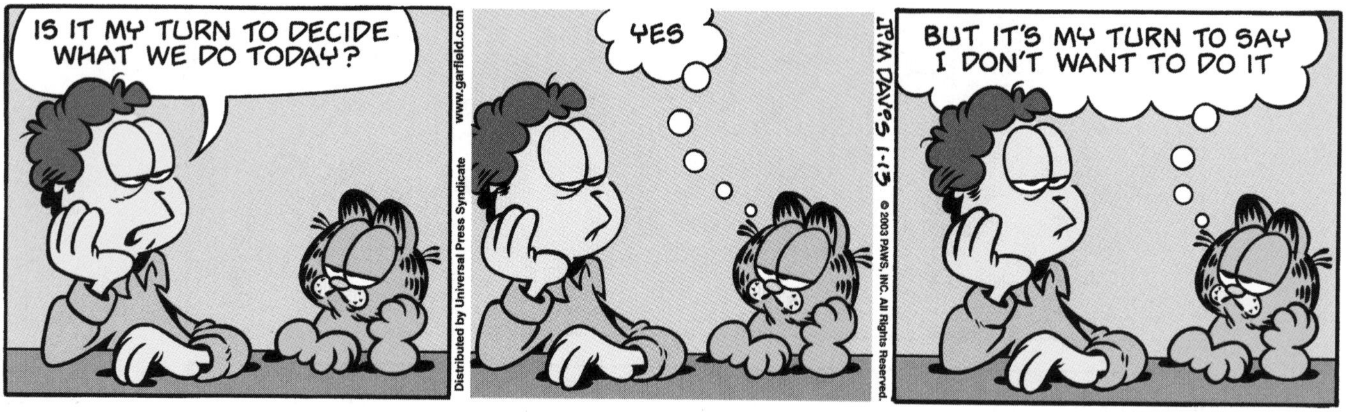
IS IT MY TURN TO DECIDE WHAT WE DO TODAY?
Distributed by Universal Press Syndicate www.garfield.com
YES
© 2003 PAWS, INC. All Rights Reserved.
BUT IT'S MY TURN TO SAY I DON'T WANT TO DO IT

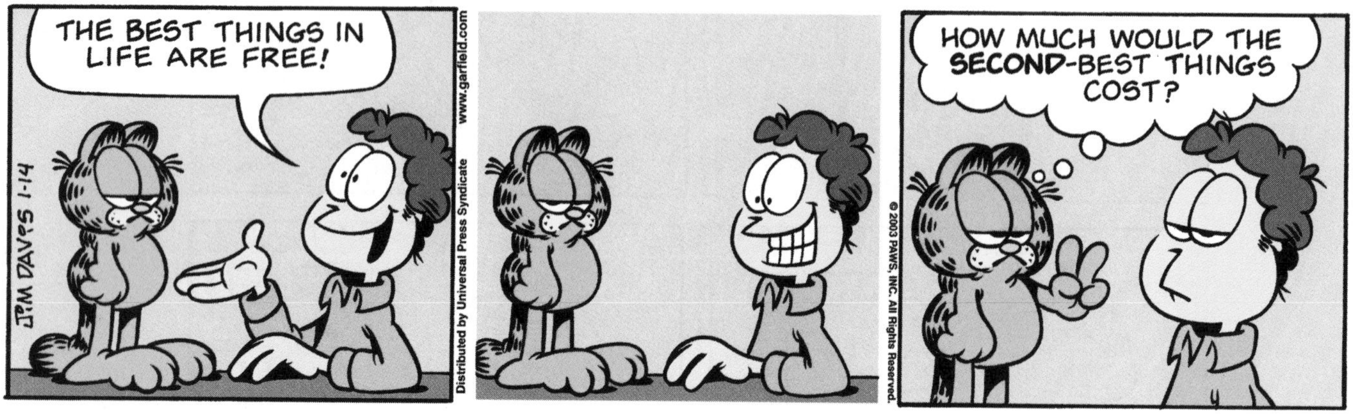
THE BEST THINGS IN LIFE ARE FREE!
Distributed by Universal Press Syndicate www.garfield.com
© 2003 PAWS, INC. All Rights Reserved.
HOW MUCH WOULD THE **SECOND**-BEST THINGS COST?

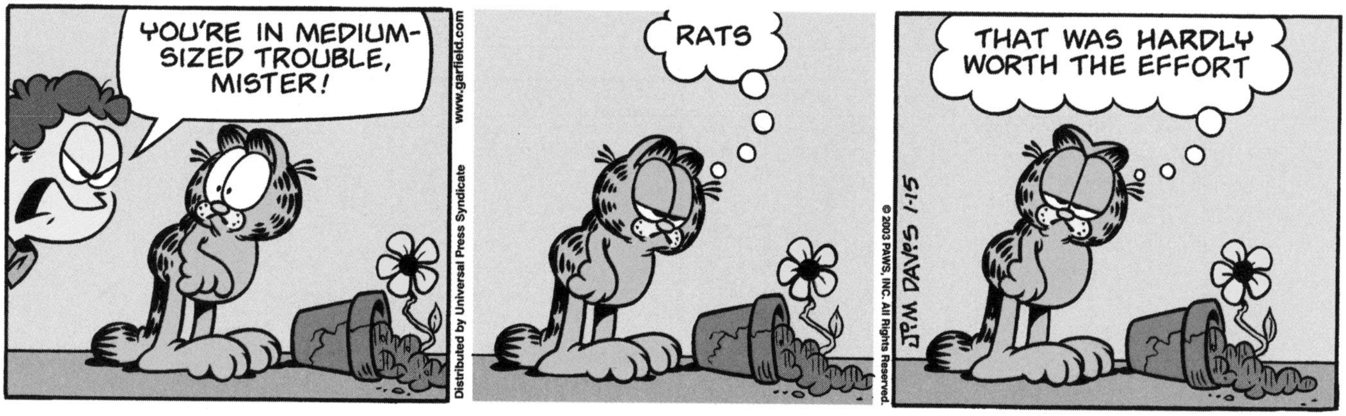
YOU'RE IN MEDIUM-SIZED TROUBLE, MISTER!
Distributed by Universal Press Syndicate www.garfield.com
RATS
© 2003 PAWS, INC. All Rights Reserved.
THAT WAS HARDLY WORTH THE EFFORT

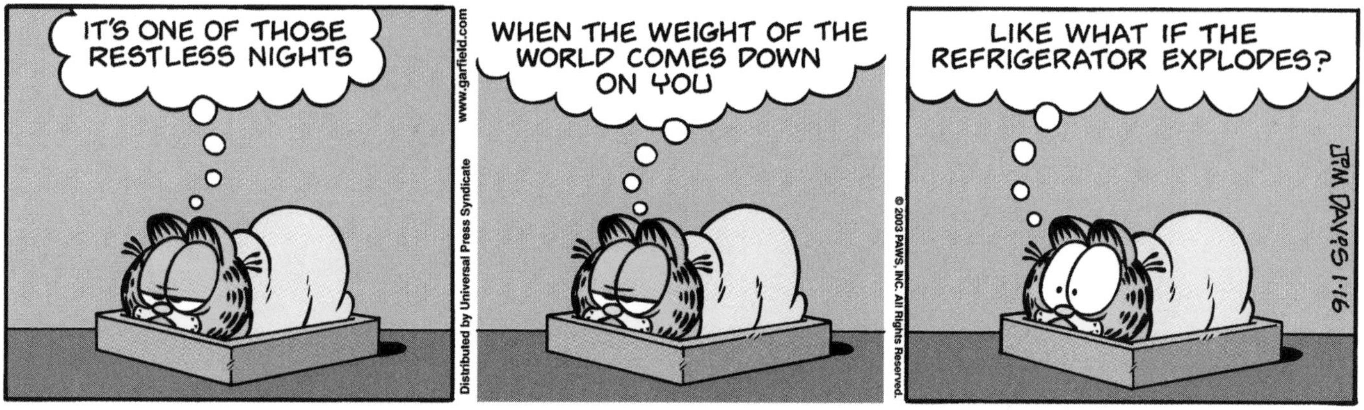
IT'S ONE OF THOSE RESTLESS NIGHTS
WHEN THE WEIGHT OF THE WORLD COMES DOWN ON YOU
LIKE WHAT IF THE REFRIGERATOR EXPLODES?
JIM DAVIS 1-16
Distributed by Universal Press Syndicate www.garfield.com
© 2003 PAWS, INC. All Rights Reserved.

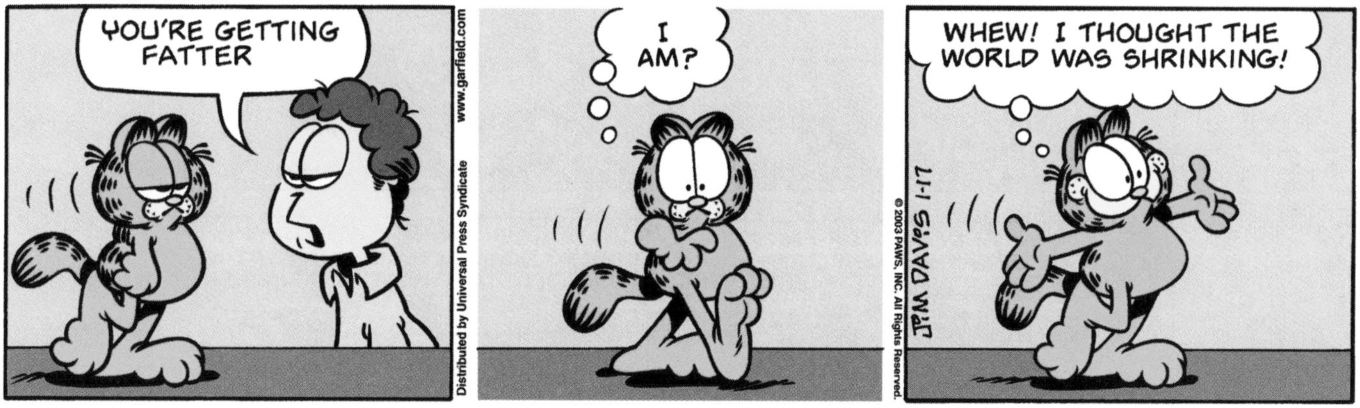
YOU'RE GETTING FATTER
I AM?
WHEW! I THOUGHT THE WORLD WAS SHRINKING!
JIM DAVIS 1-17
Distributed by Universal Press Syndicate www.garfield.com
© 2003 PAWS, INC. All Rights Reserved.

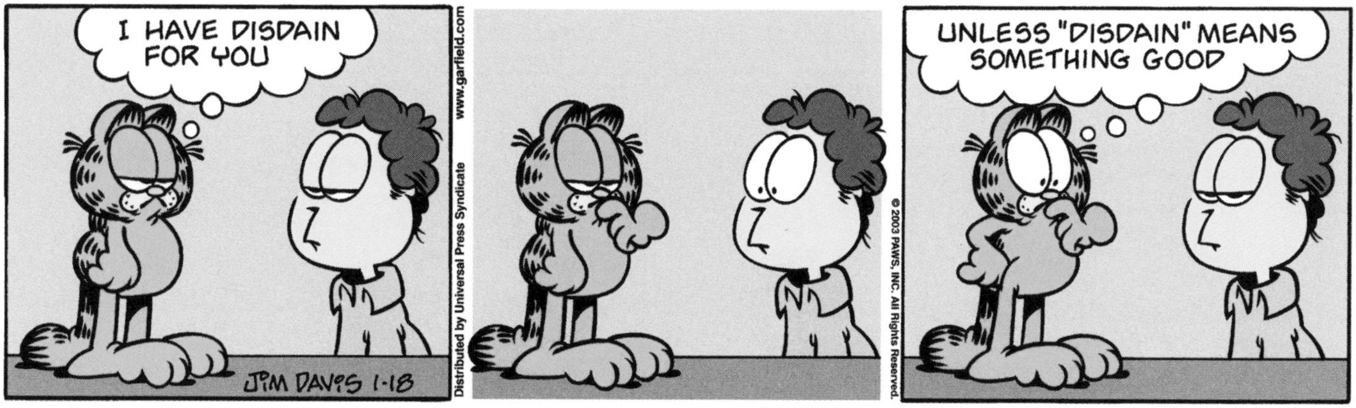
I HAVE DISDAIN FOR YOU
UNLESS "DISDAIN" MEANS SOMETHING GOOD
JIM DAVIS 1-18
Distributed by Universal Press Syndicate www.garfield.com
© 2003 PAWS, INC. All Rights Reserved.

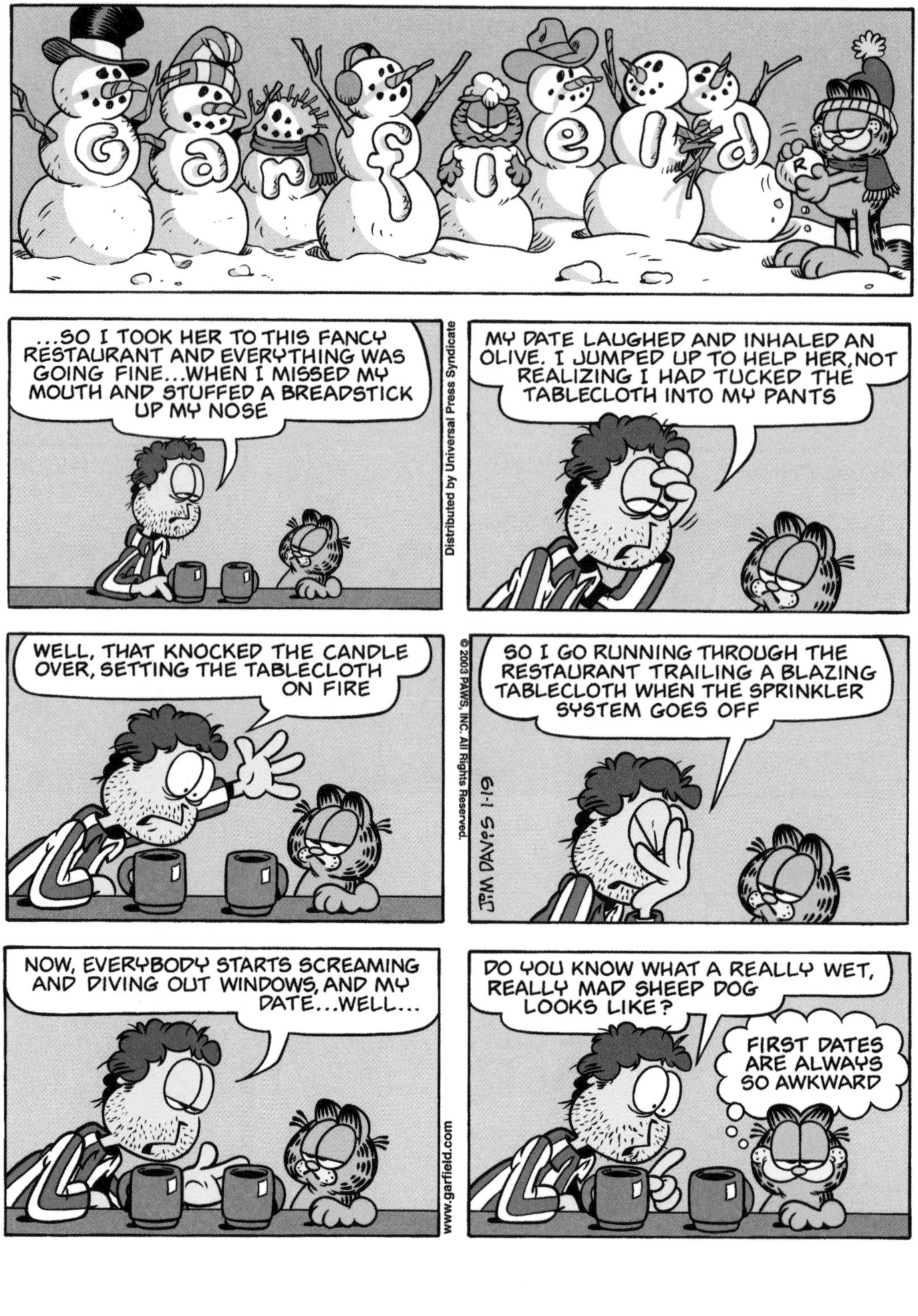
Garfield
...SO I TOOK HER TO THIS FANCY RESTAURANT AND EVERYTHING WAS GOING FINE...WHEN I MISSED MY MOUTH AND STUFFED A BREADSTICK UP MY NOSE
MY DATE LAUGHED AND INHALED AN OLIVE. I JUMPED UP TO HELP HER, NOT REALIZING I HAD TUCKED THE TABLECLOTH INTO MY PANTS
WELL, THAT KNOCKED THE CANDLE OVER, SETTING THE TABLECLOTH ON FIRE
SO I GO RUNNING THROUGH THE RESTAURANT TRAILING A BLAZING TABLECLOTH WHEN THE SPRINKLER SYSTEM GOES OFF
NOW, EVERYBODY STARTS SCREAMING AND DIVING OUT WINDOWS, AND MY DATE...WELL...
DO YOU KNOW WHAT A REALLY WET, REALLY MAD SHEEP DOG LOOKS LIKE?
FIRST DATES ARE ALWAYS SO AWKWARD
Distributed by Universal Press Syndicate
© 2003 PAWS, INC. All Rights Reserved.
JIM DAVIS 1-19
www.garfield.com

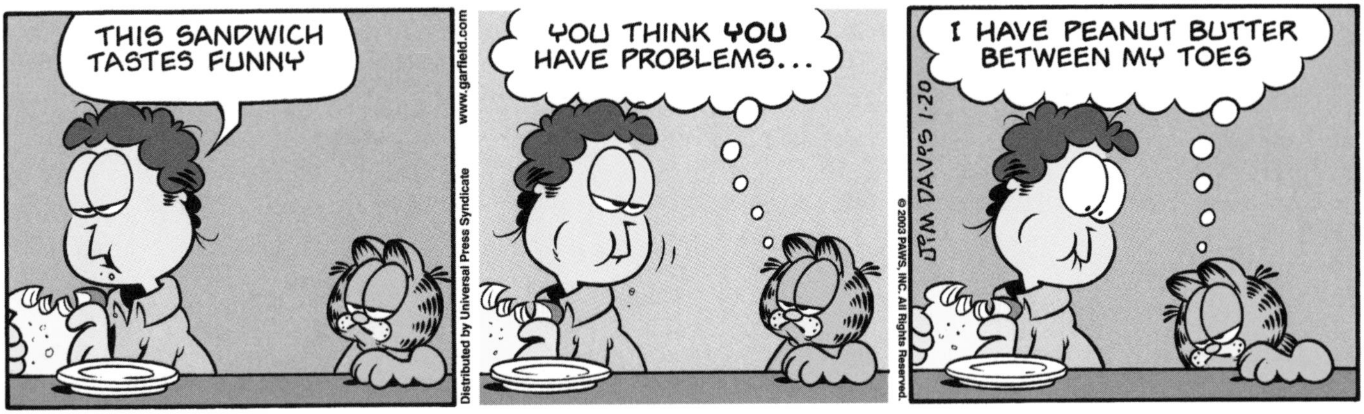
THIS SANDWICH TASTES FUNNY
YOU THINK **YOU** HAVE PROBLEMS...
I HAVE PEANUT BUTTER BETWEEN MY TOES
JIM DAVIS 1-20
www.garfield.com
Distributed by Universal Press Syndicate
© 2003 PAWS, INC. All Rights Reserved.

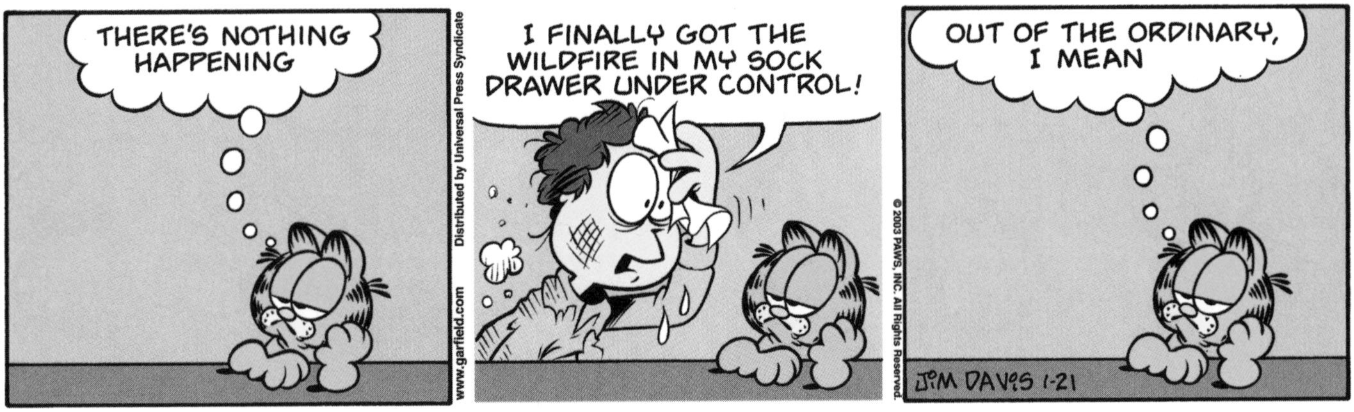
THERE'S NOTHING HAPPENING
I FINALLY GOT THE WILDFIRE IN MY SOCK DRAWER UNDER CONTROL!
OUT OF THE ORDINARY, I MEAN
JIM DAVIS 1-21
Distributed by Universal Press Syndicate
www.garfield.com
© 2003 PAWS, INC. All Rights Reserved.

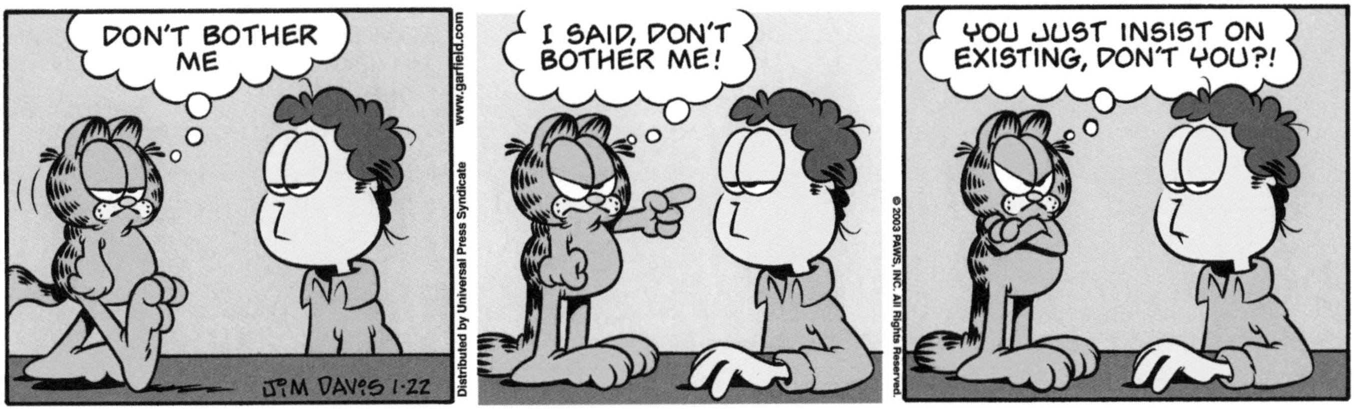
DON'T BOTHER ME
I SAID, DON'T BOTHER ME!
YOU JUST INSIST ON EXISTING, DON'T YOU?!
JIM DAVIS 1-22
www.garfield.com
Distributed by Universal Press Syndicate
© 2003 PAWS, INC. All Rights Reserved.

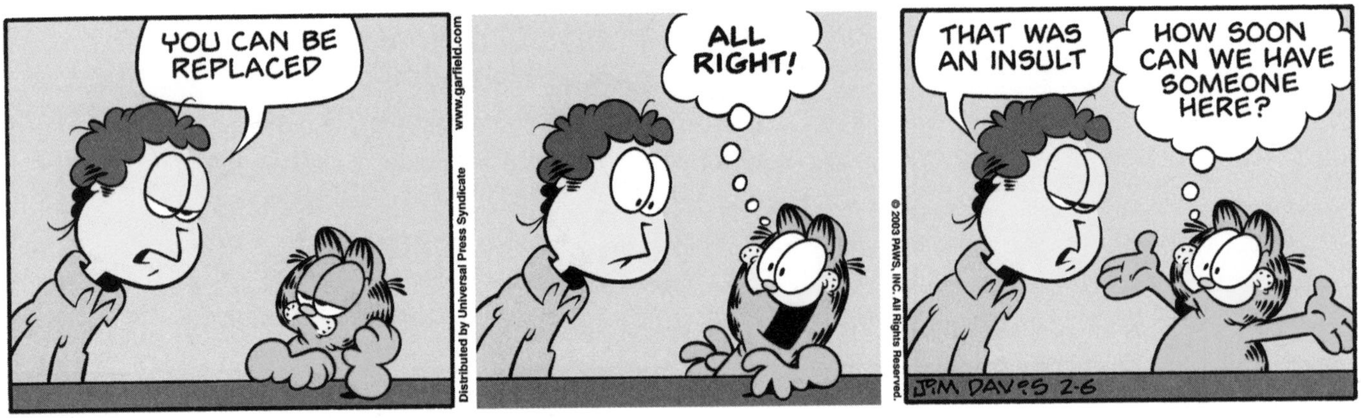
YOU CAN BE REPLACED
ALL RIGHT!
THAT WAS AN INSULT
HOW SOON CAN WE HAVE SOMEONE HERE?
www.garfield.com
Distributed by Universal Press Syndicate
© 2003 PAWS, INC. All Rights Reserved.
JIM DAVIS 2-6

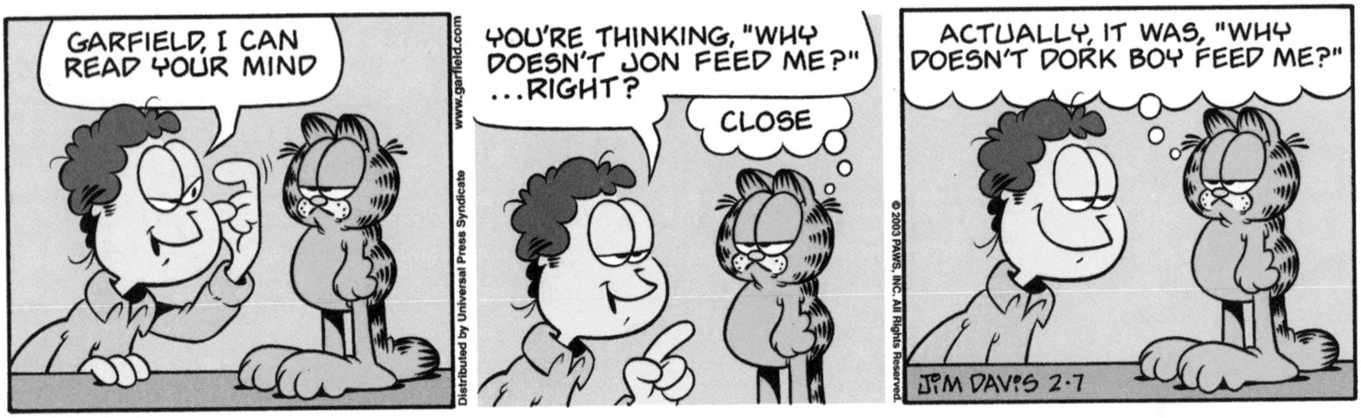
GARFIELD, I CAN READ YOUR MIND
YOU'RE THINKING, "WHY DOESN'T JON FEED ME?" ...RIGHT?
CLOSE
ACTUALLY, IT WAS, "WHY DOESN'T DORK BOY FEED ME?"
www.garfield.com
Distributed by Universal Press Syndicate
© 2003 PAWS, INC. All Rights Reserved.
JIM DAVIS 2-7

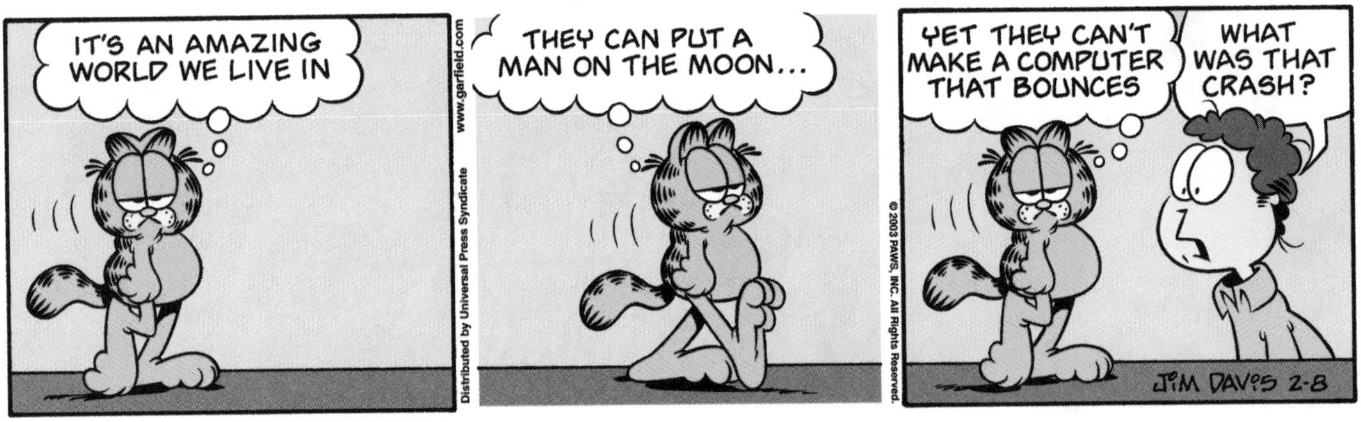
IT'S AN AMAZING WORLD WE LIVE IN
THEY CAN PUT A MAN ON THE MOON...
YET THEY CAN'T MAKE A COMPUTER THAT BOUNCES
WHAT WAS THAT CRASH?
www.garfield.com
Distributed by Universal Press Syndicate
© 2003 PAWS, INC. All Rights Reserved.
JIM DAVIS 2-8

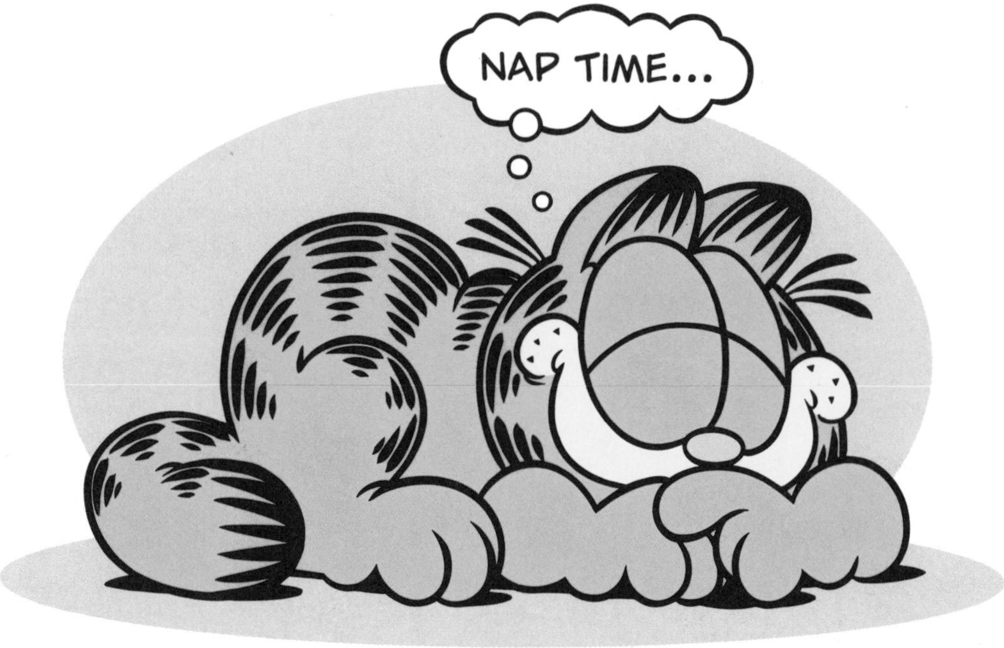
NAP TIME...

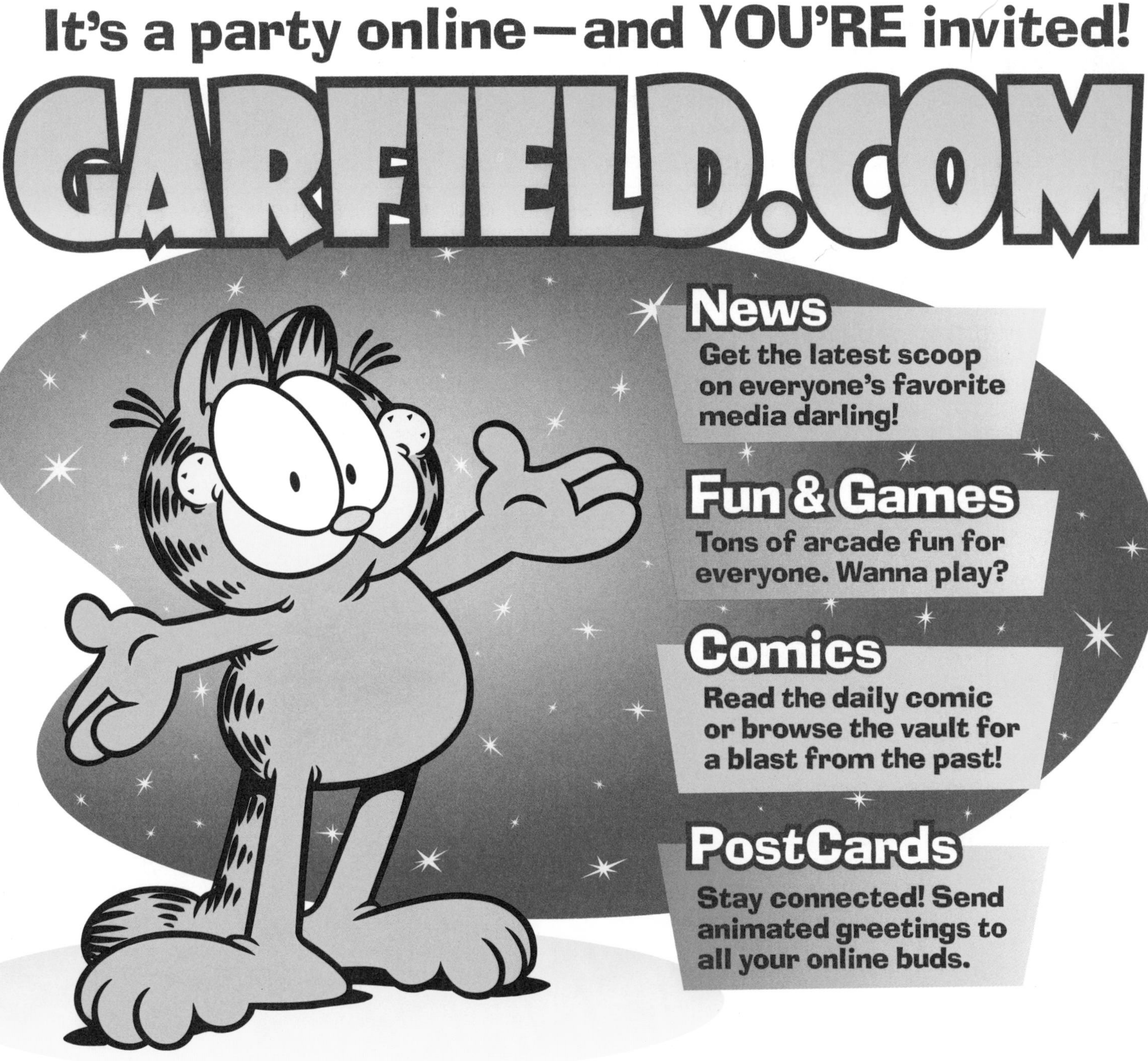
It's a party online—and YOU'RE invited!
GARFIELD.COM
News
Get the latest scoop on everyone's favorite media darling!
Fun & Games
Tons of arcade fun for everyone. Wanna play?
Comics
Read the daily comic or browse the vault for a blast from the past!
PostCards
Stay connected! Send animated greetings to all your online buds.

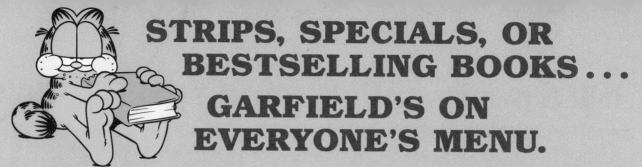

STRIPS, SPECIALS, OR BESTSELLING BOOKS...
GARFIELD'S ON EVERYONE'S MENU.

Don't miss even one episode in the Tubby Tabby's hilarious series!

New larger, full-color format!